HQ
6
1

W9-ASO-165

WOMEN TOGETHER

A History in Documents of the
Women's Movement in the United States

HQ
1426
.P34

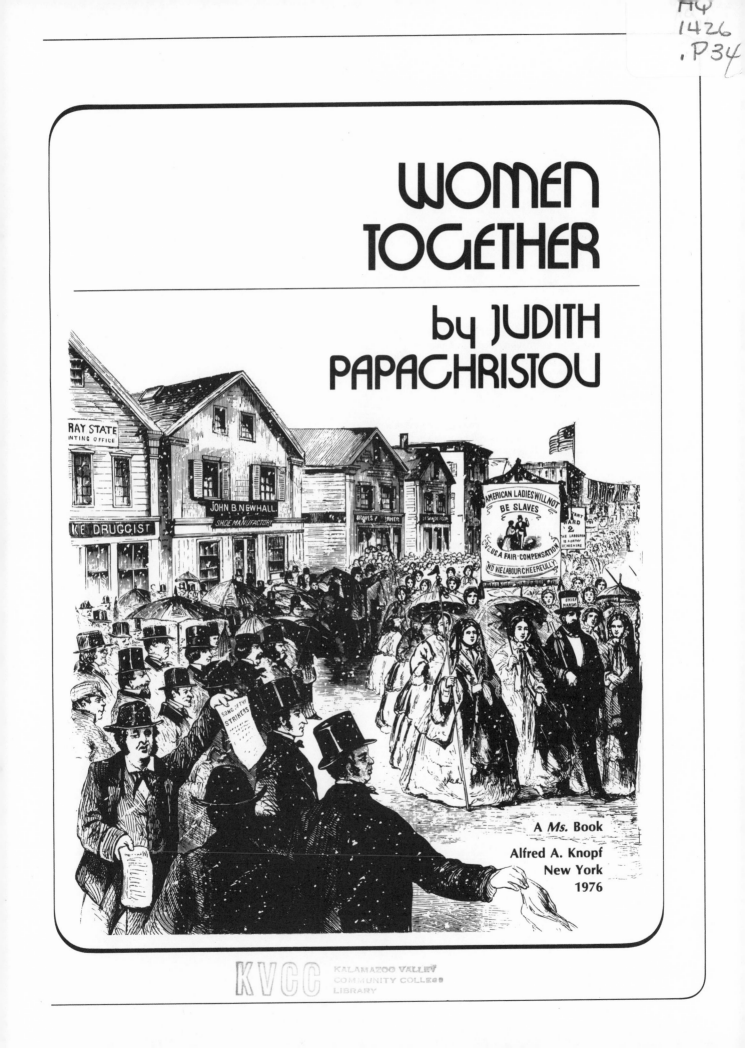

WOMEN TOGETHER

by JUDITH PAPACHRISTOU

A *Ms.* Book

Alfred A. Knopf
New York
1976

KVCC KALAMAZOO VALLEY
COMMUNITY COLLEGE
LIBRARY

32068

 THIS IS A BORZOI BOOK
PUBLISHED BY ALFRED A. KNOPF, INC.

Copyright © 1976 by *Ms.* Magazine and Judith Papachristou
All rights reserved under International and Pan-American
Copyright Conventions. Published in the United States by Alfred
A. Knopf, Inc., New York, and simultaneously in Canada by
Random House of Canada Limited, Toronto. Distributed by
Random House, Inc., New York.

Owing to space limitations, all acknowledgments of permission
to use illustrations and textual materials will be found in the back
of the book, following the Bibliography.

LIBRARY OF CONGRESS CATALOGING IN PUBLICATION DATA

Papachristou, Judith   Women together.
  "A Ms. book."
  1. Feminism—United States—History—Sources. 2. Women's
rights—United States—History—Sources. I. Title.
HQ1426.P34   301.41'2'0973   75-37709
ISBN 0-394-49429-6

MANUFACTURED IN THE UNITED STATES OF AMERICA

FIRST AMERICAN EDITION

To the women, all of them,
who lived and wrote this book.

CONTENTS

Author's Note
and Acknowledgments

The documents that have been collected and reprinted here have not been revised or corrected, except for obvious typographical errors. In most cases, their original spelling, punctuation, and grammar have been retained. All deletions from the documents, with the exception of footnotes, have been noted by ellipses, and any explanatory or clarifying additions made by the author are enclosed in brackets.

Many people helped me, in many different ways, in the writing of this book. I thank them all—my dear friends whose interest and enthusiasm for this project encouraged my own, and the many librarians who have assisted me. I am especially grateful to the staff and the Executive Office of the Research Libraries at the New York Public Library, where much of this research was accomplished and where the bulk of the illustrations in this book were obtained.

I would also like to acknowledge help, generously given, by Ellen Chesler, Jo Freeman, Barbara Gainer, Lindy Hess, Ellyn Polshek, Cintra Michaelis, Alix Kates Shulman, Gloria Steinem, Roberta Weiner, and Ellen Willis.

Special thanks go to Tician, Alexander, and Niko Papachristou for their patience and support; to my colleagues in women's studies at York College, Ellen Mintz, Gloria Waldman, and Elaine Baruch, who contributed greatly to my understanding of women's issues; to Mary Thom, whose knowledge and editorial talents are reflected in the chapter on the contemporary movement; to Regina Ryan, who edited my manuscript with understanding and who generously shared her professional skills and her lovely humanity; to Ann Close, who cheerfully and efficiently turned a manuscript into a book; and to Ronnie Eldridge, who started it all.

INTRODUCTION

This book is part of a reexamination of American history that is going on today. It focuses on American women and, most specifically, on what women in the United States have done together to change their condition and move from a position of inferiority and subservience toward equality and independence.

Through most of history, women's lives have differed from those of men in that it has been women who have given birth and nurtured and reared the new generations. They were often separated from the world of men by custom and law. They have, moreover, been cut off from the centers of power: in ancient and modern societies, politics, religion, education, and economics have been dominated by men.

History up to present times has been largely the story of the powerful and the rich, and, necessarily, the story of men. It has ignored the experience of women as it has ignored the poor or the powerless. Only recently have scholars begun to reexplore the terrain of the past to learn about the lives of ordinary people and to reevaluate their contributions.

In the first half of the nineteenth century, women in the United States (as elsewhere) were vastly inferior in status to men: they could not vote, and played no role in the political affairs of the country; they usually had no economic resources of their own and could not even control what they earned; married women had no legal existence apart from their husbands; generally, women were uneducated and considered intellectually deficient. The wives of our more affluent citizens may have benefited from the material comforts provided by their husbands, but they were subjected to a rigidly restrictive social code that made them among the most confined and isolated women in history. Yet out of their frustrations and sense of oppression, the women's movement was born.

This came about, in large part, from a gradual lowering of barriers, which permitted early-nineteenth-century women to participate in such causes as abolitionism and which led them indirectly to an awareness of the poverty of their own position and a realization of their potential strength. A few women and men had protested the inequality of American females—their subjugation and lack of opportunity and civil rights—before 1800; but it was not until around the middle of the century that the first organizations of women, specifically concerned with women's issues, began to form. The pioneering assemblage, the Seneca Falls Convention, was called in 1848 to discuss "the social, civil, and religious condition and rights of women." After the convention, women continued to come together in groups, to act publicly, and to seek change for themselves and others. This is the beginning of what can properly be called the "women's movement" in the United States.

The story of the movement is told here through historical documents—the speeches, letters, resolutions, plans for action, declarations, and other testimony of the participants themselves. The long and difficult struggle these documents reveal has taken place against the background of a century and a half of incessant social change, with old traditions and institutions continually supplanted or transformed, and Americans constantly confronted with new ways of living and working. Such leading feminists as Lucretia Mott and Elizabeth Cady Stanton lived in a nation that was agricultural, rural, and relatively homogenous in population. By the time of World War I—the era of women like Jane Addams, Carrie Chapman Catt, and Florence Kelley—the United States had become a complex industrialized urban society, with a heterogeneous people, divided by differences of race, wealth, and cultural tradition. Today, as women march and broadcast their demands for reform, the pattern of life continues to change with unsettling rapidity. Reliable methods of birth control, automation, public education, and mass communication make our lives significantly different from those of our parents and grandparents.

And yet, one surprising revelation of these documents is how many things have remained the same: "Women's Liberation" today provokes much the same kind of opposition and anger that "The Woman Question" did well over a century ago, and the goals and attitudes of feminists in the 1970s are in many respects strikingly similar to those of the 1850s.

In women's long and persistent effort to bring about changes in their status, three periods of intense activity stand out: the first began in 1848 and extended into the 1870s; the second, which saw women achieve the vote, stretched from about 1890 to 1920; and the last, the contemporary phase, began in the late 1960s. Each of these periods had its origins in a time of national reform. Before the Civil War, abolitionists agitated in behalf of the black slaves; in the Progressive era, in the early decades of the twentieth century, social workers, muckrakers, and reformers spoke out for the victims of industrialization and slum life; and in the 1950s and 1960s, protesters called attention to minority and poverty groups denied civil rights and economic opportunity. Each time, women were attracted to reform activities and joined in them, and each time, as a result of their involvement, whether as abolitionists, Progressives, or civil rights workers, they came to discover and deplore their own inferiority and demand equality and freedom for all women.

In the first phase, women fought to establish their legal existence as persons by gaining the right to own and control their own property and earnings, the right to share with their husbands in control over their children, the right to be guardians of their children in case of the husband's death, and the right to vote. They also demanded the right to an education that could prepare them for profitable and satisfying lives, and the right to work for decent pay in the jobs and professions of their choice.

From 1890 to 1920, the vote and the right to participate in public affairs were the main goals of organized women's activities; to many, woman suffrage appeared as the key to achieving all other reforms. In the popular mind, of course, this is the most familiar phase of the women's movement, although its emphasis on the vote made it the most limited in its objectives.

Like its predecessors, the contemporary phase of the movement seeks rights still denied to women. Since 1966, women have tried to end discrimination in education and employment and to gain equal treatment under the law. Through equal rights amendments to state and federal constitutions, they are trying to end all legal bases for discrimination and to achieve civil equality. Contemporary women have also expanded significantly the scope of women's rights—and, indeed, of human rights overall—with their advocacy of a general human right to develop freely, without being limited by predetermined and restrictive notions of what a woman or a man is or should be. They have also demanded the right of each woman to sexual freedom and to control over her own reproductive capacity.

Movement activity has consistently been an educative experience, raising to prominence questions about women's status and abilities. Investigating, reporting, and publicizing the facts about women in the United States, movement women have taught themselves and others. At the first women's rights convention, for example, in Seneca Falls, New York, in 1848, and at every state and national meeting thereafter, women reported and described their lack of legal and political rights, their low-quality education and training, their restricted job opportunities and pitiful wages, their confinement to a narrow sphere of experience, as well as their own inhibitions and limited aspirations.

After the Civil War, repeated failures to gain the vote provided a glaringly clear and palpable demonstration of women's second-class status. Outraged and frustrated, women learned the hard lesson that they were outside of public life, powerless to affect the world around them, and restricted to indirect, and often ineffective, means of expressing their needs.

Today, education is still an important aspect of the movement—perhaps more so than ever before. Women's organizations continue to investigate and publicize the facts of women's lives and the nature and extent of sex discrimination. The contemporary movement, moreover, is consciously involved in a process of self-education, focusing on the individual woman's perception of herself. Certainly the nineteenth-century feminist pioneers rued the lack of confidence and the low level of ambition common to females, and understood the importance of changing women as well as the laws and customs affecting them; but only in our own time has a substantial, calculated, and organized effort been launched to effect change within the individual woman. Today, indeed, self-education is seen by some as a prerequisite to all reform and by others to be at least as important as the reform of laws and institutions. In asserting that "the personal is political" and in purposefully trying to change the way women perceive themselves, the movement today encompasses individual change as both part of its strategy and one of its primary goals.

Actually, participation in the movement has often changed women of its own accord, simply by introducing them to group activity. Historically, women's lives have generally tended to be more isolated than men's, narrower in scope and often cut off from those of other women with similar needs. The movement provided a way of breaking out of this isolation and entering into the public sphere. Movement activities gave many women a practical education in fields such as economics, politics, sociology, psychology, and law that had not previously been accessible to them; and they discovered that they were capable not only of comprehending these subjects, but of mastering skills usually defined and preempted as masculine, such as speaking in public, organizing and conducting large meetings, staging demonstrations, agitating and lobbying, and planning political campaigns. In the face of persistent criticism, they discovered their inner reserves of courage and determination. Repeated failures evoked their anger and militancy. Overcoming the strictures of church and family and conquering their own doubts, women learned to be confident and to esteem themselves.

The very existence of a women's movement has from its beginning challenged traditional concepts of what a woman is and how she should behave. Circulating petitions, lobbying in legislatures, testifying before congressional committees, and marching militantly down the nations's boulevards, women have disputed the prevalent image of themselves as passive, compliant, dependent, and intellectually inferior. At the same time, feminist spokeswomen and writers directly and explicitly proclaimed women's equality with men. The movement has posed a radical challenge to the status quo, and it is quite understandable that the documents that follow should contain evidence of unending resistance and hostility.

When women first organized and spoke out, they provoked a barrage of anger and opposition. Often, the anger was expressed as ridicule. In 1848 and for decades to follow, women activists were pictured as spinsters and ugly, bitter malcontents. In the early decades of the present century, clubwomen and suffragists regularly suffered humiliation in cartoons and caricatures. Today, similarly, feminists are often regarded as foolish, unattractive, or deviant, and labeled as man-haters and bra-burners.

Opponents have consistently tried to distort the meaning of the movement. Repeatedly they have insisted that the demand for equality was, in fact, a challenge to morality; feminists were described as women with unnatural and uncontrollable sexual needs, free-lovers, libertines determined to destroy the moral foundations of society, interested only in their own sexual gratification—Eve all over again. In 1915, for example, when a bitter and difficult battle for the vote was being fought in New York State, suffragists were charged with advocating "free love," and the Empire State Suffrage Committee felt compelled to defend its sexual standards and devotion to Christian ethics. In the 1920s, the women's movement was smeared as a Communist front, and feminists were labeled "Bolshevik sympathizers" and dupes of Moscow.

Beyond the anger, ridicule, abuse, and distortion, opponents have simply refused to make the changes women have sought. Male-dominated legislatures, courts, industries, and educational institutions have failed, whether purposefully or negligently, to meet the needs of women.

It is important to realize the significance of this opposition. Those who have fought reforms for women did so because they understood that sexual equality of necessity involved changes in the institutions that controlled women's lives and maintained the status quo, like the family, the church, the schools, and, indeed, the entire economic system. They realized that a changing role for women meant a changing role for men as well, and that as women's lives altered, the entire fabric of society would have to be readjusted accordingly.

We must remember also that the women's movement has not taken place in isolation but in a complicated and ever-developing society, where changing patterns of life have created tensions between workers and employers, parents and children, immigrants and natives, blacks and whites, rich and poor. The movement, with its promise of change for men as well as women, has threatened those whose lives were already in flux and, coming at periods of general agitation for reform, has added to the strain and confusion of a growing nation; it is hardly surprising, then, that it should have brought down upon itself an enormous amount of frustration and anger.

By and large, organized women have understood and accepted the radical implications of their demands for reform. They have often, and accurately, described themselves as crusaders, fighters, and revolutionaries, and have been willing to use innovative and militant tactics. In the middle of the last century, when women found themselves in defiance of church and community merely by meeting together to protest, they went even further to demand radical change in their lives. Women today repeat the breadth and daring of the earliest feminists: they propose an end to masculine supremacy and a new concept of male as well as female nature. They challenge existing institutions and advocate change in every aspect of life—in politics, education, economics, and social relations. Coupled with this broad scope of concern is the use of new and dramatic techniques of protest and agitation. Women have actively adopted militant tactics and are experimenting with new forms of group organization and leadership.

In contrast to the radicalism of both the earliest and latest phases of the movement, the early decades of this century, the time of the big suffrage drive, seem more restrictive and moderate in tone (although some suffrage groups—the National Woman's Party, for example—pioneered in the use of militant tactics, picketing the White House, staging massive parades and demonstrations, and even going on hunger strikes). During this time, such radical feminist reformers as Charlotte Perkins Gilman and Margaret Sanger evoked a relatively weak response from women's organizations. But it is important to remember that the stand on suffrage was more radical at the time than it seems to us today. Fighting for the vote and participating in progressive reform activities, women were demanding a share of the political power monopolized by men. Those who opposed woman suffrage so tenaciously and ferociously realized what was at stake: the demand for the vote was a radical challenge to things as they were.

The documents that follow show that the women's movement, like all reform movements in American history, has never been a mass movement. In the 1870s and 1880s, probably no more than 10,000 women were at any one time directly involved with the two major suffrage organizations. By the end of the century, the Women's Christian Temperance Union, the most successful and influential nineteenth-century organization, had only 200,000 members. During the Progressive era, when public activities for women had become more acceptable, numbers grew. National suffrage organizations enrolled more than two million members, and between two and three million women were introduced to public affairs through membership in women's clubs.

Both the membership and the leadership of the movement have tended to come from the affluent middle of the population—neither from the very rich nor from the very poor; and in racial or ethnic terms, it has been, with few exceptions, native-born white women, better educated and with more leisure than most, who have filled its ranks. The movement has reflected their interests and attitudes and has concentrated on the goals most important to them. Often it has neglected the problems and needs of other women, although movement spokeswomen have usually spoken in principle for all women and proclaimed the solidarity of women in the United States as well as in the world.

Out of its close ties with abolitionism, the women's movement gained the support of black members, male and female, who played a conspicuous role in women's rights activities during the 1850s and 1860s. Most of these ties were broken by 1870, however, and from that time on, organized women remained generally cut off not only from black women but also from the growing numbers of poor white and immigrant women in the country. By the turn of the century, the white middle-class majority of the movement was generally out of touch with the poor and the most disadvantaged. Despite a belated realization of the value of solidarity during the final suffrage campaigns, and despite the humanitarian doctrines of Progressivism which impelled many middle-class women to become involved in the plight of women wage earners, sisterhood was more an abstract ideal than an operating principle.

The leaders of the contemporary movement, with their origins in the civil rights and New Left activities of the 1960s, again claim to speak for all women. While its leadership, admittedly, is still largely white and middle-class, it is now drawn from minority groups as well, and its goals—especially the attack on discrimination, the fight for legalized abortion, and the fight against the poverty of women—have come substantially to reflect the major concerns of underprivileged women.

It is difficult to compare the membership of the movement today with that of the past: organized feminist activity resumed only in the late 1960s after a long period of quiescence, and there is, in addition, the speed and efficiency—unique to our time—with which ideas can now be communicated. Today, it is easy to participate in movement activities without joining organizations. Insofar as consciousness-raising is part of the movement, for example, millions of women (and men) can be counted as participants, and women of all classes and backgrounds are involved in efforts to bring about social change.

In several ways, the documents that follow reveal similarities between the history of the women's movement and other important reform movements in the United States. Disagreements between radical and moderate women over goals and tactics, and the resulting compromises and schisms, have repeated in part the experiences of abolitionists, labor organizers and reformers, peace activists, and civil rights workers. Along with these other reform drives, the women's movement is part of a great continuing drama in which the oppressed seek the chance to be what they will. It has needed courageous and confident women to carry on the struggle in a world in which women have not been taught to be courageous or confident. Nonetheless, such women have and do exist, and the history that follows is their story.

WOMEN TOGETHER

CHAPTER ONE

THE WOMEN'S MOVEMENT IS BORN
The 1830's

If you were born a female in the early decades of the nineteenth century in America, many things about you were decided before you could walk or talk. You were a religious person, specially tuned by nature to spiritual matters; you were pure of heart, free from sensual needs. You were going to be a wife and a mother; you would be sympathetic, and would put aside your own needs and wants without hesitation to minister to the needs and wants of others.

All your interests and talents centered on the home, the family, and the church. Together they constituted your part of the world. As for the rest—what went on outside the home and the church—that was man's world, and you were ignorant of it, neither interested in it nor able to understand it. In everything connected with that world, you needed guardianship. Your father, and later your husband, was in charge of you; you could not own or control wealth by yourself; you could not sign a will or have custody of your children; you couldn't vote. You were not a whole person legally or politically.

God had made man woman's superior, and you were a subordinate member of society, without many of the freedoms and rights that men laid claim to and of which they boasted so proudly.

Hardly any women conformed to these ideals of womanhood; frontier women, black slaves, and poor women were destined to the sweat and labor of poverty as well as

to motherhood and domesticity. In a country where labor was in small supply, women worked the fields, the shops, and the home industries. Such women were neither ignorant of the ugly realities of life nor incapable of coping with them.

In the increasingly prosperous parts of the population, there were women who refused to accept this rigid prescription for their lives; they strove to break through the walls that surrounded them, to defy social convention, to seek an education, and to question and take part in the world around them. By the 1830's their numbers were increasing, and the women's movement began to take form.

WOMEN AND ABOLITIONISM

It was, strangely enough, out of her concern for others that the American woman found concern for herself. In the 1820's and 1830's, especially in New York, Pennsylvania, and New England, an exciting and contagious spirit of reform was in the air. It started in the churches and was involved at first with such Christian and humanitarian issues as temperance, peace, capital punishment, and education. In church, women became part of the reform movement.

Although some causes, like temperance and peace, seemed particularly fitting for women to take up, the cause that attracted many to its side, with compelling force and drastic repercussions, was that of the black slave in America—the most far-reaching and potentially disruptive of all reforms. It was through abolitionism that white American women realized their own inequality and began the first organized effort to change their dependent and inferior place in American life.

Four women were present at the founding of the American Anti-Slavery Society in Philadelphia in 1833. None of them signed the organizing document, but one did speak at the meeting, after receiving permission to do so. A participant,

J. Miller McKim, wrote an account of this unusual event. The speaker he described was Lucretia Mott, a Quaker minister and dedicated abolitionist.

LUCRETIA MOTT AT THE AMERICAN ANTI-SLAVERY SOCIETY

The other speaker was a woman. I had never before heard a woman speak at a public meeting. She said but a few words, but these were spoken so modestly, in such sweet tones, and yet withal so decisively, that no one could fail to be pleased. . . . She apologized for what might be regarded as an intrusion; but was assured by the chairman and others that what she had said was very acceptable. The chairman added his hope that 'the lady' would not hesitate to give expression to anything that might occur to her during the course of the proceedings.[1]

FEMALE ANTISLAVERY SOCIETIES

By the time the first national antislavery association was founded in Philadelphia, women were already involved in abolitionism; in New England they had formed several

affec? thine
Lucretia Mott.

female antislavery societies. The four women who had attended the Philadelphia meeting reconvened when it was over and proceeded to organize their own Philadelphia Female Anti-Slavery Society.

Soon societies existed in New York, Ohio, Indiana, and Illinois. The Michigan Territory could boast of one of the earliest. Most of the work women did for abolitionism they did as members of these organizations, of which there were about a hundred by the end of the 1830's.[2]

The first such society was founded by black women in Salem, Massachusetts, in 1832; similar groups followed. Most of the members of the female societies were, of course, white, reflecting the predominance of white people in the population, and they were also often the better-educated and more prosperous women of the community. A few societies, like those in Boston and Philadelphia, had black as well as white members.

After 1833, in town after town, small groups of women formed small local antislavery societies; most of them followed the pattern that is shown here in the constitution of the Philadelphia Female Anti-Slavery Society.

PHILADELPHIA CONSTITUTION

WHEREAS, more than two millions of our fellow countrymen, of these United States, are held in abject bondage; and whereas, we believe that slavery and prejudice against color are contrary to the laws of God, and to the principles of our far-famed Declaration of Independence, and recognising the right of the slave to immediate emancipation; we deem it our duty to manifest our abhorrence of the flagrant injustice and deep sin of slavery, by united and vigorous exertions for its speedy removal, and for the restoration of the people of color to their inalienable rights. For these purposes, we, the undersigned, agree to associate ourselves under the name of "THE PHILADELPHIA FEMALE ANTI-SLAVERY SOCIETY."

Article I.

The object of this Society shall be to collect and disseminate correct information of the character of slavery, and of the actual condition of the slaves and free people of color, for the purpose of inducing the community to adopt such measures, as may be in their power, to dispel the prejudice against the people of color, to improve their condition, and to bring about the speedy abolition of slavery.

Article II.

Any female uniting in these views, and contributing to the funds, shall be a member of the Society.

Article III.

The officers of the Society shall be a President, a Vice President, a Recording Secretary, a Corresponding Secretary, a

Treasurer, and Librarian, who, with six other members, shall constitute a Board of Managers, to whom shall be intrusted the business of the Society, and the management of its funds. They shall keep a record of their proceedings, which shall be laid before the Society, at each stated meeting. They shall have power to fill any vacancy that may occur in their number, till the next annual meeting. . . .

Article X.

The Managers shall meet once a month, or oftener if necessary, on a day fixed by themselves, and stated meetings of the Society shall be held on the second Fifth-day in every month. . . .

Article XII.

It is especially recommended that the members of this Society should entirely abstain from purchasing the products of slave labor, that we may be able consistently to plead the cause of our brethren in bonds. . . .[3]

In New England, within five years, there were more than forty societies. Abolitionist newspapers often carried news about them; The Liberator, *edited by William Lloyd Garrison and published in Boston, regularly did so, and its pages offer a picture of the activities and attitudes of the antislavery societies.*

"ANOTHER FEMALE SOCIETY"

East Bradford, Mass., Oct. 12, 1836

Mr. Garrison:—Knowing that you watch with deep anxiety and thrilling interest, the success of the anti-slavery cause, and hail the formation of every new society as an advancement of at least one degree, in the thermometer of public opinion; we cheerfully transmit to you (by vote of the Society) the Constitution of one formed here Saturday, Oct. 3. It commenced its existence under favorable auspices, having enrolled on its records *seventy-five* names.

We are well aware that it is tauntingly asked, by some, what has *Woman* to do with this subject? Let the suffering mothers of the South answer, as on every breeze are borne sighs and tears of bitterness wrung from them, not so much by what they endure bodily, as the rending of earthly ties, the breaking up of families, and the unknown, yet dreadful destiny of children, forever torn from them by Slavery's hateful laws. These, these cause years of sadness, and fill the soul with mental agony, almost beyond endurance, and found only in the bosom of the slave. Let the Bible answer! whose pages breathe nothing but 'peace on earth, good will to men,' and whose rewards and threatenings make known our *duty to our fellow-beings,* in language not to be misunderstood.

Let her blush to be a woman, who cannot sympathize with suffering humanity; who cannot *in* (not out of) her sphere, plead the cause of truth, of justice, and of human rights.

We trust the time is not far distant, when all our fair sisters shall see eye to eye; when unity of heart and of action shall bind in one unbroken link, all the daughters of Adam; yea, when man shall cease to be an enemy to man, to 'task him and exact his sweat'; when *self* shall cease to be the Great Diana, around which every finer feeling of the soul must cluster; and *love, unbounded love,* to God and man, fill every breast.

ELLEN B. LADD, Sec'y.[4]

"THE LADIES' FAIR"

The proposed Anti-Slavery Fair was held on Thursday, the 22nd of December. . . . Around the Hall was placed in large letters the motto: On this day did our Fathers *land* on the Rock of Freedom. Let us *stand* firmly on this Rock. . . .

There was great variety in the articles, and many of them were very handsome and tasteful. The ladies have ever regarded the pecuniary benefit derived from these sales as but *one* of several reasons in their favor. The main object is to keep the subject before the public eye, and by every innocent expedient to promote perpetual discussion. We wish to

bring Truth and Falsehood in continual *juxtaposition,* for we know full well that 'truth never came off the worse in a fair and open encounter.'

To promote this favorite object, various mottoes and devices were stamped upon the article offered for sale. Bunches of quilts bore the label, 'Twenty-five Weapons for Abolitionists.' On the wafer-boxes was written, 'The doom of Slavery is *sealed.*' On one side of the pen-wipers was inscribed, 'Wipe out the blot of Slavery'; on the other, 'Plead the cause with thy Pen.' On some needle-books was printed, 'May the use of our needles prick the consciences of slaveholders'; others were made in the form of small shoes, and on the soles was written, 'Trample not on the Oppressed.' . . . 5

FROM *HUMAN RIGHTS*

Many have done nobly, but it seems to us just now that the ladies of Boston have exceeded them all. We mean the Boston Female Anti-Slavery Society,—the most undaunted little band who met and prayed for the slave in the midst of a mob of '5000 gentlemen of property and standing' on the memorable twenty-second of October, 1835. [The reference is to a mob attack that disrupted a Female Society meeting and then seized abolitionist William Lloyd Garrison, who had to be rescued from it. The mob included so-called gentlemen as well as more ordinary people.] They have issued a second 'Right and Wrong in Boston' for 1836. We have extracted from it on the opposite page an account of the way in which they were excited to revise the laws for the protection of liberty in Massachusetts, whereby every slave, brought by his master, is free from the moment he touches her soil. They must have the credit of bringing forward the case which resulted in the honorable decision of Judge Shaw. But this is only a small part of their achievements. They have excited their sisters throughout the state to petition Congress for the abolition of slavery in the District of Columbia. As part of the result, we learn from the Liberator, that petitions have been founded, signed by upwards of *Five Thousand females.*

They have also had a fair for the sale of articles commemorative of the slave, from which they realized $550. This looks like being in earnest. Set it down that the cause *will go.* 6

After 1835, abolitionists launched a petition campaign to pressure Congress for action against slavery in the District of Columbia. The right to request government action by petition was guaranteed in the First Amendment to the Constitution and was well established in tradition. But proslavery forces were infuriated by the petitions, which implied that Congress as well as the states could legislate about slavery and which threatened to involve politicians in debates over slavery.

Women formed the bulk of the hard-working volunteer agents in the nationwide petition campaign. Led by Lucretia Mott and Lydia Maria Child, organized into regional and local committees, they set out systematically to collect signatures. Women themselves signed over half of the tens of thousands of petitions that were sent to Congress. Knocking at unknown doors, importuning and arguing with strangers about national politics, and encountering harsh disapproval and abuse, the petitioners moved along unaccustomed and dangerous paths for women.

"EXTRACTS FROM A YOUNG LADY'S JOURNAL"

[A young lady in a neighboring town, who is busily employed in circulating petitions, has sent us the following extracts from her journal, which we publish with much pleasure:]

'Well now,' said one old woman, as she returned to her room after filling her inkstand and ransacking the house for the stump of a pen, 'I don't know as I understand *that*; my *darter* says that you want the niggers and white to marry together. I didn't take it so. *Do ye?*'

'Why no—that's no business of ours. We leave all to do as they please with regard to it. This is a *petition,* asking Congress to give the slaves in the District of Columbia their freedom. I suppose you know that the colored people in the District are held as property, bought and sold like beasts, and treated very cruelly. Now what we ask is, that Congress, which 'possesses exclusive jurisdiction' there, should give all those slaves their freedom and place them under the protection of law.'

'*Well,* that's just as I thought 'twas, and I told my darter she was mistaken, but she could not believe me; I am sorry she thinks so about it.' . . .

Another woman, whom we met at the door, didn't want to have any thing to do with any paper of the kind; while her husband shouted from his easy chair in the parlour, that '*they were all opposed there to ladies doing delicate business.*'

Pray what would they have us do? . . .

A certain Mr. ——— met us at the door of his own house, and when we asked him if there were any ladies within who would like to sign such a petition, he answered in a very decided, contemptuous manner, 'NO'—without even so much as asking them. He apparently belonged to that too numerous class of men (?) who claim the right to 'possess exclusive jurisdiction in all cases whatsoever' over their wives' consciences; so we left him, and wishing him a good evening, walked on.

At one place, the father hoped there was nobody in his house who would sign such a paper; it was an insult to the public to send such papers to Congress, and a very great imposition, altogether too bad, to send young people about in that manner, on such despicable business. When we told him that we did it from choice, because we thought it our duty to do what was in our power for the oppressed, he bade us begone and to mind and never bring *such a thing to his house again.* We disclaimed all intentions of insulting any one, and told him we only wished to give them an opportunity to do their duty. He followed us to the door and dismissed us with a great deal of good advice, saying, 'It's none of your business, *galls,* and you'd better go *right straight home.'* . . .[7]

A three-day convention of female antislavery groups—the first Anti-Slavery Convention of American Women—was held in New York City in May 1837, partly to coordinate the petition campaign. More than 200 women from ten states attended the unusual event. Among the resolutions passed was one that reveals how the women regarded their own actions.

A RESOLUTION

Resolved that as certain rights and duties are common to all moral beings, the time has come to move in that sphere which Providence has assigned her, and no longer remain satisfied in the circumscribed limits with which corrupt custom and a perverted application of scripture have encircled her; therefore it is the duty of woman, and the province of woman, to plead the cause of the oppressed in our land, and do all that she can by her voice, and her pen, and her purse, and the influence of her example, to overthrow the horrible system of American slavery.[8]

The press regarded this unique occurrence with mixed feelings.

THE NATIONAL ENQUIRER

[The importance of the antislavery cause] requires a *newness* of life, activity and energy; *new* plans and modes of proceeding; *new* channels for conveyance of moral truth to the ossified heart of the oppressor. . . . Let no genuine Female Philanthropist hold back, from a timid apprehension of exceeding the limits of propriety,—of deviating from the acknowledged principles of female duty,—or of transgressing the legitimate privileges and immunities of her sex.[9]

NEW YORK *COMMERCIAL ADVERTISER*

. . . The spinster has thrown aside her distaff—the blooming beauty her guitar—the matron her darning needle—the sweet novelist her crow-quill; the young mother has left her baby to nestle alone in the cradle—and the kitchen maid her pots and frying-pans—to discuss the weighty matters of state —to decide upon intricate questions of international policy —and weigh, with avoirdupoise exactness, the balance of power.[10]

In their annual report, members of the Philadelphia antislavery society commented on the occurrence of the first antislavery convention of women. Their remarks reveal that neither unfavorable publicity nor unpleasant criticism diminished their dedication or discouraged them from "a measure so novel" as a women's convention.

PHILADELPHIA WOMEN AND THE WOMEN'S CONVENTION

A new measure for the advancement of our cause has this year been adopted by the Female Anti-Slavery Societies of this country, viz.: the holding of an "Anti-Slavery Convention of American Women." The object of this meeting was to afford the different associations an opportunity of conferring together respecting their modes of operation, and devising plans of united action; and also, that those women of America, whose souls are sickened by the oppressions that are done under the sun, might have an opportunity of together lifting up their voices, in remonstrance and entreaty, in behalf of their brethren and sisters in bonds, and of the eternal principles of justice. A measure so novel, adopted by women, would, of course, excite surprise in many minds, and from some elicit censure. This we expected; for it we were prepared; nor have the editorial rebukes, sarcasm, and ridicule, which have been awarded us, exceeded our anticipations. To calm and manly argument we would have attentively listened, and respectfully replied; but to the coarse invective and rude jesting of which we were the subject, we deem it unfit to oppose sober reasoning, or even serious expostulation. For those, who, for a little hour, found pleasant pastime in such employment, we desire no other recompense than refined tastes, and a clearer conception of the duties and privileges of rational beings. We will not here record their names—they are freely forgiven, as they would have been had their insults or injuries been multiplied a thousand fold. The immediate results of our Convention have been given to the public, and it is needless to recapitulate them. A part of its fruits will probably be seen in the increased number of memorials which will be sent to Congress during its present session. In pursuance of a plan proposed by the Convention, this Society, in the month of June, made arrangements with the Female Anti-Slavery Society of Pittsburg, to furnish every county in Pennsylvania with memorials to Congress, praying for the abolition of slavery in the District of Columbia, and the Territories of the United States, and for the abolition of the slave trade between the States. In that portion of the State allotted to us, (judging from the reports of members to whom it was entrusted,) this work has been performed as thoroughly as our means of action permitted. The number of signatures obtained in Philadelphia exceeds that of the last year by about one thousand. The benefits to the Anti-Slavery cause, arising from this department of our labor, are not to be calculated by the number of signatures appended to our memorials. We do not regard those visits as lost labor, where our request is denied, or that time wasted which is spent in unsuccessful efforts to convince persons of their duty to comply with it. Often, very often, the seed then laboriously sown, falls into good ground, and after a little season springs up, bringing forth fruit, some thirty, some sixty, some an hundred fold. Wherever our arguments find a lodgment in the mind, or our expostulations arouse the sympathies of the heart, there a victory (small though it may be) is won for the Anti-Slavery cause.[11]

The Anti-Slavery Convention of American Women met twice again, in 1838 and 1839, in Philadelphia. The 1838 meeting took place in Pennsylvania Hall, a new building that reformers had recently constructed as a forum for themselves and their controversial ideas. The first session was peaceful, but an evening assembly in the hall, where both male and female abolitionists attempted to speak, was disrupted by a wild and violent mob. The second session was accompanied by shouting and stoning, and that evening the rage of the mob exploded. Pennsylvania Hall was sacked and burned—the new symbol of abolitionism and free speech had been destroyed.

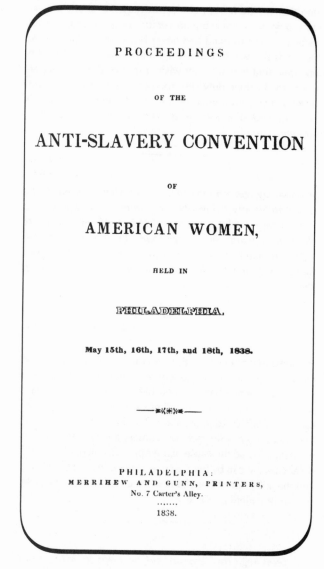

PROCEEDINGS

OF THE

ANTI-SLAVERY CONVENTION

OF

AMERICAN WOMEN,

HELD IN

PHILADELPHIA,

May 15th, 16th, 17th, and 18th, 1838.

———✳✳✳———

PHILADELPHIA:
MERRIHEW AND GUNN, PRINTERS,
No. 7 Carter's Alley.
. . . .
1838.

OTHER ABOLITIONIST ACTIVITY

Joining an antislavery society was only one way in which a woman could show her opposition to slavery and her concern for black Americans. Women contributed a substantial number of books, tracts, and articles to abolitionist literature; prominent among them were Lydia Maria Child, Catherine Beecher, Harriet Beecher Stowe, and Jane Grey Swisshelm.

Individually and often unnoticed, many other women performed acts of personal bravery. Speaking out against the slave system, befriending blacks, aiding fugitive slaves, and supporting and defending abolitionists, they defied the accepted standards of womanly behavior and took on themselves much of the anger and distrust that antislavery agitation provoked.

They also served as teachers in black schools. In Ohio, there was an active movement of young women in black communities who worked as teachers, missionaries, and social reformers, often supported by funds raised in the

East by antislavery societies. Eliza Ann Griffith, one such woman in Ohio, wrote the following letter from Mount Pleasant in May 1837.

A LETTER, 1837

Esteemed Cousins

I do not feel much in the notion of writing this evening, but I reckon if I do not take this opportunity, I shall not have any before our cousins return from their visit at Unckle George's. . . .

The Anniversary of the Ohio Anti-Slavery Society held its meetings at Short creek meeting house on the 27th 28th and 29th of last month, it was a very interesting meeting, I believe there were about two hundred and fifty delegates from the different Anti-Slavery Societies in the state and there were a great many in attendance who were not delegates, there were a hundred young women there who have been teaching coloured schools in different parts of this state there were two young women by the name of Wright have been teaching school in Chilicothe they are sisters, there were two other sisters by the name of Wright who are teaching school in Cincinnati   Axia Colburn is teaching school in Putname   Sarah Galbraith is teaching in Dayton   Emily Robinson has been teaching in Cincinnati   Phebe Weed has been teaching in Cincinnati   Emeline McConnel has been teaching in Logan County   Hannah Barker has been teaching in Brown County   I heard her say that there was not a white family within six miles of her that she could have any intercourse with   there were two young men here who have been teaching coloured schools one in Cincinnati the other in Canada, these that I have mentioned I believe are all the nigger teachers that I became acquainted with, the most of these have gone a great distance from home and have undergone a great many trials and have barely received enough to buy them provisions and some not enough there are but a few of them that could get boarding with white families some have boarded with coloured people but the most of them have rented rooms and boarded themselves   it is almost impossible for some to get rooms. Those two girls from Chilicothe were driven from place to place, some places

they could stay a week some places two weeks at others but a few days till at last there was no place they could get only as a family took them out of pity till they could find a place, all the spare time they had they tried but no place could they get except a room at the gaol, but this man who had taken them in was not willing they should go there. . . . [12]

THE GRIMKÉ SISTERS: WOMEN ATTACKED

Most of the women who dared to work for abolitionism have disappeared from history, and only a few are known today, women such as Maria Weston Chapman, Lydia Maria Child, Charlotte Forten, Lucretia Mott, Lucy Stone, Sojourner Truth, and Harriet Tubman. Among the best-known are Angelina and Sarah Grimké. The two sisters moved to Philadelphia from South Carolina, where they were members of a prominent family. Through the Quakers, they were involved with abolitionism, but their activities quickly expanded beyond the female society and church meetings of Philadelphia.

A.E. Grimké   Sarah M. Grimké

Both their firsthand knowledge of slavery as Southerners and their sex attracted attention. The Grimké sisters frequently addressed meetings organized by female antislavery groups. From the end of 1836 until March 1837, they spoke in New York and New Jersey. In the spring of 1837, they began a much-talked-about tour of New England. In Boston, for example, 550 women came to hear them in June. As their fame spread to the small towns, other women, and men too, flocked to see them and listen to their accounts and their arguments. Angelina Grimké delivered a series of subscribed lectures at the Odeon in Boston. At the same time, abolitionist newspapers were printing her writings.

The sisters became controversial as their fame and public appearances increased; any kind of publicity was dubious for a proper woman; involvement with political and economic issues was especially questionable; and their activities, particularly their speaking publicly to audiences of men and women ("promiscuous assemblies"), brought growing criticism upon them.

There had always been criticism of women who were active in abolitionism, itself a subject which elicited passionate and sometimes hysterical feelings. Even the Quakers, who permitted women to act as ministers and speak in religious meetings, questioned the propriety of some female antislavery activities. The petition campaign increased this uneasiness and aroused indignation at women who "meddled in men's affairs" and immodestly went from door to door. Some women themselves were uncertain about what they were doing. The Grimkés' fame and activities brought to a climax the doubts, abuse, sarcasm, anger, and predictions of disaster directed at women abolitionists.

As supporters (most of them fellow abolitionists) defended the Grimkés' right to speak, detractors multiplied their attacks upon the sisters' activities. Of these attacks, the official denunciation of the Congregational Church was the most important. In a pastoral letter read aloud in all its churches, the governing body of the major religion in New England criticized many of the methods and objectives of abolitionism and singled out the activity of women abolitionists for special attack.

Thus the church raised to prominence a debate that already had begun in the newspapers, pulpits, and homes: Did women have the right to speak out and participate in public affairs? What was the proper sphere for women?

Following the pastoral letter, local ministers aped the condemnation of church leaders, and church buildings were closed to the Grimkés and other antislavery speakers. In general, however, the female societies ignored the clergy's warnings and continued their work, and the sisters continued to speak. To many who flocked to their speeches, curious to see these notorious women, the issue at hand was no longer slavery alone; it was also a matter of women's rights.

Angelina Grimké's fame began with the publication of a letter she wrote to William Lloyd Garrison after reading about mob attacks on abolitionists in Boston. Garrison's plea for restraint and nonviolence, which he published in *The Liberator,* had so stirred Angelina Grimké that she wrote to him. He, in turn, was so impressed with her letter that he printed it. Grimké's letter was then reprinted in other newspapers and in pamphlet form.

In 1836, she wrote a lengthy address urging Southern women to take a stand against slavery. The American Anti-Slavery Society printed and distributed it in large numbers. Newspapers extracted it, and an edition was printed in England. The next year, the Convention of Female Anti-slavery Societies voted to publish her "Appeal to the Women of the Nominally Free States." In both documents, Grimké urged American women to assume their responsibilities and work actively against slavery.

"AN APPEAL TO THE CHRISTIAN WOMEN OF THE SOUTH"

. . . why appeal to *women* on this subject? *We* do not make the laws which perpetuate slavery. *No* legislative power is vested in *us; we* can do nothing to overthrow the system, even if we wished to do so. To this I reply, I know you do not make the laws, but I also know that *you are the wives and mothers, the sisters and daughters of those who do;* and if you really suppose *you* can do nothing to overthrow slavery, you are greatly mistaken. You can do much in every way: four things I will name. . . .

1. Read then on the subject of slavery. . . .

Read the *Bible* then, it contains the words of Jesus, and they are spirit and life. Judge for yourselves whether *he sanctioned* such a system of oppression and crime.

2. Pray over this subject. When you have entered into your closets, and shut to the doors, then pray to your father, who seeth in secret, that he would open your eyes to see whether slavery is *sinful,* and if it is, that he would enable you to bear a faithful, open and unshrinking testimony against it, and to do whatsoever your hands find to do, leaving the consequences entirely to him, who still says to us whenever we try to reason away duty from the fear of consequences, *'What is that to thee, follow thou me.'* . . .

3. Speak on this subject. It is through the tongue, the pen, and the press, that truth, is principally propagated. Speak then to your relatives, your friends, your acquaintances on the subject of slavery; be not afraid if you are conscientiously convinced it is *sinful,* to say so openly, but calmly, and to let your sentiments be known. . . .

Above all, try to persuade your husband, father, brothers and sons, that *slavery is a crime against God and man,* and that it is a great sin to keep *human beings* in such abject ignorance; to deny them the privilege of learning to read and write. . . .

4. Act on this subject. Some of you *own* slaves yourselves. If you believe slavery is *sinful,* set them at liberty, 'undo the heavy burdens and let the oppressed go free.' If they wish to remain with you, pay them wages, if not let them leave you. Should they remain teach them, and have them taught the common branches of an English education; they have minds and those minds, *ought to* be improved. . . .

But some of you will say, we can neither free our slaves nor teach them to read, for the laws of our state forbid it. Be not suprised when I say such wicked laws *ought to be no barrier* in the way of your duty, and I appeal to the Bible to prove this position. . . .

I know that this doctrine of obeying *God,* rather than man, will be considered as dangerous, and heretical by many, but I am not afraid openly to avow it, because it is the doctrine of the Bible; but I would not be understood to advocate resistance to any law however oppressive, if, in obeying it, I was not obliged to commit *sin.* If for instance, there was a law, which imposed imprisonment or a fine upon me if I manumitted a slave, I would on no account resist that law, I would set the slave free, and then go to prison or pay the fine. If a law commands me to *sin I will break it;* if it calls me to *suffer,* I will let it take its course *unresistingly.* The doctrine of blind obedience and unqualified submission to *any human* power, whether civil or ecclesiastical, is the doctrine of despotism, and ought to have no place among Republicans and Christians. . . .

But you may say we are *women,* how can *our* hearts endure persecution? And why not? Have not *women* stood up in all the dignity and strength of moral courage to be the leaders of the people, and to bear a faithful testimony for truth whenever the providence of God has called them to do so? Are there no *women* in that noble army of martyrs who are now singing the song of Moses and the Lamb? Who led the women of Israel from the house of bondage, striking the timbrel, and singing the song of deliverance on the banks of that sea whose waters stood up like walls of crystal to open a passage for their escape? It was a *woman;* Miriam, the prophetess, the sister of Moses and Aaron. . . .

Who first proclaimed Christ as the true Messiah in the streets of Samaria, once the capital of the ten tribes? It was a *woman!* Who ministered to the Son of God whilst on earth, a despised and persecuted Reformer, in the humble garb of a carpenter? They were *women!* Who followed the rejected King of Israel, as his fainting footsteps trod the road to Calvary? 'A great company of people and of *women*'; and it is remarkable that to *them alone,* he turned and addressed the pathetic language, 'Daughters of Jerusalem, weep not for me, but weep for yourselves and your children.' . . .

And who last hung round the cross of Jesus on the mountain of Golgotha? Who first visited the sepulchre early in the morning on the first day of the week, carrying sweet spices to embalm his precious body, not knowing that it was incorruptible and could not be holden by the bands of death? These were *women!* To whom did he *first* appear after his resurrection? It was to a *woman!* Mary Magdalene; Mark

xvi, 9. Who gathered with the apostles to wait at Jerusalem, in prayer and supplication, for 'the promise of the Father'; the spiritual blessing of the Great High Priest of his Church, who had entered *not* into the splendid temple of Solomon, there to offer the blood of bulls, and of goats, and the smoking censer upon the golden altar, but into Heaven itself, there to present his intercessions, after having "given himself for us, an offering and a sacrifice to God for a sweet smelling savor"? *Women* were among that holy company; Acts i, 14. . . .

Were women recognized as fellow laborers in the gospel field? They were! Paul says in his epistle to the Philippians, 'help those *women* who labored with me, in the gospel'; Phil. iv, 3. . . .

The women of the North have engaged in this work [antislavery efforts] from a sense of *religious duty,* and nothing will ever induce them to take their hands from it until it is fully accomplished. They feel no hostility to you, no

---

AN

APPEAL TO THE WOMEN

OF THE

NOMINALLY FREE STATES,

ISSUED BY AN

ANTI-SLAVERY CONVENTION

OF

AMERICAN WOMEN,

Held by adjournments from the 9th to the 12th of May, 1837.

We are thy sisters;—God has truly said,
That of one blood the nations He has made.
Oh! Christian woman, in a Christian land,
Canst thou unblushing read this great command?
Suffer the wrongs which wring our inmost heart,
To draw one throb of pity on thy part!
Our skins may differ, but from thee we claim,
A sister's privilege, and a sister's name.—*Sarah Forten.*

NEW-YORK:
WILLIAM S. DORR, PRINTER,
No. 123 Fulton-street.
::::::::::::
1837.

bitterness or wrath; they rather sympathize in your trials and difficulties; but they well know that the first thing to be done to help you, is to pour in the light of truth on your minds, to urge you to reflect on, and pray over the subject. This is all *they* can do for you, *you* must work out your own deliverance with fear and trembling, and with the direction and blessing of God, *you can do it.* . . . 13

After 1834, the church in New England had grown increasingly critical of abolitionist activities and their independence from clerical influence. The pastoral letter that was written July 28, 1837, and read from all the Congregational pulpits was one of many condemnations of Garrison and his followers. In this official denunciation, women received special attention.

"A PASTORAL LETTER TO NEW ENGLAND'S CHURCHES"

. . . We invite your attention to the dangers which at present seem to threaten the female character with wide-spread and permanent injury.

The appropriate duties and influence of woman are clearly stated in the New Testament. Those duties and that influence are unobtrusive and private, but the source of mighty power. When the mild, dependent, softening influence of woman upon the sternness of man's opinions is fully exercised, society feels the effects of it in a thousand forms. The power of woman is in her dependence, flowing from the consciousness of that weakness which God has given her for her protection, and which keeps her in those departments of life that form the character of individuals and of the nation. There are social influences which females use in promoting piety and the great objects of Christian benevolence which we cannot too highly commend. We appreciate the unostentatious prayers and efforts of woman in advancing the cause of religion at home and abroad; in Sabbath-schools; in leading religious inquirers to the pastors for instruction; and in all such associated effort as becomes the modesty of her sex; and earnestly hope that she may abound more and more in these labors of piety and love.

But when she assumes the place and tone of man as a public reformer, our care and protection of her seem unnecessary; we put ourselves in self-defence against her; she yields the power which God has given her for protection, and her character becomes unnatural. If the vine, whose strength and beauty is to lean upon the trellis-work and half conceal its clusters, thinks to assume the independence and the overshadowing nature of the elm, it will not only cease to bear fruit, but fall in shame and dishonor into the dust. We cannot, therefore, but regret the mistaken conduct of those who encourage females to bear an obtrusive and ostentatious part in measures of reform, and countenance any of

that sex who so far forget themselves as to itinerate in the character of public lecturers and teachers.—We especially deplore the intimate acquaintance and promiscuous conversation of females with regard to things "which ought not to be named"; by which that modesty and delicacy which is the charm of domestic life, and which constitutes the true influence of woman in society, is consumed, and the way opened, as we apprehend, for degeneracy and ruin. We say these things, not to discourage proper influences against sin, but to secure such reformation as we believe is Scriptural, and will be permanent. 14

DEFENSE OF FEMALE ABOLITIONISTS

Women's right to participate in political affairs had been defended in the U.S. Congress even before the Congregational Church launched its attack and widened the controversy. After 1835, as antislavery petitions flooded in to Congress (many of them objected to the annexation of Texas, a slave area), proslavery forces united to prohibit discussion of the petitions. A fierce battle developed over this effort to gag antislavery speakers. The issue of women's rights also arose; in opposing the petitions, congressmen objected to their having been circulated by women.

John Quincy Adams, the former President and a representative from Massachusetts, led the forces favoring discussion of the petitions and free debate. He also defended the right of women to participate in political activities. Using examples from religious and ancient history to demonstrate the importance of women's political contributions in the past, Adams advocated an active public role for women in an epic speech against the annexation of Texas that he delivered between June 16 and July 7, 1838.

ADAMS'S VIEWS

. . . Why does it follow that women are fitted for nothing but the cares of domestic life? for bearing children, and cooking the food of a family? devoting all their time to the domestic circle—to promoting the immediate personal comfort of their husbands, brothers, and sons? I admit that it is their duty to attend to these things. I subscribe, fully, to the elegant compliment passed upon those members of the female sex who devote their time to these duties. But I say that the correct principle is, that women are not only justified, but exhibit the most exalted virtue when they do depart from the domestic circle, and enter on the concerns of their country, of humanity, and of their God. The mere departure of woman from the duties of the domestic circle, far from being a reproach to her, is a virtue of the highest order, when it is done from purity of motive, by appropriate means, and towards a virtuous purpose. There is true distinction. The motive must be pure, the means appropriate, and the purpose good. And I say that woman, by the discharge of such duties, has manifested a virtue which is even above the virtues of mankind, and approaches to a superior nature. That is the principle I maintain, and which the chairman of the committee has to refute, if he applies the positions he has taken to the mothers, the sisters, and the daughters of the men of my district who voted to send me here.[15]

The most important defense of women's right to take part in public affairs came from women themselves. Unquestionably some were intimidated by the church's condemnation and the ridicule of others; no doubt many women retreated to the kitchen. But those who remained active and who endured the denunciations hurled at them did so with clearer understanding and stronger convictions after they were forced to justify their activities.

Following the issuance of the pastoral letter, female antislavery societies defiantly asserted their determination to continue their work. The Grimké sisters continued to travel and speak for the cause. The church's attack, rather than deterring them, acted as a stimulus. More people than ever before came to see and hear them, and they, more than ever before, claimed the right to speak out.

The following resolutions, adopted by women in Andover, Massachusetts, and the statement of the Grimkés are typical of reactions to the pastoral letter.

"ANDOVER FEMALE ANTI-SLAVERY SOCIETY"

At a meeting of the Andover Female Anti-Slavery Society held Aug. 11th, 1837, the following resolutions were offered and with the accompanying vote for publication were unanimously adopted.

Resolved, That we have seen no reason to regret the invitation which we extended to the Misses Grimke to lecture in this place; but on the contrary their efforts in behalf of emancipation have been eminently successful and encouraging to the friends of the slave.

Resolved, That we feel it is a privilege, no less than a duty, to express our sincere thanks to those noble-minded and indefatigable women for their labors of love amongst us, and that with *one mind and one heart* we join in bidding them 'GOD speed.'

Resolved, That we recommend those self-denying southern sisters to every association of females for the oppressed in our land; and we hope that every where they may be received with open arms and a welcome heart.

Resolved, That we wish to have it known that the lectures at Andover were designed for the Ladies, and that those

Gentlemen who were present must sustain the responsibility of a mixed meeting.

Voted that the above resolutions be forwarded to the Misses Grimke and also to the Liberator and the New England Spectator, for publication.

ELIZABETH W. EMERY, President
Susan Johnson, Cor. Sec.

The above communication was received by Sarah M. and Angelina E. Grimke, from their sisters in Andover, and they embrace the opportunity of informing the Anti-Slavery Societies wherever they may lecture that they are willing to bear the responsibility of holding a 'mixed meeting.' They have no wish to throw the responsibility on either their brethren or sisters. Their communications on the subject of American slavery are designed for all who are willing to give them audience. As moral and accountable beings they believe it to be their religious duty to plead the cause of the down trodden slave, and it is RIGHT to do so for the information of men as well as women.

Brookline, 8th Mo, 21st, 1837.[16]

Both Angelina and Sarah Grimké joined the debate about women's proper sphere of activity. Angelina wrote a series of letters published in The Liberator *and, beginning in July 1837, Sarah Grimké wrote fifteen letters to Mary S. Parker, president of the Boston Female Anti-Slavery Society. The* Letters on the Equality of the Sexes *were published in the New England Spectator and reprinted in other newspapers, and subsequently appeared in book form. As part of the great debate stirred up by the outcry against female abolitionists, they stand as one of the earliest and most influential statements of women's rights in the United States.*

SARAH GRIMKÉ ON THE WOMAN QUESTION

From Letter I

Here then I plant myself; God created us equal;—he created us free agents;—he is our Lawgiver, our King and our Judge, and to him, and to him alone is woman bound to be in subjection, and to him alone is she accountable for the use of those talents with which her Heavenly Father has entrusted her. One is her Master 'even Christ.

From Letter II

But I ask no favors for my sex. I surrender not our claim to equality. All I ask of our brethren is, that they take their feet from off our necks, and permit us to stand upright on that ground which God designed us to occupy. If he has not given us the rights which have, as I conceive, been wrested from us, we shall soon give evidence of our inferiority, and shrink back into that obscurity, which the high souled magnanimity of men has assigned us as our appropriate sphere.

Letter III

The Pastoral Letter of the General
Association of Congregational Ministers
of Massachusetts.

Haverhill, 7th Mo. 1837.

DEAR FRIEND,—When I last addressed thee, I had not seen the Pastoral Letter of the General Association. It has since fallen into my hands, and I must digress from my intention of exhibiting the condition of women in different parts of the world, in order to make some remarks on this extraordinary document. . . . I am persuaded that when the minds of men and women become emancipated from the thraldom of superstition and 'traditions of men,' the sentiments contained in the Pastoral Letter will be recurred to with as much astonishment as the opinions of Cotton Mather and other distinguished men of his day, on the subject of witchcraft; nor will it be deemed less wonderful, that a body of divines should gravely assemble and endeavor to prove that woman has no right to 'open her mouth for the dumb,' than it now is that judges should have sat on the trials of witches, and solemnly condemned nineteen persons and one dog to death for witchcraft.

But to the letter. It says, 'We invite your attention to the dangers which at present seem to threaten the FEMALE CHARACTER with wide-spread and permanent injury.'—I rejoice that they have called the attention of my sex to this subject, because I believe if woman investigates it, she will soon discover that danger is impending, though from a totally different source from that which the Association apprehends,—danger from those who, having long held the reins of *usurped* authority, are unwilling to permit us to fill that sphere which God created us to move in, and who have entered into league to crush the immortal mind of woman. I rejoice, because I am persuaded that the rights of woman, like the rights of slaves, need only be examined to be understood and asserted, even by some of those, who are now endeavoring to smother the irrepressible desire for mental and spiritual freedom which glows in the breast of many, who hardly dare to speak their sentiments.

'The appropriate duties and influence of women are clearly stated in the New Testament. Those duties are unobtrusive and private, but the sources of *mighty power.* When the mild, *dependent,* softening influence of woman upon the sternness of man's opinions is fully exercised, society feels the effects of it in a thousand ways.' No one can desire more earnestly than I do, that woman may move exactly in the sphere which her Creator has assigned her; and I believe her having been displaced from that sphere has introduced confusion into the world. It is, therefore, of vast importance to herself and to all the rational creation, that she should ascertain what are her duties and her privileges as a responsi-

ble and immortal being. The New Testament has been referred to, and I am willing to abide by its decisions, but must enter my protest against the false translation of some passages by the MEN who did that work, and against the perverted interpretation by the MEN who undertook to write commentaries thereon. I am inclined to think, when we are admitted to the honor of studying Greek and Hebrew, we shall produce some various readings of the Bible a little different from those we now have.

The Lord Jesus defines the duties of his followers in his Sermon on the Mount. He lays down grand principles by which they should be governed, without any reference to sex or condition:—'Ye are the light of the world. A city that is set on a hill cannot be hid. Neither do men light a candle and put it under a bushel, but on a candlestick, and it giveth light unto all that are in the house. Let your light so shine before men, that they may see your good works, and glorify your Father which is in Heaven.' I follow him through all his precepts, and find him giving the same directions to women as to men, never even referring to the distinction now so strenuously insisted upon between masculine and feminine virtues: this is one of the anti-christian 'traditions of men' which are taught instead of the 'commandments of God.' Men and women were CREATED EQUAL; they are both moral and accountable beings, and whatever is *right* for man to do, is *right* for woman.

But the influence of woman, says the Association, is to be private and unobtrusive; her light is not to shine before man like that of her brethren; but she is passively to let the lords of the creation, as they call themselves, put the bushel over it, lest peradventure it might appear that the world has been benefitted by the rays of *her* candle. So that her quenched light, according to their judgment, will be of more use than if it were set on the candlestick. 'Her influence is the source of mighty power.' This has ever been the flattering language of man since he laid aside the whip as a means to keep woman in subjection. He spares her body; but the war he has waged against her mind, her heart, and her soul, has been no less destructive to her as a moral being. How monstrous, how anti-christian, is the doctrine that woman is to be dependent on man! Where, in all the sacred Scriptures, is this taught? Alas! she has too well learned the lesson which MAN has labored to teach her. She has surrendered her dearest RIGHTS, and been satisfied with the privileges which man has assumed to grant her; she has been amused with the show of power, whilst man has absorbed all the reality into himself. He has adorned the creature whom God gave him as a companion, with baubles and gewgaws, turned her attention to personal attractions, offered incense to her vanity, and made her the instrument of his selfish gratification, a plaything to please his eye and amuse his hours of leisure. 'Rule by obedience and by submission sway,' or in other words, study to be a hypocrite, pretend to submit, but gain your point, has been the code of household morality which woman has been taught. The poet has sung, in sickly strains, the loveliness of woman's dependence upon man, and now we find it re-echoed by those who profess to teach the religion of the Bible. God says, 'Cease us from man whose breath is in his nostrils, for wherein is he to be accounted of?' Man says, depend upon me. God says, 'HE will teach us of his ways.' Man says, believe it not, I am to be your teacher. This doctrine of dependence upon man is utterly at variance with the doctrine of the Bible. In that book I find nothing like the softness of woman, nor the sternness of man: both are equally commanded to bring forth the fruits of the Spirit, love, meekness, gentleness, &c.

But we are told, 'the power of woman is in her dependence, flowing from a consciousness of that weakness which God has given her for her protection.' If physical weakness is alluded to, I cheerfully concede the superiority; if brute force is what my brethren are claiming, I am willing to let them have all the honor they desire; but if they mean to intimate, that mental or moral weakness belongs to woman, more than to man, I utterly disclaim the charge. Our powers of mind have been crushed, as far as man could do it, our sense of morality has been impaired by his interpretation of our duties; but no where does God say that he made any distinction between us, as moral and intelligent beings.

. . . . The General Association say, that 'when woman assumes the place and tone of man as a public reformer, our care and protection of her seem unnecessary; we put ourselves in self-defence against her, and her character becomes unnatural.' Here again the unscriptural notion is held up, that there is a distinction between the duties of men and women as moral beings; that what is virtue in man, is vice in woman; and women who dare to obey the command of Jehovah, 'Cry aloud, spare not, lift up thy voice like a trumpet, and show my people their transgression,' are threatened with having the protection of the brethren withdrawn. If this is all they do, we shall not even know the time when our chastisement is inflicted; our trust is in the Lord Jehovah, and in him is everlasting strength. The motto of woman, when she is engaged in the great work of public reformation, should be,—'The Lord is my light and my salvation; whom shall I fear? The Lord is the strength of my life; of whom shall I be afraid?' She must feel, if she feels rightly, that she is fulfilling one of the important duties laid upon her as an accountable being, and that her character, instead of being 'unnatural,' is in exact accordance with the will of Him to whom, and to no other, she is responsible for the talents and the gifts confided to her. As to the pretty simile, introduced into the 'Pastoral Letter,' 'If the vine whose strength and beauty is to lean upon the trellis work, and half conceal its clusters, thinks to assume the independence and the overshadowing nature of the elm,' &c. I shall only remark that it might well suit the poet's fancy, who sings of sparkling eyes and coral lips, and knights in armor clad; but it seems to me utterly inconsistent with the dignity of a Christian body, to endeavor to draw such an anti-scriptural distinction between men and women. Ah! how many of my sex feel in the dominion, thus unrighteously exercised over them, under the gentle appellation of *protection,* that what they have

leaned upon has proved a broken reed at best, and oft a spear.

Thine in the bonds of womanhood,

SARAH M. GRIMKE[17]

In 1838, Angelina Grimké was invited to address members of the Massachusetts legislature. In February, she spoke to them about ending the slave trade in the District of Columbia. Grimké was vividly aware that this was a precedent-shattering event—the first time a woman had spoken before an American legislative body—and she prefaced her speech with a defense of women's political activities.

ANGELINA GRIMKÉ'S SPEECH

MR. CHAIRMAN—

More than 2000 years have rolled their dark and bloody waters down the rocky, winding channel of Time into the broad ocean of Eternity, since woman's voice was heard in the palace of an eastern monarch, and woman's petition achieved the salvation of millions of her race from the edge of the sword. The Queen of Persia,—if Queen she might be called, who was but the mistress of her voluptuous lord,—trained as she had been in the secret abominations of an oriental harem, had studied too deeply the character of Ahasuerus not to know that the sympathies of his heart could not be reached, except through the medium of his sensual appetites. Hence we find her arrayed in royal apparel, and standing in the inner court of the King's house, hoping by her personal charms to win the favor of her lord. And after the golden sceptre had been held out, and the inquiry was made, 'What wilt thou, Queen Esther, and what is thy request? it shall be given thee to the half of the kingdom'—even then she dared not ask either for her own life, or that of her people. She *felt* that if her mission of mercy was to be successful, *his* animal propensities must be still more powerfully wrought upon—the luxurious feast must be prepared, the banquet of wine must be served up, and the favorable moment must be seized when, gorged with gluttony and intoxication, the king's heart was fit to be operated upon by the pathetic appeal. 'If *I* have found favor in thy sight, O King, and if it please the King, let *my* life be given at my petition, and *my* people at my request.' It was thus, through personal charms, and sensual gratification, and individual influence, that the Queen of Persia obtained the precious boon she craved,—her own life, and the life of her beloved people. Mr. Chairman, it is my privilege to stand before you on a similar mission of life and love; but I thank God that we live in an age of the world too enlightened and too moral to admit of the adoption of the same *means* to obtain as holy an end. I feel that it would be an insult to this Committee, were I to attempt to win their favor by arraying my person in gold, and silver, and costly apparel, or by inviting them to partake of the luxurious feast, or the banquet of wine. I understand the spirit of the age too well to believe that *you* could be moved by such sensual means—means as unworthy of you, as they would be beneath the dignity of the cause of humanity. Yes, I feel that if you are reached at all, it will not be by me, but by the truths I shall endeavor to present to your understandings and your hearts. The heart of the eastern despot was reached through the lowest propensities of his animal nature; yours, I know, cannot be reached but through the loftier sentiments of the intellectual and moral feelings.

I stand before you as a citizen, on behalf of the 20,000 women of Massachusetts, whose names are enrolled on petitions which have been submitted to the Legislature of which you are the organ. These petitions relate to the great and solemn subject of American slavery,—a subject fraught with the deepest interest to this republic, whether we regard it in its political, moral, or religious aspects. And because it is a *political* subject, it has often been tauntingly said, that *woman* has nothing to do with it. Are we aliens, because we are *women*? Are we bereft of citizenship, because we are the mothers, wives, and daughters of a mighty people? Have women *no* country—*no* interests staked in public weal—no liabilities in common peril—no partnership in a nation's guilt and shame? Let the history of the world answer these queries. Read the denunciations of Jehovah against the follies and crimes of Israel's daughters. Trace the influence of woman as a courtezan and a mistress in the destinies of nations, both ancient and modern, and see her wielding her power too often to debase and destroy, rather than to elevate and save. It is often said that women rule the world, through their influence over men. If so, then may we well hide our faces in the dust, and cover ourselves with sackcloth and ashes. It has not been by moral power and intellectual, but through the baser passions of man.—*This* domination of women *must* be resigned—the sooner the better; in the age which is approaching, she should be something *more*—she should be a *citizen;* and this title, which demands an increase of knowledge and of reflection, opens before her a new empire! I hold, Mr. Chairman, that American women have to do with this subject, not only because it is moral and religious, but because it is *political,* inasmuch as we are citizens of this republic, and as such *our* honor, happiness, and well being, are bound up in its politics and government and laws.

I stand before you as a southerner, exiled from the land of my birth, by the sound of the lash, and the pitious cry of the slave. I stand before you as a repentant slaveholder. I stand before you as a moral being, endowed with precious and inalienable rights, which are correlative with solemn duties and high responsibilities; and as a moral being I feel that I owe it to the suffering slave, and to the deluded master, to my country and the world, to do all that I can to overturn a system of complicated crimes, built up upon the broken hearts and prostrate bodies of my countrymen in chains, and cemented by the blood and sweat and tears of my sisters in bonds. . . . [18]

THE PRESS REACTS

The Boston Gazette

The Representatives' Hall was crowded yesterday with people of both sexes, 'black spirits and white,' to hear a lady from South Carolina, who rejoiceth in the name of Miss Grimke, declaim upon the subject of abolitionism. She exhibited considerable talent for a female, as an orator, appeared not at all abashed in exhibiting herself in a position so unsuitable to her sex, totally disregarding the doctrines of St. Peter, who says 'Is it not a shame for a woman to speak in public?' She belabored slaveholders and beat the air like all possessed. Her address occupied about two hours and a half in the delivery, when she gave out, stating at the close that she had a sister who was desirous to speak upon the same subject, but was prevented by ill-health. She, however, intimated that after taking breath for one day, she should like to continue the subject, and the meeting was accordingly adjourned to Friday (tomorrow) afternoon, at three o'clock, when she will conclude her speech. [19]

Boston Reformer

We should do injustice to our readers were we to pass in silence the high gratification we received in listening to Miss Grimke before the Legislative Committee in behalf of the female petitioners to the legislature in relation to the subject of petitions to Congress and Slavery generally. It was a noble day when for the first time in civilized America, a Woman stood up in a legislative Hall, vindicating the *rights of woman.* Miss Grimke deserves well of her sex and of the human kind. . . . [20]

Pittsburgh Manufacturer

Miss Grimke, of North [*sic*] Carolina, we believe, is delivering abolition lectures to members of the Massachusetts Legislature. Miss Grimke is very likely in search of a lawful protector who will take her for 'better or worse' for life, and she has thus made a bold dash among the yankee-law-makers. [21]

THE WOMAN QUESTION EVOLVES

While the churches were instrumental in stirring up the woman question, criticism from male abolitionists also contributed to the emergence of a women's movement.

There were many disagreements and differences among the abolitionists who founded the American Anti-Slavery

Society in 1833, and during the next five years, controversy over the goals and strategy of abolitionism increased and intensified. Then the issue of women's rights arose. Was it proper for women to speak out and participate conspicuously, as Angelina Grimké had done before the Massachusetts legislators? And if it was, which most believed, was it wise for men to defend their right to do so? Should they add the cause of women to the cause of the slave? Couldn't they ignore the woman question since it was sure to bring even more abuse and trouble for abolitionism? Should they reject women's rights, at this time, as a hindrance to gaining their primary goal?

These questions were hotly debated, and on several occasions they caused serious disagreement. Some abolitionists, led by Garrison and Henry C. Wright, rallied to the cause of women's rights, and gradually the subject became a symbol and a focus for disagreement on other issues, with the radicals taking the side of the women and the conservatives opposing their right to participate.

The dispute among abolitionists about the woman question first developed in New England, where it was closely connected with efforts to curtail Garrison's influence over the New England Anti-Slavery Society. Led by clergymen, the anti-Garrison forces challenged the participation of women at the annual meeting of the Massachusetts society in 1838. At issue was whether women could be members of the group.

Finding themselves in the minority, an angry group, led by several churchmen, issued the following protest.

The undersigned, being of opinion that the action of the New-England Anti-Slavery Convention now in session, inviting women to vote, debate, and aid generally as members of this body, and refusing to reconsider the vote by which it was done, is injurious to the cause of the slave, by connecting it with a subject foreign to it; injurious as a precedent for connecting with it *other* irrelevant topics; and an innovation upon our previous usage in regard to the constituent elements of the Convention; ask leave to disclaim all responsibility in regard to said proceedings, by having this PROTEST endorsed upon the records, and published with the doings of the convention.

CHARLES T. TORREY, Salem
A. A. PHELPS, Boston
THOMAS EDWARDS, Mendon
SAMUEL D. DARLING, Milford, N.H.
WILLIAM THURSTON, Bangor, Me.
GEORGE TRASK, Warren, Mass.
C. SPARRY, New York City[22]

William Lloyd Garrison boldly took his stand on women's rights (and many other controversial subjects) in the pages of The Liberator.

. . . We contend that the 'woman question,' so far as it respects the right or the propriety of REQUIRING WOMEN TO BE SILENT in Anti-Slavery Conventions, when they affirm that their consciences demand that they should speak, is not an 'irrelevant' question, but one which it is perfectly proper to discuss in such bodies, whenever the right alluded to is claimed. We are acting, it is true, under an organization for the specific purpose of abolishing slavery; but is it therefore 'irrelevant' to inquire how far we may justly go in recognizing the right of woman, as a moral being, to aid us in accomplishing our object? . . .

In what shape is the 'woman question' before us? Do any of our number propose to discuss in our Conventions, the question whether women ought to go to the polls, and vote and be voted for, for political offices? Not at all. But there are in our ranks a goodly number of females, who have borne the heat and burden of the cause, who have a keen sense of the woes and wrongs of slavery, and who are as well qualified to deliberate and act in our Conventions, as any of the other sex who are disposed to fetter and gag them. These women, many of them at least, are members of anti-slavery societies, and by the terms of our Constitution, are entitled to equal rights. Now the question, which as abolitionists, we are called upon to settle, is simply this—*Shall we, when a woman responds aye or no to a proposition which may come before us, or rises, under a conviction of duty, to express her opinion, or to pour out the feelings of her soul in relationship to the unutterable horrors of slavery,* APPLY THE GAG? Shall we tell her on the spot, or virtually by one previous action, TO STOP HER MOUTH? That is the question, and the only question; and it is by no means 'irrelevant' to 'the specific purpose' of our organization. It is a question, moreover, which must be met and decided, one way or the other. If it is said, that it was not originally expected that women would vote and speak in our Conventions, and that therefore they could not now to be permitted to do so; we reply that neither was it expected, that if they should desire to speak, they would be gagged. It has not been unusual in our meetings to call upon women to vote; and it is well known, that at the Convention which formed the American Anti-Slavery Society, women were allowed to speak. It is not *sectarianism* to contend for their right, of their own respon-

sibility, to open their mouths for the dumb; but it is the rankest sectarianism and the most consummate arrogance that would commend them to be silent when conscience and the voice of God demand that they should speak.[23]

TOWARD A WOMAN'S MOVEMENT

The woman question was kept alive by a group of dissident New England abolitionists who tried to stir up opposition to Garrison and the radical wing of the antislavery society. Finally, in 1839, a schism took place, and the dissidents formed the Massachusetts Anti-Slavery Society.

The woman question also affected the national American Anti-Slavery Society, where, as in New England, the issue of women's rights was linked with other controversies and disagreements among abolitionists during 1839 and 1840. Finally, in 1840, following the appointment of Abby Kelley to the Society's business committee, a heated and lengthy fight took place, and the national society split into two groups.

In the meantime, repercussions and echoes of the abolitionists' debate occurred in other parts of the country and the woman question spread into the press and the churches.

In 1840 in London, the world-famous Garrison distressed his hosts at an international abolitionist convention by refusing to sit with other delegates because women had been denied a place in the convention. Several American societies had sent women to the meeting, but, after a long and vehement debate, the women were barred from participating and were restricted to a special area from which they were expected to watch, silently. Among their defenders was New England abolitionist Wendell Phillips.

PHILLIPS AT THE WORLD ANTI-SLAVERY CONVENTION

. . . I would merely ask whether any man can suppose that the delegates from Massachusetts or Pennsylvania can take upon their shoulders the responsibility of withdrawing that list of delegates from your table, which their constituents told them to place there and whom they sanctioned as their fit representatives, because this Convention tells us that it is not ready to meet the ridicule of the morning papers and to stand up against the customs of England. In America we listen to no such arguments. If we had done so we had never been here as Abolitionists. It is the custom there not to admit

colored men into respectable society, and we have been told again that we are outraging the decencies of humanity when we permit colored men to sit by our side. When we have submitted to brick-bats and the tar tub and feathers in America, rather than yield to the custom prevalent there of not admitting colored brethren into our friendship, shall we yield to parallel custom or prejudice against women in Old England? We can not yield this question if we would; for it is a matter of conscience. But we would not yield it on the ground of expediency. In doing so we should feel that we were striking off the right arm of our enterprise. We could not go back to America to ask for any aid from the women of Massachusetts if we had deserted them, when they chose to send out their own sisters as their representatives here. We could not go back to Massachusetts and assert the unchangeableness of spirit on the question. We have argued it over again, and decided it time after time, in every society in the land, in favor of the women. We have not changed by crossing the water. We stand here the advocates of the same principle that we contend for in America. We think it right for women to sit by our side there, and we think it right for them to do the same here. We ask the Convention to admit them; if they do not choose to grant it, the responsibility rests on their shoulders. Massachusetts can not turn aside, or succumb to any prejudices or customs even in the land she looks upon with so much reverence as the land of Wilberforce, of Clarkson, and of O'Connell. It is a matter of conscience and British virtue ought not to ask us to yield.[24]

After the vote barring women from the abolitionist convention in London, two American women there were agitated beyond calming. Elizabeth Cady Stanton described what happened.

As Mrs. Mott [Lucretia Mott] and I walked home, arm in arm, commenting on the incidents of the day, we resolved to hold a convention as soon as we returned home and form a society to advocate the rights of women.[25]

Eight years passed before this convention, the first women's rights meeting in the United States, was held. But Stanton and Mott finally fulfilled their resolution in Seneca Falls, New York, on July 19, 1848.

Women continued to play an important role in the antislavery movement despite the controversy that developed over their participation. After 1840, they took part in the activities of the American Anti-Slavery Society, even serving on its executive committee and acting as paid agents of the Society. Especially in the newer regions of the country, across the Ohio, men and women worked together, in mixed state and local organizations, as partners in abolitionism. Black and white women contributed a major share of the hard labor as abolitionism grew during the two decades before the Civil War; they shouldered major responsibility for fund raising and shared almost all other jobs that had to be done.

Moreover, during the 1840's and 1850's, women such as Maria Chapman, Lydia Maria Child, Abby Kelley, Lucretia Mott, and Lucy Stone played a conspicuous and important role in American abolitionism, as lecturers, writers, and organizers, and their participation constituted a continuing attack on conventional ideas about women. Not content to let their example speak for itself, they used the lecture platform and antislavery publications to challenge directly the traditional view of women and to keep alive the debate on the woman question.

TEMPERANCE AND THE MOVEMENT

Abolitionism was not the only reform to attract large numbers of female followers. They also enlisted in the temperance movement—a campaign against excessive drinking.

From colonial days, Americans regularly consumed large quantities of alcoholic beverages, and, as the nation developed, a handful of reformers spoke out against the habit. By the 1830's, both the per capita consumption of liquor and the number of reformers had increased. Among the latter were many women.

Whereas opposition to slavery was essentially altruistic for the white women who joined abolitionism, women's own interests were deeply involved in temperance. For married women who were dependent upon their husbands and subject to them, there was no protection against the hardships caused by alcoholism. The drunken spouse could (and did) spend the family money as he chose, sell off his and his wife's property, apprentice their children, and assault wife and children alike. His wife was powerless to stop him, to protect herself and her children, or to escape from the marriage. With few opportunities to earn money for her own needs and no legal way to keep the money from her husband, she was the victim of intemperance. Thus, to women, temperance was a matter of women's rights as well as a religious and humanitarian reform.

There were thousands of local and state temperance societies in the 1830's and 1840's, with women's auxiliaries appended to them. The fight against drinking was ap-

Executive Committee, Philadelphia Anti-Slavery Society, 1851
(Mott, second from right, first row)

proved and often led by the clergy, and the opposition to women becoming temperance workers was less than that encountered by women abolitionists. But here, too, reform activities took them away from the hearth. Tens of thousands of women worked actively for state and local legislation to regulate or prohibit the sale of liquor. They learned techniques of group organization and political agitation, they ran petition campaigns, wrote letters and pamphlets, and appealed to lawmakers. Lucy Stone and Antoinette Brown were nationally known temperance speakers, but many lesser-known women also overcame the barriers to public speaking. In this way, temperance, like the antislavery cause, moved women into the arena of public life.

And, like abolitionism, temperance intensified their sense of women's inferiority in American life. On several occasions, at state and international conventions, leading female temperance workers were refused the right to speak. Temperance men, like abolitionists, reminded women of their proper sphere and tried to limit their participation. Temperance, like abolitionism, fed the frustration and unrest that were the root sources of the women's movement.

Among their many temperance activities, women founded and ran a newspaper. The Lily first appeared in 1848. In its opening editorial, Amelia Bloomer, whom historians have usually chosen to identify by her brief experiment in clothing reform, gently asserted women's right to do such an unusual thing as publish a newspaper.

"TO THE PATRONS OF *THE LILY*"

The first number of the LILY is to-day presented to its patrons and the public; . . .

It is WOMAN that speaks through the LILY. It is upon an important subject, too, that she comes before the public to be heard. Intemperance is the great foe to her peace and happiness. It is that, after all, which has made her home desolate, and beggared her offspring. It is that above all, which has filled to the brim the cup of her sorrows, and sent her mourning to the grave. Surely she has a right to wield the pen for its suppression. Surely she may, without throwing aside the modest retirement, which so much becomes her

sex, use her influence to lead her fellow mortals away from the destroyer's path. It is this which she proposes to do in the columns of the LILY. . . . [26]

Temperance was the main concern of The Lily, but as the years passed, women's rights received more and more attention. Tales of victimized women, like the one below, supported the contention that temperance and women's rights were intertwined.

"A HEROIC WOMAN"

Mrs. Margaret Freeland, of Syracuse, was recently arrested upon a warrant issued on complaint of Emanuel Rosendale, a rum-seller, charging her with forcing an entrance to his house, and with stones and clubs smashing his doors and windows, breaking his tumblers and bottles, and turning over his whisky barrels and spilling their contents. Great excitement was produced by this novel case. It seems that the husband of Mrs. Freeland was a drunkard—that he was in the habit of abusing his wife, turning her out of doors, etc., and this was carried so far that the police frequently found it necessary to interfere to put a stop to his ill-treatment of his family. Rosendale, the complainant, furnished Freeland with the liquor which turned him into a demon. Mrs. Freeland had frequently told him of her sufferings and besought him to refrain from giving her husband the poison. But alas! she appealed to a heart of stone. He disregarded her entreaties and spurned her from his door. Driven to desperation she armed herself, broke into the house, drove out the base-hearted landlord and proceeded upon the work of destruction.

She was brought before the court and demanded a trial. The citizens employed Charles B. Sedgwick, Esq., as her counsel, and prepared to justify her assault upon legal grounds. Rosendale, being at once arrested on complaint of Thomas L. Carson for selling liquor unlawfully, and feeling the force of the storm that was gathering over his head, appeared before the Justice, withdrew his complaint against Mrs. Freeland, paid the costs, and gave bail on the complaint of Mr. Carson, to appear at the General Sessions, and answer to an indictment should there be one found.

Mrs. Freeland is said to be "the pious mother of a fine

family of children, and a highly respectable member of the Episcopal Church.''

The *Carson League* commenting on this affair says:

''The rum-seller cowered in the face of public feeling. This case shows that public feeling will justify a woman whose person or family is outraged by a rum-seller, for entering his grocery or tavern and destroying his liquor. If the law lets loose a tiger upon her, she may destroy it. She has no other resort but force to save herself and her children. Were the women of this city to proceed in a body and destroy all the liquor of all the taverns and groceries, they would be justified by law and public opinion. Women should take this war into their hands, when men take side with the murderers of their peace.

''A tavern or grocery which makes the neighbors drunken and insane is a public nuisance, and may be pulled down and destroyed by the neighbors who are injured by it. It is worse than the plague. And if men will not put hands on it, then should the women do it. Tell us not it is property. It ceases to be property when it is employed to destroy the people. If a man lights his torch and sets about putting fire to the houses about him, any person may seize the torch and destroy it. So if a man takes a pistol and passes through the streets shooting the people, the pistol ceases to be property and may be taken from him by force and destroyed by any person who can do it. We sincerely hope that the women of the State will profit by this example, and go to destroying the liquor vessels and their contents.'' To all of which we respond AMEN.[27]

Like many women, Elizabeth Cady Stanton was active in both temperance and abolitionism. She served as president of the Woman's State Temperance Society in New York and in 1852 shocked convention members when she publicly advocated divorce as a protection against alcoholism. Stanton was certain that the temperance issue was tied to women's rights, and she worked hard to convince other women of this. In 1853, she spoke to the state temperance convention in Rochester, New York.

STANTON'S ADDRESS

. . . It has been objected to our Society that we do not confine ourselves to the subject of temperance, but talk too much about woman's rights, divorce, and the Church. It could be easily shown how the consideration of this great question carries us legitimately into the discussion of these various subjects.

We have been obliged to preach woman's rights, because many, instead of listening to what we had to say on temperance, have questioned the right of a woman to speak on any subject. In courts of justice and legislative assemblies, if the right of the speaker to be there is questioned, all business waits until that point is settled. Now, it is not settled in the mass of minds that woman has any rights on this footstool, and much less a right to stand on an even pedestal with man, look him in the face as an equal, and rebuke the sins of her day and generation. Let it be clearly understood, then, that we are a woman's rights Society; that we believe it is woman's duty to speak whenever she feels the impression to do so; that it is her right to be present in all the councils of Church and State. The fact that our agents are women, settles the question of our character on this point.

Again, in discussing the question of temperance, all lecturers, from the beginning, have made mention of the drunkards' wives and children, of widows' groans and orphans' tears; shall these classes of sufferers be introduced but as themes for rhetorical flourish, as pathetic touches of the speaker's eloquence; shall we passively shed tears over their condition, or by giving them their rights, bravely open to them the doors of escape from a wretched and degraded life? Is it not legitimate in this to discuss the social degradation, the legal disabilities of the drunkard's wife? If in showing her wrongs, we prove the right of all womankind to the elective franchise; to a fair representation in the government; to the right in criminal cases to be tried by peers of her own choosing, shall it be said that we transcend the bounds of our subject? If in pointing out her social degradation, we show you how the present laws outrage the sacredness of the marriage institution; if in proving to you that justice and mercy demand a legal separation from drunkards, we grasp the higher idea that a unity of soul alone constitutes and sanctifies true marriage, and that any law or public sentiment that forces two immortal, high-born souls to live together as husband and wife, unless held there by love, is false to God and humanity; who shall say that the discussion of this question does not lead us legitimately into the consideration of the important subject of divorce? . . . [28]

Elizabeth Cady Stanton

In several ways, women's experience in reform work during the 1830's and 1840's led to the development of a women's movement in the United States. Through reform activities, women learned about themselves. They discovered abilities and talents they had not realized and a reservoir of independence and militancy. Strong, opinionated, and able women such as the Grimké sisters, Lucretia Mott, and Abby Kelley stood as unequivocal but startling testimony to the real nature of "women's nature."

Opposition to women's participation in reform was also instructive. It made clear the conventional limits on women's role in society and the obstacles that confronted any effort to change that role.

Opposition also brought the woman question into the open and made it a public issue. Forced to defend their right to take part in public affairs, women (and their few male supporters) had to develop ideas and arguments to support a changing role for themselves in American life. Thus, out of their enlistment in the cause of the slave and the ranks of temperance came a defense of women's rights and a demand for equality that formed the basis of the emerging women's movement.

CHAPTER TWO

THE FIRST DECADE
The 1850's

Change was in the air everywhere during the decade before the Civil War. People were on the move, going west for new land and opportunity, even as far as California for gold. Cities were growing, as new kinds of work and urban life lured men and women away from the farm. Immigrants spread across the country, bringing strange languages and customs. The telegraph and the railroad were beginning to pull remote villages into the activities of the nation. Everywhere the old ways were changing, and new ones were coming in.

Slavery was still the great controversy before the Republic. Americans tensely debated whether slaves and the slave system would expand into the new territories and states of the West. For three years, the issue raged in the Kansas Territory, and the passion and violence there augured ill for the future.

Other controversies added to the tension of the times. Reformers pressed their views: freethinkers attacked hallowed religious ideas; utopian reformers called for daring new styles of living; spiritualists and temperance workers pushed their prescriptions for man's salvation and their cures for society's ills.

And, after 1848, the women's movement added to the turmoil.

Americans had been hearing about women's rights for several decades. In 1828, Frances Wright shocked lecture audiences with opinions about abolition, atheism, miscegenation, the rights of labor, and the rights of women. During the 1830's, Ernestine Rose scandalized her listeners by advocating radical social change that included a large dose of women's rights. Then the controversy over the Grimké sisters made "news" out of the woman question. In 1845, a learned and startling book, Woman in the Nineteenth Century, by Margaret Fuller, involved even more people in the controversy over women's rights.

None of this, however, constituted a women's movement.

Women's experiences in abolitionism and temperance had underlined the limits and restraints placed upon them and made their inferiority vividly clear. These experiences stirred up and brought to the surface myriad frustrations and disappointments in women's lives—and finally led them to come together to organize to change the condition of their lives.

Only then—when women decided to work together—did what can be called "the women's movement" begin in the United States. This occurred in July 1848 in Seneca Falls, in upper New York, with the first women's rights meeting. It has continued, rising and falling in intensity, for more than a century. The women's movement today is not a modern phenomenon or an isolated event; its origins go back to the middle of the 1800's and the women of that period who launched the movement.

THE FIRST WOMEN'S RIGHTS CONVENTIONS: 1848

Five women—Lucretia Mott, Martha C. Wright, Jane Hunt, Elizabeth Cady Stanton, and Mary Ann McClintock—after much serious discussion, planned the meeting in Seneca Falls to discuss "the social, civil, and religious condition and rights of women."

They put the following announcement in the Seneca County Courier, and three hundred people, mostly women, came to the historic meetings on July 19 and 20, 1848.

SENECA FALLS CONVENTION

WOMAN'S RIGHTS CONVENTION.—A convention to discuss the social, civil, and religious condition and rights of woman, will be held in the Wesleyan Chapel, at Seneca Falls, N.Y., on Wednesday and Thursday the 19th and 20th of July, current; commencing at 10 o'clock A.M. During the first day the meeting will be exclusively for women, who are earnestly invited to attend. The public generally are invited to be present on the second day, when Lucretia Mott, of Philadelphia, and other ladies and gentlemen, will address the convention.[1]

This was the first women's rights convention in history. Its speeches and discussions held the audience for two days.

REPORT

OF THE

WOMAN'S RIGHTS CONVENTION,

HELD AT

Seneca Falls, N. Y.,

JULY 19TH & 20TH, 1848.

ROCHESTER:
PRINTED BY JOHN DICK,
AT THE NORTH STAR OFFICE.
1848.

Finally, they agreed unanimously to approve a Declaration of Sentiments that had been prepared earlier by the women who organized the meeting.

The Declaration paraphrased the familiar Declaration of Independence and asserted that "all men and women are created equal." It also drew up a list of charges against men who had deprived women of their rights, their opportunities, and even their self-respect.

"DECLARATION OF SENTIMENTS"

When, in the course of human events, it becomes necessary for one portion of the family of man to assume among the people of the earth a position different from that which they have hitherto occupied, but one to which the laws of nature and of nature's God entitle them, a decent respect to the opinions of mankind requires that they should declare the causes that impel them to such a course.

We hold these truths to be self-evident: that all men and women are created equal; that they are endowed by their Creator with certain inalienable rights; that among these are life, liberty, and the pursuit of happiness; that to secure these rights governments are instituted, deriving their just powers from the consent of the governed. Whenever any form of government becomes destructive of these ends, it is the right of those who suffer from it to refuse allegiance to it, and to insist upon the institution of a new government, laying its foundation on such principles, and organizing its powers in such form, as to them shall seem most likely to effect their safety and happiness. Prudence indeed, will dictate that governments long established should not be changed for light and transient causes; and accordingly all experience hath shown that mankind are more disposed to suffer, while evils are sufferable, than to right themselves by abolishing the forms to which they were accustomed. But when a long train of abuses and usurpations, pursuing invariably the same object evinces a design to reduce them under absolute despotism, it is their duty to throw off such government, and to provide new guards for their future security. Such has been the patient sufferance of the women under this government, and such is now the necessity which constrains them to demand the equal station to which they are entitled.

The history of mankind is a history of repeated injuries and usurpations on the part of man toward woman, having in direct object the establishment of an absolute tyranny over her. To prove this, let facts be submitted to a candid world.

He has never permitted her to exercise her inalienable right to the elective franchise.

He has compelled her to submit to laws, in the formation of which she had no voice.

He has withheld from her rights which are given to the most ignorant and degraded men—both natives and foreigners.

Having deprived her of this first right of a citizen, the elective franchise, thereby leaving her without representation in the halls of legislation, he has oppressed her on all sides.

He has made her, if married, in the eye of the law, civilly dead.

He has taken from her all right in property, even to the wages she earns.

He has made her, morally, an irresponsible being, as she can commit many crimes with impunity, provided they be done in the presence of her husband. In the covenant of marriage, she is compelled to promise obedience to her husband, he becoming, to all intents and purposes, her master—the law giving him power to deprive her of her liberty, and to administer chastisement.

He has so framed the laws of divorce, as to what shall be the proper causes, and in case of separation, to whom the guardianship of the children shall be given, as to be wholly regardless of the happiness of women—the law, in all cases, going upon a false supposition of the supremacy of man, and giving all power into his hands.

After depriving her of all rights as a married woman, if single, and the owner of property, he has taxed her to support a government which recognizes her only when her property can be made profitable to it.

He has monopolized nearly all the profitable employments, and from those she is permitted to follow, she receives but a scanty remuneration. He closes against her all the avenues to wealth and distinction which he considers most honorable to himself. As a teacher of theology, medicine, or law, she is not known.

He has denied her the facilities for obtaining a thorough education, all colleges being closed against her.

He allows her in Church, as well as State, but a subordinate position, claiming Apostolic authority for her exclusion from the ministry, and, with some exceptions, from any public participation in the affairs of the Church.

He has created a false public sentiment by giving to the world a different code of morals for men and women, by which moral delinquencies which exclude women from society, are not only tolerated, but deemed of little account in man.

He has usurped the prerogative of Jehovah himself, claiming it as his right to assign for her a sphere of action, when that belongs to her conscience and to her God.

He has endeavored, in every way that he could, to destroy her confidence in her own powers, to lessen her self-respect, and to make her willing to lead a dependent and abject life.

Now, in view of this entire disfranchisement of one-half the people of this country, their social and religious degradation—in view of the unjust laws above mentioned, and because women do feel themselves aggrieved, oppressed, and fraudulently deprived of their most sacred rights, we insist that they have immediate admission to all the rights and privileges which belong to them as citizens of the United States.

In entering upon the great work before us, we anticipate no small amount of misconception, misrepresentation, and ridicule; but we shall use every instrumentality within our power to effect our object. We shall employ agents, circulate tracts, petition the State and National legislatures, and endeavor to enlist the pulpit and the press in our behalf. We hope this Convention will be followed by a series of Conventions embracing every part of the country.[2]

The convention also adopted a set of resolutions, calling for an end to women's social inferiority, for changes in the laws that oppressed them, for educational opportunities, for an end to the double standard of behavior, and for the franchise. The demand for the vote was considered the most radical and provoked heated debate. Elizabeth Cady Stanton, who had drafted the resolutions, argued for it at length, and Frederick Douglass, the well-known black abolitionist and a friend of women's rights, supported her position.

All the resolutions were adopted, although the ninth, calling for the vote, passed just barely.

SENECA FALLS RESOLUTIONS

WHEREAS, The great precept of nature is conceded to be, that "man shall pursue his own true and substantial happiness." Blackstone in his Commentaries remarks, that this law of Nature being coeval with mankind, and dictated by God himself, is of course superior in obligation to any other. It is binding over all the globe, in all countries and at all times; no human laws are of any validity if contrary to this, and such of them as are valid, derive all their force, and all their validity, and all their authority, mediately and immediately, from this original; therefore;

Resolved, That such laws as conflict, in any way, with the true and substantial happiness of woman, are contrary to the great precept of nature and of no validity, for this is "superior in obligation to any other."

Resolved, That all laws which prevent woman from occupying such a station in society as her conscience shall dictate, or which place her in a position inferior to that of man, are contrary to the great precept of nature, and therefore of no force or authority.

Resolved, That woman is man's equal—was intended to be so by the Creator, and the highest good of the race demands that she should be recognized as such.

Resolved, That the women of this country ought to be enlightened in regard to the laws under which they live, that they may no longer publish their degradation by declaring themselves satisfied with their present position, nor their ignorance, by asserting that they have all the rights they want.

Resolved, That inasmuch as man, while claiming for himself intellectual superiority, does accord to woman moral superiority, it is pre-eminently his duty to encourage her to speak and teach, as she has an opportunity, in all religious assemblies.

Resolved, That the same amount of virtue, delicacy, and refinement of behavior that is required of woman in the social state, should also be required of man, and the same transgressions should be visited with equal severity on both man and woman.

Resolved, That the objection of indelicacy and impropriety, which is so often brought against woman when she addresses a public audience, comes with a very ill-grace from those who encourage, by their attendance, her appearance on the stage, in the concert, or in feats of the circus.

Resolved, That woman has too long rested satisfied in the circumscribed limits which corrupt customs and a perverted application of the Scriptures have marked out for her, and that it is time she should move in the enlarged sphere which her great Creator has assigned her.

Resolved, That it is the duty of the women of this country to secure to themselves their sacred right to the elective franchise.

Resolved, That the equality of human rights results necessarily from the fact of the identity of the race in capabilities and responsibilities.

Resolved, therefore, That, being invested by the Creator with the same capabilities, and the same consciousness of responsibility for their exercise, it is demonstrably the right and duty of woman, equally with man, to promote every righteous cause by every righteous means; and especially in regard to the great subjects of morals and religion, it is self-evidently her right to participate with her brother in teaching them, both in private and in public, by writing and by speaking, by any instrumentalities proper to be used, and in any assemblies proper to be held; and this being a self-evident truth growing out of the divinely implanted principles of human nature, any custom or authority adverse to it, whether modern or wearing the hoary sanction of antiquity, is to be regarded as a self-evident falsehood, and at war with mankind.

Resolved, That the speedy success of our cause depends upon the zealous and untiring efforts of both men and women, for the overthrow of the monopoly of the pulpit, and for the securing to woman an equal participation with men in the various trades, professions, and commerce.[3]*

There was still much to discuss after the Seneca Falls convention. A second meeting was planned—this one to take place in a larger city, before a larger audience. The call went out for a meeting in Rochester, New York, two weeks after the Seneca Falls convention.

A CALL

The convention to discuss Woman's rights is to be held at the Unitarian church in this city to-morrow, commencing at 10 o'clock in the forenoon. An unlimited invitation to be present is extended to our citizens, and if we are rightly informed as to its objects, it will doubtless be a rich affair.[4]

After much hesitation and discussion, a woman presided over the Rochester meeting—a startling innovation. From this time on, it was standard procedure.

The Rochester meeting approved the Seneca Falls Declaration of Sentiments, and then adopted resolutions that were more forceful and specific than those agreed upon in July. The first resolution, calling for the vote, passed with

* This resolution was proposed by Lucretia Mott at the last session of the convention.

a larger majority and without the conflict it had caused at Seneca Falls. The franchise had become an accepted goal.

ROCHESTER RESOLUTIONS

1. *Resolved,* That we petition our State Legislature for our right to the elective franchise, every year, until our prayer be granted.

2. *Resolved,* That it is an admitted principle of the American Republic, that the only just power of the Government is derived from the consent of the governed; and that taxation and representation are inseparable; and therefore, woman being taxed equally with man, ought not to be deprived of an equal representation in the government.

3. *Resolved,* That we deplore the apathy and indifference of woman in regard to her rights, thus restricting her to an inferior position in social, religious, and political life, and we urge her to claim an equal right to act on all subjects that interest the human family.

4. *Resolved,* That the assumption of law to settle estates of men who die without wills, having widows, is an insult to woman, and ought to be regarded as such by every lover of right and equality.

5. *Whereas,* The husband has the legal right to hire out his wife to service, collect her wages and appropriate it to his own exclusive and independent benefit; and, whereas, this has contributed to establish that hideous custom, the promise of obedience in the marriage contract, effectually, though insidiously reducing her almost to the condition of a *slave,* whatever freedom she may have in these respects, being granted as a privilege, not as a right, therefore,

Resolved, That we will seek the overthrow of this barbarous and unrighteous law; and conjure women no longer to promise obedience in the marriage covenant.

Resolved, That the universal doctrine of the inferiority of woman has ever caused her to distrust her own powers, and paralized her energies, and placed her in that degraded position from which the most strenuous and unremitting effort can alone redeem her. Only by faithful perseverance in the practical exercise of those talents, so long "wrapped in a napkin and buried under the earth," she will regain her long-lost equality with man.

Resolved, That in the persevering and independent course of Miss Blackwell, who recently attended a series of medical lectures in Geneva, and has now gone to Europe to graduate as a physician, we see a harbinger of the day when woman shall stand forth "redeemed and disenthralled," and perform those important duties which are so truly within her sphere.

Resolved, That those who believe the laboring classes of women are oppressed ought to do all in their power to raise their wages, beginning with their own household servants.

Resolved, That it is the duty of woman, whatever her complexion, to assume, as soon as possible, her true position of equality in the social circle, the church, and the state.

Resolved, That we tender our grateful acknowledgment to

the Trustees of the Unitarian Church, who have kindly opened their doors for the use of this Convention.

Resolved, That we, the friends who are interested in this cause, gratefully accept the kind offer from the Trustees of the use of Protection Hall, to hold our meetings whenever we wish.[5]

Two such startling and unprecedented events as the meetings in Seneca Falls and Rochester did not go unnoticed. They were the biggest women's news since the Grimké sisters, and they provoked a storm of publicity. Newspaper editors were shocked, infuriated, amused, worried, and, rarely, approving.

"WOMEN OUT OF THEIR LATITUDE"

We are sorry to see that women in several parts of this State are holding what they call "Woman's Rights Conventions," and setting forth a formidable list of those Rights in a parody upon the Declaration of American Independence. . . .

The women who attended these meetings, no doubt at the expense of their more appropriate duties, act as committees, write resolutions and addresses, hold much correspondence, make speeches, etc., etc. . . . with the object in view of revolutionizing public opinion and the laws of the land, and changing their relative position in society in such a way as to divide with the male sex the labors and responsibilities of active life in every branch of art, science, trades, and professions.

Now, it requires no argument to prove that this is all wrong. Every true hearted female will instantly feel that this is unwomanly, and that to be practically carried out, the males must change their position in society to the same extent in an opposite direction, in order to enable them to discharge an equal share of the domestic duties which now appertain to females, and which must be neglected, to a great extent, if women are allowed to exercise all the "rights" that are claimed by these Convention-holders. Society would have to be radically remodelled in order to accommodate itself to so great a change in the most vital part of the compact of the social relations of life; and the order of things established at the creation of mankind, and continued *six thousand years,* would be completely broken up. The organic laws of our country, and of each State, would have to be licked into new shapes, in order to admit of the introduction of the vast change that is contemplated. In a thousand other ways that might be mentioned, if we had room to make, and our readers had patience to hear them, would this sweeping reform be attended by fundamental changes in the public and private, civil and religious, moral and social relations of the sexes, of life, and of the Government.

But this change is impracticable, uncalled for, and unnecessary. *If effected,* it would set the world by the ears, make "confusion worse confounded," demoralize and degrade from their higher sphere and noble destiny, women of all respectable and useful classes, and prove a monstrous

A Cartoonist's View of the Meeting at Seneca Falls.
Harper's New Monthly Magazine, *Nov. 1852*

A NATURAL CONSEQUENCE
MISS LUCY (blushing extensively).—Miss President and Ladies, It is my painful duty to resign my office as Corresponding Secretary of the Woman's Rights Association—for I am to be married tomorrow

PROPER PRUDENCE
MISS PRUDENCE (emphatically).—Miss President, I repeat it—No conscientious Woman will ever marry until she is in a condition to support her Husband and Children in a suitable manner

injury to all mankind. It would be productive of no positive good, that would not be outweighed tenfold by positive evil. It would alter the relations of females without bettering their condition. Besides all, and above all, it presents no remedy for the *real* evils that the millions of the industrious, hardworking, and much suffering women of our country groan under and seek to redress.[6]

"THE WOMEN OF PHILADELPHIA"

Our Philadelphia ladies not only possess beauty, but they are celebrated for discretion, modesty, and unfeigned diffidence, as well as wit, vivacity, and good nature. Whoever heard of a Philadelphia lady setting up for a reformer, or standing out for woman's rights, or assisting to *man* the election grounds, raise a regiment, command a legion, or address a jury? Our ladies glow with a higher ambition. They soar to rule the hearts of their worshipers, and secure obedience by the sceptre of affection. The tenure of their power is a law of nature, not a law of man, and hence they fear no insurrection, and never experience the shock of a revolution in their dominions. But all women are not as reasonable as ours of Philadelphia. The Boston ladies contend for the rights of women. The New York girls aspire to mount the rostrum, to do all the voting, and, we suppose, all the fighting too. . . . Our Philadelphia girls object to fighting and holding office. They prefer the baby-jumper to the study of Coke and Lyttelton, and the ball-room to the Palo Alto battle. They object to having a George Sand for President of the United States; a Corinna for Governor; a Fanny Wright for Mayor; or a Mrs. Partington for Postmaster. . . . Women have enough influence over human affairs without being politicians. Is not everything managed by female influence? Mothers, grandmothers, aunts, and sweethearts manage everything. Men have nothing to do but to listen and obey to the "of course, my dear, you will, and of course, my dear, you won't." Their rule is absolute; their power unbounded. Under such a system men have no claim to rights, especially "equal rights."

A woman is nobody. A wife is everything. A pretty girl is equal to ten thousand men, and a mother is, next to God, all powerful. . . . The ladies of Philadelphia, therefore, under the influence of the most serious "sober second thoughts," are resolved to maintain their rights as Wives, Belles, Virgins, and Mothers, and not as Women.[7]

"THE REIGN OF PETTICOATS"

The women in various parts of the State have taken the field in favor of a petticoat empire, with a zeal and energy which show that their hearts are in the cause, and that they are resolved no longer to submit to the tyrannical rule of the *heartless* "lords of creation," but have solemnly determined to demand their "natural and inalienable right" to attend the

polls, and assist in electing our Presidents, and Governors, and Members of Congress, and State Representatives, and Sheriffs, and County Clerks, and Supervisors, and Constables, etc., etc., and to unite in the general scramble for office. This is right and proper. It is but just that they should participate in the beautiful and feminine business of politics, and enjoy their proportion of the "spoils of victory." Nature never designed that they should be confined exclusively to the drudgery of raising children, and superintending the kitchens, and to the performance of the various other household duties which the cruelty of men and the customs of society have so long assigned to them. This is emphatically the age of "democratic progression," of *equality* and *fraternization*—the age when all colors and sexes, the bond and free, black and white, male and female, are, as they by

Susan B. Anthony

right ought to be, all tending downward and upward toward the common level of equality.

The harmony of this great movement in the cause of freedom would not be perfect if women were still to be confined to petticoats, and men to breeches. There must be an "interchange" of these "commodities" to complete the system. Why should it not be so? Can not women fill an office, or cast a vote, or conduct a campaign, as judiciously and vigorously as men? And, on the other hand, can not men "nurse" the babies, or preside at the wash-tub, or boil a pot as safely and as well as women? If they can not, the evil is in that arbitrary organization of society which has excluded them from the practice of these pursuits. It is time these false notions and practices were changed, or, rather, removed, and for the political millennium foreshadowed by this petticoat movement to be ushered in. Let the women keep the ball moving, so bravely started by those who have become tired of the restraints imposed upon them by the antediluvian notions of a Paul or the tyranny of man.[8]

In making news of the women's conventions, the press gave the movement the publicity it could not have made for itself. And throughout the history of the movement, to the present, this has continued. Amused or angry, editors and newscasters have called attention to the women's movement.

While the publicity in 1848 was overwhelmingly unfavorable, and undoubtedly frightened away the more hesitant and timid, the word was out. News spread to other states and other regions, so that other women learned what had taken place in New York and soon moved to act themselves.

THE MOVEMENT GROWS: A DECADE OF CONVENTIONS

The more spectacular events of the women's movement, such as the Seneca Falls meeting, have been detailed in history books, along with the names of leaders like Susan B. Anthony, Lucretia Mott, Elizabeth Cady Stanton, and Lucy Stone. But stirrings of the movement reached small towns in Ohio, New York, Massachusetts, Indiana, and Pennsylvania as well. There, thousands of unknown women began to defy tradition and overcome their own uncertainty and fears by forming small groups that agitated for women's rights throughout the 1850's.

Seneca Falls and Rochester were their inspiration and model. In 1848, for example, in South Bristol, New York, between fifteen and twenty women met weekly to exchange ideas. They elected Emily Collins as their president; they drafted a petition to the state legislature asking for woman suffrage; and they worked out a program to inform South Bristol citizens about women's rights. By 1850, local groups like this began to spring up throughout the Northern and Northwestern states.

Soon these groups were linked together by state and national associations. Some states had formal organizations, like the Ohio Woman's Rights Association; in others, local and county groups were tied together by statewide steering committees. National efforts were informally organized. In 1852, a National Woman's Rights Society was proposed, but the idea was rejected. A structured formal organization, it was argued, would be too confining and would hurt the growth of the movement. Instead, a central committee, representing members in the state organizations, was set up to coordinate activities between annual national conventions.

The mass meeting, or convention, as it was called, was the heart of the women's movement and the central mechanism for its activities, which took place mostly in the states of the North and Midwest. Here women held annual conventions; some met even more often. During the decade, so-called national conventions were held every year except 1857, attracting women from many states, mainly New England, New York, New Jersey, Pennsylvania, Ohio, and from Washington, D.C. There was no comparable activity in the Southern states, where women's rights were irretrievably associated with abolitionism and where rural life discouraged organization.

Conventions tended to follow a pattern. They were well planned and publicized; the atmosphere was usually lively. There was an air of confidence and excitement. Meetings were open to the general public, and all speakers and all ideas were generously given a forum.

In large cities, thousands came, many out of curiosity—among them loquacious opponents and crude jeerers. Usually, neither the large numbers, the hostile guests, nor the inexperience of the presiding woman upset the meetings, which were orderly and decorous. Only on occasion, as in New York City in 1853, were convention proceedings actually interrupted by a rude and angry mob.

One could expect to see and hear some of the controversial celebrities of the reform movements at the conventions. Women like Anthony, Rose, Stanton, and Stone, and men like Wendell Phillips, William Lloyd Garrison, and Frederick Douglass participated regularly.

Issues were discussed at length and with care. For the thousands attending and the greater numbers who read the detailed news accounts and published proceedings, the conventions were an introduction to new ideas about women and to a new kind of woman. Thus, they were the recruiting ground, as well as the workplace, of the women's movement.

Typically, the convention began with the publication in newspapers of an invitation, or "call," to the public. In 1850, the call to the first women's rights convention in Ohio urged women to attend.

"A CALL"

We, the undersigned, earnestly call on the women of Ohio to meet in Convention, on Friday, the 19th of April, 1850, at 10 o'clock A.M., in the town of Salem, to concert measures to secure to all persons the recognition of equal rights, and the extension of the privileges of government without distinction of sex, or color: . . .

The meeting of a convention of men to amend the Constitution of our (?) State, presents a most favorable opportunity for the agitation of this subject. Women of Ohio! we shall call upon you to come up to this work in strength and with womanly energy. Don't be discouraged at the prospect of difficulties. Remember that contest with difficulty gives strength. Come and inquire if the position you now occupy is one appointed by wisdom, and designed to secure the best interest of the human race. Come, and let us ascertain what bearing the circumscribed sphere of woman has on the great political and social evils that curse and desolate the land. Come, for this cause claims your most invincible perseverance; come in single-heartedness, and with a personal self-devotion that will yield everything to Right, Truth, and Reason, but not an iota to dogmas or theoretical opinions, no matter how time-honored or by what precedent established.[9]

The first National Woman's Rights Convention was held in October 1850, in Worcester, Massachusetts. Its call was signed by eighty-nine prominent women and men from six states. In addition to well-known movement women and abolitionist supporters, the invitation was signed by notables like William Henry Channing, A. Bronson Alcott, and Ralph Waldo Emerson.

"THE CALL"

A Convention will be held at Worcester, Mass., on the 23rd and 24th of October next, to consider the question of Woman's Rights, Duties, and Relations. The men and women who feel sufficient interest in the subject to give an earnest thought and effective effort to its rightful adjustment, are invited to meet each other in free conference at the time and place appointed. . . .

Of the many points now under discussion, and demanding a just settlement, the general question of woman's rights and relations comprehends these: Her education—literary, scientific, and artistic; her avocations—industrial, commercial, and professional; her interests—pecuniary, civil, and political; in a word, her rights as an individual, and her functions as a citizen. . . .

The signs are encouraging; the time is opportune. Come, then, to this Convention. It is your duty, if you are worthy of your age and country. Give the help of your best thought to separate the light from the darkness. Wisely give the protection of your name and the benefit of your efforts to the great work of settling the principles, devising the methods, and achieving the success of this high and holy movement. . . . [10]

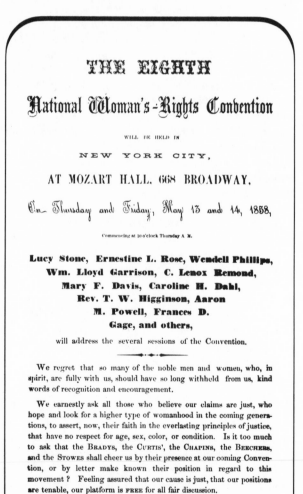

A call of a different sort brought women to a local convention in Morrow County, Ohio.

CALL TO "JOHN'S CONVENTION"

In December of 1851 I was invited to attend a Woman's Rights Convention at the town of Mount Gilead, Morrow Co., Ohio. A newspaper call promised that celebrities would be on hand, etc. I wrote I would be there. It was two days' journey, by steamboat and rail. The call was signed "John Andrews," and John Andrews promised to meet me at the cars. I went. It was fearfully cold and John met me. He was a beardless boy of nineteen, looking much younger. We drove at once to the "Christian Church." On the way he cheered me by saying "he was afraid nobody would come, for all the people said nobody would come for his asking." When we got to the house, there was not one human soul on hand, no fire in the old rusty stove, and the rude, unpainted board benches, all topsy-turvy. I called some boys playing near, asked their names, put them on paper, five of them, and said to them, "Go to every house in this town and

"Ye May Session of Ye Woman's Rights Convention." Harper's Weekly, *June 1859*

tell everybody that 'Aunt Fanny' [Aunt Fanny was Frances D. Gage, a leader in the Ohio movement] will speak here at 11 A.M., and if you get me fifty to come and hear, I will give you each ten cents.'' They scattered off upon the run. I ordered John to right the benches, picked up chips and kindlings, borrowed a brand of fire at the next door, had a good hot stove, and the floor swept, and was ready for my audience at the appointed time. John had done his work well, and fifty at least were on hand, and a minister to make a prayer and quote St. Paul before I said a word. I said my say, and before 1 P.M., we adjourned, appointing another session at 3, and one for 7 P.M., and three for following day. Mrs. C. M. Severance came at 6 P.M., and we had a good meeting throughout.

John's Convention was voted a success after all. He died young, worn out by his own enthusiasm and conflicts.[11]

CONVENTION SPEECHES

A regular part of the conventions was the prepared speeches. In an age with limited means of communication, people traveled far to see and hear the famous reformers and celebrated women who spoke at these meetings.

Thousands heard women speak in public for the first time.

Convention speeches generally offered audiences lengthy and careful analyses of women's condition in society. They dealt with subjects such as laws concerning women, the church's attitude toward women, the nature of marriage, and the relationship between economic status and personal freedom.

At the same time, the speakers offered the audience a new image of women, women who could speak with ease on the public platform, who could explore and discuss serious issues, and who strongly and confidently demanded their rights.

Paulina Wright Davis presided over the first National Woman's Rights Convention in Worcester, Massachusetts, in 1850. In her opening address, she described the movement as radical and unique.

THE PRESIDENT'S ADDRESS

The reformation we propose in its utmost scope is radical and universal. It is not the mere perfecting of a reform already in motion, a detail of some established plan, but it is an epochal movement—the emancipation of a class, the redemption of half the world, and a conforming reorganization of all social, political, and industrial interests and institutions. Moreover, it is a movement without example among the enterprises of associated reformations, for it has no purpose of arming the oppressed against the oppressor, or of separating the parties, or of setting up independence, or of severing the relations of either.

Its intended changes are to be wrought in the intimate texture of all societary organizations, without violence or any form of antagonism. It seeks to replace the worn-out with the living and the beautiful, so as to reconstruct without overturning, and to regenerate without destroying.

Our claim must rest on its justice, and conquer by its power of truth. We take the ground that whatever has been achieved for the race belongs to it, and must not be usurped by any class or caste. The rights and liberties of one human being can not be made the property of another, though they were redeemed for him or her by the life of that other; for rights can not be forfeited by way of salvage, and they are, in their nature, unpurchasable and inalienable. We claim for woman a full and generous investiture of all the blessings which the other sex has solely, or by her aid, achieved for itself. We appeal from man's injustice and selfishness to his principles and affections.[12]

Ohio was prominent in both abolitionism and women's rights. Abby Kelley, Lucy Stone, and Antoinette Brown had traveled there to speak for both causes. In 1850, Ohio women held four separate conventions to try to influence a state constitutional convention taking place at that time. Speaking at the first meeting, in Salem, Ohio, J. Elizabeth Jones described women's inferior status under the laws and then besought her audience to take action.

WOMEN OF OHIO

. . . Women of Ohio! Whose cheek does not blush, whose blood does not tingle at this cool, lawyer-like recital of the gross indignities and wrongs which Government has heaped upon our sex? With these marks of inferiority branded upon our persons, and interwoven with the most sacred relations of human existence, how can we rise to the true dignity of human nature, and discharge faithfully the important duties assigned us as responsible, intelligent, self-controlling members of society? No wonder that so many of our politicians are dough-faced serviles, without independence or manhood; no wonder our priests are time-serving and sycophantic; no wonder that so many men are moral cowards and cringing poltroons. What more could be expected of a progeny of slaves? Slaves are we, politically and legally. How can we, who, it is said, are the educators of our children,

present to this nation anything else but a generation of serviles, while we, ourselves, are in a servile condition, and padlocks are on our lips? No! if men would be men worthy of the name, they must cease to disfranchise and rob their wives and mothers; they must forbear to consign to political and legal slavery their sisters and their daughters. And, would we be women worthy the companionship of true and noble men, we must cease longer to submit to tyranny. . . .

In conclusion, we appeal to our sisters of Ohio to arise from the lethargy of ages; to assert their rights as independent human beings; to demand their true position as equally responsible co-workers with their brethren in this world of action. We urge you by your self-respect, by every consideration for the human race, to arise and take possession of your birthright to freedom and equality. Take it not as the gracious boon tendered by the chivalry of superiors, but as your *right,* on every principle of justice and equality. . . . . [13]

Lucy Stone was one of the most famous women of the time. She was an untiring abolitionist, temperance worker, and champion of women's rights. In 1855, when she married Henry Blackwell, their joint statement against the unequal relationship of men and women under the existing marriage laws was widely publicized, as was Stone's decision to maintain her own last name after marriage. She was a regular and vigorous speaker at conventions; her speech at the National Convention in Cincinnati, in 1855, would sound surprisingly familiar to a twentieth-century listener.

LUCY STONE'S SPEECH

The last speaker alluded to this movement as being that of a few disappointed women. From the first years to which my memory stretches, I have been a disappointed woman. When, with my brothers, I reached forth after the sources of knowledge, I was reproved with "It isn't fit for you; it doesn't belong to women." Then there was but one college in the world where women were admitted, and that was in Brazil. I would have found my way there, but by the time I was prepared to go, one was opened in the young State of Ohio [Oberlin College]—the first in the United States where women and negroes could enjoy opportunities with white men. I was disappointed when I came to seek a profession worthy an immortal being—every employment was closed to me, except those of the teacher, the seamstress, and the housekeeper. In education, in marriage, in religion, in everything, disappointment is the lot of woman. It shall be the business of my life to deepen this disappointment in every woman's heart until she bows down to it no longer. I wish that women, instead of being walking show-cases, instead of begging of their fathers and brothers the latest and gayest new bonnet, would ask of them their rights.

The question of Woman's Rights is a practical one. The notion has prevailed that it was only an ephemeral idea; that it was but women claiming the right to smoke cigars in the streets, and to frequent bar-rooms. Others have supposed it a question of comparative intellect; others still, of sphere. Too much has already been said and written about woman's sphere. Trace all the doctrines to their source and they will be found to have no basis except in the usages and prejudices of the age. This is seen in the fact that what is tolerated in woman in one country is not tolerated in another. In this country women may hold prayer-meetings, etc., but in Mohammedan countries it is written upon their mosques, "Women and dogs, and other impure animals, are not permitted to enter." Wendell Phillips says, "The best and greatest thing one is capable of doing, that is his sphere." I have confidence in the Father to believe that when He gives us the capacity to do anything He does not make a blunder. Leave women, then, to find their sphere. And do not tell us before we are born even, that our province is to cook dinners, darn stockings, and sew on buttons. We are told woman has all the rights she wants; and even women, I am ashamed to say, tell us so. They mistake the politeness of men for rights—seats while men stand in this hall to-night, and their adulations; but these are mere courtesies. We want rights. The flour-merchant, the house-builder, and the postman charge us no less on account of our sex; but when we endeavor to earn money to pay all these, then, indeed, we find the difference. Man, if he have energy, may hew out for himself a path where no mortal has ever trod, held back by nothing but what is in himself; the world is all before him, where to choose; and we are glad for you, brothers, men, that it is so. But the same society that drives forth the young man, keeps woman at home—a dependent—working little cats on worsted, and little dogs on punctured paper; but if she goes heartily and bravely to give herself to some worthy purpose, she is out of her sphere and she loses caste. Women working in tailor-shops are paid one-third as much as men. Some one in Philadelphia has stated that women make fine shirts for twelve and a half cents apiece; that no woman can make more than nine a week, and the sum thus earned, after deducting rent, fuel, etc., leaves her just three and a half cents a day for bread. Is it a wonder that women are driven to prostitution? Female teachers in New York are paid fifty dollars a year, and for every such situation there are five hundred applicants. I know not what you believe of God, but I believe He gave yearnings and longings to be filled, and that He did not mean all our time should be devoted to feeding and clothing the body. The present condition of woman causes a horrible perversion of the marriage relation. It is asked of a lady, "Has she married well?" "Oh, yes, her husband is rich." Woman must marry for a home, and you men are the sufferers by this; for a woman who loathes you may marry you because you have the means to get money which she can not have. But when woman can enter the lists with you and make money for herself, she will marry you only for deep and earnest affection.

I am detaining you too long, many of you standing, that I ought to apologize, but women have been wronged so long that I may wrong you a little. (Applause). A woman undertook in Lowell to sell shoes to ladies. Men laughed at her, but in six years she has run them all out, and has a monopoly of the trade. Sarah Tyndale, whose husband was an importer of china, and died bankrupt, continued his business, paid off his debts, and has made a fortune and built the largest china warehouse in the world. (Mrs. Mott here corrected Lucy. Mrs. Tyndale has not the largest china warehouse, but the largest assortment of china in the world). Mrs. Tyndale, herself, drew the plan of her warehouse, and it is the best plan ever drawn. A laborer to whom the architect showed it, said: "Don't she know e'en as much as some men?" I have seen a woman at manual labor turning out chair-legs in a cabinet-shop, with a dress short enough not to drag in the shavings. I wish other women would imitate her in this. It made her hands harder and broader, it is true, but I think a hand with a dollar and a quarter a day in it, better than one with a crossed ninepence. The men in the shop didn't use tobacco, nor swear—they can't do those things where there are women, and we owe it to our brothers to go wherever they work to keep them decent. The widening of woman's sphere is to improve her lot. Let us do it, and if the world scoff, let it scoff—if it sneer, let it sneer—but we will go on emulating the example of the sisters Grimke and Abby Kelley. When they first lectured against slavery they were not listened to as respectfully as you listen to us. So the first female physician meets many difficulties, but to the next the path will be made easy.

Lucretia Mott has been a preacher for years; her right to do so is not questioned among Friends. But when Antoinette Brown felt that she was commanded to preach, and to arrest the progress of thousands that were on the road to hell; why, when she applied for ordination they acted as though they had rather the whole world should go to hell, than that Antoinette Brown should be allowed to tell them how to keep out of it. She is now ordained over a parish in the State of New York, but when she meets on the Temperance platform the Rev. John Chambers, or your own Gen. Carey (applause) they greet her with hisses. Theodore Parker said: "The acorn that the school-boy carries in his pocket and the squirrel stows in his cheek, has in it the possibility of an oak, able to withstand, for ages, the cold winter and the driving blast." I have seen the acorn men and women, but never the perfect oak; all are but abortions. The young mother, when first the new-born babe nestles in her bosom, and a heretofore unknown love springs up in her heart, finds herself unprepared for this new relation in life, and she sends forth the child scarred and dwarfed by her own weakness and imbecility, as no stream can rise higher than its fountain.[14]

Ernestine Rose was the most exotic figure in the movement. She had been born in Poland, where her father was a rabbi and leader of the local Jewish community. When still a young girl, Rose left home alone and eventually came to the United States, where she associated herself with such controversial issues as complete religious freedom and women's rights.

Despite an accent, she was a forceful and eloquent speaker. This, plus her attractive appearance and unusual background, made her a popular figure on the lecture circuit. At women's conventions, she invariably attracted listeners and the press.

In 1851, Rose made the following speech at the second National Woman's Rights Convention, in Worcester, which was reprinted and circulated.

ERNESTINE ROSE AT WORCESTER

Ernestine Rose

. . . In the laws of the land she has no rights, in government she has no voice. And in spite of another principle, recognized in this Republic, namely, that "taxation without representation is tyranny," she is taxed without being represented. Her property may be consumed by taxes to defray the expenses of that unholy, unrighteous custom called war, yet she has no power to give her veto against it. From the cradle to the grave she is subject to the power and control of man. Father, guardian, or husband, one conveys her like some piece of merchandise over to the other. At marriage she loses her entire identity, and her being is said to have become merged in her husband. Has nature thus merged it? Has she ceased to exist and feel pleasure and pain? When she violates the laws of her being, does her husband pay the penalty? When she breaks the moral laws, does he suffer the punishment? When he supplies his wants, is it enough to satisfy her nature? . . . What an inconsistency, that from the moment she enters that compact in which she assumes the high responsibility of wife and mother, she ceases legally to exist, and becomes a purely submissive being. Blind submission in woman is considered a virtue, while submission to wrong is itself wrong, and resistance to wrong is virtue, alike in woman as in man.

But it will be said that the husband provides for the wife, or in other words, he feeds, clothes, and shelters her! I wish I had the power to make every one before me fully realize the degradation contained in that idea. Yes! he *keeps* her, and so he does a favorite horse; by law they are both considered his property. Both may, when the cruelty of the owner compels them to run away, be brought back by the strong arm of the law and, according to a still extant law in England, both may be led by the halter to the market place and sold. This is humiliating indeed, but nevertheless true; and the sooner these things are known and understood, the better for humanity. It is no fancy sketch. I know that some endeavor to throw the mantle of romance over the subject, and treat woman like some ideal existence, not liable to the ills of life. Let those deal in fancy, who have nothing better to deal in; we have to do with sober, sad realities, with stubborn facts.

Again, I shall be told that the law presumes the husband to be kind, affectionate, and ready to provide for and protect his wife. But what right, I ask, has the law to presume at all on the subject? What right has the law to intrust the interest and happiness of one being into the hands of another? And if the merging of the interest of one being into the other is a necessary consequence on marriage, why should woman always remain on the losing side? Turn the tables. Let the identity and interest of the husband be merged in the wife. Think you she would act less generously towards him, than he towards her? . . .

. . . Man forgets that woman can not be degraded without its reacting on himself. The impress of her mind is stamped on him by nature, and the early education of the mother, which no after-training can entirely efface; and therefore, the estimation she is held in falls back with double force upon him. Yet, from the force of prejudice against her, he knows it not. Not long ago I saw an account of two offenders, brought before a Justice of New York. One was charged with stealing a pair of boots, for which offense he was sentenced to six months' imprisonment; the other crime was assault and battery upon his wife; he was let off with a reprimand by the judge! With my principles, I am entirely opposed to punishment, and hold that to reform the erring and remove the causes of evil is much more efficient, as well as just, than to punish. But the judge showed us the comparative value which he set on these two kinds of *property*. But then you must remember that the boots were taken by a stranger, while the wife was insulted by her legal owner! . . .

It is high time . . . to compel man by the might of right to give woman her political, legal and social rights. . . . She will find her own sphere in accordance with her capacities, powers and tastes; and yet she will be woman still. . . . Away, then with that folly and absurdity, that a possession of her rights would be detrimental to her character; that if she is recognized as the equal to man, she would cease to be woman! Have his rights as a citizen of a republic, the elective franchise with all its advantages, so changed man's nature, that he has ceased to be man? . . .

. . . Do you not yet understand what has made woman what she is? Then see what the sickly taste and perverted judgment of man now admires in woman. Not physical and mental vigor, but a pale, delicate face; hands too small to grasp a broom, for that were treason in a lady; a voice so sentimental and depressed, that what she says can be learned only by the moving of her half parted lips; and, above all, that nervous sensibility which sees a ghost in every passing shadow, that beautiful diffidence which dare not take a step without the protecting arm of man to support her tender frame, and that shrinking mock-modesty that faints at the mention of the leg of a table. . . . Oh! the crying injustice towards woman. She is crushed at every step, and then insulted for being what a most pernicious education and corrupt public sentiment have made her.[15]

Sojourner Truth was a black woman, born a slave, who became a well-known preacher and lecturer, and stood in the forefront of the abolitionist cause. She was also an advocate of women's rights. Truth attended the First National Woman's Rights Convention, and she regularly spoke out for women's rights in her popular sermons and talks.

Close ties between abolitionism and the women's movement were common during the decade before the Civil War. Many movement leaders were also active abolitionists, and some, like Susan B. Anthony, were paid agents for the American Anti-Slavery Society. At conventions,

women repeatedly voiced their opposition to slavery and their kinship with black women. In turn, male abolitionists were among the staunchest supporters of the women. From Seneca Falls on, Frederick Douglass, the most famous black abolitionist, was a frequent convention speaker.

But it was not always simple for whites and blacks to cooperate in joint activities in a period of tension and controversy over race relations. In 1851, Sojourner Truth's appearance at an Ohio convention created a stir. Frances D. Gage was president of the convention, and she wrote down her impressions and recollections of the event.

GAGE'S REMINISCENCES OF SOJOURNER TRUTH

The leaders of the movement trembled on seeing a tall, gaunt black woman in a gray dress and white turban, surmounted with an uncouth sun-bonnet, march deliberately into the church, walk with the air of a queen up the aisle, and take her seat upon the pulpit steps. A buzz of disapprobation was heard all over the house, and there fell on the listening ear, "An abolition affair!" "Woman's rights and niggers!" "I told you so!" "Go it, darkey!"

I chanced on that occasion to wear my first laurels in public life as president of the meeting. At my request order was restored, and the business of the Convention went on.

Sojourner Truth. Leslie's, *Dec. 1869*

Morning, afternoon, and evening exercises came and went. . . . Again and again, timorous and trembling ones came to me and said, with earnestness, "Don't let her speak, Mrs. Gage, it will ruin us. Every newspaper in the land will have our cause mixed up with abolition and niggers, and we shall be utterly denounced." My only answer was, "We shall see when the time comes."

The second day the work waxed warm. Methodist, Baptist, Episcopal, Presbyterian, and Universalist ministers came in to hear and discuss the resolutions presented. One claimed superior rights and privileges for man, on the ground of "superior intellect"; another, because of the "manhood of Christ; if God had desired the equality of woman, He would have given some token of His will through the birth, life, and death of the Saviour." Another gave us a theological view of the "sin of our first mother."

There were very few women in those days who dared to "speak in meeting"; and the august teachers of the people were seemingly getting the better of us, while the boys in the galleries, and the sneerers among the pews, were hugely enjoying the discomfiture, as they supposed, of the "strong-minded." . . . When, slowly from her seat in the corner rose Sojourner Truth, who, till now, had scarcely lifted her head. "Don't let her speak!" gasped half a dozen in my ear. She moved slowly and solemnly to the front, laid her old bonnet at her feet, and turned her great speaking eyes to me. There was a hissing sound of disapprobation above and below. I rose and announced "Sojourner Truth," and begged the audience to keep silence for a few moments.

The tumult subsided at once, and every eye was fixed on this almost Amazon form, which stood nearly six feet high, head erect, and eyes piercing the upper air like one in a dream. At her first word there was a profound hush. She spoke in deep tones, which, though not loud, reached every ear in the house, and away through the throng at the doors and windows.

"Wall, chilern, whar dar is so much racket dar must be somethin' out o' kilter. I tink dat 'twixt de niggers of de Souf and de womin at de Norf, all talkin' 'bout rights, de white men will be in a fix pretty soon. But what's all dis here talkin' 'bout?

"Dat man ober dar say dat womin needs to be helped into carriages, and lifted ober ditches, and to hab de best place everywhar. Nobody eber helps me into carriages, or ober mud-puddles, or gibs me any best place!" And raising herself to her full height, and her voice to a pitch like rolling thunder, she asked. "And a'n't I a woman? Look at me! Look at my arm! (and she bared her right arm to the shoulder, showing her tremendous muscular power). I have ploughed, and planted, and gathered into barns, and no man could head me! And a'n't I a woman? I could work as much and eat as much as a man—when I could get it—and bear de lash as well! And a'n't I a woman? I have borne thirteen chilern, and seen 'em mos' all sold off to slavery, and when I cried out with my mother's grief, none but Jesus heard me! And a'n't I a woman?

"Den dey talks 'bout dis ting in de head; what dis dey call it?" "Intellect," whispered some one near. "Dat's it, honey. What's dat got to do wid womin's rights or nigger's rights? If my cup won't hold but a pint, and yourn holds a quart, wouldn't ye be mean not to let me have my little half-measure full?" And she pointed her significant finger, and sent a keen glance at the minister who had made the argument. The cheering was long and loud.

"Den dat little man in black dar, he say women can't have as much rights as men, 'cause Christ wan't a woman! Whar did your Christ come from?" Rolling thunder couldn't have stilled that crowd, as did those deep, wonderful tones, as she stood there with outstretched arms and eyes of fire. Raising her voice still louder, she repeated, "Whar did your Christ come from? From God and a woman! Man had nothin' to do wid Him." Oh, what a rebuke that was to that little man.

Turning again to another objector, she took up the defense of Mother Eve. I can not follow her through it all. It was pointed, and witty, and solemn; eliciting at almost every sentence deafening applause; and she ended by asserting: "If de fust woman God ever made was strong enough to turn de world upside down all alone, dese women togedder (and she glanced her eye over the platform) ought to be able to turn it back, and get it right side up again! And now dey is asking to do it, de men better let 'em." Long-continued cheering greeted this. " 'Bleeged to ye for hearin' on me, and now ole Sojourner han't got nothin' more to say."

Amid roars of applause, she returned to her corner, leaving more than one of us with streaming eyes, and hearts beating with gratitude. She had taken us up in her strong arms and carried us safely over the slough of difficulty, turning the whole tide in our favor. I have never in my life seen anything like the magical influence that subdued the mobbish spirit of the day, and turned the sneers and jeers of an excited crowd into notes of respect and admiration. Hundreds rushed up to shake hands with her, and congratulate the glorious old mother, and bid her God-speed on her mission of "testifyin' agin concerning the wickedness of this 'ere people."[16]

RESOLUTIONS AND GOALS

Despite the informal and loose organization of the women's movement in the 1850's, there was a surprisingly large area of consensus in the demands for change that came out of local, state, and national conventions.

Part of the standard procedure at conventions was the introduction, discussion, and adoption of resolutions. In these resolutions, women formulated their goals and gave direction to the work that took place between meetings.

Following the direction outlined at Seneca Falls and Rochester, convention resolutions affirmed women's equality with men, called for their acceptance as equals, and listed specific reforms. Consistently, they set forth demands for educational opportunities, for better jobs and pay, and for access to the professions. A common theme in the resolutions was the interrelationship of women's poor education, their poverty, and their lack of freedom.

BETTER JOBS AND EDUCATION

National Woman's Rights Convention, 1850

Resolved, That the greatest difficulty now in our path is a stinted purse; and to remove this there is but one way, for every woman interested in this reform to seek out as speedily as possible some legitimate way of getting money. Work is worship. Go, get your gold by honest toil.

Resolved, That woman must seek out a new order of employments, to secure for herself virtue and independence; marriage and the needle, heretofore her only resources, are crushing to both.[17]

Massilon, Ohio, Convention, 1852

Resolved, That in the general scantiness of compensation of women's labor, the restrictions imposed by custom and public opinion upon her choice of employments, and her opportunities of earning money, and the laws and social usages which regulate the distribution of property as between men and women, have produced a pecuniary dependence of woman upon man, widely and deeply injurious in many ways; and not the least of all in too often perverting marriage, which should be a holy relation growing out of spiritual affinities, into a mere bargain and sale—a means to woman of securing a subsistence and a home, and to man of obtaining a kitchen drudge or a parlor ornament.[18]

West Chester, Pennsylvania, 1852

Resolved, That the present position of medical organizations, precluding women from the same educational advantages with men, under pretext of delicacy, virtually acknowledges the impropriety of his being her medical attendant.

Resolved, That we will do all in our power to sustain those women who, from a conviction of duty, enter the medical profession, in their efforts to overcome the evils that have accumulated in their path, and in attacking the strongholds of vice.

Resolved, That the past actions and present indications of our medical schools should not affect us at all; and notwithstanding Geneva and Cleveland Medical Colleges closed their doors after graduating one woman each, and Harvard, through the false delicacy of the students, declared it inexpedient to receive one who had been in successful practice many years, we would still earnestly follow in peace and love where duty points, and leave the verdict to an enlightened public sentiment.[19]

New York, 1853

Resolved, That, inasmuch as universal experience proves the inseparable connection between dependence and degradation—while it is plain to every candid observer of society that women are kept poor, by being crowded together, to compete with and undersell one another in a few branches of labor, and that from this very poverty of women, spring many of the most terrible wrongs and evils, which corrupt and endanger society; therefore do we invite the earnest attention of capitalists, merchants, traders, manufacturers, and mechanics, to the urgent need, which everywhere exists, of opening to women new avenues of honest and honorable employment, and we do hereby call upon all manly men to make room for their sisters to earn an independent livelihood.

Resolved, That women justly claim an equally free access with men, to the highest means of mental, moral, and physical culture, provided in seminaries, colleges, professional and industrial schools; and that we call upon all friends of progress and upon the Legislature of New York, in establishing and endowing institutions, to favor pre-eminently those which seek to place males and females on a level of equal advantages in their system of education.[20]

At conventions and in the work done between meetings, three goals received more attention than the others. One was the revision of state personal property laws that denied women the ownership and control of their property and earnings. The next was change in child custody laws to give mothers equal guardianship rights over children, and in case of the father's death, to give the mother custody of minors and control of their property. The third objective was the vote.

PERSONAL PROPERTY RIGHTS

New York State was the first in the North to revise its laws concerning married women's property. The changes made in 1848 gave married women control of inherited property and gifts. They still, however, lacked the right to sell or will their property freely or to control their own earnings. Agitation for more reform continued through the 1850's in New York, and was echoed in most other states.

A Convention Resolution (Ohio, 1852)

Resolved, That to perfect the marriage union and provide for the inevitable vicissitudes of life, the individuality of both parties should be equally and distinctively recognized by the parties themselves, and by the laws of the land; and, therefore, justice and the highest regard for the interests of society require that our laws be so amended, that married women may be permitted to conduct business on their own account; to acquire, hold, invest, and dispose of property in their own separate and individual right, subject to all corresponding and appropriate obligations.

Resolved, That the clause of the Constitution of the State of Ohio, which declares that ''all men have the right of acquiring and possessing property,'' is violated by the judicial doctrine that the labor of the wife is the property of the husband.[21]

A Petition to State Legislators

PETITION FOR THE JUST AND EQUAL RIGHTS OF WOMEN.—The Legislature of the State of New York have, by the Acts of 1848 and 1849, testified the purpose of the people of this State to place married women on an equality with married men, in regard to the holding, conveying, and devising of real and personal property. We, therefore, the undersigned petitioners, inhabitants of the State of New York, male and female, having attained to the legal majority, believing that women, alike married and single, do still suffer under many and grievous legal disabilities, do earnestly request the Senate and Assembly of the State of New York to appoint a Joint Committee of both Houses, to revise the Statutes of New York, and to propose such amendments as will fully establish the legal equality of women with men; and we hereby ask a hearing before such Committee by our accredited Representatives.[22]

A Discussion at Convention

Mrs. ROSE [Ernestine Rose] said: As to the personal property, after all debts and liabilities are discharged, the widow receives one-half of it; and, in addition, the law kindly allows her her own wearing apparel, her own ornaments, proper to her station, one bed, with appurtenances for the same; a stove, the Bible, family pictures, and all the school-books; also, all spinning-wheels and weaving-looms, one table, six chairs, tea cups and saucers, one tea-pot, one sugar dish, and six spoons. (Much laughter). But the law does not inform us whether they are to be tea or table spoons; nor does the law make any provision for kettles, sauce-pans, and all such necessary things. But the presumption seems to be that the spoons meant are teaspoons; for, as ladies are generally considered very delicate, the law presumed that a widow might live on tea only; but spinning-wheels and weaving-looms are very necessary articles for ladies nowadays. (Hissing and great confusion). Why, you need not hiss, for I am expounding the law. These wise law-makers, who seem to have lived somewhere about the time of the flood, did not dream of spinning and weaving by steam-power. When our great-great-grandmothers had to weave every article of apparel worn by the family, it was, no doubt, considered a very good law to allow the widow the possession of the spinning-wheels and the weaving-looms. But, unfortunately for some laws, man is a progressive being; his belief, opinions, habits, manners, and customs change, and so do spinning-wheels and weaving-looms; and, with men and things, law must change too, for what is the value of a law when man has outgrown it? As well might you bring him to the use of his baby clothes, because they once fitted him, as to keep him to such a law. No. Laws, when man has outgrown them, are fit only to be cast aside among the things that were.

But I must not forget, the law allows the widow something more. She is allowed one cow, all sheep to the number of ten, with the fleeces and the cloth from the same, two swine, and the pork therefrom. (Great laughter.) My friends, do not say that I stand here to make these laws ridiculous. No; if you laugh, it is at their own inherent ludicrousness; for I state them simply and truly as they are; for they are so ridiculous in themselves, that it is impossible to make them more so.

Mrs. NICHOLS [Clarina Howard Nichols] said: As widow, too, the law bears heavily on woman. If her children have property, she is adjudged unworthy of their guardianship; and although the decree of God has made her the true and natural guardian of her children, she is obliged to pay from her scanty means to be constituted so by law.

I have conversed with judges and legislators, and tried to learn a reason for these things, but failed to find it. A noble man once gave me what he probably thought was a good one. ''Women,'' he said to me, ''can not earn as much as men!'' We say they should be allowed to earn as much. They have the ability, and the means should not be shut out from them. I have heard of another man who held woman's industrial ability at a low rate. ''His wife,'' he said, ''had never been able to do anything but attend to her children.'' ''How many have you?'' he was asked; and the answer was, ''Nine.'' Nine children to attend to! nine children cared for! and she could do nothing more, the wife of this most reasonable man. . . . Now, which is of more importance to the community, the property which that reasonable husband made, or the nine children *whom that mother* brought, with affectionate and tender toil, through the perils of infancy and youth, until they were men and women?[23]

Beginning in the 1850's, changes gradually were made in personal property laws, and by the end of the century, women had gained more economic independence under the law.

EQUAL CUSTODY RIGHTS

Resolutions like the one below, demanding equal custody over children for both parents, were also part of convention activity throughout the 1850's.

A Resolution, 1853

Resolved, That, whereas, under the common law, the father is regarded as the guardian, by nature, of his children, having the entire control of their persons and education, while only upon the death of the father, does the mother become the guardian by nature; and, whereas, by the revised statutes of New York, it is provided, that where an estate in lands shall become vested in an infant, the guardianship of such infant, with the rights, powers, and duties of a guardian in soccage, shall belong to the father, and only in case of the father's death, to the mother; and, whereas, finally and chiefly, by the revised statutes of New York, it is provided, that every father may, by his deed or last will, duly executed, dispose of the custody and tuition of his children, during their minority, "to any person or persons in possession or remainder"; therefore, do we solemnly protest against the utter violation of every mother's rights, authorized by existing laws, in regard to the guardianship of infants, and demand, in the name of common humanity, that the Legislature of New York so amend the statutes, as to place fathers and mothers on equal footing in regard to the guardianship of their children. Especially do we invite the Legislature instantly to pass laws, entitling mothers to become their children's guardians, in all cases where, by habitual drunkenness, immorality, or improvidence, fathers are incompetent to the sacred trust.[24]

As women in all states denounced laws that gave fathers more power and preferential custody over children, the pressure for reform increased. Slowly, legislators began to move toward equal child custody laws. By 1900, the inequity and injustice of custody laws had decreased significantly.

THE VOTE

Although at Seneca Falls both women and men found the idea of giving the vote to women startling and difficult to accept, the demand for the franchise—linked with a protest against taxation without representation—quickly became an important goal for women.

Resolutions calling for the vote were regularly passed at conventions.

Rochester, 1853

Resolved, That inasmuch as it is the fundamental principle of the Nation and of every State in this Union, that all "governments derive their just powers from the consent of the governed"—it is a manifest violation of the Supreme Law of the land for males to govern females without their consent; and therefore do we demand, of the people of New York, such a change in the Constitution of the State, as will secure

to women the right of suffrage which is now so unjustly monopolized by men.[25]

National Woman's Rights Convention, 1853

Resolved, That woman will soonest free herself from the legal disabilities she now suffers, by securing the right to the elective franchise—thus becoming herself a law-maker—and that to this end we will petition our respective State legislatures to call conventions to amend their constitutions, so that the right to the elective franchise shall not be limited by the word "male."[26]

MARRIAGE AND DIVORCE

One of the few controversies about goals during the first decade concerned marriage and divorce. Stanton, who played a prominent part in formulating issues within the movement, wanted a serious examination of these social institutions.

In 1852, as president of New York's women's temperance society, she dismayed the convention with this proposal:

Let no woman remain in the relation of wife with a confirmed drunkard. Let no drunkard be the father of her child. . . . Let us petition our State government so to modify the laws affecting marriage and custody of children, that the drunkard shall have no claims on wife or child.[27]

Stanton's views on marriage and divorce developed through the decade. She believed that marriage was a contractual rather than a sacred and immutable institution. Her approval of divorce, under certain circumstances, led her to favor reform of divorce laws. Conventions, too, began to consider questions relating to marriage and divorce, with Stanton and Ernestine Rose urging serious reappraisal. Finally, in 1860, at the National Woman's Rights Convention, in New York, Stanton introduced a series of resolutions on these incendiary topics.

Resolutions on Marriage and Divorce

1. *Resolved,* That, in the language (slightly varied) of John Milton, "Those who marry intend as little to conspire their own ruin, as those who swear allegiance, and as a whole people is to an ill government, so is one man or woman to an ill marriage. If a whole people, against any authority, covenant, or statute, may, by the sovereign edict of charity, save not only their lives, but honest liberties, from unworthy bondage, as well may a married party, against any private covenant, which he or she never entered, to his or her mischief, be redeemed from unsupportable disturbances, to honest peace and just contentment."

2. *Resolved,* That all men are created equal, and all women, in their natural rights, are the equals of men, and

endowed by their Creator with the same inalienable right to the pursuit of happiness.

3. *Resolved,* That any constitution, compact, or covenant between human beings, that failed to produce or promote human happiness, could not, in the nature of things, be of any force or authority; and it would be not only a right, but a duty, to abolish it.

4. *Resolved,* That though marriage be in itself divinely founded, and is fortified as an institution by innumerable analogies in the whole kingdom of universal nature, still, a true marriage is only known by its results; and, like the fountain, if pure, will reveal only pure manifestations. Nor need it ever be said, ''What God hath joined together, let no man put asunder,'' for man could not put it asunder; nor can he any more unite what God and nature have not joined together.

5. *Resolved,* That of all insulting mockeries of heavenly truth and holy law, none can be greater than that physical impotency is cause sufficient for divorce, while no amount of mental or moral or spiritual imbecility is ever to be pleaded in support of such a demand.

6. *Resolved,* That such a law was worthy [of] those dark periods when marriage was held by the greatest doctors and priests of the Church to be a work of the flesh only, and almost, if not altogether, a defilement; denied wholly to the clergy, and a second time, forbidden to all.

7. *Resolved,* That an unfortunate or ill-assorted marriage is ever a calamity, but not ever, perhaps never, a crime—and when society or government, by its laws or customs, compels its continuance, always to the grief of one of the parties, and the actual loss and damage of both, it usurps an authority never delegated to man, nor exercised by God himself.

8. *Resolved,* That observation and experience daily show how incompetent are men, as individuals, or as governments, to select partners in business, teachers for their children, ministers of their religion, or makers, adjudicators, or administrators of their laws; and as the same weakness and blindness must attend in the selection of matrimonial partners, the dictates of humanity and common sense alike show that the latter and most important contract should no more be perpetual than either or all of the former.

9. *Resolved,* That children born in these unhappy and unhallowed connections are, in the most solemn sense, of unlawful birth—the fruit of lust, but not of love—and so not of God, divinely descended, but from beneath, whence proceed all manner of evil and uncleanliness.

10. *Resolved,* That next to the calamity of such a birth to the child, is the misfortune of being trained in the atmosphere of a household where love is not the law, but where discord and bitterness abound; stamping their demoniac features on the moral nature, with all their odious peculiarities—thus continuing the race in a weakness and depravity that must be a sure precursor of its ruin, as a just penalty of long-violated law.[28]

New Yorkers were already agitated over a proposal in the

legislature for a more liberal divorce law. Stanton's resolutions caused an uproar at the convention. Some speakers questioned whether the topic should be discussed at all, and it was proposed that the resolutions be stricken from the record. After a turbulent debate, this motion was defeated. The Stanton resolutions, though not endorsed by the convention, remained in the record of its proceedings. And Stanton, Rose, and Mott received approval to testify before the New York legislative committee considering divorce reform.

DRESS REFORM

Another goal that proved controversial was dress reform. Between 1851 and 1854, several women's rights activists experimented with a new kind of clothing—the so-called Bloomer outfit, whose pantaloons and loosely fitted tunic gave women an unaccustomed freedom of movement and relieved them of the weight of voluminous long skirts with their starched slips and the discomfort of constricting stays and corsets.

Controversy over dress reform was really a disagreement

"Ladies Dress Reform Meeting at Freeman Place Chapel. Boston, Mass." Leslie's, June 1874

over tactics—one of the first to arise within the women's movement. The women who tried the new dress (their numbers included Amelia Bloomer, the Grimké sisters, Elizabeth Cady Stanton, Susan B. Anthony, Lucy Stone, Paulina Wright Davis, and Elizabeth Smith Miller) found it delightfully comfortable and liberating. They understood, as Lucy Stone wrote in a letter to Susan B. Anthony, that changing women's costume was closely related to changing their way of life.

Stone on Dress Reform

Women are in bondage; their clothes are a great hindrance to their engaging in any business which will make them pecuniarily independent, and since the soul of womanhood never can be queenly and noble as long as it must beg bread for its body, is it not better, even at the expense of a vast deal of annoyance, that they whose lives deserve respect and are greater than their garments should give an example by which woman may more easily work out her emancipation? . . .[29]

Dress reform, however, turned out to be one of the most provocative and inflammatory changes proposed by the movement. The Bloomer costume quickly became the object of ridicule both publicly and privately, and what Lucy Stone described as a "vast deal of annoyance" was a personal martyrdom for those who wore it. They were targets of cruel and painful condemnation—of criticism from the pulpit, jeers in the streets, ostracism at social gatherings. It was not long before most of those who had adopted the new costume, commencing with Stanton, reluctantly gave up wearing the trousers and put aside dress reform for other goals that seemed more important. A few, such as Elizabeth Smith Miller and Susan B. Anthony, disagreed and argued that the issue was too important to concede. Eventually, however, Anthony too forsook the Bloomer, exclaiming that she could bear no longer the emotional anguish that came with wearing it.

While concern with dress reform never completely died out—women continued to discuss and write about the importance of clothing to their condition of life—it did not become a major goal of the movement.

RADICAL CHANGES

Implicit in all convention resolutions—from those that called for the ballot to those that demanded jobs and edu-

"Two of the Fe'he males." 1851 lithograph

cation—was the demand for freedom and self-determination for women, a goal that clearly involved radical changes for men as well as women.

At the Second National Woman's Rights Convention, in Worcester, Massachusetts, in 1851, the following resolution was passed, revealing the grand vision that inspired the movement even during this early period.

A Resolution

Resolved, That we deny the right of any portion of the species to decide for another portion, or of any individual to decide for another individual, what is and what is not their proper sphere; that the proper sphere of all human beings is the largest and highest to which they are able to attain: what this is cannot be ascertained without complete liberty of choice; woman, therefore, ought to choose for herself what sphere she will fill, what education she will seek, and what employment she will follow; and not be bound to accept, in submission, the rights, education and the sphere which man thinks proper to allow her.[30]

MOVEMENT WORK

Participating in the movement meant much more than attending the conventions. An immense output of labor took place between conventions in an effort to achieve effective reform. Women were involved in preparing studies and briefs, lobbying, testifying before legislators, writing pamphlets and newspaper articles, making speeches, and collecting tens of thousands of signatures on petitions. During the decade, journals like The Lily, The Una, *the* Pittsburgh Saturday Visitor, *and the* Woman's Advocate, *published by women, offered news and information on women's rights activities.*

In some states, petition campaigns were masterpieces of strategy and organization: in New York, under Susan B. Anthony's leadership, each of the sixty counties had a captain to oversee a thorough canvassing. Canvassing was preceded by speeches which were, in turn, preceded by publicity in newspapers, on signposts, and in the churches. Pamphlets were distributed. Conventions were held at the state capital and were timed to coincide with the presentation of petitions and appearances before legislative committees.

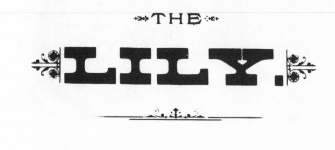

In all states, petition campaigns involved women in difficult and sustained effort. Indeed, turning movement objectives into concrete reforms was hard work, as can be seen in this report from Ohio. In 1861, J. Elizabeth Jones, who was general agent of the Ohio movement, wrote the following summary.

WORK IN OHIO

And through the earnest efforts of Mrs. Robinson, Mrs. Gage, Mrs. Wilson, Mrs. Tilden, and many others, the Legislature was petitioned from year to year for a redress of legal and political wrongs. At a later period, the indefatigable exertions of Mrs. Adeline T. Swift sustained the interest and the agitation in such portions of the State as she could reach. As the fruit of her labor, many thousands of names, pleading for equality, have been presented to the General Assembly, which labor has been continued to the present time.

Our last effort, of which I am now more particularly to speak, was commenced early in the season, by extensive correspondence to enlist sympathy and aid in behalf of petitions. As soon as we could get the public ear, several lecturing agents were secured, and they did most efficient service, both with tongue and with pen. One of these was Mrs. C. I. H. Nichols, of Kansas, formerly of Vermont; and perhaps no person was ever better qualified than she. . . .

Of another of our agents—Mrs. Cutler, of Illinois—equally as much can be said of her qualifications and her efficiency. . . .

Besides the General Agent, whose time was divided between correspondence, lecturing, and the general details of the movement, there were other and most efficient workers, especially in canvassing for signatures. We are indebted to Mrs. Anne Ryder, of Cincinnati, for much labor in this direction; and also to Mrs. Howard, of Columbus, for similar service. Miss Olympia Brown, a graduate of Antioch College, canvassed several towns most successfully—adding thousands of names to the lists heretofore obtained. Equally zealous were women, and men also, in various sections of the State. By means of this hearty co-operation, both branches of the Legislature were flooded with Woman's Rights petitions during the first part of the session—a thousand and even two thousand names were presented at a time.

Our main object this year, as heretofore, has been to secure personal property and parental rights, never ignoring, however, the right to legislate for ourselves. We were fortunate in the commencement in enlisting some of the leading influences of the State in favor of the movement. Persons occupying the highest social and political position, very fully endorsed our claims to legal equality, and rendered valuable aid by public approval of the same. We took measures at an early period to obtain the assistance of the press; and by means of this auxiliary our work has been more fully recognized, and more generally appreciated than it could otherwise have been. Without exception, the leading journals of the State have treated our cause with consideration, and generously commended the efforts of its agents.

So numerous were the petitions, and so largely did they represent the best constituency of the State, that the committees in whose hands they were placed, felt that by all just parliamentary usage, they were entitled to a candid consideration. Accordingly they invited several of us who had been prominent, to defend our own cause in the Senate chamber, before their joint Committee and such of the General Assembly and of the public, as might choose to come and listen. . . .

The change in public sentiment, the marked favor with which our cause began to be regarded in the judicial and legislative departments, encouraged us to hope that if equal and exact justice were not established, which we could hardly expect, we should at least obtain legal equality in many particulars. The Senate committee soon reported a bill, drafted by one of their number—Judge Key—and fully endorsed by all the judges of the Supreme Court, securing to the married woman the use of her real estate, and the avails of her own separate labor, together with such power to protect her property, and do business in her own name, as men possess. The last provision was stricken out and the bill thus amended passed both Houses, the Senate by a very large majority. . . . [31]

No objective received more attention than efforts to get the franchise. Women petitioned legislatures, conducted local educational campaigns, and lobbied at state capitols; the regular and hard work that was done in the 1850's was training for a long battle. As Kansas lawmakers revealed in the report below, there was little disposition to share the power of the ballot with women. The struggle would take seventy years.

REPORT OF KANSAS JUDICIARY FRANCHISE COMMITTEE

The Committee on the Judiciary, to whom in connection with the Committee on Franchise was referred the petition of sundry citizens of Kansas, "protesting against any constitutional distinctions based on difference of sex," have had the same under consideration, and beg leave to make the following report:

Your Committee concede the point in the petition upon which the right is claimed, that "the women of the State have individually an evident common interest with its men in the protection of life, liberty, property, and intellectual culture," and are not disposed to deny, that sex involves greater and more complex responsibilities, but the Committee are compelled to dissent from conclusion of petition; they think the rights of women are safe in present hands. The proof that they are so is found in the growing disposition on

the part of different Legislatures to extend and protect their rights of property, and in the enlightened and progressive spirit of the age which acts gently, but efficiently upon the legislation of the day. Such rights as are natural are now enjoyed as fully by women as men. Such rights and duties as are merely political they should be relieved from, that they may have more time to attend to those greater and more complicated responsibilities which petitioners claim, and which your Committee admit devolves upon woman.

All of which is respectfully submitted. [32]

Amelia Bloomer's labors for women's rights illustrate the movement activities that took place outside the conventions. Bloomer was well known as a temperance worker and as editor of The Lily *before she committed herself to women's rights. Her endorsement of the Bloomer costume also brought her public attention (although she did not design the baggy trousers and overblouse that were named after her, nor was she the first or the most dedicated in wearing them).*

In 1855 Bloomer had moved from New York to Council Bluffs, Iowa, where she added her dedication and experience to women's rights activities in what was then called the West. On January 8, 1856, she addressed the Nebraska House of Representatives, which had invited her to speak about a pending bill granting women the vote. Her appearance was news and was discussed in several Western papers.

AN OBSERVER COMMENTS ON BLOOMER'S SPEECH

Dear Chronotype:—I went to Omaha and spent Tuesday and Wednesday of last week. Though the thermometer ranged from twenty-seven to thirty-seven degrees below zero, which made everything as cold as an iceberg, yet there were sufficient materials for observation and mental consideration to make one regardless of the *chills* or the threatenings of old Boreas.

We peeped in to see the Legislature. Both Houses were in a fix—each repudiating the other and declining to act in concert. The cause of this we did not exactly learn; but thought it a bad start for a new Legislature in a new but prosperous territory. But they will grow wiser as they grow older, *perhaps.*

But, Mr. CHRONOTYPE, there was another feature to my observation, still more unique and curious to me. The ladies —God bless them!—are ever first and foremost in every interesting feature that springs up in society—so it was even in Omaha City. To see a lady stand before an audience, and listen to disquisitions on "Woman's Rights," was something full of interest, and on Tuesday night I was gratified for my first time. Mrs. Amelia Bloomer, who had been formerly invited by members of the Legislature and others, arrived at the door of the State House, at 7 o'clock P.M., and, by the gallantry of General Larimer, a passage was made for her to the stand. The house had been crowded for some time with eager expectants to get a glimpse of the Bloomer Costume, and listen to the arguments which were to be adduced as the fruitage of female thought and research. We all had been

Amelia Bloomer. The Lily, Sept. 1851

packed into the house who could possibly find a place for the sole of the foot. Mrs. Bloomer arose amidst cheers. We watched her closely and saw that she was perfectly self-possessed—not a nerve seemed to be moved by excitement, and the voice did not tremble. She arose in the dignity of a true woman, as if the importance of her mission so absorbed her thoughts that timidity or bashfulness were too mean to entangle the mental powers. She delivered her lecture in a

pleasing, able, and, I may say, eloquent manner, that enchained the attention of her audience for an hour and a half. A *man* could not have beat it.

In mingling with the people the next day, we found that her argument had met with favor. As far as property rights were concerned all seemed to agree with the lady, that the laws of our country were wrong, and that Woman should receive the same protection as man; but the idea of enfranchising Woman met with some disfavor. All we have time to say now is that Mrs. B's arguments on Woman's Rights are unanswerable. We may doubt the policy for woman to vote, but who can draw the lines and say that *naturally* she has not a right to do so? Mrs. Bloomer, though "little body," is among the great women of the United States; and her keen, intellectual eye seems to flash fire from a fountain that will consume the stubble of old theories until Woman is placed in her true position in the enjoyment of equal rights and privileges.—Her only danger is in asking too much.

Respectfully,
ONEIDA[33]

OPPOSITION

Throughout the decade, a steady stream of abuse and ridicule was poured upon the women who dared to speak out for their rights. Undoubtedly, many were in this way intimidated and kept from participating. Those who were not deterred needed a large reservoir of courage and determination.

Criticism came from many sources. Clergymen continued to denounce any departure from women's "proper sphere," and politicians disparaged their claim to political power. Newspapers, which were rapidly increasing in number and influence, were among the loudest critics of the movement.

THE SYRACUSE *DAILY STAR*

Our usual amount of editorial matter is again crowded out this morning by the extreme quantity of gabble the Woman's Righters got off yesterday. Perhaps we owe an apology for having given publicity to the mass of corruption, heresies, ridiculous nonsense, and reeking vulgarities which these bad women have vomited forth for the past three days. Our personal preference would have been to have entirely disregarded these folks *per signe de mepris,* but the public appetite cries for these novelties and eccentricities of the times, and the daily press is expected to gratify such appetites; furthermore, we are of opinion that reporting such a Convention as this, is the most effectual way of checking the mischief it might otherwise do. The proceedings of these three days' pow-wow are a most shocking commentary upon themselves, and waken burning scorn for the participants in them. . . . [34]

THE NEW YORK *HERALD*

The assemblage of rampant women which convened at the Tabernacle yesterday was an interesting phase in the comic history of the nineteenth century.

We saw, in broad daylight, in a public hall in the city of New York, a gathering of unsexed women—unsexed in mind all of them, and many in habiliments—publicly propounding the doctrine that they should be allowed to step out of their appropriate sphere, and mingle in the busy walks of every-day life, to the neglect of those duties which both human and divine law have assigned to them. We do not stop to argue against so ridiculous a set of ideas. We will only inquire who are to perform those duties which we and our fathers before us have imagined belonged solely to women. Is the world to be depopulated? Are there to be no more children? Or are we to adopt the French mode, which is too well known to need explanation?

It is almost needless for us to say that these women are entirely devoid of personal attractions. They are generally thin maiden ladies, or women who perhaps have been disappointed in the endeavors to appropriate the breeches and the rights of their unlucky lords; the first class having found it utterly impossible to induce any young or old man into the matrimonial noose have turned out upon the world, and are now endeavoring to revenge themselves upon the sex who have slighted them. The second having been dethroned from their empire over the hearts of their husbands, for reasons which may easily be imagined, go vagabondizing over the country, boring unfortunate audiences with long essays lacking point or meaning, and amusing only from the impudence displayed by the speakers in putting them forth in a civilized country. They violate the rules of decency and taste by attiring themselves in eccentric habiliments, which hang loosely and inelegantly upon their forms, making that which we have been educated to respect, to love, and to admire, only an object of aversion and disgust. A few of these unfortunate women have awoke from their momentary trance, and quickly returned to the dress of decent society; but we saw yesterday many disciples of the Bloomer school at the Tabernacle. There was yesterday, and there will be to-day, a wide field for all such at the Tabernacle. . . . [35]

LEGISLATORS RESPOND, ALBANY *REGISTER*

Mr. Foote, from the [New York State] Judiciary Committee, made a report on Women's Rights that set the whole House in roars of laughter:

"The Committee is composed of married and single gentlemen. The bachelors on the Committee, with becoming diffidence, have left the subject pretty much to the married gentlemen. They have considered it with the aid of the light they have before them and the experience married life has given them. Thus aided, they are enabled to state that the ladies always have the best place and choicest titbit at the table. They have the best seat in the cars, carriages, and sleighs; the warmest place in the winter, and the coolest place in the summer. They have their choice on which side of the bed they will lie, front or back. A lady's dress costs three times as much as that of a gentleman; and, at the present time, with the prevailing fashion, one lady occupies three times as much space in the world as a gentleman.

"It has thus appeared to the married gentlemen of your Committee, being a majority (the bachelors being silent for the reason mentioned, and also probably for the further reason that they are still suitors for the favors of the gentler sex), that, if there is any inequality or oppression in the case, the gentlemen are the sufferers. They, however, have presented no petitions for redress; having, doubtless, made up their minds to yield to an inevitable destiny.

"On the whole, the Committee have concluded to recommend no measure, except that as they have observed several instances in which husband and wife have both signed the same petition. In such case, they would recommend the parties to apply for a law authorizing them to change dresses, so that the husband may wear petticoats, and the wife the breeches, and thus indicate to their neighbors and the public the true relation in which they stand to each other." [36]

SUPPORT

The movement also had its friends. Many men, especially reform leaders, steadfastly supported the women; they served on committees, spoke at conventions, and contributed experience, money, and confidence. In some newspapers, women's activities received serious and objective treatment. A few showed outright sympathy.

REPORT FROM BOSTON

The hall was crammed at ten cents a head, and the meeting [a women's rights meeting, organized by Boston women, and held in May 1859] of no little interest. The speeches were excellent in the main, and the whole affair a success. Hundreds went away, unable to obtain admittance. The audience was three quarters ladies, among whom we recognized not a few well-known in the first circles of the city and its vicinity. [37]

NEBRASKA *NEWS*

Last evening Mrs. AMELIA BLOOMER delivered a lecture at the State House in this city, on the question of Woman's right of franchise. The Hall of Representatives in which she spoke, was crowded to overflowing. The lady was listened to with marked interest and attention. We think all persons of candor, whatever their opinions may be in relation to the views of Mrs. BLOOMER, will at least acknowledge, that she is certainly a most pleasing and logical speaker, and that she handled the subject with great ability.[38]

The most consistent newspaper support in the 1850's came from the abolitionist press. Frederick Douglass, who edited The North Star, *used its pages to support the rights of women.*

AN EDITORIAL

THE RIGHTS OF WOMEN.—One of the most interesting events of the past week, was the holding of what is technically styled a Woman's Rights Convention at Seneca Falls. The speaking, addresses, and resolutions of this extraordinary meeting were almost wholly conducted by women; and although they evidently felt themselves in a novel position, it is but simple justice to say that their whole proceedings were characterized by marked ability and dignity. . . .

. . . While it is impossible for us to go into this subject at length, and dispose of the various objections which are often urged against such a doctrine as that of female equality, we are free to say that in respect to political rights, we hold woman to be justly entitled to all we claim for man. We go farther, and express our conviction that all political rights which it is expedient for man to exercise, it is equally so for woman. All that distinguishes man as an intelligent and accountable being, is equally true of woman; and if that government only is just which governs by the free consent of the governed, there can be no reason in the world for denying to woman the exercise of the elective franchise, or a hand in making and administering the laws of the land. Our doctrine is that ''right is of no sex.'' We therefore bid the women engaged in this movement our humble Godspeed.[39]

The women's movement remained lively and controversial throughout the decade. Its implications for change in the relationships between men and women and in all social institutions concerned everyone and aroused many. Yet it was a minor issue of the times, overshadowed by the controversy over slavery that grew more threatening with each year.

When the decade ended, the women's movement was still young. Many issues and problems remained unexamined and unsolved. They would stay so until the country had experienced four terrible years of war.

CHAPTER THREE

DEFEAT, CONFLICT, AND SCHISM

1865-1869

The organized women's movement came to a dead stop with the outbreak of the Civil War. Although Susan B. Anthony and Elizabeth Cady Stanton challenged the wisdom of putting aside the fight for women's rights, there seemed more urgent work for women to do in a country stricken by war. No national conventions were held during the war, and agitation for women's rights all but ceased after 1861.

However, the war itself was important in changing women's lives, taking many out of the confines of the home and the church and revealing to them and to others surprising reserves of resourcefulness and self-confidence. For the burdens of the Civil War, the deadliest in our history, fell upon governments that were unprepared and unequipped for the severity and length of the struggle, and by the thousands, women stepped forward to perform critical services that government neglected.

Through local aid societies, in North and South, they set up and ran hospitals, provided nursing services, collected medical equipment, sewed, knitted, and cooked for servicemen from their communities, aided their families, and raised the funds to finance their own activities. In the Union, this work was coordinated and directed by the Sanitary Commission, staffed and directed largely by

"Lady Clerks Leaving the Treasury Department at Washington."
Harper's Weekly, Feb. 1865

women. To support its activities and those of local groups, women found themselves speaking at public meetings, writing letters to newspapers, organizing the distribution of funds, and managing staffs of workers.

Throughout the country, women went to work doing "men's jobs," managing businesses, farms, and plantations in the face of rising prices and serious shortages of goods. Both the Union and the Confederacy hired women to staff the bureaus that grew and multiplied as the war persisted.

Women continued to champion the cause of the slave during the war years. Many black and white women volunteered to teach and aid refugees and freedmen and -women. Leading feminist abolitionists like Anthony, Stanton and Lucy Stone scrutinized and criticized government policies, demanding effective emancipation and, after 1863, joined together in the National Women's Loyal League, to work for passage of an amendment that would abolish slavery throughout the country. Organized by Anthony, the League collected more than 400,000 signatures petitioning for the Thirteenth Amendment.

The years of the war contributed to the changing image of American women. Anna Dickinson was the most famous female orator of the period, attracting large crowds to her speeches on abolitionism and military and political affairs. But she was not the only one. Increasing numbers of women took to writing and publishing their ideas, stirred to express themselves by the tumultuous and dramatic events around them. The war, in general, made women more conspicuous, as it brought thousands into the public sphere. Indeed, grave concern was expressed about their apparent "strong-mindedness" and independence.

Finally, the long struggle was over, and in 1865, the Thirteenth Amendment, which prohibited slavery in the United States, was approved by Congress and ratified in the states. Slavery was abolished, and abolitionists who had struggled long and hard rightfully felt triumphant. It seemed that the crusade was over. But it was not. More fighting lay ahead to secure and protect the rights of the freed people.

From the 1830's, women had linked their own subjection with that of the slaves, and now, in the years after the war, when abolitionists, Republicans, and the freedmen rallied to secure equal rights for black Americans, women expected the same for themselves. In particular, they expected that the efforts to give the vote to freedmen would be expanded to include the vote for women. They were wrong.

In Congress, in state legislatures, and at state constitutional conventions, changes were being considered to accommodate the new status of Afro-Americans. Doors formerly closed to black people were slowly opening. And, as each one opened, with the passage of a federal amendment or a change in a state constitution, women rushed forward, hoping to pass through with the ex-slaves. Often, the door was closed on them both. It always closed on the women.

Woman suffrage was overwhelmingly rejected in the 1860's. And among those who helped to close the doors were some men who had been allies and comrades in abolitionism. The disappointment and frustration of these early efforts to gain the vote were great, and out of them grew the first major controversy within the women's movement. It was a serious conflict which eventually split the movement in two and polarized it for two decades.

Trouble began in the fall of 1865, when proposals for a Fourteenth Amendment to the Constitution were being drafted.

THE FOURTEENTH AMENDMENT

The Fourteenth Amendment was intended to give citizenship, and its privileges and immunities, to the freed slaves. Among these was the right to vote, and the amendment proposed to penalize states that denied the ballot to black

Anna E. Dickinson. Leslie's, Oct. 1873

voters. Its second section provided that when a state refused the franchise to black voters, it lost representation in Congress.

Several different versions of the amendment were introduced into Congress. A few women, alerted by Elizabeth Cady Stanton and Susan B. Anthony, immediately realized that the way in which the black voter was defined in the second section would affect them. The Constitution, as then worded, did not mention sex in discussing voters. The women set out to influence the wording of the amendment, hoping to gain the enfranchisement of women or, at the least, to prevent the adoption of language that would exclude women by describing voters as "male."

A LETTER TO THE PRESS

To the Editor of the Standard—Sir:—Mr. Broomall, of Pennsylvania; Mr. Schenck, of Ohio; Mr. Jenckes, of Rhode Island; Mr. Stevens, of Pennsylvania, have each a resolution before Congress to amend the Constitution.

"Mrs. E. Cady Stanton." Leslie's, Dec. 1868

Article 1st, Section 2d, reads thus: "Representatives and direct taxes shall be apportioned among the several States which may be included within this Union according to their respective number."

Mr. Broomall proposes to amend by saying "male electors," Mr. Schenck "male citizens," Mr. Jenckes "male citizens," Mr. Stevens "legal voters." There is no objection to the amendment proposed by Mr. Stevens, as in process of time women may be made "legal voters" in the several States, and would then meet that requirement of the Constitution. But those urged by the other gentlemen, neither time, nor effort, nor State Constitutions could enable us to meet, unless, by a liberal interpretation of the amendment, a coat of mail to be worn at the polls might be judged all-sufficient. Mr. Jenckes and Mr. Schenck, in their bills, have the grace not to say a word about taxes, remembering perhaps that "taxation without representation is tyranny." But Mr. Broomall, though unwilling to share with us the honors of Government, would fain secure us a place in its burdens; for while he apportions representatives to "male electors" only, he admits "all the inhabitants" into the rights, privileges, and immunities of taxation. Magnanimous M.C.!

I would call the attention of the women of the nation to the fact that under the Federal Constitution, as it now exists, there is not one word that limits the right of suffrage to any privileged class. This attempt to turn the wheels of civilization backward, on the part of Republicans claiming to be the Liberal party, should rouse every woman in the nation to a prompt exercise of the only right she has in the Government, the right of petition. To this end a committee in New York have sent out thousands of petitions, which should be circulated in every district and sent to its Representative at Washington as soon as possible.

ELIZABETH CADY STANTON.[1]
New York, January 2, 1866.

Even before Congress began its consideration of the proposed amendment, Anthony and Stanton organized a national petition campaign. They hoped, by the pressure of thousands of signatures, to influence Congress.

A PETITION

—To the Senate and House of Representatives:—

The undersigned women of the United States, respectfully ask an amendment of the Constitution that shall prohibit the several States from disfranchising any of their citizens on the ground of sex.

In making our demand for Suffrage, we would call your attention to the fact that we represent fifteen million people —one-half the entire population of the country—intelligent, virtuous, native-born American citizens; and yet stand outside the pale of political recognition. The Constitution classes us as "free people," and counts us whole persons in the basis of representation; and yet are we governed without our consent, compelled to pay taxes without appeal, and punished for violations of law without choice of judge or juror. The experience of all ages, the Declarations of the Fathers, the Statute Laws of our own day, and the fearful revolution through which we have just passed, all prove the uncertain tenure of life, liberty, and property so long as the ballot—the only weapon of self-protection—is not in the hand of every citizen.

Therefore, as you are now amending the Constitution, and, in harmony with advancing civilization, placing new safeguards round the individual rights of four millions of emancipated slaves, we ask that you extend the right of Suffrage to Woman—the only remaining class of disfranchised citizens—and thus fulfill your constitutional obligation "to guarantee to every State in the Union a Republican form of Government." As all partial application of Republican principles must ever breed a complicated legislation as well as discontented people, we would pray your Honorable Body, in order to simplify the machinery of Government and ensure domestic tranquillity, that you legislate hereafter for persons, citizens, tax-payers, and not for class or caste. For justice and equality your petitioners will ever pray.[2]

ing the whole number of persons in each State, excluding Indians not taxed. But when the right to vote at any election for the choice of electors for President and Vice-President of the United States, Representatives in Congress, the Executive and Judicial officers of a State, or the members of the Legislature thereof, is denied to any of the *male* inhabitants of such State, being twenty-one years of age, and citizens of the United States, or in any way abridged, except for participation in rebellion, or other crime, the basis of representation therein shall be reduced in the proportion which the number of such *male* citizens shall bear to the whole number of *male* citizens twenty-one years of age in such State. [Italics added.][3]

Friends rallied to the women in a brief and unsuccessful campaign over the Fourteenth Amendment. Unfortunately, supporters were in the minority, and the amendment, which was approved by Congress in 1866 and ratified by the states in 1868, specifically granted suffrage to males. For the first time, the Constitution explicitly defined voters as men; women's struggle for political equality had suffered a major defeat.

THE FOURTEENTH AMENDMENT

SECTION 2. Representatives shall be apportioned among the several States according to their respective numbers, count-

THE EQUAL RIGHTS ASSOCIATION

After the Fourteenth Amendment, another opportunity to obtain the vote arose. A bill was before Congress enfranchising black men in the District of Columbia. Senator Edgar Cowan, from Pennsylvania, proposed a revision of the bill that would extend the vote to women as well. Support was quickly organized for Cowan's amendment. The agitation resulted in the first debate in Congress concerning female suffrage, the prototype for countless others. But the defeat was overwhelming: the vote was 39–9 in the Senate, and 74–49 in the House for a similar bill. There-

"Congressional Pests—Lady Lobbyists Importuning Senators at the Capitol, Washington, D.C."
Leslie's, *Mar. 1869*

after, whenever the charter of government for the District was revised, women demanded to vote in the nation's capital. But this door stayed shut tight.

Suffrage was the main concern at the first National Woman's Rights Convention after the war, which took place in 1866. Although the assemblage heard reports and discussed issues concerning women and education, religion, labor, and state laws, the vote dominated the meeting. With no opposition, the convention voted to merge with other groups seeking the vote for freedmen, and the American Equal Rights Association was formed.

Between 1866 and 1869, this group of women and men was in the forefront of the fight for women's rights. Whenever an opportunity appeared, they sallied forth, with boundless energy and optimism. At the same time, but with less publicity, local and state woman suffrage groups were being formed throughout the country. These groups often sent representatives to the Equal Rights Association, linking local efforts with the national campaign.

Members of the American Equal Rights Association were, in large part, the same women and men who had fought the abolitionist and women's rights battles before the Civil War. Many of them were well known as reformers. They were experienced agitators and well acquainted with the criticism and abuse that came their way. Newspaper comment, like the one below, was familiar fare for the supporter of unpopular causes.

NEW YORK *WORLD*

Mummified and fossilated females, void of domestic duties, habits and natural affections; crack-brained, rheumatic, dyspeptic, henpecked men, vainly striving to achieve the liberty of opening their heads in presence of their wives; self educated, oily-faced, insolent, gabbling negroes, and Theodore Tilton, make up less than a hundred members of this caravan called, by themselves, the American Equal Rights Association.[4]

At the first anniversary meeting of the Association, Henry Ward Beecher, well-known clergyman and reformer, made a speech reflecting the group's commitment to the vote for women as well as black men.

BEECHER'S SPEECH

. . . I am not a farmer, but I know that spring comes but once in the year. When the furrow is open is the time to put in your seed, if you would gather a harvest in its season.

Now, when the red-hot plowshare of war has opened a furrow in this nation, is the time to put in the seed. If any say to me, ''Why will you agitate the woman question when it is the hour for the black man?'' I answer, it is the hour for every man and every woman, black or white. The bees go out in the morning to gather the honey from the morning glories. They take it when they are open, for by 10 o'clock they are shut, never to open again. When the public mind is open, if you have anything to say, say it. If you have any radical principles to urge, any higher wisdom to make known, don't wait until quiet times come, until the public mind shuts up altogether.

We are in the favored hour; and if you have great principles to make known, this is the time to advocate them. Therefore say whatever truth is to be known for the next fifty years in this nation, let it be spoken now—let it be enforced now. The truth that I have to urge is not that women have the right of suffrage—not that Chinamen or Irishmen have the right—not that native born Yankees have it—but that suffrage is the inherent right of mankind. . . . I do not put back for a single day the black man's enfranchisement. I ask not that he should wait. I demand that this work should be done, not upon the ground that it is politically expedient now to enfranchise black men; but I propose that you take expediency out of the way, and put a principle which is more enduring in the place of it—manhood and womanhood suffrage for all. That is the question. . . . [5]

THE KANSAS CAMPAIGN: 1867

Kansas was the first battleground for the Equal Rights Association. In 1867, voters there were offered two separate proposals to change the state constitution: one would enfranchise the black man (the Fourteenth Amendment to the Federal Constitution was not ratified until July 1868); the other would give the vote to women.

All the weapons of persuasion were used in Kansas: speeches, debates, sermons, letters to newspapers, pamphlets, and rallies supported the vote for blacks and for women. Starting in the spring and continuing until election day, a steady stream of experienced campaigners traveled West. Anthony, Stanton, and Stone joined a large contingent of Kansas suffragists, crisscrossing the state as they went from meeting to meeting.

Early in the campaign, in April 1867, Henry Blackwell, who was in Kansas with his wife, Lucy Stone, described their experiences in a letter.

A LETTER

Dear Friends, E. C. Stanton and Susan B. Anthony:

You will be glad to know that Lucy and I are going over the length and breadth of this State speaking every day, and sometimes twice, journeying from twenty-five to forty miles daily, sometimes in a carriage and sometimes in an open wagon, with or without springs. We climb hills and dash down ravines, ford creeks, and ferry over rivers, rattle across limestone ledges, struggle through muddy bottoms, fight the high winds on the high rolling upland prairies, and address the most astonishing (and astonished) audiences in the most extraordinary places. To-night it may be a log school house, tomorrow a stone church; next day a store with planks for seats, and in one place, if it had not rained, we should have held forth in an unfinished court house, with only four stone walls but no roof whatever.

The people are a queer mixture of roughness and intelligence, recklessness and conservatism. One swears at women who want to wear the breeches; another wonders whether we ever heard of a fellow named Paul; a third is not going to put women on an equality with niggers. One woman told Lucy that no decent woman would be running over the country talking nigger and woman. Her brother told Lucy that "he had had a woman who was under the sod, but that if she had ever said she wanted to vote he would have pounded her to death!" . . .

I think we shall probably succeed in Kansas next fall if the State is thoroughly canvassed, not else. . . .

We must have Mrs. Stanton, Susan, Mrs. Gage, and Anna Dickinson, this fall. Also Ben Wade and Carl Schurz, if possible. We must also try to get 10,000 each of Mrs. Stanton's address, of Lucy Stone's address, and of Mrs. Mills' article on the Enfranchisement of Women, printed for us by the Hovey Fund.

Kansas is to be *the battle ground* for 1867. *It must not be allowed to fall.*

The politicians here, except Wood and Robinson, are generally "on the fence." But they dare not oppose us openly. And the Democratic leaders are quite disposed to take us up. If the Republicans come out against us the Democrats will take us up. Do not let anything prevent your being here September 1 *for the campaign,* which will end in November. There will be a big fight and a great excitement. After the fight is over Mrs. Stanton will never have *use* for *notes* or *written* speeches any more.

Yours truly,

Henry B. Blackwell[6]

Despite Blackwell's optimism in the spring, the equal rights campaigners got little help in Kansas. Local newspapers and the New York papers that were influential in the state were reluctant or chary in their support. Most crucial was the role of the Republican Party. Most Republicans, at this time, believed it in the interests of their party to gain the vote for the black man. In Kansas, they feared hurting the cause of the black man by linking it with that of woman suffrage. Therefore, the Republicans in Kansas generally

turned their back on the women, leaving them adrift and friendless. Olympia Brown, a female minister and a stalwart movement worker, described what took place.

OLYMPIA BROWN'S REMINISCENCES

. . . I went to Kansas, through an arrangement made by Lucy Stone with leaders of the Republican party there, whereby they were to furnish comfortable conveyance over the State with a lady as traveling companion, and also to arrange and preside over all the meetings; these were to be Republican meetings in which it was thought best that a woman should present the claims of the woman suffrage

Olympia Brown

amendment, which had been submitted to the vote of the men of the State by a strongly Republican Legislature.

The Kansas Republicans so far complied with their part of this arrangement that on my arrival, the 1st of July, I found appointments made and thoroughly advertised for the whole of July and August; two lectures for every week day, and a preaching service for every Sunday. As it proved, these appointments were at great distances from each other, often requiring a journey of twenty, thirty, forty, and even fifty miles across a country scarcely settled at all, to reach some little village where there would be a school-house or some public building in which a meeting could be held. All were eager to hear, and the entire settlement would attend the lecture, thus giving an astonishingly large audience in proportion to the size of the place.

The country was then new and public conveyances few, and the Republicans having failed to furnish the stipulated carriage and escort, the speaker was dependent almost entirely upon the people in each little place for the means to pursue the journey. Many a time some kind man, with a genuine chivalry worthy of the days of knighthood, has left his half-mown field or his sorghum boiling in the kettle, to escort the woman suffrage advocate to the next appointment; and although the road often seemed long and perilous and many an hour was spent in what appeared a hopeless endeavor to find our way over the almost trackless prairie, yet somehow we always came to the right place at last; and I scarcely recollect an instance of failure to meet an appointment from July 1st to Nov. 5th.

In those four months I traveled over the greater part of Kansas, held two meetings every day, and the latter part of the time three meetings every day, making in all between two and three hundred speeches, averaging an hour in length; a fact that tends to show that women can endure talk and travel at least, as well as men; . . .

It is deemed, in certain quarters, wicked heresy to complain of or criticise the Republican party, that has done so much in freeing the slaves and in bringing the country victoriously through the war of the rebellion; but if there is to be any truth in history we must set it down, to stand forever a lasting disgrace to the party that in 1867, in Kansas, its leaders selfishly and meanly defeated the woman suffrage amendment.

As the time for the election drew nigh, those political leaders who had been relied upon as friends of the cause were silent, others were active in their opposition. The Central Committee issued a circular for the purpose of preventing loyal Republicans from voting for woman suffrage; not content with this, the notorious I. S. Kalloch, and others of the same stripe, were sent out under the auspices of the Republican party to blackguard and abuse the advocates of woman's cause while professedly speaking upon "manhood suffrage." And Charles Langston, the negro orator, added his mite of bitter words to make the path a little harder for women, who had spent years in pleading the cause of the colored man.

And yet, with all the obstacles which the dominant party could throw in our way; without organization, without money, without political rewards to offer, without any of the means by which elections are usually carried, we gained one-third of all the votes cast! Surely it was a great triumph of principle; and had the leading Republicans, even one or two of them, stood boldly for the measure which they themselves had submitted, Kansas might have indeed been a "free State"; the first to enfranchise women; the advance guard in the great progressive movements of the time; and her leading politicians might have gone down in history as wise, far-seeing statesmen who loved principles better than office, and who gained the rewards of the world because they sought "first the kingdom of God and His righteousness." . . . [7]

In the Kansas campaign, the seemingly endless dedication and determination of the equal-righters collided head on with a mass of disinterest as well as opposition. The injustice of denying the vote to half the population was indisputable and painful to the tireless campaigners. The voters felt differently. On election day, close to 20,000 of the 30,000 voting said no to woman suffrage and refused the vote to the blacks as well.

THE STRUGGLE IN NEW YORK

The fight in Kansas overlapped another major effort of the Equal Rights Association, in New York State, where a convention was planned to revise the state constitution. Here, too, the Association saw an opportunity to push against the barriers to universal suffrage.

The first step in New York was to have women vote in a special election that would select the delegates to the constitutional convention. Failing to achieve that, in 1867 the Association organized an elaborate program of petitions, conventions, public speeches, and publications, directed at the convention members who would propose revisions in the state's constitution for the voters.

The committee preparing suffrage changes for consideration of the convention was headed by Horace Greeley, editor of the Tribune, *who was no friend of woman suffrage at the time. Before Greeley's committee made its recommendations, Anthony and Stanton presented it with petitions and spoke in Albany.*

Nonetheless, the committee rejected all the pleas for woman suffrage, and in its report to the convention, on June 28, 1867, recommended against giving the vote to women.

REPORT OF THE STANDING COMMITTEE ON THE RIGHT OF SUFFRAGE

Your committee does not recommend an extension of the elective franchise to women. However defensible in theory, we are satisfied that public sentiment does not demand and would not sustain an innovation so revolutionary and sweeping, so openly at war with a distribution of duties and functions between the sexes as venerable and pervading as government itself, and involving transformations so radical in social and domestic life. Should we prove to be in error on this head, the Convention may overrule us by changing a few words in the first section of our proposed article.

Nor have we seen fit to propose the enfranchisement of boys above the age of eighteen years. The current ideas and usages in our day, but especially in this country, seem already to set too strongly in favor of the relaxation, if not total overthrow of parental authority, especially over half-grown boys. With the sincerest good-will for the class in question, we submit that they may spend the hours which they can spare from their labors and their lessons more usefully and profitably in mastering the wisdom of the sages and philosophers who have elucidated the science of government, than in attendance on midnight caucuses, or in wrangling around the polls.

ALBANY, June 28, 1867.

HORACE GREELEY, *Chairman,* WM. H. MERRILL, LESLIE W. RUSSELL, GEO. WILLIAMS.[8]

When the convention accepted the committee's recommendations, the fight was over. The Equal Rights Association had suffered defeat in New York.

DEMOCRATS AND REPUBLICANS

One more effort was made by the Equal Rights Association: Susan B. Anthony was authorized to attend the Democratic Party convention in July 1868 "to press upon the delegates the propriety of embracing woman suffrage within their resolves."

This was a controversial and somewhat ironic move, since the Democrats had not only been less sympathetic than Republicans to female suffrage but had also been the defenders of slavery. However, the Republican Party had failed to support women in Kansas, and its most recent suffrage platform, adopted at the 1868 Chicago convention, endorsed the vote for freedmen but evaded any commitment to female suffrage.

Stanton and Anthony had not been hesitant to express their disappointment and anger at the Republican Party, in Kansas and in New York, and they initiated the idea of seeking help from the Democrats. In contrast, many of the members of the Equal Rights Association, still regarding the Republicans as the party of reform and humanitarianism, were uneasy about Anthony's mission to the Democratic Party convention.

Having arranged to address the Democrats, Anthony, accompanied by Stanton and two other women, walked into Tammany Hall on July 4, 1868, and took seats on the platform. The all-male crowd stared at them in amazement. Newspaper reports offer a picture of what happened next.

THE *SUN*

The Chairman—I have a memorial from the Woman's Suffrage Association, with the request that it be handed to the Committee on Resolutions. (Laughter, cheers, "Hear, hear," and cries of "Read.")

The Chairman—I may mention that this document is signed by Susan B. Anthony. (Renewed cheers and laughter.)

The communication was then read.[9]

THE CHICAGO *REPUBLICAN*

Susan B. Anthony appeared to the convention like Minerva, goddess of wisdom. Her advent was with thunders, not of applause, but of the scorn of a degenerate masculinity. The great Horatio said, with infinite condescension, that he held in his hand a memorial of the women of the United States. The name of Miss Anthony was greeted with a yell such as a Milton might imagine to rise from a conclave of the damned. "She asked to plead the cause of her sex; to demand the enfranchisement of the women of America—the only class of citizens not represented in the government, the only class without a vote, and their only disability, the insurmountable one of sex." As these last significant words, with more than significant accent and modulation, came from the lips of the knightly, the courtly Horatio, a bestial roar of laughter, swelling now into an almost Niagara chorus, now subsiding into comparative silence, and again without further provocation rising into infernal sublimity, shook the roof of Tammany. Sex—the sex of women—was the subject of this infernal scorn; and the great Democratic gathering, with yells and shrieks and demoniac, deafening howls, consigned the memorial of Susan B. Anthony to the committee on resolutions.[10]

Failure to enlist the Democratic Party in the cause of women's rights was no surprise; nor was the scorn and laughter with which men received the plea for the vote. Some observers even regarded the episode with optimism.

ELIZABETH CADY STANTON'S COMMENTS

. . . what of it? She [Anthony] has been laughed at twenty years, and cares no more for the laugh of the heedless world than for the popping of a chestnut in a farmer's fire. When we held our first convention in 1848, the press of the country laughed, from Maine to Louisiana. The journals of every section and party were filled with ridicule and the grossest personalities; and yet, how changed to-day. . . . Sooner or later they must come to "Woman's Suffrage," and sit down in their national councils with both women and black men. So let them laugh on for the good time of "equal rights to all" is close at hand.[11]

FROM THE NEW YORK *NEWS*

The appearance of a female delegate in a national party Congress, such as that of Miss Anthony in the late Conven-

"The Cincinnati Convention.—Mrs. Laura de Force Gordon, of California, and Miss Susan B. Anthony, of New York, being escorted to their seats on the platform." Leslie's, May 1872

tion held in this city, marks an era in the woman's rights movement. The acceptance and reading of her address is the first sign of recognition, in a political sense, that woman has received from any of the great parties of the day. . . .[12]

CONTROVERSY OVER THE FIFTEENTH AMENDMENT

A serious difference of opinion within the Equal Rights Association hovered in the background during the struggles in Kansas and New York. In 1869, it came to the fore: Should the Association support the Fourteenth Amendment, an amendment that advanced the cause of black men but harmed the cause of all women?

In July 1868, before the Association was forced to resolve its disagreements on the question, the Fourteenth Amendment was ratified. But the issue rose again in another way. In January 1869, Congress debated another amendment to the Constitution that directly prohibited states from depriving black men of the vote (as Kansas had done in 1867 and as Nevada had done in a new constitution). Suffrage was again a national issue, and women tried to get the wording of the new amendment revised so that the states could not deny citizens the right to vote on the basis of sex as well as race.

THE PROPOSED AMENDMENT

Restrictions on denial of vote. 1. The right of citizens of the United States to vote shall not be denied or abridged by the United States or by any State on account of race, color,

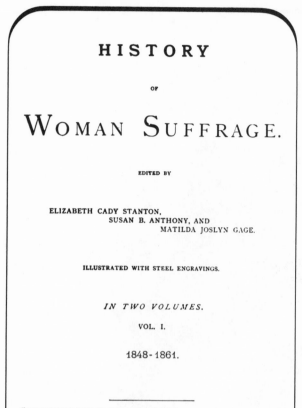

HISTORY

OF

WOMAN SUFFRAGE.

EDITED BY

ELIZABETH CADY STANTON,
SUSAN B. ANTHONY, AND
MATILDA JOSLYN GAGE.

ILLUSTRATED WITH STEEL ENGRAVINGS.

IN TWO VOLUMES.

VOL. I.

1848-1861.

" GOVERNMENTS DERIVE THEIR JUST POWERS FROM THE CONSENT OF THE GOVERNED."

NEW YORK:
FOWLER & WELLS, PUBLISHERS
753 BROADWAY.
1881.

The "History of Woman Suffrage" was the result of years of labor by my sister Susan B. Anthony, and was sincerely believed by her to be the richest and best legacy she could leave to the coming generation

Mary S. Anthony

April 2-1827— June 4-1906

[the revision would add "sex" here] or previous condition of servitude.

2. The Congress shall have power to enforce this article by appropriate legislation.[13]

Again they lost. Congress, enmeshed in Reconstruction politics, approved the Fifteenth Amendment, without revision, and on February 26, 1869, sent it on to the states for ratification.

The question was clear, unavoidable, and difficult: Should the Association work for ratification of an amendment that aided the freedmen—an amendment that most Republicans considered a crucial component of their reconstruction plans for the nation—but rejected the rights of women?

The debate within the Equal Rights Association grew in intensity after the upsetting experiences in Kansas and New York. For the entire country, it was a time of tension and disagreement. Bitter conflicts had developed over Reconstruction in Congress, and in February 1868, in a fury over Reconstruction policy, the House of Representatives voted to impeach President Andrew Johnson; only one vote in the Senate kept the President in office.

From the end of 1867, optimism and unity had been fading in the women's movement as well. The harmony that graced its first decade was gone. Disappointment and outrage, weariness and anger overcame the frustrated campaigners for equal rights, and they turned against each other.

Disagreement over the Fifteenth Amendment polarized the Association, and two factions emerged. One was led by the old abolitionist comrades of the women's movement—William Lloyd Garrison, Wendell Phillips, and Frederick Douglass—and was composed largely of New Englanders. Claiming it was the "negro's hour," they argued that female suffrage had to wait its time lest a linking of the two causes jeopardize that of the freedman. They advocated support of the Fifteenth Amendment and, later, a separate Sixteenth Amendment for female suffrage.

The other faction was led by Anthony and Stanton. They rejected the suggestion that women wait patiently for their rights and opposed ratification of the Fifteenth Amendment.

After January 1868, Stanton was a co-editor and Anthony the business manager of a newspaper dedicated to women's rights and other reforms. The Revolution, as it was called, was an important battleground in the developing controversy over the Fifteenth Amendment.

During the Kansas campaign, smarting at the failure of Republican newspapers and politicians to aid woman suffrage, Anthony and Stanton had accepted help from and joined forces with George Francis Train. Train was a controversial figure. A financier, a Democrat, he supported

"George Francis Train in Court, Refusing Bail."
The Daily Graphic, New York, Mar. 1873

diverse causes such as the eight-hour day, paper money, woman suffrage, and Irish independence. He was outspokenly prejudiced against black people. In Kansas, his flamboyant appearances and effective speeches attracted attention for woman suffrage and earned him the gratitude of Anthony and Stanton. During the campaign, he offered them money with which to start a newspaper, and The Revolution *was begun.*

In its columns, Anthony and Stanton developed the ideas that crystallized into their opposition to the Fifteenth Amendment.

FROM *THE REVOLUTION*

Manhood Suffrage? Oh! no, my friend, you mistake us; we have enough of that already. We say not another man, black or white, until woman is inside the citadel. What reason have we to suppose the African would be more just and generous than the Saxon has been? Wendell Phillips pleads for black men; we for black women, who have known a degradation and sorrow of slavery such as man has never experienced.[14]

How insulting to put every shade and type of manhood above our heads, to make laws for educated, refined, wealthy women. Horace Greeley thinks that Patrick and Sambo would appreciate the ballot more highly than the women of "THE REVOLUTION."[15]

. . . while the enfranchisement of all men hastens the day for justice to her, it makes her degradation more complete in the transition period. It is to escape the added tyranny, persecutions, insults, horrors, that will surely be visited upon woman, in the establishment of an aristocracy of sex in this republic, that we raise our indignant protest against this wholesale desecration of woman in the pending amendment, and earnestly pray the rulers of this nation to consider the degradation of disfranchisement. Our republican leaders see that it is a protection and defence for the black man, giving him new dignity, self-respect, and making his rights more sacred in the eyes of his enemies.[16]

Train's contributions to The Revolution, *literary and financial, were limited and short-lived, but while they lasted, they fed the fire of controversy developing within the Equal Rights Association. His comments, like the one be-*

The Revolution.

PRINCIPLE, NOT POLICY: JUSTICE, NOT FAVORS.—MEN, THEIR RIGHTS AND NOTHING MORE: WOMEN, THEIR RIGHTS AND NOTHING LESS.

low, inflamed many old abolitionists and friends of the newly freed slaves.

TRAIN ADVOCATES EDUCATED SUFFRAGE

What is Educated Suffrage? Let all vote, male and female, black and white, when they are educated to know what a vote is. That is Educated Suffrage. But the voter who waits outside the poll for a mule, under the impression that the paper he dropped into the box was an order for said article, ought not to be allowed to impeach a President! . . . 17

The Revolution was also a forum for those who disagreed with the Anthony-Stanton position.

LETTERS TO THE EDITOR

. . . Suppose it takes a generation to settle this woman question (it will not, for the battle was half fought by the abolitionists), shall the loyal disfranchised men whose right to the ballot is already in the arena of politics be kept out of their inheritance all that time, because we are despoiled of ours? Some of them are educated, wealthy, living continually the lives of noble men, shall we say to them, stand back, turn again into the rugged paths of proscription? We forbid you to go higher because we cannot go! I cannot for a moment imagine you endorsing the recent repudiation of colored suffrage by Connecticut, Ohio, and those states to which it has been submitted, and yet the result accords with your philosophy. Woman's claim to the ballot is not ripe for settlement in those states at present, therefore must the colored man still endure his degradation, still chafe at the tyranny and injustice of his political oppressor . . . how can we make any invidious distinctions, or cast the slightest obstacle in the path of any human soul struggling to be free. . . .

J. ELIZABETH JONES 18

DEAR MRS. STANTON: I get "THE REVOLUTION" regularly and like it very much, I think it is a good paper. I think it is a *very good paper;* and if it is, I know it will bear criticising, so I propose to say a few words to that effect, which were prompted to my mind some time since. It is just this and nothing more. Don't "pitch in" to the *Standard* so fiercely. The woman's movement has no better friend than Wendell Phillips. But is the negro so far removed from the power of tyranny as to be able to part with his last fast friend? I think not. Mr. Phillips is a clear-headed man, and for statesmanship the country cannot show his equal. Why, he can see farther ahead with his *eyes shut* than some of our Congressmen could with Ross's telescope! So say those who know him best, and the fulfilment of his predictions for the past thirty years go far to prove the truth of the assertion. Why cannot reformers labor together side by side, each in their own specialty, knowing that each is helping the other. As I see the human race, we are all one vast *chain-gang,* and no person or clan can advance one step without moving the whole body. Consequently every successful effort to elevate mankind must elevate womankind. I am a woman, and need my rights as much as any woman, but I am not a *chattel slave,* and I would not ask a friend of the slave to give me one hour of time that can be advantageously used in ridding the country of the remains of that curse. I sometimes think it rather *cheeky* to ask a *man* to advocate our cause. I canvassed a town of three thousand inhabitants not long since to get signers to a petition for female suffrage. But five married women in the town would sign it. Some were afraid of offending their husbands, and others were treated *so well* by their husbands that they were ashamed to ask for privileges! I made up my mind, then, that there was one thing certain in this life beside death, and that was, that neither God or the Courts will ever answer prayers until the prayers are presented *personally.* Thanks to the noble men who volunteer to aid us; but I have no hope of seeing woman as a class elevated to her true position except so far and so fast as she steps forward and demands what belongs to her. *Women* must labor among *women.* Female lecturers who are counted by hundreds in this country must take up the subject and *hold it up* until all women are blessed with an open vision. It is a question of time only. *It is to be.* God has decreed it and the angels are superintending the work. So speed "THE REVOLUTION." Don't fail to have the *Anti-Slavery Standard* and the *Banner of Light* among your exchanges. They are our true allies.

SUBSCRIBER.[19]

GONFLIGT DEEPENS

Other differences and disagreements hardened the lines that were dividing the Equal Rights Association into two groups. From the start, Lucy Stone and others had objected to Anthony's decision to accept help from George Francis Train, and members of the Association continued to deplore Stanton and Anthony's relationship with him.

The controversy over Train was part of a larger disagreement concerning the relation between the women's movement and the two political parties. Many equal-righters saw the tie with Train, who was a Democrat, as a repudiation of the Republican Party, and this they could not accept, especially when the country was engaged in a bitter partisan battle over Reconstruction policies and the Republican Party seemed to champion the rights of the freed slaves.

GARRISON ATTACKS TRAIN

Jan. 4, 1868.

Dear Miss Anthony:

In all friendliness, and with the highest regard for the woman's rights movement, I cannot refrain from expressing my regret and astonishment that you and Mrs. Stanton should have taken such leave of good sense as to be travelling companions and associate lecturers with that crack-brained harlequin and semi-lunatic, Geo. Francis Train. You may, if you choose, denounce Henry Ward Beecher and Wendell Phillips (the two ablest advocates of woman's rights on this side of the Atlantic), and swap them off for the nondescript Train, but in thus doing, you will only subject yourselves to merited ridicule and condemnation, and turn the movement which you aim to promote into unnecessary contempt. The nomination of this ranting egotist and low blackguard for the presidency, by your audiences, shows that he is regarded by those who listen to him as on a par with poor demented Mellen and Daniel Pratt, "the Great American Traveller."

The colored people and their advocates have not a more abusive assailant than this same Train, especially when he has an Irish audience before him, to whom he delights to ring the changes upon "nigger, nigger, nigger," *ad nauseam.* He is as destitute of principle as he is of sense, and is fast gravitating toward a lunatic asylum. He may be of use in drawing an audience, but so would be a kangaroo, a gorilla, or a hippopotamus. . . .

Your old outspoken friend,

WILLIAM LLOYD GARRISON.[20]

STANTON DEFENDS TRAIN

To Our Radical Friends.

We occasionally receive letters from Republicans and Abolitionists criticizing our affiliation with Democrats. They say, "Your paper is admirable, and if you would only 'drop Train' your subscribers would pour in by the hundreds, and all your *old friends* would rally round you and make your paper a complete success."

. . . Before advising us to throw aside the generous services of our new found friends, look at the position of the Woman's Rights cause in this country before the Kansas election. Republicans and abolitionists alike ignored the question, claiming that this was "the negro's hour." Even Wendell Phillips told us before all Israel and the sun, on our own platform, that fashion was more to woman than the right of suffrage, after clearly showing the day before, on the anti-slavery platform, that without the ballot a man was but a slave. Republicans ignored us because they feared Woman's Suffrage was more than their party could carry; and abolitionists because they feared it would lessen the black man's chance of enfranchisement to make any demand for the woman by his side.

Our three most radical papers—the *Tribune,* the *Independent,* and the *Standard*—were closed against us. We could not get an article in either, pointing out the danger of reconstruction on the old basis of caste and demanding the recognition of woman in the new government.

Seeing the danger on all sides of the nation crystallizing again on the old principle of caste, with an aristocracy of sex, the most narrow, hateful, and dangerous on which a government was ever based—seeing that the women of virtue, wealth and character in this country were to be made the subjects of every vicious, ignorant, degraded type of manhood, we unfurled the new banner to the breeze, "immediate and unconditional enfranchisement for the women of the republic." Democrats saw the logic of our position, and echoed it. They presented our petitions when republicans laughed them to scorn, and plead our cause in the State and national councils, and franked our documents from one end of the Union to the other. The women of St. Louis sent George Francis Train to Kansas, because neither Horace Greeley, Theodore Tilton or Wendell Phillips proposed to go. He labored there faithfully for weeks, often speaking three times a day, and the result of the election was 9,000 votes for Woman's Suffrage. Some deny the credit of this vote to Mr. Train, but we were on the spot and saw the wonderful power he exerted over a class of voters whom none of our other speakers could reach. As soon as we stated to him the necessity of an organ for our thought, he pledged himself at once that the long-wished for "REVOLU-TION" should no longer be postponed. He then travelled through nine States in the Union, announcing "THE REVOLU-TION" in his speeches wherever he went, thus successfully heralding us before we were born.

Now, it seems to us, in the full tide of our success, quoted and recognized by the press on both Continents, that warnings and criticisms, or any patronizing professions of interest, come with rather a bad grace from those who have maintained a stolid silence on our question to this hour. It was the utter desertion of our cause by those to whom we had a right to look for aid, that forced us to our present affiliations.

So long as we are enabled to proclaim our principles, it matters not who helps to do it. We regard the enfranchisement of woman as the most important question of the age, and we are determined to keep it before the nation, and to this end we will accept aid from any quarter, affiliate with any man, black or white, Jew or Gentile, saint or sinner, democrat or republican. . . . All this hue and cry about Train *is a mere cover, a sham.* The real trouble is, he has made it possible for us to utter the thoughts that radicals wish to hold in abeyance until the black man is safe beyond a peradventure, and Grant is enthroned in the White House. . . .   E. C. S.[21]

REPORT OF THE AMERICAN EQUAL RIGHTS ASSOCIATION ANNUAL MEETING, MAY 14, 1868

FREDERICK DOUGLASS deprecated the seeming assertion of Rev. O. B. Frothingham, that one good cause was in opposition to another. I champion the right of the negro to vote. It is with us a matter of life and death, and therefore can not be postponed. I have always championed woman's right to vote; but it will be seen that the present claim for the negro is one of the most *urgent* necessity. The assertion of the right of women to vote meets nothing but ridicule; there is no deep seated malignity in the hearts of the people against her; but name the right of the negro to vote, all hell is turned loose and the Ku-klux and Regulators hunt and slay the unoffending black man. The government of this country loves women. They are the sisters, mothers, wives and daughters of our rulers; but the negro is loathed. Women should not censure Mr. Phillips, Mr. Greeley, or Mr. Tilton, all have spoken eloquently for woman's rights. We are all talking for woman's rights, and we should be just to all our friends and enemies. There is a diffrence between the Republican and Democratic parties.

OLYMPIA BROWN: What is it?

FREDERICK DOUGLASS: The Democratic party has, during the whole war, been in sympathy with the rebellion, while the Republican party has supported the Government.

OLYMPIA BROWN: How is it now?

FREDERICK DOUGLASS: The Democratic party opposes impeachment and desires a white man's government.

Frederick Douglass

OLYMPIA BROWN: What is the difference in *principle* between the position of the Democratic party opposing the enfranchisement of 2,000,000 negro men, and the Republican party opposing the emancipation of 17,000,000 white women?

FREDERICK DOUGLASS: The Democratic party opposes suffrage to both; but the Republican party is in favor of enfranchising the negro, and is largely in favor of enfranchising woman. Where is the Democrat who favors woman suffrage? (A voice in the audience, "Train!") Yes, he hates the negro, and that is what stimulates him to substitute the cry of emancipation for women. The negro needs suffrage to protect his life and property, and to ensure him respect and education. He needs it for the safety of reconstruction and the salvation of the Union; for his own elevation from the position of a drudge to that of an influential member of society. If you want women to forget and forsake frivolity, and the negro to take pride in becoming a useful and respectable member of society, give them both the ballot.

OLYMPIA BROWN: Why did Republican Kansas vote down negro suffrage?

FREDERICK DOUGLASS: Because of your ally, George Francis Train!

OLYMPIA BROWN: How about Minnesota without Train? The Republican party is a party and cares for nothing but party! It has repudiated both negro suffrage and woman suffrage.

FREDERICK DOUGLASS: Minnesota lacked only 1,200 votes of carrying negro suffrage. All the Democrats voted against it, while only a small portion of the Republicans did so. And this was substantially the same in Ohio and Connecticut. The Republican party is about to bring ten States into the Union; and Thaddeus Stevens has reported a bill to admit seven, all on the fundamental basis of constitutions guaranteeing negro suffrage forever.

OLYMPIA BROWN again insisted that the party was false, and that now was the time for every true patriot to demand that no new State should be admitted except on the basis of suffrage to women as well as negros. . . . [22]

There was a conspicuous difference in the style and tone of the two rival factions developing within the Equal Rights Association. The Stanton-Anthony group was usually more angry, strident, and impetuous than the other, which, by comparison, was patient, persuasive, and cautious. Concerning the Fifteenth Amendment, for example, the Stanton-Anthony faction insisted belligerently: Women first! We will not step aside or wait for anyone. While the others, mainly New Englanders, said they would wait: Women's turn will come in time.

Behind these differences lay even more serious disagreement. Many members of the Association, including Lucy Stone and other Bostonians, were irritated by The Revolution, *apart from Train's connection with it. Stanton, as co-editor with reformer Parker Pillsbury, opened the columns of* The Revolution *to almost every idea and reform from its first issue in January 1868. Its pages hosted calls for economic reform, supported the labor union movement, and condemned capitalist greed. As for women's issues, anything that concerned women, any reform, any subject, found a home in* The Revolution. *Subjects that could not be discussed elsewhere, shocking ideas and proposals, were aired in the paper.* The Revolution *and its enthusiastic staff championed the cause of working women; they condemned their low wages, listed job opportunities for women, and aided the formation of working women's associations. Critics of* The Revolution *deplored this catholicity and objected to the confusion of woman suffrage with other, even more controversial, issues.*

In the future, it would become clear that the two factions represented the radical and moderate sides of the women's movement. Stanton and Anthony were the more radical feminists, rejecting all aspects of women's inferiority and demanding not only legal and political reform but sweeping social and economic changes to insure justice and equality for women. Out of the New England group emerged a more moderate feminist position that aimed at piecemeal reform and gradual change to give women equal rights.

The direction in which the Stanton and Anthony group was heading is best illustrated by a sampling of the contents of The Revolution *during this period.*

A CALL FOR POLICEWOMEN

[Commenting on an article from the *Tribune* about a woman who was arrested for "having manifested too much emotion on the sudden death of her child from starvation," *The Revolution* wrote the following:]

Women must look to man for care and protection. He is the judge of the proper degree of emotion the agonized mother may manifest for a starving dying child. . . . Do we not need a company of police of noble women uniformed and paid by the state, to secure to the unhappy and unfortunate of our own sex comfort and protection? We protest against the dynasty of force. [23]

A CALL FOR DRESS REFORM AND MORE

He [man] not only prescribes woman's sphere but how she shall dress in that sphere. Now one of the rights we claim for women is to wear a bifurcated garment and be sailors and soldiers and whatever they choose. [24]

WORK FOR WOMEN

. . . Working women, throw your needles to the winds; press yourselves into employments where you can get better pay; dress yourselves in costume, like daughters of the regiment, and be conductors in our cars and railroads, drive hacks. If your pettitcoats stand in the way of bread, virtue and freedom, cut them off. . . . Woman's dress keeps her out of a multitude of employments where she could make good wages. We heard of a family of daughters out West who, being left suddenly to depend on themselves, decided to ignore all woman's work at low wages, so they donned male attire. One went to work in a lumber yard, one on a steamboat, one drove a hack in a Western city, and in a few years with economy they laid up enough to buy a handsome farm where they now live in comfort as women.

Mrs. Bickerdyke, who followed Sherman through his entire campaign, taking care of sick soldiers, has built a large hotel at Salina, Kansas, which she intends to manage entirely herself. If women are to have a place in this world they must get right out of the old grooves and do new and grand things. We have looked through the eye of a needle long enough. It is time for "THE REVOLUTION." [25]

Prostitution and venereal disease were widespread at this time, but the subjects were rarely discussed in print and more rarely discussed by women. In The Revolution, *they received serious consideration. Below, Stanton writes about a bill regulating prostitution being considered in the New York State legislature.*

PROSTITUTION

. . . This bill, as presented in our daily journals last winter, section by section, is a disgrace to the decency and humanity of the nineteenth century. . . . Whoever will examine it carefully, section by section, will find that it is not a bill to suppress prostitution, but to legalize it.

It requires every young girl who leads this miserable life, to register her name in a book, kept by the police, and thus announce prostitution as her profession. Think of the hardening effect of this shameless act on the young victim—oft repenting, resolving a better life—never confessing even to herself that she chooses this means of support—now compelled by legislators, who should be the protectors of public virtue, deliberately to admit that henceforth prostitution is to be her profession. Having registered her name, she is to be under the constant supervision of a Board of Health, *composed of men!* to be watched and kept for the safety and convenience of the depraved and licentious of their own sex. "The duties of the Board are similar to those conferred upon the medical authorities in Paris." What man who has transgressed the immutable laws of nature, and suffers the inevitable penalties, would consent thus to register *his* name, though old in crime?

Yet is it nothing to virtuous, healthy, high-toned women that men come to them from the by-ways of vice, to poison the family purity and peace, to stamp the scars of God's curse on the brow of infancy, and make lazar-houses of all our homes? What father in the state of New York would consent to such legislation for his young and erring daughter? We ask for all the daughters of the state the same protection and consideration that we desire for our own. Let our rulers consider that to-day they may be legislating for the frail ones of their own household, as it is from the gay and fashionable throng that vice recruits for its palsied ranks her most helpless victims.

Moreover, this bill is grossly inconsistent. After legalizing prostitution, registering the names of its victims, providing hospitals for their treatment, why make it a crime to rent them a house where they can follow their profession? If the public good requires this annual holocaust of womanhood, why fine those who keep or let these pleasure palaces for the accommodation of those who make the laws? If our rulers at Albany are to make vice respectable by legalizing prostitution, affixing the seal of the state to such a bill of abominations as the one before us, why suppose that the "medical authorities" of New York, the Board of Health or the Metropolitan Police (all men of like temptation with our rulers) will exercise a wise supervision in suppressing crime sanctioned by the state? Oh! men of New York, the best legislation you can give us for the suppression of prostitution is to make woman independent, educate your daughters for self-support, make it respectable for all classes of women to labor, and open to them all the honorable and profitable posts of life.

So long as woman is dependent on man, she will be the victim of his lust. "Give a man a right," says Alexander Hamilton, "over my subsistence, and he has a right over my whole moral being." . . .

For twenty years we have asked the men of this state to give us the "ballot," that great moral lever by which woman can be raised from the depths of her degradation and made to assert herself in the world of thought and action. To-day we demand it as the best "bill for the suppression of prostitution" that our rulers can present to the people of this state for their thoughtful consideration.[26]

CONCERNING RAPE AND THE LAW

Editor of THE REVOLUTION . . .

It seems now to be almost a matter of course that such tragedies [rapes] are to occur weekly, and they excite no comment unless accompanied by the murder of the victim. And because we and our daughters are comparatively safe, is no reason that we should neglect the welfare of such women as are constantly exposed to danger. We must not suffer this country to become a place unsafe for a woman to be alone in; we must force men to guard us against such a state of things, by stringent legislation. This is a question that will not wait until we become of sufficient value in the political world to obtain what we want because men need our votes—we must do something about it *now,* and what we must do is to make the punishment of such crimes so sure and severe that they will be committed at the risk of the criminal's life.

The objection that the evidence obtainable in such cases would not warrant a death sentence, would hold equally against every other punishment; a judge has no more right to commit a man to jail for a year on insufficient evidence, than he would have to sentence him to be hanged. The real difficulty lies in the fact that men do not consider this crime worthy of death, and it should be our duty, for our own sakes and that of others, to impress on the country that it *is* worthy of death, that the man who commits such an outrage on a woman, does her an injury incalculably greater than if he had murdered her in any most brutal manner.

Will you help us so far as you can, by the circulation of a petition to the Legislatures of the various states? If every subscriber to THE REVOLUTION could have one, we should secure a sufficient number of names before December to show how deep and general a feeling I express.

A WOMAN[27]

"SWAPPING WIVES"

Two men and two women in Salisbury, Mass., not well mated in marriage, have exchanged partners by a mutual and harmonious agreement all round. They were respectively married at first in 1856 and 1862. Last year they all went before a lawyer and made and gave the new pledges and perfected the exchange. Since then both partnerships have been happy and harmonious. But a meddlesome community has just interfered and arrested all four, who, not able or willing to give sureties for appearance to court, are now in jail. The neighborhood could and did tolerate their matrimonial discords and contentions in a false union, for years. But their felicity, in the new and apparently real marriage, it could not endure. . . . [28]

ON MARITAL RELATIONS

. . . A wife's duty ceases the moment a man is abusive—the moment she discovers him to be untrue, and it is a sin against God, against self-respect, against the community to bear children for such a scamp, to place herself in a position to be enfeebled by disease and sent to an untimely grave as hosts of pure, noble women have been. Anything is preferable to such a life—the workshop, the factory, the poorhouse, even! . . . [29]

THE MOVEMENT IS DIVIDED

After Congress approved the Fifteenth Amendment, in February 1869, the controversy among the equal-righters reached its peak. The amendment was before the states for ratification. What should the Association do? A faction had coalesced around Anthony and Stanton that agreed to stand firm against the Fifteenth Amendment. The Garrison-Douglass position, attracting most of its adherents from New England, demanded full support for the amendment.

Tension and anger had been accumulating, and in May 1869, at the annual meeting of the Equal Rights Association, they exploded in a long debate that exposed the serious division of opinion. Efforts to remove Anthony and Stanton from office in the Association and the tone of the debate also revealed the deep personal antagonisms that had developed.

REPORT OF THE EQUAL RIGHTS ASSOCIATION

The Committee on Organization reported the officers of the society for the ensuing year.*

STEPHEN FOSTER [an abolitionist and old Garrisonian] . . . He objected, to certain nominations made by the

* *President*: Lucretia Mott. *Vice-Presidents at Large*:—Mrs. Elizabeth Cady Stanton and Ernestine L. Rose. *Vice-Presidents for the States*:—John Neal, Maine; Armenia S. White, New Hampshire.

committee for various reasons. The first was that the persons nominated had publicly repudiated the principles of the society. One of these was the presiding officer.

Mrs. STANTON:—I would like you to say in what respect.

Mr. FOSTER:—I will with pleasure; for, ladies and gentlemen, I admire our talented President with all my heart, and love the woman. (Great laughter.) But I believe she has publicly repudiated the principles of the society.

Mrs. STANTON:—I would like Mr. Foster to state in what way.

Mr. FOSTER:—What are these principles? The equality of men—universal suffrage. These ladies stand at the head of a paper which has adopted as its motto Educated Suffrage. I put myself on this platform as an enemy of educated suffrage, as an enemy of white suffrage, as an enemy of man suffrage, as an enemy of every kind of suffrage except universal suffrage. *The Revolution* lately had an article headed "That Infamous Fifteenth Amendment." It is true it was not written by our President, yet it comes from a person whom she has over and over again publicly indorsed. I am not willing to take George Francis Train on this platform with his ridicule of the negro and opposition to his enfranchisement.

Mrs. MARY A. LIVERMORE:—Is it quite generous to bring George Francis Train on this platform when he has retired from *The Revolution* entirely?

Mr. FOSTER:—If *The Revolution*, which has so often indorsed George Francis Train, will repudiate him because of his course in respect to the negro's rights, I have nothing further to say. But it does not repudiate him. He goes out; it does not cast him out.

Miss ANTHONY:—Of course it does not.

Mr. FOSTER:—My friend says yes to what I have said. I thought it was so. I only wanted to tell you why the Massachusetts society can not coalesce with the party here, and why we want these women to retire and leave us to nominate officers who can receive the respect of both parties. The Massachusetts Abolitionists can not co-operate with this society as it is now organized. If you choose to put officers here that ridicule the negro, and pronounce the Amendment infamous, why I must retire; I can not work with you. You can not have my support, and you must not use my name. I can not shoulder the responsibility of electing officers who publicly repudiate the principles of the society. . . .

Mr. DOUGLASS [Frederick Douglass]:—I came here more as a listener than to speak, and I have listened with a great deal of pleasure to the eloquent address of the Rev. Mr. Frothingham and the splendid address of the President. There is no name greater than that of Elizabeth Cady Stanton in the matter of woman's rights and equal rights, but my sentiments are tinged a little against *The Revolution*. There was in the address to which I allude the employment of certain names, such as "Sambo," and the gardener, and the bootblack, and the daughters of Jefferson and Washington, and all the rest that I can not coincide with. I have asked what difference there is between the daughters of Jefferson and Washington and other daughters. (Laughter.) I must say that I do not see how any one can pretend that there is the same urgency in giving the ballot to woman as to the negro. With us, the matter is a question of life and death, at least, in fifteen States of the Union. When women, because they are women, are hunted down through the cities of New York and New Orleans; when they are dragged from their houses and hung upon lamp-posts; when their children are torn from their arms, and their brains dashed out upon the pavement; when they are objects of insult and outrage at every turn; when they are in danger of having their homes burnt down over their heads; when their children are not allowed to enter schools; then they will have an urgency to obtain the ballot equal to our own. (Great applause.)

A VOICE:—Is that not all true about black women?

MR. DOUGLASS:—Yes, yes, yes; it is true of the black woman, but not because she is a woman, but because she is black. (Applause.) Julia Ward Howe at the conclusion of her great speech delivered at the convention in Boston last year, said: "I am willing that the negro shall get the ballot before me." (Applause.) Woman! why, she has 10,000 modes of grappling with her difficulties. I believe that all the virtue of the world can take care of all the evil. I believe that all the intelligence can take care of all the ignorance. (Applause.) I am in favor of woman's suffrage in order that we shall have all the virtue and vice confronted. Let me tell you that when there were few houses in which the black man could have put his head, this wooly head of mine found a refuge in the house of Mrs. Elizabeth Cady Stanton, and if I had been blacker than sixteen midnights, without a single star, it would have been the same. (Applause.)

MISS ANTHONY:—The old anti-slavery school say women must stand back and wait until the negroes shall be recognized. But we say, if you will not give the whole loaf of suffrage to the entire people, give it to the most intelligent first. (Applause.) If intelligence, justice, and morality are to have precedence in the Government, let the question of woman be brought up first and that of the negro last. (Applause.) While I was canvassing the State with petitions and had them filled with names for our cause to the Legislature, a man dared to say to me that the freedom of women was all a theory and not a practical thing. (Applause.) When Mr. Douglass mentioned the black man first and the woman last, if he had noticed he would have seen that it was the men that clapped and not the women. There is not the woman born who desires to eat the bread of dependence, no matter whether it be from the hand of father, husband, or brother; for any one who does so eat her bread places herself in the power of the person from whom she takes it. (Applause.) Mr. Douglass talks about the wrongs of the negro; but with all the outrages that he to-day suffers, he would not exchange his sex and take the place of Elizabeth Cady Stanton. (Laughter and applause.)

MR. DOUGLASS:—I want to know if granting you the right of suffrage will change the nature of our sexes? (Great laughter.)

MISS ANTHONY:—It will change the pecuniary position of woman; it will place her where she can earn her own bread. (Loud applause.) She will not then be driven to such employments only as man chooses for her. . . .

MISS COUZINS [Phoebe Couzins, a young law student from Missouri] said:—MRS. PRESIDENT AND LADIES: . . . While feeling entirely willing that the black man shall have all the rights to which he is justly entitled, I consider the claims of the black woman of paramount importance. I have had opportunities of seeing and knowing the condition of both sexes, and will bear my testimony, that the black women are, and always have been, in a far worse condition than the men. As a class, they are better, and more intelligent than the men, yet they have been subjected to greater brutalities, while compelled to perform exactly the same labor as men toiling by their side in the fields, just as hard burdens imposed upon them, just as severe punishments decreed to them, with the added cares of maternity and household work, with their children taken from them and sold into bondage; suffering a thousandfold more than any man could suffer. . . .

The advocates of the XVth Amendment tell us we ought to accept the half loaf when we can not get the whole. I do not see that woman gets any part of the loaf, not even a crumb that falls from the rich man's table. . . .

The Anti-Slavery party declares that with the adoption of the XVth Amendment their work is done. Have they, then, been battling for over thirty years for a fraction of a principle? If so, then the XVth Amendment is a fitting capstone to their labors. Were the earnest women who fought and endured so heroically with them, but tools in the hands of the leaders, to place "manhood suffrage" on the highest pinnacle of the temple dedicated to Truth and Justice? And are they now to bow down, and worship in abject submission this fractional part of a principle, that has hitherto proclaimed itself, as knowing neither bond nor free, male nor female, but one perfect humanity?

The XV. Amendment virtually says that every intelligent, virtuous woman is the inferior of every ignorant man, no matter how low he may be sunk in the scale of morality, and every instinct of my being rises to refute such doctrine, and God speaking within me says, No! eternally No! . . .

MRS. HARPER [Frances Harper, black poet and abolitionist]: — . . . When it was a question of race, she let the lesser question of sex go. But the white women all go for sex, letting race occupy a minor position. She liked the idea of working women, but she would like to know if it was broad enough to take colored women?

MISS ANTHONY and several others: Yes, yes.

MRS. HARPER said that when she was at Boston there were sixty women who left work because one colored woman went to gain a livelihood in their midst. (Applause) If the nation could only handle one question, she would not have the black women put a single straw in the way, if only the men of the race could obtain what they wanted. (Great applause). . . . 30

After the debate and discussion, the Association voted whether to endorse the Fifteenth Amendment. The majority, including many members from New England suffrage groups, gave the Amendment their support.

Immediately after the meeting, the dissident group, led by Anthony and Stanton, met to form a new organization dedicated to woman suffrage. They called themselves the National Woman Suffrage Assocation.

The Equal Rights Association had suffered a mortal blow and it soon disappeared. In November 1869, the women who supported the Fifteenth Amendment and many of the men who had been in the Association formed another group—the American Woman Suffrage Association.

Thus, after four years of hard work for the vote, the women's movement was defeated, frustrated, and divided into two.

KVCC KALAMAZOO VALLEY COMMUNITY COLLEGE LIBRARY

CHAPTER FOUR

DIVISION AND REUNION

1869-1890

Continuing differences between the two national woman's rights organizations formed in 1869—the American Woman Suffrage Association and the National Woman Suffrage Association—kept them separate for two decades. The Fifteenth Amendment was ratified by the states early in 1870 and was no longer a divisive issue. But many of the other disagreements that had plagued the parent Equal Rights Association, differences that stayed beneath the surface during the struggle over the Fifteenth Amendment, arose after 1870. And although both groups were committed to suffrage as the primary reform for women and often worked together for the vote, each maintained its own distinct approach within the women's movement.

The differences between the two associations were most pronounced at the level of their leadership, where personal antagonism reinforced ideological and tactical clashes. The rank-and-file members were often in state and local suffrage groups, and geographic distance kept them somewhat removed from many of the conflicts which took place in the East at the top.

The period of the 1870's and 1880's, in which the two groups functioned independently, was a difficult time for

Lucy Stone

both. Years of civil war and the postwar ordeal of Reconstruction had left the country with a yearning for harmony and a preoccupation with economic development. Interest in reform had died out. Distrust of agitation and fear of change had made many Americans unusually cautious and conservative. The women's movement, controversial and disturbing as ever, struggled just to keep itself moving forward. During this period, the combined membership of the National and American associations was probably never more than ten thousand.[1] Most members came from Northern and Western states, but by the 1870's this small membership included Southerners as well. The National, for example, counted more than a third of its vice-presidents from the South.

The American Woman Suffrage Association (hereafter called the "American") was the more moderate of the two. Among its leaders were Julia Ward Howe, Mary A. Livermore, Lucy Stone, Henry B. Blackwell, Thomas W. Higginson, and the well-known minister Henry Ward Beecher.

In the struggle over the Fifteenth Amendment, the American faction had refused to put women's claim for the vote ahead of the black man's; it had also renounced George Francis Train, objected to Anthony and Stanton's belligerency, and criticized their involvement with issues other than suffrage. At its first convention, in November 1869, in Cleveland, Ohio, the new organization reiterated its primary commitment to woman suffrage, and through the decades that followed, the American remained foremost a woman suffrage organization. It had a cautious strategy: The American would not be sidetracked by other issues. It would concentrate on suffrage, avoiding extraneous and controversial subjects that might antagonize possible supporters.

The American departed from the loose, informal structure that had characterized the women's movement thus far. It was a carefully organized national group, to which state suffrage associations were affiliated, and the presidents of state groups were ex officio vice-presidents of the national organization. Conventions of the American Woman Suffrage Association were meetings of officially accredited delegates from member groups. The open convention, at which all speakers and ideas had the floor, was rejected.

As a suffrage organization, the American was committed to gaining the vote for women by changing state laws and constitutions, and most of its activities took place within the individual states, not in Washington. Its annual conventions, in cities such as Philadelphia, Indianapolis, and St. Louis, helped to tie together the national organization and the groups in the states.

In January 1870, the American began to publish The Woman's Journal. Throughout the 1870's and 1880's, the paper played an important part in coordinating suffrage efforts in the country, and after the death of The Revolution in 1872 was the major source of women's news.

Male suffragists were prominent in the American association, and they functioned as equal and trusted allies. The Woman's Journal was financed and partly run by men. Men were officers of the Association, and together Henry B. Blackwell and Lucy Stone formed its hard-working core.

As a reform organization, the American was consistently conservative. Its leaders, as determined and dedicated as any others, tried to be politic. They believed that persuasion, education, patience, and hard work would serve their cause best.

The National Woman Suffrage Association took a more radical stance than the American. It grew out of opposition to the Fifteenth Amendment when Anthony and Stanton gave priority to women's rights over black men's. From the start, the "National" (as it will be called here) was more aggressive and demanding than the American. "Women first" was the gist of their refusal to support the Fifteenth Amendment as well as of their willingness to accept help from George Francis Train and other Democrats.

After the split in 1869, the National insisted on defining women's rights broadly. It attacked and demanded change in all aspects of American life that concerned women and refused to limit its agitation to the vote, although the National agreed with the American that suffrage was the fundamental reform women needed. As a result, National spokeswomen were associated with issues like wages and working conditions of women and marriage and divorce laws. These subjects, the National argued, could not be ignored or postponed even though they were controversial.

The National was more casually organized than the American. Individuals could join the association and officers of suffrage organizations could affiliate their organizations to the national group. Officers elected at the annual convention and representatives of state groups made up a National Executive Committee. In effect, the National was a loose assemblage of individuals and state and local suffrage groups who chose to associate themselves with National politics and personalities.

A faithful core of leaders—women like Susan B. Anthony, Elizabeth Cady Stanton, Laura Curtis Bullard, Paulina Wright Davis, Matilda Joslyn Gage, and Isabella Beecher Hooker—labored to coordinate and organize the National's activities. Initially, a large proportion of New Yorkers formed the National association, but other women, especially Westerners, joined as time went on.

National leaders tried several approaches to gain the vote for women, all of them aimed at enfranchising all women, at the same time, through federal action. Consequently, Washington was the focus of National activities, and annual conventions were held there.

Conventions of the National Woman Suffrage Association were open meetings, often exuberant and confident, and provided a forum for new and sometimes shocking ideas. In May 1872, The Revolution, early abandoned by Train, ceased publication for lack of funds. Without a regular voice, National leaders relied on the annual conventions, together with frequent speeches and writings of its more famous leaders, to mobilize women and to broadcast its views.

Unlike the American, the National had little room for men, of whom it was suspicious. The conflict with male abolitionists over the Fifteenth Amendment and the consistent rejection of women's efforts to get the vote led the National leadership to view men as its opponents. Men could not serve as officers of the organization and they never played as important a part in National activities as they did in the American, although some male supporters did participate and cooperate with the National.

Especially during the 1870's, the National was more belligerent, aggressive, and impatient than the American. The Stone-Blackwell leadership advocated and performed hard work to educate and persuade Americans to grant women the vote. They believed they were more likely to succeed if they were temperate, judicious, and respectable. The Anthony-Stanton forces were angry and impatient. They bristled at compromise and conciliation and refused to demand less than equality. Heady with determination and confidence, they were impolitic and, at least at first, felt willing to take on the world, if necessary, to have justice done.

AMERICAN VS. NATIONAL: ONE ISSUE OR MANY

During the 1870's, the greatest contrast between the two wings of the movement lay in the American's concentration on suffrage and the National's exploration of almost all aspects of women's lives and experience, although it, too, considered the vote the primary reform.

The American focus on suffrage was in part a strategic decision. Any reader of The Woman's Journal knew that the American leadership ultimately wanted more than political equality for women and welcomed other reforms. But it was a mistake, they believed, to scatter their forces, especially on controversial reforms; the vote was the key.

The Woman's Journal.

ANNOUNCEMENT FOR 1872.

A WEEKLY NEWSPAPER.

THE WOMAN'S JOURNAL,

Devoted to the interests of WOMAN, to her educational, industrial, legal and political Equality, and especially to her RIGHT OF SUFFRAGE.

**Published Every Saturday by its Proprie-
tors, in Boston, Chicago and St. Louis.**
JULIA WARD HOWE, LUCY STONE, HENRY B.
BLACKWELL and T. W. HIGGINSON, *Editors.* MARY
A. LIVERMORE, *Corresponding Editor.*

St. Louis Address, FANNY HOLY, Insurance Exchange Building, Room 18, corner Fifth and Olive st.

OPINIONS OF THE PRESS.

THE WOMAN'S JOURNAL.—The friends of Woman
Suffrage who wish to keep the issue clear from en-
tangling alliances with other reforms and the endless
host of individual whims and vagaries—who would
pursue it with the same singleness of aim that marks
the movement in England, and the temperance and
other special reforms in this country, have established
a weekly paper, the WOMAN'S JOURNAL, published
in Boston and Chicago, and edited by Mrs. Livermore,
Mrs. Lucy Stone, Mrs. Julia Ward Howe, Mr. Wm.
Lloyd Garrison and Mr. T. W. Higginson, assisted by
accomplished friends of the cause. The WOMAN'S
JOURNAL is a fair and attractive paper in appearance;
while the variety and spirit of its articles, and the dignity, self-respect, good-humor and earnestness of its
tone, will show how profoundly mistaken are those
who suppose that folly and extravagance are necessarily characteristic of the discussion of the question.
The JOURNAL is indispensable to those who would
truly understand the character of the movement and
measure its progress.—*Harper's Weekly.*

TERMS :

$2.50 a year, *invariably in advance.* Single copy 6
cents.

CLUB RATES :

Any person sending five subscribers will receive a
sixth copy FREE. Ten copies will be forwarded on re-
ceipt of $20.00.
Specimen copies sent on receipt of two-cent stamp
for postage.
Liberal terms to canvassers.
For sale and subscriptions received by THE NEW
ENGLAND NEWS CO., 41 Court street, Boston, and
THE AMERICAN NEWS CO., 119 Nassau street, New
York.
RATES OF ADVERTISING—One square of eight
lines, first insertion, $1.00; subsequent insertion, 50
cents. Business notices 20 cents per line. The price
for advertising is uniform and inflexible.

BOSTON OFFICE—3 Tremont Place, rear of Tremont
House, and second door from Beacon street.

All communications for the WOMAN'S JOURNAL,
and all letters relating to its editorial management,
must be addressed to HENRY B. BLACKWELL.
Letters containing remittances, and relating to the
business department of the paper, must be addressed
to the WOMAN'S JOURNAL, Boston.

*At the second annual meeting of the American Woman
Suffrage Association, Thomas W. Higginson, first vice-
president, explained the American's position.*

THE AMERICAN POSITION

. . . Early in the movement in behalf of women the broad
platform of "woman's rights" was adopted. This was all
proper and right then, but the progress of reform has developed the fact that suffrage for woman is the great key that
will unlock to her the doors of social and political equality.
This should be the first point of concentrated attack. When
a fortress is about to be carried by an army, each soldier does
not select a separate brick and push at that, but the commander selects one point and concentrates his whole force
upon it. Once in, he can dictate his own terms of peace.
Suffrage is not the *only* object, but it is the *first,* to be attained. When we gave our Association that name we escaped a vast deal of discussion and argument, for its object
cannot be misunderstood. It is because to the sex the ballot
symbolizes everything, that we give it that name. (Applause.)
But after that is gained there will be worlds yet to conquer.
If the conservatives think that because it is called the Woman
Suffrage Association it has no further object, they are greatly
mistaken. Its purpose and aim are to equalize the sexes in all
the relations of life; to reduce the inequalities that now exist
in matters of education, in social life and in the professions
—to make them equal in all respects, before the law, society
and the world. Through it we see the end, although it may
be afar off. With this burden upon our shoulders we cannot
carry all the other ills of the world in addition, we must take
one thing at a time. Suffrage for woman gained, and all else
will speedily follow. Upon the labor question we do not
advocate or oppose the eight-hour movement, but we claim
that if a man works eight hours his wife must not be made
to work eight hours and a quarter. In relation to the law of
marriage and divorce, as soon as there is no difference between the rights of man and woman in all the States, then
our work in that direction is finished. In the countries of
Europe, England for instance, the difference between man
and woman as to divorce is so vast as to be an insult to
woman, and one of the chief causes of her degradation. The
object of reform is to secure absolute equality, and when
that is attained our work is done. But we need not fear that
after the accomplishment of suffrage there will be nothing
else for us to do before the great end is reached. We are in
the work for life, in one form or another. The anti-slavery
societies have been dissolved, their work being accomplished, and yet their members find plenty to do. And so we,

after we have succeeded in securing suffrage for woman, will join in new movements and carry on the work of progress. [2]

While it lasted, The Revolution *exemplified the National Association's willingness to involve itself with a wide variety of reforms and concerns. For the two years in which* The Revolution *was the only movement publication, and an influential one, it dismayed its critics within the movement—and continued to do so until it ceased publication.*

In 1868, an enthusiastic subscriber wrote the following letter to the paper.

"TO *THE REVOLUTION*"

Auburn, Oregon, July 14, 1868

"The Revolution" came in good time, and we are very much pleased with its appearance. . . . It exceeds our anticipation in every respect. I hope it will have as extensive a circulation as its merits demand. It should be in every family.

Auburn is a small mining camp of about one hundred men and twenty-five women. There is but one woman here who has had courage enough to take the paper. Two married men have subscribed for their wives, the rest are single men. The paper has created quite an excitement here, because of its views on Woman's Rights. Some of the men think that women have too many rights now and are in favor of curtailing rather than increasing them.

I shall circulate the paper in other towns in this vicinity, and do what I can for the cause in Eastern Oregon. Some of our republican friends object to the paper, as opposed to the union party. We have very little opportunity to know the truth of many things we hear of our public men. . . . [3]

Freedom of movement for women; defense of George Sand; compensation for housework. Were these extraneous issues? red flags that aroused hostility and hurt the suffrage cause? For the first time, they were aired in The Revolution.

"HAVE WOMEN ANY RIGHT IN A HOTEL?"

It is a frequent boast of Americans that a woman may travel alone across the length and breadth of our country, not only without danger of insult, but that she is sure of receiving from every one she meets the greatest courtesy and kindness; ready assistance in any little difficulty or perplexity is offered her by all gentlemen, since it is taken for granted that a woman is entitled to all respect and courtesy until, by her own conduct, she forfeits her claim to receive it.

But this general principle, so creditable to both the men and women of America, is not accepted by the hotel proprietors of our country. A single woman shrinks from presenting herself at one of these temporary sojourns; for if she does not receive insult in words, she has to pass a critical survey from the officials, who scan her from head to foot, in attempting to decide for themselves whether she is or is not a respectable woman, while her blood tingles in every vein with her shame and indignation at this mute investigation of her moral character.

No single man has to pass this crucial test of immaculate purity before a room is assigned him, nor can we believe that it is the high standard of morality of hotel-proprietors which leads to this scrutiny of single women. There is little investigation of the character of a woman accompanied by a man who visits a hotel, even if her appearance and manners are of a suspicious sort; and many of our large hotels have an unenviable reputation of sheltering fast women with their paramours. . . . [4]

"A WORD ABOUT GEORGE SAND"

One of the most painful results of women's slavery and degradation is their cruelty and faithlessness to one another, seen alike in the highest and lowest orders.

The slaves of the South could have conquered their own freedom years ago had they at any time been united in their attempted insurrections; but one of their own number invariably betrayed them to the enemy.

Just so with women; whenever the brave and far-seeing strike any blow for their emancipation and enfranchisement, the timid, cautious and time-serving of their sex invariably betray them.

A recent item in the *Woman's Journal* illustrates this assertion. Mrs. Stowe who, with her late writings, has brought the blush to more cheeks than any writer of the age, attempts with the scratch of her pen to annihilate the author of *Consuelo,* whose great soul felt the depths of woman's degradation in a joyless, unclean marriage relation, and who bravely sundered the unholy tie with her own hand, thus sanctifying her own sorrows to the multitude, making herself a beacon light to warn the young and the unwary from the dangerous coasts where she was wrecked.

George Sand has done a grander work for women, in her pure life and bold utterances of truth, than any woman of her day and generation; while Mrs. Stowe has been vacillating over every demand made for her sex, timidly watching the weathercock of public sentiment, and ridiculing the advance guard, who, the world said, had blundered; . . . she [Sand] has pointed her guns at the stronghold of her slavery—a relation enforced by the state and sanctified by the church—called Christian marriage, that makes woman the abject slave of her husband. When women first demanded suffrage in this country, where was Mrs. Stowe? While the thousands of wives of drunkards, licentious men, tyrants and criminals call aloud to-day for deliverance from all these degrading, abominable relations, where is Mrs. Stowe?

Behold her, Bible in hand, proclaiming to these unhappy ones, "a woman hath not power over her own body, but the husband."[5]

"OUR WOMEN PAUPERS"

It would, perhaps, startle the most of us if suddenly in the midst of a festive social occasion, or when seated in a crowded railway car, or in church, at a lecture, or in some other assembly of people, a whisper should reach our ears, "More than half these women present are paupers!" . . .

"What, these well dressed women paupers!" you exclaim. Yes! Probably nine-tenths of those gaily apparelled ladies could not dispose of even so small a sum of money as ten dollars without first asking for it from the purseholder of the family, and stating for what uses it was intended. . . .

The sensitiveness, the humiliation with which a woman approaches her husband for money, none but a woman can know. She feels, indeed, that it is her right, for if her servants earn their wages and they are paid cheerfully, to how much more are her untiring and unflagging services entitled. In every department of household labor, the good wife and mother takes her share. In every emergency she must be prepared to act. All day long and often into the night she toils for her household. . . . For services such as hers, were she to be taken by death from her family, her husband would be obliged to pay a good salary, but he considers her food and necessary clothing an all-sufficient recompense for her life-long work.

Do you say that her love for her family should sweeten her toil and be all the reward she should ask? No doubt she would find the daily routine of her cares unendurable were it not for the unfailing affection which stimulates her to exertions, but has not her husband the same motives to incite him to action in his business . . . ?

Among the happiest women we have known, we may reckon the writers, singers, artists, lecturers, milliners and dressmakers, who have contributed to the maintenance of their families. They have been invariably the tenderest of wives and the most devoted of mothers—happy in the exercise of their talents, and in the pecuniary advantages which their families have reaped from their labors.

But all women cannot, nor should they desire to enter the arena of daily business with men—nor would they, were their home services regarded, as they deserve to be, of equal value with the out-door labors of the husband and father.

. . . Women have borne in silence this position of paupers, smothering the indignation and humiliation they have felt in it—growing hard and bitter under the wrong, and yet making no attempt to right it. It is time that all this was changed—that a woman should become not only in name, but in fact, the equal partner of her husband in the money

which he amasses, and that at least whatever may be said as to her participation in business matters, that she should be consulted with regard to the household expenditures. A woman who is fit to be a wife and a mother ought at least to be capable of giving advice on the money matters of the home. Wives should claim this share in the household economy, and in order to exercise the right judiciously, they should inform themselves of the state of their husband's affairs, and graduate their expenditures accordingly.[6]

After the demise of The Revolution, *the National used its conventions and other women's meetings along with the speeches and publications of its spokeswomen to disseminate its ideas and opinions.*

Conventions of the National Woman Suffrage Association continued through the 1870's and 1880's to discuss the controversial issues that had helped to split the movement in 1869. Subjects like prostitution, marriage and divorce laws, and religion came under scrutiny at annual meetings. Convention resolutions consistently demanded legal, economic, social, and religious changes, as well as the vote.

The National's leaders, like other women in the movement, were regular speakers on the lecture circuits. In an era without radios and cheap daily newspapers, lecturers were a popular and important means of communication. To the National, which suffered even more than the American from lack of funds, the lecture tour offered a way of raising money and spreading ideas. Elizabeth Cady Stanton was an unusually successful and busy podium speaker. She used her opportunity to make clear that not one issue but many were involved in women's drive for equality. Her lecture on marriage and divorce, delivered on many occasions, was popular and controversial. The American's leaders found Stanton's willingness to discuss such issues—and on occasion to talk with groups of women about pregnancy and abortion—especially irritating. The lecture on marriage and divorce, as presented to the 1870 National convention, reveals how Stanton's ideas had developed since she proposed divorce as a solution for intemperance to an outraged women's meeting in 1853.

STANTON ON MARRIAGE AND DIVORCE

All this talk about the indissoluble tie and the sacredness of marriage, irrespective of the character and habits of the husband, is for its effect on woman. She never could have been held the pliant tool she is to-day but for the subjugation of her religious nature to the idea that in whatever condition she found herself as man's subject, that condition was ordained of Heaven; whether burning on the funeral pile of her husband in India, or suffering the slower torture of bearing children every year in America to drunkards, diseased, licen-

The Revolution.

PRINCIPLE, NOT POLICY: JUSTICE, NOT FAVORS.

VOL. I.—NO. 1. NEW YORK, WEDNESDAY, JANUARY 8, 1868. $2.00 A YEAR.

The Revolution;

THE ORGAN OF THE

NATIONAL PARTY OF NEW AMERICA.

PRINCIPLE, NOT POLICY—INDIVIDUAL RIGHTS AND
RESPONSIBILITIES.

THE REVOLUTION WILL ADVOCATE:

1. IN POLITICS—Educated Suffrage, Irrespective of Sex or Color; Equal Pay to Women for Equal Work; Eight Hours Labor; Abolition of Standing Armies and Party Despotisms. Down with Politicians—Up with the People!

2. IN RELIGION—Deeper Thought; Broader Idea; Science not Superstition; Personal Purity; Love to Man as well as God.

3. IN SOCIAL LIFE.—Morality and Reform; Practical Education. not Theoretical; Facts not Fiction; Virtue not Vice; Cold Water not Alcoholic Drinks or Medicines. It will indulge in no Gross Personalities and insert no Quack or Immoral Advertisements, so common even in Religious Newspapers.

4. THE REVOLUTION proposes a new Commercial and Financial Policy. America no longer led by Europe. Gold like our Cotton and Corn for sale. Greenbacks for money. An American System of Finance. American Products and Labor Free. Foreign Manufactures Prohibited. Open doors to Artisans and Immigrants. Atlantic and Pacific Oceans for American Steamships and Shipping; or American goods in American bottoms. New York the Financial Centre of the World. Wall Street emancipated from Bank of England, or American Cash for American Bills. The Credit Foncier and Credit Mobilier System, or Capital Mobilized to Resuscitate the South and our Mining Interests, and to People the Country from Ocean to Ocean, from Omaha to San Francisco. More organized Labor, more Cotton, more Gold and Silver Bullion to sell foreigners at the highest prices. Ten millions of Naturalized Citizens DEMAND A PENNY OCEAN POSTAGE, to Strengthen the Brotherhood of Labor; and if Congress Vote One Hundred and Twenty-five Millions for a Standing Army and Freedman's Bureau, cannot they spare O e Million to Educate Europe and to keep bright the chain of acquaintance and friendship between those millions and their fatherland?

Send in your Subscription. THE REVOLUTION, published weekly, will be the Great Organ of the Age.

TERMS.—Two dollars a year, in advance. Ten names ($20) entitle the sender to one copy free.

ELIZABETH CADY STANTON, }
PARKER PILLSBURY, } EDS.

SUSAN B. ANTHONY,
Proprietor and Manager.
37 Park Row (Room 17), New York City,
To whom address all business letters.

KANSAS.

THE question of the enfranchisement of woman has already passed the court of moral discussion, and is now fairly ushered into the arena of politics, where it must remain a fixed element of debate, until party necessity shall compel its success.

With 9,000 votes in Kansas, one-third the entire vote, every politician must see that the friends of "woman's suffrage" hold the balance of power in that State to-day. And those 9,000 votes represent a principle deep in the hearts of the people, for this triumph was secured without money, without a press, without a party. With these instrumentalities now fast coming to us on all sides, the victory in Kansas is but the herald of greater victories in every State of the Union. Kansas already leads the world in her legislation for woman on questions of property, education, wages, marriage and divorce. Her best universities are open alike to boys and girls. In fact woman has a voice in the legislation of that State. She votes on all school questions and is eligible to the office of trustee. She has a voice in temperance too; no license is granted without the consent of a majority of the adult citizens, male and female, black and white. The consequence is, stone school houses are voted up in every part of the State, and rum voted down. Many of the ablest men in that State are champions of woman's cause. Governors, judges, lawyers and clergymen. Two-thirds of the press and pulpits advocate the idea, in spite of the opposition of politicians. The first Governor of Kansas, twice chosen to that office, Charles Robinson, went all through the State, speaking every day for two months in favor of woman's suffrage. In the organization of the State government, he proposed that the words " white [male" should not be inserted in the Kansas constitution. All this shows that giving political rights to women is no new idea in that State. Who that has listened with tearful eyes to the deep experiences of those Kansas women, through the darkest hours of their history, does not feel that such bravery and self denial as they have shown alike in war and peace, have richly earned for them the crown of citizenship.

Opposed to this moral sentiment of the liberal minds of the State, many adverse influences were brought to bear through the entire campaign.

The action of the New York Constitutional Convention; the silence of eastern journals on the question; the opposition of abolitionists lest a demand for woman's suffrage should defeat negro suffrage; the hostility everywhere of black men themselves; some even stumping the State against woman's suffrage; the official action of both the leading parties in their conventions in Leavensworth against the proposition, with every organized Republican influence outside as well as inside the State, all combined might have made our vote comparatively a small one, had not George Francis Train gone into the State two weeks before the election and galvanized the Democrats into their duty, thus securing 9,000 votes for woman's suffrage. Some claim that we are indebted to the Republicans for this vote; but the fact that the most radical republican district, Douglass County, gave the largest vote against woman's suffrage, while Leavenworth, the Democratic district, gave the largest vote for it, fully settles that question.

In saying that Mr. Train helped to swell our vote takes nothing from the credit due all those who labored faithfully for months in that State. All praise to Olympia Brown, Lucy Stone, Susan B. Anthony, Henry B. Blackwell, and Judge Wood, who welcomed, for an idea, the hardships of travelling in a new State, fording streams, scaling rocky brinks, sleeping on the ground and eating hard tack, with the fatigue of constant speaking, in school-houses, barns. mills, depots and the open air; and especially, all praise to the glorious Hutchinson family-- John, his son Henry and daughter, Viola--who, with their own horses and carriage, made the entire circuit of the state, singing Woman's Suffrage into souls that logic could never penetrate. Having shared with them the hardships, with them I rejoice in our success.

E. C. S.

THE BALLOT—BREAD, VIRTUE, POWER.

THE REVOLUTION will contain a series of articles, beginning next week, to prove the power of the ballot in elevating the character and condition of woman. We shall show that the ballot will secure for woman equal place and equal wages in the world of work; that it will open to her the schools, colleges, professions and all the opportunities and advantages of life; that in her hand it will be a moral power to stay the tide of vice and crime and misery on every side. In the words of Bishop Simpson—

" We believe that the great vices in our large cities will never be conquered until the ballot is put in the hands of women. If the question of the danger of their sons being drawn away into drinking saloons was brought up, if the mothers had the power, they would close them ; if the sisters had the power, and they saw their brothers going away to haunts of infamy, they would close those places. You may get men to trifle with purity, with virtue, with righteousness ; but, thank God, the hearts of the women of our land—the mothers, wives and daughters—are too pure to make a compromise either with intemperance or licentiousness."

Thus, too, shall we purge our constitutions and statute laws from all invidious distinctions among the citizens of the States, and secure the same civil and moral code for man and woman. We will show the hundred thousand female teachers, and the millions of laboring women, that their complaints, petitions, strikes and protective unions are of no avail until they hold the ballot in their own hands; for it is the first step toward social, religious and political equality.

tious men, at the expense of her own life and health and the enfeebling of both the mind and body of her progeny. Women would not live as they now do in this enlightened age in violation of every law of their being, giving the very heyday of their existence to the exercise of one animal function, if subordination to man had not been made through the ages the cardinal point of their religious faith and daily life. It requires but little thought to see that . . . the indissoluble tie was found to be necessary in order to establish man's authority over woman. The argument runs thus:

Men all admit that if two cannot be agreed they must part. This may apply to partners in business, pastor and people, physician and patient, master and servant, and many other relations in life; but in the case of parent and child, husband and wife, as their relations cannot be dissolved, there must be some alternate authority to decide all matters in which they cannot agree, hence man's headship. These cases should be distinguished, however; the child is free to act on his own opinions, by law, at a certain age, and the tie is practically dissolved between him and the parent so soon as he earns his own bread. The child is under the parent's control only during its minority; but the wife's condition is perpetual minority, life-long subjection to authority, with no appeal, no hope on the indissoluble tie theory. The practical effect of this is to make tyrants of men and fools of women. There never was a human being yet on this footstool godlike enough to be trusted with the absolute control of any living thing. Men abuse each other. Look in your prisons, jails, asylums, battle-fields and camps, they abuse their horses, dogs, cats. . . . They abuse their own children, and of course they will abuse their wives, taught by law and gospel that they own them as property, especially as a wife can vex and thwart a man, as no other living thing can.

It is sheer folly at this age of the world to waste ink or words on marriage as an indissoluble tie and on the husband's divinely ordained authority, for woman's growing self-respect and keen perception of the drift of these dogmas enable her at last to see that the long and weary bondage her sex has endured through the centuries was based in the beginning on these twin heresies. . . .

Together we suffer, together let us work for the new civilization now dawning upon us.

The day is breaking! It is something to know that life's ills are not showered upon us by the Great Father from a kind of Pandora's box, but are the results of causes that we have the power to control. By a knowledge and observance of law, the road to health and happiness opens before us: a joy and peace that passeth all understanding shall yet be ours and Paradise regained on earth. When marriage results from a true union of intellect and spirit—when mothers and fathers give to their holy offices even the preparation of soul and body that the artist gives to the conception of his poem, statue or landscape, then will marriage, maternity and paternity acquire a new sacredness and dignity, and a nobler type of manhood and womanhood will glorify the race.[7]

Toward the end of 1870, a serious effort was made to unite the National and American associations into a women's union. But they could not reconcile their disagreements over "extraneous" issues. The American objected strongly to Stanton's willingness to challenge contemporary attitudes toward marriage and divorce. It believed her personal opinions, which were radical and unconventional, were not the prevailing views within the women's movement even though the public assumed they were. And it felt that her views aroused anger against the movement and hurt the suffrage cause.

The controversy developed in The Revolution *and* The Woman's Journal.

THE NATIONAL'S VIEW

Shall We Go a Solitary Path?

Two cannot walk together except they be agreed.

Heretofore, in favoring a union of the two national societies for woman's enfranchisement, THE REVOLUTION has acted on the theory that both were equally faithful to the woman's movement.

But late utterances in *The Woman's Journal* and elsewhere notify us of the painful fact that the Boston managers of the American Woman Suffrage Association have abandoned nine-tenths of the woman question, and are devoting themselves only to the other one-tenth; in other words, have surrendered the most vital or social phase of the reform to its more superficial or political. Their plan of campaign is to cut off all "side issues" and to "stick to the one point":— the "side issues" being such trifles as wages, education, property, marriage, and divorce; and the "one point" being the ballot.

This is like abandoning one's self to the spoon at breakfast, and forgetting the coffee, sugar, and milk which it is to stir up. . . .

We are wholly opposed to the Boston attempt to distil our whole great question into a single drop. The woman question is more than a demand for suffrage. Whoever says it is not, is either a new convert, if a woman, or (more ignorant still) if a man. We do not expect men to understand the woman's movement—except some solitary, rare spirit here and there, like John Stuart Mill. Our chief hopes of such clergymen as the Rev. Thomas Higginson is, that when they lend their sacred but clumsy hands to the woman's cause they will not actually mark it with a bruise. . . .

But, great as suffrage is in itself, it is only a fragment of the reform on which the hopes of woman depend—a reform whose true foundations do not rest on the surface of her citizenship, but in the heart of her womanhood.

We have said before, and we repeat it with renewed emphasis, that the woman question—the very question which the *Woman's Journal* and the American Woman Suffrage Association ought to discuss in all its phases, and which they have no right to evade in any—is a question covering the whole range of woman's needs and demands, woman's rights and wrongs, woman's opportunities and enterprises—including her work, her wages, her property, her education, her physical training, her social status, her political equality, her marriage, and her divorce.

Finally, if we cannot, in arranging the wedding of the two societies, secure to the united organization its rightful dowry of all these questions, we hereby forbid the banns. . . . [8]

THE AMERICAN'S VIEW

Many of the better class of newspapers, favorable to Woman Suffrage, as well as many prominent and faithful workers for this great end, fail to comprehend why there are two National Woman Suffrage Associations.

Last spring, Mr. Theodore Tilton announced his determination to merge the two in one. He evidently believed that by some trick of moral legerdemain this might be done. . . . But the quiet, resolute, persistent purpose of the American Woman Suffrage Association has baffled him. It will not be rubbed into any other. It declines to be "merged." Those who organized the "American" were not children. They knew what they were about. They had a purpose in forming that Association. And they insist that it shall remain intact, unmerged, to work out the purpose for which it was formed—rejecting Mr. Tilton's proposition to "merge," at its last annual meeting at Cleveland [1870], by a vote of 113 to 47. . . .

When the vote was taken, a majority of all the delegates present, a large majority of the aggregate votes of the auxiliary State societies, and an overwhelming majority of the votes of the States represented, were cast against the appointment of a Conference Committee [to consider merger] and in favor of the following resolutions:—

Resolved, That the primary object of the American Woman Suffrage Association is to secure the ballot for woman, and its general objects include the establishment of her equality and rights in all directions.

Resolved, That the ballot for woman means stability for the marriage relation, stability for the home, and stability for our republican government.

Resolved, That the American Woman Suffrage Association heartily invites the cooperation of all individuals and all State societies who feel the need of a truly national association on a delegated basis, which shall avoid side issues and devote itself to the main question of suffrage.

This settles the question of fusion for the coming year and, we hope, forever. If a real difference exists between the principles and methods of the two societies, as we believe, it will grow more evident as time goes by. Each will gather around its standard the class who naturally belong to it, and each will lose the support of those whose principles and convictions it fails to represent.

Be this as it may, the question of divorce has no business in a Woman Suffrage meeting. It has no more to do with Woman Suffrage than with Manhood Suffrage. Woman stands to-day equal with man as regards divorce. There is not a single State from Maine to California where a husband can obtain a divorce from his wife for any cause which would not equally entitle a wife to obtain a divorce from her husband if the case was reversed. During the existence of the marriage, a wife is subjected to cruel legal disabilities. But, as regards its dissolution, husband and wife stand equals before the law.

Henceforth let both societies agree neither to combine, compromise, nor quarrel. Let each seek to surpass the other in worthy work, and criticize each other only by creating a nobler representation of the Woman's Cause.

H.B.B.[9]

SEX REARS ITS UGLY HEAD: THE WOODHULL AFFAIR

Sex was an even more incendiary subject than marriage and divorce. Actually, there were only small differences on the subject between leaders of the National and the American. While Stanton was unusual in her willingness to discuss prostitution, pregnancy, abortion, and birth control as women's issues, she did so only occasionally. Neither she nor other prominent leaders defined these as primary concerns, and they did not explore such issues in depth. Both the bold Stanton and the more cautious Stone were restricted by Victorian mores and modesty. Neither the National nor the American took any official stand on sex-related issues, and neither group condoned a relaxation of contemporary sexual standards.

Nonetheless, from its beginning, the women's movement encountered detractors who insisted that women's rights were simply a disguise for sexual license. (This attack would be made again during the great suffrage battle of the 1910's, and again in the 1970's.) Women who deviated from the traditional paths were destined for lives of sin; in seeking equality, women were heading for immorality. And disagreements did arise as the women pondered how best to respond to these attacks.

In 1868, at an Equal Rights Association meeting, Mary A. Livermore introduced a resolution that was typical of one response to charges of "free love" (as sexual freedom was then labeled), and an interesting debate followed.

A RESOLUTION AND DEBATE

Resolved, That while we recognize the disabilities which the legal marriage imposes upon woman as wife and mother, and while we pledge ourselves to seek their removal by putting her on equal terms with man, we abhorrently repudiate Free Loveism as horrible and mischievous to society, and disown any sympathy with it.

Mrs. LIVERMORE said that the West wanted some such resolution as that in consequence of the innuendoes that had come to their ears with regard to their striving after the ballot.

Mrs. HANAFORD spoke against such inferences not only for the ministers of her own denomination, but the Christian men and women of New England everywhere. She had heard people say that when women indorsed woman suffrage they indorsed Free Loveism, and God knows they despise it. Let me carry back to my New England home the word that you as well as your honored President, whom we love, whose labor we appreciate, and whose name has also been dragged into this inference, scout all such suggestions as contrary to the law of God and humanity.

LUCY STONE: I feel it is a mortal shame to give any foundation for the implication that we favor Free Loveism. I am ashamed that the question should be asked here. There should be nothing said about it at all. Do not let us, for the sake of our own self-respect, allow it to be hinted that we helped forge a shadow of a chain which comes in the name of Free Love. I am unwilling that it should be suggested that this great, sacred cause of ours means anything but what we have said it does. If any one says to me, "Oh, I know what you mean, you mean Free Love by this agitation," let the lie stick in his throat. You may talk about Free Love, if you please, but we are to have the right to vote. To-day we are fined, imprisoned, and hanged, without a jury trial by our peers. You shall not cheat us by getting us off to talk about something else. When we get the suffrage, then you may taunt us with anything you please, and we will then talk about it as long as you please.

ERNESTINE L. ROSE: We are informed by the people from the West that they are wiser than we are, and that those in the East are also wiser than we are. If they are wiser than we, I think it strange that this question of Free Love should have been brought upon this platform at all. I object to Mrs. Livermore's resolution, not on account of its principles, but on account of its pleading guilty. When a man comes to me and tries to convince me that he is not a thief, then I take care of my coppers. If we pass this resolution that we are not Free Lovers, people will say it is true that you are, for you try to hide it. . . . We have been thirty years in this city before the public, and it is an insult to all the women who have labored in this cause; it is an insult to the thousands and tens of thousands of men and women that have listened to us in our Conventions, to say at this late hour that we are not Free Lovers.

SUSAN B. ANTHONY repudiated the resolution on the same ground as Mrs. Rose, and said this howl came from those men who knew that when women got their rights they would be able to live honestly; no longer be compelled to sell themselves for bread, either in or out of marriage.[10]

Victoria Woodhull. Leslie's, Aug. 1874

The entrance of Victoria Woodhull into the movement forced the two associations to consider the issue of sexual mores.

Starting in May 1870, Woodhull and her sister Tennessee Claflin edited a small newspaper in New York City, Woodhull & Claflin's Weekly, *in which they revealed their unorthodox views on subjects like spiritualism, women's rights, and sexual freedom for men and women. Most scandalous of these was Woodhull's advocacy of a single sexual standard for women and men. Her views and the reputation of the two sisters who boldly and adventurously defied social convention brought them a great and growing notoriety.*

As an advocate of full equality, Woodhull was an ardent agitator for the vote for women. In January 1871, she was invited to Washington to address the Senate Judiciary Committee on women's rights. There she spoke at length, arguing impressively that women, as citizens, actually had the vote under the provisions of the Fourteenth and Fifteenth amendments; and she urged Congress to pass legislation overtly recognizing what she declared was already implicit in the Constitution.

Several National leaders listened as Woodhull clearly and precisely presented her views, and they invited her to repeat the speech, which they later printed and distribu-

ted at the National convention which was then meeting in Washington.

Four months later, in May 1871, Elizabeth Cady Stanton invited Woodhull to speak again, this time before a convention in New York. Woodhull's address again concerned the ballot. She made a strong and aggressive demand for the vote.

FROM WOODHULL'S SPEECH TO THE NATIONAL CONVENTION

. . . And yet men deny women the first and greatest of all the rights of citizenship, the right to vote.

Under such glaring inconsistencies, such unwarrantable tyranny, such unscrupulous despotism what is there left women to do but to become the mothers of the future government.

We will have our rights. We say no longer by your leave. We have besought, argued and convinced, but we have failed; *and we will not* fail.

We will try you *just once more.* If the very next Congress refuse women all the legitimate results of citizenship; if they indeed merely so much as fail by a proper declaratory act to withdraw every obstacle to the most ample exercise of the franchise, then we give here and now, deliberate notification of what we will do next. . . .

We shall proceed to call another convention expressly to frame a new constitution and to erect a new government, complete in all its parts, and to take measures to maintain it as effectually as men do theirs. . . .

We mean treason; we mean secession, and on a thousand times grander scale than was that of the South. We are plotting revolution; we will overslough this bogus republic and plant a government of righteousness in its stead, which shall not only profess to derive its power from the consent of the governed, but shall do so in reality. . . . [11]

Victoria Woodhull's association with the National Woman Suffrage Association dismayed many women for whom her articulate and passionate dedication to woman suffrage could not counterbalance her reputed commitment to, and practice of, Free Love. A court hearing in New York during 1871 resulted in extensive press publicity about Woodhull's unconventional personal life. And newsmen could not resist the spectacle of the notorious Woodhull seated on the National platform between the redoubtable Lucretia Mott and Elizabeth Cady Stanton.

Then, in November 1871, in Steinway Hall in New York, Woodhull delivered a speech on the "Principles of Social Freedom," proclaiming beyond doubt that she advocated and practiced Free Love. The speech was presented again in Boston and repeated across the country, where Woodhull attracted and shocked lecture audiences. For those who could not manage to hear the outrageous proposals in person, the speech was eventually reprinted.

A CIRCULAR

FREEDOM! FREEDOM! FREEDOM!
IN ITS LAST ANALYSIS:
THE SOCIAL RELATIONS
If it is good in the Religious and Political sphere
who shall dare deny that it is good in
THE SOCIAL SPHERE?

For the express purpose of silencing the voices and stopping the pens of those who, either ignorantly or willfully, persistently misrepresent, slander, abuse and vilify her on account of her outspoken advocacy of, and supreme faith in, God's first, last and best law,

VICTORIA C. WOODHULL
WILL SPEAK AT
STEINWAY HALL,
MONDAY, NOVEMBER 20,
AT EIGHT P.M., ON
"THE PRINCIPLES OF SOCIAL FREEDOM"
INVOLVING THE QUESTION OF
FREE LOVE, MARRIAGE, DIVORCE AND PROSTITUTION

She wishes it to be distinctly understood that freedom does not mean anarchy in the social relations any more than it does in religion and politics; also that the advocacy of its principles requires neither abandoned action nor immodest speech.

HORACE GREELEY, GOVERNOR HAWLEY,
of Connecticut and the Boston Exclusive [illegible]

are specially invited to seats on the platform. All her lesser defamers should secure front seats. [12]

FROM WOODHULL'S SPEECH ON SOCIAL FREEDOM

. . . To love is a right *higher* than Constitutions or laws. It is a right which Constitutions and laws can *neither give* nor take, and with which they have nothing whatever to do, since in its *very* nature it is forever independent of both Constitutions and laws, and exists—comes and goes—in *spite* of them. Governments might just as well assume to determine how people shall exercise their right to *think* or to say that they shall not think at all, as to assume to determine that they shall not love, or how they may love, or that they shall love.

The proper sphere of government in regard to the relations of the sexes, is to enact such laws as in the present conditions of society are necessary to *protect each* individual in the *free* exercise of his or her *right* to love, and also to protect each individual from the forced interference of *every other* person, that would compel him or her to submit to *any* action which is against their *wish* and *will.* If the law do this it fulfills its duty. If the law do not afford this protection, *and worse still,* if it *sanction* this *interference* with the rights of an individual, then it is *infamous* law and worthy only of the *old-time* despotism: since individual tyranny forms *no* part of the guarantee of, or the right to, individual freedom.

It is therefore a strictly legitimate conclusion that where there is *no* love as a basis of marriage there should be *no* marriage, and if that which was the *basis* of a marriage is taken away that the *marriage* also ceases from that time, statute laws to the contrary notwithstanding. . . .

I repeat a frequent reply: "I am [a Free Lover]; and I can honestly, in the fullness of my soul, raise my voice to my Maker, and thank Him that I *am,* and that I have had the strength and the devotion to truth to stand before this traducing and vilifying community in a manner representative of that which shall come with healing on its wings for the bruised hearts and crushed affections of humanity."

And to those who denounce me for this I reply: "Yes, I am a Free Lover. I have an *inalienable, constitutional* and *natural* right to love whom I may, to love as *long* or as *short* a period as I can; to *change* that love *every day* if I please, and with *that* right neither *you* nor any *law* you can frame have *any* right to interfere. And I have the *further* right to demand a free and unrestricted exercise of that right, and it is *your* duty not only to *accord* it, but, as a community, to see that I am fully understood, for I mean *just* that, and nothing less! . . . 13

Stanton and Anthony had consistently defended Woodhull against the increasing attacks against her place in the movement—as they had earlier defended their ties with George Francis Train. And Stanton persisted in associating the National with Woodhull even after the scandalous Steinway Hall speech. Woodhull's opponents deplored her life style and her freewheeling iconoclasm and feared both

From Thomas Nast

would alienate women from the movement. Stanton insisted; she invited Woodhull to the annual National convention in January 1872 and publicly praised her.

STANTON DEFENDS WOODHULL

Mrs. Woodhull's speeches and writings on all the great questions of national life are beyond anything yet produced by man or woman on our platform. What if foul-mouthed scandal, with its many tongues, seeks to defile her? Shall we ignore a champion like this? Admit for the sake of argument that what all men say of her is true—though it is false—that she has been or is a courtesan in sentiment and practice. When a woman of this class shall suddenly devote herself to the study of the grave problem of life, brought there by profound thought or sad experience, and with new faith and hope struggle to redeem the errors of the past by a grand life in the future, shall we not welcome her to the better place she desires to hold? There is to me a sacredness in individual experience that it seems like a profanation to search into and expose. Victoria C. Woodhull stands before us to-day a grand, brave woman, radical alike in political, religious and social principles. Her face and form indicate the complete triumph in her nature of the spiritual over the sensuous. The processes of her education are little to us; the grand result is everything. . . .

When I think of the merciless and continued persecution of that little woman by the entire press of this nation, I blush for humanity. . . . In reading the reports of her Steinway speech, I could see nothing so monstrously immoral on which to base the severe editorial comments of our journals. It seems to me that the Legislatures of our several States, in granting eighteen causes for divorce, and in their bills to license prostitution by the State, are more legitimate targets for the press of a nation than one suffering woman who has been most unjustly scarified in her own flesh by the iron teeth of the law. . . .

Now I think we had better agree to fight this battle just as our fathers and husbands have their two revolutions—enroll all that are loyal to the principle. How much of an army should we have had for the rebellion if every man who came to enroll himself had been asked, Do you smoke, chew, drink, steal, lie, swear? Are you low-bred, illiterate or licentious? If so, you cannot fight for freedom. Was it not just this element we swept into the army? And were not they the better for suffering and dying for a noble cause? . . . 14

As Woodhull's ties with the National and her association with the women's movement expanded, American leaders in Boston grew increasingly distressed. At their convention in May 1871, a resolution was introduced asserting that the ballot for women meant "stability for the marriage relation, stability for the home and stability for our representa-

tive form of government.[15] *Another resolution responded even more directly to Woodhull.*

THE AMERICAN'S RESPONSE TO WOODHULL

Resolved . . . That the claim of woman to participate in making the laws she is required to obey, and to equality of rights in all directions, has nothing to do with special social theories, and that the recent attempts in this city and elsewhere to associate the woman suffrage cause with the doctrines of free love, and to hold it responsible for the crimes and follies of individuals, is an outrage upon common sense and decency, and a slander upon the virtue and intelligence of the women of America.[16]

By the spring of 1872, Woodhull's efforts to involve the National association in her own presidential ambitions (she was the candidate of a new political party) led to a separation between them. By this time, Anthony had grown doubtful of the soundness of Woodhull's judgment. Eventually, Stanton, too, agreed to sever relations with her.

In the public mind, however, Victoria Woodhull was still associated with the women's movement, and when, soon after the break, she became part of the most sensational scandal of the day, the movement was adversely affected.

At a convention of the National Association of Spiritualists in September 1872, Woodhull, in her farewell speech as president of the association, accused Henry Ward Beecher, one of the country's best-known preachers and president of the American Woman Suffrage Association, of an adulterous affair with one of his own parishioners, Elizabeth Tilton. Elizabeth Tilton was the wife of Theodore Tilton, New York newspaper editor, reformer, and friend of women's rights. After the denunciation, Woodhull was accused of slander. In November, in the columns of her Weekly, *she defended her actions, decrying the hypocrisy of those, like Beecher, who agreed with her rejection of traditional marriage and who practiced free love, but who would not take a public stand, and had, in fact, joined in the outcry against Woodhull. She then reprinted in* Woodhull & Claflin's Weekly *a newspaper interview which she hoped would "relate in formal terms, for the whole public, the simple facts of the case as they have come to my knowledge. . . . "*

THE BEECHER-TILTON SCANDAL

The Detailed Statement of the Whole Matter by Mrs. Woodhull

Reporter.—"I confess, then, I cannot understand why you of all persons should have any fault to find with Mr. BEECHER, even assuming everything to be true of him which I have hitherto heard only vaguely hinted at."

Mrs. Woodhull.—"I have no fault to find with him in any such sense as you mean, nor in any such sense as that in which the world will condemn him. . . .

"The fault I find with Mr. BEECHER is of a wholly different character, as I have told him repeatedly and frankly, and as he knows very well. It is, indeed, the exact opposite to that for which the world will condemn him. I condemn him because I know, and have had every opportunity to know, that he entertains, on conviction, substantially the same views which I entertain on the social question; that, under the influence of these convictions, he has lived for many years, perhaps for his whole adult life, in a manner which the religious and moralistic public ostensibly, and to some extent really, condemn; that he has permitted himself, nevertheless, to be over-awed by public opinion, to profess to believe otherwise than as he does believe, to have helped to maintain for these many years that very social slavery under which he was chafing, and against which he was secretly revolting both in thought and practice; and that he has, in a word, consented, and still consents to be a hypocrite. The fault with which I, therefore, charge him, is not infidelity to the old ideas, but unfaithfulness to the new. . . . "

Reporter.—"You speak very confidently, Mrs. WOODHULL, of Mr. BEECHER's opinions and life. Will you now please to resume that subject, and tell me exactly what you know of both?"

Mrs. Woodhull.—"I had vaguely heard rumors of some scandal in regard to Mr. BEECHER, which I put aside as mere rumor and idle gossip of the hour, and gave to them no attention whatever. . . .

"It was brought up subsequently, in an intimate conversation . . . by Mrs. PAULINE WRIGHT DAVIS, without any seeking on my part, and to my very great surprise. Mrs. DAVIS had been, it seems, a frequent visitor at Mr. TILTON's house in Brooklyn—they having long been associated in the Woman's Rights movement—and she stood upon certain terms of intimacy in the family. . . . She called, as she told me, at Mr. TILTON's. Mrs. TILTON met her at the door and burst into tears, exclaiming: 'Oh, Mrs. DAVIS! have you come to see me? For six months I have been shut up from the world, and I thought no one ever would come again to visit me.' . . .

"Mrs. TILTON confessed to Mrs. DAVIS the intimacy with Mr. BEECHER, and that it had been of years' standing. She also said that she had loved Mr. BEECHER before she married Mr. TILTON, and that now the burden of her sorrow was greatly augmented by the knowledge that Mr. BEECHER was untrue to her. She had not only to endure the rupture with her husband, but also the certainty that, notwithstanding his repeated assurance of his faithfulness to her, he had recently had illicit intercourse, under most extraordinary circumstances, with another person. . . .

"I next heard the whole story from Mrs. ELIZABETH CADY STANTON."

Reporter.—"Indeed! Is Mrs. STANTON also mixed up in this affair? Does she know the facts? How could the matter have been kept so long quiet when so many people are cognizant of it?"

Mrs. Woodhull.—" . . . This grand woman did indeed know the same facts, and from Mr. TILTON himself. . . . Mrs. STANTON continued and repeated to me the sad story, which it is unnecessary to recite, as I prefer giving it as Mr. TILTON himself told it me, subsequently, with his own lips."

Reporter.—"Is it possible that Mr. TILTON confided this story to you? It seems too monstrous to be believed!"

Mrs. Woodhull.—"He certainly did. And what is more, I am persuaded that in his inmost mind he will not be otherwise than glad when the skeleton in his closet is revealed to the world, if thereby the abuses which lurk like vipers under the cloak of social conservatism may be exposed and the causes removed. Mr. TILTON looks deeper into the soul of things than most men, and is braver than most. . . . "

Reporter.—"Do you not fear that by taking the responsibility of this *expose* you may involve yourself in trouble? Even if all you relate should be true, may not those involved deny it *in toto,* even the fact of their having made the statements?"

Mrs. Woodhull.—"I do not fear anything of the sort. . . . I believe it is my duty and my mission to carry the torch to light up and destroy the heap of rottenness, which, in the name of religion, marital sanctity, and social purity, now passes as the social system. I know there are other churches just as false, other pastors just as recreant to their professed ideas of morality—by their immorality you know I mean their hypocrisy. I am glad that just this one case comes to me to be exposed. This is a great congregation. He is a most eminent man. When a beacon is fired on the mountain the little hills are lighted up. This exposition will send inquisition through all the churches and what is termed conservative society."

Reporter.—"You speak like some weird prophetess, madam."

Mrs. Woodhull.—"I am a prophetess—I am an evangel—I am a Saviour, if you would but see it; but I too come not to bring peace, but a sword."

Mrs. WOODHULL then resumed saying: "Mr. TILTON first began to have suspicions of Mr. BEECHER on his own return from a long lecturing tour through the West. He questioned his little daughter, privately, in his study regarding what had transpired in his absence. 'The tale of iniquitous horror that was revealed to me was,' he said, 'enough to turn the heart of a stranger to stone, to say nothing of a husband and

"The Beecher–Tilton Case." Leslie's, *Aug. 1874*

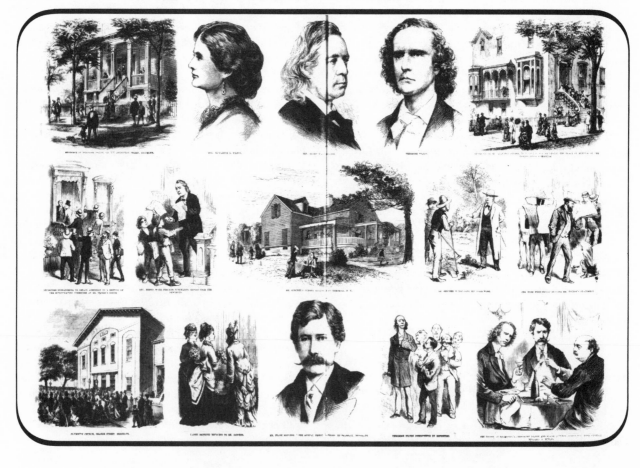

WOODHULL & CLAFLIN'S WEEKLY.

PROGRESS! FREE THOUGHT! UNTRAMMELED LIVES!
BREAKING THE WAY FOR FUTURE GENERATIONS.

VOL. 2—No. 23.—WHOLE No. 49.   NEW YORK, APRIL 22, 1871.   PRICE TEN CENTS.

VICTORIA C. WOODHULL & TENNIE C. CLAFLIN
EDITORS AND PROPRIETORS.

CONTENTS OF THIS NUMBER.

THE FIRST WOMAN BALLOT.

The Fourteenth Amendment has Begun its Work.

WHO WILL STOP IT?

The pioneer woman voter is Mrs. Nannette B. Gardner, and she lives in Detroit, Mich. She succeeded in registering her name week before last, and on Tuesday, the 4th of April, she cast the first vote for a State officer deposited in an American ballot-box by a woman for the last half century. Some time since, by the way, a number of ladies, of St. John, Mich., succeeded in getting themselves registered, but they were not permitted to vote. Why was this? However, as to the pioneer. We quote at length from the Detroit *Post*:

"Mrs. Gardner arrived at the polls of the First Precinct of the Ninth Ward at about half-past 10 o'clock, in a carriage accompanied by her son, a lad of ten years, Mrs. Starring and Mrs. Giles B. Stebbins. Barely a dozen bystanders were present at the voting place, and the larger part of these were laboring men. No demonstration, whatever followed the appearance of the ladies, the men remaining quiet and civil, and contenting themselves with comments *sotto voce* on this last political development, and with speculations as to how the newly enfranchised would vote. Mrs. Gardner presented herself at the polls with a vase of flowers and also a prepared ballot, which she had decorated with various appropriate devices. The inspectors asked the questions in regard to name and residence usually put to all applicants, and her name being found duly registered her ballot was received and deposited in the box without any further proceedings whatever. There was no argument, no challenging no variation from the routine traversed by each masculine exerciser of the elective franchise. Mrs. Gardner voted, as we understand, for the Republican candidates generally, with one Democrat and one lady. After the vote was deposited she presented the vase of flowers to the inspectors, and also handed them a large picture representing a large crowd of women in darkness just entering the portals of an arch inscribed "Liberty", and upon which an eagle was perched. The gates were held open by Columbia and the Goddess of Justice. The foremost woman held in her hands a scroll inscribed "The Fourteenth Amendment." To the right were imps of darkness fleeing away, some with barrels of whisky. On the left was pictured the Capitol of Washington, with men crowding its steps, cheering, etc. Streams of light flowed upon them, while, with the exception of this and the foreground, the picture was darkness intensified. The following lines appeared underneath:

"We come, free America, five millions strong,
 In darkness and bondage for many years long
 We've marched in deep silence, but now we unroll
 The Fourteenth Amendment, which gives us a soul
 Glory, Glory, Hallelujah, glory, etc.,
 As we go marching on."

COLUMBIA—"Welcome, beloved daughters,
 Take your places beside my sons."

After the vote had reached its resting-place there was a faint attempt at hurrah among some of those present, but this was frowned down by the others as tending to interfere with the solemnity of the occasion. The ladies then left the voting places and matters resumed their usual appearance thereabouts.

THE COSMO-POLITICAL PARTY.

NOMINATION FOR PRESIDENT OF THE U. S., IN 1872.

VICTORIA C. WOODHULL

SUBJECT TO

RATIFICATION BY THE NATIONAL CONVENTION.

WEDDING PRESENTS OF THE PRINCESS LOUISE.

EMERALDS AND DIAMONDS IN PROFUSION.

THE BRIDEGROOM'S PRESENTS.

HER TROUSSEAU.

The following presents were given to her Royal Highness the Princess Louise on the occasion of her marriage to the Marquis of Lorne:

FROM HER MOTHER, QUEEN VICTORIA.

A very large and fine emerald, set with brilliants as a centre of bracelet; another as centre of necklace; a very fine opal and brilliant necklace, with five large opals, set round with brilliants and connected by a diamond chain; a large drop brooch, with two very fine opals, set round with brilliants; a pair of opal and diamond earrings to correspond; a richly-chased, silver-gilt dessert service, consisting of one centre, two sides and four corner ornaments.

FROM THEIR ROYAL HIGHNESS THE PRINCE AND PRINCESS CHRISTIAN.

A beautifully-chased silver-gilt tea and coffee service, containing the following pieces: Coffee-pot, two tea-pots, one sugar basin, one hot milk jug, one cream ewer, in case.

FROM THEIR ROYAL HIGHNESSES, PRINCE ARTHUR, PRINCE LEOPOLD AND PRINCESS BEATRICE.

Two diamond daisy flowers mounted as hair-pins.

FROM HER ROYAL HIGHNESS THE DUCHESS OF CAMBRIDGE.

A silver-gilt ink-stand in the shape of a shell.

FROM HIS ROYAL HIGHNESS THE DUKE OF CAMBRIDGE.

A richly-engraved silver salver.

FROM THE DUKE AND DUCHESS OF ARGYLE.

A tiara formed of a band of emeralds and diamonds, surmounted by a scroll-work also of emeralds and diamonds.

FROM THE MARQUIS OF LORNE.

A beautiful pendant ornament, with a large and fine sapphire, mounted with brilliants and pearls and pearl-drop; the centre forms a bracelet.

FROM THE CLAN CAMPBELL.

A necklace composed of pearls and diamonds, from which is suspended a locket of oval form, with pendant. The centre of the locket is formed by a large and extremely beautiful Oriental pearl, surrounded by a closely-set row of diamonds of large size and great brilliancy. The outer border also consists of large diamonds, but set in such a manner as to give an appearance of lightness very seldom obtained

in ornaments of a similar description. The pendant, the characteristic portion of the jewel, is suspended by an emerald sprig of bog myrtle (the Campbell badge), and bears in the centre the galley of Lorne, composed of sapphires on a * pavé* of diamonds; the border, also of sapphires and diamonds, bears the inscription, "*Ne obliviscaris.*"

FROM THE LADIES AND GENTLEMEN OF HER MAJESTY'S HOUSEHOLD.

One large single candelabrum for five lights; four smaller ditto for three lights each; a very complete toilet service in silver-gilt, with the cipher and coronet engraved on each article.

FROM THE QUEEN'S HOUSEHOLD

A silver tea and coffee service, with table mounted in silver.

FROM THE BRIDESMAIDS.

A very handsome gold bracelet, with rubies and diamonds.

FROM THE DUKE OF ROXBURGH.

A silver-gilt tea-kettle to correspond with the service presented by their Royal Highnesses Prince and Princess Christian.

FROM THE DUCHESS OF BUCCLEUCH.

A richly chased antique pattern silver toilet casket.

FROM THE COUNTESS OF MACCLESFIELD.

A case of silver-gilt coffee-spoons.

OTHER PRESENTS.

In addition to the above, and numerous other presents, a very large and handsome silver tankard has been presented to Lord Lorne by Eton. It is richly chased all over with battle subjects, after LeBrun; the handle formed of satyrs. The black base on which it stands has two inscription plates. On one are engraved the arms of Eton College, and on the other "Presented to the Marquis of Lorne on his marriage, by the present Members of his old School.—Eton, 1871."

His Highness the Maharajah Duleep Singh's gift was a very fine specimen of a Lahore pendant, with 12 large emerald drops, and composed of Indian basque diamonds from the collection of the renowned Runjeet Singh, once the mighty ruler of the Punjaub. It was arranged with a massive gold chain, and inclosed in a white velvet casket bearing the coronet and letter L.

Earl Russell's gift was a very beautiful pearl and torquoise bracelet, of Abyssinian design. The Countess's present to the Marquis of Lorne was a beautiful carbuncle and pearl handkerchief ring; the Hon. E. F. Leveson Gower, M. P., giving his lordship an elegant gold spring cigar-cutter of novel design.

Not the least interesting item of this happy event are those beautiful *souvenirs de marriage*, yclept in English bridesmaids' gifts. Her Royal Highness's talent as an artist is well known, and upon this occasion she has brought to bear her excellent good taste in a design at once simple, pure and ele-

father.' It was not the fact of the intimacy alone, but in addition to that, the terrible orgies—so he said—of which his house had been made the scene, and the boldness with which matters had been carried on in the presence of his children—'These things drove me mad,' said he, 'and I went to ELIZABETH and confronted her with the child and the damning tale she had told me. My wife did not deny the charge nor attempt any palliation. She was then *enceinte,* and I felt sure that the child would not be my child. I stripped the wedding ring from her finger. I tore the picture of Mr. BEECHER from my wall and stamped it in pieces. Indeed, I do not know what I did not do. . . .'

"Free Love." Leslie's, *Apr. 1870*

FREE LOVE AND WOMEN'S RIGHTS.

LADY CUSTOMER—"*Mr. Smith—ah, ah—have you any Her-books?*"
BOOKSELLER—(Slightly surprised)—"HER-*books, ma'am? I really——*".
LADY CUSTOMER—"*Ah, well, you naughty men call them Hymn-books. But, as we of the angelic sex are resolved on freeing ourselves from the chains imposed on us by tyrant man, we want Her-books in future!*" [Bookseller faints.]

"I went as I have said to see her [Elizabeth Tilton] and found her, indeed, a wretched wreck of a woman, whose troubles were greater than she could bear. She made no secret of the facts before me. Mr. BEECHER's selfish, cowardly cruelty in endeavoring to shield himself and create public opinion against Mr. TILTON, added poignancy to her anxieties. She seemed indifferent as to what should become of herself, but labored under fear that murder might be done on her account. . . .

"I attempted to show him [Tilton] the true solution of the imbroglio, and the folly that it was for a man like him, a representative man of the ideas of the future, to stand whining over inevitable events connected with this transition age and the social revolution of which we are in the midst. I told him that the fault and the wrong were neither in Mr. BEECHER, nor in Mrs. TILTON, nor in himself; . . .

"I assumed at once, and got a sufficient admission, as I always do in such cases, that he was not exactly a vestal virgin himself; that his real life was something very different from the awful 'virtue' he was preaching, especially for women, as if women could 'sin' in this matter without men, and men without women, . . . that, in a word, neither Mr. BEECHER nor Mrs. TILTON had done any wrong, but that it was he who was playing the part of a fool and a tyrant; that it was he and the factitious or manufactured public opinion back of him, that was wrong; that this babyish whining and stage-acting were the real absurdity and disgrace. . . . I tried to show him that a true manliness would protect and love to protect; would glory in protecting the absolute freedom of the woman who was loved, whether called wife, mistress, or by any other name, and that the true sense of honor in the future will be, *not to know even* what relations our lovers have with any and all other persons than ourselves— as true courtesy never seeks to spy over or to pry into other people's private affairs.

"I believe I succeeded in pointing out to him that his own life was essentially no better than Mr. BEECHER's, and that he stood in no position to throw the first stone at Mrs. TILTON or at her reverend paramour. I showed him again and again that the wrong point, and the radically wrong thing, if not, indeed, quite the only wrong thing in the matter, was *the idea of ownership in human beings, which was essentially the same in the two institutions of slavery and marriage.* Mrs. TILTON had in turn grown increasedly unhappy when she found that Mr. BEECHER had turned some part of his exuberant affections upon some other object. There was in her, therefore, the same sentiment of the real slaveholder. Let it be understood *that whosoever is true to himself or herself is thereby, and necessarily, true to all others,* and the whole social question will be solved. *The barter and sale of wives stands on the same moral footing as the barter and sale of slaves.* The god-implanted human affections cannot and will not, be any longer subordinated to these external, legal restrictions and conventional engagements. *Every human being belongs to himself or herself by a higher title than any which, by surrenders or arrangements or prom-*

ises, he or she can confer upon any other human being. Self-ownership is inalienable. Those truths are the latest and greatest discoveries in true science. . . . "[17]

The Beecher-Tilton scandal and the events that followed Woodhull's revelations were nationwide news. Beecher publicly declared his innocence; Tilton took the matter to the courts; investigations and trials ensued. Woodhull and Tennessee Claflin were arrested several times before they eventually were tried and found not guilty of printing obscene literature. Statements to the press by all concerned, publication of private letters, interviews with friends and witnesses, subsidiary libel suits—all fed the nation's prurient appetites.

COMMENTS OF THE PRESS UPON THE SCANDAL

Tilton Blameless and Beecher Not to Be Prejudged.

(From the Utica *Observer.*)

While we cannot find it in our hearts to blame Mr. Tilton, we do not wish to be understood as prejudging Mr. Beecher. The whole world will listen with broad, generous sympathy to every word he may utter in his own defense. But he can not afford to remain silent. It is against the terrible suggestions of his own written words that Henry Ward Beecher must vindicate himself.

Scandal like Death Loves a Shining Mark.

(From the Chicago *Inter-Ocean.*)

The talk of the entire country is about the letter of Theodore Tilton, made public yesterday. Unless indications are to be taken for naught, it means the conviction of Mr. Beecher of what at least was a grave indiscretion, and, perhaps, a crime. No matter what his sin may be, it cannot alter the fact that his influence in favor of patriotism and practical Christianity has been more widely felt and productive of more good than that of any other public man in America. Mr. Beecher is human; a man subject to temptation as others are. If the cruel and sceptical reflect upon this they might be able to say "to err is human, to forgive, divine"; and admit that all his long life devoted to noble deeds should not be forgotten in the one error which he may have committed. . . .

Regretting the Revival Yet Excusing Tilton.

(From the Detroit *Free Press.*)

. . . The revival of this scandal is to be regretted; but it is useless to insist that if Mr. Tilton's story is true he is bound to withhold it. . . . For years he has borne, and most of the time with patience, the stigma of slandering his pastor. If this stigma has been unjust, society has no right to demand that he endure it quietly because his attempt to remove it may injure society. His reputation is as dear to him doubtless as Mr. Beecher's is either to himself or his friends, and it is his right to vindicate it if he can, whatever may be the consequences so far as others are concerned. Nor is it his right only; it is his duty. Sad as it would be to lose that confidence in our fellowmen upon which so much of life's happiness is based, it would be sadder still to retain it if it is ill founded and misplaced, and he who knows that in any instance it is so is bound to destroy the illusion.

Endorsing Mrs. Woodhull, Whom Tilton Repudiates.

(From the Chicago *Post*.)

There can no longer be any doubt as to the substantial correctness of the Woodhull's scandal. The cry of agonizing confession—"I will plead for myself. I even wish I were dead"—proves it beyond all controversy.

But the original sin was a comparatively small matter. It was the after crimes of perversion and falsehood, to save himself, of slander and insinuation to injure Tilton, and, finally, of an attempt to rid the country of the witnesses against him, that will do most for Beecher's hurt. It is the moral depravity that four years of persistent and superlatively wicked deceit must indicate that will shock his admirers more than all the rest. Such turpitude in a man who has stood so high, who has breathed so many glowing words of truth, will be hard to believe in. But it seems it does exist. . . .

Faith in Human Nature Gone.

(From the Louisville *Courier Journal*.)

. . . This Beecher business is enough to shatter one's faith in human nature, and will do a deal of mischief in proportion as it disturbs the hold of a less vigorous and self preserving faith. . . . The desecration of the altar is a sin for which there should be no atonement in this world; for it is the source not merely of physical corruption, but steals like a slow poison through the very bosom of the church, to blight and wither its fresh and wholesome life.[18]

For several years, the Beecher-Tilton scandal continued to be news, and both the National and the American association were indelibly marked by it. Whatever fears or hesitations potential recruits may have had about joining the battle for women's rights were magnified by these events, since they appeared to confirm the popular charge that woman activists were of loose morals. Moreover, the episode solidified the separation of the associations and delayed their unification. In 1875, Lucy Stone wrote the following in a letter to a friend.

LUCY STONE'S LETTER

We sh'n't unite with her [Susan B. Anthony]. After all the experience we had of her wild alliance . . . all sorts of misbehaving things. She can speak well and if she would only let vagaries alone, could do a great work. But you can never tell what she will do.[19]

Seventeen years after the Beecher-Tilton scandal, Alice Stone Blackwell was in New England on a lecture tour. She related a conversation with a woman with whom she boarded in a letter to her mother, Lucy Stone.

ALICE STONE BLACKWELL'S LETTER

She [Mrs. Griffin] spoke of the Woodhull matter and said it set the cause back 20 years, and that to this day the country people all around here can't believe that women want suffrage for anything but free love. She says unless the other association has entirely given up the advocacy of that, she thinks it is a pity to unite, for fear they may break out again just at the wrong time. . . . [20]

TOWARD REUNION OF THE MOVEMENT

Despite the persistent disagreements and tensions that kept the American and National associations apart for twenty years, there was always a large area of agreement between them. Both organizations deplored the subjugation and inferiority that burdened women in American life; both sought equality and dignity for women; both understood that the achievement of women's equality involved profound social change; and both agreed that the ballot was the key to change.

As the years passed, their differences began to lessen and pale, and the possibilities for reunion grew steadily greater. Since both organizations expended most of their energy on suffrage activities, National and American spokeswomen often found themselves working side by side. While the American concentrated on gaining the vote through individual state campaigns and the National sought reform at the federal level, neither organization was rigid or stingy in its suffrage work. National leaders traveled to states where a suffrage battle was on to join in the campaign, and the

American regularly sent representatives to congressional hearings to support efforts to gain the vote by amending the Constitution. And although the separation of organizations remained clear at the top level, many state suffrage groups and individual women participated in the work of both the American and the National, and the lines distinguishing them were often blurred.

In July 1876, members of the American joined with the National to demonstrate for women's rights at the celebration of the country's Centennial. Women went to Philadelphia, where, after being denied an official place in the proceedings, they marched in to interrupt a July 4th ceremony and present a Declaration of Rights for Women. Newspapers reported the disruption to the rest of the country.

A NEWSPAPER REPORT

There was yet another incident of the Fourth, in Independence Square. Immediately after the Declaration of Independence had been read by Richard Henry Lee, and while the strains of the "Greeting from Brazil" were rising upon the air, two ladies pushed their way vigorously through the crowd and appeared upon the speaker's platform. They were Susan B. Anthony and Matilda Joslyn Gage. Hustling generals aside, elbowing governors, and almost upsetting Dom Pedro [the emperor of Brazil and guest of honor] in their charge, they reached Vice-President Ferry, and handed him a scroll about three feet long, tied with ribbons of various colors. He was seen to bow and look bewildered; but they had retreated in the same vigorous manner before the explanation was whispered about. It appears that they demanded a change of programme for the sake of reading their address.[21]

Unable to speak at the ceremony, the women went outside, where Anthony read aloud and distributed copies of the Declaration to the large crowd. The Centennial demonstration illustrated that the differences that separated the National and American were not as large as the differences that lay between the women's rights movement and the men who celebrated the Centennial of American democracy.

With the passage of time, the National Woman Suffrage Association changed in ways that decreased its differences with the American. The National became increasingly preoccupied with suffrage and gave less and less attention to other issues. Moreover, as the National lost its youth, it lost its daring. The tone of belligerency and spirit of radicalism faded, although this narrowing of interests and tendency toward conservatism did not truly reflect the views of Anthony and Stanton. Stanton, especially, retained the freedom and daring of thought that were always hers. But she was no longer able to command the support of the Association on all issues.

In the middle 1880's, a conflict arose over religion and the role of the churches that illustrates well what was happening within the National. Clergymen had been among the major opponents of the women's movement from its beginning. Women, like Sarah Grimké in the 1830's, saw that religious dogma contributed to and supported their subjection, and dared to dispute religious teaching. In 1885, Clara Bewick Colby wrote a set of resolutions on the subject, and Elizabeth Cady Stanton introduced and recommended them to the National convention.

RESOLUTIONS ABOUT RELIGION

WHEREAS, The dogmas incorporated in the religious creeds derived from Judaism, teaching that woman was an afterthought in creation, her sex a misfortune, marriage a condition of subordination, and maternity a curse, are contrary to the law of God as revealed in nature and the precepts of Christ; and,

WHEREAS, These dogmas are an insidious poison, sapping the vitality of our civilization, blighting woman and palsying humanity; therefore,

Resolved, That we denounce these dogmas wherever they are enunciated, and we will withdraw our personal support from any organization so holding and teaching; and,

Resolved, That we call upon the Christian ministry, as leaders of thought, to teach and enforce the fundamental idea of creation that man was made in the image of God, male and female, and given equal dominion over the earth, but none over each other. And further we invite their cooperation in securing the recognition of the cardinal point of our creed, that in true religion there is neither male nor female, neither bond nor free, but all are one.[22]

A vigorous discussion followed in which some convention members objected to being embroiled in a pointless controversy about church dogma, and others disputed Colby's contention about the teachings of the church. Eventually, the convention decided to reject the resolutions.

The next year, Stanton wrote to the Executive Committee of the National recommending that the Association work on the subject of religion and try to change the church's attitude toward women and enlist the clergy in support of suffrage. She drafted resolutions similar to Colby's the year before to present to the convention. The Executive Committee's debate over Stanton's proposals reveals their differences.

DISCUSSION OF THE NATIONAL EXECUTIVE COMMITTEE

Mrs. Helen M. Gougar (Ind.) moved that the resolution be laid upon the table, saying: "A resolution something like this came into the last convention, and it has done more to cripple my work and that of other suffragists than anything which has happened in the whole history of the woman suffrage movement. . . . We can not afford to antagonize the churches. Some of us are orthodox, and some of us are unorthodox, but this association is for suffrage and not for the discussion of religious dogmas. I can not stay within these borders if that resolution is adopted, from the fact that my hands would be tied. I hope it will not go into open convention for debate.

Mrs. PERKINS (O.): I think we ought to pay due consideration and respect to our beloved president [Stanton]. I have no objection to sending missionaries to the churches asking them to pay attention to woman suffrage; but I do not think the churches are our greatest enemies. They might have been so in Mrs. Stanton's early days, but to-day they are our best helpers. If it were not for their cooperation I could not get a hearing before the public. And now that they are coming to meet us half way, do not throw stones at them. I hope that resolution, as worded, will not go into the convention.

Mrs. MERIWETHER (Mo.): I think the resolution could be amended so as to offend no one. The ministers falsely construe the Scriptures. We can overwhelm them with arguments for woman suffrage—with Biblical arguments. . . .

Mrs. SHATTUCK (Mass.): We did not pass the resolution of last year, so it could not have harmed anybody. But I protest against this fling at masculine interpretation of the Scriptures.

Mrs. MINOR (Mo.): I object to the whole thing—resolution and letter both. I believe in confining ourselves to woman suffrage.

Mrs. COLBY (Neb.): I was on that committee of resolutions last year and wrote the modified one which was presented, and I am willing to stand by it. I have not found that it hurts the work, save with a few who do not know what the resolution was, or what was said about it. . . .

Mrs. GOUGAR: I think it is quite enough to undertake to change the National Constitution without undertaking to change the Bible. I heartily agree with Mrs. Stanton in her idea of sending delegates to church councils and convocations, but I do not sanction this resolution which starts out —"The greatest barrier to woman's emancipation is found

in the superstitions of the church." That is enough in itself to turn the entire church, Catholic and Protestant, against us.[23]

Finally, the committee did introduce Stanton's views to the National convention, but the convention rejected them. Stanton, undeterred, moved on alone, developing her ideas on religion and other subjects, and writing and speaking to spread them. But she no longer represented the National Woman Suffrage Association.

As the National was growing older and more sedate, the American Woman Suffrage Association also changed. During the quarrel about the Fifteenth Amendment in the 1860's, Anthony's willingness to accept support from Democrats and her criticism of Republicans had widened the gap between the factions in the Equal Rights Association and contributed to the formation of two separate associations. Since then, countless pilgrimages to Republican Party conventions to seek endorsement of woman suffrage had shown the American's disappointed leaders that the Republican Party was not to be the champion of women's rights as they had once expected. Time revealed that a Democrat was as likely to support suffrage as a Republican. There were few of either. Eventually, the American's leaders concluded that suffrage should take precedence over other political issues, that they owed no loyalty to the Republican Party, and that friendship for women's rights should be accepted wherever it was proffered.

The American moved closer to the Anthony-Stanton position in another way as well. Once, the American leaders had vehemently repudiated George Francis Train for his racism and objected to Stanton's willingness to sacrifice the black man's progress for woman's. But shortly after taking this stand, the American moved in a similar direction.

Testifying before a Massachusetts legislative committee in 1881, Henry Blackwell suggested publicly that the enfranchisement of women could put to rest fear of black voters in the South and worry about the increasing numbers of foreign (and non-Protestant) voters in the North.

BLACKWELL'S TESTIMONY

. . . When we consider that the illiteracy of the State is mostly foreign and female, it follows that four-fifths of all our women voters will be Americans and Protestants. While therefore I am not in favor of curtailing the political rights of any class of citizens nor afraid of the influence of Catholicism, I state for the benefit of those who differ from me that the result of Woman Suffrage here and now would be to elevate the standard of intelligence, and to Americanize the politics of the State. Upon the basis of Manhood Suffrage the

American majority is 138,000, but upon the basis of Universal Suffrage it would be 350,000. The women of Massachusetts have been educated in our free schools, are readers of our newspapers and constitute nearly three-fourths of all our church members.

We need the women at the polls and in the legislature to protect the interests of the home. . . .

We need a wider Suffrage to curtail the growing power of monopolies, and to break up the despotisms of political "rings." In the nation we need the women to obliterate the lines of sectionalism, which are kept up by the dread which intelligence and property feels of a government controlled by ignorance and poverty. . . . If all women, white and black, voted, the white majority of the South would equal the entire white vote on the basis of Manhood Suffrage. There are eight million whites and four million blacks, south of Mason and Dixon's line. In other words, there are as many white women as all negroes, men and women. With Woman Suffrage, the color line would disappear in the South, and the class line would disappear in the North, because the power would be securely lodged in the intelligence of both sections.[24]

During the 1880's and 1890's, the columns of The Woman's Journal often carried views similar to those Blackwell expressed in 1881. In supporting efforts to get the vote for women in Kentucky, the American leader made this argument.

BLACKWELL IN *THE WOMAN'S JOURNAL*

. . . there are . . . in Kentucky 250,000 women who can read and write intelligently. If allowed to vote, they would neutralize all the illiterate voters, black and white, and would leave a surplus of 150,000 educated women to add to the 278,000 educated male voters. Who can fail to see what a refining and elevating influence, what a power for intelligence, for purity, for honesty, and for public good, would be gained by adding 250,000 thoughtful, educated, patriotic daughters of Kentucky to the voting constituency? . . .

If Kentucky will take this step, every Southern State will follow her. She will settle at once and forever the political problems, otherwise insoluble, of race and illiteracy. She will remove every temptation to resort to force or fraud, to bribery or corruption, in order to carry elections. Women are made the helpmeets of men, their best friends and most trusty allies; women only wait to be asked and will come when they are called, not as office-seekers or office-holders, but as a great reserved force for order, for social well-being, and for a higher civilization.

The North needs this example and would follow Kentucky. The North, in her cities and manufacturing towns, is often controlled by hordes of illiterate and brutal men, many

of whom cannot even speak our language, but all of them voters. Yet, in every Northern city, the educated women outnumber the illiterate men, the American women outnumber the men of foreign birth. . . .

Thus the enfranchisement of women who can read and write in the State of Mississippi would convert the present negro voting majority of 22,024 into a *white* voting majority of 45,116; and would increase the present educated voting majority of 15,450 into an *educated* voting majority of 129,-414. It would solve the problem of the illiterate vote by giving ample political control to the intelligent class.[25]

Thus, the American leadership, which had insisted in 1869 that it was "the negro's hour" and that women must wait, had now changed their views drastically. By 1890, not only were they arguing that giving the vote to women would increase the number of educated and informed voters but they also were evaluating the notion of an educational qualification for all voters. Such an educational qualification would be an obvious means of disfranchising blacks and immigrants. When George Francis Train proposed this, in 1868, the idea was rejected in horror by the same people who, twenty years later, were willing to consider gaining the vote for women at the expense of the political rights of others.

REUNION

The American Woman Suffrage Association and the National Woman Suffrage Association united in 1890. There were many reasons for the merger. The passage of time had brought changes. The Beecher-Tilton scandal of 1872 was receding slowly into history. Anthony and Stanton, whose ideas and political activities were once shocking and infuriating, had become familiar and almost respectable figures. Similarly, many of the demands and beliefs of the women's movement seemed less outrageous and threatening than they had earlier in the century. However, despite the fact that the country was becoming more accustomed to the movement, women did not flock to join either of the two associations. What many did join instead was a new organization, the National Woman's Christian Temperance Union, formed in 1874. While the suffrage organizations were at a standstill with about ten thousand members combined, the NWCTU expanded both its activities and its recruiting. By 1890, it had about 200,000 members.

Ironically, although the National and the American remained small, the opponents of woman suffrage became more vocal and better organized. At Seneca Falls in 1848, some women present had objected to including the franchise in their demands, and since then women as well as men continued to oppose the vote for their own sex. In

1882, the first major organization of such women appeared in Boston. Similar "antis" were organized in other states and territories. Male opposition, moreover, received a powerful boost. In 1881, the NWCTU officially endorsed the ballot for women, and this link between woman suffrage and temperance marshaled the strength and resources of the liquor interests against the women. Whenever the movement made a few gains, this served to stimulate the growth of new opponents.

It was clear, to leaders within both the National and the American, that their strategies needed re-evaluation. Thirty years of hard work and unending devotion seemed to have achieved little. National leaders admired the American's carefully organized procedures and its concern with educating the public to win support for suffrage. American leaders, after countless separate suffrage campaigns in the states, realized that federal action, as advocated by the National, could save them from unending and repetitive work in the states.

Tempers had cooled, and many of the personal antagonisms of the 1860's and 1870's were gone. A reunited suffrage movement, in the form of the National American Woman Suffrage Association, was the result in 1890.

The formation of the National American Woman Suffrage Association was a triumph of the more conservative and narrow tendencies within the two associations. This was vividly illustrated at the National-American's convention in 1896.

Since the rejection of her religious views by the National in 1886, Elizabeth Cady Stanton had continued to write and speak out on her own. Independently, she agitated for divorce reform and attacked religion as a major source of women's troubles. In 1895, with help from some friends, she published The Woman's Bible, a commentary and analysis of Biblical attitudes toward women. In response to its publication, the following resolution was proposed at the National American Woman Suffrage Convention in 1896.

A RESOLUTION

This association is non-sectarian, being composed of persons of all shades of religious opinion, and has no official connection with the so-called "Woman's Bible" or any theological publication.[26]

A long debate ensued, in which Anthony deplored the timidity and narrowness of the resolution, which she believed to threaten the Association's vitality.

ANTHONY'S REMARKS

The one distinct feature of our association has been the right of individual opinion for every member. We have been beset at each step with the cry that somebody was injuring the cause by the expression of sentiments which differed from those held by the majority. The religious persecution of the ages has been carried on under what was claimed to be the command of God. I distrust those people who know so well what God wants them to do, because I notice it always coincides with their own desires. All the way along the history of our movement there has been this same contest on account of religious theories. Forty years ago one of our noblest men said to me: "You would better never hold another convention than allow Ernestine L. Rose on your platform;" because that eloquent woman, who ever stood for justice and freedom, did not believe in the plenary inspiration of the Bible. Did we banish Mrs. Rose? No, indeed!

Every new generation of converts threshes over the same old straw. The point is whether you will sit in judgment on one who questions the divine inspiration of certain passages in the Bible derogatory to women. If Mrs. Stanton had written approvingly of these passages you would not have brought in this resolution for fear the cause might be injured among the *liberals* in religion. In other words, if she had written *your* views, you would not have considered a resolution necessary. To pass this one is to set back the hands on the dial of reform.

What you should say to outsiders is that a Christian has neither more nor less rights in our association than an atheist. When our platform becomes too narrow for people of all creeds and of no creeds, I myself can not stand upon it. Many things have been said and done by our *orthodox* friends which I have felt to be extremely harmful to our cause; but I should no more consent to a resolution denouncing them than I shall consent to this. Who is to draw the line? Who can tell now whether these commentaries

Elizabeth Cady Stanton

may not prove a great help to woman's emancipation from old superstitions which have barred its way?

Lucretia Mott at first thought Mrs. Stanton had injured the cause of all woman's other rights by insisting upon the demand for suffrage, but she had sense enough not to bring in a resolution against it. In 1860 when Mrs. Stanton made a speech before the New York Legislature in favor of a bill making drunkenness a ground for divorce, there was a general cry among the friends that she had killed the woman's cause. I shall be pained beyond expression if the delegates here are so narrow and illiberal as to adopt this resolution. You would better not begin resolving against individual action or you will find no limit. This year it is Mrs. Stanton; next year it may be I or one of yourselves who will be the victim.

If we do not inspire in women a broad and catholic spirit, they will fail, when enfranchised, to constitute that power for better government which we have always claimed for them. Ten women educated into the practice of liberal principles would be a stronger force than 10,000 organized on a platform of intolerance and bigotry. I pray you vote for religious liberty, without censorship or inquisition. This resolution adopted will be a vote of censure upon a woman who is without a peer in intellectual and statesmanlike ability; one who has stood for half a century the acknowledged leader of progressive thought and demand in regard to all matters pertaining to the absolute freedom of women.[27]

Among those who spoke in favor of the resolution were Blackwell and Stone and Carrie Chapman Catt and Anna Howard Shaw. Catt and Shaw belonged to the new leadership of the National-American. They would guide it after the turn of the century, as the old generation of leaders died out. Their support of the Bible resolution revealed their views as well as the future direction of the organization.

The resolution repudiating Stanton's book was passed, although the vote was close. Its passage was symbolic of the changes that conflict, disunion, and the passage of time had made. Fifty years before, the women's movement began in a spirit that was fearless and optimistic. It had grown into a cautious and restrained adulthood.

CHAPTER FIVE

THE WOMAN'S CHRISTIAN TEMPERANCE UNION

1874-1898

The National Woman's Christian Temperance Union, formed in 1874, was the forerunner of several major national women's organizations which hundreds and thousands, and eventually millions, of women joined around the turn of the century. Unlike the two national suffrage associations, and after 1890 the National-American Association, the new women's groups attracted members easily and grew rapidly, in the South as well as in the North and West. Increasing numbers of women were seeking access to the world outside the home, but, put off by the faint aura of scandal and radicalism that surrounded the suffrage groups, they preferred to join the WCTU and other newcomers on the national scene.

For many women, especially those living in cities and towns, life had changed dramatically during the last quarter of the nineteenth century. Educational opportunities were increasing. For the wives of more prosperous citizens, housework was beginning to be lightened by cheap immigrant labor and technological advances. The use of birth control and changing styles of life were shrinking the size of the middle-class family and with it the hard work of child rearing. Education and less work meant greater freedom and enabled many women to venture outside the home and to seek ways to participate in man's world. Since there were few jobs available for middle-class women and many prejudices against their working, employment was not the

"Women's Whisky War in Ohio: Procession of Ladies of Springfield Entering Zischler's Saloon."

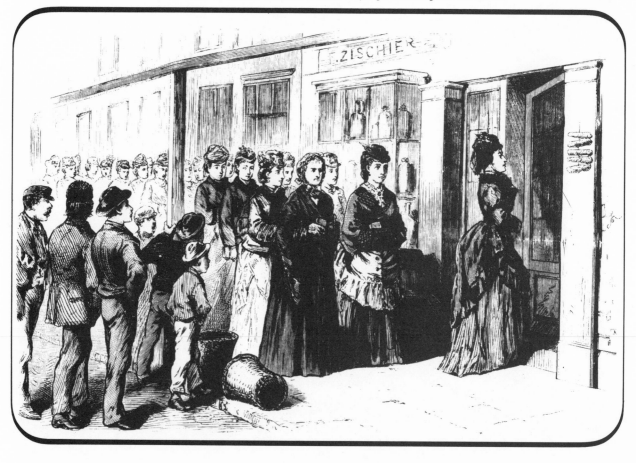

way out of the kitchen. For many women, organizations were the answer. Even farm women, cut off from the benefits of urban life, enjoyed some of the advantages of group activities as women's auxiliaries accompanied the growth of the Patrons of Husbandry. During the 1860's and 1870's, membership in the Grange, as it was popularly called, meant companionship as well as a broadening of ideas and interests for rural women. Of the new women's organizations developing during the end of the century, the National Woman's Christian Temperance Union was perhaps the best known and certainly one of the most successful.

FORMATION OF THE WCTU

The WCTU grew out of a seemingly spontaneous explosion of temperance activity that shook up the Ohio towns of Hillsboro and Washington Court House, and Fredonia, New York, during 1873 and 1874. In a lengthy report, the Fayette County Herald, *a weekly paper published in Washington Court House, described the crusade against intemperance launched by the women in that Ohio town.*

THE BALL OPENED!
A DETACHMENT OF WOMEN MARCHING THE STREETS OF WASHINGTON!
PRAYER AND SINGING IN THE SALOONS!
A PRAYER MEETING SEVEN HOURS LONG, ETC!
LIQUOR EMPTIED INTO THE STREETS!

. . . The meeting Thursday evening [December 25, 1873] was one of deep interest and feeling. After prayer and singing, the committee on appeal presented the following for adoption:

"Knowing as you do, the fearful effects of intoxicating drinks, we, the women of Washington, after earnest prayer and deliberation, have decided to appeal to you to desist from this ruinous traffic, that our husbands and sons be no longer exposed to this terrible temptation, and that we may no longer see them led into those paths that go down to ruin, and bring both soul and body to destruction.

We appeal to the better instincts of your hearts in the name of desolated homes, blasted hopes, ruined lives, widowed hearts; for the honor of our community; for our prosperity; for our happiness; for our good name as a town; in the name of God, who will judge you, as well as ourselves; for the sake of your souls, which are to be saved or lost, we beg, we implore you to cleanse yourselves from this heinous

"Open-air Prayer-Meeting in Front of Dotze's Saloon, Springfield, Ohio." Leslie's, *Feb. 1874*

sin, and place yourselves in the ranks of those who are striving to elevate and ennoble themselves and their fellow-men: and to this we ask you to pledge yourselves.''

After twice reading, the appeal was adopted, and many prayers and earnest words uttered, and the meeting adjourned to meet Friday morning. . . .

[When the meeting convened again, copies of this appeal were ordered printed.]

Now came the most interesting movement of this meeting. More than forty of our best women in the community were to go forth on their errand of mercy. There was much trembling of heart, much taking hold of God, much crying and supplication in prayer. . . .

Down the central aisle of the church marched those women to their work, while the brethren continued in prayer . . . , to appeal face to face in their various places of business, to those men who are at work selling liquor.

At one place they were met with a ''God bless you, ladies,'' and an immediate signing of the appeal.

Thirteen places in all were visited, with the proprietors of which the following exercises were held:

1. Singing; 2. Prayer; 3. Singing; 4. Prayer; 5. Reading of appeal; 6. Promise to call again.

The novel procession created the wildest excitement on the streets, and was the subject of conversation to the exclusion of all other subjects.

The work of the ladies was thoroughly done. Not a den escaped. Into the front door, filling the front room and back room too. Prayer, followed by Bible arguments in answer to the excuses of men. Down into the cellar, everywhere they go with the same eloquent plea. . . .

Saturday morning . . . It was agreed that the brethren would stay in Church and pray for God's blessing on the ladies. . . . This prayer-meeting continued for seven hours. . . .

Monday, December 29th, 1873. - Promptly at 9 A.M., a still larger attendance at the Presbyterian Church announced that the enthusiasm was still on the increase. . . . a straight course taken for the establishment of Messrs. Anderson and Keller, all the bells in towns pealing out a grand anthem of praise. . . . the following order of exercises was carried out.

1. Singing; 2. Prayer by Rev. A. C. Hurst; 3. Singing; 4. Rolling out of whiskey barrels; 5. Pouring out of liquor.

An ax was placed in the hands of the women who suffered most, and swinging through the air came down with ringing blows, bursting the heads and flooding the gutters of the street. One good woman putting her soul into every blow, struck but once for a barrel, splashing Holland Gin and old Bourbon high into the air, amid the shouts of the immense multitudes. Four casks and one barrel were forced open, and the proprietors all the time giving a hearty consent. . . .

The temperance meeting on Monday was fairly red-hot with enthusiasm. The report of the committee of visitation was read and the temperance pledge signed by a large number of men and boys. Such singing, hearty applause, cries

of ''good, good'' were never heard before in Washington. . . . [1]

The example of the women in Washington Court House and other towns in Ohio and New York proved contagious, and for six months or so, all over the country, similar groups of reformers prayed, marched, demonstrated, and even destroyed property to pressure saloon owners to close their doors, individual drinkers to abstain, and legislators to pass prohibition laws. The temperance movement, subdued by years of Civil War, had revived with a vengeance.

The National Woman's Christian Temperance Union was formed in Cleveland in November 1874 to harness and direct the interest and passion aroused by the temperance issue. In less than twenty years, the organization, with state and local unions, represented more than 200,000 women; it was now the most influential women's organization in the country.

From the beginning, the WCTU, in contrast to the suffrage organizations, was blessed with many ingredients for success. Local temperance groups were often led by wives of prominent citizens and generally had a sympathetic press. They also enjoyed wholehearted approval and help from the churches. In the South, a stronghold of restraints on middle-class women, respectable wives and mothers hurried to join the Union. For it was respectable; unlike the response to the vote and political issues, no one questioned that alcoholism and its effects on the home were women's business. Because women were seen as guardians of the family's morality and religious life, involvement in the WCTU was an acceptable activity: it was, as its president, Annie Wittenmyer, declared, in addressing a national convention, a religious experience.

PRESIDENT'S ADDRESS

. . . We have been called by the Spirit of the Lord to lead the women of the world in a great and difficult reform movement, and thousands in our own, and other lands, are looking to us with hope and expectation. The drink system is the common enemy of women the world over, and the plans we inaugurate, will be eagerly sought after by the women of all civilized nations, and as the success of all moral reforms depends largely upon women, the world will halt, or move in its onward march towards millennial glory, as *we* halt or march. Every consideration that could move a true patriotic soul conspires to stimulate us for the work. As we prize our loved ones; our homes, our American institutions, our Sabbaths; our Church altars; as we love our country and our God, let us be true in this time of our grandest opportunity. In view then, of the great responsibilities that rest upon us, let us be thoughtful and prayerful, and during the hours we are together here, walk softly before the Lord, that we may catch the whisper of his Spirit, and be guided in our works. I trust that the atmosphere of this meeting will be prayer. This Society was born of prayer, and must be nurtured and sustained by prayer. . . . [2]

FROM TEMPERANCE TO SUFFRAGE

Foremost among the assets of the WCTU was Frances E. Willard, who led the national organization from 1879 until 1898. Her wide variety of talents was important in the spectacular growth of the Union. She was a skilled administrator and organizer, and supervised the development of a complex federation of local and state unions into a powerful organization. Under her leadership, the WCTU became a major publisher, producing millions of printed pages annually. Her appreciation of publicity and the dramatic character she gave to the Union made her the most famous and admired woman of the 1880's and the WCTU the best-known women's organization.

When Willard addressed Union members, she did so as the beloved commander of a great crusade. To her, the WCTU was an "army" and a "sisterhood"; as an emblem members wore a knot of white ribbon that in an almost literal sense tied them together. In the following address, she greets delegates to the 1883 annual meeting of the NWCTU.

PRESIDENT'S ADDRESS

Dearly Beloved Friends:

In contemplation of this Assembly, its purpose and relationships, any words save those of prayer or hymn, or from God's Holy Word, seem unworthy [of] the occasion. You who are here gathered from every quarter of this vast republic, are not self-constituted, but elected delegates, with a great constituency behind you, and chosen leaders of the chief army that battles for the mightiest reform of any age, in the country where that reform has achieved its most splendid victories. This is your character to-day in the eyes of intelligent christendom. Your purpose would confederate all sections, unite all parties and unify all creeds for the destruction of humanity's most ancient and most accursed foe. Your relationships are to Christ's church, that of defender; to the home, that of protector; to the nation, that of purifier. You represent a mysterious movement known as the "Crusade," divinest manifestation of God's Spirit since tongues of fire sat on the saints at Pentecost. . . .

In less than two months we shall celebrate the Tenth Anniversary of the Crusade. In less than three weeks (November 18) we shall have completed nine years since

our National Union was organized at Cleveland. Then the light of the gospel temperance movement was nebulous; now it shines in the steady blaze of stars and constellations. . . . Then we were raw recruits, now we are soldiers drilled and disciplined; then we crusaded in saloons but now in halls of legislation; then we thought only of cure, now we are occupied with prevention; then we wept, now we rejoice. Then we said, "God be pitiful," now we say "God, be praised!" Then we *called* ourselves a National Union, now we *are* National in very deed. Then we were friends, now we are sisters. [3]

Although temperance was the first and main object of her life's work, Willard was a woman of wide interests and expanding vision. She perceived a complex relationship between temperance and other social and economic issues, and it was she who led the membership of the WCTU into activities other than temperance. Of these, woman suffrage became the most important.

In 1876, Willard began a cautious campaign to convince Union members of the link between temperance and the ballot. That year, she proposed to an Illinois convention a rather mild resolution that read:

Resolved, That we will pray and labor for the early dawning of that day when the mothers and daughters of America shall have a voice in the decision by which the door of the rum-shop is opened or shut beside their homes. [4]

The resolution provoked great opposition. Many temperance women did not agree that voting was a woman's business, even voting in a local election in which a community could decide to prohibit the sale of alcoholic drinks. Still more members feared that associating suffrage with temperance would lose public and church support for the movement.

To overcome the conservatism and doubts within the Union, Willard emphasized that the ballot was needed as a means of protecting the home and the family, a function which was, beyond question, women's responsibility. Over and over again, in speeches and in her writings, she argued for the ballot as a means of "Home Protection."

A MANUAL FOR HOME PROTECTION

"Home Protection" is the general name given to a movement already endorsed by the W.C.T. Unions of eight states, the object of which is to secure for all women above the age of twenty-one years the ballot as one means for the protection of their homes from the devastation caused by the legalized traffic in strong drink.

Let us remember that in giving prominence to this branch of work, we are but *transferring the crusade from the saloon to the sources whence the saloon derives its guaranties and safeguards.* Surely, this does not change our work from sacred to secular! Surely, that is a short-sighted view which says: "It was womanly to plead with saloon-keepers not to sell; but it is unwomanly to plead with law-makers not to legalize the sale and to give us power to prevent it."[5]

A HOME PROTECTION SPEECH

. . . Dear Christian women who have crusaded in the rum shops, I urge that you begin crusading in halls of legislation, in primary meetings, and the offices of excise commissioners. Roll in your petitions, burnish your arguments, multiply your prayers. Go to the voters in your town—procure the official list and see them one by one—and get them pledged

Yours for Home Protection,
Frances E. Willard.
Jan. 30, 1889

to a local ordinance requiring the votes of men and women before a license can be issued to open rum-shop doors beside your homes; go to the Legislature with the same; remember this may be just as really Christian work as praying in saloons was in those other glorious days. Let us not limit God, whose modes of operation are so infinitely varied in nature and in grace. I believe in the correlation of spiritual forces, and that the heat which melted hearts to tenderness in the Crusade is soon to be the light which shall reveal our opportunity and duty as the Republic's daughters.

Longer ago than I shall tell, my father returned one night to the far-off Wisconsin home where I was reared; and, sitting by my mother's chair, with a child's attentive ear, I listened to their words. He told us of the news that day had brought about Neal Dow and the great fight for prohibition down in Maine, and then he said: "I wonder if poor, rum-cursed Wisconsin will ever get a law like that?" And mother rocked a while in silence in the dear old chair I love, and then she gently said:

"YES, JOSIAH, THERE'LL BE SUCH A LAW OVER THE LAND SOME DAY, WHEN WOMEN VOTE."

My father had never heard her say so much before. He was a great conservative; so he looked tremendously astonished, and replied, in his keen, sarcastic voice: "And pray how will you arrange it so that women shall vote?" Mother's chair went to and fro a little faster for a minute, and then, looking not into his face, but into the flickering flames of the grate, she slowly answered: "Well, I say to you, as the apostle Paul said to his jailor, 'You have put us into prison, we being Romans, and you must come and take us out.'"

That was a seed-thought in a girl's brain and heart. Years passed on, in which nothing more was said upon this dangerous theme. My brother grew to manhood, and soon after he was twenty-one years old he went with his father to vote. Standing by the window, a girl of sixteen years, a girl of simple, homely fancies, not at all strong-minded, and altogether ignorant of the world, I looked out as they drove away, my father and my brother, and as I looked I felt a strange ache in my heart, and tears sprang to my eyes. Turning to my sister Mary, who stood beside me, I saw that the dear little innocent seemed wonderfully sober, too. I said: "Don't you wish we could go with them when we are old enough? Don't we love our country just as well as they do?" and her little frightened voice piped out: "Yes, of course we ought. Don't I know that? but you mustn't tell a soul—not mother, even; we should be called strong-minded."

In all the years since then I have kept these things, and many others like them, and pondered them in my heart; but two years of struggle in this temperance reform have shown me, as they have ten thousand other women, so clearly and so impressively, my duty, that

I HAVE PASSED THE RUBICON OF SILENCE

and am ready for any battle that shall be involved in this honest declaration of the faith that is within me. . . .

Ah, it is women who have given the costliest hostages to fortune. Out into the battle of life they have sent their best beloved, with fearful odds against them, with snares that men have legalized and set for them on every hand. Beyond the arms that held them long, their boys have gone forever. Oh! by the danger they have dared; by the hours of patient watching over beds where helpless children lay; by the incense of ten thousand prayers wafted from their gentle lips to Heaven, I charge you give them power to protect, along life's treacherous highway, those whom they have so loved. Let it no longer be that they must sit back among the shadows, hopelessly mourning over their strong staff broken, and their beautiful rod; but when the sons they love shall go forth to life's battle, still let their mothers walk beside them, sweet and serious, and clad in the garments of power. . . . [6]

In 1877, the national convention adopted a resolution favoring municipal suffrage for women, which, in effect, gave WCTU approval to women voting in local elections in which, in many states, voters could choose to prohibit the sale of alcoholic beverages in their communities.

Finally, in 1881, in the face of considerable reluctance and opposition, members adopted a resolution that made the national Union the most formidable proponent of equal suffrage in the country.

THE SUFFRAGE RESOLUTION

Believing that it is the part of wisdom to place temperance legislation upon the firm foundation of Constitutional law, both State and National, that shall prohibit the manufacture and sale of intoxicating beverages; and recognizing the fact that the varying conditions of communities must, in a large measure, determine our line of action, wisdom dictates the do-every-thing-policy—constitutional amendment, where the way is open for it; Home Protection, when Home Protection is the strongest rallying cry; equal franchise, where the vote of woman joined to that of men can alone give stability to Temperance legislation.[7]

As a result, local and state unions could and did participate in the suffrage campaigns that were being conducted in the states, and national Union representatives joined the efforts being made in Washington to obtain a Sixteenth Amendment to the Constitution to give women the vote.

The WCTU added its huge membership, its respectability, and its organizational and public relations skills to the suffrage movement. In 1879, Willard's Home Protection Manual *was published to guide local and state unions in suffrage agitation. In addition to carefully developed argu-*

ments for giving the ballot to women, the manual contained detailed "how to" information for political workers.

PLANS FOR PETITION WORK

**Home Protection Petition to the
National or State Legislature.**

This will include the following methods:

1. A committee to be appointed by the State W.C.T.U. and called the "Home Protection Committee." (As a rule, the president should be its chairman.) The petition is to be drafted by this committee, acting under legal advice, and every detail relating to its circulation and presentation controlled by them.

2. A special committee, to be chosen also by the State Union, whose duty it is to secure a separate Home Protection Fund (by private subscription) to pay for documents,

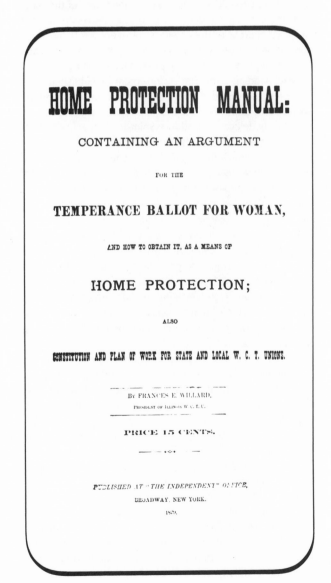

HOME PROTECTION MANUAL:

CONTAINING AN ARGUMENT

FOR THE

TEMPERANCE BALLOT FOR WOMAN,

AND HOW TO OBTAIN IT, AS A MEANS OF

HOME PROTECTION;

ALSO

CONSTITUTION AND PLAN OF WORK FOR STATE AND LOCAL W. C. T. UNIONS.

By FRANCES E. WILLARD,
PRESIDENT OF ILLINOIS W. C. T. U.

PRICE 15 CENTS.

PUBLISHED AT "THE INDEPENDENT" OFFICE,
BROADWAY, NEW YORK.
1879.

printing, postage, and amanuenses bills, also a clerk, who will send out all documents and receive and classify all letters and signatures. . . . (N.B.—We found it easier to raise money for this work than for any other ever undertaken by our Unions.)

3. Petitions and documents (this Manual furnishes a sufficient variety) containing facts and arguments for Local Option and Home Protection to be sent out from the central office to every editor in the state, with a printed letter, carefully prepared by the committee, urging him to publish the petition and extracts from the documents and to give the movement his personal endorsement. As the campaign progresses, notes, incidents, news, etc. to be sent, on printed slips, to every editor and leading newspaper correspondent. (Send 30 cents to Geo. P. Rowell, New York, for list of all the editors in any state.) The leading journalists to be personally visited by influential delegations of men and women and their support requested. This "press work" must be carefully assigned to capable women in all leading towns of the state.

4. The petition and documents to be sent to each minister of every church, to the president of every temperance organization and of *every society in the state,* and to each postmaster, separate forms of printed letters being prepared for each leading class. The endorsement by published resolutions of all religious and philanthropic bodies is to be sought; and to this end the best men and women are to be specifically delegated to address ministers' meetings and societies in every locality, also conferences, synods, and conventions of county, district, and state. The names of all these persons can be readily obtained in large cities from directories or at the publishing houses of their respective organs, and for the smaller towns by calling at the city headquarters of the various organizations, as indicated in the directories.

5. Conventions in every congressional district, and, if possible, in every county; as many first-class speakers in the field as the people will support; special sermons (for which in the "Letter to Ministers" earnest and respectful request has been made); Union meetings on Sabbath evenings; parlor meetings for the more conservative in towns and cities.

6. Delegations to visit Catholic bishops and priests, urging their co-operation . . .

7. Each town and village to be *districted,* and women to go from house to house, store to store, and office to office. This enlists most brains, hearts and hands, and, hence, this is the right arm of the service. Nothing will compensate for neglect here. . . . The "Home Protection" documents, copies of "Our Union," "Miss Colman's Leaflets," and "The Juvenile Temperance Banner," and other temperance literature, must be furnished, to be distributed according to their discretion. . . .

9. There must be but one "Headquarters," one person to whose address all orders for petitions and documents and all the signatures obtained are sent. State precise date when all petitions must be returned, with signatures, to headquarters, and *do not change that date.* These signatures must be at once and gratefully acknowledged by printed postal. Ad-

dresses of all persons who gather up signatures or specially interest themselves in the work must be kept in the Home Protection Directory at headquarters, and will be invaluable for present reference and in future work. The autograph signatures to the petition may be pasted and ironed smooth on white cloth, half a yard wide, bound on one side with blue and on the other with red braid, wound on a roller, and tied with white ribbon. If practicable, classify by towns, and keep a tabulated book account of them.

10. *At the Capital.*—*Before the legislature assembles* a committee of gentlemen and ladies, residents of the capital, will be required to prepare for the coming of [the] Home Protection Committee.

Women's Local Petition for the Temperance Ballot.

In many towns the municipal authorities could, if they would, adopt a special ordinance, by which women might vote on the question of license. A petition asking for this should be thoroughly circulated, every person of legal age being given the opportunity to sign, and should be presented to the council by a strong delegation, after having first been read and expounded at a great public meeting of the people. The following may serve as a form of petition:

To the Mayor and Council of———:

We, the undersigned, men and women of———, believe that women should be granted a voice in deciding whether we are to have dram-shops among the institutions of our village; and we earnestly desire that provision shall be made, by special ordinance, for a vote on the question of legalizing the liquor traffic, and that in such vote women be invited to share.

NAMES OF MEN OVER 21.	NAMES OF WOMEN OVER 21.

(With slight changes, this will apply to counties and states under local option laws.)

If they will not grant this, do not say, in dolorous accents, "It was of no use, and we'll not try again"; but faithfully use your two best weapons, the printed and the spoken word, seasoned with prayer. Throng the primaries where the fathers are again chosen; work up the sentiment; toil on the election day; and place men in their stead who will grant what your petition asked. Or, if not successful the first year, try again the second. With the motto "*The W.C.T.U. never surrenders,*" success is sure.

Petition Against Games, Screens, Etc. in Saloons.

Good work can be done with the following, especially in cities:

To the Honorable Mayor and Board of Aldermen:

We, the undersigned, respectfully and earnestly request the adoption of an ordinance requiring saloon-keepers to take the paint off their window-panes and the screens from before their doors; also that the front door shall be their only means of entrance or of exit, and that no chairs or tables shall be allowed within their walls; and, further, that this ordinance shall be faithfully executed.

To the foregoing might be added the banishing of all games and billiard-tables from the saloons, also the prohibiting of the sale of liquor to minors and closing on the Sabbath. If thought best, some one specification might be made the subject of petition.[8]

The contributions of the Women's Christian Temperance Unions to the suffrage cause did not go unnoticed. Writing to The Woman's Journal, *in 1883, an observer from Osage, Iowa, said the following:*

LETTER TO *THE WOMAN'S JOURNAL*

. . . The W.C.T.U. of this State is making Woman Suffrage its main subject of work and discussion. I attended the District Convention of that body, in the fourth congressional district, held at Charles City in September. I could not help comparing its tone on that subject with the first one I attended five years ago. At that time one must have been brave indeed who should say suffrage even in a whisper, (though some of us did say it aloud.) If one spoke of it, she was hushed up as quickly as possible. In selecting delegates the President of our Union then said:—"We must be sure and not send a delegate who is an advocate of Woman Suffrage, for it will not do at all to have it understood that we endorse that." So they sent one who was not tainted with that dreadful heresy. This fall they sent as delegate one who has always been a strong suffragist, and one whom they knew was on the programme for a paper on "The Ballot for Woman as Related to the Temperance Work." I think the other delegates must have been chosen in the same way, for I felt as if it was a Woman Suffrage Convention. There were but one or two speakers who did not advocate the ballot for women. Mrs. Jane A. McKinney, District President and State Superintendent of the Suffrage work, is doing good service for the cause.

I believe that within the year every W.C.T.U. in the State of Iowa will be a *working* Suffrage Society. They are already organized for work, and in many places can do more efficient work than any other society. The death of the Prohibitory Amendment has converted thousands of women to see

"New York—Scene at the Woman's Temperance Convention." Once a Week, 1891

the pressing need of the ballot in the hands of women. This work in the W.C.T.U. has been one of the great educators. No woman can work for temperance a year without seeing how utterly powerless women are without the ballot. God speed the day when we shall have it![9]

In 1891, Alice Stone Blackwell reported about the national WCTU convention for the Journal. She commented on the size and the enthusiasm of the crowd and concluded with this observation:

REPORT OF NWCTU CONVENTION

. . . One woman asked another, as they stood in the surging crowd that filled the vestibule of Tremont Temple, "Why cannot we have audiences like this at suffrage meetings?" The other answered, in the words of Lucy Stone, "Because it is so much easier to see a drunkard than it is to see a principle." Nevertheless, multitudes of women who began by seeing only the drunkard are learning through the WCTU to look beyond him to the principle. For this reason, if for no other, all advocates of equal rights have cause to say, "God bless the WCTU!"[10]

THE WCTU AS A SCHOOL FOR WOMEN

The Women's Christian Temperance Unions offered American women a gentle and respectable transition from the home to a larger world as it involved them in stimulating and provocative public issues. As Willard's own social and economic views developed, she carefully guided the membership of the Union to expand its involvement beyond temperance work. WCTU resolutions, committee work, publications and speeches provided a sympathetic introduction for thousands of women to the labor movement, to welfare issues, to prison reform, to education reform, to the peace movement, to the kindergarten movement, and to many others.

In contrast to the controversial suffrage organizations, the national Union, under the guise of the Home Protection banner, led hundreds of thousands of women out of their "impoverished lives" with relatively little opposition. It provided them with an education in large-scale organization activities, in parliamentary procedures, in techniques of political pressure and agitation, and in group action. The enormous success of the temperance movement at this time (about half the population was legally "dry" by 1910) attests to the skills that women had mastered.

GLIMPSES OF FIFTY YEARS.

The Autobiography

OF

AN AMERICAN WOMAN

BY

FRANCES E. WILLARD.

WRITTEN BY ORDER OF THE NATIONAL WOMAN'S CHRISTIAN
TEMPERANCE UNION.

INTRODUCTION BY HANNAH WHITALL SMITH.

"*Nothing makes life dreary but lack of motive.*"

PUBLISHED BY THE
Woman's Temperance Publication Association.

H. J. SMITH & CO.
CHICAGO,   PHILADELPHIA,   KANSAS CITY,   OAKLAND, CAL.
General Agents for United States, Canada, Australia, Sandwich Islands.

Frances Willard clearly understood that the WCTU was a school for women, a device for broadening their lives. In her 1885 presidential address, she made this observation.

. . . [the temperance movement] is God's way out of the wilderness for half the human race. In its glowing crucible, the dross of sectional enmity is being rapidly dissolved; the trifling occupations, the narrow aims, the paralizing indolence of women are barriers burned away by its all-conquering heat while their once impoverished lives are expanded into wide areas of gracious strength and heavenly magnanimity.[11]

As the years passed, Willard came to regard temperance as part of a general movement toward equality and dignity for all people. She saw it not as an isolated reform or as a cure-all, but as part of a complex of social reforms, among which was the women's suffrage movement. In a presidential address, she explained her views.

WILLARD'S BROAD VIEW OF TEMPERANCE

. . . The greatest movement known to history is this new correlation and attuning each to other, of a more complete humanity equalized upon the Christ-like basis of "there shall be no more curse." The temperance reform is its necessary forerunner, for while the race-brain is bewildered it cannot be thought out. The labor reform is another part, for only under co-operation can material conditions be adjusted to a non-combatant state of society, and every yoke lifted from the laboring man lifts one still heavier from the woman at his side. The equal suffrage movement is still another part, for a government organized and conducted by one half of the human unit, a government of the minority, by the minority, for the minority, must always bear unequally upon the whole. The social purity movement could only come after its heralds, the three other reforms I have mentioned, were well under way, because alcoholized brains would not tolerate its expression; women who had not learned to work would have lacked the individuality and intrepidity required to organize it, and women perpetually to be disfranchised could not have hoped to see its final purposes wrought out in law. But back of all were the father and mother of all reforms—Christianity and education—to blaze the way for all these later comers. . . .

The W.C.T.U. is doing no work more important than that of reconstructing the ideal of womanhood. . . . Woman is becoming what God meant her to be and Christ's gospel necessitates her being, the companion and counsellor, not the incumbrance and toy, of man. To meet the new creation, how grandly men themselves are growing; how considerate and brotherly, how pure in word and deed! The world has never yet known half the amplitude of character and life to which men will attain when they and women live in the same world. It doth not yet appear what they shall be, or we either, for that matter, but in many a home presided over by a Prohibition voter and a White Ribbon worker, I have thought the heavenly vision was really coming down to terra firma. . . . [12]

Throughout her career, each step that Willard took away from exclusively temperance work provoked opposition and challenged her leadership and diplomatic skills. In the 1890's, she was personally involved in partisan politics and her own interest and commitment to socialism developed. Now, intemperance seemed to her less the cause and more the symptom of other problems.

These views were very different from those of her uneasy, though still loyal, constituency. Criticism and disagreement disturbed the national Union; factions and unrest developed. When Frances Willard died in 1898, a retreat began from the adventures into social reform that she had inspired. Soon the Union narrowed its interests until it became, once again, a temperance organization and nothing more.

CHAPTER SIX

THE FIRST SUFFRAGE DRIVE

Apart from temperance, the main objective of the women's movement was suffrage, and most of its activities were directed toward gaining the vote. The work for the ballot was prodigious—and unsuccessful. Between 1870 and 1910, 527 separate efforts were made to persuade state legislatures or state constitutional conventions to submit the question of woman suffrage to the voters. Few succeeded: there were only 17 occasions when the issue reached the ballot. Before 1900, only two campaigns for referendums in which the voters had a chance to accept woman suffrage were successful—one in Colorado in 1893 and the other in Idaho in 1896. (Wyoming, in 1890, and Utah, in 1896, came into the Union with female suffrage in their constitutions, and without large-scale efforts.)

Nineteen campaigns were launched to convince Congress to approve a federal suffrage amendment. Nineteen times they failed. The only accomplishment in Washington was the temporary formation of special congressional committees to consider the subject of woman suffrage; on occasion, a favorable report was issued by such a committee.

Over 300 separate moves were made to gain official support from political parties at their state and national conventions. Most of them failed; only third parties were willing to risk endorsement of the vote for women.

"Washington, D.C.—The Judiciary Committee of the House of Representatives Receiving a Deputation of Female Suffragists, January 11th—A Lady Delegate Reading Her Argument in Favor of Woman's Voting, on the Basis of the Fourteenth and Fifteenth Constitutional Amendments." Leslie's, Feb. 1871

The work involved in these efforts was staggering. It fell upon a relatively small number of women and a handful of male supporters. The two major suffrage organizations, the American Woman Suffrage Associaton and the National Woman Suffrage Association, took the lead in organizing and directing the suffrage drive. Throughout the country, state and local suffrage organizations, some affiliated with the National or the American, others acting independently, joined in the work. After 1881, the National Woman's Christian Temperance Union also joined, and the members of its state and local unions swelled the infantry of suffrage workers.

Close ties developed between the WCTU and the suffrage organizations. In state and federal work, temperance and suffrage workers labored side by side. Frances Willard herself joined the American and was an associate editor of The Woman's Journal. *She also became an influential friend and colleague of Susan B. Anthony. Alice Stone Blackwell and Anna Howard Shaw, leading figures in suffrage work, were officers of the NWCTU.*

The suffrage cause gained not only the friends and the resources of the temperance movement but also its enemies. The liquor interests automatically associated woman suffrage with prohibition, and they mobilized well-financed and well-organized opposition to the ballot for women. Other interest groups opposed to municipal reform believed that temperance, woman suffrage, and municipal reform were all part of the same threat. Thus the link between suffrage and temperance had both positive and negative effects on the struggle for the vote.

TWO STRATEGIES

There were two basic approaches used by the suffrage groups to get the vote. One strategy, advocated and often led by the American Woman Suffrage Association, aimed at gaining suffrage through state action and involved separate campaigns in the states. The other strategy, which the National Association advocated, strived to enfranchise all women at one stroke by federal action.

National and American leaders argued the advantages of each approach.

ANTHONY EXPLAINS THE NATIONAL'S STRATEGY

. . . I do not wish to see the women of the thirty-eight States of this Union compelled to leave their homes to canvass each one of these, school district by school district. It is asking too much of a moneyless class. The joint earnings of the marriage co-partnership in all the States belong legally to the husband. It is only that wife who goes outside the home to work whom the law permits to own and control the money she earns. Therefore, to ask of women, the vast majority of whom are without an independent dollar of their own, to make a thorough canvass of their several States, is asking an impossibility.

We have already made the experiment of canvassing four States—Kansas in 1867, Michigan in 1874, Colorado in 1877, Nebraska in 1882—and in each, with the best campaign possible for us to make, we obtained a vote of only one-third. One man out of every three voted for the enfranchisement of the women of his household, while two out of every three voted against it. . . .

We beg, therefore, that instead of insisting that a majority of the individual voters must be converted before women shall have the franchise, you will give us the more hopeful task of appealing to the representative men in the Legislatures of the several States. You need not fear that we shall get suffrage too quickly if Congress submits the proposition, for even then we shall have a long siege in going from Legislature to Legislature to secure the vote of three-fourths of the States necessary to ratify the amendment. It may require twenty years after Congress has taken the initiative step, to obtain action by the requisite number, but once submitted by Congress it always will stand until ratified by the States.[1]

BLACKWELL DEFENDS THE AMERICAN'S STRATEGY

. . . While petitioning Congress for a sixteenth amendment does good as a means of agitation, the real work lies with the State Legislatures, and can be effected most directly by State Suffrage societies. Every intelligent man and woman knows that an amendment to the Federal Constitution is practically possible only under two conditions:—either public sentiment everywhere must be overwhelmingly strong in its favor, or else, a part of the States being practically unanimous, the opposing States must withdraw from Congress, and go to war, in which case, an amendment can be carried through by the States that remain. Neither case is likely to occur. The Supreme Court of the United States has decided that Suffrage is not a national, but a State affair—that "women are citizens, and as such, are capable of being endowed with Suffrage by appropriate State legislation. . . . [2]

THE FEDERAL APPROACH: WOMEN TRY TO VOTE

The first step in trying to gain suffrage through federal action involved interpreting the Constitution, as it was then worded, to include women as voters. The Constitu-

tion did not specifically deny the vote to women. It did grant and guarantee it to "citizens." Suffragists proposed that women were "persons" and "citizens," and were, therefore, entitled to the vote under the Constitution.

Women in the National Association worked hard to get this interpretation of the Constitution accepted, and they heartily agreed with Victoria Woodhull, who argued before a Senate committee, in January 1871, that the Fourteenth and Fifteenth amendments actually gave the vote to women.

Up to 1875, a lot of effort was expended in this approach. Women petitioned and lobbied in Washington yearly, trying to persuade Congress to pass a declaratory act instructing election officials to register women voters. In addition, women went to the courts for corroboration of their interpretation of the Constitution. And to publicize and test their claim to the vote, the National Woman Suffrage Association encouraged women to go to the polls and try to cast a ballot.

MESSAGE FROM THE NATIONAL ASSOCIATION

Women should attempt to qualify and attempt to vote in every State election or otherwise, according to opportunity. This action not only serves the purpose of agitation of the whole question of suffrage, but it puts upon men, our brothers, the onus of refusing the votes of their fellow citizens, and compels them to show just cause for such proceeding. If it could be well understood that every woman who believes that she has a right to vote, would actually test her right by an appearance at the polls before and at the next Presidential election, the question as to nominees for that office would contain a new element, and the views and preferences of this large constituency would receive serious consideration at the hands of president-makers in both the great parties of the country.[3]

In Vineland, New Jersey, women tried to vote as early as 1868. By 1872, about 150 women in eleven states and the District, including a few in the South, had gone to the polls to confront puzzled registration and election officials. Several of these episodes eventually ended up in the courts. Much publicity accompanied the march of the women to the voting tables, but none as much as Susan B. Anthony's in her hometown, Rochester, New York, in 1872.

A LETTER FROM SUSAN B. ANTHONY

ROCHESTER, November 5, 1872.
DEAR MRS. STANTON: Well, I have been and gone and done it! positively voted the Republic ticket—straight—this A.M. at seven o'clock, and *swore my vote in, at that;* was registered on Friday and fifteen other women followed suit in this ward, then in sundry other wards some twenty or thirty women *tried* to *register,* but all save two were refused. All my three sisters voted—Rhoda De Garmo, too. Amy Post was rejected, and she will immediately bring action against the registrars; then another woman who was registered, but vote refused, will bring action for that—similar to the Washington action. Hon. Henry R. Selden will be our counsel; he has read up the law and all of our arguments, and is satisfied that we are right, and ditto Judge Samuel Selden, his elder brother. So we are in for a fine agitation in Rochester on this question. . . .

How I wish you were here to write up the funny things said and done. Rhoda De Garmo told them she wouldn't swear nor affirm, "but would tell them the truth," and they accepted that. When the Democrats said that my vote should *not* go in the box, one Republican said to the other, "What do you say, Marsh?" "I say put it in." "So do I," said Jones; "and we'll fight it out on this line if it takes all winter." Mary Hallowell was just here. She and Sarah Willis tried to register, but were refused; also Mrs. Mann, the Unitarian minister's wife, and Mary Curtis, sister of Catharine Stebbins. Not a jeer, not a word, not a look disrespectful has met a single woman.

If only now *all the Woman Suffrage women* would work to *this* end of *enforcing the existing Constitutional supremacy of National law* over State law, what strides we might make this very winter! But I'm awfully tired; for five days I have been on the constant run, but to splendid purpose; so all right. I hope you voted too.

Affectionately,
SUSAN B. ANTHONY.[4]

Anthony was accused of having voted "knowingly, wrongfully and unlawfully" and was brought to trial. The episode in itself was newsworthy, but Anthony and her supporters traveled furiously about New York State, capitalizing on the publicity to promote their contention that the Fourteenth Amendment gave women the vote, and winning considerable sympathy for the cause.

NEWSPAPER REPORTS

The Rochester Evening Express

. . . The Pittsburg Leader, among others, disgraces itself by a scurrilous report of what "the gay old girl said to a reporter;" and the New York World, of course, waxed very funny in its account of the late convention. These gibes at Miss Anthony's personal appearance, unwillingness to tell her age, "fishy eyes," etc., are read by her friends in Rochester with indignation and with contempt for the press which will publish such misrepresentations as truth.

One Comment on Anthony's Attempt to Vote

All Rochester will assert—at least all of it worth heeding—that Miss Anthony holds here the position of a refined and estimable woman, thoroughly respected and beloved by the large circle of staunch friends who swear by her common sense and loyalty, if not by her peculiar view. . . . She is no "sour old maid," our Miss Anthony, nor are the young men shy of her when she can find time to accept an invitation out; genial, cheery, warm-hearted, overflowing with stories and reminiscences, utterly fearless and regardless of mere public opinion, yet having a woman's delicate sensitiveness as to anything outré in dress or appearance.[5]

The Boston Transcript

The last work came on the New York Calendar; a person is discovered to have voted who had no right to; this is believed to be the first case of the kind ever heard of in New York, and its heinousness is perhaps aggravated by the fact that the perpetrator is a woman, who, in the vigorous language of the Court, "must have known when she did it that she was a woman." We await in breathless suspense the impending sentence.[6]

The New York Commercial Advertiser

There is perplexity in the northern district of New York. It was in that jurisdiction that Miss Susan B. Anthony and sundry "erring sisters" voted at the November election. For this they were arrested and indicted. The venue was laid in Monroe county and there the trial was to take place. Miss Anthony then proceeded to stump Monroe county and every town and village thereof, asking her bucolic hearers the solemn conundrum, "Is it a crime for a United States citizen to vote?" The answer is supposed generally to be in the negative, and so convincing is Sister Anthony's rhetoric regarded that it is supposed no jury can be found to convict her. Her case has gone to the jurymen of Monroe, in her own persuasive pleadings, before they are summoned. The district-attorney has, therefore, postponed the trial to another term of the court, and changed the place thereof to Ontario county; whereupon the brave Susan takes the stump in Ontario, and personally makes known her woes and wants. It is a regular St. Anthony's dance she leads the district-attorney; and, in spite of winter cold or summer heat, she will carry her case from county to county precisely as fast as the venue is changed. One must rise very early in the morning to get the start of this active apostle of the sisterhood.[7]

AN

ACCOUNT OF THE PROCEEDINGS

ON THE

TRIAL OF

SUSAN B. ANTHONY,

ON THE

Charge of Illegal Voting,

AT THE

PRESIDENTIAL ELECTION IN NOV., 1872,

AND ON THE

TRIAL OF

BEVERLY W. JONES, EDWIN T. MARSH

AND WILLIAM B. HALL,

THE INSPECTORS OF ELECTION BY WHOM HER VOTE WAS RECEIVED.

ROCHESTER, N. Y.:

DAILY DEMOCRAT AND CHRONICLE BOOK PRINT, 3 WEST MAIN ST.

1874.

Anthony's trial created more furor. Judge Hunt denied her the right to testify in her own defense, ruled that the Fourteenth Amendment was inapplicable, and informed the jury that "there is no question for the jury and that the jury should be directed to find a verdict of guilt."[8] Hunt then rejected a request for a new trial, and the courtroom scene ended in this way:

AN ACCOUNT OF THE TRIAL

. . . JUDGE HUNT—(Ordering the defendant to stand up), "Has the prisoner anything to say why sentence shall not be pronounced?"

MISS ANTHONY—Yes, your honor, I have many things to say; for in your ordered verdict of guilty, you have trampled under foot every vital principle of our government. My natural rights, my civil rights, my political rights, my judicial rights, are all alike ignored. Robbed of the fundamental privilege of citizenship, I am degraded from the status of a citizen to that of a subject; and not only myself individually, but all of my sex, are, by your honor's verdict, doomed to political subjection under this, so-called, form of government.

JUDGE HUNT—The Court cannot listen to a rehearsal of

arguments the prisoner's counsel has already consumed three hours in presenting.

MISS ANTHONY—May it please your honor, I am not arguing the question, but simply stating the reasons why sentence cannot, in justice, be pronounced against me. Your denial of my citizen's right to vote, is the denial of my right of consent as one of the governed, the denial of my right of representation as one of the taxed, the denial of my right to a trial by a jury of my peers as an offender against law, therefore, the denial of my sacred rights to life, liberty, property and—

JUDGE HUNT—The Court cannot allow the prisoner to go on.

MISS ANTHONY—But your honor will not deny me this one and only poor privilege of protest against this high-handed outrage upon my citizen's rights. May it please the Court to remember that since the day of my arrest last November, this is the first time that either myself or any person of my disfranchised class has been allowed a word of defense before judge or jury—

JUDGE HUNT—The prisoner must sit down—the Court cannot allow it.

MISS ANTHONY—All my prosecutors, from the 8th ward corner grocery politician, who entered the complaint, to the United States Marshal, Commissioner, District Attorney, District Judge, your honor on the bench, not one is my peer, but each and all are my political sovereigns; and had your honor submitted my case to the jury, as was clearly your duty, even then I should have had just cause of protest, for not one of those men was my peer; but, native or foreign born, white or black, rich or poor, educated or ignorant, awake or asleep, sober or drunk, each and every man of them was my political superior; hence, in no sense, my peer. Even, under such circumstances, a commoner of England, tried before a jury of Lords, would have far less cause to complain than should I, a woman, tried before a jury of men. Even my counsel, the Hon. Henry R. Selden, who has argued my cause so ably, so earnestly, so unanswerably before your honor, is my political sovereign. Precisely as no disfranchised person is entitled to sit upon a jury, and no woman is entitled to the franchise, so, none but a regularly admitted lawyer is allowed to practice in the courts, and no woman can gain admission to the bar—hence, jury, judge, counsel, must all be the superior class.

JUDGE HUNT—The Court must insist—the prisoner has been tried according to the established forms of law.

MISS ANTHONY—Yes, your honor, but by forms of law all made by men, interpreted by men, administered by men, in favor of men, and against women; and hence, your honor's ordered verdict of guilty, against a United States citizen for the exercise of *"that citizen's right to vote,"* simply because that citizen was a woman and not a man. . . . As . . . the slaves who got their freedom must take it over, or under, or through the unjust forms of law, precisely so, now, must women, to get their right to a voice in this government, take it; and I have taken mine, and mean to take it at every possible opportunity.

JUDGE HUNT—The Court orders the prisoner to sit down. It will not allow another word.

MISS ANTHONY—When I was brought before your honor for trial, I hoped for a broad and liberal interpretation of the Constitution and its recent amendments, that should declare all United States citizens under its protecting aegis—that should declare equality of rights the national guarantee to all persons born or naturalized in the United States. But failing to get this justice—failing, even, to get a trial by a jury *not* of my peers—I ask not leniency at your hands—but rather the full rigors of the law.

JUDGE HUNT—The Court must insist—

(Here the prisoner sat down.)

JUDGE HUNT—The prisoner will stand up.

(Here Miss Anthony arose again.)

The sentence of the Court is that you pay a fine of one hundred dollars and the costs of the prosecution.

MISS ANTHONY—May it please your honor, I shall never pay a dollar of your unjust penalty. All the stock in trade I possess is a $10,000 debt, incurred by publishing my paper—*The Revolution*—four years ago, the sole object of which was to educate all women to do precisely as I have done, rebel against your man-made, unjust, unconstitutional forms of law, that tax, fine, imprison and hang women, while they deny them the right of representation in the government; and I shall work on with might and main to pay every dollar of that honest debt, but not a penny shall go to this unjust claim. And I shall earnestly and persistently continue to urge all women to the practical recognition of the old revolutionary maxim, that "Resistance to tyranny is obedience to God."

JUDGE HUNT—Madam, the Court will not order you committed until the fine is paid.[9]

Anthony stuck by her statement that she would "never pay a dollar of your unjust penalty," but nothing was done about it. No further charges were brought, and Anthony was denied the opportunity of taking her case to a higher court.

The Revolution;

THE ORGAN OF THE

NATIONAL PARTY OF NEW AMERICA.

PRINCIPLE, NOT POLICY—INDIVIDUAL RIGHTS AND RESPONSIBILITIES.

The United States Supreme Court eventually did rule on women's claim to vote under the Constitution. In 1872, Virginia L. Minor, president of the Missouri suffrage association, and her husband, attorney Francis Minor, filed suit against Reese Happerstett, a St. Louis registrar, for refusing to permit Virginia Minor to register as a voter. The case was eventually carried to the Supreme Court, which delivered its opinion in 1874, rejecting the contention that women, as citizens, necessarily enjoyed the right of suffrage. This decision effectively ended the movement's employment of this strategy.

MINOR V. HAPPERSTETT

From the Plaintiff's Argument

. . . We hold that the adoption of the XIV. Amendment put an end to it and placed the matter beyond controversy. The history of that Amendment shows that it was designed as a limitation on the powers of the States, in many important particulars, and its language is clear and unmistakable. "No State shall make or enforce any law which shall abridge the privileges and immunities of citizens of the United States." Of course all the citizens of the United States are by this protected in the enjoyment of their privileges and immunities. Among the privileges, that of voting is the highest and greatest. To an American citizen there can be none greater or more highly to be prized; and the preservation of this privilege to the citizens of the United States respectively is, by this Amendment, placed under the immediate supervision and care of the Government of the United States, who are thus charged with its fulfillment and guaranty. . . . The State of Missouri, therefore, is estopped from longer claiming this right to limit the franchise to "males," as a State prerogative; and the Supreme Court of Missouri should have so declared, and its failure to do so is error; because, by retaining that word in the State Constitution and laws, not this plaintiff only, but large numbers of other citizens of the United States are "abridged" in the exercise of their "privileges and immunities as citizens of the United States," by being deprived of their right or privilege to vote for United States officers, as claimed by the plaintiff in her petition. . . .

From the Court's Opinion

There is no doubt that women may be citizens. . . .

If the right of suffrage is one of the necessary privileges of a citizen of the United States, then the Constitution and laws of Missouri confining it to men are in violation of the Constitution of the United States as amended, and consequently void. The direct question is, therefore, presented whether all citizens are necessarily voters. . . .

Certainly if the courts can consider any question settled, this is one. For near ninety years the people have acted upon the idea that the Constitution, when it conferred citizenship, did not necessarily confer the right of suffrage. If uniform

Virginia L. Minor

Myra Bradwell

practice long continued can settle the construction of so important an instrument as the Constitution of the United States confessedly is, most certainly it has been done here. Our province is to decide what the law is, not to declare what it should be. . . .

Being unanimously of the opinion that the Constitution of the United States does not confer the right of suffrage upon any one, and that the Constitutions and laws of the several States which commit that important trust to men alone are not necessarily void, we affirm the judgment. . . . [10]

In 1870, the state of Illinois denied an application by Myra Bradwell to practice law.

A LETTER FROM THE ILLINOIS SUPREME COURT

State of Illinois, Supreme Court, Third Grand Division, Clerk's Office, Ottawa, Oct. 6, 1869.

Mrs. Myra Bradwell—*Madam* : The court instruct me to inform you that they are compelled to deny your application for a license to practice as an attorney-at-law in the courts of this State, upon the ground that you would not be bound by the obligations necessary to be assumed where the relation of attorney and client shall exist, by reason of the disability imposed by your married condition—it being assumed that you are a married woman.

Applications of the same character have occasionally been made by persons under twenty-one years of age, and have always been denied upon the same ground that they are not bound by their contracts, being under a legal disability in that regard.

Until such disability shall be removed by legislation, the court regards itself powerless to grant your application.

Very respectfully, your obedient servant,
N. L. Freeman. [11]

Bradwell brought a suit which eventually reached the United States Supreme Court. She argued that Illinois had violated the privileges granted her in the Constitution and protected by the Fourteenth Amendment. The court ruling, which is extracted here, rejected her contention.

BRADWELL V. ILLINOIS

The Supreme Court Ruling

. . . In regard to that amendment counsel for plaintiff in this court truly says that there are certain privileges and immunities which belong to a citizen of the United States as such; otherwise it would be nonsense for the XIV. Amendment to prohibit a State from abridging them, and he proceeds to argue that admission to the bar of a State of a person who possesses the requisite learning and character is one of those which a State may not deny.

In this latter proposition we are not able to concur with counsel. We agree with him that there are privileges and immunities belonging to citizens of the United States, in that relation and character, and that it is these, and these alone, which a State is forbidden to abridge. But the right to admission to practice in the courts of a State is not one of them. The right in no sense depends on citizenship of the United States. . . .

From a Concurring Opinion

The claim that, under the XIV. Amendment of the Constitution, which declares that no State shall make or enforce any law which shall abridge the privileges and immunities of citizens of the United States, the statute law of Illinois, or the common law prevailing in that State, can no longer be set up as a barrier against the right of females to pursue any lawful employment for a livelihood (the practice of law included), assumes that it is one of the privileges and immunities of women as citizens to engage in any and every profession, occupation, or employment in civil life.

It certainly can not be affirmed, as a historical fact, that this has ever been established as one of the fundamental privileges and immunities of the sex. On the contrary, the civil law, as well as nature herself, has always recognized a wide difference in the respective spheres and destinies of man and woman. Man is, or should be, woman's protector and defender. The natural and proper timidity and delicacy which belongs to the female sex evidently unfits it for many of the occupations of civil life. The constitution of the family organization, which is founded in the divine ordinance, as well as in the nature of things, indicates the domestic sphere as that which properly belongs to the domain and functions of womanhood. The harmony, not to say identity, of interests and views which belong, or should belong, to the family institution is repugnant to the idea of a woman adopting a distinct and independent career from that of her husband. [12]

THE FEDERAL APPROACH: A CONSTITUTIONAL AMENDMENT

By 1875 the Minor and Bradwell decisions had made it clear that the existing Constitution did not give sufficient protection to women's rights and that the Fourteenth Amendment strategy would not succeed. At this point, the federal approach changed to focus upon securing a woman suffrage amendment to the Constitution. Led at first by the National Woman Suffrage Association, the struggle for a constitutional amendment was long and hard, and eventually enlisted all suffrage groups. For forty-five years, the federal amendment remained an unfulfilled objective of the women's movement.

In 1875, the National Association's plan was to have bills introduced into the House and the Senate each year by friends of woman suffrage. Moreover, each year women labored to collect signatures for petitions that were submitted to Congress to demonstrate support for the bills proposing an amendment.

AN APPEAL FOR PETITION WORKERS

To the Women of the United States:

Having celebrated our centennial birthday with a national jubilee, let us now dedicate the dawn of the second century to securing justice to women. For this purpose we ask you to circulate a petition to congress, just issued by the National Association, asking an amendment to the United States Constitution, that shall prohibit the several States from disfranchising citizens on account of sex. We have already sent this petition throughout the country for the signatures of those men and women who believe in the citizen's right to vote.

To see how large a petition each State rolls up, and to do the work as expeditiously as possible, it is necessary that some person in each county should take the matter in charge, urging upon all, thoroughness and haste. . . . The petitions should be returned before January 16, 17, 1877, when we shall hold our Eighth Annual Convention at the capital, and ask a hearing before congress. . . .

Constituting, as we do, one-half the people, bearing the burdens of one-half the national debt, equally responsible with man for the education, religion and morals of the rising generation, let us with united voice send forth a protest against the present political status of woman, that shall echo and reëcho through the land. In view of the numbers and character of those making the demand, this should be the largest petition ever yet rolled up in the old world or the new; a petition that shall settle forever the popular objection that "women do not want to vote."

ELIZABETH CADY STANTON, *President.*
MATILDA JOSLYN GAGE, *Chairman Executive Committee.*
SUSAN B. ANTHONY, *Corresponding Secretary.*
Tenafly, N. J., November 10, 1876.[13]

A FORM OF PETITION

To the Senate and House of Representatives in Congress assembled:

The undersigned citizens of the United States, residents of the State of———, earnestly pray your honorable bodies to adopt measures for so amending the constitution as to prohibit the several States from disfranchising United States citizens on account of sex.[14]

The annual January conventions of the National Association were held in Washington and helped to focus attention on the pending legislation in Congress. State delegations traveled to the capital to lobby with their congressmen. Prominent women, sometimes supported by male speakers, testified at length before the Senate and House committees that were considering the proposed amendment. In 1879, although the Senate committee rejected the amendment as usual, a minority of the committee issued a report that contained one of the first expressions of congressional sentiment favorable to woman suffrage.

FROM THE MAJORITY REPORT

First—If the petitioners' prayer be granted it will make several millions of female voters.

Second—These voters will be inexperienced in public affairs.

DECLARATION OF RIGHTS

OF THE

WOMEN OF THE UNITED STATES

BY THE

NATIONAL WOMAN SUFFRAGE ASSOCIATION.

JULY 4th, 1876.

WHILE the Nation is buoyant with patriotism, and all hearts are attuned to praise, it is with sorrow we come to strike the one discordant note, on this hundredth anniversary of our country's birth. When subjects of Kings, Emperors, and Czars, from the Old World, join in our National Jubilee, shall the women of the Republic refuse to lay their hands with benedictions on the nation's head? Surveying America's Exposition, surpassing in magnificence those of London, Paris, and Vienna, shall we not rejoice at the success of the youngest rival among the nations of the earth? May not our hearts, in unison with all, swell with pride at our great achievements as a people; our free speech, free press, free schools, free church, and the rapid progress we have made in material wealth, trade, commerce, and the inventive arts? And we do rejoice, in the success thus far, of our experiment of self-government. Our faith is firm and unwavering in the broad principles of human rights, proclaimed in 1776, not only as abstract truths, but as the corner stones of a republic. Yet, we cannot forget, even in this glad hour, that while all men of every race, and clime, and condition, have been invested with the full rights of citizenship, under our hospitable flag, all women still suffer the degradation of disfranchisement.

The history of our country the past hundred years, has been a series of assumptions and usurpations of power over woman, in direct opposition to the principles of just government, acknowledged by the United States at its foundation which are:

First. The natural rights of each individual.

Second. The exact equality of these rights.

Third. That these rights, when not delegated by the individual, are retained by the individual.

Fourth. That no person can exercise the rights of others without delegated authority.

Fifth. That the non-use of these rights does not destroy them.

And for the violation of these fundamental principles of our Government, we arraign our rulers on this 4th day of July, 1876,—and these are our

ARTICLES OF IMPEACHMENT.

BILLS OF ATTAINDER have been passed by the introduction of the word "male" into all the State constitutions, denying to woman the right of suffrage, and thereby making sex a crime—an exercise of power clearly forbidden in Article 1st, Sections 9th and 10th of the United States Constitution.

Third—They are quite generally dependent on the other sex.

Fourth—They are incapable of military duty.

Fifth—They are without the power to enforce the laws which their numerical strength may enable them to make.

Sixth—Very few of them wish to assume the irksome and responsible duties which this measure thrusts upon them.

Seventh—Such a change should only be made slowly and in obedience to a general public demand.

Eighth—There are but thirty thousand petitioners.

Ninth—It would be unjust to impose "the heavy burden of governing, which so many men seek to evade, on the great mass of women who do not wish for it, to gratify the few who do."

Tenth—Women now have the sympathy of judges and juries "to an extent which would warrant loud complaint on the part of their adversaries of the sterner sex."

Eleventh—Such a change should be made, if at all, by the States. Three-fourths of the States should not force it on the others. In any State in which "any considerable part of the women wish for the right to vote, it will be granted without the intervention of congress."

FROM THE MINORITY REPORT

. . . Our conclusion, then, is that the American people must extend the right of suffrage to woman or abandon the idea that suffrage is a birth-right. The claim that universal suffrage will work mischief in practice is simply a claim that justice will work mischief in practice. Many honest and excellent persons, while admitting the force of the arguments above stated, fear that taking part in politics will destroy those feminine traits which are the charm of woman, and are the chief comfort and delight of the household. If we thought so we should agree with the majority of the committee in with-holding assent to the prayer of the petitioners. . . . The violence, the fraud, the crime, the chicanery, which, so far as they have attended masculine struggles for political power, tend to prove, if they prove anything, the unfitness of men for the suffrage, are not the result of the act of voting, but are the expressions of coarse, criminal and evil natures, excited by the desire for victory. The admission to the polls of delicate and tender women would, without injury to them, tend to refine and elevate the politics in which they took a part. When, in former times, women were excluded from social banquets, such assemblies were scenes of ri-baldry and excess. The presence of women has substituted for them the festival of the Christian home.[15]

Until 1882, Congress sent bills proposing a suffrage amend-ment to standing committees of the House and the Senate for their consideration. In 1882, both houses set up special Select Committees on Woman Suffrage, and in that year, both committees reported favorably on the amendment. Other years witnessed other favorable reports, and in 1887

the first floor debate and vote on a woman suffrage amendment took place in the Senate.

The amendment was still far from a reality, but constant labor and persistent effort had evoked response.

THE AMERICAN APPROACH: WORK IN THE STATES

While the struggle for a federal amendment was going on in the capital, in Illinois, Iowa, Indiana, Nebraska, Michi-gan, Kansas, Idaho, South Dakota, Colorado, Oregon, and Rhode Island, hundreds of repetitious and exhausting cam-paigns were fought to win the vote within the states. In some, the fight was a regular event in the legislature. In others, suffragists had a hard time even raising the issue.

For suffrage workers, there was always a campaign go-ing on somewhere in the country. As soon as one was over, there was another to wage. And the heaviest burdens fell upon state and local suffrage groups and temperance un-ions, although local workers could count on help from both the National and the American. The American, con-vinced that the vote would be won in the states, played a leading role in coordinating and aiding state activities.

The Woman's Journal provided news, so that state workers could learn what was going on in other parts of the coun-try. Its pages were full of advice and information as it followed each state campaign in detail.

"SUGGESTIONS FOR STATE WORK."

The following excellent suggestions of the Indiana Woman Suffrage Association are equally applicable to all the States. We commend them to consideration every where.

H.B.B.

Organizing Societies.

The method of organization must be governed by circum-stances to some extent. In some localities it is best to call a public meeting, in others to invite the friends of the move-ment to a quiet conference. Both women and men should be members and co-operate, and the society should be or-ganized on as broad and liberal basis as is possible. If but half a dozen will unite, organize and go on, others will soon come. Let the membership fee be small.

Public Meetings.

Hold public meetings frequently. Occasionally have a lec-ture from some one who will draw a large crowd. But utilize

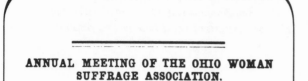

ANNUAL MEETING OF THE OHIO WOMAN SUFFRAGE ASSOCIATION.

The annual meeting of the Ohio Woman Suffrage Association will be held in the Opera House, Columbus, on the 15th and 16th of February, 1872.

As interests of great moment are to be considered, as well as the annual election of officers, it is to be hoped that there will be a full representation of all the societies in the State. Able speakers will be present, and we earnestly solicit the hearty coöperation of all who are like-minded with us.

HANNAH M. T. CUTLER, Pres.
REBECCA A. S. JANNEY, Chair. Ex. Com.
COLUMBUS, Jan. 14, 1872.

From The Woman's Journal, *Aug. 29, 1882*

your own talent, encourage your young men and women to speak, read essays and debate on the question. Hold public celebrations of the birthdays of eminent women, and in that way interest many who would not attend a pronounced suffrage meeting.

Parlor Meetings.

Persons who can not be induced to attend a public meeting will often accept an invitation to a parlor conference, social or entertainment, where woman suffrage can be made the subject of an entertaining paper or an earnest conversation. Cultured women and men who have "given the matter no thought" can be interested through a paper presenting the life and work of such women as Margaret Fuller, Abigail Adams, Lucretia Mott, etc.

Circulation of Literature.

A strong effort should be made in this direction. Every suffrage society should own a copy of the "Woman Suffrage History," of Mrs Robinson's "Massachusetts in the Woman Suffrage Movement," of T. W. Higginson's "Common Sense for Women," of John Stuart Mill's "Subjection of Women" and of Frances Power Cobbe's "Duties of Women." These will furnish ammunition for arguments and debates. Suffrage tracts can be obtained from the WOMAN'S JOURNAL Company, at fifteen cents per hundred, and should be scattered

broadcast. As the campaign develops, tracts particularly applicable to this State will be issued by the Central Committee at low rates. Newspapers advocating suffrage should be extensively read and circulated.

Press Work.

Advocate suffrage through the columns of your local papers. Send them brief communications, short, pithy extracts, and few will refuse to publish. So far as is practicable make it to the interest of papers to favor the amendment.

Petitions.

Circulate petitions for presentation to the next legislature. Have the signature of men and women of legal age written in separate columns. Keep the original copy to send to your member when the legislature convenes, and send a copy to the Central Committee.

Political Work.

Women can exert great influence by attending the primary meetings and County and District Conventions, and urging in whatever manner seems best, the selection of candidates for the legislature, who will, with or without instructions from the Convention, agree to the submission of the suffrage amendment. We urge women to interview the legislative candidates and to work and to influence the voters of their families and acquaintances to work for the election of members favorable to the amendment.[16]

The American often sent organizers into a state that was embarking on a suffrage drive. These devoted and experienced women traveled across the country and traversed many states during the 1870's and 1880's, advising local suffrage groups on strategy, setting up speakers' programs, organizing petition campaigns, and distributing enormous quantities of suffrage literature. Rarely could women find the money to compensate these tireless workers for their exhaustive physical as well as political labors. Margaret Campbell, for example, organized for the American in more than twenty states and territories. In this letter, she describes her work in Nebraska in 1882.

LETTER FROM MARGARET CAMPBELL

EDITOR JOURNAL:—I have now been traveling nearly two months in Nebraska. I have passed through sixteen counties, and have traveled quite generally over about half that number. I am constantly surprised to see the great growth the state has made during the last six years. The little places which were then just beginning to build up, and consisted of a station-house and one or two buildings more, with a few huts or dug-outs scattered over the prairies between the stations, are now quite flourishing towns. Where then I saw only bare plains, without a tree or house, I see to-day fine groves and comfortable farm-houses and in many places fruit trees growing. Great fields of rye, wheat, oats and barley are now ready for the harvest. In some places the rye is already cut. The corn suffered from the cold wet weather in the early part of the season, but is now growing finely, and bids fair to yield a bountiful crop. It can be truly said of Nebraska, "the desert blossoms as the rose." . . . If the crops are gathered in without loss this year, the farmers of this state will make up for the misfortunes of the past, and take fresh courage. It will make a great difference with the vote upon the adoption of the suffrage amendment next fall. If there is a good crop everybody will feel glad, and men will be more likely to vote right.

I have traveled by rail where it was possible, but in order to reach the people one must go miles away from railroads. Up to the present time, I have traveled two hundred and eighty-five miles by team across the country, mostly by private conveyance. In many places, women drive me from one precinct to another, sometimes in single buggy, and sometimes with a span of fine horses. In some cases men took their teams from the field and went willingly to take me on to my next appointment, refusing any pay for their services. When I offered pay, they said, "Come again; come again." In almost all the places visited, I have found the greatest liberality in entertainment. The railroad companies have given half-fare permits when they have been asked to do so. The meetings have been well attended, except in two places where there was sufficient reason for failure. The ministers of all denominations come to our help; not every one, but a majority of them. The editors are many of them advocating the adoption of the amendment; but of late, some who had been in favor have taken the wrong side, and will oppose the measure with what strength they have. There are men in both political parties who favor the amendment, and some who oppose it. It is not a party question.

From what I have seen and heard in the state, I feel confident the amendment can be carried. If every person who believes in equality of rights would contribute one dollar to help the hard workers in this state, there would be no lack of means, which is now one great trouble here. The women are trying to raise the means to publish the *Western Women's Journal* every week from the first of August till the election. It is to be hoped that they will find help in this time of need.

MARGARET W. CAMPBELL.[17]
Hastings, Neb., July 11, 1882.

Lucy Stone and Henry B. Blackwell were at the heart of the American's work. They edited the Journal, *worried about Association finances, and painstakingly held on to the long and fragile ties that reached out from their center in Boston to the rest of the country. Here, Henry Blackwell writes from Michigan about the coming election in which voters will decide on a woman suffrage amendment to the state constitution.*

A LETTER FROM BLACKWELL

Election day in Michigan is at hand; the most important day, in its possibilities, that has dawned upon America since the Declaration of Independence. The day approaches when the men of Michigan, by their votes, will establish or defeat Impartial Suffrage and Equal Rights for women. . . .

In one way the probability of success could be greatly increased. Let the friends of Suffrage everywhere procure affirmative tickets, (Woman Suffrage—Yes), and be present at every poll in Michigan from sunrise to sunset. Offer the Woman Suffrage ticket to all comers Above all, let every woman who values liberty and justice, be there with the tickets, and let her respectfully ask each voter to cast his ballot for the enfranchisement of her sex.

Remember that the Woman Suffrage Amendment is submitted separately. It stands or falls alone. Even if the new Constitution is defeated, a majority given for the Woman Suffrage Amendment will incorporate it in the old Constitution. Therefore ask even the opponents of the new Constitution, while they vote against that, to vote nevertheless for the Woman Suffrage Amendment.

Remember, also, that we do not need a majority of all the voters of Michigan to carry the Suffrage Amendment, but only a majority of the votes actually cast upon this special question. For instance, if only 1000 men vote for Woman Suffrage, it will carry, provided only 999 vote against it. Thus every indifferent voter will help us. "He who is not against us is for us." Therefore, ladies, ask every voter if he will not vote for us, at least not to vote against us.

Let no woman feel that it is unwomanly to go near the polls and offer the tickets. You are not asking for yourselves, but for all women and for a great principle. You represent Womanhood, now crippled, dwarfed, degraded by political disfranchisement. The ballot in the hands of Woman means equal opportunities, equitable laws, public respect, a fair day's wages for a fair day's work. It means moral and political reform, and a purer, nobler Civilization. If the women of

Michigan could only realize the value of Woman Suffrage to man, to woman and to society, we should not need to remind them to go to the polls next election day; they could not and would not stay away. H. B. B.[18]

Margaret Campbell and her husband were campaigning in Colorado in 1874 when Lucy Stone wrote this letter to her. It illustrates the hardships experienced both by the workers in the states and by those who labored to support their activities.

LUCY STONE TO MARGARET CAMPBELL

I think of you with the five-cent loaf and ten cents' worth of meat a day for you two brave people, and the tears are in my eyes. But it is by just such sacrifice that the world will be saved. . . .

I wish I could rest. I am so tired to-day, body and soul, it seems as though I should never feel fresh again. I have been trying to get advertisements for the *Woman's Journal* to eke out its expenses. Yesterday I walked miles; to picture stores, crockery stores, to "special sales," going up flight after flight of stairs only to find the men out, or not ready to advertise. And for all my day's toil I did not get a cent; and when I came home at night, it was to find the house cold, the fire nearly out in the furnace, and none on the hearth; and it seemed as if the tiredness of a whole life came into my essence. I don't often complain, or feel like complaining, but I do wish there was some way of carrying on the *Woman's Journal* without such a hard, constant tug. If only the housekeeping would go on without so much looking after![19]

LIMITED SUFFRAGE

The repeated failure of women's efforts to gain the vote by state constitutional amendment or by popular referendums led them to try another tactic. By narrowing their objective from the right to vote in all kinds of elections to the right to vote only in some kinds of elections, women sought changes that state legislatures could accomplish simply by revising the election laws.

In the 1880's, close tries were made in New England, New York, Indiana, Illinois, Michigan, Iowa, and Kansas for municipal suffrage—the right to vote in city, village, or town elections in the state. In 1894 in Iowa and in 1887 in Kansas, women got the right to vote in local elections, with help from both the American and the National associations. The Woman's Christian Temperance Union provided a large part of the force behind the drive for municipal suffrage, because the vote was closely tied to

temperance—in many states local elections could determine whether or not the area would be wet or dry.

Women sought other kinds of limited suffrage, ranging from the right to vote for electors in Presidential elections to school suffrage, by which they gained the vote in the election of school officials and in deciding on school issues. They were most successful in gaining school suffrage, and by 1890 could vote in school elections in nineteen states. It appeared that men would allow women to participate in public affairs only when, as in the case of schools, it seemed related to their role as mothers.

On January 27, 1881, at a public hearing of the Massachusetts legislature's Joint Special Committee on Woman Suffrage, Henry Blackwell presented the American's arguments for limited suffrage.

BLACKWELL'S SPEECH ON LIMITED SUFFRAGE

. . . We ask, first of all, for Presidential Suffrage for women, because it is the most conspicuous and important form of Suffrage, is common to all the States, and is regulated by the provisions of the Federal Constitution, which is the supreme law of the land, irrespective of State laws or constitutions. Article 2, Section 2, gives entire control of this matter to the State Legislatures: "Each State shall appoint in such manner as the Legislature thereof may direct a number of electors equal to the whole number of Senators and Representatives to which the State may be entitled in the Congress." This power is unqualified and unlimited. In some States, even up to 1860, the Legislature chose the Presidential electors in joint session. You have the legal right to choose them, or to delegate your power to women only, or to men only as at present. The objection to Woman Suffrage most commonly urged is that women do not want to vote. Give us Presidential Suffrage and we will abide the issue. Every woman in this State, last fall, had a preference for Garfield, or for Hancock, or for Weaver, or for Dow. Give them an opportunity of expressing it in 1884.

Next we ask for full Municipal Suffrage for women because that too is in your power to grant. Before you ask the people to change the State constitution it seems reasonable that you should use the powers you already possess in the same direction. Until a recent period the qualifications for voting in town meetings and municipal affairs were easier and more liberal than those for State officers. A simple change in our election laws is all we need to enable women to vote on all domestic questions such as schools, police, liquor-selling, roads, charities and local taxation. In cities they might vote for mayor and aldermen and council and school committee; in towns for selectmen and all other town officers. This covers a large and most important field of political interest. One branch of it—School Suffrage—has been extended to women, but in its present isolated and restricted form it fails to bring out a large vote. This is inevitable. It is the same with men also in special elections. The best possible way to amend the School Suffrage law so as to enlist a general interest among women is to extend it, by giving them full Municipal Suffrage in accordance with the advice of Governor Talbot. Your legal right to do so has been conceded by the enactment of School Suffrage. The women of England already have and exercise Municipal Suffrage. To men who are doubtful of the wisdom of Woman Suffrage, one great argument for this step will be that it is tentative and not irrevocable. If it works badly a Legislature elected by men alone can repeal it. If it works well the Constitution can afterwards be amended. It can be carried by a majority of both houses. . . . [20]

OTHER ACTIVITIES

Although most of the resources of the women's movement were devoted to suffrage during the last three decades of the century, women continued to work for other changes. In addition to temperance legislation, in groups and individually they sought more and better education for women, revision of property and child custody laws, and equity in job opportunities and pay. And gradually, they were successful in many of these efforts: by the beginning of the twentieth century, married women could own and control their own property in three quarters of the states; in nine states and the District of Columbia they had won equal guardianship rights over their children.

They were kept regularly informed about other women's activities by women's publications. With the death of The Revolution, The Woman's Journal *became the major source for news about women that could not be found anywhere else. The* Journal *followed women's struggle for change on every front, and reported their successes and failures in detail. It reported what women in other countries were doing as well. From its pages, readers derived a sense of connection with other women, in the United States and the rest of the world.*

Moreover, participation in movement activities was itself a cause of change. In temperance and suffrage work, women discovered skills and abilities in themselves and in other women that they had not recognized before. Rank-and-file workers in women's causes proved women's fitness for activities traditionally reserved to men and their ability to act in man's sphere.

The women's movement also contributed toward a changing popular image of women. Anthony, Stanton, and Stone, for example, were well-known national figures by the end of the century. Frances Willard, who combined a religious nature with a strong political bent, was a popular

heroine. Their examples made it very clear that women were not necessarily ignorant, dependent, passive, or weak.

As the news article below illustrates, movement leaders had slowly won a degree of respect and admiration that contrasted strongly with the abuse and ridicule once heaped upon them. In 1879, Susan B. Anthony lectured in Indiana and received this accolade.

ON SUSAN B. ANTHONY

Miss Anthony's lecture was full of fine passages and strong appeals, and replete with well-stated facts in support of her arguments. She has wonderful command of language, and her speech at times flows with such rapidity that no reporter could do her justice or catch a tithe of the brilliance of her sayings. Moreover, there are not one half of our public men who are nearly so well posted on the political affairs of our country as she, or who, knowing them, could frame them so solidly in argument. If the women of the nation were half so high-minded or even half so earnest, their title to the franchise might soon be granted.[21]

The common ideas about what women could do and what they should do was changing. One of Elizabeth Cady Stanton's most popular lectures, delivered to large audiences

Susan B. Anthony

Elizabeth Cady Stanton and her daughter, Harriot. from a daguerreotype 1856.

throughout the country during the 1870's, was entitled "Our Young Girls." On the surface, it did not seem to be a political speech, but its message was the message of the women's movement.

"OUR YOUNG GIRLS"

They are the music, the flowers, the sunshine of our social life. How beautiful they make our homes, churches, schools and festive scenes. . . . Who can see a bevy of young girls tripping home from school without pausing to watch their graceful motions, pretty faces. . . . See how they romp, play with hoops and balls, with sled and skates, wash their brothers faces in the snow, and beat them in a race on yonder pond. These boys & girls are one to-day in school, at play, at home, never dreaming that one sex was foreordained to clutch the stars, the other but to kiss the dust. But watch awhile and you will see these dashing, noisy, happy, healthy girls grow calm, pale, sad. . . . And why? They have awakened to the fact that they belong to a subject, degraded, ostracised class: that to fulfill their man appointed sphere, they can have no individual character, no life purpose, personal freedom, aim or ambition. They are simply to revolve around some man. . . . The world will talk to you of the duties of wives & mothers & housekeepers, but all these incidental relations should ever be subordinated to the greater fact of womanhood. You may never be wives, or mothers, or housekeepers, but you will be women, therefore labor for the grander, more universal fact of your existence.[22]

CHAPTER SEVEN

ASSOCIATIONISM AND REFORM

1890-1920

The development of the Woman's Christian Temperance Unions and the success of the Grange among rural women during the last quarter of the nineteenth century heralded an era in which American women joined together to form a multitude of clubs, leagues, societies, and associations. Between 1890 and 1920, this "associating" tendency reached fulfillment as millions of women organized into thousands of separate groups.

Clubs sprang up in small towns and cities in all the states. One of the earliest was the Sorosis Club, formed in New York in 1868 by a group of women, mainly writers and journalists, to promote "agreeable and useful relations among women of literary, artistic, and scientific tastes."[1] In other large cities, professional and well-educated women formed groups that soon became involved in civic and educational issues.

While many women's groups were related to church activities, like the prayer circles and the Dorcas societies that flourished at this time, generally the club movement was nonreligious and nonsectarian. The vast majority of the groups were simply local literary and social clubs established by the wives of the solid citizens of the nation's cities and towns. Unlike religious and farm groups, they were completely independent of male organizations.

There were several national women's organizations before 1890, most notably the suffrage organizations, the National Woman's Christian Temperance Union, and the Association of Collegiate Alumnae, formed in 1882. After 1890, associationism led to many new nationwide groups, which attracted large memberships. The Daughters of the American Revolution was founded in 1891, the National Council of Jewish Women in 1896, the National Association of Colored Women in 1896, the National Congress of Mothers in 1897, and the Young Women's Christian Association in 1906, and others continued to appear.

The associationism behind the proliferation and expansion of women's organizations reflected the changing economic and social character of the country—and of the women themselves. Industrialization, which had been progressing slowly from the early part of the century, speeded up considerably after the Civil War with the unprecedented immigration from Europe and Asia and transformed America. By 1900 the United States was unquestionably an industrial society, with the beginnings of an overseas empire and its expanding wealth concentrated in the hands of a relatively small group of men. Although a spiderweb of railroad and telegraph lines tied the sprawling nation together, the population was a complex mixture of religions, races, and cultural backgrounds. The hardships of the new industrialism encouraged a belligerent labor movement, and severe agricultural depression begat political radicalism. More than one-third of the population lived in cities, to which they had come, bewildered and expectant, from either faraway lands or the farms and small towns of old rural America.

For most people, the world in which they found themselves was different from the one they had grown up expecting. The way they lived and worked was often unrelated to the experiences of their parents and grandparents. This was especially true of women, and most particularly of women living in the cities. For them, changes that had begun after the Civil War continued to occur with dazzling rapidity, so that by 1900, their condition was radically different from what it had been at the time of Seneca Falls, in 1848.

Many of the legal and educational inequalities that had handicapped women before the Civil War were fading away, and the suffocating hold of Victorian mores and manners had begun to loosen. The pale and passive lady was being replaced by a more vigorous and outspoken woman. For the educated woman—and her numbers were growing—the professions were slowly opening and job opportunities were increasing, if she had a large supply of determination and stamina and was unmarried.

For married women, alternatives also increased as birth control and divorce became more common. By 1900, the national fertility rate, which had been declining since 1810 among the middle and upper classes, had been almost halved. The divorce rate increased more than two and one half times between 1890 and 1920. Together, these changes made marriage less rigid a status and less burdensome an occupation. Other factors also lightened the labors of housewifery and motherhood; immigrant labor provided cheap household servants, machines and food processing decreased domestic chores, and a small family meant relatively smaller responsibilities. Moreover, urban life offered women and men a kind of freedom that had not existed in closed rural society.

Even the poor woman who labored sixty hours a week for a pittance benefited from more social freedom than she had ever had before. But the major beneficiaries of the leisure and freedom of industrialism and urbanism were the wives of the prospering middle class. These women, by the millions, found themselves with unused energies. Educated, curious about the world around them, but without a comfortable place in it, what were they to do? Associationism offered them an answer.

NEW ORGANIZATIONS

Unlike the suffrage organizations or the Woman's Christian Temperance Unions, most of the new clubs and societies, local and national, were content, at first, with offering members companionship and an introduction to literature and other cultural activities. Only on occasion, before 1890, did they muddy their hands in public affairs, and this occurred in the larger cities. In Boston, the New England Women's Club agitated to get females on the school board; in Chicago, the Women's Club campaigned for police matrons for women prisoners. Some societies, such as the Association for the Advancement of Women, dedicated themselves to the improvement of women's lives, but it, like most of the early clubs and societies, was not involved in political activities.

As a result, the new clubs were less controversial, less intimidating, and more popular than the suffrage groups. Although some diehards insisted that women still belonged at home, by and large there was support rather than opposition for the women who decided to join. The new organizations were generally calm and respectable, as the following early press comment reveals. Here the reporter makes a favorable contrast between an annual meeting of the Association for the Advancement of Women and the usual suffrage conventions.

FROM THE SYRACUSE *DAILY JOURNAL*

Heretofore many of the great assemblages of women in this country have had three distinct characteristics: acidity, vituperation and "give-me-that-ballot or die!" But it is not so in this Woman's Congress; the real spirit of the gathering . . . is expressed in the words: "Whatsoever ye would that others should do unto you, do ye unto them." No not force, but love is the motive power of these wives and mothers.[2]

The Association for the Advancement of Women was one of the national organizations formed after the Civil War.

It began when Sorosis Club members in New York sponsored a call for a national meeting.

A CALL FOR A CONGRESS OF WOMEN

To meet a pressing demand for interchange of thought and harmony of action among women interested in the advancement of their own sex, we issue this Call for a Congress of Women, to be held in the City of New York.

At this Conference we hope to found an Association for the Advancement of Women, at the annual gatherings of which shall be presented the best ideas and the most advantageous methods of our foremost thinkers and writers. Therefore, we solicit the presence or responsive work of all accordant associations of women—of Women Preachers, Teachers, Professors, Physicians, Artists, Lawyers, trading Capitalists, Editors, Authors, and practical Philanthropists, those who by their example inspire others not only to covet the best gifts, but to labor earnestly for them. . . .

Those whose names are appended to this Call will constitute the first membership. Application for membership may be made to any signer of this Call. A preliminary meeting of signers only will be held at 7.30 P.M. on Tuesday, Oct 14, at No. 332 West Twenty-Third Street, for organization. The subsequent sessions will be held at the Hall of the Union League, Madison Avenue and Twenty-Sixth Street, on the three following days, at 10:30 A.M. and 7.30 P.M.

Sarah H. Adams, Boston, Mass.

A. A. Allen, Alfred University, Alfred, N.Y.

Marie Andrief, New York City.[3]

At its first meeting in 1873, the Association agreed to seek "practical methods for securing to women higher intellectual, moral and physical conditions and thereby to improve all domestic and social relations."[4] In practice, the Association, with its annual Woman's Congress, was like the thousands of small clubs throughout the country. It served as a forum for the exchange of ideas among women and offered them an opportunity for self-improvement and an outlet for associationism.

REPORT OF A SUPPLEMENTAL WOMAN'S CONGRESS IN ST. PAUL

Our meeting took place in one of the smaller public halls of the city. The president and members of the New Century Club, and many ladies from St. Paul were there to greet us. At 10:00 A.M., Mrs. Julia Ward Howe called the meeting to order, and after a few timely words, telling of the character and aims of the Association, introduced Mrs. Mitchell, from

Denver, Col., who read a scholarly paper on "Art." Mrs. Adams, from Dubuque, Ia., spoke for about five minutes on the "Influence of Woman in Art." Mrs. Howe then read her paper on "Aliens in America." Mrs. Colby, from Nebraska, read a critique of Ibsen's "Doll's House." . . .

In the afternoon meeting, Mrs. Wolcott, from Dedham, Mass., read her paper "On the Necessity of Keeping Close to Nature in Education." Miss Octavia W. Bates, from Detroit, Michigan, read her paper on "Women in Colleges." Mrs. Maude Howe Elliott, from Massachusetts, read the report of the vice-president from New York. Dr. E. V. Mark, from Baltimore, Md., read a paper on "La Grippe," and Miss Ripley read a paper on "The Wise Economy of Time and Strength as a Part of Education." After some informal discussion on the papers, by several ladies from St. Paul and Minneapolis, the supplementary Congress closed its sessions....[5]

WOMEN'S CLUBS AND REFORM

Several efforts were made to organize the thousands of clubs scattered throughout the states by the end of the century. Frances Willard and Susan B. Anthony, alert to the political potential within the clubs, were instrumental in forming the National Council of Women in 1888. Its aim was to organize local groups into national societies and then unite the national societies to work for specific goals. In 1895, the National Council represented about 700,000 members of national organizations such as the National-American Woman Suffrage Association, the National Woman's Christian Temperance Union, the Women's National Press Association, and the National Free Baptist Women's Missionary Society.

Even more successful and longer-lived was the General Federation of Women's Clubs formed in 1890. Its original goal was less ambitious than the National Council's since it proposed merely to organize the profusion of women's clubs into local, state, and national groups in order to "compare methods of work and become mutually helpful."[6] The General Federation of Women's Clubs had a ready-made constituency, and since existing clubs lost none of their autonomy or character in affiliating in state and national federations, they were quick to join; in this way an immense number of groups throughout the country were linked together. By 1910, almost a million women were members of the General Federation of Women's Clubs, and by 1916, nine thousand clubs and two million women belonged to the organization.

After 1900, associationism merged with another major tendency of the time—an outburst of reform activity. This reform spirit was a response to many problems and tensions—to the growing concentration of corporate power

GENERAL FEDERATION BULLETIN

MRS. FELIX T. McWHIRTER
President Indiana State Federation of Women's Clubs

NATIONAL·OFFICIAL·ORGAN OF THE GENERAL · FEDERATION OF WOMEN'S·CLUBS

Vol. X. TROY, N. Y., APRIL, 1912 No. 1

and wealth, to corruption in municipal and state governments, to dreadful poverty in the cities, to the suffering of farmers, to appalling labor conditions and unrest, to widespread prostitution, and to rapidly changing life styles. Progressivism, as this reform movement is called, sought specific legislative and constitutional changes to achieve its major objectives: the preservation of economic individualism, the protection and advancement of political democracy, and humanitarian reform. The list of specific Progressive reforms was long; it included antitrust legislation, woman- and child-labor laws, settlement house programs, prohibition, free public libraries, pure food and drug legislation, clean streets, the use of the initiative and referendum, direct election of senators, and woman suffrage.

The Progressive impulse, with few exceptions, was reforming, conservative, and moderate. Progressives aimed to give the country a good scrubbing behind the ears. They did not seek radical revision of economic, political, or so-

cial institutions. Indeed, Progressives often rose to the defense of these basic institutions which, in their eyes, were being altered by industrialism. As such, Progressivism appealed to middle-class Americans, who found its goals, its spirit of service to the community, and its cleansing, missionary character attractive and exciting as well as comfortable.

Participation in the Progressive movement led many women and men into new activities. Investigative journalism expressed the outrage of writers at unfair business practices, slum life, and degrading labor conditions, and their books and articles stirred readers to work for reform. Many well-educated and relatively prosperous young women were attracted to settlement house work in the slums, where they were introduced to the disturbing realities of life. Dynamic and clever leaders, such as Jane Addams and Lillian Wald, connected settlement house work with the main currents of political reform activity.

Most of the women who worked in the Progressive cause did so through existing women's organizations which, like the General Federation of Women's Clubs, expanded their activities to include reform work. Some new organizations were formed precisely for the purpose of enabling women to carry on Progressive reform activities, organizations such as the National Federation of Settlements, the National Women's Trade Union League, and the National Consumers' League.

Thus, through clubs and organizations, women were enrolled in the great reform movement of the time. They formed the bulk of the workers who did the hard and unglamorous tasks that lay behind municipal and state reform campaigns. Nationally, women were the major force behind reforms such as the Pure Food and Drug Act (passed in 1906) and the Child Labor Act (1916).

THE GENERAL FEDERATION OF WOMEN'S CLUBS

At its 1896 convention, the General Federation of Women's Clubs proclaimed that "bodies of trained housekeepers shall constitute those guardians of the civic housekeeping of their respective communities,"[7] officially endorsing the expansion of club activities beyond literary and educational subjects. And, as the GFWC became increasingly involved with Progressive reforms, it repeatedly stressed that the role of women, as the protectors of home and family, gave them ample justification for such activities.

Some of the reforms supported by the GFWC were directly connected with the home and seemed, beyond question, to be the concern of women, like pure food and drug legislation and weights and measures laws. But soon,

the interests of the Federation expanded far beyond issues related to domesticity. Between 1890 and 1910, the General Federation of Women's Clubs conventions passed resolutions authorizing state and local clubs to study and work for improvements in public education, municipal government reforms, child labor laws, civil service reform, prison reform, highway safety, conservation, prohibition, and protective labor legislation for working women. At its 1914 convention, the Federation adopted resolutions that dealt with such diverse subjects as support of the merit system, calls for dress reform, attacks on prostitution, and for the first time the endorsement of woman suffrage.

1914 GFWC RESOLUTIONS

. . . Whereas, The question of the political equality of men and women is to-day a vital problem under discussion throughout the civilized world; therefore,

Resolved, That the General Federation of Women's Clubs gives the cause of political equality for men and women its moral support by recording its earnest belief in the principles of political equality, regardless of sex. . . .

Resolved, That the General Federation recommends to the various State Federations and local clubs that they adopt active measures toward securing increased appropriations for their state and city boards of health.

Resolved, That this Convention recommends State Federations to urge their respective universities to consider the establishment of university extension work for the prevention of disease.

Resolved, That the General Federation co-operate with the Children's Bureau in the promotion of health education by advocating the employment of nurses for rural communities; and be it further

Resolved, That the Children's Bureau be requested to issue a leaflet containing simplified information for the use of mothers in the instruction of children in sex-hygiene.

Resolved, That the General Federation approves legislation in the various states and municipalities which requires the reporting of venereal diseases to boards of health, as are other infectious and contagious diseases.

Resolved, That the General Federation approves the abatement and injunction law which makes it possible, without complicated process of law, to rid a city of houses of ill-fame, such as is successfully in operation in Iowa and ten other states.

Resolved, That this Convention, in full recognition of the rights and privileges of the individual, places itself on record as heartily in favor of the movement for simple, becoming and modest designs in women's clothes.

Resolved, That the General Federation of Women's Clubs endorses the movement of social organization as promoted by the federal and state departments of agriculture, and recommends to each State Federation the encouragement and the co-operation with said federal and state departments in promoting rural social organization bearing chiefly on woman's work.

Resolved, That the State Chairmen of the Civics Committees be asked to initiate in their states efforts to secure legislation for opening the schools and other public buildings as social centers for public discussion.

Whereas, Owing to the expiration of the Burton Franchise, further spoliation threatens Niagara Falls, from which already one-third power has been diverted; therefore, be it

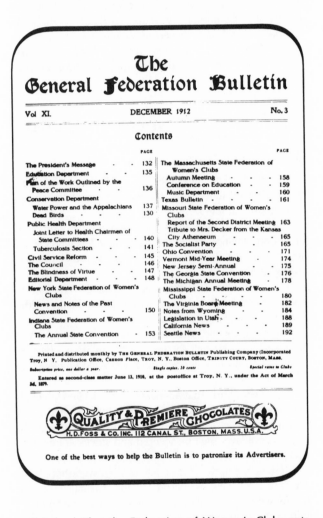

The
General Federation Bulletin

Vol XI.   DECEMBER 1912   No. 3

Contents

	PAGE		PAGE
The President's Message	132	The Massachusetts State Federation of	
Education Department	135	Women's Clubs	
Plan of the Work Outlined by the		Autumn Meeting	158
Peace Committee	136	Conference on Education	159
Conservation Department		Music Department	160
Water Power and the Appalachians	137	Texas Bulletin	161
Dead Birds	130	Missouri State Federation of Women's	
Public Health Department		Clubs	
Joint Letter to Health Chairmen of		Report of the Second District Meeting	163
State Committees	140	Tribute to Mrs. Decker from the Kansas	
Tuberculosis Section	141	City Athenaeum	165
Civil Service Reform	145	The Socialist Party	165
The Council	146	Ohio Convention	171
The Blindness of Virtue	147	Vermont Mid-Year Meeting	174
Editorial Department	148	New Jersey Semi-Annual	175
New York State Federation of Women's		The Georgia State Convention	176
Clubs		The Michigan Annual Meeting	178
News and Notes of the Past		Mississippi State Federation of Women's	
Convention	150	Clubs	180
Indiana State Federation of Women's		The Virginia Board Meeting	182
Clubs		Notes from Wyoming	184
The Annual State Convention	153	Legislation in Utah	188
		California News	189
		Seattle News	192

Printed and distributed monthly by THE GENERAL FEDERATION BULLETIN Publishing Company (Incorporated) Troy, N Y. Publication Office, Cannon Place, TROY, N. Y., Boston Office, TRINITY COURT, BOSTON, MASS.

Subscription price, one dollar a year.   Single copies, 10 cents   Special rates to Clubs

Entered as second-class matter June 13, 1910, at the postoffice at Troy, N. Y., under the Act of March 14, 1879.

QUALITY & PREMIERE CHOCOLATES
H. D. FOSS & CO. INC. 112 CANAL ST., BOSTON, MASS. U.S.A.

One of the best ways to help the Bulletin is to patronize its Advertisers.

Resolved, That the Federation of Women's Clubs puts itself on record as urging legislation which will prevent any greater diversion of power from Niagara, and urges each State Federation to watch federal legislation now pending on this subject.

Resolved, That we recommend to the local clubs support of the campaign for the reduction of fire waste, with especial reference to the fire hazard of the home and the protection of women and children in factories and places of assemblage, and that we advocate fire-exit drills.

Whereas, The liquor traffic is responsible for three-quarters of the crime, vice, misery in this country; be it

Resolved, That the women of the General Federation

place themselves on record as opposed to the liquor traffic and in favor of such federal or states laws as will tend to eradicate this evil.

Resolved, That a sub-committee be created, under the Department of Education, for the improvement of rural schools. . . . [8]

Federation activities went far beyond convention resolutions. On all levels, nationally and in state and local communities, GFWC members were active reformers, urged on by their leaders and by the GFWC's monthly Bulletin *(later called the* Magazine*). This open letter from the Federation's board of directors was a clear call to action in 1903.*

OPEN LETTER
FROM THE BOARD OF DIRECTORS

So long as children six years of age are employed in mills and factories in any part of the United States, and there is the crying need for uniform laws regarding child labor; so long as six hundred million dollars is wasted every year in housekeeping in America for want of knowledge of household economics; so long as women who live in mountains or on prairies are hungry for books and art; so long as there is need of the creation of general sentiment for national irrigation bills that homes for women and children may be created and preserved; so long as the most vital work of social betterment can only bring results by cooperation—can it be that any club can say it has no responsibility in the larger work, that it is enough that it dust its own room? Or if it take a hand in the world outside its own door, can it wisely say it proposes to sweep in any direction it desires?[9]

Certain issues and reforms were singled out for concentrated effort, and prominent among them were matters concerning working women and children. The Magazine *educated club members about the conditions under which children and women labored in agriculture and industry in the United States, and it explained and urged reforms to change them. Articles, like this one by Agnes Peterson, superintendent of the Minnesota Department of Labor's Bureau of Women and Children, were common fare for GFWC readers.*

"WOMEN INSPECTORS
FOR WOMEN AT WORK"

We have employed in the different industries of the United States a wage earning army of women, numbering about 8,000,000. Each year will add to this number and when we consider that about 50 per cent. of these women are under the age of twenty-one years, we realize the need of doing all we can to protect and help them.

The problem of woman's work does not lie in the fact that it is new, for she has always worked, but that her old tasks are being performed in a new place, by a new method. . . . this change and the demand for woman labor in the industrial world, has not been because it was best for her, or because she wished it, but because woman's labor is cheap labor, and that industry might profit in dollars and cents. . . .

Only a few have fitted themselves for their work by special training. As yet women in industry are not able to look out for their own interests as men do. Organization will make this possible, but today the larger majority are young, are inexperienced, are poorly paid, and are too busy, too weary and too ignorant to think of much else than be on the alert for something to live on, so are not thoughtful students of the conservation of health and industrial conditions. They are slow to organize and are not watchful in behalf of their own interests.

Leisure is possible to a large number of women because these other women work in great numbers in factory, store and other establishments. It is therefore the duty of women with more leisure and influence to aid them. Public opinion can do anything—it is therefore one's duty to mold public opinion to the needs which surround them, our sisters. They are especially in need of two things; the general introduction of vocational training in our schools so that they may enter the industrial world as skilled workers and good laws regulating their employment in this same industrial world—laws as to hours, sanitation, pay and inspection by women. . . .

It is your duty to force public opinion to a realization of the fact that the lack of uniformity of labor laws is a great handicap in the improvement of conditions. It is your duty to explain that uniform laws will only be made possible by federal legislation.

Most of the States have recognized the need of factory inspection. . . .

Twenty-two States have recognized the need of women in this work and have placed women on their staff as inspectors. . . . In none of these States, however, are there enough

women inspectors to do all there is to do. I, therefore, . . . make the recommendation that each State Federation take the initiative and see to it that for every 25,000 women employed in the industries of their respective State at least one woman inspector be provided. . . . [10]

Following up a series of resolutions concerning working women and children adopted in convention in 1898, the Federation's Committee on Industrial Problems Affecting Women and Children issued two circular letters to clubs urging them to organize themselves in order to investigate their states' labor laws and to work for industrial progress.

"FIRST CIRCULAR LETTER"

My Dear Madam Secretary:

At the Biennial meeting of the General Federation of clubs, held in Denver, June, 1898, the following resolutions were unanimously adopted:

"Believing that right and justice demand that women of larger opportunities should stand for the toilers who cannot help themselves, we therefore beg leave to present the following resolutions:

"Resolved, First, That the United States Government be asked to establish a system of postal savings banks for the benefit of small wage earners.

"Resolved, Second, That no child under fourteen years of age be employed in mill, factory, workshop, store, office, or laundry, and no boy under sixteen years old employed in mines.

"Resolved, Third, That adequate school facilities, including manual training, should be provided in the United States for every child up to the age of fourteen years, and also that good school laws shall be secured and strictly enforced in every community.

"Resolved, Fourth, That in mill, factory, workshop, laundry, and mercantile establishment, the maximum working day for women and children shall not exceed eight hours, or forty-eight hours per week.

"Resolved, Fifth, That so far as possible, uniform labor legislation shall be secured throughout the different States.

"Resolved, Sixth, That each club in this Federation shall appoint a standing committee whose special duty it shall be to inquire into the labor conditions of women and children in that particular locality. That each State Federation shall appoint a similar committee to investigate its State labor laws, and those relating to sanitation and protection for women and children. That it also shall be the duties of these committees to influence and secure enforcement of labor ordinances and State laws of this character. That these committees at specified times shall inform their organizations of all conferences and conventions in the interest of social and industrial progress, also that the General Federation shall appoint a committee of five members, whose duty it shall be to collect the reports of the above mentioned work and present the results at the next biennial." . . .

Recognizing this necessity, and in compliance with the resolutions of the General Federation, the undersigned [members of the committee of five] urge that your club at once appoint a committee of those who are interested in the subject, and that their names and addresses be forwarded to the Chairman of the General Committee with such suggestions and information as may apply to your own particular locality.

Upon receipt of these names and addresses a second circular will be sent to all local committees containing such advice and help as the General Committee can offer, and arranging as nearly as may be a uniform course of investigation and study.

Meanwhile the local committees are advised to discuss the resolutions adopted by the Federation, and determine whether their application would make any change in their own community.[11]

"SECOND CIRCULAR LETTER"

. . . The work of the Consumers' League is recommended for study and emulation. The League has been successful in New York and Boston, and branches have been established in Philadelphia and Chicago. Information concerning it may be obtained from Mrs. Florence Kelley, National Secretary.

To effectually study social questions, the importance of changing your point of view cannot be too strongly urged. Therefore your committees are advised to,

(*a*) Subscribe for a labor or reform paper, to become familiar with the wants and desires of those who are struggling for better conditions.

(*b*) Attend meetings of working people, especially during times of strikes, and visit as students conventions and conferences held in the interest of any reform.

(*c*) Induce the public Library Boards to purchase books and periodicals dealing with industrial and economic subjects.

In conclusion, we remind the committees that this subject is now engaging the attention of the best, keenest and brightest minds. The vitality and life of all argument depend upon a knowledge of it. It provokes discussion and awakens interest as no other subject can. To be unacquainted with it is to be behind the times; to be familiar with it is to have the key to the current world-wide movements now impending.

PASSIE FENTON OTTLEY.
ANGIE H. HUME.
MARIE YOUNG.
CORINNE S. BROWN, Chairman.[12]

Through state federations and in small-town clubs, women responded to the Federation's calls for action, as the following reports show.

GFWC LEGISLATIVE REPORTS

Pennsylvania— . . . It may be noted, with satisfaction to child labor reform workers, . . . that the bill commented upon at length in the May *Magazine,* thanks to a most determined Governor, is now a law. . . . All workers between fourteen and sixteen who are restricted to a nine-hour day, must attend continuation schools for eight hours per week, which time must be deducted from their fifty-one-hour week. No boy under twenty-one may engage in night messenger service; and the minimum age for street trades is twelve years. Children on the stage are included in the no night work provisions.

Arkansas—Arkansas reports the passage of a Minimum Wage Law, providing that experienced women workers shall receive a compensation of not less than $1.25, apprentices not less than $1.00, for a day of nine hours; and appropriation to take advantage of Smith-Lever Federal Fund for domestic science and agricultural extension work.

Nevada—Miss Bird Wilson, chairman of Legislative Committee, thinks the women of Nevada didn't secure results commensurate with their efforts, but reports four good measures passed:

1. Mothers' Pensions.

2. Change in inheritance laws, by which the mother now receives one-half of estate of a deceased child dying unmarried, whereas formerly the father received it all. The mother now has one-half in her own name and right.

3. A bill providing for establishment of kindergartens by School Trustees in all communities where there are twenty-five children of kindergarten age, on petition of parents.

4. Teachers' Pensions.

Tennessee—The Legislature of Tennessee in recess; but during its first half, passed the two measures most strongly advocated by club women, viz.: providing a reformatory for girls, and making women eligible to serve on boards of education and charities.

Maine—Mrs. George F. French, Legislative Chairman, has clear ideas and convictions, which she by no means fears to express. She writes: . . .

We helped to secure:

1. A State reformatory for women.

2. Fifty-four-hour week for women and children under sixteen.

3. Workmen's Compensation Act.

4. Registration of nurses.

Missouri—M. P. Cayce, Legislative Chairman, writes that . . . among the successful social legislation advocated were the following:

A State-wide Juvenile Court Bill.

An Injunction and Abatement Act.

Segregation of Feeble-Minded.

A Mothers' Pension Act (vetoed because so amended as to be of little value).

Public school centers.

Women police officers . . .

Iowa—Secured an eight-hour day for working children under sixteen.

An act enabling cities to establish and maintain play grounds. Provision for free treatment of maimed and deformed poor children. A re-enactment of a more stringent injunction and abatement law—the first having been declared unconstitutional.

Rhode Island—State Federation worked for and secured an appropriation for traveling library work. And assisted in securing a measure regulating street trades.

Illinois and Michigan—Are endeavoring to increase the minimum age for working children to sixteen and fifteen respectively, and with prospects of success—which gives rise to many "I told you so's" from employers, who claim that child labor reformers never know when to stop. . . .13

"NEW MEXICO WOMEN ACTIVE"

. . . The board meeting in May recommended only two bills for support, the Traveling Library bill and a bill creating a state Board of Charities and Corrections. The Civil Department has inaugurated a movement to secure school buildings for social centers. . . .

The Literature, Library and Reciprocity Department has assisted in starting several libraries, secured lists of suitable books for small libraries, and maintains a bureau of reciprocity for exchange of papers among the clubs of the Federation.

The Civic and Public Health departments are active in the usual sanitation and uplift work and the Public Health Department is working with the Albuquerque Woman's Club for a better babies' show during the State Fair at Albuquerque.14

Neither all the members nor all the clubs within the General Federation participated in reform activities. Some clubs shunned issues such as labor legislation and preferred to spend their energies on less controversial goals, supporting local cultural events or aiding schools and libraries. Others talked about reform but were unable to organize themselves for action. Many clubs remained simply social and literary groups. The GFWC's Magazine continued to publish articles about literature and the dramatic arts which ran side by side with discussions of such contrasting subjects as the practice of using convict labor.

But no matter what the level of participation, the vast majority of club women had been brought out of the narrow sphere of home and family into the real and troubled world around them.

BLACK WOMEN'S ORGANIZATIONS

Although the club movement, drawing its members mainly from the more prosperous groups in the country, was overwhelmingly white and Protestant, a vigorous and important club life existed among Afro-American women during the period between 1890 and 1920. Like their white counterparts, these clubs were established and led by the better-educated and more affluent black women. Black women's organizations were not new. Northern women had formed antislavery societies in the 1830's, and North and South, black women frequently came together in church societies and circles. But the clubs formed after the upheaval of the Civil War had subsided and as the new century began were larger, and almost all of them were nonreligious and nonsectarian. Among the earliest and most successful of the new women's clubs were the Harper Woman's Club of Jefferson County, Missouri, founded in 1890, the Woman's League of Washington, D.C., 1892, and the Woman's Era Club of Boston, 1893.

From the outset, because of the experiences of black women and the facts of racial prejudice and injustice in the country, there were important differences between the Afro-American clubs and the white groups. While black women turned to their clubs for companionship and for self-improvement, as white women did, they also saw such organizations as a means of improving racial conditions and as a way to repudiate the humiliating and prevalent stereotype of black women as immoral and uncivilized.

In 1895, Josephine St. Pierre Ruffin, a leader in the club movement, addressed a conference of club members on the need for a union of black clubs. She discussed many reasons for joining together and then added this statement.

FROM JOSEPHINE ST. PIERRE RUFFIN'S SPEECH

I have left the strongest reason for our conferring together until the last. All over America there is to be found a large and growing class of earnest, intelligent, progressive colored women, women who, if not leading full useful lives, are only waiting for the opportunity to do so, many of them warped and cramped for lack of opportunity, not only to do more but to *be* more; and yet, if an estimate of the colored women of America is called for, the inevitable reply, glibly given, is, "For the most part ignorant and immoral, some exceptions, of course, but these don't count."

Now for the sake of the thousands of self-sacrificing young women teaching and preaching in lonely southern backwoods, for the noble army of mothers who have given birth to these girls, mothers whose intelligence is only limited by their opportunity to get at books, for the sake of the fine cultured women who have carried off the honors in school here and often abroad, for the sake of our own dignity, the dignity of our race, and the future good name of our children, it is "mete, right and our bounden duty" to stand forth and declare ourselves and principles, to teach an ignorant and suspicious world that our aims and interests are identical with those of all good aspiring women. Too long have we been silent under unjust and unholy charges; we cannot expect to have them removed until we disprove them through *ourselves.* It is not enough to try to disprove unjust charges through individual effort, that never goes any further. Year after year southern women have protested against the admission of colored women into any national organization on the ground of the immorality of these women, and because all refutation has only been tried by individual work the charge has never been crushed, as it could and should have been at the first. Now with an army of organized women standing for purity and mental worth, we in ourselves deny the charge and open the eyes of the world to a state of affairs to which they have been blind, often willfully so, and the very fact that the charges, audaciously and flippantly made, as they often are, are of so humiliating and delicate a nature, services to protect the accuser by driving the helpless accused into mortified silence. It is to break this silence, not by noisy protestations of what we are not, but by a dignified showing of what we are and hope to become that we are impelled to take this step, to make of this gathering an object lesson to the world. For many and apparent reasons it is especially fitting that the *women* of the race take the lead in this movement, but for all this we recognize the necessity of the sympathy of our husbands, brothers and fathers.

Our woman's movement is woman's movement in that it is led and directed by women for the good of women and men, for the benefit of *all* humanity, which is more than any one branch or section of it. We want, we ask the active interest of our men, and, too, we are not drawing the color line; we are women, American women, as intensely interested in all that pertains to us as such as all other American women; we are not alienating or withdrawing, we are only coming to the front, willing to join any others in the same work and cordially inviting and welcoming any others to join us.[15]

Several efforts were made in the 1890's to federate the black women's groups scattered across the nation. They culminated in 1896 in the formation of the National Association of Colored Women. Its first president was Mary Church Terrell and its official publication was a newspaper, The Woman's Era, *edited by Josephine Ruffin. In less than twenty years after its beginning, there were twenty-eight state federations, more than a thousand clubs, and over 50,000 women in the National Association of Colored Women.*

The Association sponsored activities intended to uplift and improve black home life. Through Mothers' Congresses and Mothers' Clubs, it taught the rudiments of domestic science and child care to poor black women. Writing to Mary Church Terrell in 1899, Emma Prickett described the work of women in Waugh, Alabama.

LETTER FROM AN ALABAMA CLUB

Mrs. President,
Ladies of the Association:—

We beg leave to submit the following report:
The Mt. Meigs Woman's Club has been organized for two years. The object of the Club is to make better the home life of our plantation women. In doing this, we get at the founda-

Mary Church Terrell

tions of most social evils, and they rise, as it were, unconsciously upon a higher plane of living.

We realize more and more the importance of home training, and confidence which should exist in the home between mother and daughter. In view of this fact the Mt. Meigs Club brings to-gether in a mutual way the mother and daughter. We discuss the mother's duty to daughter and home and daughter's duty to mother and home and other subjects of like importance.

We have committees appointed to attend to outside work, such as caring for sick, organizing other clubs in different localities.

Summing up the work of our Club in a few words we would say much good has been accomplished even among the women themselves. . . . [Their] homes are neat and clean, pictures on their walls, flowers growing in the yards, strings no longer are wrapped around the hair, and an air of contentment and a love of home seems to surround their little homes.[16]

The clubs were always concerned with the pressing needs of black people, the most impoverished and neglected of the nation's poor. Local clubs as well as state and national federations performed social services for the black community as diverse as were its needs. In New York City, as in other large Northern centers, women set up the White Rose mission to aid young girls migrating North, finding them rooms, training, and jobs. Women's clubs pioneered in setting up day-care centers for working mothers, in sponsoring schools and homes for the aged, and in all communities where there was a black woman's club, they were involved in education and health work.

The variety of activities is illustrated in this report to the NACW from the Phillis Wheatley Club of New Orleans, dated January 10, 1898.

REPORT OF THE PHILLIS WHEATLEY CLUB

The Phillis Wheatley Club of N.O. was the outcome of the realization among our women that something must be done to elevate our race and that we as women should exercise some executive ability. A few earnest women under the guidance of Mrs. S. F. Williams organized the club October 9, 1894. As it is in all things the beginning of the club was small. The club was divided into several committees viz: Temperance, Social Purity and Anti-Tobacco, Philanthropy and Prison Work, Night Schools, Literature, Law and History, Law Schools, Fireside Schools and Suffrage Committees. . . .

In the Nurse Training Dept. eight nurses have been registered under the tuition [?] of Drs. Martinet and Newman. One of these nurses, Mrs. M. E. Williams, on the comple-

tion of her course successfully passed the examination as midwife before the State Medical Board of Louisiana and is now practicing her profession. Many of these nurses were in constant demand during the last visitation of Yellow Fever. . . . Since the organization much good has been done by these committees. Sewing [?] and Night Schools were established. The prison work has progressed finely. The committee makes weekly visits to the prison distributing reading matter among the inmates and encouraging the attendance of religious services. . . . Shoes and clothing have been distributed among the poor. Some needy ones have been sent to various Homes. Two needy members of the club have been assisted.

The one great object towards which the members have bent their efforts was the establishment of a Sanitorium and Training School for Nurses. We realized the necessity of *trained* nurses, since all professions are now calling for trained hands. Many of our old nurses were deprived of work because they did not hold certificates from a Training School. We needed the Sanitorium in connection with our Medical School to give the students that practice which is such a necessary adjunct to theory. Our colored doctors are not allowed to practice in our city hospitals, not even in the colored wards. Colored patients are not received in their pay wards and we saw that the establishment of such an institution would cover a multitude of needs.

After much hard work under our able Pres. the hope was realized and on Oct. 31, 1898 the doors of the Sanitorium were thrown open to the public. . . . We have a free clinic daily for the poor. . . . We have expended as running expenses for the eight months the sum of six hundred and twenty dollars. The money for the establishment of the institution was raised through the donations of generous friends and of the public. Our budget committee succeeded in obtaining from the city an appropriation of $240 annually. . . . Our membership has reached 97. We have very small dues of 5 cents monthly and have brought in all good moral women so that our work is purely humanitarian and in no way a social affair. We work for the masses and urge individual advancement. We have a Board of Managers composed of the officers and ten members of the club to act as an advisory board in the management of the Sanitorium. We have great hopes for the future of our work and sincerely trust that we may be successful.

Cordially,
Phillis Wheatley Club
S. F. Williams, president[17]

In view of the inadequate public educational facilities for Afro-Americans, the educational work of the clubs was extremely important. While pressuring for improvements in public education, they often established their own facilities. Clubs supported industrial training programs for women and men, and much work was expended setting up kindergartens, which were seen both as a means of educating the young child and as a help to working mothers.

As president of the NACW, Mary Church Terrell solicited funds from wealthy patrons to support club kindergarten work. In 1901 she wrote to Mrs. Stuyvesant Fish.

A FUND-RAISING LETTER

Dear Madam:

The colored women of the country are trying to do something to improve the condition of our people. We feel that by reaching our children at an early age, we shall be able to do the most good. We are trying therefore to establish kindergartens for them especially in the South. A few such schools have already been founded and great good has been accomplished. We are sorely in need of funds to carry on our work and I take the liberty of appealing to you for aid. I have read of your generous interest in all good works and I entertain the hope that this may enlist your sympathy. If you establish a kindergarten in a southern city, we shall name it for you, if you will permit us to do so. The cost will not be great and it will do untold good to the poor little barbarians who need it most. . . . . [18]

Despite such carefully worded appeals, shortages of money for educational projects constantly frustrated the ambitions of the clubs, but determined and resourceful, the club women of the National Association of Colored Women kept moving forward. The National Association Notes kept members informed of each other's activities, as in this 1902 report.

KINDERGARTEN WORK

The Kindergarten work in Rome [Georgia] was begun during the summer of 1900. We had only a few blocks and such material as the little ones could get from their homes.

We sat on the floor during work time, and played picnic when lunch time came. Fortunately, I owned an instrument, and this helped us a great deal in our morning skips, songs and other exercises.

It was fall before a kitchen table could be procured. The legs were sawed off, and it answered our purpose. A friend donated a dozen chairs. With this scanty supply we have been able to do some creditable work.

Mrs. C. S. Sharp, President of the Woman's Club of Rome (white), gave 50 cents per month to buy materials for the children to use during the occupation period.

Part of the time we have charged 10 cents a week—very little of this was collected. As funds have been so very low, the fuel, room and necessary articles we have furnished. This

has been our work for two years. It has been uphill work, sometimes, but our Kindergarten has come to stay.

We are contemplating an afternoon school for young women in service. Although the work for the present must be charitable, I believe much good can be done. We shall teach these young women the common English branches, plain sewing, cooking and house work.

Yours sincerely,

ANNA S. INGRAHAM [19]

Strong ties were created between middle-class and poor black women by the clubs' commitment to welfare services within the black community. The black women's club movement, for example, was in the vanguard of the battle against lynching, inspired in large part by the work of Ida B. Wells Barnett.

Barnett was an experienced journalist, and one of the most outspoken black Americans in calling for resistance to

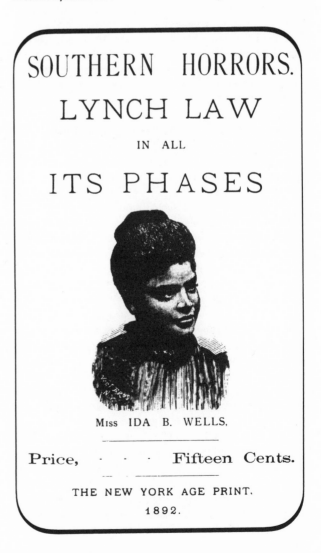

SOUTHERN HORRORS.

LYNCH LAW

IN ALL

ITS PHASES

MISS IDA B. WELLS.

Price, - - - Fifteen Cents.

THE NEW YORK AGE PRINT.

1892.

discrimination and opposition to the lynching and mob violence that were the most flagrant manifestations of racism. To the shock and consternation of many, she spoke out directly and boldly against lynching, which she publicized and analyzed as a factor in race relations. The excerpt that follows is from Barnett's first pamphlet on lynching, entitled Southern Horrors; *it was printed in 1892.*

ON LYNCHING

One by one the Southern States have legally (?) disfranchised the Afro-American, and since the repeal of the Civil Rights Bill nearly every Southern State has passed separate car laws with a penalty against their infringement. The race regardless of advancement is penned into filthy, stifling partitions cut off from smoking cars. All this while, although the political cause has been removed, the butcheries of black men at Barnwell, S. C., Carrolton, Miss., Waycross, Ga., and Memphis, Tenn., have gone on; also the flaying alive of a man in Kentucky, the burning of one in Arkansas, the hanging of a fifteen year old girl in Louisiana, a woman in Jackson, Tenn., and one in Hollendale, Miss., until the dark and bloody record of the South shows 728 Afro-Americans lynched during the past 8 years. Not 50 of these were for political causes; the rest were for all manner of accusations from that of rape of white women, to the case of the boy Will Lewis who was hanged at Tullahoma, Tenn., last year for being drunk and "sassy" to white folks.

These statistics compiled by the Chicago "Tribune" were given the first of this year (1892). Since then, not less than one hundred and fifty have been known to have met violent death at the hands of cruel bloodthirsty mobs during the past nine months.

To palliate this record (which grows worse as the Afro-American becomes intelligent) and excuse some of the most heinous crimes that ever stained the history of a country, the South is shielding itself behind the plausible screen of defending the honor of its women. This, too, in the face of the fact that only *one-third* of the 728 victims to mobs have been *charged* with rape, to say nothing of those of that one-third who were innocent of the charge. A white correspondent of the Baltimore Sun declares that the Afro-American who was lynched in Chestertown, Md., in May for assault on a white girl was innocent; that the deed was done by a white man who had since disappeared. The girl herself maintained that her assailant was a white man. When that poor Afro-American was murdered, the whites excused their refusal of a trial on the ground that they wished to spare the white girl the mortification of having to testify in court.

This cry has had its effect. It has closed the heart, stifled the conscience, warped the judgment and hushed the voice of press and pulpit on the subject of lynch law throughout this "land of liberty." Men who stand high in the esteem of the public for christian character, for moral and physical courage, for devotion to the principles of equal and exact justice to all, and for great sagacity, stand as cowards who fear to open their mouths before this great outrage. They do not see that by their tacit encouragement, their silent acquiescence, the black shadow of lawlessness in the form of lynch law is spreading its wings over the whole country.

Men who, like Governor Tillman, start the ball of lynch law rolling for a certain crime, are powerless to stop it when drunken or criminal white toughs feel like hanging an Afro-American on any pretext.

Even to the better class of Afro-Americans the crime of rape is so revolting they have too often taken the white man's word and given lynch law neither the investigation nor condemnation it deserved.

They forget that a concession of the right to lynch a man for a certain crime, not only concedes the right to lynch any person for any crime, but (so frequently is the cry of rape now raised) it is in a fair way to stamp us a race of rapists and desperadoes. They have gone on hoping and believing that general education and financial strength would solve the difficulty, and are devoting their energies to the accumulation of both.

The mob spirit has grown with the increasing intelligence of the Afro-American. It has left the out-of-the-way places where ignorance prevails, has thrown off the mask and with this new cry stalks in broad daylight in large cities, the centres of civilization, and is encouraged by the "leading citizens" and the press.[20]

Barnett's newspaper articles, speeches, and pamphlets aroused black and white alike. Barnett herself contributed much to the changing image of black women, as did the club women whom she inspired to work for the betterment of the black community. In this way, women's clubs served a dual purpose: for women, they were part of the process of emerging from the sphere of domesticity into the larger world; they were also an important mechanism in the development of race consciousness and union among black Americans.

From their origins in the nineteenth century, black women's organizations have continued to increase in number and size. In 1935, the National Council of Negro Women was established. Led by Mary McLeod Bethune, it was formed to coordinate national organizations of black women. Today, there are more than twenty affiliated groups and over three-quarters of a million members associated with the Council.

RADICAL CHANGE VERSUS REFORM

At the same time that millions of women were participating in public affairs through associations and the Progressive movement, a small number of women were involved

PARLIAMENTARY USAGE
FOR WOMEN'S CLUBS

By Mrs. Emma A. Fox

Is the authority of the General Federation of Women'sClubs and of more than half of the State Federations. It is designed for beginners as well as for the most advanced.

Price, sixty-five cents, postpaid

Orders may be sent to

THE
FEDERATION
MAGAZINE

25 W. 42d Street
New York

in more direct and radical challenges to women's economic and social position.

Some of these were socialists who joined political organizations, worked as labor organizers, agitated for revolutionary changes, and demanded freedom and dignity for all women and all men. Others, influenced less by Marx and more by the social and psychological ideas of writers such as Sigmund Freud, Havelock Ellis, and Ellen Key, focused on social and sexual institutions. They rejected the traditional roles that determined the lives of both women and men, called for sexual equality, challenged the value of compulsory monogamy, and advocated birth control.

Among these were such figures as Ella Reeve Bloor, Emma Goldman, Margaret Sanger, Crystal Eastman, and Henrietta Rodman. Charlotte Perkins Gilman was the best-known radical feminist philosopher in the United States. In a widely read book, Women and Economics, published in 1898, she analyzed the subjection and underdevelopment of American women, affirmed that economic equality was the key to freedom, and called for radical changes in family and child care to liberate women for work.

The challenges to traditional economic and social institutions made by radical women and men did not go unnoticed. Their books and articles were published and discussed; their lectures and speeches drew curious audiences. Their personal lives, which often diverged from conventional sexual and family patterns, were widely talked about and criticized. Their morality was attacked by defenders of the status quo.

Many women involved in radical change also participated in the organized women's movement. They worked in the suffrage drive, published in The Woman's Journal, and supported the work of the National Women's Trade Union League. However, the reforms that constituted the radical feminist program—such as an amendment to end all forms of discrimination against women, the legalization and spread of birth control, the adoption of liberal and uniform divorce laws, greater sexual freedom for women, changes in the child care system—had to wait decades before they became goals of the women's movement. But radical feminist ideas did influence individual women and led many to support and work for birth control and divorce reform outside of their more cautious organizations.

Despite the moderation of their views, accomplishments and significance of women's organizations at this time should not be undervalued, for associationism was both a response to changing times and a cause of further change. The clubs offered women relatively easy and exciting access to the fringes of men's sphere of activity and authority. Moreover, they gave millions of women training in organization, planning, political agitation, and public speaking, and they created new bonds between women, other than those of family and church. While this had been true of the nineteenth-century religious missionary societies and the temperance and suffrage organizations, it was more pronounced and widespread in the club life of the twentieth century.

No doubt, the average clubwoman was still often conservative or timid, but dynamic and outspoken leaders provided new examples of admired and acceptable female behavior. And gradually the involvement of women in subjects recently considered "unwomanly" became a matter of course. The members of the Young Women's Christian Association, for example, received a monthly publication that contained a full page of legislative news, reporting the content and progress of bills in Congress and state legislatures. It was clear that women were expected to think about such matters, to understand them, to have opinions about them, and even to do something about them. This had never been clear before.

CHAPTER EIGHT

A BRIEF HISTORY OF WAGE-EARNING WOMEN
1820-1914

At the same time that middle-class women found their work as housewives and mothers decreasing and their material and social freedom expanding, other women were joining the ranks of wage earners in increasing numbers. By 1900, one out of every five women in the country worked for wages, and women comprised about 20 percent of the nation's work force.

Actually, although the churches and women's magazines in the nineteenth century had preached that woman's place was in the home and the nursery, where she was portrayed as a gentle, immaculate, and somewhat delicate presence, the realities of life were very different for almost all women. From the earliest days of American history, women had worked, and worked hard. The country had always suffered from a serious shortage of labor— and it needed the labor of women, as wives of free men, as indentured servants, and as slaves.

Well into the nineteenth century, women's unpaid labor in the home was complicated, arduous, and endless. Families were large. Relatively few manufactured products were available, and most of the goods needed and consumed at home had to be made there. The burden of housework was doubly hard on the frontier and in new settlements, but even in the Southern states, where a slave labor system prevailed, slaveowners' wives had difficult and continuing responsibilities managing elaborate and complex households.

From colonial days, women also worked for wages and other remuneration. Before the spread of factories, they manufactured goods at home, playing an important part in cottage industries that produced such items as cloth and clothing. They also worked outside the home for wages, as agricultural hands, laundresses, domestic servants, milliners, teachers, inn or boardinghouse keepers, and cooks.

As the factory system spread in the early decades of the nineteenth century, the employment of women and children as factory workers became common. By 1831, in the cotton mills of New England, 80 percent of the workers were women, and until 1870 female operatives outnumbered males in this major industry. In the middle of the century, one out of every four U.S. factory workers was a woman. And she was likely to be working in the textile, shoe, clothing, or printing industries of the North and Northeast. There were relatively few factories in the South and West, and they seldom employed female workers.

Like their male counterparts in the pioneer days of industrialization, women wage earners often labored twelve hours a day, six days a week. The owners and managers of New England factories, among the most important in the country, spouted paternalistic and benevolent-sounding phrases about the young farm women who worked their mill machines; but in the 1840's they demanded eleven-and-a-half hours of labor a day during the winter. After April, the workday lengthened to thirteen-and-a-half hours; and the machines stopped only at mealtimes— which lasted half an hour. There was, however, one way in which the experience of working women was consistently different from that of men: they were always paid less.

Nineteenth-century wage-earning women were on their own. The small organized women's movement was made up predominantly of women who did not earn wages, and after the Civil War its preoccupation with suffrage and temperance left little but rhetoric for the working woman. Male workers looked on female workers much in the way they regarded black and immigrant men entering the work force. They saw them as competition for jobs and resented their willingness to work for the lowest pay. Moreover, they found working women particularly infuriating since they believed that women really belonged at home, as wives and mothers, and not in the work force. Thus, women wage earners got little sympathy and less assistance from their fellow workers, either the few who were unionized or the masses who were not.

In many ways, the working women were ill equipped to look out for their own interests and to handle the problems they encountered. Like male workers at the time, women had only meager knowledge of labor organization and the techniques of resistance and collective bargaining. And they were doubly handicapped by custom and by training that induced women to be passive, undemanding, and unaggressive. Most women themselves, as well as men, believed that they belonged at home, where they could perform their natural roles as wives and mothers. And

OPPOSITE: "The Shoemakers' Strike in Lynn, Mass.—Procession, in the Midst of a Snow Storm, of Eight Hundred Woman Operatives Joining in the Strike of Firemen." Leslie's, Mar. 1860

many looked on their employment as temporary, accidental, or abnormal.

Sometimes, however, powerful imperatives—pitiful wages, unbearable working conditions, an endless workday—drove them to action. Through the century, women workers repeatedly organized themselves and rebelled against their conditions. In outbursts of anger, factory women walked off jobs; they came together to form associations for self-help; and they lobbied and agitated for relief. Their early unions and associations were short-lived, but a fiery determination, a strong spirit of independence, and a lot of fight lie in their history.

THE FIRST STRIKE

Working women's organizations were formed early in the nineteenth century. In 1825, tailoresses in New York established a union; in Philadelphia, by the 1830's, an organization was created to represent women wage earners in many different trades and occupations.

The first strike of women wage earners took place in Dover, New Hampshire, in 1828, when cotton mill owners issued a set of new regulations for workers. The young Yankee women working the mill machines found these provisions unacceptable.

FACTORY REGULATIONS

First. No person shall be admitted within the yard, except on business, without permission from an agent.

Second. The bell to call the people to their work will be rung five minutes and tolled five minutes; at the last stroke the entrance will be closed and a fee of 12 1/2 cents exacted of any one for whom it may be opened.

Third. No person can be allowed to leave work without permission from their overseer.

No talking can be permitted while at work, except on business.

Spirituous liquor, smoking nor any kind of amusement will be allowed in the workshops, yards, or factories.

Fourth. To preserve the present high character of our profession and give the enemies of domestic manufactures no cause of exaltation, a strictly moral code is required for every one. Gambling, drinking, or any other debaucheries will procure the immediate and disgraceful dismissal of the individual.

Fifth. Self-respect, it is expected, will induce every one to be as constant in attendance on some place of divine worship as circumstances will permit.

Sixth. All those that faithfully perform their duty, have prevented as far as possible the waste or destruction of the company's property, and wish to leave their employment, by giving fourteen days notice of their intention, receive a certificate that they are regularly discharged at their own request.[1]

———

The fine of 12 1/2 cents for lateness amounted to one-third of a day's wages. Hundreds of women found this penalty and the other restrictions obnoxious. They joined together to protest.

The newspapers reacted to the unusual event of a women's strike with disdainful amusement.

FROM PHILADELPHIA'S *NATIONAL GAZETTE*

The late strike and grand public march of the female operatives in New Hampshire exhibit the Yankee sex in a new and unexpected light. By and by the governor may have to call out the militia to prevent a gynecocracy.[2]

FROM THE *MECHANICS' FREE PRESS*

. . . [The strike] formed the subject of a squib, probably for more than half the newspapers from Maine to Georgia. The circumstance of three or four hundred girls or women marching out of their factory in a procession and firing off a lot of gunpowder, and the facetious advertisement of the factory agent for two or three hundred better behaved women made, altogether, a comical story quite worth telling.[3]

———

The Dover strike lasted a few days, and then the women returned to work. Six years later, eight hundred women were mobilized to strike at Dover again.

ORGANIZATION AND RESISTANCE

Despite their reputation as benevolent working places for young women from good homes, the textile factories in Lowell, Massachusetts, experienced a strike in February 1834, when the mill owners announced a 15 percent cut in wages. The striking mill workers issued this proclamation.

THE LOWELL PROCLAMATION

UNION IS POWER.—Our present object is to have union and exertion, and we remain in possession of our own unquestionable rights. We circulate this paper, wishing to obtain the names of all who imbibe the spirit of our patriotic ancestors, who preferred privation to bondage and parted with all that renders life desirable—and even life itself—to produce independence for their children. The oppressing hand of avarice would enslave us, and to gain their objective they very gravely tell us of the pressure of the times; this we are already sensible of and deplore it. If any are in want of assistance, the ladies will be compassionate and assist them, but we prefer to have the disposing of our charities in our own hands [In this strike, as in others, the strikers set up a fund to help those in need], and as we are free, we would remain in possession of what Kind Providence has bestowed upon us, and remain daughters of freemen still.

All who patronize this effort we wish to have discontinue their labor until terms of reconciliation are made.

Resolved, that we will not go back into the mills to work unless our wages are continued to us as they have been.

Resolved, that none of us will go back unless they receive us all as one.

Resolved, that if any have not money enough to carry them home that they shall be supplied.

Let Oppression shrug her shoulders
  And a haughty tyrant frown

And little upstart Ignorance
  In mockery look down

Yet I value not the feeble threats
  Of Tories in disguise,
While the flag of Independence
  O'er our noble nation flies.[4]

The Lowell strike, like many early efforts at protest, was short-lived and unsuccessful. The strike leaders were not rehired, while most of the striking women went back to work, at reduced wages.

In 1836, the Lowell mill owners permitted the boarding-houses, where the workers lived, to raise the price of board, effectively reducing the women's wages by more than 12 percent. Another strike was the result.

During the 1840's, work conditions continued to deteriorate and work loads increased in most of the New England mills. In response, women wage earners often organized themselves to protest or strike, and labor unrest

The Lighter Side: "Procession of Lady 'Strikers' to the Chowder Party at Lynn."
Leslie's, *Apr. 1860*

became a more familiar part of the New England land-scape.

In 1844, five mill workers in Lowell set up an organization to work for the ten-hour day. This Lowell Female Reform Association was one of the most influential of the early women's labor groups. In one year, about five hundred women joined, and branches in other mill towns began to imitate their work. Led by Sarah Bagley, the Lowell association published tracts, gave lectures, and took the lead in petitioning and lobbying for a state law establishing a ten-hour workday. Their agitation provoked the first government investigation of working conditions, and the appearance of Sarah Bagley and other working women before the Massachusetts legislature in 1845 was a unique event.

Speaking before a Special Committee on Hours of Labor, the Lowell women testified about conditions in the mills. Despite their touching appeal, the Massachusetts legislature rejected the call for a ten-hour law.

TESTIMONY OF LOWELL MILL WORKERS

The first petitioner who testified was Eliza R. Hemmingway. She had worked 2 years and 9 months in the Lowell Factories; 2 years in the Middlesex, and 9 months in the Hamilton Corporations. Her employment is weaving,—works by the piece. The Hamilton Mill manufactures cotton fabrics. The Middlesex, woollen fabrics. She is now at work in the Middlesex Mills, and attends one loom. Her wages average from $16 to $23 a month exclusive of board. She complained of the hours for labor being too many, and the time for meals too limited. In the summer season, the work is commenced at 5 o'clock, A.M., and continued till 7 o'clock, P.M., with half an hour for breakfast and three quarters of an hour for dinner. During eight months of the year, but half an hour is allowed for dinner. The air in the room she considered not to be wholesome. There were 293 small lamps and 61 large lamps lighted in the room in which she worked, when evening work is required. These lamps are also lighted sometimes in the morning.—About 130 females, 11 men, and 12 children (between the ages of 11 and 14) work in the room with her. She thought the children enjoyed about as good health as children generally do. The children work but 9 months out of 12. The other 3 months they must attend school. Thinks that there is no day when there are less than six of the females out of the mill from sickness. Has known as many as thirty. She, herself, is out quite often, on account of sickness. There was more sickness in the Summer than in Winter months; though in the Summer, lamps are not lighted. She thought there was a general desire among the females to work but ten hours, regardless of pay. Most of the girls are from the country, who work in the Lowell Mills. The average time which they remain there is about three years. She knew one girl who had worked there 14 years. Her

health was poor when she left. Miss Hemmingway said her health was better where she now worked, than it was when she worked on the Hamilton Corporation.

She knew of one girl who last winter went into the mill at half past 4 o'clock, A.M. and worked till half past 7 o'clock P.M. She did so to make more money. She earned from $25 to $30 per month. There is always a large number of girls at the gate wishing to get in before the bell rings. On the Middlesex Corporation one fourth part of the females go into the mill before they are obliged to. They do this to make more wages. A large number come to Lowell to make money to aid their parents who are poor. She knew of many cases where married women came to Lowell and worked in the mills to assist their husbands to pay for their farms. The moral character of the operatives is good. There was only one American female in the room with her who could not write her name.

Miss Sarah G. Bagley said she had worked in the Lowell Mills eight years and a half,—six years and a half on the Hamilton Corporation, and two years on the Middlesex. She is a weaver, and works by the piece. She worked in the mills three years before her health began to fail. She is a native of New Hampshire, and went home six weeks during the summer. Last year she was out of the mill a third of the time. She thinks the health of the operatives is not so good as the health of females who do house-work or millinery business. The chief evil, so far as health is concerned, is the shortness of time allowed for meals. The next evil is the length of time employed—not giving them time to cultivate their minds. She spoke of the high moral and intellectual character of the girls. That many were engaged as teachers in the Sunday schools. That many attended the lectures of the Lowell Institute; and she thought, if more time was allowed, that more lectures would be given and more girls attend. She thought that the girls generally were favorable to the ten hour system. She had presented a petition, same as the one before the Committee, to 132 girls, most of whom said that they would prefer to work but ten hours. In a pecuniary point of view, it would be better, as their health would be improved. They would have more time for sewing. Their intellectual, moral, and religious habits would also be benefited by the change.

Miss Bagley said, in addition to her labor in the mills, she had kept evening school during the winter months, for four years, and thought that this extra labor must have injured her health.[5]

In Pennsylvania, women were involved in a fierce struggle for the ten-hour day. A state law prohibited cotton factories from requiring more than ten hours of work a day, but factory owners in Pittsburgh closed their doors to women who would not work for twelve hours and hired those who agreed to do so.

The women who had been shut out of their jobs were furious. Their protest, as described in the Pittsburgh Daily Commercial Journal, *reveals the depth of their anger.*

A NEWSPAPER REPORT

We visited the scene of excitement at about 12 o'clock, M. . . . A dense mass of men, women, and children were collected around the front gate of the factory—facing toward the Allegheny—with the avowed intention of taking summary vengeance on the delinquents who had gone to work, so soon as they should get out for dinner.

Tired of waiting, and their passions constantly becoming more excited—demonstrations toward breaking open the gate were at last made.

An axe was procured, and a woman seizing hold of it commenced hewing away with true Amazonian vehemence and vigor.

The gate was of pine, and would soon have yielded to the energetic exertions of this young woman but for the protection afforded by an iron bar, which we were told secured it on the inside. . . .

Suddenly a cry arose that several women and children had been scalded from the engine room, and yells of vengeance were heard on all sides. . . .

As if by common consent, a rush was made to storm the factory. A platoon of women were in front as a sort of forlorn hope, followed by a storming party of men, who kept up a continuous cheer as the whole column moved on to the assault.

The scene at this moment was exciting in the extreme. The girls in front acted for the time as pioneers and commenced tearing away the boards from the fence so as to make a breach, through which their storming columns could enter.

Protected by a hurricane of brickbats, mud, and stones, these warriors made great progress, and in a short time a breach was made which the general in command (whoever he was) pronounced practicable. "Now, men!" "hurra!" "give 'em h—ll!" and yells utterly indescribable by any combination of letters, announced the onset upon this second Molina del Rey.

The sheriff of the county, John Forsyth, esq.; the owners of the mill, clerks, and a detachment of the Allegheny police were inside and they prepared manfully to resist the attack.

Placing themselves opposite the breach they awaited the charge.

One moment of calm preceded the bursting of the storm, and then a general volley of brickbats and bludgeons commenced the grand movement of the day.

The authorities made a gallant stand, but in vain. In a minute they began to waver, and finally broke and retired from the disastrous encounter. . . .

The scene of uproar and confusion inside the yard now baffled description.

Stones and brickbats were flying in every direction and the windows in that part of the building were soon entirely destroyed. . . .

We left the ground about 3 o'clock, when it appeared that the operatives had completely triumphed. The sheriff had abandoned the ground, as had also the police. The factory appeared to be completely in the power of the operatives, and they had it all their own way. . . .

We offer no comments upon the proceedings of yesterday. Our whole duty is discharged when we state the facts of the case.[6] . . .

Some of the strikers were arrested; thirteen were found guilty. In less than two months the ten-hour day was the rule in Pittsburgh's cotton mills, but wages were reduced one-sixth to compensate for the manufacturers' loss.

INDUSTRIALIZATION AND CHANGE

During the Civil War, labor shortages and economic hardships opened areas of employment usually closed or barely accessible to women. Many were hired to work in the expanding bureaus of the Union and Confederate governments; the Treasury, War, and Post Office departments took on large numbers of female workers. Some even managed to retain these jobs after the war was over. New factory jobs opened, too, as arsenals and textiles factories ground out war supplies; these jobs proved more difficult to hold on to when the war emergency had passed.

Before the war, a quarter of the nation's elementary and secondary schoolteachers were women. During the war, many reluctant school boards, unable to find a male teacher, hired women. Soon they dominated the profession; by 1880, sixty percent of the country's schoolteachers were female. Teaching remains to this day primarily a female occupation.

In the decades after the Civil War, the economic life of the United States changed dramatically. The 1880's and 1890's were a period of spectacular industrial expansion. Immigrants and rural Americans migrated to the cities, finally ending the long labor drought. The number and proportion of people in industrial jobs escalated.

The position of women in the economy changed in several important ways. By 1900, one of every five women worked for wages. But the proportion of women in manufacturing jobs had dropped; while women constituted 25 percent of all factory workers in 1850, they were only 19 percent in 1900. Those who did work in factories were mainly in the textile and garment industries of the North. Industrialization did begin to change the patterns of life in the South during the last three decades of the 1800's, and the number of women working in factories in Southern states tripled.

By the turn of the century, women generally were holding the lowest-paying and least-skilled jobs. Almost two million of the five million who worked for wages were domestic laborers; others toiled as saleswomen, clerks, typists, and stenographers. The most prestigious of the common occupations for women were teaching and nursing.

Before the great acceleration of industrialization, the women who worked outside the home for wages were not easily distinguished from those who did not. The bulk of the factory workers in New England were daughters of Yankee farmers who left home for the factory for several reasons. Money, of course, was a strong motive, but they also came for excitement, adventure, and release from the confinement of rural life. Their families were not conspicuously poorer or socially very different from the majority of the population. And in a country without clear or fixed class lines, in which the distance from poor to rich was

relatively small, factory experience did not alter women's place in society very much. Most female wage earners expected to return to traditional womanly work—housewifery and child rearing—and did. During the century, the Yankee mill women were joined by immigrant laborers, and by the end of the century, they had all but been replaced by them. Indeed, by 1900, a disproportionately high number of the women who worked outside the home for wages were immigrant women or Afro-Americans. Forty-one percent of all black women worked in 1900, in contrast to 17 percent of white women. Over a million black women labored, mainly as agricultural workers and domestic servants. Immigrant women and their daughters comprised the majority of factory women, especially in the textile and clothing industries, although in the South, the increase in female operatives was made up of black women.

In contrast to the factory woman before the Civil War, who typically was young, unmarried, and native-born, by 1900 the woman wage earner was a poor woman, often not of Anglo-Saxon background; she worked out of necessity and, especially if she was black, might well continue to work even after marriage and childbirth.

Changes in wealth and social stratification had taken place. Poor people were poorer in relative terms than they had been before the war, while the middling classes were relatively wealthier. The rich were fewer but greater in wealth. There was, therefore, a great economic distance between working women and those women who were included in the middle class of their fathers and their husbands. In addition, immigration and the end of slavery had left the country tense with prejudice and conflict, and social distances were added to the economic ones that separated rich from poor.

One thing had not changed for working women during the nineteenth century, and that was the disparity between their wages and men's. In 1900, it remained enormous, as it had always been. In the printing industry, for example, the median wage for men was $14 a week; for women, it was $5. Overall, women earned 53 percent of what men earned in the same jobs.

U.S. Bureau of the Census Report on Women Wage Earners

TABLE VI.—PER CENT IN EACH OCCUPATION GROUP AND IN SELECTED OCCUPATIONS OF FEMALE BREADWINNERS 15 YEARS OF AGE AND OVER, FOR THE UNITED STATES (AREA OF ENUMERATION), CLASSIFIED BY RACE AND NATIVITY, 1890 AND 1900.

[From Special Reports of the Census Office: Statistics of Women at Work, 1900, page 161.]

Occupation	Native white — Both parents native		Native white — One or both parents foreign-born		Foreign-born white		Negro		Total	
	1890	1900	1890	1900	1890	1900	1890	1900	1890	1900
All occupations	100.0	100.0	100.0	100.0	100.0	100.0	100.0	100.0	100.0	100.0
Agricultural pursuits	14.6	15.0	1.7	2.3	4.4	4.8	41.2	39.8	16.0	16.2
Agricultural laborers	3.8	5.0	.4	.6	.4	.6	35.5	33.5	9.8	9.9
Professional service	16.2	15.1	9.2	9.9	2.6	3.0	1.0	1.3	8.4	8.6
Teachers and professors in colleges, etc.	12.7	11.4	7.5	7.8	1.8	2.0	.9	1.2	6.6	6.5
Domestic and personal service	32.6	30.4	30.5	30.0	59.7	53.6	54.5	55.8	42.8	40.2
Barbers and hairdressers	.1	.1	.1	.2	.1	.1	.1	.1	.1	.1
Boarding and lodging house keepers	1.3	1.7	.5	.9	1.3	1.7	.2	.3	.9	1.2
Hotel keepers	.2	.3	.1	.1	.2	.2	(a)	(a)	.1	.2
Housekeepers and stewardesses	3.6	4.3	1.5	2.6	2.6	3.5	.9	.8	2.3	2.9
Janitors and sextons	(a)	.1	.1	.2	.2	.3	.1	.1	.1	.2
Laborers (not specified)	.6	1.2	.4	.6	.6	1.0	4.6	6.3	1.4	2.2
Laundresses	1.5	2.3	1.6	2.6	4.2	5.0	17.3	18.6	5.8	6.6
Nurses and midwives	1.3	2.4	.8	1.7	1.7	3.1	.6	1.6	1.1	2.2
Servants and waitresses	23.8	17.7	25.3	20.9	48.4	38.0	31.2	27.8	30.9	24.2
Other domestic and personal service	.2	.2	.2	.3	.4	.6	.7	.6	.2	.3
Trade and transportation	7.7	12.5	11.1	17.6	4.5	7.2	.3	.3	6.0	9.9
Agents	.3	.4	.1	.2	.1	.2	(a)	(a)	.1	.2
Bookkeepers and accountants	1.1	2.0	1.4	2.7	.3	.7	(a)	.3	.7	1.5
Clerks and copyists	2.4	2.3	3.2	2.9	.8	.9	(a)	(a)	1.7	1.7
Merchants and dealers (except wholesale)	.6	.6	.7	.7	1.6	1.7	.1	.1	.7	.7
Packers and shippers	.1	.4	.4	.8	.1	.3	(a)	(a)	.2	.4
Saleswomen	1.7	3.4	3.7	3.9	.9	2.0	(a)	(a)	1.5	2.9
Stenographers and typewriters	1.0	2.5	.9	3.0	.2	.7	(a)	(a)	.6	1.7
Telegraph and telephone operators	.3	.7	.4	.8	.1	.2	(a)	(a)	.2	.4
Other persons in trade and transportation	.2	.4	.3	.5	.4	.5	.1	.1	.2	.4
Manufacturing and mechanical pursuits	29.0	27.0	47.6	40.1	28.8	31.4	3.0	2.8	26.8	25.1
Bookbinders	.2	.3	.9	.8	.2	.2	(a)	(a)	.3	.3
Boot and shoe makers and repairers	1.1	.8	1.9	1.5	.6	.6	(a)	(a)	.9	.8
Box makers (paper)	.3	.3	.9	.8	.2	.3	(a)	(a)	.3	.3
Confectioners	.1	.1	.3	.3	.2	.2	(a)	(a)	.1	.2
Glovemakers	.2	.2	.1	.3	.2	.2	(a)	(a)	.1	.1
Gold and silver workers	.1	.1	.2	.3	.1	.1	(a)	(a)	.1	.1
Paper and pulp mill operatives	.2	.1	.5	.4	.4	.3	(a)	(a)	.2	.2
Printers, lithographers, and presswomen	.5	.5	.4	.6	.1	.1	(a)	(a)	.3	.3
Rubber-factory operatives	.1	.1	.4	.3	.2	.3	(a)	(a)	.1	.2
Textile-mill operatives	4.2	4.5	10.0	7.4	10.2	9.7	.1	(a)	5.7	5.0
Carpet-factory operatives	.2	.1	.5	.3	.4	.3	(a)	(a)	.3	.2
Cotton-mill operatives	1.7	2.1	3.0	1.9	5.2	5.1	(a)	(a)	2.3	2.1
Hosiery and knitting-mill operatives	.6	.7	1.0	1.0	.5	.7	(a)	(a)	.5	.6
Silk-mill operatives	.3	.5	1.2	1.1	.7	.8	(a)	(a)	.6	.6
Woolen-mill operatives	.6	.4	2.1	1.1	1.4	1.1	(a)	(a)	.9	.6
Other textile-mill operatives	.9	.6	2.1	1.9	2.0	1.7	(a)	(a)	1.2	.9
Textile workers	19.9	16.3	26.3	21.1	13.7	14.8	2.3	2.1	15.8	13.8
Dressmakers	9.9	8.4	13.3	10.5	6.6	6.5	.9	1.1	7.8	6.8
Hat and cap makers	.2	.1	.4	.3	.2	.2	(a)	(a)	.2	.1
Milliners	2.7	2.5	2.3	2.6	1.0	1.1	(a)	(a)	1.6	1.7
Seamstresses	5.3	3.4	5.3	3.8	2.8	3.0	1.3	1.0	3.9	2.9
Shirt, collar, and cuff makers	.4	.7	.9	1.1	.4	.6	(a)	(a)	.4	.6
Tailoresses	1.2	.8	3.4	2.2	2.5	2.9	(a)	(a)	1.7	1.3
Other textile workers	.5	.8	.4	.7	.6	.3	(a)	(a)	.3	.4
Tobacco and cigar factory operatives	.5	.8	1.0	1.0	.9	1.2	.5	.4	.7	.8
Other manufacturing and mechanical pursuits	1.7	2.8	4.4	5.6	1.9	3.5	.1	.2	1.9	3.0

a Less than one-tenth of 1 per cent.

WOMEN AND THE LABOR MOVEMENT

A national labor movement took form in the United States after the Civil War as increasing numbers of men and women went into industrial jobs. But women, despite their part in the work force, were not in the mainstream of the emerging movement. More than thirty national trade unions developed soon after the war. Only two of them, the printers' and cigar makers' unions, reluctantly permitted women to join. Women were, however, represented in the National Labor Union, a forum for the growing body of organized workers.

In all, a very small proportion of women wage earners were organized, and most of these were in short-lived women's unions, unaffiliated with any other groups and usually formed to work for specific short-range goals. Such women's unions were formed by burnishers, laundresses, seamstresses, shoemakers, and umbrella sewers. Of these, the most successful were the Collar Laundry Union in Troy, New York, the New York Women's Typographic Society, and the Daughters of St. Crispin, the longer-lived shoemakers' union, which eventually had several branches.

Women wage earners also organized into rather loosely formed working women's associations and societies that tried to aid all working women in a city or town. These associations, sometimes with community support, offered job information, housing advice, legal aid, and even food for those who came too close to starvation. In the first fifteen years of its operations, the New York Working-women's Protective Union, one of the most active in the North, went to court six thousand times to aid women who had been cheated of their wages, and it found employment for 37,000 of the 124,000 who came seeking jobs.

There was one exception to the exclusion of women from the center of the labor movement. Between 1881 and 1890, women wage earners enjoyed an unusual offer of friendship and support from the Knights of Labor. The Knights, shunning the use of the strike, set out on a utopian and humanitarian quest to remake American society, by organizing all "toilers," skilled and unskilled, industrial, agricultural, and domestic workers, black and white, male and female. It was the first important labor organization to encourage the organization of women wage earners.

The motivation behind the Knights of Labor's support of women wage earners was a combination of practical and idealistic considerations. In 1881, Terence V. Powderly, General Master Workman of the Knights, and its moving spirit, explained his views on the relationship between working men and working women in this report to the members.

POWDERLY ON WOMEN WORKERS

. . . The working man has struggled down through the centuries for a recognition of his toil, and within the last ten

"New York City.—The Uptown 'New York Herald' Office—Servant Girls Writing Advertisements for Situations." Leslie's, Dec. 1874

"The Great Fire in Boston.—The Association for the Relief of Unemployed Workingwomen in Session at the Park Street Church." Leslie's, Dec. 1872

years has received more of recognition than ever before. But, while securing that recognition for himself he has selfishly ignored the woman worker, and she, through the same necessities which compelled him to part with his labor at a sacrifice, is now obliged to do the same by hers. The only logical result of that is it eventually reduces the wages of all, for the work of the future will be done by far more delicate hands than the past ever saw manipulating the implements of labor. The rights of the sexes are coequal. Their privileges should be the same, and I can see no reason why woman should not be entitled to share in giving to the world its products as well as man. Her compensation should be the same as that which man receives, and if for no other reason the selfishness of man should come to the rescue by aiding woman to command the same price for labor done as that which man receives. To do this the men of this Order must take more of an interest in the affairs of the women workers, and must give more support than heretofore to every effort put forth by the women of the land to place their labor upon an equity with that of the men. . . .

Equity draws no lines of difference between the sexes. Our Order is based upon equity and must do the same in order to make the words "equal pay for equal work" a living truth. . . . Only those who will work for small wages are employed in many occupations. It is not an uncommon thing to see whole factories in which women, children and old men are employed. . . . Unity of purpose, strength of will and a determination not to part for trifles wins not only battles on the tented field alone, but on the broad field of labor as well. These elements will eventually win for the working man the right to control the machine which now makes woman the medium through which man's wages are reduced. We must assist to elevate her, or through her helplessness she will make it impossible for man to help either her or himself. Shorn of sentiment and viewed in its proper light, the problem which woman presents to her sister woman is not the question of the rights of woman, nor yet the rights of man—it is the rights of humanity.[7]

Under Powderly's influence, the Knights of Labor eventually set up 190 local assemblies (or unions), which an estimated 50,000 women joined during the period of the Knights' greatest activity—between 1881 and 1886. Many women in the union seized the opportunity offered them to act in their own interests: they participated as delegates at the General Assemblies, conducted a survey of the hours and wages of working women, and publicized their need for equal treatment. On the recommendation of a committee of women, Leonora M. Barry, herself a mill worker, was appointed General Investigator for women's work. With impressive energy and ability, for three years Barry investigated working conditions, publicized her findings, and labored for the formation of women's assemblies.

At the 1888 General Assembly, Barry delivered the General Investigator's Report. The document provides a picture of the staggering amount of work Barry performed, traveling, speaking, and organizing. It also gives a picture of the jobs women held, the conditions under which they worked, and the frustrations that followed Barry's efforts to organize them.

REPORT OF THE GENERAL INVESTIGATOR OF WOMAN'S WORK AND WAGES

. . . With your other servants I herewith submit my annual report, with such suggestions and recommendations as my observations and judgment warrant me in believing to be for the best interest of all concerned. Ere I have concluded many may say I have done more lecturing than investigating. I have neglected neither wherever I found an opportunity to carry them out. I found by repeated trial and failure that to investigate the condition of women as thoroughly as I could wish was, as a Knight of Labor, simply impossible, as not only did employers refuse me the opportunity, but cautious friends of the employed warned them against ever holding conversation with the General Investigator, lest some error be made public for which they would receive blame and consequent discharge. . . .

My understanding of the duties implied in my office was that I was to do every thing in my power that would in my judgment have a tendency to educate and elevate the workingwomen of America and ameliorate their condition. Therefore, when I spoke to a public audience of American citizens, exposing existing evils and showing how, through the demands of Knighthood, they could be remedied, I felt that I was fulfilling the duties of my office. When I found a body of workingmen who were so blind to what justice demanded of them on behalf of women as to pass unanimously a resolution excluding women from our organization, I felt I was performing a sacred duty toward women by trying to enlighten those men and showing their mistake. When I found an opportunity of laying before other organizations of women the cause of their less fortunate sisters and mould a favorable sentiment, I felt I was doing that which is an actual necessity, as woman is often unconsciously woman's oppressor. With these, my honest convictions, I place my work of the past year in your hands, ready and willing to accept your decision and abide by the same. . . .

. . . During our stay at Minneapolis I addressed two public meetings, visited the Woman's Local, whose numerical strength and progress in the work of Knighthood was

sufficient evidence of the clear brain and honest heart of its members. From October 22 to 31 I filled an engagement under the auspices of D. A. 72 at Toledo, Ohio. There are two Locals of women in this city. Few are organized from the many industries in which they are employed, such as tailoring, knitting mills, box factories, pin factory, etc. The earnestness and activity of the officials of D. A. 72 will surely have its reward. After my address in Findlay, Ohio, a Woman's Local was organized. November 18 I delivered an address in Allentown, Pa. Here I found women employed in shoe, silk, shirt, stocking and cigar factories, none of which were organized, except about half of the three hundred employed in the silk mill. It is stated on good authority that of the eight hundred people employed in this factory about one hundred and fifty are children under 14 years of age— another proof of the great need of a State factory inspection law in the Keystone State, many parts of which is known as the Europe of America by the products of its cheap labor. . . .

December 7 to 20 filled dates with D. A. 68 of Troy, N. Y. There is not a city in the Empire State, excepting New York City, which stands so much in need of thorough organization as Troy. Women are employed principally in manufacturing shirts, collars, cuffs, and laundrying, with one or two knitting mills. In the shirt industry Troy has a governing influence throughout the State. This is also true of laundrying. At the first inception of the Order in Troy women flocked into the Order until their membership numbered thousands, but closely following their connection with the Order came the Ide's strike and lockout, with which all our members are familiar. Had the strike been successful, they might have remained members until disappointed in some other demand; its injudicious precipitation and consequent failure caused disruption in their ranks, although a faithful few still remain at the helm. . . .

On January 30 held a meeting of hatworkers in Brooklyn.

On February 10 held a public meeting at Harrisburg, Pa. One Woman's Local Assembly in the city, which was not as flourishing as it should be, owing, it was claimed, to some injudicious and illegal action on the part of some men, officials at the time of its formation.

On February 11 and 12, Mahanoy City. One Woman's Local was organized in this place, composed of the bright, intelligent, earnest wives, daughters and sisters of the miners of this locality, who, seeing the injustice done those whose welfare was identical with their own, determined to give their womanly support and influence toward securing justice at the hands of the coal barons of the Schuylkill Valley. But they met with opposition, bitter and unfounded, from a source from which they ought to look for support and encouragement, and the effect was suicidal to their brightest and best hopes.

On February 13 visited Columbia, Pa. February 15 visited Elkhart, Ind.; one Local of women in this city, very earnest but not very progressive. February 18, Elgin, Ill. The extensive watch factory known as the Elgin Watch Factory is situated here and employs about 2,000 women and girls, who, as far as I could learn, received fairly good wages and fair treatment. Quite a large number of the women were organized. There are also one or two milk-canning factories, in which women are employed, receiving very small wages. February 21 visited a Woman's Local in Chicago. February 23 held a public meeting at Pullman, Ill. This plant employs 8,050 people, about 75 of whom are women. The output per day is 27 cars. A large number of the men are organized, but none of the women, although they work at etching glass, painting, varnishing and upholstering, at all of which they receive fair wages. . . .

February 29, Chicago. Held a public meeting. This was my last and also my most successful meeting in this city. Chicago is a good field for organizers and educators, but with deep regret it must be admitted that up to the time of my visit both these important matters were neglected, especially in the interest of women. Being very sick while there I was unable to do much by way of investigation. However, I visited the manufacturing house of Marshall Field & Co.; the operatives worked on the top floor, but went up and down by way of elevator; room was nice, clean, warm and well-lighted. . . .

In a large retail store known as "The Fair" children of all ages from apparently nine years up to fifteen, are employed. Each was well drilled in the parrot-like answer to the query, "How old are you?" "Past fourteen." The older employes refused to give any information whatever about their wages or the system under which they worked. Another establishment had one of its departments in a basement, where salesmen and women, who were largely in the majority, worked all day with incandescent lights, not one ray of sunshine or fresh air, except such as was circulated through the rooms by means of pipes in the side. Here again I tried to glean some information, but failed, finding at least some women who did not love to talk. I was told on good authority that the reason for this was the employer would go to each girl in turn and tell her that, owing to her superior qualities, he would pay her more than any other, naming the amount, but upon condition that she would not mention it to her neighbor. Thus each imagined herself more favored than others and no confidences were exchanged, when in reality all got the same, the prevailing wages being from $2.50 to $5 per week, the highest ranging from $6 to $10, according to experience. There are employed in Chicago, including domestics, 80,000 women and girls at following industries: Shirtmakers, laundresses, children's shirt operatives, cloakmakers, buttonmakers, bookbinding, corsetmakers, furriers, regalias and costumes, shoeworkers, dressmakers, gents' neckwearmakers, cigarmakers (some factories being run exclusively by women), suspendermakers, tobaccoworkers, type-writers, printing-office operatives, hosiery and knit goods, gloves and mittens, 1,000 employed in tinshops, including many small girls, painters and decorators on china, glass, etc., coreworkers in iron and brass foundries, millinery, scouring, dying and feather cleaning, paper-box facto-

ries, paper-bag factory, confectionery, rag and junk shops (this work is mostly done by foreigners; it is very filthy and all done piece-work), photographers, actresses, gilders, waiters, cooks and the professions make up the army of women wage-workers. The injustice, wrongs and indignities which many of them suffer has been ably and truthfully told through the columns of the Chicago *Times*. . . .

On March 14, 15 and 16 held public meetings in Cleveland, Ohio; quite a number of women organized here, but only a small percentage of the number employed. In the various trades (cloak and shirtmaking being the prevailing industry) a great deal of dissatisfaction seemed to exist on account of small wages and arbitrary dealing. A seal plush cloak, selling from $40 to $75, is made by the cloakmakers of this city for 80 cents and $1 apiece, one being a day's work for an expert operative. . . .

On May 2 and 3 I was at Sandy Hill, N. Y., and from May 5 to 9 at Cohoes, N. Y., (D. A. 104). The unsuccessful termination of a strike in the Harmony Cotton Mills of that city caused the almost total disruption of the woman's organization; and it is a pity that such is the fact, as there is no city in the Union more in need of organized effort on the part of workwomen to protect themselves from wrongs that are suicidal to life, liberty and happiness. The effect of the employment of foreign labor, child labor, together with cutdowns and fines, the large number of married women who are obliged to seek employment to support their families owing to the inability, incapacity or dissipation of their husbands, is seen in the fact that in twelve years the reduction in the wages of the cotton operatives of Cohoes has been 45 per cent. by actual cut-downs—to say nothing of the injustice of holding back their earnings by shortage in measurement. And in this twelve years the amount of work required of the individual has been increased. The number of women employed in the six cotton mills, known as the Harmony Mills, and conducted by Garner & Co., is 1,617—married women, 500; single, 1,117—about 250 of whom are widows' children, (321 from 11 years of age and upward). Notwithstanding the repeated and continuous efforts of the State Factory Inspector, through the conniving of parents and employers the child-labor law is violated. The large number of women and children employed is owing chiefly to there being no work for men at living wages. Fines are reported to be excessively large. In the twenty-one woollen mills of Cohoes the number of women employed is 2,449; children, from 12 years upward, 117.

The box-making industry of this city employs 90 women —married, 5; single, 85; widows, 4; children, from 12 to 16 years, 25. In all three of these industries the prevalence of diseases among women is very great, being mostly of consumption and complaints peculiar to women only, brought on by constant confinement and close application to their work, defective sanitary condition, and inability through small wages to secure sufficient home comforts. The effect of all this on future generations will be a progeny wanting in development and health of body and mind. . . .

From June 25 to 30 stayed at Dubuque, Iowa. There are two Woman's Locals here, neither of which are very strong in membership, owing largely to some internal dissension, which was handled in turn by Local, State and General Officers; and, as is usually the case where so much handling takes place, was not settled at all. Since my visit one Local has died a natural death, from the same disease that has killed many others—selfishness and struggle for self-aggrandizement and personal supremacy. Aside from this the falling off in membership of the old Local was just such ingratitude and lack of appreciation as has been displayed by thousands of others throughout the land, as through organization they had received innumerable benefits. The principal industry here employing women is the overall factories. Previous to organization the operatives were fined 25 cents per week for machine power; compelled to buy their own thread; pay for the needles used in the machine, and also for the oil they put on their machine. Since and through organization all this has been done away with, which was equal to an increase of 15 per cent. They are paid 85 to 90 cents and $1.25 per doz.; weekly pay from $6 to $7.50. Fire escapes have also been put upon both sides of the factories. All claimed their general condition to be above the average. . . .

It has been intimated that the Woman's Department was started on sentiment. Well, if so, it has turned out to be one of the most thoroughly practical departments in the Order. Without egotism I can safely say it has done as much effective work in cheering, encouraging, educating and instructing the women of this Order in the short year of its existence as was done by the organization in the whole time of women's connection with it previous to its establishment. Ten thousand organized women to-day look to the Woman's Department for counsel, advice and assistance. It is their hope, their guiding star; and the free and full outpouring of sorrow-stricken and heavy-laden hearts, not alone of women and girls, but their heart-broken parents, that comes to the Woman's Department for consolation and comfort cannot be recorded here because that would be a breach of sacred confidence. . . .

There have come to the Woman's Department, from November 1, 1887, to October 1, 1888, 537 applications for my presence, 213 of which have been filled by actual service, and all others answered from the office. Communications requesting advice and information, 789, all of which have been answered by the faithful and efficient Secretary, Mary A. O'Reilly, whom I made no mistake in appointing, or the General Executive Board in indorsing, and to whom the Woman's Department owes a goodly share of its success. Circulars, written and printed, sent out, 1,900—pertaining to Beneficial Department and information blanks. Telegrams received and answered, 97. The number of women in the Order at present, as nearly as can be enumerated, is between 11,000 and 12,000 and represent the following trades: Tailoresses, tobacco-workers, clerks, shoe-workers, waiteresses, printers, glass-packers, domestics, textile-workers, dressmakers, farmers, school teachers, laun-dresses, watch-casemakers, students, authoresses, editors, rubberworkers, agents, music teachers, milliners, operators, typedressers, eyletmakers, hatters, tackmakers and squib-makers. . . . [8]

At its peak, the Knights of Labor had about 600,000 members. But it began to weaken after 1886. By the early 1890's, it was almost defunct. Most of the women's assemblies collapsed. All that remained was an introduction to national unionization and a brief exploration of the idea that all working men and women were interdependent.

The failure of the Knights of Labor and the subsequent rise of the American Federation of Labor as the major national labor organization had important consequences for the working woman. In contrast to the Knights, who, under Powderly's grand vision, aimed at radical changes in the country's economic and social institutions, the AFL, founded in 1881, had narrower goals. Its main concern was to increase its members' share of economic benefits within the existing economic and social framework. Had the Knights succeeded (a rather remote possibility), American history probably would have been drastically different, and with it the condition of American women. The success of the AFL augured little change and improvement for women wage earners.

Whereas the Knights believed that both practical and humanitarian considerations argued for the unionization of women wage earners, the leaders of the American Federation of Labor did not. Instead, they generally supported the view that women belonged at home, as wives and mothers, and not in the factories, as competitors. The Federation, therefore, was generally slow to aid or encourage the formation of women's trade unions.

Moreover, the American Federation of Labor was a federation of unions of relatively skilled and overwhelmingly white workers, organized by trades. Women, by and large, were among the most unskilled workers in the country. Often they were employed in seasonal jobs and often they were black. Thus the AFL did not come into contact with the mass of women wage earners (or the mass of male workers either).

A few women's trade unions did affiliate with the American Federation of Labor, and at national conventions the Federation endorsed the concept of equal pay for equal work for men and women, favored woman suffrage, supported protective legislation for women workers, and called for the organization of female wage earners. In practice, the Federation did little positive work toward unionizing women workers and in many instances actually opposed it. At the federal level, the AFL denied charter requests from women's unions, while member unions did little to accommodate themselves to the needs of women workers in their trade. By and large, then, the rise of the

The Milliner

The Straw Braider

The Artificial Flower Maker

The Type Rubber

The Umbrella Maker

The Washerwomen

American Federation of Labor did not appreciably change the condition of women wage earners at the turn of the century.

When the new century began, most of the five million female workers were unorganized and unaware of the strength that lay in their numbers. They were cut off from the male labor movement and, as we will see later, from the major national women's organizations. Moreover, they were also separated from each other by differences of race, religion, cultural background, and training. They constituted a vulnerable and cheap labor supply—bewildered farm girls forced to find work in the cities, European peasant women learning new ways of life and language, and growing numbers of black women looking northward for a better life.

In the years after 1900, conditions worsened noticeably for these millions of women workers and for men, too: prices continually went up, wages often shrank, and working conditions remained primitive and unregulated. The work experiences of millions of people were unpublished chapters of misery.

A few personal records of the experiences of this era remain. In 1905, Dorothy Richardson published an account describing her ordeals in the unskilled labor market of New York City. Coming from a small rural town, Richardson joined the heterogeneous throng of women who flooded the job market. Her story, which is briefly excerpted here, provides a dramatic insight into the lives of the women who struggled for survival in the cities of industrial America.

RICHARDSON'S "LONG DAY"

[The writer had recently found a job in a box factory.] . . . During my five minutes' absence the most exciting event of the day had occurred. Adrienne, one of the strippers, had just been carried away, unconscious, with two bleeding finger-stumps. In an unguarded moment the fingers had been cut off in her machine. Although their work does not allow them to stop a moment, her companions were all loud in sympathy for this misfortune, which is not rare. Little Jennie, the unfortunate girl's turner-in and fellow-worker for two years, wept bitterly as she wiped away the blood from the long, shining knife and prepared to take the place of her old superior, with its increased wage of five dollars and half a week. The little girl had been making only three dollars and a quarter, and so, as Henrietta remarked, "It's a pretty bad accident that don't bring good to somebody."

"Did they take her away in a carriage?" Henrietta asked of Goldy Courtleigh, who had stopped a moment to rest at our table.

OPPOSITE:
From Life in New York by William Burns

"Well, I should say! What's the use of getting your fingers whacked off if you can't get a carriage-ride out of it?" . . .

The order on which we worked was, like most of the others on the floor that day, for late-afternoon delivery. Our ruching-boxes had to be finished that day, even though it took every moment till six or even seven o'clock. Saturday being what is termed a "short-day," one had to work with might and main in order to leave at half-past four. . . . Lunch-time found us still far behind. Therefore we did not stop to eat, but snatched bites of cake and sandwich as hunger dictated, and convenience permitted, all the while pasting and labeling and taping our boxes. Nor were we the only toilers obliged to forgo the hard-earned half-hour of rest.

The awakening thunder of the machinery burst gratefully on our ears. It meant that the last half of the weary day had begun. How my blistered hands ached now! How my swollen feet and ankles throbbed with pain! Every girl limped now as she crossed the floor with her towering burden, and the procession back and forth between machines and tables began all over again. Lifting and carrying and shoving; cornering and taping and lacing—it seemed as though the afternoon would never wear to an end.

The whole great mill was now charged with an unaccustomed excitement—an excitement which had in it something of solemnity. There was no sign of the usual mirth and hilarity which constitute the mill's sole attraction. There was no singing—not even Angelina's "Fatal Wedding." No exchange of stories, no sallies. Each girl bent to her task with a fierce energy that was almost maddening in its intensity.

Blind and dizzy with fatigue, I peered down the long, dusty aisles of boxes toward the clock above Annie Kinzer's desk. It was only two. Every effort, human and mechanical, all over the great factory, was now strained almost to the breaking point. How long can this agony last? How long can the roar and the rush and the throbbing pain continue until that nameless and unknown something snaps like an overstrained fiddle-string and brings relief? The remorseless clock informed us that there were two hours more of this torture before the signal to "clean up"—a signal, however, which is not given until the last girl has finished her allotted task. At half-past two it appeared hopeless even to dream of getting out before the regular six o'clock.

The head foreman rushed through the aisles and bawled to us to "hustle for all we were worth," as customers were all demanding their goods.

"My God! ain't we hustling?" angrily shouted Rosie Sweeny, a pretty girl at the next table, who supplied most of the profanity for our end of the room. "God Almighty! how I hate Easter and Christmas-time! Oh, my legs is 'most breaking," and with that the overwrought girl burst into a passionate tirade against everybody, the foreman included, and all the while she never ceased to work. . . .

By four o'clock the last box was done. Machines became mute, wheels were stilled, and the long black belts sagged into limp folds. Every girl seized a broom or a scrub-pail, and hilarity reigned supreme while we swept and scrubbed for the next half hour. . . .

[Richardson also worked in a laundry.]

. . . "Shakers Wanted.—Apply to Foreman" was the first that caught my eye. I did n't know what a "shaker" was, but that did not deter me from forming a sudden determination to be one. . . . I found the "Pearl Laundry," a broad brick building, grim as a fortress, and fortified by a breastwork of laundry-wagons backed up to the curb and disgorging their contents of dirty clothes. Making my way as best I could through the jam of horses and drivers and baskets, I reached the narrow, unpainted pine door marked, "Employees' Entrance," and filed up the stairs with a crowd of other girls— all, like myself, seeking work.

At the head of the stairs we filed into a mammoth steam-filled room that occupied an entire floor. The foreman made quick work of us. Thirty-two girls I counted as they stepped up to the pale-faced, stoop-shouldered young fellow, who addressed each one as "Sally," in a tone which, despite its good-natured familiarity, was none the less businesslike and respectful. At last it came my turn.

"Hello, Sally! Ever shook?"

"No."

"Ever work in a laundry?"

"No; but I'm very handy."

"What did you work at last?"

"Jewel-cases."

"All right, Sally; we'll start you in at three and a half a week, and maybe we'll give you four dollars after you get broke in to the work.—Go over there, where you seen them other ladies go," he called after me as I moved away, and waved his hand toward a pine-board partition. Here, sitting on bundles of soiled linen and on hampers, my thirty-two predecessors were corralled, each awaiting assignment to duty.

. . . the foreman appeared in the door, and we trooped out at his heels. Down the length of the big room, through a maze of moving hand-trucks and tables and rattling mangles, we followed him to the extreme rear, where he deposited us, in groups of five and six, at the big tables that were ranged from wall to wall and heaped high with wet clothes, still twisted just as they were turned out of the steam-wringer. An old woman with a bent back showed me the very simple process of "shaking."

"Jist take the corners like this,"—suiting the action to the word,—"and give a shake like this, and pile them on top o' one another— like this," . . .

For the first half-hour I shook napkins bearing the familiar legend—woven in red—of a ubiquitous dairy-lunch place, and the next half-hour was occupied with bed-linen bearing the mark of a famous hostelry. During that time I had become fairly accustomed to my new surroundings, and was now able to distinguish, out of the steamy turmoil, the general features of a place that seethed with life and action. All the workers were women and girls, with the exception of the fifteen big, black, burly negroes who operated the tubs and the wringers which were ranged along the rear wall on a platform that ran parallel with and a little behind the shakers' tables. The negroes were stripped to the waist of all save a thin gauze undershirt. There was something demoniacal in their gestures and shouts as they ran about the vats of boiling soap-suds, from which they transferred the clothes to the swirling wringers, and then dumped them at last upon the big trucks. The latter were pushed away by relays of girls, who strained at the heavy load. The contents of the trucks were dumped first on the shakers' tables, and when each piece was smoothed out we—the shakers—redumped the stacks into the truck, which was pushed on to the manglers, who ironed it all out in the hot rolls. So, after several other dumpings and redumpings, the various lots were tied and labeled.

Meanwhile a sharp, incessant pain had grown out of what was in the first ten or fifteen minutes a tired feeling in the arms—that excruciating, nerve-torturing pain which comes as a result of a ceaseless muscular action that knows no variation or relaxation. . . .

The work was now under full blast, and every one of the hundred and twenty-five girls worked with frenzied energy as the avalanche of clothes kept falling in upon us and were sent with lightning speed through the different processes, from the tubs to the packers' counters. Nor was there any abatement of the snowy landslide—not a moment to stop and rest the aching arms. Just as fast as the sweating negroes could unload the trucks into the tubs, more trucks came rolling in from the elevator, and the foaming tubs swirled perpetually, swallowing up, it would seem, all the towels and pillow-cases and napkins in Greater New York. . . .

In the excruciating agony of the hours that followed, the trucks became a veritable anodyne for the pains that shot through my whole body. Leaning over their deep sides was a welcome relief from the strained, monotonous position at the tables. . . .

The day was terrifically hot outdoors, and with the fearful heat that came up through the floor from the engine-room directly under us, combined with the humidity of the steam-filled room, we were all driven to a state of half-dress before the noon hour arrived. The women opened their dresses at the neck and cast off their shoes, and the foreman threw his suspenders off his shoulders, while the colored washers paddled about on the sloppy floor in their bare black feet.

"Don't any men work in this place except the foreman?" I asked Mrs. Mooney, who had toiled a long time in the "Pearl" and knew everything.

"Love of Mary!" she exclaimed indignantly; "and d' ye think any white man that called hisself a white man would work in sich a place as this, and with naygurs?"

"But we work here," I argued.

"Well, we be wimmin," she declared, drawing a pinch of snuff into her nostrils in a manner that indicated finality.

"But if it is n't good enough for a man, it is n't good enough for us, even if we are women!" I persisted.

She looked at me half in astonishment, half in suspicion

at my daring to question the time-honored order of things. Economics could make no appeal to her intelligence, and shooting a glance out of her hard old black eyes, she replied with a logic that permitted no gainsaying.

"Love of Mary! if yez don't like yer job, ye can git out. Sure and we don't take on no airs around here!"9

Between 1900 and 1914, the number of strikes and the number of workers joining unions increased greatly. For women, the period was one of unprecedented labor activity. The strikes took place mainly in the garment industry, a major employer of female labor, and one that was characterized by unrestrained exploitation and abuse of its workers. In 1909, some shirtwaist workers in New York City went on strike. Their numbers swelled as other workers voted to join them. This newspaper story describes the unusual event.

"WAISTMAKERS VOTE GENERAL STRIKE"

NEW YORK, Nov. 23, 1909
Thirty thousand ladies' waistmakers, driven to desperation by the intolerable conditions prevailing in their trade, voted to go on a general strike last night at four enormous mass meetings which packed Cooper Union, Astoria Hall, Beethoven Hall and Manhattan Lyceum.

For weeks these weary men and women—70 per cent of them are women—debated the advisability of rebelling against long hours, low wages and brutal treatment at the hands of the bosses and their foremen, of pitting their numbers against the wealth of their masters. For weeks they weighed the awful trials of a strike in the balance against their present miserable lot, and unanimously they decided to strike.

The decision to strike was first reached at the Cooper Union meeting which was addressed by Samuel Gompers, president of the AFL.

Gompers was given an ovation when he was introduced by Chairman B. Feigenbaum. The vast crowd rose to its feet and cheered him very enthusiastically for several minutes.

"A man would be less than human," said Gompers, in opening, "if he were not impressed with your reception. I want you men and women not to give all your enthusiasm for a man, no matter who he may be. I would prefer that

you put all of your enthusiasm into your union and your cause." . . .

Appealing to the men and women to stand together, he declared: "If you had an organization before this, it would have stood there as a challenge to the employers who sought to impose such conditions as you bear.

"This is the time and the opportunity, and I doubt if you let it pass whether it can be created again in five or ten years, or a generation. I say, friends, do not enter too hastily but when you can't get the manufacturers to give you what you want, then strike. And when you strike, let the manufacturers know you are on strike!

"I ask you to stand together," said Gompers in conclusion, "to have faith in yourselves, to be true to your comrades. If you strike, be cool, calm, collected and determined. Let your watchword be: Union and progress, and until then no surrender." . . .

Clara Lemich, who was badly beaten up by thugs during the strike in the shop of Louis Leiserson, interrupted Jacob Panken just as he started to speak, saying: "I want to say a few words." Cries came from all parts of the hall. "Get up on the platform!" Willing hands lifted the frail little girl with flashing black eyes to the stage, and she said simply: "I have listened to all the speakers. I would not have further patience for talk, as I am one of those who feels and suffers from the things pictured. I move that we go on a general strike!"

As the tremulous voice of the girl died away, the audience rose en masse and cheered her to the echo . . . [and voted the general strike.]10

Similar strikes took place in the garment industries of Philadelphia and Chicago. Together they added up to the largest strike of women workers in American labor history. During the strikes more women than ever before joined the garment workers union, and by 1920 almost one-half of the women in the clothing trades were organized. Through these organizations—the Amalgamated Clothing Workers and the International Ladies' Garment Workers Union—women finally entered into the mainstream of the labor movement.

But progress for working people was ponderously slow; in 1914, only 10% of all industrial workers were unionized; and only 5% of the women in factory jobs were organized. More than 98% of all women wage earners remained unorganized to face the difficulties and hardships of their situation alone.

CHAPTER NINE

TIES BETWEEN WOMEN: CLASS, RACE, ETHNICITY, AND THE WOMEN'S MOVEMENT

1850-1920

During most of its history, the organized women's movement made few efforts to strengthen the bonds between all women and to minimize the economic, social, and racial differences that tended to separate them from one another. The membership of most movement organizations was overwhelmingly white, and the women came from relatively prosperous families and were relatively well educated. Their ties with other women—with black women, with poor women, and with immigrant women—were often fragile and sometimes nonexistent. While the rhetoric of sisterhood was usually a part of the women's movement, only on occasion did the organized women's movement reach out to understand and accommodate the needs and attitudes of less fortunate women. Around the turn of the century, a fear of labor and farm radicalism and heightened racial and class prejudice afflicted many Americans, and this demolished even the rhetorical solidarity among women. As the twentieth century began, middle-class women viewed poor women—black, white, and immigrant—as significantly different from themselves. With few exceptions, no common need caused them to rise above this outlook.

In the earliest years close ties with abolitionism seemed to nurture a sense of kinship between women and slaves, and especially with female slaves. The prominence of black leaders like Frederick Douglass and Sojourner Truth in early women's rights activities reflected an often-voiced belief that women and black Americans would march side by side toward equality. But this unusual picture of racial harmony and cooperation soon clouded over.

During the struggle over the Fourteenth and Fifteenth amendments after 1865, the women's movement split apart over its relationship to the black movement. While Lucy Stone and other women's-righters agreed with male abolitionists that women should step aside and allow the black man to pass ahead of them and get the vote, Elizabeth Cady Stanton, Susan B. Anthony, and many other women refused to do so. They would not postpone the fight for women's equality, and they opposed expanding the rights of black men rather than acquiesce in the continued disfranchisement of women. Though it was not apparent then, a serious separation between the women's movement and black women had begun.

The separation deepened with each passing decade, for the times were destructive of solidarity between black and white. During the decades after Reconstruction, the emphasis on reconciling North and South allowed the deep racist prejudices and antagonisms of the country to surface. The compassion and humanitarianism for black Americans that the "war against slavery" had engendered evaporated with frightening rapidity. This was the era in which the devices of segregation were perfected in both North and South, putting the lie to much of the idealism in American life. The Supreme Court nodded approval at schemes to disfranchise black voters. After 1890, the number and frequency of lynchings moved toward record dimensions.

Within the women's movement, the racism of the country echoed clearly. The Young Women's Christian Association was segregated. At its 1900 convention, the General Federation of Women's Clubs denied delegate status to Josephine St. Pierre Ruffin. Ruffin, a well-known and respected New Englander, was there to represent the Woman's Era Club, a black group in Boston. Two years later, after considerable and bitter debate over the Ruffin incident, the GFWC reaffirmed its racist policy.

NAWSA AND RACIAL ISSUES

In 1898, Mary Church Terrell, president of the National Association of Colored Women, spoke at the National American Woman Suffrage Association's convention about "The Progress and Problems of Colored Women." The next year, one of these problems was brought to the attention of the convention by this resolution:

Resolved, That colored women ought not to be compelled to ride in smoking cars, and that suitable accommodations should be provided for them.[1]

Lottie Wilson Jackson, a Michigan delegate to the convention and a light-complexioned black American, proposed the resolution and spoke for it. Minutes of the meeting report that she said the following:

. . . in some parts of the South it was almost impossible for respectable colored women to travel, because of the filthy state of the cars, and the insults to which they were exposed from the rough company into which they were thrown. The Pullman cars had been their only refuge from such conditions, and it was now proposed to exclude them from these. There was a great work to be done among the ignorant colored women which could only be done for them by more intelligent women of their own race, and it was important that educated colored women should not be hindered from working for the improvement and moral elevation of their less fortunate sisters. In traveling for the Association of colored women to which she belonged, she had found the condition of the cars in some parts of the country almost intolerable.[2]

Southern delegates at the meeting objected strongly to the resolution. They disputed Jackson's contention that there was segregation on the railroads, and they deplored the resolution as an irritant to the healing wounds of the War Between the States.

Finally, Susan B. Anthony ended the debate with a statement that is summed up below by the convention reporter. It contained a sad admission from the old and once fearless fighter for women's equality.

SUSAN B. ANTHONY'S STATEMENT

No one will doubt that I am true to the colored people. I am true to both the races the blood of which is mingled in Mrs. Jackson's veins. But what I want to say to you is this: We women are a helpless, disfranchised class. Our hands are tied. While we are in this condition, it is not for us to go passing resolutions against railroad corporations or anybody else.[3]

Earlier in the discussion, Alice Stone Blackwell had argued that an injustice to any woman, anywhere, was the concern of the convention. But, with apparent relief, Anthony's statement ended the discussion, and the women voted to table Jackson's resolution.

THE SOUTHERN STRATEGY OF THE SUFFRAGE MOVEMENT

After 1890, expediency and political strategy joined with racism to enlarge the breach between the women's movement and black women.

Many years earlier, while attempting to recruit Southern members for the American Woman Suffrage Association, Henry Blackwell had argued persuasively that the enfranchisement of women in the South would increase the white vote sufficiently to counteract the influence of black voters. After 1890 and during the height of the suffrage struggle, this argument was a major theme in the National American Woman Suffrage Association's efforts to attract and satisfy the growing number of Southern suffragists and to win support from Southern politicians for a suffrage amendment to the Constitution.

The National American Woman Suffrage Association's 1903 convention was held in New Orleans, in good part to help attract Southern suffragists. Just before the April meeting, the New Orleans Times-Democrat *wrote an editorial attacking NAWSA's racial views (and Anthony's in particular), as objectionable to Southerners. A letter from NAWSA officers to the newspaper followed.*

NAWSA'S VIEW ON THE "COLOR QUESTION"

March 18, 1903

To the Editor of the *Times-Democrat*:

The article in this morning's *Times-Democrat*, entitled "Woman Suffrage in the South," contains some remarks that are evidently based on a misapprehension.

. . . Like every other national association, it [the NAWSA] is made up of persons of all shades of opinion on the race question, and on all other questions except those relating to its particular object. The Northern and Western members hold the views on the race question that are customary in their sections. The Southern members hold the views that are customary in the South. The doctrine of State's rights is recognized in the National Association, and each auxiliary State Association arranges its own affairs in accordance with its own ideas and in harmony with the customs of its own section.

Individual members, in addresses made outside the National Association, are of course free to express their views on all sorts of extraneous questions, but they speak for themselves as individuals, and not for the Association. . . .

The National American Woman Suffrage Association is seeking to do away with the requirement of a sex qualification for suffrage. What other qualifications shall be asked for, it leaves to each State. The Southern women most active in the National Association have always, in their own States, emphasized the fact that granting suffrage to women who can read and write, and who pay taxes, would insure white supremacy without resorting to any methods of doubtful constitutionality. The Louisiana State Suffrage Association asks for the ballot for educated and tax-paying women only, and its officers believe that in this lies "the only permanent and honorable solution of the race question." Most of the Suffrage Associations of the Northern and Western States ask for the ballot for all women, though Maine and several other States have lately asked for it with an educational or tax qualification. . . .

SUSAN B. ANTHONY.
CARRIE CHAPMAN CATT.
ALICE STONE BLACKWELL.
LAURA CLAY.
KATE M. GORDON.
HARRIET TAYLOR UPTON.
ANNA H. SHAW.[4]

Two Southerners, Laura Clay of Kentucky and Kate M. Gordon from Louisiana, held influential positions in NAWSA between 1896 and 1910. In 1903, NAWSA convention participants in New Orleans heard a major address by Belle Kearney of Mississippi on "The South and Woman Suffrage." After surveying the contributions of the South in American history, Kearney spoke about the present:

KEARNEY'S SPEECH ON THE SOUTH

. . . The people of the South have remained true to their royal inheritance. To-day the Anglo-Saxon triumphs in them more completely than in the inhabitants of any portion of the United States—the Anglo-Saxon blood, the Anglo-Saxon ideals, continue the precious treasure of 2,000 years of effort and aspiration. . . .

To-day one third of the population of the South is of the negro race, and there are more negroes in the United States than there are inhabitants in "Mexico, the third Republic of the world." In some Southern States the negroes far outnumber the whites, and are so numerous in all of them as to constitute what is called a "problem." . . .

The world is scarcely beginning to realize the enormity of the situation that faces the South in its grapple with the race question which was thrust upon it at the close of the Civil War, when 4,500,000 ex-slaves, illiterate and semi-barbarous, were enfranchised. Such a situation has no parallel in history. . . . The South has struggled under its death-weight for nearly forty years, bravely and magnanimously.

The Southern States are making a desperate effort to maintain the political supremacy of Anglo-Saxonism by amendments to their constitutions limiting the right to vote by a property and educational qualification. . . .

The present suffrage laws in the different Southern States can be only temporary measures for protection. Those who are wise enough to look beneath the surface will be compelled to realize the fact that they act as a stimulus to the black man to acquire both education and property, but no incentive is given to the poor whites; for it is understood, in a general way, that any man whose skin is fair enough to let the blue veins show through, may be allowed the right of franchise.

The industrial education that the negro is receiving at Tuskegee and other schools is only fitting him for power, and when the black man becomes necessary to a community by reason of his skill and acquired wealth, and the poor white man, embittered by his poverty and humiliated by his inferiority, finds no place for himself or his children, then will come the grapple between the races.

To avoid this unspeakable culmination, the enfranchisement of women will have to be effected, and an educational and property qualification for the ballot be made to apply, without discrimination, to both sexes and to both races. It will spur the poor white to keep up with the march of progression, and enable him to hold his own. The class that is not willing to measure its strength with that of an inferior is not fit to survive.

The enfranchisement of women would insure immediate and durable white supremacy, honestly attained; for, upon unquestionable authority, it is stated that "in every Southern State but one, there are more educated women than all the illiterate voters, white and black, native and foreign, combined." As you probably know, of all the women in the South who can read and write, ten out of every eleven are white. When it comes to the proportion of property between the races, that of the white outweighs that of the black immeasurably. The South is slow to grasp the great fact that the enfranchisement of women would settle the race question in politics. . . . [5]

Kearney's speech was followed by "great applause" and comments by Carrie Chapman Catt, NAWSA president, that made it clear that there was room for Southern white supremacy under the umbrella of woman suffrage.

CATT ON THE RACE PROBLEM

. . . Almost every day questions are sent up here as to our position on the race question. The woman question, as such, has nothing to do with the Negro question. Here is a letter just sent up by a New Orleans woman: "We are afraid, if we come into your Association, that colored clubs may some day be let in, and that we shall find ourselves obliged to meet colored women on a footing of equality." I think I have heard that the South believes in State rights. The National American W. S. A. recognizes them. Louisiana has the right to regulate the conditions of membership for Louisiana; it has not the right to regulate them for Massachusetts, nor has Massachusetts for Louisiana. It is perfectly safe for you to come in on that basis.

Miss Kearney is right in saying that the race problem is the problem of the whole country, and not that of the South alone. The responsibility for it is partly ours. But if the North shipped slaves to the South and sold them, remember that the North has sent some money since then into the South to help undo part of the wrong that we did to you and to them. Let us try to get nearer together, and to understand each other's ideas on the race question, and let us try to solve it together.[6]

In 1913, suffragists organized a parade in Washington, D.C., as part of a program to arouse interest in a federal suffrage amendment and rejuvenate suffrage activity. Ida B. Wells Barnett, a black woman, was president of a Chicago suffrage club. But National American Woman Suffrage Association officials, organizing the march, asked Barnett not to walk with the Illinois delegation, fearing that a mixture of black and white women would alienate Southern suffragists.

The next year, in response to pressure from Southern states'-righters within NAWSA, the Association transferred its support from the traditional federal suffrage amendment to a new proposal, the Shaforth-Palmer amendment, which put the initiative and the power to establish woman suffrage in state referendums, rather than in congressional action. Although NAWSA's affair with Shaforth-Palmer lasted only one year, it was illustrative of the strong pull of expediency and NAWSA's susceptibility to Southern views and Southern attitudes as it strove for Southern support for woman suffrage.

The National American Woman Suffrage Association was not alone in condoning, or even promoting, racist sentiments in the struggle for woman suffrage. Other suffrage organizations and other women's organizations that endorsed the vote for women behaved similarly. The National Woman's Party was formed as a result of a schism within NAWSA; the women who left the older suffrage group were more radical in the tactics and strategy they used in pursuit of the vote, but they too were willing to capitalize on racism, as a flyer distributed by the National Woman's Party illustrates.

Officers of the National American Woman Suffrage Association developed a "Winning Plan," in which they carefully calculated the votes needed to gain approval in Congress for the suffrage amendment and the states in which they were likely to gain such votes. They understood clearly that some Southern votes were necessary for the amendment to pass. In 1919, these calculations were uppermost when a black women's organization, the Northeastern Federation of Women's Clubs, applied for membership in the National American Woman Suffrage Association.

In March, the following letter was sent to the president of the New England group. It is an eloquent and persuasive request for the black women to wait in their application for membership until the suffrage struggle had succeeded, and

its arguments, based on political expediency, are ironically reminiscent of the request white women received in 1868 to wait until the black man had achieved the vote.

A PLEA FOR PATIENCE

Miss Elizabeth C. Carter,
Pres. Northeastern Fed. of Women's Clubs,
New Bedford, Mass.

My dear Miss Carter:

Mrs. Carrie Chapman Catt, president of the National Woman Suffrage Association, has been talking with me in reference to the application of the Northeastern Federation of Women's Clubs for co-operative membership and has asked me to write you my views. She feels that as I am not an officer of the association I can do this simply as a friend. My father and mother were Abolitionists, and before and during the Civil War their doors were always open to the colored people. They were in favor of woman suffrage before there was any movement for it. I have helped it since I was in my twenties. . . .

I write you these things to show you my sympathy and interest for the colored race, and its women especially have

Flyer

Will The Federal Suffrage Amendment Complicate The Race Problem?

A little study will prove that the national enfranchisement of women will IN NO WAY complicate the race problem.

In all of the fifteen Southern States, except Mississippi and South Carolina, THE WHITE WOMEN GREATLY OUTNUMBER THE NEGRO WOMEN.

In nine of these States, THE WHITE WOMEN OUTNUMBER THE TOTAL NEGRO POPULATION.

There are in the Southern States 2,017,286 MORE WHITE WOMEN THAN NEGRO MEN AND WOMEN PUT TOGETHER.

The following table taken from the Census of 1910 proves this statement. The figures are for the total population of the States named. They may be found on page 100 of the Abstract of the 1910 Census.

STATES	Total Negro Population	White Women	Negro Women	Preponderance of White over Negro Women
Maryland	232,250	533,567	117,501	416,066
Virginia	671,096	685,446	340,554	344,892
North Carolina	697,843	745,659	358,262	387,397
South Carolina	835,843	335,617	427,765	-92,148
Georgia	1,176,987	707,314	596,724	110,590
Florida	308,669	211,089	147,307	63,782
Mississippi	1,009,487	384,055	506,692	-122,636
Alabama	908,282	602,941	460,488	142,453
Tennessee	473,088	841,810	239,378	602,432
Kentucky	261,656	997,918	130,164	867,754
Arkansas	442,891	544,606	219,568	325,038
Louisiana	713,874	460,626	360,050	100,576
Texas	691,049	1,533,411	345,108	1,188,303
Missouri	157,452	1,528,376	76,963	1,451,413
West Virginia	64,173	549,491	27,566	521,925
Total	8,644,640	10,661,926	4,354,089	6,307,837

In Mississippi and South Carolina, where negro women outnumber white women, negro men outnumber white men. There is no more reason why the presence of negro women should debar women from voting, than the presence of negro men debars men from voting.

Mississippi imposes a heavy educational qualification; South Carolina both an educational and a property qualification. If women voted, these qualifications would apply to women exactly as to men.

A FEDERAL SUFFRAGE AMENDMENT MERELY FORBIDS THE DISFRANCHISEMENT OF A WOMAN ON THE SOLE GROUND THAT SHE IS A WOMAN.

There are to-day, in all our States, widely-varying voting qualifications—some wise; some unwise. Women did not frame these qualifications; and since women are disfranchised, they cannot change them. They merely ask that where a woman measures up to the standard required of a man, she may not be debarred from voting because she is a woman.

This will not make our electoral arrangements perfect, but it will remedy THEIR MOST GLARING INJUSTICE, THE ALMOST COMPLETE DISCRIMINATION AGAINST WOMEN.

NATIONAL LITERATURE HEADQUARTERS
NATIONAL WOMAN'S PARTY
Lafayette Sq., Washington, D. C.

no stronger friend than myself. . . . It would be impossible for me to give any advice that I did not believe to be for their highest welfare and in this spirit I am asking your Federation to withdraw *temporarily* its application for admission to the National American Suffrage Association.

The situation in regard to the Federal Amendment has now reached its climax and without that amendment there will not be universal woman suffrage in your lifetime. Until within a few years the Southern members of Congress have stood like a solid wall against it and have been sustained by the women of their States. Through reason, argument, logic and diplomacy every Southern State Suffrage Association now supports the Federal Amendment. With this backing 56 Southern Representatives voted for it when it was carried in the Lower House, Jan. 10, 1917. In March, 1914, three Democratic Senators voted for it; in October, 1918, 12; in February, 1919, 13. These figures show the remarkable progress in Southern sentiment.

This Federal Amendment has now become a question of cold, hard politics. Even if the Republican members of Congress should stand solidly for it they have not the two-thirds necessary to carry it, but eight from the six States represented by your Federation are unalterably opposed to it. Some Democratic votes are absolutely essential to carry it and most of these must come from the South. Without the consent of some Southern Legislatures it positively cannot be ratified after it has been submitted. In the closing days of the last session Senator Jones, chairman of the Suffrage Committee, offered the amendment with a change in the enabling act which Senator Gay of Louisiana was willing to accept, and if a vote could have been secured it would have carried, but the Republicans prevented a vote.

Such is the situation. Many of the Southern members are now willing to surrender their beloved doctrine of State's rights, and their only obstacle is fear of "the colored woman's vote" in the States where it is likely to equal or exceed the white woman's vote. It has been the policy of the leaders of the National Association to meet this foreboding with silence. It has never yielded one inch of its original position taken when it was founded fifty years ago: "The right of suffrage shall not be denied or abridged on account of *sex*." This was its first demand, this is the exact wording of the Federal Amendment today. It has refused to assist in any way the effort of the women of any State for a white women's franchise, a taxpaying women's franchise or anything except universal suffrage. The proposed Federal Amendment applies to colored women exactly as it applies to white women. If it fails, both alike will remain disfranchised.

Two-thirds of both houses of the new Congress are pledged to vote for this amendment. There is every indication that it will be adopted early in the session. The opponents are not leaving a stone unturned to defeat it and if the news is flashed throughout the Southern States at this most critical moment that the National American Association has just admitted an organization of 6,000 colored women, the enemies can cease from further effort—the defeat of the amendment will be assured. It is for the Northeastern Federation of Women's Clubs to determine whether admission as a co-operative member of the association at the present time is worth to it the sacrifice of the Federal Amendment, or whether it cannot afford to delay its application until this crisis has passed. Many personal sacrifices have been made during the last three-score years by those who have carried on the struggle for woman suffrage. Can you not accept this as the one laid upon you?

With high appreciation and sincere friendship,

Cordially yours,[7]

CONCERN FOR WOMEN WORKERS

Just as the women's movement began in the 1850's with an avowed solidarity between white and black women, so too did its early years see a strong concern and interest in the problems of wage-earning women. For several decades, women's rights conventions and activities called attention to the hardships suffered by working women and demanded equal pay for equal work, educational and occupational training for better jobs for women, and the ballot as a means to economic independence.

By the end of the nineteenth century, however, things had changed. The large majority of working-class women were no longer native-born whites, they were immigrant and black, and this strained and weakened the ties between the organized women's movement and wage-earning women. While some women responded to the humanitarian pull of Progressivism and socialism by championing the poor and the oppressed and by working for reforms for working women, others, especially those in the forefront of the suffrage drive, responded for a while to the attractions of expediency, racism, and nativism, repudiating the interests of their wage-earning sisters.

Writing in 1837 on the condition of women, Sarah Grimké examined the lives of the more affluent and "fortunate" women who she found actually were stunted in growth and floundering about in empty or meaningless activities. She also wrote about poor women, those who worked for wages and those who labored as slaves.

SARAH GRIMKÉ
WRITES ABOUT WORKING WOMEN

There is another way in which the general opinion, that women are inferior to men, is manifested, that bears with tremendous effect on the laboring class, and indeed on al-most all who are obliged to earn a subsistence. Whether it be by mental or physical exertion—I allude to the disproportionate value set on the time and labor of men and of women. A man who is engaged in teaching, can always, I believe, command a higher price for tuition than a woman —even when he teaches the same branches, and is not in any respect superior to the woman. This I know is the case in boarding and other schools with which I have been acquainted, and it is so in every occupation in which the sexes engage indiscriminately. As for example, in tailoring, a man has twice, or three times as much for making a waistcoat or pantaloons as a woman, although the work done by each may be equally good. In those employments which are peculiar to women, their time is estimated at only half the value of that of men. A woman who goes out to wash, works as hard in proportion as a wood sawyer, or a coal heaver, but she is not generally able to make more than half as much by a day's work. The low remuneration which women receive for their work, has claimed the attention of a few philanthropists, and I hope it will continue to do so until some remedy is applied for this enormous evil. I have known a widow, left with four or five children, to provide for, unable to leave home because her helpless babes demand her attention, compelled to earn a scanty subsistence, by making coarse shirts at 12 1-2 cents a piece, or by taking in washing, for which she was paid by some wealthy persons 12 1-2 cents per dozen. All these things evince the low estimation in which woman is held.[8]

In her concern for the underpaid and overworked wage earner, Grimké set the pace for the next four decades of the women's movement.

At the second women's rights convention, held in Rochester, New York, in 1848, participants listened to a report by Sarah Owen that described women's place in the working world.

FROM A REPORT ON WORKING WOMEN

I am informed by the seamstresses of this city, that they get but thirty cents for making a satin vest, and from twelve to thirty for making pants, and coats in the same proportion. Man has such a contemptible idea of woman, that he thinks

"New York City.—New Labor Employment Bureau, Under the Direction of the Commissioners of Charities and Correction." Leslie's, Mar. 1870

she can not even sew as well as he can; and he often goes to a tailor, and pays him double and even treble for making a suit, when it merely passes through his hands, after a woman has made every stitch of it so neatly that he discovers no difference. Who does not see gross injustice in this inequality of wages and violation of rights?[9]

At Rochester, those present also passed the following resolution.

A RESOLUTION

Resolved, That those who believe the laboring classes of women are oppressed ought to do all in their power to raise their wages, beginning with their own household servants.[10]

This was frequently the pattern at the many women's rights conventions that followed Seneca Falls and Rochester. Throughout the 1850's and into the post-Civil War period, conventions heard reports and analyses concerning the wages and labor of women and adopted resolutions calling for remedy and reforms.

Elizabeth Cady Stanton and Susan B. Anthony were especially interested in women wage earners, and they repeatedly pointed to the link between women's political and legal inferiority and their economic dependence. They believed that the plight of poor working women was inseparable from their disabilities as women. And in several specific ways, Stanton and Anthony tried to aid women wage earners, to the dismay, sometimes, of their more conservative critics.

The Revolution—which described itself as the friend of labor and foe of capital—regularly devoted space to the problems of laboring women, listed new job opportunities, and commented and published reports on women's wages and working conditions.

FROM *THE REVOLUTION*

WOMAN'S WORK AND WAGES.—Fifty cents the dozen pair is now the price in this city for making common overalls. It is time for *Revolution.*[11]

Higgins and Co. of this city, manufacturers of carpet, have lately discharged all their old hand-loom weavers, who are men, and taken in girls. Why is this? It is because women are paid but about half the price of men for the same work. Is *Revolution* not needed here?[12]

With the approval of the National Woman Suffrage Association, Anthony and Stanton helped in setting up a Working Woman's Association in New York. They supported it and similar groups in other cities that tried to provide employment information and to encourage women to form unions and press for better working conditions. But both Anthony and Stanton believed that the vote was the most effective way to improve the lives of working women, and suffrage work dominated their activities. In one of Anthony's most popular lectures, "Woman Wants Bread, Not the Ballot!" she reiterated this idea in major cities in the country.

ANTHONY ON THE BALLOT AND WOMEN'S WAGES

. . . Disfranchisement means inability to make, shape or control one's own circumstances. The disfranchised must always do the work, accept the wages, occupy the position the enfranchised assign to them. The disfranchised are in the position of the pauper. . . .

Governments can not afford to ignore the rights of those holding the ballot, who make and unmake every law and law-maker. It is not because the members of Congress are tyrants that women receive only half pay and are admitted only to inferior positions in the departments. It is simply in obedience to a law of political economy which makes it impossible for a government to do as much for the disfranchised as for the enfranchised. Women are no exception to the general rule. As disfranchisement always has degraded men, socially, morally and industrially, so today it is disfranchisement that degrades women in the same spheres. . . .

There are many women equally well qualified with men for principals and superintendents of schools, and yet, while three-fourths of the teachers are women, nearly all of them are relegated to subordinate positions on half or at most two-thirds the salaries paid to men. The law of supply and demand is ignored, and that of sex alone settles the question. If a business man should advertise for a book-keeper and ten young men, equally well qualified, should present themselves and, after looking them over, he should say, "To you who have red hair, we will pay full wages, while to you with black hair we will pay half the regular price"; that would not be a more flagrant violation of the law of supply and demand

than is that now perpetrated upon women because of their sex. . . . It is in order to lift the millions of our wage-earning women into a position of as much power over their own labor as men possess that they should be invested with the franchise. This ought to be done not only for the sake of justice to the women, but to the men with whom they compete; for, just so long as there is a degraded class of labor in the market, it always will be used by the capitalists to checkmate and undermine the superior classes. . . . [13]

During the last decades of the nineteenth century, the breadth and fire of the old women's rights organizations diminished, and suffrage became the consuming interest of both the American Woman Suffrage Association and the National Woman Suffrage Association. Their ties with wage-earning women grew weaker. Conventions listened sympathetically to descriptions of the deplorable state of laboring women, as did women in the great Woman's Christian Temperance Union gatherings, but all that came of such disturbing information were resolutions like this one that emphasized the importance of the vote.

Resolved, That we call the attention of the working women of the country to the fact that a disfranchised class is always an oppressed class and that only through the protection of the ballot can they secure equal pay for equal work. [14]

EXPEDIENCY AND PREJUDICE AMONG WOMEN

At the same time that racism and expediency were separating white and black women, many suffragists alienated themselves from immigrant and wage-earning women as well.

Ever since Seneca Falls, women had demanded the vote simply out of justice, noting in addition that their moral and gentle nature would be a good influence on politics. But around the turn of the century, suffragists developed a new strategy that emphasized the possible good results of enfranchising women rather than women's right in principle to the vote.

In 1900, Susan B. Anthony told a convention of the Bricklayers' and Masons' International Union why it was important for them to help women to get the vote.

ANTHONY'S SPEECH

Women should vote for the sake of the home. By working to give your wives and daughters the ballot you would be working to double the representation of the home in the government; for the lowest men—the men who make up the slum vote—these men seldom have homes and women in them whose votes could be added to theirs. It is the honest, hardworking men, with homes and families, those who have done the most to build up this country, and who are the bone and sinew sustaining it today, who have the most to gain from women's getting the ballot. But the best argument of all is justice—the sister should have the same rights as her brother, the wife as her husband, the mother as her son . . . [15]

The innuendoes in Anthony's speech were not difficult to understand. Clearly, she suggested that some voters were superior to others, that slum dwellers (the most recently arrived immigrants) constituted the least able voters, that the wives of the men "who have done the most to build up this country" would strengthen the political power of their husbands with the ballot, and that immigrant women would not vote. During the 1890's and 1900's, suffrage leaders explored these ideas, and in their campaign for the vote placed more and more emphasis on the results rather than the morality of giving the ballot to women. It was a strategy that recognized and encouraged the fears and prejudices rife in the United States at that time—racial antagonism, hostility to foreigners, and fear of labor unrest.

Closely connected with the suggestion that many women would be better voters than some men ("the men who make up the slum vote," for example) was the idea of establishing educational requirements for voting. At its 1893 convention, National American Woman Suffrage Association delegates approved a resolution that shows its interest in the idea.

NAWSA RESOLUTION

. . . without expressing any opinion on the proper qualifications for voting, we call attention to the significant facts that in every state there are more women who can read and write than all the illiterate male voters; more white women who can read and write than all negro voters; more American women who can read and write than all foreign voters; so that the enfranchisement of such women would settle the vexed question of rule by illiteracy, whether of home-grown or foreign-born production. [16]

Southern states were already experimenting with property and literacy requirements as devices for disfranchising black voters; and now suffrage leaders examined the idea of an educational qualification for all voters. Such a requirement, they saw, might well ease the way for woman

The Woman's Journal.

VOL. XXV. BOSTON, SATURDAY, NOVEMBER 3, 1894. No. 44.

The Woman's Journal.

FOUNDED BY LUCY STONE.

A Weekly Newspaper, published every Saturday in BOSTON, devoted to the interests of woman—to her educational, industrial, legal and political equality, and especially to her right of suffrage.

EDITORS:
H. B. BLACKWELL,
ALICE STONE BLACKWELL.

ASSISTANT EDITORS:
FLORENCE M. ADKINSON,
CATHARINE WILDE.

OCCASIONAL CONTRIBUTORS.
JULIA WARD HOWE,
MARY A. LIVERMORE,
MRS. H. M. T. CUTLER,

BOSTON OFFICE—No. 3 Park Street, where copies are for sale and subscriptions received.

SUBSCRIPTION.

Per Annum,	$2.50
First year on trial,	1.50
Single copies,	.05
CLUB RATES—Five copies one year,	$10.00

Checks and drafts and post-office orders should be made payable to the WOMAN'S JOURNAL. Letters containing remittances should be addressed to Box 3638, or to the office of the WOMAN'S JOURNAL, 3 Park Street, Boston, Mass. Registered letters or Express Co.'s money orders may be sent at our risk. Money sent in letters not registered will be at the risk of the sender.

J. B. MORRISON, Advertising Manager.

IN THE TIME OF THE AFTER-MATH.

BY HARRIET PRESCOTT SPOFFORD.

Though flame and spice and flower
Are fallen and dead,
Yet mantling all the sphere
Of fragrance fled
Some unknown country's airs
Strange sweetness shed,
And fulness of content
Broods overhead.

For far a-field the soul
In quiet goes
Where wrapt in azure bloom
The distance glows.
Where redder droops the leaf
Than any rose,
And softer than the west
The south wind blows.

Down dim depths droops the moon
His golden barque—
And if the mist comes chill,
The night comes dark,
The great sky has no star,
The hill no spark,
Yet from the outer vast
What music, hark!

EDITORIAL NOTES.

The coming week will mark an era in the woman suffrage movement. Kansas is, of course, the storm centre, on which all eyes and hearts are fixed. Whatever the immediate result in Kansas, the cause cannot fail to receive a tremendous impetus from the political activity of women in ten State campaigns.

Next week we shall publish a summary of facts regarding the women voters, the women candidates and the woman suffrage question as involved in the State elections next Tuesday. Its preparation has proved a greater task than we expected. We have on our table eight piles of clippings and papers representing eight States (not including Utah or New York) where the woman question in some form is a prominent factor in this election.

At Montpelier, Vt., Oct. 31, 1894, a bill was introduced into the House entitled "an act to enable women to become voters under certain conditions." It provides that all women residents of the State over twenty-one years of age may vote at all town meetings, provided they take the freeman's oath and pay a poll tax the same as a man. They shall be eligible to hold all offices in the gift of the people, and be subject to all the duties of men, except bearing arms. They cannot take the freeman's oath unless they are willing to swear that they do not favor anarchy, nihilism or socialism. The act shall not become a law unless a majority of the women in the State so elect.

These two last-named provisions are unreasonable and of doubtful constitutionality. They were probably introduced by opponents, and should be struck out before the bill is enacted. But we are glad to know that Vermont is moving in the matter.

We continue this week the discussion of an educational qualification for suffrage; William Lloyd Garrison and Frederick Douglass in the negative, Mrs. Elizabeth Cady Stanton in the affirmative. It may have been wise and necessary in the reconstruction to extend suffrage to colored men without restrictions, and yet it may be equally wise and necessary now to require an educational qualification in the case of women. Circumstances alter cases, and the circumstances are different.

In Chicago 30,000 women have registered to vote for trustees of the State University. Throughout the entire State large numbers have done the same. No one in Illinois ought ever again to say "Women do not want to vote." If the case were reversed, and men were asked to vote only for a single State officer, probably not half that number could have been induced to register.

A banquet was given, Oct. 29th, at the Sherman House, Chicago, to Dr. Julia Holmes Smith, Professor Rena Michaels Atchison, and Mrs. Lucy L. Flower, the three Cook County women nominated by the three political parties of Illinois for trustees of the State University. Mrs. Mary E. Holmes, president of the State Equal Suffrage Association, presided. The program and toasts were as follows:

"Realizing the Hopes of Twenty Years Ago," James B. Bradwell.

"The Present Campaign," Miss Mary H. Krout.

"Need of Women in Municipal Politics," Rev. Charles Martyn.

"Our Candidate," Dr. Sarah Hackett Stevenson.

"Foreign-Born Women Citizens Want the Ballot," Mrs E. C Evald.

"Taxation Without Representation," Clarence S. Darrow.

"Relation of Equal Suffrage to Party Politics," Rev Celia Parker Woolley.

"The First Nominee," Hon. Samuel Dickie.

In an opinion rendered last week at the request of Gov. McKinley, Attorney-General Richards held that women are not eligible as notaries public in Ohio. The question is brought up anew since women have been given the right to vote in school elections. By the constitution, electors are made eligible to office. But Attorney-General Richards holds that the suffrage given to women by the new Ohio law is a limited one, and not such as to make them eligible to office generally. They are as eligible to the office of governor as to the office of notary public. He adds that in his opinion it would be a good thing if a woman were eligible to appointment as notaries public.

"Overmeyer versus Overmeyer" is the latest political sensation in Kansas. This man is now the Democratic candidate for governor, and a violent opponent of woman suffrage. But the ghost of his old speeches, when he was a Republican, has risen to plague him. He then said:

> Women of Kansas, God has given you a grand opportunity to demand equality and justice before the law. It is your right to demand that you are permitted to labor for the welfare of your State. I have always been in favor of woman suffrage simply because I deem it unwise and unjust to disfranchise an entire class of human beings. This question of female suffrage on which our platform is plain and outspoken is one of the live issues of the time. It has ceased to be a theory, for wherever it has been tried it has proved a success. I am aware of the existence of prejudice among a certain class against female suffrage, but I fail to find a single well-founded argument in opposition to it.

In North Dakota the Republicans, Populists and Prohibitionists have all declared for woman suffrage. Dr. Cora Smith Eaton writes from Grand Forks:

> There has never before been so much interest in this State in woman suffrage. The Democrats alone refused to consider the matter, and treated it quite insultingly in their convention.

For nearly a month a German girl, who left the city of her birth to come to Chicago, has been detained by the immigration officials at Ellis Island, New York, and a petition is being prepared for presentation to John G. Carlisle, Secretary of the Treasury, asking that she be permitted to land. The girl is Louise Heusinger, and her case is a notable one, because when Dr. Senner, Commissioner of Immigration at New York, refused to permit her to land and ordered that she be sent back to Germany, he rendered a decision without precedent. Louise, who is twenty-five years old, was left an orphan in the City of Chemnitz. For several years she made a living as a domestic. A year or so ago Louise became engaged to Max Luther, a young mechanic of Chemnitz. The banns were published in church and the wedding day set, but the lover ran away. The girl has but one relative in the world, and that is Mrs. Minna Mueller, No. 116 Fremont Street, Chicago. Mrs. Mueller went to Germany to look after her sister, and decided to bring her to Chicago and give her a home. They landed in New York Sept. 27, on the steamer *Spree*, but Commissioner Senner refused to permit the girl to continue her journey and ordered her back to Germany.

The Commissioner's action is based solely on the condition of the girl. Mrs. Mueller hurried to Chicago and procured ample bonds to guarantee that her sister would never become a public charge. This did not satisfy the Commissioner, and he refused to change his ruling. There is no law that applies to the case except the statute excluding women of immoral character, and the girl's friends offered testimony to prove that her character was of the best. The offered testimony was rejected, and the friends have determined to appeal to Secretary Carlisle. The petition has been signed by numerous friends of the Mueller family, and also bears the signature of Mayor Hopkins, Collector M. J. Russell, Collector Mize, and Postmaster Hesing. The appeal will be forwarded to the Secretary by Immigration Inspector Bradsby. If women were voters Dr. Senner would cease to be commissioner.

The Lutheran Women's Missionary convention, in session recently at Topeka, Kan., adopted the following:

> Believing that the admonition of our Lord, "Go work in My vineyard," applies with special force to the women in the churches of to-day, We realize that we can do most acceptable service to the Master by being able to praise Him; also that we can do more efficient work in making the world, nation, State and home fit places for His indwelling by being able to express our opinion so that it may be counted in helping to choose those who are to make and enforce the laws; therefore
>
> *Resolved*, That we are in favor of the amendment now pending in our State, granting equal suffrage to women; and we urge all, both men and women, to labor unceasingly to that end till the adoption thereof.

"Solitary confinement for eighteen consecutive days in a dark cell seven feet long, four feet wide, and six feet high, with double doors four inches apart, ventilated only by twelve small holes the size of a finger tip, with eight ounces of dry bread and a pint and a half of water once a day." This is not in the torture-chambers of the Inquisition, or in the dungeons of the Sultan or the Czar, but in the Boston House of Correction, in the year of our Lord, 1894! The above is a literal description given before the Boston Board of Aldermen last week by William A. Witham, an officer of the institution, and published in the Boston daily papers without note or comment. In one case it is known to have driven a prisoner insane. It is time that the women of Boston should have municipal suffrage to put a stop to such frightful cruelty.

SUFFRAGE FAIR NOTES.

A great many people are at work for the Fair, but it is almost impossible to get them to report in detail what they are doing.

A young lady in Cambridge announces that she has collected a barrel of rose-haws and another of laurel and bayberries, to aid in the decorations.

The Chelsea League suggests that gifts of potted plants for the Fair would be very acceptable.

A great quantity of hydrangeas are promised.

The Waltham League, already actively at work for the Fair, has had its vigor stimulated by the circulation of a local "remonstrance." Thus our friends the enemy help us.

The Boston League table will be devoted to 25 cent packages. Contributions for this table are invited by Miss Whiting, who is actively working for it.

It is suggested that night-clothing for children is always salable.

A lady who wears six and a quarter gloves wants a pair of black silk knitted mittens, and will buy them for the benefit of the Fair if some one will knit her a pair.

Another lady writes: "Can you get some one to make me a drawer sachet (heliotrope)? I would like the top in silk or satin, the suffrage color, 17 by 36 inches. I have seen them tufted in silk or worsted. I shall be ready to pay for it whenever it is ready for me."

Many friends are ready to buy their supply of groceries at the Fair, if contributions of such articles can be secured from the dealers.

The Hyde Park League has reorganized and taken up work with energy. It is preparing to have a doll's table.

Remember that it is only a month before the Fair opens, and send in word what you are doing, for the encouragement of others.

Every Friday some one will be present at the parlors of the Association, No. 3 Park Street, to confer with any friends who would like to help. Come one, come all!

DR. BUCKLEY ON EQUAL SUFFRAGE.

Dr. Buckley says the fact that women constitute two-thirds of our church members and less than one-fifth of our criminals is no proof that women are better than men. But unless it can be shown that they are decidedly worse than men, why should they be excluded from suffrage?

Dr. Buckley says the suffragists claim that women will always vote against war. No sensible suffragist ever made so sweeping a claim. When there is a principle involved, or when they think there is, women have often encouraged their men to fight to the uttermost. But all through nature the male animal is more belligerent than the female; and it may be fairly expected that the women's vote would generally be against wars of mere conquest and aggression.

Dr. Buckley says the higher education leads to a wish for suffrage "only when the normal dissimilarity in the constitution of the sexes . . . is ignored or neglected." This dissimilarity is one of the strongest arguments for equal suffrage. If women were forbidden to sing in church choirs, there would be a good argument for their admission if it could be shown that women singers had voices as beautiful as those of male singers, and voices of the same quality. But the argument would become much stronger when it was shown that the women had voices not only as beautiful as those of men, but of a distinctly different quality—that they were able not merely to increase the volume of sweet sound, but to bring in soprano and alto to enrich the harmony. Because women are different from men, they look at public questions from a somewhat different standpoint. They feel certain abuses more keenly; the moral and humanitarian aspects of certain questions appeal to them more strongly. They will bring to the ballot box not merely an added number of good and patriotic voters, but voters of a different and valuable kind.

Dr. Buckley then gives a list of what he regards as "insurmountable objections."

First, he says, if women are admitted, it must be all women indiscriminately. Why so? Maine and Wyoming have lately adopted an educational qualification for all their voters. The tendency seems to be in that direction. There is nothing to prevent any State from extending suffrage to women with an educational qualification, if it seems best.

Dr. Buckley here throws in, parenthetically, the misstatement that "jury duty is a concomitant of the ballot." But doctors, lawyers, ministers and about twenty other classes of men are exempt from jury duty, without being excluded from the ballot. There would be no difficulty in securing exemption for women, when there was any good reason for it. Often the presence of women on the jury would be desirable. Some lawyers, not in favor of woman suffrage, have expressed the opinion that in cases of attempted blackmail, women on the jury would be especially valuable as a protection to men unjustly accused. A pretty but unprincipled plaintiff can sometimes pull the wool over the eyes of a jury of men when a jury of her own sex would see through her at once. In cases where actual wrong had been done to women or girls, the presence of women on the jury would be likely to secure more certain and adequate punishment. In several of our Western States women have served, and they made excellent jurors.

Dr. Buckley's next insurmountable objection is "the physiological and pathological reasons." But the physiological constitution of women in the United States is not materially different from what it is in England and Canada, in Wyoming, and other places where women have been exercising the suffrage for many years, without perceptible damage to their health.

A. S. B.

CONCERNING WOMEN.

MRS. MINA S. WHITE, a white ribboner of Taylorville, is the nominee for school superintendent in Christian County Ill., on the Republican ticket.

MRS. AMES, wife of Sheriff Ames, of Belvidere, Ill., is deputy sheriff of Boone County, and fearlessly takes charge of insane persons and prisoners in transit.

MISS STERLING has a model farm at Aylesford, Nova Scotia, to which she brings destitute children from Scotland and educates them to trades. She has a grist-mill, saw-mill, and various workshops on the place, and generally has about a hundred little waifs in training for useful lives. Miss Sterling made an interesting address lately at a woman suffrage meeting in St. John, N. B.

MRS. ORMISTON CHANT and other earnest women have been making a vigorous attempt to prevent some of the London music halls, which serve as places of assignation, from securing licenses from the County Council. The license of one of the most objectionable of these places, the "Empire," has been revoked. All the many diverse theories on the abolition or restraint of the social evil are having an airing in the London daily press.

MRS. LOUISA PARSONS HOPKINS, who lately resigned from the Boston Board of School Supervisors on account of impaired health, has published a strong endorsement of the recent protest against the overcrowding of the public schools. Mrs. Hopkins says: "Much of the wear and tear of the work of supervision was the demand of these conditions upon one's sympathies, and the baffling of all efforts to alleviate the trouble. I hope the subject will be agitated until good rooms are provided, which will satisfy all the disappointed parents and accommodate all the children of the city. It is not, in my judgment, important that the schoolhouses and schoolrooms be elaborate and costly in structure, but that they should be made healthful and ample in all their appointment is imperative." This is sound common sense.

MARGARET MACDONALD, a nineteen-year-old girl, station agent for the Lehigh Valley Railroad at Warrior Run, Pa., lately saved an express train from being telescoped by a runaway engine on a down-grade by her quickness and presence of mind. The train had stopped to take on an invalid passenger, when she heard the noise of an approaching engine. Supposing it to be a train, she ordered the passenger train to start at full speed without waiting for the passenger. The order saved the train, for, although the runaway engine overtook it at the foot of the grade, the train was then under such headway that the shock was almost imperceptible. Miss MacDonald applied for the place as station agent when her brother who held it resigned, a year ago. She was refused at first, on account of her sex; but while waiting to get a man agent, the company allowed her to run the office, and she attended to the duties so well that she has since been made the regular agent. The station is an important one, being at the foot of the heavy mountain grade, where the single track diverges into many.

MRS. JOSEPHINE SHAW LOWELL, who has been chosen as the New York women's leader in their crusade against Tammany, comes of a family noted for their interest in philanthropic and reform work. Her grandfather, Robert Gould Shaw, endowed an asylum for sailor's children. Her father, Francis George Shaw, was interested in the Brook Farm experiment. Her brother, Colonel Robert G. Shaw, organized the first colored regiment. Both he and her husband fell in battle during the Civil War. Mrs. Lowell began her work in the Sanitary Commission, and, when left a widow, devoted herself to good works. She was the first woman on the New York State Board of Charities and Correction, receiving her appointment from Governor Tilden in 1876, and it was through her efforts that the Charity Organization Society was founded in 1881, and that matrons were placed in police station houses. She has always been interested in work for working girls. Last year, during the distress among the poor, she, with several others, started the East Side Relief Committee. In 1884 she published a book on "Public Relief and Private Charity," and she has written much on these subjects for magazines and reviews. Although connected highly in Boston and New York, she cares far less for society than for work, and her two passions are books and philanthropy.

suffrage, since, together, the vote for women and an educational qualification for all voters would assure that white middle-class women would vote while a great many black and immigrant women and men would be denied the vote because of illiteracy. In this way, those women who advocated educated suffrage were willing to barter away the votes of millions of women and men to gain the ballot for themselves.

The greatest interest in educated suffrage occurred between 1890 and 1905. The columns of The Woman's Journal *often contained articles such as this by Stanton.*

STANTON JUSTIFIES EDUCATED SUFFRAGE

. . . It seems to me the proposition for "educated suffrage" made and reiterated in the WOMAN'S JOURNAL, is preeminently wise and timely. A law providing that after 1898 those who vote must be able to read and write the English language would be an immense advantage to the individual and the State. With the ignorant and impecunious from the Old World landing on our shores by hundreds every day, we must have some restrictions of the suffrage for our own safety and for their education before they take part in the administration of the government. Every man of them should be compelled to read and write the English language before they are allowed to register themselves as voters. This would be a double blessing—to them and to the State. . . .

The proposition, as stated in the WOMAN'S JOURNAL, involves no injustice to women, but provides that all educated men and women shall vote on the same basis. True, we cannot take the suffrage from the ignorant men who already exercise it, not because they prize it so highly, but because no political party dare make the experiment. . . .

The greatest block in the way of woman's enfranchisement, is the fear of the "ignorant vote" being doubled. Wise men see what a strain it is on our institutions today, and object to any further experiment in that direction. I do not see that the ignorant classes need the suffrage more than the enlightened, but just the reverse. When a vessel is in danger on a stormy sea, we need skill and intelligence on the bridge and at the wheel, to protect those who are ignorant of the science of navigation. Just so in the State we need the highest intelligence and morality to govern a nation with justice and wisdom.

"The first desire of every enlightened mind," says Matthew Arnold, "is to take part in the great work of government."[17]

The National American Woman Suffrage Association never officially endorsed an educational qualification for voting, although the speeches of its leaders and the response of convention members suggest that there was considerable

sympathy for the measure. And an informal vote taken at the 1903 convention revealed that almost all the NAWSA delegates present supported it.

Carrie Chapman Catt, who was president of NAWSA and a forceful and influential leader, frequently spoke at conventions in favor of restricted suffrage.

CATT CALLS FOR EDUCATIONAL QUALIFICATION

Does it not seem that the time has come when in defense of good government we must unite in the establishment of an educational qualification for the ballot, in all the States where it does not exist, and that this qualification shall be severe enough to represent a sufficient amount of understanding to guarantee a fitness of good citizenship? One may well ask, why punish the ignorant and the poor for the crimes of the intelligent and the rich and common justice will answer, why, indeed? But it is surely no punishment to take away a vote which is only bartered away to the first "ward heeler." It is true that it is far from demonstrated that illiterate voters are necessarily all "floaters," but there is sufficient

PROCEEDINGS

of the Thirty-Fourth Annual Convention

of the

National

American Woman Suffrage

Association,

held at Washington, D. C.,

February 14th, 15th, 16th, 17th, 18th,

1902.

EDITED BY

ALICE STONE BLACKWELL,
HARRIET TAYLOR UPTON.

testimony to lead us to the conclusion that their removal from the constituency would take away a great source of temptation, while it would impose no wrong on them. A few months or years of effort would enable them to qualify themselves for the suffrage, no matter how exacting the qualification might be made.[18]

Support for educated suffrage was by no means unanimous among suffragists. Here Harriot Stanton Blatch joins the debate and takes issue with her famous mother, Elizabeth Cady Stanton.

"AN OPEN LETTER TO MRS. STANTON"

BASINGSTOKE, ENG., NOV. 25, 1894

My honored Mother: A few days since, you wrote asking my opinion of a letter of yours in the WOMAN'S JOURNAL of Nov. 3. As you represent a growing body of opinion in America, and addressed the wide constituency of the JOURNAL, I beg leave to express my thoughts in an equally public way. . . .

People are ever raising to themselves fetiches to worship in government, as in every thing else. No sooner is one Golden Calf,—as, for instance, that it is only the man with a money-bag who has a stake in the country,—been torn down, than another is erected. The idea of restricting the suffrage to those who can read and write is another fetich. Now, my dear mother, if you have the heart to re-read the letter in which you invite us to fall down and worship this fetich, you will find that throughout you imply that if a person can *read and write,* he is "enlightened" and "educated," and if he cannot read and write, he is "ignorant." I am sure, if you will frankly appeal to your knowledge of the world, you will be forced to admit that many a person who could satisfy even you in the "intelligence" of his reading, nay, more, who could satisfy a board of examiners of his collegiate accomplishments, is lamentably ignorant; while many a man, without a sign of the 3 Rs about him, is gifted with the sterling commonsense and abiding honesty which the school of life's experience teaches.

But you go still further, and call every American citizen who was born in Europe, and who cannot read or write the *English* language, an "ignorant foreigner." Perhaps you forgot that the nations of Europe have their public school systems. Take Germany, for instance; probably not a son of the Fatherland arrives in New York who has not had quite as good a common school education as the average man of the proletariat born in the United States. . . .

I do say that the proletariat, whether able to read or not, can give a more valuable opinion than any other class upon such a question, for example, as the housing of the poor. As our ability to feel our own needs is not bounded by our linguistic accomplishments, neither should our power to *remedy* them through government be so bounded. Because you overlook the fact that the conditions of the poor are so much harder than yours or mine, you are led to argue that "the ignorant classes do not need the suffrage more than the enlightened, but just the reverse." Every working man needs the suffrage more than I do, but there is another who needs it more than he does, just because conditions are more galling, and that is the working woman.

You warn us that "Wise men see what a strain it (the ignorant vote) is on our institutions." . . . The heaviest strain on American institutions was the Civil War and all the upheaval that preceded it; but surely the "ignorant vote" was not then the disturbing cause. And has not a government by an aristocracy of "intellect" been tried? Why, my dear mother, right in our own country a government of the "educated" ruled over a wide area for generations. Before the war, the whole southern section of the United States was ruled by its men who could "read and write." They had it all their own way, and what did they do with their power? No, no, we are ever vainly trying to get morals and character out of intellect, but they grow on quite other soil. . . .

But do not understand that, if it were possible to separate the truthful, the upright, the conscientious and the loving from their weaker fellowmen, I would advocate a government of an aristocracy of the moral; for I would not, and on this ground, that government is not the end of man, but merely a method of expressing collective thought, and achieving concerted action. And the thought is not collective if any human being capable of thought is excluded. . . .

Yours ever devotedly,

HARRIOT STANTON BLATCH[19]

Among those who dissented from the National American Woman Suffrage Association's flirtation with limited suffrage was Jane Addams. Addams was an official of NAWSA, and an ardent suffragist, but she was also a leader in the settlement house movement, where her involvement with immigrant slum dwellers convinced her that they, like other women, needed the ballot.

ADDAMS ON THE BALLOT FOR ALL WOMEN

The Russian Jewish women are always grumbling because there are no covered markets in Chicago. They look upon the buying of food for their families as a matter of importance: they are anxious that it should be wholesome, and with them the food question is associated with very ancient ceremonials. They do not like to take home their meat all grimy and dusty. They say such dirty markets would never be allowed in Russia. We are accustomed to hearing

women are being brought to the wish for the ballot in a thousand ways, not through any theory, but as the result of their own practical experience. . . .

Around us there are many factories that employ young girls in running dangerous machinery, making tin cans, etc. Our women collected a long list of bad accidents, the loss of fingers and of hands. They went before a committee of the Legislature, and told the results of their investigations. The committee seemed impressed, and promised to recommend legislation calling for the use of guards on the machines. But a deputation of business men went to the Legislature after us, and destroyed all the effect of our hearing. They had votes, and they succeeded in preventing the needed legislation.[20]

BUILDING SOLIDARITY AMONG WOMEN

Emphasis on suffrage had distracted many organized women from understanding and supporting the needs of wage-earning, immigrant, and black women; and after 1890, flirtation with the idea of limited suffrage had the same effect. Interest in an educational qualification began to fade around 1905, and eventually it died out, but the episode was important within the women's movement, since while it lasted, it tended to separate middle- and working-class women.

However, at the same time that prejudice and expediency were causing women to turn away from one another, other forces were operating to draw them together. Most important was the spirit of Progressivism with its concern for injustice and its far-reaching humanitarianism. And as Progressivism spread, interest in limited suffrage faded and concern for the oppressed and less fortunate grew. Muckraking journalists, socially aware novelists, reformers crusading for change, added to the strikes and protests of the discontented themselves and the disturbing arguments of socialists, shook up the complacency of middle-class Americans in the years before the Great War. In spite of themselves, people became more aware of the agonies of slum life, the horrors of industrialization, and the corruption of their governments.

Influential women leaders, like Jane Addams and social worker Florence Kelley, hoped to harness the aroused sympathies of women to bring about change and reform, and spoke directly to middle-class women. Just as Frances Willard had introduced WCTU members to the world outside their homes, so now did the General Federation of Women's Clubs educate its members to the realities of child labor and contemporary factory conditions. It called on them to agitate for a federal investigation of the working conditions of women and children, and then to lobby for remedial legislation. The activities of the Women's Trade

Jane Addams

Chicago compared unfavorably with New York and Boston, but when it is compared unfavorably with Russia, we feel mortified.

The Italian women are greatly dissatisfied because there is no public wash-house. In their own country they always washed the clothes together, either at a stream or in a village wash-house, and they talked and had a great deal of laughter and fun while they did it. They find it very dull to do their washing alone, and very uncomfortable to have to hang the wet clothes up to dry among their families, in a small room. But they have no votes, and they cannot get attention for their perfectly reasonable and legitimate wish for a municipal wash-house.

Then there is the burning question of fire-escapes. A woman with young children was very much troubled because her tenement had no fire escape. She came to Hull House to ask us to put one on. We advised her to have her husband see the alderman from our ward, who had scattered promises of fire-escapes right and left, before he was elected. She answered, ''But my husband is away at work for months at a time, and when he is at home he is not as much afraid of fire as I am, and he does not understand as well as I do how helpless the children would be if there was a fire.'' That woman was from the interior of Sicily, and there is no more conservative woman anywhere than can be found in the interior of Sicily; but at the end of our talk she said, ''Well, if I had a vote, I believe I should get a fire-escape.'' So

Union League also brought greater awareness and understanding of the problems of working women to middle-class women and stressed the importance of the vote in improving labor conditions.

Within the suffrage movement, important changes took place. Several new independent suffrage groups formed after 1910—like the Women's Political Union in New York, led by Harriot Stanton Blatch, and the Illinois State Woman Suffrage Party—were sympathetic to working women and made great efforts to enlist them in the suffrage movement. Women wage earners, in turn, proved to be enthusiastic and active in their support of suffrage. Similarly, black women's organizations joined the suffrage effort.

As the National American Woman Suffrage Association moved away from its dalliance with educated suffrage, it, too, awakened to the problems of working women. In 1909, for example, NAWSA president Anna Howard Shaw spoke at a rally supporting the New York shirtwaist-makers' strike.

The Woman's Journal *reported the 1909–10 garment workers' strikes in detail. The sympathy of the editors was apparent. And as the* Journal *grew more deeply involved in the trials of laboring people, it also grew more insistent that the ballot would be their salvation. In this article, the* Journal *relates to woman suffrage a disastrous fire in the Triangle Shirtwaist factory.*

"NEW YORK'S FIRE HORROR"

Not only New York but the whole country has been shocked by the conflagration last week in the work-rooms of the Triangle Shirt-Waist Company. This was the firm in whose shop the great strike of the shirt-waist makers began. It started because the Triangle Company dismissed all those of their girls who had joined a union. During the strike this firm is said to have caused the arrest of more than 300 pickets and strikers. It was charged with hiring prostitutes to annoy the striking girls, besides employing thugs to attack them. After the strike, it made some concessions, but later became an "open shop" again.

When the fire broke out last week, it was found that the ten-story building was a fire-trap; that the single fire-escape went down into an inner court and was wholly inadequate; and that the doors opened inward and were kept locked. More than 140 workers, mostly women and girls, were either burned to death or lost their lives by jumping from the eighth and ninth stories. . . . There has been a universal outcry of horror; but will anything be done? Not long ago a like accident, on a smaller scale, took place in Newark, N.J. There was an outcry then; but the courts decided that no one could be punished. It seems uncertain now whether anyone

can be proved to be legally guilty in connection with this appalling disaster. It is said that hundreds of other buildings where multitudes of people work every day are in just as risky a condition. One thing is clear—either the building laws are inadequate or their enforcement is not what it should be.

After the Newark disaster, the New Jersey suffragists pointed out that they had been going up to the Legislature for years, asking for more effective factory legislation and a larger number of inspectors, and had been told practically—and in one case verbally—that women ought to mind their own business and not come bothering the legislators about men's affairs. Napoleon once expressed his disapproval of women's meddling in politics. A famous Frenchwoman answered, "Sire, when women are liable to have their heads cut off, it is natural that they should wish to know the reason why." When women are liable to be burned alive by hundreds, it is natural that a growing number of them should wish for a vote in making the laws and choosing the officers who are to enforce them. Meanwhile the anti-suffragists will continue to ask, "Am I my sister's keeper?"

A.S.B.[21]

Adding to the idea that working women needed the ballot, suffragist and socialist Jessie Ashley argued in the Journal *that the suffrage movement needed the working women.*

A CALL TO WOMEN OF ALL CLASSES

. . . For the most part the handsome ladies [in a recently held suffragist march] are well satisfied with their personal lot, but they want the vote as a matter of justice, while the fluttering, jammed-in subway girls are terribly blind to the whole question of class oppression and of sex oppression. Only the women of the working class are really oppressed, but it is not only the working class woman to whom injustice is done. Women of the leisure class need freedom, too. All women, of whatever class, must become conscious of their position in the world; all must be made to stand erect and become self-reliant, free human beings. . . .

Is there a common camp from which we can all march to demand the ballot? We who believe in the power and the destiny of the working class know that no possible common ground exists when the exercise of the ballot is an issue; the working man, jammed like the girls into the subway trains, should not vote as does the owner of the subway train, nor should the fluttering girls vote as would the handsome ladies. Upon this point there can be no room for doubt.

But is it impossible for all women to work together to uproot an injustice common to all? Is there no way to bring this about? Surely there should be. We must be rid of mere lady-likeness, we must succeed in making the oppressed class of women the most urgent in the demand for what all must have. When we have brought this about, we women

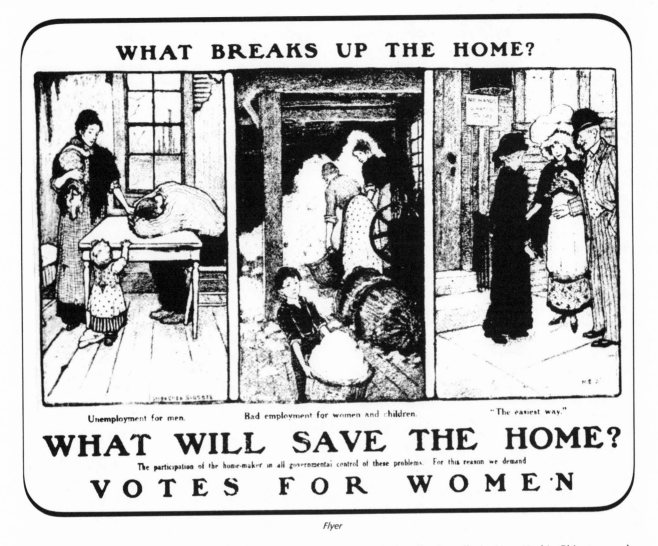

WHAT BREAKS UP THE HOME?

Unemployment for men.   Bad employment for women and children.   "The easiest way."

WHAT WILL SAVE THE HOME?

The participation of the home-maker in all governmental control of these problems. For this reason we demand

VOTES FOR WOMEN

Flyer

shall be irresistibly strong. But, while we lack enthusiasm and the consecration that can be derived only from the knowledge of great wrongs, we shall continue to show a certain amount of weakness; and great wrongs are not suffered by the handsome ladies as a class, but they are suffered by the working class as a whole. If the working girls ever become really alive to their situation, they will throw themselves into the fight for the ballot in overwhelming numbers, and on that day the suffrage movement will be swept forward by the forces that command progress.[22]

Practical considerations also worked to counteract the effects of the limited-suffrage episode. Leaders of the National American Woman Suffrage Association realized that the votes of the large cities (many of them immigrant and labor votes) were as necessary for achieving the suffrage amendment as Southern votes. They responded, moreover, to the growing interest in suffrage from black and wage-earning women.

A 1912 suffragist rally in New York's Chinatown, described in The Woman's Journal, *was one of many signs of the changes taking place.*

"RALLY IN CHINATOWN"

Some very active work has been carried on this summer in the Third Assembly District of the Borough of Manhattan by the Woman Suffrage Party. . . . Beginning at St. Mark's Place we have moved south through the district until last Tuesday we held a stirring meeting near the southern boundary of the district, which is at the corner of Mott and Pell streets. This includes rough sections of the city, and Chinatown is one of the roughest. Many good friends warned us against going there, but our party, which aims to reach every section, sternly disallowed that any street, by-way, court or alley shall be closed to us. We suffragists are implacably against restricted districts of any kind. . . . We expected a polyglot and varied crowd at the meeting at Mott and Pell streets. We took with us literature in Yiddish, Italian, and notices were written in Chinese. We were sure the politicians from the surrounding district political clubs would come out. We knew that many voters would be there whom we could reach, and many grafters whom we could not reach; that many a white-faced despairing woman would hear our message, that many struggling mothers and children would listen to us, that many of the respectable merchants and business men, both American and Chinese, who want better conditions, would welcome us, and that some of the social workers of the district would co-operate—to make our meeting successful. But we were not prepared to see the great orderly throng that greeted us. Many efficient police officers were stationed about, and any slight disturbances were immediately quelled.

For instance, while Mrs. Jean White, dressed in Chinese costume, was talking to the great crowd in Chinese, telling them the latest news she had received by letter from China about the suffrage movement there and showing them pictures of the Chinese suffragists, a flashlight picture went off with a great explosion, causing alarm in a crowd always on the lookout for the violence which breaks out ever and again in that much abused and exploited district. However, when I announced to the startled crowds the cause of the report, the police quickly restored order. . . .

In my speech I tried to emphasize . . . that Chinamen are not responsible for the conditions in Chinatown, but that they have been exploited as a cover for a remunerative center for vice. The crowd being still friendly and attentive, questions were asked for. Some hostile, some intelligent questions were asked and answered by Mr. Crosby and myself. Then the auto started, some riding and some afoot, the Woman Suffrage Party waved good-by to their audience and left, feeling that the network of sympathy and understanding which is being spread everywhere had here been woven more closely between the suffragists and their "constituents."[23]

THE YWCA

The activities of the Young Women's Christian Association also helped improve relations between working and middle-class women. When it began, before the Civil War, the "band of Christian girls uniting in the name of Jesus" defined their purpose as follows:

They shall seek out especially young women of the operative class, aid them in procuring employment and in obtaining suitable boarding places, furnish them with proper reading matter, establish Bible classes and meetings for religious exercises at such times and places as shall be most convenient for them during the week, secure their attendance at places of public worship on the Sabbath, surround them with Christian influences and use all practicable means for the increase of true piety in themselves and others.[24]

Before the formation of the national YWCA in 1906, associations in New York, Boston, Hartford, and elsewhere had programs staffed largely by middle-class women that offered job information, reliable and inexpensive boarding-houses, vocational and domestic training classes, and some nursery facilities for the children of working mothers.

Although its original religious purpose—to lead the young and vulnerable working girl to Christ—was never lost, the YWCA was influenced by the reform spirit during the Progressive era. It set up a Federation of Industrial Clubs to give wage earners their own organization within the Y, and the Federation, in turn, expanded the Y's activities and interests. In addition, the national Young Women's Christian Association became an active supporter of protective legislation for women and children, and it cooperated with other Progressive organizations in agitating for these reforms.

The following resolution, adopted at the 1911 convention of the YWCA, reveals how the organization introduced its members to the social and industrial problems of the day and helped, in this way, to bridge the gap between women of different classes.

YWCA RESOLUTION

Inasmuch as the utterly inadequate wages paid to thousands of young women throughout the country often hamper the work of the Association as a great preventive agency, and as the white slave traffic is admitted to be closely related to the lack of living wage, the Association recognizes its responsibility as an influential unit in the body of Christian public opinion, and accordingly it is recommended:

a) That the Association shall seek to educate public opinion regarding the need of establishing a minimum living wage and of regulating the hours of labor compatible with the physical health and development of wage earners.

b) That the Association shall declare its belief in the right of a woman over sixteen years of age in good health, working a full day, to a living wage which shall insure her the possibility of a virtuous livelihood.

c) That the Association, recognizing the necessity of legislation for the regulation of hours and wages of wage earners in industry and trade hereby expresses its sympathy with the great purpose of securing the determination by law of a minimum living wage for women.

d) That the Association, while endeavoring to improve the industrial condition of the working girl, shall point steadfastly to a higher standard of faithful service and achievement for the worker and of justice and consideration for the employer.[25]

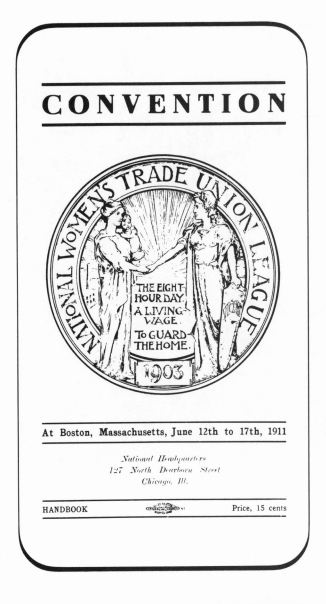

CONVENTION

NATIONAL WOMEN'S TRADE UNION LEAGUE

THE EIGHT HOUR DAY. A LIVING WAGE. To GUARD THE HOME.

1903

At Boston, Massachusetts, June 12th to 17th, 1911

National Headquarters
127 North Dearborn Street
Chicago. Ill.

HANDBOOK   Price, 15 cents

THE NWTUL

Two new organizations—the National Women's Trade Union League and the National Consumers' League—were important in creating new ties between middle-class and wage-earning women.

The National Women's Trade Union League was founded in 1903 by a group of working women, social reformers, and settlement house workers who decided, in the middle of an American Federation of Labor convention they were attending, to form an independent organization that would "assist in the organization of women wage workers into trade unions."[26] They were responding to their own conviction that unionization was the key to improvement for working women and to the rather pale performance by the AFL in supporting unionization for women.

Membership was open to anyone "who will declare himself or herself willing to assist those trade unions already existing, which have women members and to aid in the formation of new unions of women wage workers."[27] While the membership of the League was a mixture of working and middle-class women, at first its leadership was dominated by middle- and upper-class women, such as Margaret Dreir Robins and Ellen Henrotin. But by 1910 working women played an increasingly important part in the organization. Women like Mary Anderson, who had been a shoe worker, and Rose Schneiderman, who had been a cap maker, and many others sacrificed their few hours of leisure and even more scarce dollars for the NWTUL. And by 1920, most of the leadership were or had been wage earners.

The organization began with three leagues, in Boston, Chicago, and New York. About ten years later, there were eleven local leagues tied together into the National Women's Trade Union League.

The first great work of the National Women's Trade Union League was its unflagging support of striking garment workers during the massive labor protests in 1909 and 1910. The New York strike, a three-month-long uprising of tens of thousands of workers, was the biggest strike of women up to that time. And the Women's Trade Union League made important contributions to its strength. League members joined picket lines, obtained legal aid, raised funds for bail and for relief, enrolled new members in the International Ladies' Garment Workers Union, and provided the union with an infantry of secretarial and clerical volunteers. League members organized a huge rally and worked hard to spread understanding and sympathy for the strike. The more affluent and prestigious women among them exploited their own resources and influence to protest the brutal mistreatment of the strikers by the police and to create an atmosphere in which the strike was tolerated, if not approved, by the public. The support of Trade Union League women also served to bolster the courage of the girls and women who ran the risk of imprisonment and starvation in joining the strike.

In Chicago, in a similar strike, the Women's Trade Union League repeated the same difficult labors; members also ran a commissary for distributing relief supplies and sat, with union leaders and management, at the negotiating table.

As Women's Trade Union Leagues spread into different cities and states, the League was able to assist in every important strike involving women workers. National League leaders rushed from aiding brewery workers in Milwaukee to helping the corset makers in Bridgeport, carrying with them the techniques and know-how of labor organization and protest.

The job of interpreting the needs and objectives of laboring people to the middle class—so important during the strikes—became a major function of the League. League representatives worked hard on the lecture platform; they

Rose Schneiderman Organizing for the WTUL

spoke to women's clubs; they urged the General Federation of Women's Clubs to action; they addressed national suffrage conventions. The NWTUL published its own magazine, Life and Labor, *and League members regularly wrote articles for other publications. At the same time, League activities were directed toward working women as well, calling their attention to the advantages of unionization and urging them to organize.*

NWTUL HANDBOOK

Laundry Workers

Do you know through how many pairs of hands your shirt or shirtwaist must pass, and with how many different twists and turns from the time you take it to the laundry to the time it reaches you again immaculately clean and perfectly laundered? How would you like to iron a shirt a minute? Think of standing at a mangle just above the wash room with the hot steam pouring up through the floor for ten, twelve, fourteen and sometimes seventeen hours a day! Sometimes the floors are made of cement and then it seems as though one were standing on hot coals, and the workers are dripping with perspiration. In some of the non-union factories the girls work for three dollars and three-fifty a week, and the work is so hard and so exhausting that you seldom find a woman who has been able to work long at the trade. Perhaps you have complained about the chemicals used in the washing of your clothes, which cause them to wear out quickly, but what do you suppose is the effect of these chemicals upon the workers? They are standing ten, twelve, fourteen and seventeen hours a day in intense heat, breathing air laden with particles of soda, ammonia and other chemicals! Is it any wonder that these workers become physical wrecks in a very short time, just because you and I never count the cost? The Laundry Workers' Union is the one way out of these difficulties. In one city it has reduced the hours of work from eighteen and twelve to nine hours, and has increased the wages fifty per cent, and in another city the union has reduced the hours of work from eighteen and twelve to nine, and increased the wages from $15.00 a month to $9.00 a week, minimum wage, and $15.00 a week average wage.

Human Hair Workers

A large majority of human hair factories are in old, badly lighted buildings, often in low-windowed attics, where the air is laden with tiny particles of hair and where the girls work long hours by artificial light for poor pay. Sometimes conditions are even worse. In one work room the family dinner of macaroni was found on the same cook stove with a bubbling boiler of disinfecting hair, for work is often taken home at night. In Greater New York alone about 5,000 workers are employed in this trade, considerably over half being women and children. The work for women is divided into three classes—Rat, Weft, and Wig. "Rats" are considered the most unhealthy work in the girls' department, for it is almost impossible for a rat-maker to keep the particles of hair from escaping, and she literally breathes hair as well as works it. The average wage for this work is $6.00 to $7.00. Wig-making is the most difficult branch of work in the entire trade, and it takes a year to learn it. It is very hard on the eyes. The average wage paid is $5.00, and the highest $12.00. Most girls are employed at weft work. This consists in making a fringe by knotting strands of hair on to a string. This is then stitched by machine into switches and fronts. A skilled worker knots over three miles of hair in a year. She is paid according to her skill, 6 cents to 12 cents a yard. The union is trying to bring about better sanitary conditions, shorter hours of work and an increase in wages.

Straw and Felt Hat Making

Imagine that you are bending over a hat machine all day; that your foot is on a treadle run by electricity, your eyes upon two rows of straw braid that are racing, racing, racing as fast as electricity can urge them on. Your duty is to keep the two edges of the straw braid just lapping—not too much, but just enough—and at the same time to turn your work so that the product will be a perfectly shaped, symmetrical hat. If you are working on a "Merry Widow" it will perhaps take you twice as long to finish it, and it will be much harder to handle than if it is a small hat. Strangely, you are not likely to get any more money for the "Merry Widow" than for the smaller hat. If you are making a straw hat, you may work all winter (straw hats are made in winter, you know) before you learn your trade well. Then about Easter time you will find yourself, and all the other workers in the shop, in a grand rush to fill orders for styles that have caught on this season. You will work long into the evening; by Saturday night you may have earned thirty dollars for six days' (and nights'!) work; but very likely the next week you will earn but ten dollars; the next week five; the next week you may be told that there are no more straw hats to be made this season, and you are out of work because you have permitted your employers in the name of Fashion to make your trade a seasonal one. Join the Straw and Felt Hat Workers' Union, which is trying to establish a longer season and a shorter day.

The Sewing Trades

Have you ever seen a needle making 2,200 stitches a minute? And would you like to be sewing a shirt or a petticoat at a machine with a needle stitching 2,200 times a minute? Supposing a thread breaks, or a point of the needle breaks, and you do not discover it in time—your shirt or your petticoat is ruined. And rather than have that happen you watch

Life and Labor

A MONTHLY MAGAZINE

FEBRUARY, 1919

What Organization Means to the Woman Barber

By Blanche Johnson

Organizer Central Labor Council of Seattle

THE woman engaged in barbering as a means of livelihood is beset with numerous difficulties and temptations, more so, perhaps, than in any other line of work.

She is originally attracted to the trade by the high wages advertised by the barber colleges, with the guarantee of a position to all students entering the college. This guarantee is usually not lived up to, and the woman graduate is, therefore, forced to hunt her own position, taking whatever she can secure regardless of location. Perhaps she has spent her last dollar to learn the trade, and so must of necessity lay aside her personal views and preferences in order to live. As time goes on she is again and again met in her work with trials wherein she must either smother her resentment or change her occupation. She realizes that she has paid a considerable sum to learn the trade, and it is doubtful whether or not she can secure another position in some other line of work. And so she perforce chooses the first alternative.

Generally speaking, the woman barber is paid on a straight percentage basis, which is termed "piece work" in other lines of occupation and is considered one of the most injurious conditions under which to labor, bringing unlimited worry lest the output be insufficient to bring an adequate income, and in time causing the individual to suffer a nervous collapse. This often results in permanent injury, and at best invariably takes months for even a temporary cure.

This basis of compensation has a tendency to affect the morals of the woman worker. She must let pass, apparently unnoticed, offensive remarks which she would ordinarily resent, because she realizes that her earning capacity, which means her bread and butter, indeed her very existence, is controlled by her customers. She must at all times be courteous and ready to attend to the wants of her patrons. They, on the other hand, take little thought, perhaps, as to the value of her time and frequently loiter, as the villagers do in a country store, to relate experiences and talk of things in general.

Another form of temptation, which may be attributed in its entirety to the method of compensation, is grafting. While some employers forbid this practice, others encourage it. The more work a woman can secure from a customer, the more wages she receives and the more profit accrues to the employer. This is usually made possible by hurrying through the work on other customers. Usually it is the transient who is the victim of this graft.

Because of the uncertainty of the trade, there are perhaps hours throughout the day when the woman worker is idle. Although she receives no compensation for this time, she is compelled to be on duty, and as the shops are open from morning until night, with only one shift of workers, her condition is indeed deplorable. In some shops a day off, besides Sunday, is granted, but this does very little to relieve the tired nerves, inasmuch as the majority of the women engaged in this work are married and probably have children who need attention, besides other work which accumulates throughout the rest of the week to dispose of.

There is also another thing which has handicapped the women barbers in Seattle—

February, 1919

that needle and that thread and you never lift your eyes from your work. And if you should be sewing in a non-union factory you will be sewing and watching the needle for ten, twelve, fourteen hours, and your eyes will ache with the strain and your back will ache. But we are so proud of our machine that we think and think how we may improve it. And one day we discover that we can make our machine carry two needles and even ten needles at the same time, and we can make it run still faster, so that each needle will make 4,400 stitches a minute. And now, if you are sewing tucks in a waist or petticoat, you are watching ten needles run at 4,400 stitches a minute—watching to see if a thread breaks, or the point of any one of the ten needles snaps. And they dance up and down like flashes of steel or lightning, and your eyes smart with the strain. But we are improving machinery—not eyes! And sometimes you feel as if the machine were running away from you, and your effort to control it makes your whole body ache. Let us go on supposing that you are running this new and wonderful machine. Have your wages increased with the stitches per minute? You are now producing from twice to twenty times as much as with the old machine; you are putting into your sewing many times greater eye ache and nerve strain. Are your wages keeping pace? Why, no! Just the same average wage of

$5.00 to $6.00 a week—in a non-union factory. Isn't it strange? Is it right?

But not all sewing is done by these racing machines; some of it can be done by hand, some by the old foot-power machine. And because you and I with all other women know how to use our needles the employer finds us easily. And, if we are mothers he knows he can find us in our homes, as he found our neighbor across the way; and then we are a convenience; for by permitting the employer to use our home for his workshop we save him the cost of rent, the cost

of fuel, the cost of light. You and I want our home for the husband and the children, but our neighbor's husband has been ill long; she is pressed hard by poverty and her need is great; she turns her home into her employer's workshop, and he calls her "a home finisher." Under her deft fingers men's coats, pants, vests become finished. If she works till midnight and coaxes her little boy to sew on buttons she can "finish" a dozen pants a day, and for this work, and for the rent and light and fuel saved her employer, she receives 30 cents a day—and another "sweat shop" has been established. . . .

But, in union there is strength! If you stand with your sisters and your brothers you can control the conditions that are bad; you can create conditions that are good. Join the union of your trade. Join the International Ladies' Garment Workers. Join the United Garment Workers of America. The Union has abolished child labor wherever it controls the trade, has established the eight hour day, and in some cities the forty-four hour week; sanitary conditions are insisted upon; where over-time is demanded time and a half is paid in wages, while the general wage has been increased over fifty per cent. Demand the Union Label.[28]

Like other Progressive organizations, the Women's Trade Union League tried to bring about reform through legislative action as well as by unionization. At its national convention, the NWTUL committed itself to support of specific legislative measures, and League members lobbied and agitated for them in the states and in Washington. The objectives listed below were agreed upon by a League committee after its 1911 convention as legislative goals of the WTUL.

NWTUL LEGISLATIVE GOALS

1. The eight-hour day.
2. Elimination of night work.
3. Protected machinery.
4. Sanitary workshops.
5. Separate toilet rooms.
6. Seats for women and permission for their use when the work allows.
7. Prohibition of the employment of pregnant women two months before and after child-birth.
8. Pensions for working mothers during the lying-in-period.
9. Factory inspection laws which make possible the enforcement of labor laws. An increased number of women inspectors . . . and the inspectors to be men and women with a practical knowledge of the work, under civil service.
10. In the states where women workers are to be examined for physical fitness, women physicians be employed.
11. A minimum wage commission to create wage boards for each industry having an equal representation of employers and workers and representation from the public.
12. To provide adequate fire protection in factories, stores and offices, including compulsory fire drills.
13. Employers' Liability Law and compensation for industrial accident.
14. Banking laws for the protection of the savings of the workers. Weekly payment of wages, and prohibition of payment of wages by check.
15. Control and supervision of employment agencies, and abolition of the vampire system [a system in which workers were forced to make regular payments in order to keep their jobs].
16. The enactment of a law making it compulsory . . . when advertising for employees in time of strike, to state in such advertisement that a strike is going on. . . .
17. The initiative, referendum and recall.
18. Amendment to the child labor law that the certificate of employment shall not be granted unless the child has passed on examination in the labor laws of the State.[29]

The NWTUL was also an active advocate of the vote for women. The organization believed that suffrage would be of particular value to working women, since it would in-

crease their influence upon lawmakers and would help to achieve the kinds of legislative changes listed above.

As a result, the NWTUL set up a suffrage department in 1908 and worked hard for the ballot, lecturing, writing, and campaigning in the cause. League members encouraged working-class women to join the suffrage movement, urged unions to support the ballot, and aided the efforts of the National American Woman Suffrage Association as well as other suffrage organizations.[30]

In 1913, the NWTUL established a training school to prepare women workers for leadership roles in the labor movement, and increasing numbers of wage earners began to participate in the leadership of the League itself.

From this time, League activities concentrated more and more on legislative reform and educational work rather than on union organizing. Its commitment to laboring women, however, remained, and when, after World War I, many women lost the jobs they had been able to get during the war years, the NWTUL came to their aid. One incident of this kind occurred in December 1918, when the National War Labor Board ordered the dismissal of 150 women conductors of the Cleveland Street Railway Company at the request of Division 268 of the Amalgamated Association of Street and Electric Railway Employes. The NWTUL declared this an infringement of the rights of working women and filed a protest. The following article in the League's magazine, Life and Labor, describes this incident and the NWTUL's efforts to help women streetcar conductors in both Cleveland and Detroit.

"THE WOMAN STREET CAR CONDUCTOR —SHALL SHE HAVE FAIR PLAY?"

Essential facts in the case of the women street car conductors of Cleveland, according to a representative of the National Women's Trade Union League who made inquiry on the ground, are as follows:

(1) The women did not displace any men on the cars of Cleveland when they took jobs as conductors. They were first employed on the cars in August, when the U. S. Employment Service was advertising the fact that there was a shortage of 36,000 men for the conduct of essential industries in that section of Ohio alone.

(2) The women are not now keeping men out of such jobs. This statement is proved by the fact that the Cleveland Street Railway was not at the time of the recent strike, and is not now, as LIFE AND LABOR goes to press, running all its cars, because it has not the crews. The men's attitude is simply a demand for a monopoly of the street car occupations.

(3) The women conductors of Cleveland are all self-supporting women, two-thirds of them supporting also children or parents. Twenty-six have husbands or sons in the Army.

(4) The women conductors are competent. They were trained for their work in a training school established by the company because the men refused to teach them. The women were employed at the same wages the men receive and are subject to all other conditions applicable to the men.

(5) The women applied for membership in Division 268 of the Amalgamated Association of Street Railway Employes, which has a closed shop agreement with the Cleveland company. But the Amalgamated, both local and national officers, refused to admit the women as members, because to do so would extend to the women protection against dismissal.

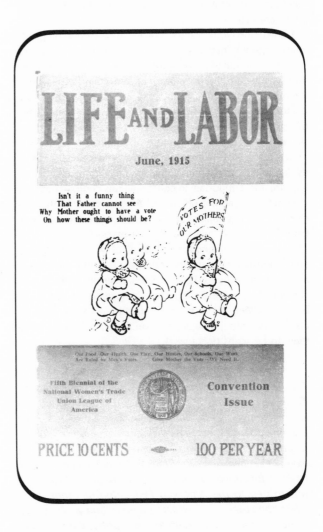

(6) The women conductors' work in Cleveland is primarily the work of cashiers. The doors of the cars open and close with an automatic device upon pressure of a button, or else by a light lever which requires but the turn of a hand. The car barns are clean and comfortable, with separate waiting rooms for men and women, the women's department being fitted up neatly as a sitting room and rest room, with a matron in charge. There are a dozen kinds of work historically accepted as "a woman's job" which are harder physically, more disagreeable and associated with more undesira-

ble surroundings than is the work of the women conductors. . . .

At the hearing on the case in Washington in November, the women were given to understand by the Board that a final hearing would be held at some subsequent date, when they would again have opportunity to appear. On December 3, the Mayor of Cleveland, and he alone, was heard, and the National War Labor Board took action upon the basis of his statements and his request alone.

On December 21 it was announced from the Washington headquarters of the League that the women conductors have filed a motion for a reopening, or rather, a final hearing of their case before the Board. . . .

Trade union women and suffragists are also watching with intense interest developments in a similar situation in Detroit, regarding the outcome of both cases as vital in their effect upon women's rights in industry. In Detroit, as in Cleveland, the union men threatened to strike unless the women conductors were discharged by January 1. The case has been brought before the War Labor Board, and hearings, it was stated, would be completed after the holidays. . . .

According to Chairman Taft's rulings as to the limits of evidence in the Detroit case, the issue which he terms "perhaps the most important in construing this contract (i.e., the contract between the union and the company) is the women's right to continue in employment when the supply of labor becomes adequate to fill their places."

This raises the fundamental issue of women's right to equal industrial opportunity with men, trade union women point out, and they add, puts it squarely up to the Amalgamated Association once more to choose, on the one hand, between giving the women conductors a square deal by taking them into the union, and, on the other hand, forcing them to be scabs or starve.[31]

The success and contributions of the National Women's Trade Union League in the history of the laboring woman are difficult to assess. With the perspective of time, the League's changing emphasis from unionization of women to protective legislation for women workers appears to have weakened its commitment to labor agitation. The NWTUL functioned in the midst of a complex of forces. It was related to the American Federation of Labor, from which the League derived some support and access to the center of labor organization in the country. On the other hand, it was hampered by the AFL's weak commitment, if not opposition, to the organization of women workers. The struggle that ensued after World War I, when male unions led the effort to fire women hired during the war, makes it clear that the affiliation of the NWTUL with the AFL was of dubious advantage.

The NWTUL represented women in craft positions. And like the American Federation of Labor, it ignored the bulk of unskilled and lowest-paid women workers, many of whom were black and domestic laborers. It was an organi-

zation that, like most Progressive groups, sought reform and was ultimately concerned with moderate and gradual change. The National Women's Trade Union League did not seek radical change for women workers either as workers or as women.

While there were many things the NWTUL did not accomplish, its positive effects were important. It did, along with the National Consumers' League, contribute a major share of the work behind the drive for protective legislation for working women and children, and whatever the long-range results of this legislation, at the time it constituted a humanitarian and constructive impulse that cannot be denigrated.

Moreover, the Trade Union Leagues, like the National Consumers' League, helped to draw middle-class women and working-class women closer together. In view of the divisive power of racism and nativism, this contribution of the NWTUL stands up well against the test of time.

THE NATIONAL CONSUMERS' LEAGUE

During the 1890's, consumers' leagues were founded in New York, Pennsylvania, Massachusetts, and Illinois with the specific intention of involving the consumers—that is, the middle class—in the plight of the workers.

The leagues were based on the assumption that if consumers were educated about the labor conditions under which products were made and sold, they would form a progressive force, pressuring employers and governments for reform. Josephine Shaw Lowell, later president of the National Consumers' League, was head of the Consumers' League of New York City when she explained the views of the women in New York who formed the first league.

LOWELL ON THE DUTY OF CONSUMERS

. . . the responsibility for some of the worst evils from which producers suffer rests with the consumers, who seek the cheapest markets regardless of how cheapness is brought about. It is, therefore, the duty of consumers to find out under what conditions the article they purchase are produced and distributed and to insist that these conditions shall be wholesome and consistent with a respectable existence on the part of the workers.[32]

In 1899, the four leagues that had been set up joined together to form the National Consumers' League. It grew quickly—in three years there were sixty-four branches in twenty states—and its membership, most of which was

The Consumer's Conscience

By MRS. FREDERICK NATHAN
President of the Consumers' League of New York City

middle-class women, continued to grow during the Progressive era.

Consumers' leagues, like many other Progressive organizations, believed firmly in the power of education, and so regarded the task of informing the public as one of their most important functions. In pursuit of their objectives, league spokeswomen were hard and faithful convention speakers and regular contributors to newspapers and magazines. This article, published in the General Federation of Women's Clubs Magazine, *was typical of efforts to spread the word about consumer responsibility. Its author, Maud Nathan, was president of the New York league and of the National Consumers' League.*

"THE CONSUMER'S CONSCIENCE"

. . . Women hold the household purse strings in the majority of families; they spend a large part of the family income for food, clothing, household utensils and decorations. It is therefore very largely in the power of organized womanhood to raise the standard of productive and distributive industry in the various communities. They can help to abolish sweat shop conditions, by creating a demand for articles bearing the label of the National Consumers' League which guarantees that the garments have been made in wholesome factories that have been inspected, where short hours prevail, where labor laws are not violated, where no children under sixteen years of age are employed and where no night work is exacted. Surely the benefit to the consumers through the use of the label is obvious. For garments made in living rooms of tenement houses may contain germs of infectious disease and are not necessarily any cheaper in price.

Organized women can also materially lessen the exhaustion, the toxic fatigue of workers, if they set their faces against rush orders and against procrastinated shopping hours.

Conscientious consumers can spare delivery clerks and shorten their hours by declining to receive goods delivered after the close of the working day; they can refrain from shopping on Saturdays, and thus help to forward the movement to establish a general holiday for recreation once a week other than the day used by the majority as a day of rest. During the hot summer months this is particularly important, when many a salesgirl faints from the strain of standing all day in a close atmosphere.

While it is true that hours of labor are in general getting shorter for working men as the years go by, there seems to be a tendency to increase the hours for women in certain trades. For instance, the canners of New York State perennially endeavor to get legislation enacted permitting them to employ women longer hours than are those employed in other trades. If exception be made in favor of canners, then candy manufacturers and manufacturers of other essential products would claim the same exemption from the law. . . . If organized women demanded the canned goods of those manufacturers who have obeyed the law, the rest of the canners would soon discover that it is more profitable to obey than to violate the law.

In "Marcella," Mrs. Humphrey Ward's novel which depicts the heroine engaged in social service work, we find this significant phrase: "Attack wealth as wealth, possessions as possessions, and civilization is undone. But bring the force of the *social conscience* to bear as keenly, as ardently as you may upon the separate activities of factory and house, farm and office, and from the result we obtain a richer individual freedom."[33]

After its formation in 1899, the National Consumers' League made its first investigative inquiry into labor conditions. This study, of the manufacture of women's and children's cotton underwear, was typical of its later activities. League members researched conditions in factories and stores; they publicized their findings; they pressured employers to shorten hours, to devise safe machinery, to raise wages; and they appealed to state and local government to enforce existing laws.

When products were manufactured by child labor or in home sweatshops, the NCL tried to publicize these facts and to get legislation passed to prohibit these practices. Below are excerpts from a lengthy NCL study of the conditions in textile mills in Passaic, New Jersey. Written by Agnes De Lima, the study focused on one hundred women night workers employed in the various textile factories in Passaic.

"WOMEN NIGHT WORKERS IN PASSAIC"

To quote directly from the latest report of the investigator [for NCL] following a night inspection on June 17, 1920:

The mill is conspicuously lacking in anything that might contribute to the health and efficiency of its workers. Accommodations as elementary as dressing rooms, rest rooms, adequate washing facilities and seats for women are no-where to be found. Surrounded by a brick wall, some 15 feet high, the plant resembles nothing so much as a mediaeval fortress. It is laid out principally in great sheds, hundreds of feet long, one story high, lighted only by skylights, and jammed to capacity with heavy machines whose combined noise is deafening. The effect of this, together with the heat and humidity, the constant standing and the high speed demanded of the operatives was evident. The workers looked beaten and crushed. That they could keep up the pace under these conditions through the long night seemed impossible. . . .

The one hundred night workers [studied by the NCL] represented the leading textile industries of Passaic. . . . They were largely engaged in one of the spinning processes, although there were carders, packers and weavers also among them.

Only four of the one hundred women were unmarried, and 92 of the married women had children. Of the four childless married women, one had lost two children, and another was recovering from a miscarriage. Five of the women were widowed. The average number of children was three in a family, though thirty-nine had four children or more; three had six, and six had seven children each. The women were mainly between twenty-five and forty years of age, and over half the children were under seven. Forty-one mothers had no children over that age, and in only four families were there no children as young as seven. Most had babies of one, two and three years.

It is the young married women with young children who work on the night shift. They are driven to it by the low wages of their husbands, and they choose night work in order to be with their children by day, fearing with reason the neglect and ill treatment the little ones receive at the hands of paid caretakers. The women, thus, are condemned to from eighteen to twenty hours of daily toil, for clearly no mother with three, four, five or six children can secure much rest by day.

The most casual questioning reveals how cruelly limited are the sleeping or resting hours of these night working moth-ers. . . . Not one of the hundred women visited reported getting eight hours sleep daily. Over two-thirds slept no more than five hours daily, forty not more than four. The seventeen who said they slept between six and seven hours thought they had "plenty" of rest. Most of the women took their rest during the day, getting up to prepare meals, to do other necessary housework, or to look after the children. Most of them did their main sleeping in the forenoon. None seemed entirely to undress but went to bed half clad, ready to jump up at any emergency. Interruptions are constant and insistent. Several women were found with a baby or two in bed with them, the only method apparently of keeping the little ones quiet and out of mischief. . . . The women's wages were comparatively high, allowance being made for

the generally accepted assumption that a woman has only herself to support, but the men's wages, on a family basis, were low. . . .

The conclusion therefore is inescapable that night work for women . . . is fostered by the low wage scale for men, coupled with a comparatively high wage level for women, which tempts them to enter the industry. Could a more ingenious device be contrived for lowering the vitality of the wage earners than to pay men so little that their wives, during their child bearing years, must spend their nights at the most exhausting kind of factory toil and their days at the no less exacting and insistent duties of motherhood?

The following excerpts from the investigator's records are typical of conditions found:

Mrs. S., a weaver, has three black rooms in a rear flat on the second floor of what was once a cottage. The sagging porch overflows with pale, sickly children who live inside. Seven of them belong to Mrs. S., who is still nursing the youngest, only a few months old. She earns from $19 to $24 weekly, seldom more; her husband makes $25 in a lumber yard. Worn and haggard, she sat there, the child pulling at her breast. Her mother, who interpreted, said "she never sleeps,—how can she with so many children?" She works up to the last moment before her babies come, and as soon as they are a month old. Mrs. L. who lives below in the same house, has just stopped work because she was pregnant, and although the boss had told her she could stay, she found the reaching on the heavy spinning machine too hard. Three children, ranging in ages from five to twelve years, sickly and forlorn must be cared for, and a tubercular husband, unable to work steadily, who brings in only $12 a week. During the interview he sat in a huddled heap in one corner. Two babies had died, one because she had gone to work too soon after its birth and lost her milk. She fed him tea and bread, "so he died." She was now planning—though obviously unfit for heavy work—to do day's cleaning to tide the family over the present "emergency." . . .

Mr. B was at home during his noon hour, hastily getting dinner for himself and five children so that his wife could sleep. The neglected home and children, the dejected man trying to help out, showed their struggle. He earns $25 a week in the mill, and she $17-18. "The baby," he said, "is sick most of he time and cranky. Most time he cries, mother no can sleep." A child of seven or eight, dressed in rags, with broken shoes on her little bare feet wandered about the room. Her wasted, sickly face was fixed upon her father while he was talking. Perhaps the most poignant thing is the expression in the faces of the children of these toiling mothers.

Mrs. V. lives in a dilapidated row of small frame buildings bordering on the Dundee Silk Throwing Works. The hall-ways are black and squalid, the bedrooms tiny and almost as black as the halls. The stairways seem in perpetual danger of collapse. Mrs. V. is a carder in a large woolen mill. The work is heavy and coarse, and she gets very tired before the night is over from the constant standing and carrying heavy spools. Her husband makes $22 in the same mill; she earns from $15 to $19. On the day of the visit she was wearily doing a big washing. Her two children, two and four years old, dirt and sores on their livid faces, sat dully in a corner. They seemed almost as weary and lifeless as their mother, lacking entirely the animation and gaiety almost inextinguishable in childhood.

A wretched creature was discovered on Sixth Street, living with her husband, a feebleminded daughter of fourteen and a younger child of three in one black bedroom, rented from another family. The woman was obviously afflicted with syphilis which had nearly destroyed her nose and palate, so that she could scarcely enunciate. She is a weaver making about $25 a week; her husband makes $20 in a rubber factory. It seems incredible that the mill authorities would employ a person so diseased as to be a serious menace to her fellow workers. . . . [34]

After studying working conditions in factories and stores, the consumers' leagues produced lists of recommended manufacturers for the use of consumers. They also designed a label that stamped finished products with the League's approval, functioning, much as a union label worked, to allow consumers to discriminate between products on the basis of their method of production.

In order to stamp his goods with the NCL label of approval, the manufacturer had to conform to a list of conditions which were set forth in a contract.

"FORM OF AGREEMENT BETWEEN THE NATIONAL CONSUMERS' LEAGUE AND THE MANUFACTURERS"

. . . That said Manufacturer agrees to maintain said factory under conditions approved by said League, among which conditions the following are especially agreed to, viz.:

1. That all provisions of the State Factory Law and rulings of the State Wage Commission are to be complied with.

2. That the label is to be used by said Manufacturer only when all stitched goods, sold by the Manufacturer, are made on premises previously approved by the League.

(a) Said Manufacturer agrees to furnish said League with addresses of all premises where any part or parts of stitched goods sold by him are made.

(b) Said Manufacturer furthermore agrees that no stitched goods nor any part thereof be manufactured, altered or repaired in a room or apartment any part of which is used as a dwelling, nor in any room directly connected therewith.

3. (a) That standards approved by the League with regard to cleanliness, sanitation, lighting and ventilation shall be maintained on the premises at all times.

(b) That such physical conditions shall be maintained on premises as will not give rise to fire, and will minimize the spread of fire, and that safe egress shall be provided to accommodate all workers.

4. That no girl under the age of sixteen years shall be employed, or permitted or suffered to work on such premises.

5. That no female shall be employed, or suffered or permitted to work in said factory between the hours of 10 P.M. and 7 A.M.., nor longer than nine hours in any one day, except for the purpose of making one shorter work day, in which case the hours shall not exceed ten in any one day, nor fifty-four hours in any one week.

6. (a) That entrance to the premises for purposes of inspection shall be granted at any time to the League's accredited investigator.

(b) That all records of hours and wages shall be accessible to any investigator duly accredited by the League, no information so gathered to be made public in so far as it involves the name of the individual firm.

7. That said Manufacturer shall immediately notify said League if a strike or lockout occur in his factory, it being understood that the League reserves the right to suspend the use of its label during such strike or lockout.

The license hereby granted to the Manufacturer by the League may be revoked by the League whenever in its opinion the Manufacturer has violated any of the conditions of this agreement or whenever, for any reason or cause, the League desires such revocation. Written notice of such revocation of license shall be given by registered mail to the Manufacturer at the address given below, and all rights of the Manufacturer to use the label shall terminate thirty days after his receipt of such notice. . . . [35]

The National Consumers' League joined with other Progressive groups to lobby for labor legislation in Washington and in the states. It was a major force behind the movement for child labor legislation and minimum wage and hour laws for women. When these protective labor laws were challenged in the state courts and, in eight instances, in the Supreme Court, the National Consumers' League organized and funded the legal defense. Louis D. Brandeis and, later, Felix Frankfurter served as counsels for the League. It was Brandeis who defended Oregon's minimum hour law for women in the Supreme Court, and it was NCL members who collected much of the data incorporated in Brandeis' brief.

On February 19, 1903, the Oregon legislature had passed a law prohibiting the employment of women for more than 10 hours a day in factories and laundries. A violation of the law had resulted in a trial and conviction. The defendant, a man named Muller, appealed the conviction to the Supreme Court of Oregon, which upheld the decision. Muller then went before the U.S. Supreme Court, where he argued that the Oregon law violated his rights under the Fourteenth Amendment and conflicted with the Constitution since it did not apply equally to all persons but ordained different treatment for women workers than for male workers.

The famous decision, based on Brandeis' argument, seemed to open the way for protective labor legislation and for better days for wage-earning women: the court ruled that differences between the sexes justified different treatment under the law.

FROM THE OPINION OF THE SUPREME COURT OF THE UNITED STATES

In the Case of Muller v. State of Oregon

Delivered by MR. JUSTICE BREWER, February 24, 1908

. . . . .

That woman's physical structure and the performance of maternal functions place her at a disadvantage in the struggle for subsistence is obvious. This is especially true when the burdens of motherhood are upon her. Even when they are not, by abundant testimony of the medical fraternity continuance for a long time on her feet at work, repeating this from day to day, tends to injurious effects upon the body, and as healthy mothers are essential to vigorous offspring, the physical well-being of woman becomes an object of public interest and care in order to preserve the strength and vigor of the race.

Still again, history discloses the fact that woman has always been dependent upon man. He established his control at the outset by superior physical strength, and this control in various forms, with diminishing intensity, has continued to the present. As minors, though not to the same extent, she has been looked upon in the courts as needing especial care that her rights may be preserved. Education was long denied her, and while now the doors of the school-room are opened and her opportunities for acquiring knowledge are great, yet even with that and the consequent increase of capacity for business affairs it is still true that in the struggle for subsistence she is not an equal competitor with her brother. Though limitations upon personal and contractual rights may be removed by legislation, there is that in her disposition and habits of life which will operate against a full assertion of those rights. She will still be where some legislation to protect her seems necessary to secure a real equality of right. Doubtless there are individual exceptions, and there are many respects in which she has an advantage over him;

but looking at it from the viewpoint of the effort to maintain an independent position in life, she is not upon an equality. Differentiated by these matters from the other sex, she is properly placed in a class by herself, and legislation designed for her protection may be sustained, even when like legislation is not necessary for men and could not be sustained. It is impossible to close one's eyes to the fact that she still looks to her brother and depends upon him. Even though all restrictions on political, personal, and contractual rights were taken away, and she stood, so far as statutes are concerned, upon an absolutely equal plane with him, it would still be true that she is so constituted that she will rest upon and look to him for protection; that her physical structure and a proper discharge of her maternal functions—having in view not merely her own health, but the well-being of the race—justify legislation to protect her from the greed as well as the passion of man. The limitations which this statute places upon her contractual powers, upon her right to agree with her employer as to the time she shall labor, are not imposed solely for her benefit, but also largely for the benefit of all. Many words cannot make this plainer. The two sexes differ in structure of body, in the functions to be performed by each, in the amount of physical strength, in the capacity for long-continued labor, particularly when done standing, the influence of vigorous health upon the future well-being of the race, the self-reliance which enables one to assert full rights, and in the capacity to maintain the struggle for subsistence. This difference justifies a difference in legislation and upholds that which is designed to compensate for some of the burdens which rest upon her.

We have not referred in this discussion to the denial of the elective franchise in the State of Oregon, for while that may disclose a lack of political equality in all things with her brother, that is not of itself decisive. The reason runs deeper, and rests in the inherent difference between the two sexes, and in the different functions in life which they perform.

For these reasons, and without questioning in any respect the decision in *Lochner* v. *New York,* we are of the opinion that it cannot be adjudged that the act in question is in conflict with the Federal Constitution, so far as it respects the work of a female in a laundry, and the judgment of the Supreme Court of Oregon is

Affirmed.[36]

Florence Kelley, president and guiding force of the National Consumers' League, was a peripatetic speaker in the campaign for child labor laws and minimum wage laws. She addressed groups as diverse as the National Convention of Charities and Correction and the General Federation of Women's Clubs during her lecture tours.

Kelley was also an outspoken advocate of the ballot for women, which she believed was intrinsically connected with the condition of working women and children. In 1905, she spoke to members of the National American

Florence Kelley

Woman Suffrage Association on the relationship between child labor and woman suffrage.

KELLEY ON CHILD LABOR AND WOMAN SUFFRAGE

We have, in this country, two million children under the age of sixteen years who are earning their bread. They vary in age from six and seven years (in the cotton mills of Georgia) and eight, nine and ten years (in the coal-breakers of Pennsylvania), to fourteen, fifteen and sixteen years in more enlightened States.

No other portion of the wage earning class increased so rapidly from decade to decade as the young girls from fourteen to twenty years. Men increase, women increase, youth increase, boys increase in the ranks of the breadwinners; but no contingent so doubles from census period to census period (both by per cent. and by count of heads), as does the contingent of girls between twelve and twenty years of age. They are in commerce, in offices, in manufacture.

To-night while we sleep, several thousand little girls will be working in textile mills, all the night through, in the deafening noise of the spindles and the looms spinning and weaving cotton and woolen, silks and ribbons for us to buy.

In Alabama the law provides that a child under sixteen years of age shall not work in a cotton mill at night longer than eight hours, and Alabama does better in this respect than any other Southern State. North and South Carolina and Georgia place no restriction upon the work of children at night; and while we sleep little white girls will be working to-night in the mills in those States, working eleven hours at night.

In Georgia there is no restriction whatever! A girl of six or

seven years, just tall enough to reach the bobbins, may work eleven hours by day or by night. And they will do so to-night, while we sleep.

Nor is it only in the South that these things occur. Alabama does better than New Jersey. For Alabama limits the children's work at night to eight hours, while New Jersey permits it all night long. Last year New Jersey took a long backward step. A good law was repealed which had required women and [children] to stop work at six in the evening and at noon on Friday. Now, therefore, in New Jersey, boys and girls, after the 14th birthday, enjoy the pitiful privilege of working all night long.

In Pennsylvania, until last May it was lawful for children, 13 years of age, to work twelve hours at night. A little girl, on her thirteenth birthday, could start away from her home at half past five in the afternoon, carrying her pail of midnight luncheon as happier people carry their midday luncheon, and could work in the mill from six at night until six in the morning, without violating any law of the Commonwealth.

If the mothers and the teachers in Georgia could vote, would the Georgia Legislature have refused at every session for the last three years to stop the work in the mills of children under twelve years of age?

Would the New Jersey Legislature have passed that shameful repeal bill enabling girls of fourteen years to work all night, if the mothers in New Jersey were enfranchised? Until the mothers in the great industrial States are enfranchised, we shall none of us be able to free our consciences from participation in this great evil. No one in this room to-night can feel free from such participation. The children make our shoes in the shoe factories; they knit our stockings, our knitted underwear in the knitting factories. They spin and weave our cotton underwear in the cotton mills. Children braid straw for our hats, they spin and weave the silk and velvet wherewith we trim our hats. They stamp buckles and metal ornaments of all kinds, as well as pins and hat-pins. Under the sweating system, tiny children make artificial flowers and neckwear for us to buy. They carry bundles of garments from the factories to the tenements, little beasts of burden, robbed of school life that they may work for us.

We do not wish this. We prefer to have our work done by men and women. But we are almost powerless. Not wholly powerless, however, are citizens who enjoy the right of petition. For myself, I shall use this power in every possible way until the right to the ballot is granted, and then I shall continue to use both.

What can we do to free our consciences? There is one line of action by which we can do much. We can enlist the workingmen on behalf of our enfranchisement just in proportion as we strive with them to free the children. No labor organization in this country ever fails to respond to an appeal for help in the freeing of the children.

For the sake of the children, for the Republic in which these children will vote after we are dead, and for the sake of our cause, we should enlist the workingmen voters, with us, in this task of freeing the children from toil.[37]

The National Consumers' League, which has continued to function up to the present, was typical of Progressivism in its faith in education, the democratic process, and the humanitarian impulse. It was, moreover, a moderate reform organization, seeking legislative and judicial change to regulate and adjust economic practices. It left unchallenged the economic relationships and the economic system that produced those practices.

Within the women's movement also, the NCL was a moderate force. While it pressed hard for improvements in women's wages and working conditions, it did so somewhat as a protector of abused and exploited women, rather than as the champion of women's right to full equality in the world of work.

Nonetheless, its motives and its accomplishments were important. The NCL helped to bring about protective labor laws for women and children and did increase consumers' awareness of the human suffering that lay behind industrial production. It also served to introduce large numbers of middle-class women to the realities of working-class life and to the idea that they, who lived very different lives, were, in some way, connected with working-class women. Although the connection was seen, then, in terms that were protective, almost paternalistic, nonetheless a connection was made where none had been before. And in this way, the National Consumers' League, like the National Women's Trade Union League, did work against the divisive forces of class, race, and ethnicity.

CHAPTER TEN

THE FINAL SUFFRAGE DRIVE

Suffrage was the major objective of the women's movement during the first two decades of the twentieth century, and the passage of the Nineteenth Amendment in 1920 was a triumph for the multitude of women's organizations that had faithfully maintained the struggle for the ballot. In the forefront were the National American Woman Suffrage Association and its affiliated state suffrage organizations, and the National Woman's Party, but a host of independent suffrage groups, women's clubs, and reform organizations like the National Women's Trade Union League played an important part in the battle.

Suffrage had been a primary objective for women since the movement began. By the 1870's and 1880's, it was the dominant goal of both the National Woman Suffrage Association, which worked for an amendment to the Federal Constitution, and the American Woman Suffrage Association, which labored for changes within individual states. With support from state and local suffrage groups and from the Woman's Christian Temperance Union, the National and the American fought hard for the vote, each in its own way, but both were unsuccessful. In 1890, when they merged to form the National American Woman Suffrage Association, it was hoped that factionalism within the suffrage movement would end and a unified and coordinated drive for the vote would begin. However, the suffrage movement remained tired and colorless; and despite the rush of millions of women into clubs of all kinds, NAWSA's membership was less than 100,000 in 1910.

After the 1890 reunion, most of NAWSA's suffrage work took place in the states. In South Dakota, Kansas, Colorado, California, Idaho, Oregon, Washington, New Hampshire, and New York, the old war horses of the movement, like Anthony and Blackwell, and younger leaders, like Anna Howard Shaw and Carrie Chapman Catt, backed up by a faithful membership, repeated familiar campaign routines, trying to persuade state legislatures to put woman suffrage on the ballot or to convince voters to approve it by referendum.

Failures overshadowed the few accomplishments (Colorado in 1893 and Idaho in 1896) and the National-American fell into the doldrums. Factionalism and personality clashes marred the reunion; the great leaders died off, and the familiar arguments and campaign techniques seemed stale and weak.

However, there were signs, after 1910, that the suffrage movement would see better days. Defeats continued, of course, in New York, Massachusetts, Pennsylvania, New Jersey, Ohio, Wisconsin, Michigan, the Dakotas, Nebraska, and Missouri. But significant victories occurred in Washington (1910) and California (1911), and some close losses nurtured the hope that other victories were near at hand. In the important California campaign, suffrage workers revealed some of the flexibility and imagination that would soon combine with their usual energy and dedication to revitalize the struggle for the ballot. Moreover, in the South, the suffrage movement, which had been slow to develop during the nineteenth century, was gaining in numbers and organizations; Southerners became more active and prominent in the National-American.

"Progress of Woman's Rights in Kansas."
New York Tribune, Aug. 11, 1911

There were other causes for optimism. After 1910, many new suffrage groups sprang up independent of the sluggish NAWSA, and they displayed a refreshing vigor and style. Moreover, non-suffrage organizations—like church groups, labor unions, socialist groups, and even the major political parties in some states—began to endorse and work for the ballot for women. Progressives, male and female, were committed to political democracy, and they advocated woman suffrage. They also believed that the enfranchisement of women would help them achieve other Progressive reforms. Organizations like the General Federation of Women's Clubs, the National Women's Trade Union League, the National Association of Colored Women, and the National Consumers' League made important contributions to the suffrage drive.

Prominent throughout the gamut of organizations supporting woman suffrage were the increasing numbers of female college graduates. By the last decade of the nineteenth century, women, educated in women's colleges in the South and the East, joined with the graduates of the coeducational institutions of the Middle and Far West, to make up an unusually energetic, well-informed, and able component of the suffrage force.

NEW BLOOD FOR THE SUFFRAGE MOVEMENT

Among the most active and influential of the new and independent suffrage organizations was the Women's Political Union in New York. Harriot Stanton Blatch, daughter of Elizabeth Cady Stanton, returned to New York in 1902 after living in England for many years. There she had witnessed the dramatic activities of the English suffragists: these women were carrying on a militant protest campaign, heckling anti-suffrage speakers, assembling in defiance of the law, disrupting public meetings, breaking windows, and even setting fires. Moreover, under the leadership of Emmeline Pankhurst, they had enlisted British factory workers in the suffrage cause through the Women's Franchise League. The New York suffrage movement seemed lifeless by comparison. Blatch set out to invigorate it, to politicize it, and to expand it to include working-class women.

In 1907, at a mass meeting to which labor unions were specifically invited, Blatch launched the Equality League of Self-Supporting Women, which became the Women's Political Union three years later, and which attracted 20,-000 working-class women to its membership. One of the League's first activities was to testify in Albany before the Joint State Judiciary Committee in support of a resolution to give the vote to women by striking the word "male" from the definition of a voter in the state constitution. For the first time, the speakers testifying for suffrage were wage-earning women. Mary Duffy of the Overall Workers' Union and Clara Silver from the Buttonhole Workers' Union delivered the following addresses in 1907.

MARY DUFFY'S SPEECH IN ALBANY

Trade unionism is not very popular with some of you; but, gentlemen, it is the only protector we working women have. Why, that law to protect women from night work which

"The Type Has Changed."
New York Tribune, Feb. 24, 1911

some of your friends worked so hard to pass has just been declared unconstitutional. We have no votes to change the constitution. We must depend on our union to protect us. . . .

Miss Schneiderman, who wanted to come here to-day, but could not leave the city, sent you a message by me. Rose Schneiderman is a cap maker. She is a Russian, but has been a long time in America. She told me to tell you how we women who are born in America or have lived here a long time and have learned to understand the laws of this country feel when we see some man from Europe who knows nothing of free government and is too old to learn just put right over our heads.

And, gentlemen, this shows in our working life. That man learns his lesson quickly, and thinks himself superior to every woman. . . . He won't take his place in any organization according to his ability, but wants to push in and lead, when he is not up to it. . . .

In some of the clothing trades almost all the workers a little time ago were women, and women who had been born in America, or who had lived here a long time. They were self-respecting women, and skilled in their trade. Then came foreign men. They knew nothing about the country or the conditions here, but the State told them they knew everything better than any woman. Well, in such unions we women have a tough job bringing the men up to our standard. The State has much to answer for in filling those men full of conceit. . . .

Two million of the . . . men in the National Federation of Labor . . . have declared that they want us working women to be their equals in the State. And I bring you this resolution from the Central Federated Union in New York asking you to help us get the vote. . . .

CLARA SILVER'S SPEECH TO LEGISLATORS

I came to this country some twenty years ago. I had been trained for the tailoring trade. And I had had some training in politics, too. My home was in Birmingham, and my father and mother often took me to hear John Bright. I can remember as a child standing in a crowd on the platform, packed in tight, and listening to our great orator. And when I was older, I joined the other women and canvassed for our candidate. . . .

My mother was a great politician. Some people think that doesn't do for wives and mothers; they say it makes us neglect the home. Well, my home was always neat and orderly. And my mother is living today, a hale and hearty old lady of over eighty with nine sons and three daughters. Politics and home life seem to me to be a pretty good combination.

Perhaps, to think of things outside themselves makes both men and women stronger and more self-reliant. Anyway, I notice it is more difficult to organize women in my trade in New York than in England. In my union, that is the needle-workers, the women are almost all foreigners. They come from places in Europe where even the men don't know much about suffrage or liberty of any kind. Such women are rather meek, willing to submit to anything the boss asks. And these women are not good housekeepers and mothers. My experience teaches me that it is the upright and downright woman that makes the best home and the best worker. The meek woman is ready to knuckle under to anything, for she has not self-respect.

We working women are often told that we should stay at home and then everything would be all right. But we can't stay at home. We have to get out and work. I lost my husband. He was a diamond setter, a fine workman, and he earned good money, but he fell ill and was ailing for a long time. I had to go back to my trade to keep the family together. Gentlemen, we need every help to fight the battle of life, and to be left out by the State just sets up a prejudice against us. Bosses think and women come to think themselves that they don't count for so much as men. I think that the ladies who just asked you not to give them suffrage lack self-respect. I was sorry to hear them speak of women as

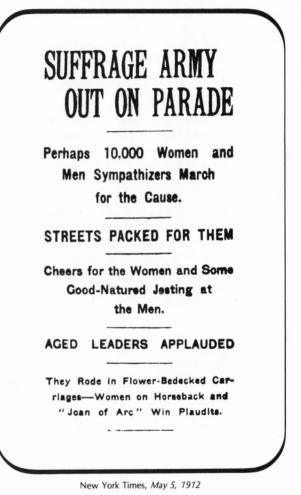

SUFFRAGE ARMY OUT ON PARADE

Perhaps 10,000 Women and Men Sympathizers March for the Cause.

STREETS PACKED FOR THEM

Cheers for the Women and Some Good-Natured Jesting at the Men.

AGED LEADERS APPLAUDED

They Rode in Flower-Bedecked Carriages—Women on Horseback and "Joan of Arc" Win Plaudits.

New York Times, *May 5, 1912*

they did in front of men. They seem to look for all the vices and not the virtues of their sisters. . . . [1]

Other activities of the Equality League of Self-Supporting Women were equally innovative and even more sensational. In 1910, the League organized the first suffrage parade. Although it shocked New Yorkers, it impressed other suffrage workers, and the parade became a regular event in many cities as suffragists used it as a device to publicize their struggle for the vote.

As it attracted new members, the Equality League branched out into politics, supporting the nomination of pro-suffrage politicians, questioning candidates, working to defeat its foes, and setting up a system of poll watchers at election time. New York, as this editorial comment from The New York Times suggests, was somewhat dismayed.

EDITORIAL COMMENT ON LEAGUE ACTIVITIES

The foxes have holes, and birds of the air have nests, but the politician has no hiding place when the suffragists get after him. They have advanced their lines, they have narrowed the circle around their enemy. They have been contenting themselves with demanding of candidates whether they were for or against suffrage. Now they have gone a step further, and are demanding of politicians who are not candidates whether or not they will support a candidate who does not believe in suffrage. This marks an advance in the reign of terror. . . . This fiendish addition to the troubles of the politicians is not the work of the suffragists in general, it is only fair to add. It is the invention of that corps headed by Mrs. Harriot Stanton Blatch. . . . Mrs. Blatch's independent cavalry have committed more deviltries in the way of harassing the enemy than all the other forces put together. . . . If women get the vote in this State, interest will not center so much on what Dr. Shaw and the reasonable suffragists do with it as on the use the Blatchian sharp-shooters make of it. They are afraid of nothing; they want what they want when they want it; and they have perfected an organization which will come in handy for other purposes when they have got the vote.[2]

In Albany, two female "silent sentinels" stood at the door of the Judiciary Committee room to publicize the lobbying efforts of the Women's Political Union. Parading, stumping upstate, lobbying, and pressuring political candidates, WPU work came to a head in New York's 1915 referendum campaign. Despite defeat, the techniques of the WPU survived, to be used by women in other states and in Washington, D.C.

NEW TACTICS IN SUFFRAGISM -THE CONGRESSIONAL UNION

The strategy of achieving woman suffrage by amendment of the Federal Constitution had been neglected for work in the states since the formation of the National-American in 1890. On Capitol Hill, the amendment, although intro-

Flyer

duced faithfully at each session of Congress, had not been debated in either house since 1887; it lay in congressional committees covered with dust. In 1913, the dust began to fly as a result of the work of Alice Paul and Lucy Burns, who headed NAWSA's Congressional Committee. They, like Blatch in New York, had learned their suffragism in England. Now, in Washington, they set out to revitalize the effort for the federal amendment.

Their first objective was to publicize the federal amendment by a variety of attention-getting activities. Paul and Burns began with an immense parade of women the day before Woodrow Wilson's inauguration as President in March 1913. Many in the huge crowds that had gathered in the capital were incensed at the intrusion of women into the presidential celebration, and the parade became a riot as mobs of spectators disrupted the orderly march. Finally, troops were called in to restore quiet.

In April, women delegates from each congressional dis-

trict marched to Capitol Hill on the opening day of a special session of Congress. In May, Paul and Burns organized demonstrations in the states; and then, with much fanfare, women presented a huge petition to the Senate in July.

The work of the Congressional Committee succeeded in gaining publicity for the federal amendment. And in Congress, the amendment was revived and debated during 1913, the first time in 26 years! And the dramatic techniques that Blatch, Burns, and Paul had introduced—the parades, outdoor rallies, mass demonstrations—became a regular part of the new suffrage movement.

In 1913, still heading the National-American's Congressional Committee, Paul and Burns formed a new organization, the Congressional Union, to work exclusively for a federal amendment. Their insistence on federal work, at the sacrifice of work in state campaigns, led to repeated disagreements between them and other NAWSA officials. Personal friction also grew, and ties between the National American Woman Suffrage Association and the Congressional Union were severed during 1914. NAWSA's effort to woo Southern states-righters who opposed a blanket federal enactment of woman suffrage by endorsing the Shaforth-Palmer amendment only multiplied disagreements between the two groups. The Congressional Union continued its work as an independent suffrage organization, and from then on, side by side, each in its own way, the Congressional Union and the National-American made up the vanguard of the final suffrage drive.

In 1914, Burns and Paul proposed that the Congressional Union actively oppose Democrats, as members of the majority party, who were running for election to Congress. Union members adopted the proposal that Alice Paul described to them.

PAUL'S ARGUMENT FOR POLITICAL ACTIVITY

. . . The point is first, who is our enemy and then, how shall that enemy be attacked?

We are all, I think, agreed that it is the Democratic Party which is responsible for the blocking of the Suffrage Amendment. Again and again that Party has gone on record through the action of its leaders, its caucus, and its committees so that an impregnable case has been built up against it. We now lay before you a plan to meet the present situation.

We propose going into the nine Suffrage States and appealing to the women to use their votes to secure the franchise for the women of the rest of the country. All of these years we have worked primarily in the States. Now the time has come, we believe, when we can really go into national politics and use the nearly four million votes that we have to win the vote for the rest of us. Now that we have four

million voters, we need no longer continue to make our appeal simply to the men. . . .

. . . We would issue an appeal signed by influential women of the East addressed to the women voters as a whole asking them to use their vote this one time in the national election against the Democratic Party throughout the whole nine States. Every one of these States, with one exception, is a doubtful State. Going back over a period of fourteen years, each State, except Utah, has supported first one Party and then another. Here are nine States which politicians are thinking about and in these nine States we have this great power.[3]

Officials of the National American Woman Suffrage Association were angered by the plan, which, they contended, directly violated NAWSA's nonpartisan policy. Paul and Burns disagreed.

PAUL AND BURNS DEFEND THEIR PLAN

This policy is entirely non-partisan, in that it handles all Parties with perfect impartiality. If the Republicans were in power, we would regard them in their capacity as head of the Government as responsible for the enfranchisement of

Alice Paul

women. If the Progressives or Socialists should become the majority Party, and control the machinery of Congress, we would claim from them the right to govern ourselves, and would hold them responsible for a refusal of this just demand.

Today the Democrats are in power. They control the executive office, the Senate, and the House. They can, if they will, enfranchise women in the present session; their refusal to do so establishes a record which must necessarily be taken into consideration by women when the Party seeks the re-indorsement of the people at the polls.[4]

With this conflict over partisan political activity, the split between the two groups widened; and chances for reunification of the movement disappeared when the Congressional Union put its new strategy into effect.

The Congressional Union's 1914 campaign against Democrats in the nine states in which women could vote attracted national publicity as well as many new members for the Union. Through its own weekly paper, The Suffragist, *the Congressional Union kept members informed of activities.*

"REPORT FROM SUFFRAGE TRAIN GOING WEST"

Here we are—all bound for the field of battle. Miss McCue, Miss Whittemore and I are together. . . . We have put up signs in each car that there will be a meeting tonight in the observation car, and that we will speak on the record of the Democratic Party in Congress and Woman Suffrage. There is much interest. We have sold ten *Suffragists* today on board the train, secured new subscribers to the *Suffragist,* and contributions for the campaign.[5]

"C.U. ACTIVITY IN COLORADO"

Friday afternoon, Mrs. Lucius M. Cuthbert, a daughter of ex-Senator Hill, gave us a drawing-room meeting in her beautiful Denver home. She invited representative women from all Parties to come and hear of the work of the Union, to which invitation about one hundred women responded. One Democratic lady came up to me after the meeting and said, "I had no idea you women had been so rebuffed by my Party. I am convinced that my duty is to the women first, and my Party second." Another: "You have almost convinced me that we women must stand together on this national issue." And so it went. . . . Offers of help, loans of furniture, and general expressions of eagerness to aid were made on every side. The meeting was a splendid success, judging

from the large number of women who joined the Union and the generous collection which was given.[6]

"MEETINGS IN KANSAS"

The meeting at Lebanon was especially well advertised. The moving picture shows had run an advertising slide; the Wednesday prayer meeting had announced my coming, and the Public Schools had also made announcements to their pupils. The Ladies' Aid Society invited me to speak in the afternoon, while they were quilting; and thus another anti-Suffrage argument was shattered; for quilting and politics went hand in hand.

At Phillipsburg the meeting was on the Court House green. It is fifty-seven miles from Phillipsburg to Osborne and the trip has to be made by freight. I was on the road from six-thirty o'clock in the morning until three P.M. About a dozen passengers were in the caboose on the freight, and we held a meeting and discussion which lasted about forty-five minutes. Upon reaching Osborne at three o'clock I found about one hundred people assembled for an auction sale in the middle of the street. Cots, tables, and chairs were to be offered at sacrifice prices. The temptation to hold a meeting overcame fatigue. I jumped into an automobile nearby and had a most interested crowd until the auctioneer came.[7]

As the Congressional Union expanded, state groups were set up to carry on its work. For a second campaign against Democrats in 1916, the Union organized the National Wo-

The Suffragist, *Oct. 1916*

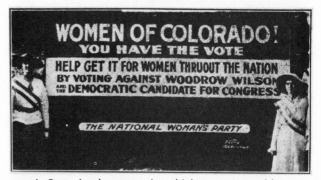

man's Party in the states in which women could vote, hoping to divert women's votes from Wilson, running for re-election, and from other Democratic candidates.

THE SUFFRAGIST REPORTS ON CAMPAIGN ACTIVITIES

While speaking and organizing have received great attention in the effort to turn votes from the National Democratic ticket, all other means of reaching the voter have been

FIVE CENTS

The Suffragist

WEEKLY ORGAN OF THE
CONGRESSIONAL UNION FOR WOMAN SUFFRAGE

APRIL 8, 1916

The Woman's Party
for
"Suffrage First"

Our Hat in the Ring

adopted in addition. The moving picture houses, in particular, have been made the means of winning converts. Upon thousands of screens have been thrown the slogans of the Woman's Party calling upon the women voters to vote against Wilson because "he kept us out of suffrage."

Billboarding and banners across the street have also been used lavishly by the Woman's Party throughout the suffrage states. In Kansas, Illinois, Arizona and Colorado particular emphasis has been placed upon this method of appeal.

Perhaps none of the various campaign devices used by the Woman's Party has attracted more attention and been more efficacious in arousing the latent wrath of the Democrats than the street banners with their conspicuous, clarion call to the women voters to "vote against Wilson."

In Chicago, where a dozen immense street signs were thrown to the breeze in various parts of the "Windy City," several of the big streamers met with an untimely end. One of them, placed in a prominent business block in "the loop," so aroused passing Democrats that many of them went in to complain to the proprietor of the building, who had previously given his ready consent to the hanging of the Woman's Party emblem. He was so pestered by the steady stream of worried Democrats that he ordered the banner removed. . . .

Another important phase of the Woman's Party activities which in its results is proving most effective in winning votes away from Wilson is the literature campaign. Leaflets and folders, appeals, cartoons and dodgers of various sorts have been distributed broadcast in an effort to reach the voting women. Many of them live on ranches or in rural districts where it has not been possible for speakers to reach them personally. In these cases literature has taken the place of speakers.

A comprehensive text book has been prepared by Miss Lucy Burns, giving a complete survey of the record of the Democratic party on national suffrage and reasons why women should not vote to return that party to power. This was sent, early in the campaign, to the editors throughout all the suffrage states.[8]

"DODGERS" FROM THE 1916 CAMPAIGN

Women Voters!
You have the vote.
Help get it for all American women by voting against Wilson.
He opposes National Woman Suffrage.

Women Voters!
Wilson opposes suffrage in Congress where he has great power.
He votes for it in New Jersey where he knows it will fail.

After the Civil War the negroes were given the vote.

Women were told to *wait*—that this was the negro's hour.
In 1916 the Democratic party advocates political freedom for Filipinos and Porto Ricans.
President Wilson tells voteless women still to wait.

Women Voters!
Why does Wilson seek votes *from* women when he opposes votes *for* women?
Do not send to the White House a Man who is against National Woman Suffrage.
National Woman's Party.

We are against Wilson.
Why?
Because he is against National Woman Suffrage.
Vote against Wilson for the sake of the voteless women of the East.[9]

Wilson carried all but two of the suffrage states in 1916, and after his re-election, the Congressional Union's activities centered once again in Washington. Here Union members pressured and hounded members of Congress to gain support for the amendment, missing no opportunity to push or cajole. On Valentine's Day, 1916, congressmen received greetings from women living in their districts.

VALENTINES FROM THE UNION

TO CONGRESSMAN EDWARD STEVENS HENRY, HOUSE RULES COMMITTEE

H is for Hurry—
   Which Henry should do.

E is for Every —
   Which includes women too.

N is for Now—
   The moment to act.

R is for Rules—
   Which must bend to the fact.

Y is for You—
   With statesmanlike tact.

TO CONGRESSMAN THOMAS SUTLER WILLIAMS, HOUSE JUDICIARY COMMITTEE

Oh, will you will us well, Will,
As we will will by you,
If you'll only will to help us
Put the Amendment through!

TO CONGRESSMAN EDWARD WILLIAM POU, HOUSE RULES COMMITTEE

The rose is red,
The violet's blue,
But VOTES are better
Mr. Pou.[10]

As head of the party in power, President Wilson was, of course, one of the main targets of their efforts. The Union regularly asked for opportunities to discuss the suffrage amendment with the President and also tried to goad him into action by techniques like the one described below.

"HANG SUFFRAGE BANNER AS PRESIDENT SPEAKS"

Carefully Planned Demonstration in the Capitol Fails to Interrupt Wilson's Address

Special to The New York Times

WASHINGTON, Dec. 5.—While legislators and gallery spectators looked on in amazement, a large yellow banner bearing the words, "Mr. President, what will you do for woman suffrage?" was unfurled before President Wilson as he read his annual address in the hall of the House of Representatives today.

A delegation representing the Congressional Union for Woman Suffrage staged the sensational incident. Without warning the banner was rapidly strung out along the railing of the public gallery, almost directly in front of the rostrum, from which the President was reading the message.

The affair was carefully planned. This was shown by the fact that at the very instant the banner was unfurled, a messenger from the Congressional Union headquarters appeared suddenly at the door of the press gallery of the House and shoved into a doorkeeper's hands copies of an article about the banner and the women responsible for its display.

The President caught only a glimpse of the big streamer. Those immediately in front of Mr. Wilson say he smiled just a little, but there was no break in the reading of his address.

James Griffin, one of the assistant doorkeepers of the House, moved quickly from his place on the floor toward the offending banner. Twice he jumped in an effort to haul it down. On a third attempt he was successful. He gave the banner a vigorous jerk, and it was pulled out of the hands of the six women who held it.[11]

PICKETING THE WHITE HOUSE

In January 1917, after one of several fruitless meetings with Wilson, the Congressional Union commenced picketing the White House. For one and a half years, two teams of "silent sentinels" (eventually more than a thousand women were involved) stood at the White House entrance gates every day in summer and winter. Enduring jeers and abuse, they stood there staunchly, holding up banners demanding the vote.

A short time later, in April 1917, the United States entered World War I. The National Woman's Party (the Congressional Union had just been reorganized and renamed) announced it would continue to work for the amendment despite the war.

"WHY THE SUFFRAGE STRUGGLE MUST CONTINUE"

. . . In our national convention in March, our members, though differing widely on the duty of the individual in war, were unanimous in voting that in event of war the National Woman's Party, as an organization, should continue to work for political liberty for women and for that alone, believing, as the convention resolution stated, that in so doing the organization "serves the highest interest of the country." . . .

Never was there greater need of work for internal freedom in this country. At the very moment when democracy is increasing among nations in the throes of war, women in the United States are told that attempts at electoral reforms are out of place until war is over. The Democrats have decided in caucus that only war measures shall be included in their legislative program and have announced that they will take up no new subjects unless the President considers them of value for war purposes. Suffrage has not yet been included under this head. . . . No "war measure" that has been suggested would contribute more toward establishing unity in the country, than would the giving of suffrage to all the people. It will always be difficult to wage a war for democracy abroad while democracy is denied at home.[12]

With the United States at war, the picketers, already acquainted with taunts and hostile curiosity, faced a cre-

President Wilson Says, "Godspeed to the Cause"

scendo of anger. The banners they held, like the one below that greeted a mission of Russian allies, enraged chauvinist spectators.

BANNERS FOR THE RUSSIAN MISSION

PRESIDENT WILSON AND ENVOY ROOT ARE DECEIVING RUSSIA. THEY SAY, "WE ARE A DEMOCRACY, HELP US WIN THE WORLD WAR SO THAT DEMOCRACY MAY SURVIVE."

WE, THE WOMEN OF AMERICA, TELL YOU THAT AMERICA IS NOT A DEMOCRACY. TWENTY MILLION AMERICAN WOMEN ARE DENIED THE RIGHT TO VOTE. PRESIDENT WILSON IS THE CHIEF OPPONENT OF THEIR NATIONAL ENFRANCHISEMENT.

HELP US MAKE THIS NATION REALLY FREE. TELL OUR GOVERNMENT IT MUST LIBERATE ITS PEOPLE BEFORE IT CAN CLAIM FREE RUSSIA AS AN ALLY.[13]

Other banners simply repeated Wilson's own words on democracy, deploring the obvious contradiction between what the President said and the disfranchisement of American women.

BANNERS QUOTING WILSON

I TELL YOU SOLEMNLY, LADIES AND GENTLEMEN, WE CANNOT POSTPONE JUSTICE ANY LONGER IN THESE UNITED STATES, AND I DON'T WISH TO SIT DOWN AND LET ANY MAN TAKE CARE OF ME WITHOUT MY HAVING AT LEAST A VOICE IN IT . . .

WE SHALL FIGHT FOR THE THINGS WE HAVE ALWAYS HELD NEAREST OUR HEARTS—FOR DEMOCRACY, FOR THE RIGHT OF THOSE WHO SUBMIT TO AUTHORITY TO HAVE A VOICE IN THEIR OWN GOVERNMENT[14]

It was more than some bystanders could endure. They pushed their fists through the banners, grabbed them, tore them apart, and stomped on them. Sometimes the attackers struck the picketers as well. National Woman's Party members quietly and quickly replaced both banners and picketers.

For several weeks, the police stood by, watching. Finally they acted: they began to arrest the picketers, who later were charged with obstructing the sidewalk.

There were mixed reactions to these extraordinary events. Although most newspapers followed the arrests and the subsequent trials and imprisonment of the suffragists, many editors and other commentators were in no mood to question the assertion that the women had vi-

olated the law, nor were they inclined to grapple with the implications of these events in a nation engaged in a war "to save the world for democracy."

Some, however, were outspokenly sympathetic to the women and critical of both the police and the Wilson Administration, as witness, for example, this article in the Boston Journal.

THE BOSTON *JOURNAL* COMMENTS ON THE ARRESTS

That higher authorities than the Washington police were responsible for the amazing policy of rough house employed against the suffrage pickets has been suspected from the very beginning. Police power in Washington is sufficient to protect a handful of women against a whole phalanx of excited or inspired government clerks and uniformed hoodlums, if that power were used.

. . . In our nation's capital, women have been knocked down and dragged through the streets by government employees—including sailors in uniform. The police are strangely absent at such moments, as a rule, and arrive only in time to arrest a few women. . . .

Perhaps the inscriptions on the suffrage banners were not tactful. . . . But right or wrong, the suffragists at Washington are entitled to police protection, even though in the minds of the Administration they are not entitled to the ballot. . . . All this suffrage shouting in Washington has as its single object the attainment of President Wilson's material support for equal suffrage. . . .

President Wilson's word would carry the question into Congress. . . .

Would there be any harm in letting Congress vote on a suffrage resolution? That would end the disturbance and it would make our shield of national justice somewhat brighter.

It looks like President Wilson's move.[15]

BRUTALIZED FOR SUFFRAGE

The first group of women arrested in June for obstructing the sidewalk were pardoned despite their refusal to cooperate in court. But during the summer and fall, as picketing and rioting continued, more arrests were made. Eventually 218 women were arrested and 97 of them were sent to jail. (All the sentences—some were for days, some for weeks, and some for months—were later invalidated by the courts.)

It was a sensational episode. The women, many of whom were wealthy, professional, or prominent women, had been accused only of blocking the sidewalk. Now they were in jail. Although the war news dominated the front pages, the arrests and the events that followed them excited the country. (Paul and Burns's desire to attract attention for suffragism had succeeded beyond their expectations.)

Some observers, like the two below, probed behind the sensationalism to worry about the meaning of the events.

FROM THE ST. PAUL *DAILY NEWS*

The day's news contains two items of deep significance in this war of ours—this war for democracy.

No. 1. A judge of the supreme court of New York upholds the right of a citizen of the United States to criticize the government.

No. 2. A police judge in Washington, the capital city of the nation, sentences sixteen women to serve sixty days each in the workhouse for criticizing the government.

Regardless of whether or not we agree with the women, we can only regard their arrest as a petty display of intolerance of criticism, and an abridgment of fundamental rights of an American citizen. The police of Washington have heretofore, on other occasions, exercised a similar arrogance and defiance of the rights of citizenship.

The American people will not be filled with greater enthusiasm for a war for democracy abroad which begins with the suppression of democracy at home.

And, which is perhaps of graver import, this rank encroachment on the rights of citizens peacefully to petition their President, will, if it goes unrebuked, greatly encourage petty officials in many parts of the country to larger exercise of their tendency to suppress by force all who do not happen to agree with their conception of freedom, justice, liberty and democracy.[16]

LETTER TO THE EDITOR OF THE NEW YORK *WORLD*

As an eye-witness of recent events in Washington, permit me to add a word to the discussion which has been stirred up by your editorial entitled "Lawbreakers, Not Martyrs."

The pickets were tried on the charge of "obstructing traffic" and "unlawful assemblage." They denied the charge and brought evidence to support their denial. In addition, they frankly told the judge that their arrest was a "frame-up;" that he had decided their case before he had heard it; that they were so certain that he had his sentence of guilty ready-made that they had brought their bags with them to court; that throughout the trial he had shown such bitter prejudice that every element of judicial fairness had been absent. To the amazement of those somewhat familiar with courts, the judge showed no resentment at such statements; he smiled indulgently.

Five lawyers, among them men of national legal reputation, witnessed the proceedings. All agreed that the verdict was contrary to the weight of the evidence, that the sentence was excessive and that the judge had given such unmistakable evidence of bias that the case should have been thrown out of court. . . .

Policemen engaged in the arrest told the writer of this letter that the arrest should not have been made, and excused themselves from all responsibility, saying, "We acted under orders." . . .

Refusing to pay their fines because they believed themselves "not guilty," the sixteen pickets went to the workhouse. The President pardoned them either because they were not lawbreakers or because, in spite of their lawbreaking, he was sorry for their plight. In the absence of any explanatory statement the pardon was susceptible of either interpretation. Either the pickets were lawbreakers and the President kind, or the pickets were not lawbreakers and the President just. . . . [17]

The arrest of large numbers of respectable women and their incarceration in the workhouse were themselves startling events. But subsequent stories of physical abuse, the forced feeding of Alice Paul and others, and the much-publicized "Night of Terror" tinged the suffragists with martyrdom.

THE LAWRENCE, MASS., *TELEGRAM*

No matter if it is war time it does not seem right to treat American women who have petitioned for the suffrage in the manner in which the women militants who have been released from Occoquan jail [in Virginia] have been treated.

If only one or two of the women prisoners in that jail told the stories of brutal and inhuman treatment meted out to them the public would be inclined to believe that it was a case of hysteric imaginings on the part of gently reared women. . . .

But when thirty or more women all practically agreed in telling similar stories of deliberate attempts to break down their spirit by threats and rough usage in jail the American public is reluctantly forced to the conclusion that some one in authority in Washington blundered grievously in permitting such conduct on the part of jail officials.

According to Mrs. Eunice Dana Brannan, wife of John Winters Brannan, president of Bellevue and Allied hospitals, of New York, her experience in Occoquan prison, where she was confined for her picketing activities, was extremely brutal. . . .

Mrs. Brannan describes the scene that took place in the reception room on Nov. 14, following the arrests, after 41 women of the National Women's party had picketed the White House gates on Nov. 10. She added that when a demand was made to see the Superintendent the women were attacked by guards, and that Mrs. Lewis, who had acted as spokesman, was seized, lifted from her feet, and thrown through the door. Mrs. Brannan added:

"I saw three men seize Miss Burns, twisting her arm behind her, and then two other men grasp her shoulders. There were six to ten guards in the room and many others collected on the porch—40 to 50 in all. These all rushed in. Instantly the room was in havoc. The guards fell upon us. I saw Miss Lincoln, a slight young girl, thrown to the floor. Mrs. Nolan, a delicate old lady of 73, was mastered by two men. The furniture was overturned and the room was a scene of havoc. The whole group of women were thrown, dragged and hurled out of the office, down the steps and across the road and field to the administration building where another group of bullies was waiting for us. The women were thrown down roughly on benches. I was thrown, with four others, in a cell with a narrow bed and dirty blankets. The chair was immediately taken out."

That sounds more like Russia under the czar than like America.[18]

"THAT NIGHT OF TERROR," NOVEMBER 14, 1917

As Described by Mrs. Mary A. Nolan

. . . When Mrs. Gould and Miss Younger asked Florida women to go to Washington to help, I volunteered. I am seventy-three, but except for my lame foot I was well. . . .

I picketed three times with these splendid women, carrying a purple, white and gold suffrage flag. The third time we spent the night in the House of Detention because we refused to give bail. . . .

They ran through that "trial" rapidly the next day. We did not answer them or pay any attention. We knew, of course, that we would all be convicted and sentenced for months, just as the hundred and more other women who had done this thing for suffrage. . . .

It was about half past seven at night when we got to Occoquan workhouse. A woman was standing behind a desk when we were brought into this office, and there were six men also in the room. Mrs. Lewis, who spoke for all of us, refused to talk to the woman—who, I learned, was Mrs. Herndon—and said she must speak to Mr. Whittaker, the superintendent of the place.

"You'll sit here all night then," said Mrs. Herndon. I saw men beginning to come up on the porch through the window. But I didn't think anything about it. Mrs. Herndon called my name, but I did not answer. "You had better answer or it will be the worse for you," said one man. "I'll take you and handle you, and you'll be sorry you made me," said another. The police woman who came with us begged us to answer to our names. We could see she was afraid.

Suddenly the door literally burst open and Whittaker rushed in like a tornado; some men followed him. We could see the crowds of them on the porch. They were not in uniform. They looked as much like tramps as anything. They seemed to come in—and in—and in. One had a face that made me think of an orang-outang. Mrs. Lewis stood up—we had been sitting and lying on the floor; we were so tired—but she had hardly began to speak, saying we demanded to be treated as political prisoners when Whittaker said:

"You shut up! I have men here glad to handle you. Seize her!" I just saw men spring toward her and some one screamed, "They have taken Mrs. Lewis," when a man sprang at me, and caught me by the shoulder. I am used to being careful of my bad foot and I remember saying, "I'll come with you; don't drag me; I have a lame foot." But I was jerked down the steps and away into the dark. I didn't have my feet on the ground; I guess that saved me. I heard Mrs. Cosu, who was being dragged after me, call, "Be careful of your foot."

It was very black. The other building as we came to it, was low and dark. I only remember the American flag flying above because it caught the light from a window in a wing. We were rushed into a large room that we found opened on a long hall with brick dungeons on each side. "Punishment cells" is what they call them. They are dungeons. Mine was filthy; it had no window save a little slit at the top and no furniture but a sheet-iron bed and an open toilet flushed from outside the cell.

In the hall outside was a man called Captain Reems. He had on a uniform and was brandishing a stick as thick as my

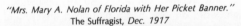

"Mrs. Mary A. Nolan of Florida with Her Picket Banner."
The Suffragist, *Dec. 1917*

fist and shouting as we were shoved into the corridor. "Damn you, get in here!" I saw Dorothy Day brought in. She is a very slight girl. The two men were twisting her arms above her head. Then suddenly they lifted her up and banged her down over the arm of an iron bench—twice. As they ran me past she was lying there with her arms out, and I heard one of the men yell, "The ——— suffrager! My mother aint no suffrager. I'll put you through ———."

At the end of the corridor they pushed me through a door. I lost my balance and fell on the iron bed. Mrs. Cosu struck the wall. Then they threw in two mats and two dirty blankets. There was no light but from the corridor. The door was barred from top to bottom. The walls were brick cemented over. It was bitter cold. Mrs. Cosu would not let me lie on the floor. She put me on the couch and stretched out on the floor. We had only lain there a few minutes trying to get our breath when Mrs. Lewis, doubled over and handled like a sack of something, was literally thrown in by two men. Her head struck the iron bed and she fell.

We thought she was dead. She didn't move. We were crying over her as we lifted her to the bed and stretched her out, when we heard Miss Burns call: "Where is Mrs. Lewis?"

Mrs. Cosu called out, "They've just thrown her in here." We were roughly told by the guard not to dare to speak again, or we would be put in straight-jackets. We were so terrified we kept very still. Mrs. Lewis was not unconscious; she was only stunned. But Mrs. Cosu was desperately ill as the night wore on. She had a bad heart attack, and then vomiting. We called and called. We asked them to send our doctor because we thought she was dying; there was a woman guard and a man in the corridor, but they paid no attention. A cold wind blew in on us from the outside, and we all lay there shivering and only half conscious until early morning. . . .

I was released on the sixth day, and passed the dispensary as I came out. There were a group of my friends, Mrs. Brannan and Mrs. Morey and several others. They had on coarse striped dresses and big grotesque heavy shoes. I burst into tears as they led me away, my term having expired. I didn't want to desert them like that, but I had done all I could.[19]

FROM "THE PRISON NOTES OF ROSE WINSLOW"

Smuggled to Friends from the District Jail

Alice Paul is in the psychopathic ward. She dreaded forcible feeding frightfully, and I hate to think how she must be feeling. I had a nervous time of it, gasping a long time afterward, and my stomach rejecting during the process. I spent a bad restless night, but otherwise I am alright. The poor souls who fed me got liberally besprinkled during the process. I heard myself making the most hideous sounds, like an animal in pain, and thought how dreadful it was of me to make such horrible sounds. . . . One feels so forsaken

Ryan Walker, in *The New York Call*

"'Women First' Is the Rule of Civilization."
The Suffragist, *Dec. 1917*

when one lies prone and people shove a pipe down one's stomach. . . .

We still get no mail; we are "insubordinate." It's strange, isn't it: if you ask for food fit to eat, as we did, you are "insubordinate"; and if you refuse food you are "insubordinate." Amusing. I am really all right. If this continues very long I perhaps won't be. I am interested to see how long our so-called "splendid American men" will stand for this form of discipline. . . .

All the officers here know we are making this hunger strike that women fighting for liberty may be considered political prisoners; we have told them. God knows we don't want other women ever to have to do this over again.[20]

By the end of 1917, the arrested women had been released on the recommendation of the Administration. However, in the summer of 1918, more arrests were made, and suffragists were jailed again. Early in 1919, when Woman's Party volunteers burned copies of Wilson's speeches and an effigy of the President himself, they were jailed once more, even as the amendment for which they had fought so devotedly was close to passage.

NAWSA AND THE FINAL STRATEGY

The success of Paul and Burns and the Congressional Union in attracting women to their lively campaigns in 1913 and 1914 contrasted sharply with the tired and static condition of the National American Woman Suffrage Association, which patiently repeated its suffrage work in the states. But in 1915, new leadership in NAWSA and a mounting interest in suffrage in the country gave life and vigor to the old suffrage organization.

In 1915, Carrie Chapman Catt, who had headed NAWSA earlier in the century, was elected president once again. With characteristic energy and decisiveness, Catt surrounded herself with able and dedicated assistants, and proceeded to reorganize the national as well as the state associations. She brought professionalism, political savvy, and planning to the National-American. Relations between national officials and state associations were clearly defined; national programs were enunciated with precision, and state organizations, having been honed and tuned according to crisp directives, were ready to comply. By 1917, the National-American was a well-oiled and intelligently led political organization which, according to Catt, had close to two million members.

Appreciating the value of Paul and Burns's dramatic techniques, NAWSA also worked to gain publicity for suffrage through massive rallies, parades, and other public events. But, in contrast to the Congressional Union and later the National Woman's Party, the National-American shunned confrontation and militancy and concentrated, instead, on persuasion, public education, and gradual conversion. This strategy (whose roots went back to the old American Woman Suffrage Association's emphasis on education and persuasion) had always guided NAWSA's activities. In 1912, for example, this circular letter was sent by NAWSA to clergymen in important suffrage states.

A LETTER TO CLERGYMEN

Dear Sir:

"Mothers' Day" is becoming more and more observed in the churches of our land, and many clergymen on that day are delivering special sermons, calling attention to the Mother's influence in the Home. . . .

In view of the fact that in the moral and social reform work of the churches the Mothers and Women of the churches are seeking to correct serious evils that exist in our cities as a menace to the morals of their children outside the home and in view of the fact that church women are finding that much of their effort is ineffective and of no value because they are denied the weapon of Christian warfare, the ballot, . . . we ask of you, will you not in justice to the Mothers of your church choose for your topic on "Mothers' Day" some subject bearing on "The need of the Mother's influence in the State?"

Women are recognized as the most religious, the most moral and the most sober portion of the American people. Why deny them a voice in public affairs when we give it for the asking to every ignorant foreigner who comes to our shores?

The women have always been the mainstay and chief supporters of the churches and in their struggle for their civil liberty. Should not their clergymen or Christian brothers sympathize with them and "Remember those in bonds as bound with them" and help them in their struggle? On behalf

Carrie Chapman Catt

of the church work committee representing Christian Mothers in every State in the Union, I would be pleased to know if you will be one to raise your voice on "Mothers' Day" in favor of the extension of the Mother's influence in our land "to help those women that labored with you in the Gospel?"

Very truly yours,[21]

In its dealings with political parties, the tactics of the National American Woman Suffrage Association were the opposite of the Congressional Union's. As the Union, and later the Woman's Party, campaigned against the Democrats and Wilson, NAWSA reaffirmed its nonpartisan position. When the Woman's Party gave up negotiating with Wilson and began to hector and taunt him, eventually burning copies of his speeches and his effigy, Catt was involved in a calculated and patient effort to win his support, by first gaining his ear and then persuading him of the political advantages of supporting the amendment.

Catt's strategy regarding Wilson was apparent as early as 1915, when she headed New York State's suffrage campaign, and it is clearly revealed in this press release issued by the Empire State Campaign Committee.

"MRS. CATT'S VIEWS ON HECKLING PRESIDENT WILSON"

I believe I can speak authoritatively of 99.9% of the hundreds of thousands of suffragists of the Empire State when I declare that they unqualifiedly condemn the attempt made yesterday to harry the President. The great majority of American suffragists have had no sympathy with "the militant tactics'' of the small British group called suffragettes even when applied across the sea and will not welcome the introduction of those methods here, and especially by British women.

Suffragists as well as all other citizens realize that no president since Lincoln has had such serious and delicate problems to solve, nor responsibilities so significant as Mr. Wilson. . . . We are distressed that any person in the name of our cause should have attempted to intrude upon his peace of mind. . . .

Although the denial of the vote to American women is a monstrous injustice, there is neither sense nor logic in harrying the President over it.[22]

When the country went to war in 1917, NAWSA announced itself ready to help the government, in spite of the pacifism of many of its members. And when National Woman's Party picketers made front-page news, NAWSA was quick to repudiate their activities and to assure the public (and the Wilson Administration) that NAWSA was neither associated with nor sympathetic toward such tactics. Nor did NAWSA officials join the ranks of those who protested the imprisonment and mistreatment of the picketing suffragists.

"MRS. CATT ASSAILS PICKETS"

Mrs. Carrie Chapman Catt, President of the National American Woman Suffrage Association, said yesterday afternoon that the women who were doing the picketing in Washington had made a psychological mistake.

"The pickets," Mrs. Catt said, "make the psychological mistake of injecting into this stage of the suffrage campaign tactics which are out of accord with it. Every reform, every change of idea in the world passes through three stages—agitation, argument, and surrender. We have passed through the first two stages and entered into the third. The mistake of the pickets is that they have no comprehensive idea of the movement and are trying to work this first stage in the third. We stand on the threshold of final victory, and the only contribution these women make to it is to confuse the public mind.[23]

In contrast to the antagonism that grew out of Woman's Party tactics, the patient and polite pressure exerted in Washington by NAWSA's leaders resulted in a friendly, and even cooperative, relation with the Administration. The following letter, written to President Wilson in 1917 by Helen H. Gardener, one of Catt's chief assistants, was typical of the cordial correspondence between NAWSA and the White House.

A LETTER TO PRESIDENT WILSON

May 10, 1917

The President of the United States,
The Honorable Woodrow Wilson,

My dear Mr. President:

When Mrs. Catt and Dr. Shaw were called west they left with me instructions to do whatever I thought best in their absence to further the securing of a Committee on Woman Suffrage in the House of Representatives.

I conferred with Speaker Clark who is willing to do what he can to help us secure such a Committee. . . .

The matter now seems to hinge upon the attitude of Mr. Pou, Chairman of the Rules Committee, who, *I am told,* says that he will report favorably "if the President approves of the creation of such a committee at this time."

If I might assure him that you do so approve, it would, we think, lead to the granting of the *only* request that the National American Woman Suffrage Association has made of this session of the Congress and secure to us the machinery

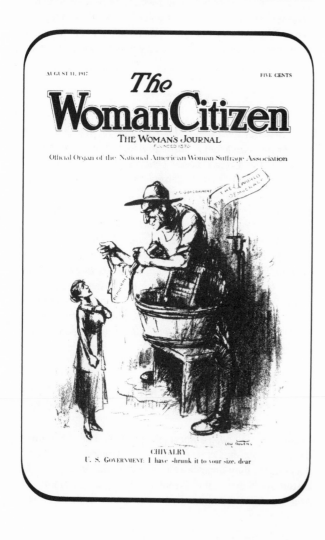

AUGUST 11, 1917   FIVE CENTS

The WomanCitizen

THE WOMAN'S JOURNAL
FOUNDED 1870

Official Organ of the National American Woman Suffrage Association

CHIVALRY
U. S. GOVERNMENT: I have shrunk it to your size, dear

of future work for which we have plead in vain for years.

Surely, Mr. President, the women of the country—half of the population—are not asking too much when they urge that they have a committee in the House of Representatives to which they may go freely with their problems and their pleas. . . .

Is it asking too much, Mr. President, at this time to urge you to make known to Mr. Pou that you would approve of this bit of machinery in the interest of the women of America?

I am assuming that you would approve of such a committee for it seems to me, as a student of your work and career, that it is in line with your progressive democracy. . . .

Yours sincerely,
Helen H. Gardener[24]

Wilson replied to Gardener's letter that he would write to Chairman Pou, and on May 14 he did so, telling Pou that he approved the formation of a suffrage committee, which seemed both wise and fair to the "best women" involved in the suffrage cause.[25]

Both the National-American and the National Woman's Party believed that an amendment to the Constitution was the most practical and fair method of achieving suffrage. But NAWSA insisted that lobbying in Washington was premature unless it was supported by work in the states, where the approval of voters and state legislators was essential to the eventual passage of the amendment.

In a letter to NAWSA assembly district leaders in New York, written while she was head of New York's 1915 suffrage referendum campaign, Catt explains the importance of state work.

CATT ON WORK IN THE STATES

To Assembly District Leaders:

Two up-state Campaign District Chairmen have complained that workers for the Congressional Union are seriously handicapping their work [in the referendum campaign]. One County Leader and two captains have resigned with a view to working with that organization: . . . it is important that all our leaders should know the facts concerning the Federal amendments so as to be prepared for any predatory raids upon our organization and campaign.

A Federal amendment must be ratified by the legislatures of three-fourths of the states, which means that 36 states must vote for, and that 12 may vote against. Ever since the Civil War the South has clung tenaciously to the doctrine of States Rights and has never yet endorsed anything in Congress which conflicts with that idea. The South may get away from that notion some time, but suffrage agitation in that part

of the country is many years behind that of the North and there is not a ghost of a chance that the real southern legislatures will ratify a Federal amendment even if submitted.

Formerly the southern group numbered fifteen. Take away Texas and Missouri as westernized, and Kentucky and Tennessee as northernized, and consider these four as possible in the list of states to ratify our amendment, and there remain eleven iron-bound southern states which for a long time to come will not ratify a Federal amendment. It follows then that the suffrage amendment when submitted must be ratified by all the New England States, all the Middle States and by New York and Pennsylvania, one or both. Only one state outside of this southern group can go against the amendment and still give us a chance to win.

No legislature in New York or in any other Eastern state has ever had more than one-third of its members who believed in suffrage; in New York it has usually been about one-fourth. Submission of our question [in a referendum to the voters] is merely throwing the responsiblity on the voters and most of our legislative members will use their influence to defeat it at the polls, whereas, the ratification of a Federal amendment means that the members will vote for suffrage per se not only for our own state but for all states.

5 cents a copy
Sept. 29, 1917

THE Woman Citizen

THE WOMAN'S JOURNAL FOUNDED 1870

"SHE HAS GIVEN ME TO DEMOCRACY; GIVE DEMOCRACY TO HER"

Official Organ of the National American Woman Suffrage Association

Imagine a Federal amendment submitted now. How could we secure its endorsement by our Legislature? Only by doing what we are now doing; working up a big sentiment in the constituency of each man. As yet that sentiment has not become noticeable enough to have brought the majority over. It doubtless would involve going into the elections with the effort to elect favorable members. The difficulty of an unenfranchised class attempting to persuade political parties to give up the men of their choice, needs only to be tried to be appreciated.

In the event we should lose in our campaign [they did, but in 1917, they won] and if no way is open for immediate or early resubmission, then in my judgment, we should turn our guns upon Congress and work for a Federal amendment; but while working for it we will have to work also upon the Legislature which will be called upon to ratify it. Any one who has observed with care the development of our movement within the last five years will realize that the task is quite difficult to secure that ratification in Albany as to secure the ratification at the polls. We may come in finally by the Federal route; but whether we do or not it is good common sense to do our utmost to carry the general election while the referendum is on rather than to postpone action to some uncertain date in the future. If we fail, every vote we have made will serve again in the constituency of the legislature. . . .

Most cordially yours,
CARRIE CHAPMAN CATT
Chairman[26]

As NAWSA president, Catt developed this strategy further, and in 1916, NAWSA leaders approved a ''Winning Plan'' devised by Catt.

CATT'S WINNING PLAN

. . . National Boards must be selected hereafter for one chief qualification—the ability to lead the national fight. There should be a mobilization of at least thirty-six state armies [after congressional approval an amendment needed the approval of three quarters of the states—or thirty-six states], and these armies should move under the direction of the national officers. They should be disciplined and obedient to the national officers in all matters concerning the national campaign. This great army with its thirty-six, and let us hope, forty-eight divisions, should move on Congress with precision, and a will. . . . More, those who enter on this task, should go prepared to give their lives and fortunes for success, and any pusillanimous coward among us who dares to call retreat, should be courtmartialled.

Any other policy than this is weak, inefficient, illogical, silly, inane, and ridiculous! Any other policy would fail of success. . . .

When a general is about to make an attack upon the enemy at a fortified point, he often begins to feint elsewhere in order to draw off attention and forces. If we decide to train up some states into preparedness for campaign, the best help which can be given them is to keep so much ''suffrage noise'' going all over the country that neither the enemy nor friends will discover where the real battle is. . . .

We should win, if it is possible to do so, a few more states before the Federal Amendment gets up to the legislatures. . . . A southern state should be selected and made ready for a campaign, and the solid front of the ''anti'' south broken as soon as possible.

Some break in the solid ''anti'' East should be made too. If New York wins in 1917 the backbone of the opposition will be largely bent if not broken. . . .

By 1920, when the next national party platforms will be adopted, we should have won Iowa, South Dakota, North Dakota, Nebraska, New York, Maine and a southern state. We should have secured the Illinois law in a number of other states.

With these victories to our credit and the tremendous increase of momentum given the whole movement, we should be able to secure planks in all platforms favoring the Federal Amendment (if it has not passed before that time) and to secure its passage in the December term of the 1920 Congress.

It should then go to the legislatures of thirty-nine states which meet in 1921, and the remaining states would have the opportunity to ratify the amendment in 1922. If thirty-six states had ratified in these two years, the end of our struggle would come by April 1, 1922, six years hence. . . . [27]

Prodigious work by an army of women carried out the ''Winning Plan.'' Although NAWSA was in the forefront of the struggle, the efforts of the National Woman's Party and the less spectacular but crucial work of other suffrage and reform organizations contributed to the changing sentiment within the country and the Congress. Seventy years of agitation, argumentation, and activity seemed to be reaching a climax. Arguing that woman suffrage was a ''war measure,'' suffragists capitalized on the democratic sensitivity aroused by the World War. Bolstered by Progressivism, they argued that enfranchisement would bring a better world.

Opposition was well organized and financed, but so was the suffrage movement by this time. When the amendment finally cleared congressional hurdles in 1919, more than a year ahead of the schedule in Catt's plan, NAWSA had the organization and the resources needed in the states to achieve ratification.

By 1918, Wilson finally agreed that suffrage was not being achieved in the states, as he preferred, and he made his first move in Congress in favor of the amendment on January 9. The President conferred with the chairman of *the House Committee on Suffrage, who then issued this obtuse statement to the country:*

The committee found that the President had not felt at liberty to volunteer his advice to members of Congress in the important matter [the suffrage amendment], but when we sought his advice he very frankly and earnestly advised us to vote for the amendment as an act of right and justice to the women of the country and of the world. [28]

Its meaning was sharp and clear. The President, leader of the Democratic Party, had conveyed to his party in Congress his support of the suffrage amendment.

The next day, January 10, 1918, the House passed the amendment. In September, as the bill came before the Senate, Wilson appeared before that body to appeal for woman suffrage.

WILSON'S APPEAL FOR WOMAN SUFFRAGE

The unusual circumstances of a world war in which we stand and are judged in the view not only of our own people and our own consciences but also in the view of all nations and peoples will, I hope, justify in your thought, as it does in mine, the message I have come to bring you. I regard the concurrence of the Senate in the constitutional amendment proposing the extension of the suffrage to women as vitally essential to the successful prosecution of the great war of humanity in which we are engaged. I have come to urge upon you the considerations which have led me to that conclusion. . . .

This is a peoples' war and the peoples' thinking constitutes its atmosphere and morale, not the predilections of the drawing room or the political considerations of the caucus. If we be indeed democrats and wish to lead the world to democracy, we can ask other people to accept in proof of our sincerity and our ability to lead them whither they wish to be led nothing less persuasive and convincing than our actions. . . . They are looking to the great, powerful, famous Democracy of the West to lead them to the new day for which they have so long waited; and they think, in their logical simplicity, that democracy means that women shall play their part in affairs alongside men and upon an equal footing with them. If we reject measures like this, . . . they will cease to believe in us; they will cease to follow or to trust us. They have seen their own Governments accept this interpretation of democracy,—seen old Governments like that of Great Britain, which did not profess to be democratic, promise readily and as of course this justice to women, though they had before refused it, the strange revelations of this war having made many things new and plain, to governments as well as to peoples.

Are we alone to refuse to learn the lesson? Are we alone to ask and take the utmost that our women can give,—service and sacrifice of every kind,—and still say we do not see what title that gives them to stand by our sides in the guidance of the affairs of their nation and ours? We have made partners of the women in this war; shall we admit them only to a partnership of suffering and sacrifice and toil and not to a partnership of privilege and right? . . .

. . . I tell you plainly, as the commander-in-chief of our armies and of the gallant men in our fleets, as the present spokesman of this people in our dealings with the men and women throughout the world who are now our partners, as the responsible head of a great government . . . I tell you plainly that this measure which I urge upon you is vital to the winning of the war and to energies alike of preparation and of battle.

And not to the winning of the war only. It is vital to the right solution of the great problems which we must settle, and settle immediately, when the war is over. We shall need then a vision of affairs, which is theirs, and, as we have never needed them before, the sympathy and insight and clear moral instinct of the women of the world. The problems of that time will strike to the roots of many things that we have not hitherto questioned, and I for one believe that our safety in those questioning days, as well as our comprehension of matters that touch society to the quick, will depend upon the direct and authoritative participation of women in our counsels. We shall need their moral sense to preserve what is right

New York Times, *Jan. 10, 1918*

WILSON BACKS AMENDMENT FOR WOMAN SUFFRAGE

Victory on House Vote Today Expected as Result of His Belated Conversion.

CONFERS WITH DEMOCRATS

Then President Throws Support to Resolution "as an Act of Justice."

DEMOCRATS WERE ALARMED

Feared Reprisals at Polls in Suffrage States—House Republicans in Line.

and fine and worthy in our system of life as well as to discover just what it is that ought to be purified and reformed. Without their counsellings we shall be only half wise.

That is my case. This is my appeal. Many may deny its validity, if they choose, but no one can brush aside or answer the arguments upon which it is based. The executive tasks of this war rest upon me. I ask that you lighten them and place in my hands instruments, spiritual instruments, which I do not now possess, which I sorely need, and which I have daily to apologize for not being able to employ.[29]

THE NINETEENTH AMENDMENT

Despite the President's eloquence, the Senate failed by two votes to pass the Amendment. But the tide had turned, and on June 4, 1919, Congress finally approved the Nineteenth Amendment.

By August 26, 1920, it had been ratified by the states and was proclaimed part of the Constitution.

THE NINETEENTH AMENDMENT

The right of citizens of the United States to vote shall not be denied or abridged by the United States or by any State on account of sex.

Congress shall have power to enforce this Article by appropriate legislation.[30]

———

With the adoption of the Nineteenth Amendment, a struggle of seventy years came to an end. That struggle, which started at Seneca Falls in 1848, grew, from the daring aspiration of a handful of women and a few men, to a major political campaign, enlisting millions. By the last decade of the suffrage struggle, every major women's organization rallied to the fight. As its momentum increased, participants felt themselves part of a great army, marching together, as in a crusade. It was a huge common effort, suffused with passion and conviction, and it created a strong and unusual unity among many women, a feeling of connectedness such as they had rarely experienced.

The suffrage struggle was much more than the demand for the vote. From the start, the demand for the ballot was also a demand for a place in what had always been the world of men. In calling for political equality, women were challenging men's exclusive control over that sphere of public activity—the world outside of the home and the church—where important power and influence lay and where decisions that affected women were made.

The demand for the vote, therefore, was more than an issue of political democracy; it implied a different role for women in American society.

Many of the women who fought so long and hard for suffrage understood this, although the full implications of enfranchisement remained unarticulated, almost suppressed. Nonetheless, many of the men who opposed woman suffrage understood and perceived the real meaning of women's claim to the vote. Those who insisted, for example, that woman suffrage meant prohibition for the country were saying, in effect, that with the ballot women would have power to affect public affairs and in ways they did not agree with. In a country ideologically committed to political democracy, the continued and passionate opposition of men to woman suffrage can only be understood by realizing what the vote symbolized for women and what it meant, potentially, for the place of women in the nation.

CHAPTER ELEVEN

ACTION, REFORM, AND QUIESCENCE

1920-1950

There were many reasons to expect that the passage of the woman suffrage amendment in 1920 was the beginning, rather than the end, of a period of growth and accomplishment for the women's movement. Yet, before the decade had passed, an inactivity and quiescence began that lasted for forty years. And although important changes happened to women during those forty years, women together, acting in reform organizations, played a relatively minor part in directing and controlling the forces of change.

There were few indications of this in 1920. The struggle for the Nineteenth Amendment had aroused women's interest and energy and utilized their talents and passions as never before. The tendency to come together in groups and the reforming zeal of Progressivism seemed robust. In the South, where both associationism and reform had been slow to develop, many reform activities were taking place, as women investigated labor conditions, tried to secure protective laws for female and child labor, and sought to improve racial relations. New national organizations were set up, among them two that are active at present—the National Federation of Business and Professional Women's Clubs established in 1919 and the American Association of University Women, formed when two groups of college alumnae merged in 1921.

Despair over the horrors of World War I and pessimism over the Versailles Treaty involved many women activists in international affairs. The age-old view that war was man's business and that women had an innate affinity for peace had justified their attraction to the peace movement, even in the nineteenth century. Now many women joined existing peace organizations. In 1919, Jane Addams headed a newly organized Women's International League for Peace and Freedom. In the mid-1920's Carrie Chapman Catt founded the Committee on the Cause and Cure of War.

The habit of cooperation among women's groups seemed well established and enabled them to assemble a unified and powerful political force. Together, for example, the National Women's Trade Union League, the National American Woman Suffrage Association, the General Federation of Women's Clubs, the Daughters of the American Revolution, and others demanded and pressured for a women's division in the federal Department of Labor. The establishment of the Women's Bureau by Congress in 1920 seemed to symbolize the vitality of the women's movement and to foretell an active future.

In 1919, anticipating the demise of suffrage organizations after the vote was won, Carrie Chapman Catt called for a new organization of women. Its founders hoped that the two million members of the National American Woman Suffrage Association would move into the new League of Women Voters, which would educate and prepare them for an active political life as well as provide women with the machinery for achieving their goals.

THE WOMEN'S JOINT CONGRESSIONAL COMMITTEE

The Women's Joint Congressional Committee exemplifies the women's movement in the early 1920's. It was, in effect, a coalition of the major national women's organizations that pooled their resources and influence to act as a women's lobby in Congress. Formed in 1920, the WJCC began its campaign for reform in high spirits of confidence and cooperation. The Committee described its aims and purposes in a formal declaration.

WOMEN'S JOINT CONGRESSIONAL COMMITTEE

Aims and Purposes

The Women's Joint Congressional Committee now in its second year serves as a clearing house for organizations engaged in promoting in Congress legislation of especial interest to women.

Many organizations maintain national headquarters or legislative offices in Washington for the purpose of keeping in touch with Federal legislation and conveying to members of Congress the sentiments of their constituents and to the members of the organizations the record of their Congressmen on approved legislation. . . .

The Joint Committee prevents duplication of effort and enables these organizations to unite in support of legislation. . . .

The Joint Congressional Committee does not separately endorse legislation. Its members bring to it the endorsements of their respective organizations. When any measure has received the endorsement of five member organizations, a subcommittee, composed of representatives of all the organizations which have endorsed the legislation, is formed to work for the enactment of that measure by Congress. This subcommittee chooses its own officers, is responsible for its own publicity and works without involving organizations that have not endorsed the measure.

No organization joining the committee is committed to any policy except that of cooperation wherever possible.

At present the legislative measures receiving active support are:

The Towner-Sterling Department of Education bill.

The bill for independent citizenship of married women.

The Capper-Focht bill, for compulsory education and school attendance in the District of Columbia.

The Fess bill for increased home economics appropriation.

The Fess-Capper bill for physical education.

The Sterling-Lehlback reclassification bill.

Officers

Chairman—Mrs. Maud Wood Park, National League of Women Voters.

Vice Chairman and Treasurer—Mrs. Ellis Yost, Women's Christian Temperance Union.

Secretary—Mrs. Arthur C. Watkins, National Congress of Mothers and Parent-Teacher Associations.

Member Organizations

American Association of University Women—Mrs. Raymond B. Morgan

American Home Economics Association—Miss Gertrude Van Housen.

General Federation of Women's Clubs—Miss Lida Hafford.

Girls' Friendly Society in America—Miss M. A. Ingle.

National Congress of Mothers and Parent-Teacher Associations—Mrs. Arthur C. Watkins.

National Consumers' League—Mrs. Florence Kelley.

National Council of Jewish Women—Mrs. Alexander Wolf.

National Council of Women—Mrs. Glen Levin Swiggett.

National Federation of Business and Professional Women—Miss Mary Stewart.

National League of Women Voters—Mrs. Maud Wood Park.

National Women's Christian Temperance Union—Mrs. Ellis A. Yost.

National Women's Trade Union League—Miss Ethel Smith.

National Board of the Young Women's Christian Association—Mrs. Samuel MacClintock.

Service Star Legion—Mrs. Max Mayer.[1]

Two of the reform goals endorsed by members of the WJCC received the most attention: a constitutional amendment prohibiting child labor and the Sheppard-Towner bill, which would provide federal funds to the states to set up instructional programs for maternity and infant care by such means as public health and visiting nurse programs and educational conferences on child care.

The bill, amended in Congress, provided the states with about one and a quarter million dollars a year, for six years; it was a small beginning, financially, in light of the high maternity and infant mortality rates in the United States, but it was a large change in the federal government's welfare role. Securing passage of the Sheppard-Towner bill was a challenge, and the WJCC and every member organization worked vigorously for its passage. With support from women's magazines and with a mammoth outpouring of effort, they made Sheppard-Towner into a major legislative issue.

"WE COULDN'T AFFORD A DOCTOR"

By Anne Martin

The Third Article in Good Housekeeping's Campaign for the Sheppard-Towner Maternity Bill

She went into the Textile mills in Providence when she was twelve. She had worked there ever since, first to increase her father's and then her husband's insufficient wages. Her hours were from five in the afternoon till one in the morning. Her work was done standing at a machine during the whole eight hours, except for half an hour off for some food. She went home at one o'clock and slept till six, when she rose to cook breakfast and get her husband off to the mills and her children off to school.

"We Couldn't Afford a Doctor"

GOVERNMENT BUREAUS REPORT 23,000 AMERICAN MOTHERS AND 125,000 BABIES DIED IN ONE YEAR BECAUSE OF LACK OF PROPER CARE!

Uncle Sam is aroused at last! How much longer will the Congress delay?

"I always feel tired," she said. She looked it. Her hair was gray; she was thin and undersized and seemed fifty instead of thirty-five. She had borne six children, and another was coming very soon. With stoicism she told how she had always worked in the mill up to the last day and had usually managed to return within a few days after the birth of her baby, so as to continue earning money. One baby was still-born; three were too feeble at birth to live more than a few days; two had managed to survive. Owing to her run-down condition she could not nurse any of them, she said, but could not have nursed them anyway, as she had to keep on at the mill.

She worked at night because it enabled her to "see the children some in the daytime," and to do the family washing, cooking, and sewing. She made over, for both the children and herself, old clothes which were sent by a relative. She had not had a new dress in eight years, or a vacation in twelve. The family earnings barely sufficed for the most meager supply of food and a place in which to live.

"I do not see how we can pay the doctor for coming for the next baby," she said. "He charges fifteen dollars and only comes once. The midwife will come eight times for eight dollars, but of course she doesn't know as much as the doctor. The housework always goes to pieces, though my husband cooks and does the best he can. But the children always get sick when I am sick, and everything in the house gets dirty, and we get in debt, so having babies is getting to be a horror to me."

The wife of a homesteader in Montana left the ranch with her husband in December, two weeks before confinement, and after a seventy-mile automobile drive to the railroad traveled over one hundred miles by train to the nearest hospital. They started back before the baby was three weeks old, in bitter winter weather. They knew this was unwise, but the hospital expenses were heavy, and the mother was worried about the other children, who had been left alone on the ranch. Owing to bad roads and a snow-storm, they were four days and nights driving the last seventy miles. One night they had to spend in the open.

"We intended to go to the hospital again for my next baby," said this Montana mother, "but the terrible expense of my last baby got us into debt, and then I couldn't get away in time because all the autos in the neighborhood were being used for sheep-shearing."

She was attended only by a midwife in this next confinement and suffered serious complications which caused the death of the baby.

These stories, as told to representatives of the Federal Children's Bureau, are typical of many thousands of others in the industrial cities and rural districts of the United States. Is it surprising that we have one of the highest infant death-rates in the world, that more babies die every year in the United States, under normal conditions and in proportion to the number born, than in almost any other country, great or small?

The facts are simple and tragic. Of the 2,500,000 babies born yearly in this country, at least a quarter of a million—one out of every ten babies born—die within the first twelve months of birth. Foreign countries long ago adopted government measures to save the lives of babies, and have thereby lowered the death-rate. France loses only one out of thirteen babies born; Australia and Sweden one out of fourteen; Norway, one out of seventeen; New Zealand, which through its most effective provisions for rest and medical and nursing care for the mother before and after childbirth, has achieved the lowest baby death-rate of any country in the world, loses only one out of twenty. . . .

Our government has made no provision for the protection of maternity and infancy, although the fact that the child's chance of life and future health is greatly increased by rest and care for the mother has become a matter of general knowledge. . . . [2]

Success came to these early efforts of the Women's Joint Congressional Committee: the Sheppard-Towner bill was passed by Congress in 1921, and the proposed constitutional amendment prohibiting child labor, which received similar support from the WJCC, won congressional approval in 1924.

ORGANIZING FOR BIRTH CONTROL

Among the new national organizations formed in the early 1920's was the American Birth Control League; it was the major proponent for the improvement and legalization of birth control during the decade.

Although the practice of birth control was common among more affluent and educated people and was increasing among working-class people, it was far from being as reliable or as widespread as it could have been. A series of federal laws, known as the Comstock laws, classified birth control literature as obscene and prohibited its distribution, while twenty-two states had laws that hampered both the spread of information and the use of contraceptives. Despite the growing practice of birth control, there was little public discussion of contraception, much haranguing against it, and considerable ignorance and avoidance of the subject by doctors and scientists. Embarrassment, ignorance, and confusion all hampered an informed and rational attitude toward the control of human fertility.

In 1915, the first U.S. birth control organization, the National Birth Control League, was formed in New York by a group of women, inspired by the arrest of Margaret Sanger and her husband, William Sanger, for violation of the laws against birth control literature. The League's objectives, as stated in a Declaration of Principles, were to make contraceptive information available by repealing the restrictive laws.

PRINCIPLES OF THE NATIONAL BIRTH CONTROL LEAGUE

The object of the Birth Control League is to help in the formation of a body of public opinion that will result in the repeal of the laws, National, State or local, which make it a criminal offense, punishable by fine or imprisonment, or both, to print, publish or impart information regarding the control of human offspring by artificial methods of preventing conception.

The Birth Control League holds that such restrictive laws result in widespread evil. While they do not prevent contraceptive knowledge of a more or less vague or positively harmful character being spread among the people, these repressive laws do actually hinder information that is reliable and has been ascertained by the most competent medical and scientific authorities, being disseminated systematically among those very persons who stand in greatest need of it.

This League specifically declares that to classify purely scientific information regarding human contraception as obscene, as our present laws do, is itself an act affording a most disgraceful example of intolerable indecency.

Information, when scientifically sound, should be readily available. Such knowledge is of immediate and positive individual and social benefit. All laws which hamper the free and responsible diffusion of this knowledge among the people are in the highest degree pernicious and opposed to the best and most permanent interests of society.[3]

From 1915 on, the birth control movement grew, spurred by Margaret Sanger, whose writings, lectures, and activities dramatized and publicized the subject as never before. In 1916, Sanger, her sister, Ethel Byrne, and Fania Mindell set up the first U.S. birth control clinic in Brownsville, Brooklyn. Police action, the arrest of Byrne and Sanger, Byrne's trial, imprisonment, and forced feeding, made front-page news of a subject that ordinarily was avoided by the daily newspapers. By 1917, about twenty birth control leagues had been formed in the country to fight the laws against contraception.

In 1921, Sanger organized the American Birth Control League. (In the meantime, the differences and divisions that had developed among birth control advocates had brought about the demise of the National Birth Control League.) By 1926, there were more than 37,000 members in the American Birth Control League. The League had state affiliates, among the most active of which were those in Illinois, Ohio, California, Michigan, and Texas. About ninety percent of their members were women, and most of these women were white, native-born, married, and educated. Many of them came to the birth control movement after experience in suffrage and other reform work.

Margaret Sanger

The ABCL was carefully organized and well run. Its professional staff, nearly all of whom were women, labored hard to carry out the aims and principles enunciated by the League.

PRINCIPLES AND AIMS OF THE AMERICAN BIRTH CONTROL LEAGUE

Principles

The complex problems now confronting America as the result of the practice of reckless procreation are fast threatening to grow beyond human control.

Everywhere we see poverty and large families going hand in hand. Those least fit to carry on the race are increasing most rapidly. People who cannot support their own offspring are encouraged by Church and State to produce large families. Many of the children thus begotten are diseased or feeble-minded; many become criminals. The burden of supporting these unwanted types has to be borne by the healthy elements of the nation. Funds that should be used to raise the standard of our civilization are diverted to the maintenance of those who should never have been born.

In addition to this grave evil we witness the appalling waste of women's health and women's lives by too frequent pregnancies. These unwanted pregnancies often provoke the crime of abortion, or alternatively multiply the number of child workers and lower the standard of living. . . .

We hold that children should be

1. Conceived in love;

2. Born of the mother's conscious desire;

3. And only begotten under conditions which render possible the heritage of health.

Therefore we hold that every woman must possess the

power and freedom to prevent conception except when these conditions can be satisfied. . . .

Instead of being a blind and haphazard consequence of uncontrolled instinct, motherhood must be made the responsible and self-directed means of human expression and regeneration.

These purposes, which are of fundamental importance to the whole of our nation and to the future of mankind, can only be attained if women first receive practical scientific education in the means of Birth Control. That, therefore, is the first object to which the efforts of this League will be directed.

Aims

THE AMERICAN BIRTH CONTROL LEAGUE aims to enlighten and educate all sections of the American public in the various aspects of the dangers of uncontrolled procreation and the imperative necessity of a world program of Birth Control.

The League aims to correlate the findings of scientists, statisticians, investigators and social agencies in all fields. To make this possible, it is necessary to organize various departments:

RESEARCH: To collect the findings of scientists, concerning the relation of reckless breeding to delinquency, defect and dependence.

INVESTIGATION: To derive from these scientifically ascertained facts and figures, conclusions which may aid all public health and social agencies in the study of problems of maternal and infant mortality, child-labor, mental and physical defects and delinquence in relation to the practice of reckless parentage.

HYGIENIC AND PHYSIOLOGICAL instruction by the Medical profession to mothers and potential mothers in harmless and reliable methods of Birth Control in answer to their requests for such knowledge.

STERILIZATION of the insane and feeble-minded and the encouragement of this operation upon those afflicted with inherited or transmissible diseases, with the understanding that sterilization does not deprive the individual of his or her sex expression, but merely renders him incapable of producing children.

EDUCATIONAL: The program of education includes: The enlightenment of the public at large, mainly through the education of leaders of thought and opinion—teachers, ministers, editors and writers—to the moral and scientific soundness of the principles of Birth Control and the imperative necessity of its adoption as the basis of national and racial progress.

POLITICAL AND LEGISLATIVE: To enlist the support and co-operation of legal advisors, statesmen and legislators in effecting the removal of state and federal statutes which encourage dysgenic breeding, increase the sum total of disease, misery and poverty and prevent the establishment of a policy of national health and strength.

ORGANIZATION: To send into the various States of the Un-

ion field workers to enlist the support and arouse the interest of the masses, to the importance of Birth Control so that laws may be changed and the establishment of clinics made possible in every State.

INTERNATIONAL: This department aims to co-operate with similar organizations in other countries to study Birth Control in its relations to the world population problem, food supplies, national and racial conflicts, and to urge upon all international bodies organized to promote world peace, the consideration of these aspects of international amity. . . . [4]

To educate the nation and to develop support for revision of birth control laws, the American Birth Control League sent its speakers out to talk to women's clubs, social workers, doctors' organizations, to any group that would listen. It also published a monthly, The Birth Control Review, *edited by Sanger, that kept local and state groups informed about League activities, work in other countries, and current thinking on subjects like eugenics, sexuality, and marriage. In the states and in Washington, leagues lobbied throughout the 1920's for legislative change, but they had little success.*

In 1923, Sanger set up a "Clinical Research Bureau" in New York; it was a birth control clinic, usually known as the Sanger clinic, in which she hoped to promote research about contraception as well as provide contraceptive services under direction of a physician to those who needed them. Elsewhere in the country, birth control advocates also tried to establish public clinics. The women who were in the forefront of these efforts found themselves hampered by laws that proscribed contraception unless it was medically necessary to save a woman's life, by a medical profession that was timid and ignorant, and by powerful opposition from the churches. Clinic work was most successful in California and Illinois. By 1926, there were several active birth control clinics in both states. In 1930, there were approximately thirty clinics in the country and most of them, with the exception of hospital clinics, were staffed by women volunteers and women doctors.[5]

REPORT OF ILLINOIS BIRTH CONTROL CLINIC

In 1923, when the League decided to open a free clinic, we had wonderful plans and high hopes which were all dashed by the refusal of the Health Commissioner to grant us the necessary license. . . . We temporarily abandoned the idea of a free clinic and opened a Medical Center which does not require a license as it is operated as a private office, a small fee being charged to each patient. . . .

. . . We opened in February, 1925, a second office at ——— Street, known as Medical Center No. 2. Each Center has a secretary and our Medical Staff consists of the Director, Dr. ——— and three physicians . . . all of whom have given devoted service.

There is a commonly accepted picture of our Birth Control work which represents us as standing in the midst of clamoring crowds, distributing information indiscriminately to all comers and handing leaflets and tracts destined to fall into the hands of high school children and unmarried girls, thereby doing unlimited harm. The true picture is very different. Our offices, one on the inside court of the ——— Building, the other in a small house on a quiet West Side street, have very little publicity. We do not advertise. It is difficult to get any notice of our work in the newspapers. It is not spectacular enough. The result is that our patients come slowly. We have had to build up a practice.

The first Medical Center was opened July 7, 1924, and during the first three months we had sixty patients, mostly sent to us by a few social agencies. In October we had some newspaper notices and our numbers jumped to seventy-four in one month. In November we had one hundred and twenty. From July seventh to date, ten months, we have had in all five hundred and forty patients. It may be interesting to hear some of the data on the first five hundred cases.

We are constantly asked what nationalities we reach. It would be simpler to say what nationalities we do not reach. The exact figures are as follows:

American	252	Slovakian	4
Polish	58	Canadian	2
Hebrew	42	Lithuanian	2
German	35	Austrian	2
Colored	26	Spanish	2
Bohemian	15	Belgian	1
Italian	14	Croatian	1
Swedish	11	Greek	1
English	8	Swiss	1
Irish	7	Dutch	1
Norwegian	5	Russian	1
Scotch	4	Mexican	1
Hungarian	4		

Of these,
304 were Protestants, or 6/10ths were Protestants
147 were Catholics
  3 were Greek Orthodox, or 3/10ths were Catholics
46 were Jewish, or 1/10th Jewish

Women of all ages have come, from 16 to 40, the largest number (152) being between the ages of twenty-five and thirty. The young girls under twenty are not school girls, they are rather weary, discouraged little mothers with two or three children, who seem to us entitled to information which will give them a few years' rest in which to recuperate before they bear more children.

So much has been said about the selfishness of women and the growing desire of the modern woman to leave her home and go into industry that it is rather a surprise to find

BIRTH CONTROL REVIEW
Dedicated to Voluntary Motherhood

Fifteen Cents

JULY

How Shall We Change The Law?
—Page 8

Must She Always Plead in Vain?
"You are a nurse—can't you tell me? For the children's sake—help me!"
—Hard Facts, page 12

1919

that 464 of the 500 patients gave their occupation as "Housewife" and only 36 were engaged in work outside their homes. . . .

In almost every case, the women were working to support their families because their husbands were either ill, or drank, or gambled. In a few cases the young couple were just married and living in one or two rooms and were both obliged to work in order to support themselves and of course felt that they must postpone all thought of children until they had saved enough to take care of them.

It is impossible to classify the occupation of the husbands. They cover practically every employment. . . .

. . . The reasons given for wishing information are as difficult to classify as are the occupations of the men. In almost every case, the foundation of the trouble is economic but there are usually other complications. For instances:

Four children in four years.
Instrumental deliveries—contracted pelvis and goitre.

Caesarean operation always necessary.

Wants to wait until stronger before having any more.

Wants children but husband is just starting in business.

Six children—all tubercular.

No home, husband traveling musician.

Nine miscarriages in ten years—retroversion—cannot carry to term.

It is also very interesting to note that we have had five cases of sterility, the women willing to do anything if only they might have children. . . . [6]

FIRST ANNUAL REPORT OF LOS ANGELES MOTHERS CLINIC ASSOCIATION

. . . The objects of Los Angeles Mothers Clinic Association are expressed in its by-laws as follows:

"The purpose of this organization is to establish in the City of Los Angeles a Mothers Clinic, and to undertake other enterprises for imparting to applicants advice and instruction for protecting the life and health of mothers and insuring, as far as possible, the mental and physical vigor of their off-spring, such purpose to be carried out in conformity with the laws of the State of California."

The present report represents not a full year's activities, but only activities from April 1, 1925 to December 31, 1925, —a period of nine months.

Following is a statistical statement of the work of the clinic:

Number of patients who applied 251

Number of patients who have received information and instruction 146

Number of patients who have not yet received infor-mation and instruction pending investigation of their cases 19

Number of patients from whom information and in-struction has been withheld for various reasons 86

Mothers Clinic has quickly established itself in the estima-tion of other medical and social agencies in this city as a useful addition to existing organizations.

On the one hand, various medical and social agencies

"Her Legal Status." Birth Control Review, May 1919

have referred patients to Mothers Clinic, and on the other hand they have co-operated by assisting patients referred by Mothers Clinic to them. . . . [7]

Although contraception was unquestionably a woman's issue, offering her more freedom and control over her life, this was not the main argument made by the birth control advocates. In the 1920's, they talked about social reform, about healthier and better-loved children, about eradicating poverty, and improving the species by eliminating feeblemindedness and hereditary disease. At a time when the country passed its most restrictive immigration law, proponents of birth control understood its appeal to nativists and racists who assumed incorrectly that immigrants and blacks were uninterested in family limitation. But the women's issue was there: the rank-and-file workers of the birth control movement were women; and its leaders and movers were predominantly women.

In 1920, Sanger wrote a popular book about birth control called Woman and the New Race. *Discussing the necessity and advantages of controlling reproduction, she said:*

The basic freedom of the world is woman's freedom. A free race cannot be born of slave mothers. . . . No woman can call herself free who does not own and control her body. No woman can call herself free until she can choose consciously whether she will or will not be a mother. . . . Look at it from any standpoint you will, suggest any solution you will, conventional or unconventional, sanctioned by law or in defiance of law, woman is in the same position, fundamentally, until she is able to determine for herself whether she will be a mother and to fix the number of her offspring. This unavoidable situation is alone enough to make birth control, first of all, a woman's problem. On the face of the matter, voluntary motherhood is chiefly the concern of the woman.[8]

Despite its obvious importance for women, the movement for birth control received little official support from women's organizations in the 1920's. While many of the women who worked for birth control were also members of organizations like the League of Women Voters and the General Federation of Women's Clubs, these organizations and most others refused to endorse the struggle for contraceptive information and generally shied away from the subject of family limitation. In 1920, officials of the General Federation, despite a strong show of interest among members, refused to discuss a birth control resolution at its biennial convention and recommended, instead, that the subject was one for study by local clubs. The National Woman's Party and the League of Women Voters also resisted moves within their organizations to give support to the birth control movement.

Clearly, the leaders of groups like the League and the Woman's Party understood the relevance of birth control for women's lives, but they also saw the mass of opposition and resistance to contraception in the country; they feared the subject could divide members along religious lines; and they recognized that the subject was extremely uncomfortable and embarrassing to many women. Their decision to avoid the birth control issue was not unlike their avoidance of other controversial issues concerning women. It reflected a conservatism that would soon overcome the reform spirit within the women's movement.

In contrast, the National Women's Trade Union League, at its convention in 1922, passed the following resolution:

Whereas the effect of certain laws of the United States, both State and Federal, is to withhold contraceptive information from the women of the working classes, while it is in most cases readily available to the well to do; and

Whereas it is important that in this, as in other matters, the best scientific information should be available to the people's need, regardless of their economic standing: Therefore be it

Resolved, That we, the National Women's Trade Union League, in convention assembled, go on record as opposed to all laws, State and Federal, which in effect establish censorship over knowledge which, if open to one, should be open to all who care to secure it.[9]

THE DECLINE OF REFORM

In 1922, the Women's Joint Congressional Committee was described as "The Most Powerful Lobby in Washington . . . the Public Welfare Lobby Backed by Seven Million Women."[10] Yet, only a few years later, the WJCC was on the defensive, its membership was rapidly draining away, and its influence was disappearing. The exhilarating congressional victory of 1924 for a child labor amendment turned to ashes when the proposal reached the states; and by 1928, the once-powerful WJCC was unable to rescue the Sheppard-Towner bill with its scanty appropriation for maternity and infancy care when it came up for renewal.

The changing fortunes of the WJCC, the plunge from optimism and strength in the early 1920's to weakness and defeat after the mid-1920's, reflected a decline in the political activity of women and in the women's movement itself.

By the 1930's, there were only about 100,000 members in the League of Women Voters, far less than the two million claimed by the National American Woman Suffrage Association. The General Federation of Women's Clubs left the Women's Joint Congressional Committee in 1928 and, turning away from politics, involved itself in home economics and literary meetings. The Daughters of the American Revolution, briefly an auxiliary of the WJCC and supporter of the Sheppard-Towner bill, in 1927 condemned the bill as a Bolshevik device to destroy the family and set about purging itself of any such strange taints and deviations.

The unity, the passion for a better world, and the heady involvement of women in public affairs had gone. What had happened?

The decline in the women's movement was closely related to the decline of Progressivism and the rise of a conservative political climate in the country. Years of war and a troublesome postwar period full of strikes and disruptions fostered a yearning for tranquillity. The success of the Communists in Russia and Eastern Europe caused disquiet, and foreboding, and nostalgia for the good old days.

The reform spirit—with its insistence on change and its disturbing discontent—was at odds with the national mood. And so was the women's movement, which had been in the vanguard of reform and which, by its very existence, testified to a changing role for women and a changing society.

For those reformers who still had fight left in them, the situation was discouraging. After a seventy-year battle for the vote, the results of the first elections in which women voted were disappointing. Illinois was the only state that counted its voters by sex in 1920. But using its figures as a base, analysts estimated that approximately 40 percent of the women voted who could have in this first election, while over 70 percent of the eligible male voters exercised their right. It seemed clear that most women had not rushed to the polls. Those who did, appeared to have voted the way their husbands had. In subsequent elections, there was little support for women candidates and no sign of a women's bloc determined to change the world at the ballot box.

In retrospect, women's hesitation and reluctance to vote can be seen as predictable. At the time, Rose Schneiderman, president of the National Women's Trade Union League, commented: "For so many hundreds of years they [women] haven't been held responsible for anything outside their own households. Naturally, it is hard to get them to accept responsibility for something which will affect a state, or the entire nation."[11] But most suffragists and reformers, who had expected dramatic change from women voters, were not consoled by such observations.

Also disappointing were the actions of the Supreme Court, which twice struck down child labor legislation and in 1923 found Washington, D.C.'s minimum wage law for women unconstitutional. In the states, too, much of the hard work expended by Progressives was nullified in the courts. Together these decisions threatened precisely the kind of reform and change that had been the foundation of the Progressive movement and a major goal of women's political activity.

Moreover, despite years of struggle and effort, less than 3 percent of working women in the country had been unionized by the mid-1920's, while wages, hours, and working conditions remained exploitative. Efforts to turn the consumer into a force for reform and a support for unionization had also failed. Instead, advertising and prosperity were seducing consumers away from any concern about labor conditions.

For all the sacrifice, devotion, and commitment, the world was the same as, maybe even worse than, it had ever been. And the job of improving it seemed more difficult and complex than ever to those who still wanted to try.

Many of the old fighters were undaunted and, like Florence Kelley, Jane Addams, and Margaret Dreir Robins, continued the battle for reform. Through the 1920's and into the 1930's women were in the vanguard of welfare reform and the peace movement. But around them, their organizations shrank in size and effectiveness. Some, like the National Consumers' League and the National Women's Trade Union League, which had never been mass membership groups and which were exceptionally vulnerable targets in the 1920's suffered more than others. Younger women were uninterested in joining, and older members turned away. For the middle-class women, who made up the bulk of the women's organizations, associationism and reform had lost their appeal.

Technology and prosperity, in the form of vacuum cleaners, canned foods, and ready-made clothing, continued to liberate women from household work. But as their role as producers and processors in the home shrank, advertising and the proliferation of manufactured goods enlarged their job as consumers. There was more to buy, more money with which to buy it, and a beguiling new advertising industry, all of which turned the housewife into a purchasing agent and made shopping a time-consuming and complicated activity. The expansion of alternatives in clothing and cosmetics offers a good example, but there were many others.

Since the turn of the century, women had gained more personal freedom, as urban life changed social patterns and as Victorianism faded. Where once they had to justify activities outside the home and the church—club women were engaged in "civic housekeeping" and temperance workers were involved in "home protection"—and needed the security and support of groups of women to do so, by the 1920's much had changed. Women needed neither an excuse nor a crowd in order to leave home and children for a foray into the outside world. This was a time, also, of increasing individualism, of self-concern, and of sexual discovery. There seemed room for all of this within the apparently flexible boundaries of domestic life. There was, consequently, less need for and less interest in collective activities and in social reform.

THE RED SMEAR ATTACK

The conservative climate of the 1920's weakened the women's movement not only by decreasing interest in change

and reform but also by supporting a direct attack on women's organizations.

The Bolshevik Revolution in Russia in the fall of 1917
aroused deep apprehension in Europe and in America.
When the new government refused to collapse—despite
repeated predictions and assurances in the West that it
would—and seemed vigorous enough to spread its influence westward after 1919, the apprehension swelled. Labor unrest in the United States and a wave of big strikes
finally ignited fear and tension, and a "Red Scare" followed—a wave of hatred and persecution against unions,
foreigners, minorities, socialists, pacifists, and eventually
against feminists.

Two aspects of women's activities were particularly irritating to the superpatriots and defenders of the status quo
who stoked the Red Scare fires: their advocacy of welfare
legislation such as the Sheppard-Towner bill that provided
for instruction in maternity and infant care and of labor
legislation that involved government regulation of business; and the participation of women in a growing international peace movement.

There were, however, more subtle aspects to the attack
on women. In their description of women's organizations
as Bolshevist (or at best dupes of the Bolsheviks), the National Association of Manufacturers, the American Medical
Association, the Daughters of the American Revolution,
and other, shorter-lived groups insisted that the Sheppard-
Towner bill, along with birth control, was a device for
destroying the family; they saw in the child labor amendment a plot for the nationalization of children and the
elimination of parental influence. Beneath this foolishness
lay both the practical interests of these defenders of the
status quo and their sense that a serious threat to traditional male-female relations and the family system lurked
behind the façade of women's organizations and the social
changes that were slowly taking place. Ironically, these
frightened opponents detected radical implications in the
women's movement that most women activists were
themselves reluctant to explore at the time.

As part of the attack on women's organizations, a chart
was prepared, within the War Department, which described a menacing interlocking directorate of women's
organizations whose purposes were to weaken the de-
fenses of the country and prepare it for a Bolshevik take-
over. This "Spider-Web" chart and the poem that was
attached to it were originally printed and distributed by the
U.S. Chemical Warfare Service. This elicited strong protests
from women's groups, and the government soon stopped
its circulation of the chart. Both the chart and the poem,
however—and hostile articles as well—appeared in the
Dearborn Independent, published by Henry Ford; and both
were also printed in a number of pamphlets published
elsewhere.

OPPOSITE:
"Spider Web" chart. Dearborn Independent

THE SPIDER-WEB POEM

Miss Bolsheviki has come to town,
With a Russian cap and a German gown,
In women's clubs she's sure to be found,
For she's come to disarm America.

She sits in judgment on Capitol Hill
And watches appropriations bills
And without her O.K., it passes—NIL
For she's there to disarm America.

She uses the movie and lyceum too,
And alters text-books to suit her view,
She prates propaganda from pulpit and pew,
For she's bound to disarm America.

The male of the species has a different plan
He uses the bomb and the fire brand,
And incites class hatred wherever he can
While she's busy disarming America.

His special stunt is arousing the mob,
to expropriate and hate and kill and rob,
While she's working on her political job
AWAKE! AROUSE!! AMERICA!!![12]

FROM THE *DEARBORN INDEPENDENT*

. . . the two most conspicuously propaganda organizations
affiliated with the National Council of Women are the Na-
tional League of Women Voters and the Women's Interna-
tional League of Peace and Freedom. Mrs. Maud Wood
Park, president of the National League of Women Voters, is
a vice-president of the National Council of Women. Mrs.
Park is said to have great influence over Mrs. Thomas G.
Winter, president of the General Federation of Women's
Clubs, herself a vice-president of the National Council of
Women. . . .

All of the principal women's organizations maintain legislative representatives in Washington and the astute Mrs. Park
some time ago organized what is known as the "Congressional Committee," of which she is chairman and of which
Mrs. A. C. Watkins is secretary.

This "Women's Bloc," as it is called, can in co-operation
with the radicals in Congress practically dictate our legislation, and our women, comprising the vast membership of
these organizations, women who would quickly resent being
called Socialists or Bolsheviki, are blithely passing resolutions and voting for a program that was inaugurated by

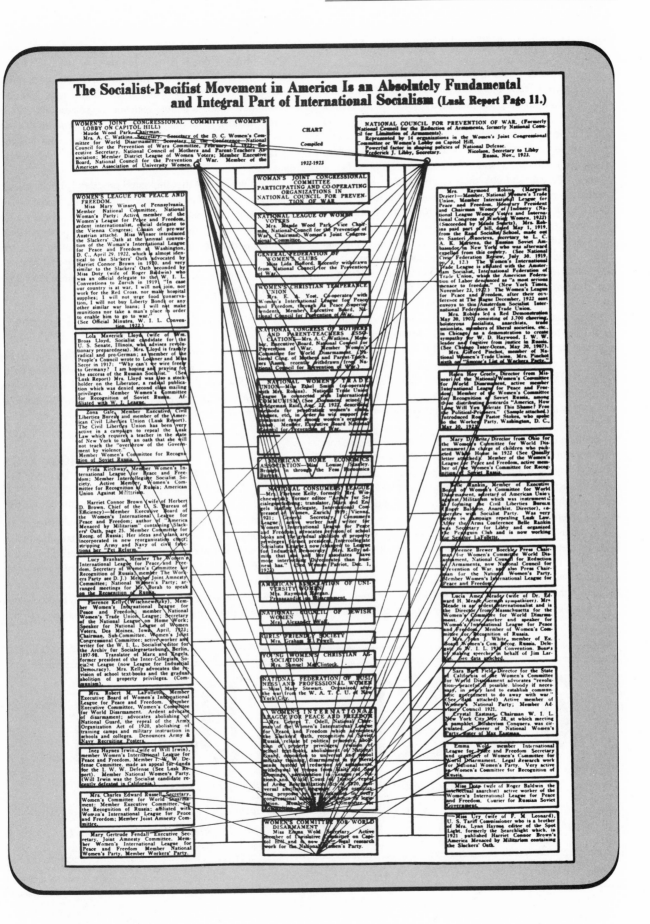

The Socialist-Pacifist Movement in America Is an Absolutely Fundamental and Integral Part of International Socialism (Lusk Report Page 11.)

Madam Alexandria Kollontay in her Soviet "Department of Child Welfare" in Russia. . . .

Mrs. Raymond Robbins, formerly president of the National Women's Trade Union League, an organization which the Lusk Committee reports "adopted resolutions in favor of the Soviet government," and a contributor to the Rand School of Social Science where socialist leaders are trained, is one of the socialist women promoting pacifist and welfare propaganda. Miss Mary Anderson, chief of the United States Women's Bureau and chairman of the Industrial Relations Committee in the National Council, issued a call for a WORLD CONGRESS OF WORKING WOMEN, which met at Washington, November 6, 1919, and adopted the name International Federation of Working Women, of which Mrs. Robbins was made president. This congress gave special attention to "legislative reforms for the purpose of protecting maternity." The *Woman Citizen* magazine, the official organ of Mrs. Carrie Chapman Catt, reports that plans were recommended to secure state grants to mothers for each child born and to secure free medical, nursing and surgical care during maternity and, in addition, an allowance for the support of the mother and child during the maternity period. At the World Congress of Working Women they also advocated that there be organized an INTERNATIONAL LABOR OFFICE OF THE LEAGUE OF NATIONS BUREAU to collect information on best methods of maternity care.

The heart of everyone is touched by an appeal to care for mothers and babies. *The radicals find it easy to build their bureaucracy by selecting such obvious heart appeals* because by such means they sweep the uninformed to the polls unknowingly to vote away individual freedom and Constitutional Government. . . .

It gives us food for thought when the leading women in both the Democratic and Republican parties are members of the League of Women Voters which organization is admittedly working for pacifism and internationalism and is sworn to uphold the non-partisan movement among women.

Rather clever of the women! They tap the treasuries of both the Democratic and Republican parties for funds with which to break down party machinery. Not long ago Mrs. Harriet Taylor Upton, of the Republican National Committee and Mrs. Emily Newell Blair, of the Democratic National Committee, made a lecture tour for the League of Women Voters, almost, if not quite, together. And a story of this trip was printed in a Sunday Washington paper with authenticated interviews from each, together with their photographs.

When we realize that this same program is being carried out by women in European countries as well, and that the program in our country is backed by these women who manipulate all of the committees from the great national political parties to the humblest church societies, and that they are lobbying for a program identical with that promulgated by Madam Alexandria Kollontay, the director of welfare in Soviet Russia, what are we to think? . . . [13]

The Woman Patriots was an organization that played an active part in the red smear, attacking the Women's Bureau, the Sheppard-Towner Act, and the women's groups involved in Progressive reform. Its publication, The Woman Patriot, *printed articles such as this:*

"HOW REDS ARE ORGANIZING WOMEN"

By Donald Alexander

How carefully the Russian communists have laid their plans to undermine the Government of the United States by means of the "boring from within" process is disclosed by documents which have come into the possession of the government authorities during the last few months. . . . Within the last few days another important document has been discovered which discloses the detailed instructions given to the

The Woman Patriot

Dedicated to the Defense of The Family and The State

AGAINST Feminism and Socialism

Published Twice a Month by The Woman Patriot Publishing Co., 726 14th Street, N. W., Washington, D. C.

Entered as second-class matter April 26, 1918, at the post office at Washington, D. C., under the Act of March 3, 1879

Vol. 7, No. 3   WASHINGTON, D. C., FEBRUARY 1, 1923   10 Cents a Copy

Russian agents in this country for winning American *women* to communism. . . .

Under the plan of campaign outlined for Communists of the United States by their Moscow headquarters every effort must be made by female Communists here to obtain membership in women's clubs and social organizations throughout the country, working within the ranks of their fellow club members for the eventual overthrow of Society, and of the United States Government. . . .

"Communist women should become members of the feminine organizations of their communities, such as social clubs, sewing circles, etc. Entertainments should be offered to which their fellow club members should be invited, and discussions of social problems should in every instance be staged. Those who express any degree of discontent with society or the government *should be admired and cultivated by their Communist hosts.* In this way many female organizations can be gradually developed into *units of Communism,* from which those who never can be brought to a belief in our principles will either voluntarily withdraw or can be cast out." . . . [14]

The attack continued into the 1920's and engaged powerful forces. In 1926, John H. Edgerton, president of the National Association of Manufacturers, delivered a speech that revealed some of the subtler aspects of smear tactics. By strange logical constructions, Edgerton related women's activities for Progressive reform, especially their work for protective legislation for working women, with a rise of divorce and deterioration of the American home. Edgerton criticized women for spending their efforts on legislation such as eight-hour laws and minimum wage laws which were a "pestiferous interference with the processes of natural law." He urged them, instead, to work on protecting the home and preserving motherhood and to beware of the Communist influences that had led them away from their true responsibilities. The speech, which is excerpted below, was printed by the National Association of Manufacturers as a pamphlet, and copies of it were distributed throughout the country, as were other, similar attacks.

EDGERTON SPEECH ON PROTECTING AMERICAN WOMANHOOD

. . . The restoration of the American home is the greatest need of the hour; and if among your society and club women, the leisure classes, and many of the social workers themselves you can and will destroy or change the conditions that are choking the divorce courts with their filthy spawn and converting our homes into mere eating and sleeping places, you will be rendering, in my judgment, the largest and most vital service to the nation. . . .

A very careful study and investigation by you ladies of your multitude of organizations and their power machinery will show you pretty clearly, I think, that one Madame Kollontai, whose headquarters are at Moscow but whose parish is the world, is exercising a very large if not a dominating influence upon at least some of the major activities of at least some of your organizations.

It is to be recalled that this woman, according to reliable information, is now sojourning with husband number eight. And there are many other facts about her that the innocent and uninformed should know. Those who are really in search of truth may find it—and I shall be happy to aid in the quest.

Perhaps some of you know as well as I that the program of those for whom the woman of many husbands speaks is the successive nationalization of the children, the women, and industry—and those are some of the so-called ideals for which they would foment a world revolution and in the service of which they are in devious, insidious ways flooding America and other countries with their hellish propaganda.

The tragedy of it lies in the fact that many innocent Americans are carrying around in their clothes the deadly germs of these insufferably alien theories and don't know it. They are made to believe that they are crusaders for defenseless women and innocent childhood. . . .

I can not believe that the womanhood of our country is willing to accept from such a woman as Madame Kollontai or her admirers any theory or advice concerning women or children; or that the masses of our women would become the conscious carriers of those alien doctrines of Communism, socialism, paternalism and other variegated isms that are so poisonous to the peculiarly American system as devised by the founders of our government.

Never was it so impressively important for good Americans of all classes and sexes to be on their guard against enemies within and without.

We should keep thoroughly informed as to the influences that control our various organizations, the personal records, and habits of thought and action of their leaders, whoever they are or seem to be.

When Samson yielded his strength to Delilah's shears, she became the first victim of his impotency.[15]

The accused fought back as best they could.

"LIES-AT-LARGE"

By Carrie Chapman Catt

The First in a Series of Articles About Certain Patriotic Citizens Who See Certain Other Patriotic Citizens Through a Red Haze of Fear

A singular thing is happening in this country. A group of men and women have wrought themselves up to an almost apoplectic state of mind with sheer fright over the expected coming of the Bolsheviki. The group appears to be composed of irredentist anti-suffragists [The Woman Patriots contained many old opponents of suffrage], groups of the D.A.R. and other patriotic societies, some elderly army and navy men and scattered scared souls here and there. . . . It is seemingly well financed and venomous to an astonishing degree. They take themselves seriously and perform as though they actually believe what they say. It is indeed a revelation that men and women of a civilized land can hate so ardently, think so falsely, or stoop so low to give a vicious kick at those they hate. . . .

Many senators, representatives, clergymen, authors, correspondents and most public speakers are enumerated among the red and dangerous, according to the literature. Tons of it are distributed by the anxious at doors of clubs, dinners, theatres, lecture halls, churches, each telling the reader of the horrors of the conspiracy in our midst. Tons of lies passed out by American citizens charging other American citizens at least as honest, intelligent and patriotic as themselves, with near treason.

It astonishes, amuses and shames the nation. . . .

It is safe to say that in the women's organizations listed as dangerous and deceitful, even Diogenes with his lamp could not find a Bolshevik. Whoever says they are red, *lies*. I know very many of the men and women listed and advertised as red. Those who write and print these tales about them *lie*. To be sure, they say I am red, too. Therefore, let me add I am not a Bolshevik, Communist (nor even a Socialist), and whoever charges me with leanings in that direction *lies*. More, whoever circulates by word of mouth or the distribution of literature any of the above lies, disobeys the law of God, "Thou shalt not bear false witness." . . .

"Even Diogenes with His Lamp Could Not Find a Bolshevik in the Women's Organizations Listed as Dangerous."
The Woman Citizen, *June 1927*

Some say, sue, sue, sue! Sue whom? No one can sue the Government for its printing office policy, nor the Senate, and the senator is immune. Your Government may destroy its own citizens and these citizens are powerless to defend themselves. If there is some one to provide the lies and a senator weak or malicious enough to read the lies into the *Record*, the process may continue indefinitely. . . .

This organized or federated group dealing in lies favors war and opposes all proposals for peaceful settlements of disputes including arbitration. . . .

The group opposes the abolition of child labor. It does not defend the employment of children in factories; it merely denounces those who condemn such practices as red. They have widely announced that the Child Labor Amendment was written in Moscow and prescribed by the Bolsheviki. . . .

The group opposes the Maternity Act. This, too, it seems, was ordered in Moscow. The deaths of mothers at maternity in this country was far above the mortality in other lands. The act had its origin in the desire to correct this unfortunate condition and to save the lives of mothers and babies. It appears that the reds always begin with special care of babies!

The group once opposed woman suffrage, and at least two-thirds of the silly mess used now for circulation is only revamped material broadcast in press and on platform with the intention of showing that woman suffrage was the program of Socialism, . . . [16]

THE NATIONAL WOMAN'S PARTY

The red-baiting attacks were harmful. They discouraged women from joining and caused others to abandon the organizations that were under fire. Moreover, the assaults encouraged timidity and conservatism within the organizations and stifled the reform impulse. Because of this, the red smear also contributed to a breakdown of the coalition that once made the Women's Joint Congressional Committee a powerful force. The General Federation of Women's Clubs left the WJCC, the DAR turned against it; those who remained were far from unanimous in responding to the attack upon them.

At the same time, the unity that had developed during the reform years suffered even greater damage from differences within the movement. Unlike the irrational and frenzied accusations of The Woman Patriots and their like, the issues raised by the reorganized National Woman's Party were substantive and real.

The National Woman's Party had ruffled the movement earlier during its conflict with the National American Woman Suffrage Association concerning suffrage tactics and strategy. At that time, although suffrage was the com-

mon goal, NAWSA officials repudiated any connection with the NWP and its aggressive and impatient activities for the vote. Now, in the 1920's, with the common goal achieved, other differences arose between the NWP and most of the other national women's groups.

In 1921, the NWP was reorganized, still under Alice Paul's commanding influence. At a time when the Women's Joint Congressional Committee was trying to channel organized women's activities toward specific reform legislation, the NWP announced that suffrage had not ended women's inferior position, and it dedicated itself to exclusively feminist goals.

In contrast to the moderate reform goals of organized women during the Progressive era, the NWP's Declaration of Principles, adopted in 1922, was a jarring demand for an end to all forms of discrimination against women, to the double standard in sex behavior, and to sexual exploitation. It called for full equality under the law and real equality within the family, a challenge to conventional views about marriage and family relations. Among its radical principles, the NWP included demands such as these:

THAT women shall no longer be the governed half of society, but shall participate equally with men in the direction of life. . . .

THAT women shall no longer be barred from the priesthood or ministry, or any other position of authority in the church, but equally with men shall participate in ecclesiastical offices and dignities.

THAT a double moral standard shall no longer exist, but one code shall obtain for both men and women.

THAT exploitation of the sex of women shall no longer exist, but women shall have the same right to the control of their persons as have men.

THAT women shall no longer be discriminated against in treatment of sex diseases and in punishment of sex offenses, but men and women shall be treated in the same way for sex diseases and sex offenses. . . .

THAT a women shall no longer be required by law or custom to assume the name of her husband upon marriage, but shall have the same right as a man to retain her own name after marriage.

THAT the wife shall no longer be considered as supported by the husband, but their mutual contribution to the family maintenance shall be recognized.

THAT the headship of the family shall no longer be in the husband alone, but shall be equally in the husband and wife. . . .

IN SHORT—THAT WOMAN SHALL NO LONGER BE IN ANY FORM OF SUBJECTION TO MAN IN LAW OR IN CUSTOM, BUT SHALL IN EVERY WAY BE ON AN EQUAL PLANE IN RIGHTS, AS SHE HAS ALWAYS BEEN AND WILL CONTINUE TO BE IN RESPONSIBILITIES AND OBLIGATIONS.[17]

Many of the reforms sought by women's organizations during the 1920's were directly related to women's own condition, such as the Sheppard-Towner Act for maternity care, hour and wage legislation for wage-earning women, and the Cable Act, which made a woman's citizenship independent of her husband's. (Before 1922, a woman automatically got her husband's citizenship upon marriage, so that an American who married a foreigner simply lost her American citizenship.) The work of the General Federation of Women's Clubs for revision of state marriage and divorce laws and the efforts of the American Birth Control League also were clearly involved with women's issues. But women's organizations also sought reforms, such as child labor prohibition and disarmament and international peace machinery, that were not simply women's concerns. In contrast, the NWP dedicated itself to exclusively feminist goals and confronted head on the full range of non-political discrimination that made women second-class citizens, despite the vote.

Other differences between the NWP and the majority of women's organizations were readily apparent. Spokeswomen for the Party often used a militant and aggressive tone that interdicted the kind of easy collaboration between male and female reformers that characterized the Progressive era.

Prominent among the outspoken members of the NWP was Alva Smith Belmont, who served as president after 1921. Divorced from a Vanderbilt and married to Oliver H. Belmont, she diverted her wealth to the Party treasury. Below, in an article written for the Ladies' Home Journal, Belmont expresses her views on women's future role.

"WOMEN AS DICTATORS"

By Mrs. O. H. P. Belmont

The end of the dictatorship of the world by men alone is in sight. We women have lived long enough in the cramped confines of a misfit social structure. We have been forced to sit still too long. We have been powerless for such an endless time that we have accumulated enough stored-up energy to shape any structure to our will.

We know we can manage the house. We can reconstruct it. We can put on a left wing and a right wing. We can add a sun porch to let in the light. We could even tear the house down if we liked—and I think men know that too.

The time has come to take this world muddle that men have created and strive to turn it into an ordered, peaceful, happy abiding place for humanity. In its present condition the world is its own worst indictment against the sole dictatorship of men. Men have always obstructed and suppressed the intellect of one-half of the human race. They have always worked for themselves. That is not sufficient. The error lies here.

By excluding women men have interfered for too long with the development, interests and intelligence of humanity. Men have always kept women in subjection. To acknowledge them as equals would have destroyed their own pedestals. They have opposed an even partially woman-governed world, fearing a limitation of their own undisputed freedom. Men have insisted not only that we live in a man-governed world but that we worship in a man-dominated church; and we can no longer accept this.

We are going to make the necessary changes, but not for the sake of women alone. I have no nearsighted idea that what is done for women and children is not to the advantage of men also. In short, we are not working against men, for women, when we speak of women as dictators; we are working for the human race.

The day is not far off when the Woman's Party, of which I am president, will be strong enough to impose any measure it may choose. . . .

Women have got to stop being followers. They will never get anywhere unless they begin to initiate. Perhaps there is something very glorious about being a helpmate, but if so it's time some man shared that glory. And if there is something very glorious about being a starter, an initiator, a leader, it's time women shared that too.

Alva Belmont

Personally, I think it would be far better for women to stay out of all parties and away from all elections, if they can find no other medium of expression than the existing decrepit man-dominated parties.

If you are elected to office by a party you are responsible to that party, and I do not want to see any woman elected to a man's party. I do not want to see any woman in the Senate as a Republican or a Democrat.

The strength of man has always been in the union of men, and the weakness of woman in her lack of union. It is necessary to make women realize that until they have achieved some sort of solidarity they will never be able to impose their will upon the state.

Men have always tried to isolate women, to keep them as creatures apart. Men have always put women in houses, shut them away behind walls, kept them for themselves, detained them apart from the community. Men used to put women in a harem; now they put them in a home. But the home, like the harem, has considered its own interests rather than the interests of the community, and in so doing it has jeopardized its well-being instead of fostering it. The home, like the individual, is insufficient when it stands alone.

If a man commits an indiscretion all other men protect him. If a woman is at fault other women, instead of protecting her, are often the first to condemn. Women in the past have been afraid to lose the respect or the admiration or the love of men by opposing their wishes. In the last few years the suffragists have demonstrated that women do not lose the admiration of the worthwhile men by expressing their own individualities. On the contrary, it has been my experience that the modern man finds the intelligent, socially conscious, individualistic woman a more companionable person than her frightened sister who fears to speak or move lest she offend him. Women gain far more than they lose by an attitude of independence. . . .[18]

THE GREAT DEBATE OVER THE EQUAL RIGHTS AMENDMENT

Soon after its reorganization, the National Woman's Party resolved to end women's inequality by the passage of state equal rights laws and a federal equal rights amendment which would prohibit all forms of discrimination on the basis of sex. Thus, the NWP committed itself to a blanket, sweeping revision of existing statutes, rather than step-by-step elimination of discriminatory laws and customs. An equal rights amendment to the Federal Constitution became the overriding objective of the Party (and remained so into the 1970's). Although the NWP did instigate lawsuits in state courts against specific examples of sex

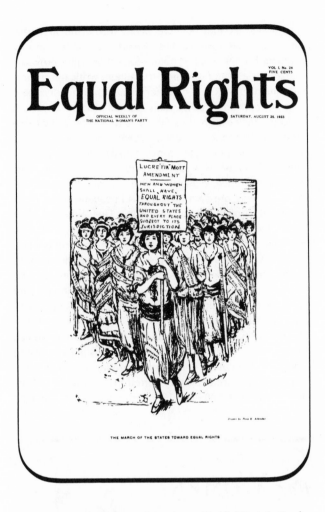

THE MARCH OF THE STATES TOWARD EQUAL RIGHTS

discrimination, other goals suggested in the Party's Declaration of Principles, such as divorce reform or the dissemination of birth control information, received hardly any attention.

In December 1923, the first of many bills for a federal amendment was introduced in Congress. Nicknamed the Lucretia Mott amendment, it read:

Men and women shall have equal rights throughout the United States and every place subject to its jurisdiction.

The Equal Rights Amendment split the women's movement in two. If enacted, the amendment probably would have invalidated the special laws protecting women workers, since these laws (for example, a law prohibiting the employment of women for more than ten hours a day in certain industries) clearly treated women differently from men. Because of this, the major national women's organizations officially opposed the Equal Rights Amendment and organized a campaign to prevent its passage.

A great debate over the ERA took place during the 1920's before legislative committees, in popular magazines, at political conventions, and at every important gathering of organized women. Although the NWP was small—its membership never reached 10,000—many of its members were articulate, well educated, and influential. Under Alice Paul's firm guidance, they agitated for the ERA with the bluntness and single-mindedness that they had displayed during the suffrage struggle.

The opposing organizations marshaled their experienced troops. Old antagonisms from suffrage days revived, and a considerable amount of personal hostility inflamed the issue. But the disagreement was mainly substantive. Much of the controversy was over the question of whether protective labor legislation aided or hindered working women.

"SHOULD THERE BE LABOR LAWS FOR WOMEN?"

During the last legislative session there was heated discussion, all over the country, of the question of the complete equality of the sexes. One side favored the removal from our statute books of all laws applying to women alone, insisting that women can and should take their places alongside men, neither asking for favors nor accepting restrictions. The other side rested its case upon the unalterable fact that life requires of women duties from which men are exempt, and asked that laws be framed accordingly. Needless to say, the question was not settled last year; it will buzz in legislative halls, state and national, again this winter. If you will read these two articles you will have no difficulty in deciding which side you favor.

NO: Rheta Childe Dorr

Author of "What Eight Million Women Want"

. . . The whole question of restrictive legislation applied to adult women workers is obscured by a fogginess of thought, a confusion of ideas and arguments, based on propaganda rather than on facts. Back of the whole question lie ages of prejudice against any freedom for women, any acknowledgment of their right to function as independent, self-determining citizens. To deal with it properly requires cool thinking, clear intelligence. . . .

My first protest is against classing grown women with children under the law. Practically all laws limiting hours of work, prohibiting night work, and providing for a minimum wage are enacted for women and minors. I say "practically" just to be on the safe side. As a matter of fact, it is the routine thing to class woman labor with child labor or with adolescent boy and girl labor.

The reason given is that the vast majority of "females in gainful occupations" are girls of tender years, temporary invaders of industry, pathetic flitters between the schoolroom and the matrimonial altar. . . . the last census gave the number of women, eighteen and over, in industry as

7,593,709. Nearly two million of these adult women workers were married. These wage-earners are not children. Why interfere with their right to earn the highest possible wage by putting them under the police power of the State? All the arguments in favor of such a policy boil down to one sentimental aphorism, "Women are women." Different from men. Weaker. More susceptible to accidents and to industrial diseases. Helpless under exploiting employers, defenceless after dark. Above all, they are . . . mothers or potential mothers. . . .

All so-called protective legislation is based on this "women are women" argument. It was the basis and foundation of the celebrated Brandeis brief supplied by the Consumers' League in defence of the Nine Hour Law in Oregon. . . . I recommend to all club women who desire to be fair in this matter of restrictive legislation to read a new book, "Protective Legislation," by Elizabeth Faulkner Baker, Ph. D., instructor in economics, Barnard College, Columbia. . . .

In cautious and scientific fashion Dr. Baker puts her finger on the real disability under which most wage-earning women, at a disadvantage with wage-earning men, labor. The women do a thing which would speedily break down the health and strength of the average man. They carry on two jobs, wage-earning and housework. Young women living at home are expected to do their share of housework after hours, and they not infrequently sew, mend, and wash and iron their own clothes. Everybody expects this of women. Even in the best homes for working girls provision is made as a matter of course for laundry work and sewing. Imagine a Y. M. C. A. hotel for men with a laundry and a sewing room for tired workers! As for married women in industry, they usually do a full day's work after going home from toil. In Fall River, Mass., when I myself was working there as a ring spinner, the conventional hour for hanging out the week's wash was eleven o'clock at night. The more intelligent women, especially those who are "unprotected" and can therefore earn high wages in superior jobs, never dream of carrying this double burden. They either hire their heavy work done, or they invest in labor-saving devices— vacuum cleaners, electric washing machines, and the like. But great numbers of poorly paid women, kept down to the lower ranks in most trades, still work long hours at home because of poverty, seasonal trades, legal prohibition against working overtime in seasonal trades, and always the fear of unemployment. . . .

The futility of conserving family life by barring women from certain trades, and limiting their hours in most, is also shown in the cutting and polishing trades. In a number of states women are altogether barred from these. New York laws, enacted in 1889 and 1903, prohibited all females (and

males under eighteen) from working in factories where operation in emery, stone, "or any abrasive where articles of the baser metals or iridium are manufactured." This was done in spite of strong protests of men workers, who declared that the danger in these trades was common to both men and women, and what was needed was not sex discrimination, but laws compelling employers to place blowers behind the grinding and buffing lathes. Women over twenty-one may now be employed for limited hours, but only in wet grinding and under special rules of the Industrial Board. Men are not so protected, and when they have coughed themselves to death their women are at liberty to support the families, but only during fifty-four hours a week and during daylight hours.

What I am trying to urge, in this short article, is that unequal wages and bad factory conditions, and not special laws for adult women workers, are the things in which we all should interest ourselves. Sex has nothing to do with the case. . . . When we limit women's opportunities to work, we simply create more poverty, and we postpone the day when equal pay for equal work will be universal. Without equal work there can be no equal pay, nor anything like a fair field for men and women alike.

Instead of dry statistics I want to give GOOD HOUSEKEEPING readers just a few instances of the cruelty wrought by classing women with children and adolescents, and preventing grown women from exercising their Constitutional right freely to contract. If my stories are all of New York women, it is because I live in New York City and know working conditions there.

Mrs. A. is a printer, an expert in every branch of the trade. By the time she was old enough to marry another printer, she was a skilled linotype operator and a member of the union. Her husband died, leaving her with two children to support. In 1913 she was earning, in the composing room of the *New York Times,* about $60 a week, enough to pay for a comfortable little apartment and a capable maid. Mrs. A. worked at night because the *Times* is a morning paper. But she had had her eight hours' sleep by the time the children got home from school, and she did not leave the house until long after they were in bed. One night, when she reported for work she was astonished to find a young man at her machine.

"New night law for women's just gone into effect," explained the foreman. "Mean to say you didn't know the uplifters were pushing it through the Legislature? Darned shame. Nothing you can do but look for a job on the day side somewhere." . . .

This New York law prohibiting women from working at night originally affected practically all women except those in the learned professions, actresses, office charwomen, and domestic servants. Even women reporters and editors on morning papers were ordered away from their desks. Gradually a few groups were exempted, against protests from the welfare workers, who urged that the favored wage-earners ought to be willing to sacrifice their jobs for the sake of the weakest workers. In other words, to sacrifice all the victories

women have won in their long industrial struggle from menial work to independent positions.

Among women who never gained exemption are waitresses. Miss N. is a waitress in a Child's restaurant in the theater district. Formerly she worked on the night shift, where wages are higher and tips much more liberal than on the day shift. Miss N.'s average income, tips and all, was around $32 a week. On this she supported without difficulty herself and her invalid mother. Under the present law she is not allowed to work after eight o'clock at night, at which time men come on to enjoy the good wages and the generous tips she once received from theater-goers. . . .

These are [two] stories out of hundreds I could tell. I wish I had space to include the story of the women in city transportation, the thousands in half a dozen American cities who substituted for men as conductors, drivers, guards, and ticket sellers during the War. Not all the men displaced were drafted. A large number left their work for the enormous wages offered in shipyards and munitions works. The women who were taken on by the street and suburban electric railroads were drawn from factory trades, and although the sentimentalists shuddered at seeing them in such unusual places, most of them were really better off than they had ever been. The improvement in their health, due to ten hours a day in the open air, plus good wages and interesting work, was a wonder to all beholders. In New York City wages were as high as $30 a week. The companies installed new toilets and rest rooms and promised to keep the women on after the war. It was too good to be true, of course. In 1919 the welfare advocates pushed through the Legislature a fifty-four-hour law and a prohibition against night work for the transportation workers. Ninety-six percent of the nearly 3000 women in Greater New York immediately lost their jobs, only a small number of ticket sellers escaping the general slaughter. . . .

I don't want a single woman to relax her war against the crime of child labor, or against the exploitation of adolescent boys and girls. I want them only to turn their intelligence and their great influence in favor of better working conditions and safeguarding of hazardous trades for both men and women. For it takes healthy men as well as healthy women to rear a healthy race. . . .

YES: Mary Anderson

Chief of Women's Bureau,
Department of Labor

. . . This difference between the practical and the theoretical woman is coming to be a serious matter in its effects upon the interests of the great mass of women wage-earners.

So we have over-articulate theorists attempting to solve the working women's problems on a purely feministic basis, with the working woman's own voice far less adequately heard. And these over-articulate, highly theoretical feminists are talking about things and conditions entirely outside their own experience or knowledge. More facts about industry and women in industry are what we need, and less abstract feminist theorizing.

I am convinced that we can not, and we should not, attempt a ruthless application of abstract principle to women's industrial problems. The woman problem in industry is equally a labor problem. Equal rights and equal opportunities for women workers can not be separated from the question of industrial justice for all workers. Above all things, "rights" must be interpreted for women workers as something concrete, and we must start with the world where it is today—not where it might have been had present industrial conditions existed from the beginning.

And now to a specific situation that confronts us:

In two of our great industrial states, New York and Illinois, women are working hard to secure laws which will reduce the present 9-hour and 10-hour working days of women in factories and workshops to 8 per day or 48 per week. Working women are leaders in the movement in both states, so this is not a reform instigated by "outsiders."

The question is a vital one because the shorter working day is the most essential thing in the lives of industrial workers. It means opportunities for life and self-development which are shut out by the whir of the machinery and the routine of the factory job at which the day is spent. It means also more efficiency on the job and better service to the employer. . . .

Today all the states but one have some kind of labor law for women, and about four million women are directly affected by such laws. Indirectly, the better standards of employment thus secured influence the hours of work and the wages or salary of practically all the nearly nine million gainfully occupied women in the United States. Some of the laws are weak—permitting an 11-hour day in North Carolina, for example, and a 10-hour day in 16 states. But other states have gone far above this standard, and 9 of them have an 8-hour day or 48-hour week, while three more with a 9-hour day have a 48-hour week. Thirteen states have minimum wage laws for women, 16 have night work laws, others have laws requiring seats in stores, or otherwise lightening the conditions of employment for women. All such laws penalize employers, not the employees, for failure to conform to the standards. . . . Such labor laws are to employers a code for fair play in industry. For the workers and the community as a whole, they are primarily public health provisions. This entire body of law, however, is now under attack by certain ultra-feminists who argue that because the laws do not apply to men as well as women, they constitute a discrimination against women and a handicap to women's economic advance. It is not the provisions of the laws they are opposed to, they say, but merely the limitation to women, and to demonstrate this they propose to amend pending 8-hour bills to make them apply to "all persons."

For my own part, I believe in the laws because, for one thing, I know the meaning *and the feeling* of industrial fatigue. I know because throughout those years of my life in the factory I worked 10 hours a day, six days a week, stitch-

ing shoes; drawing $12 in my pay envelope after that amount of toil. . . . Reasonable hours for the industrial worker mean all the difference between health, vigor, the capacity for enjoyment on the one hand, and on the other the horrors of exhaustion, physical ruin and fear of the human scrap-heap. . . .

There are other hour regulations, however, of which night work laws are a more controversial example. They prohibit the employment of women on night shifts. It may be admitted, I think—I for one will admit—that the night work laws are easily capable of misapplication, and the most judicious care should be taken in the drafting of them. Since they have in view fundamentally the health and efficiency of the worker, and night work is usually a hardship, there is no question but that means of avoiding it are desirable for men and women *both*. Not equally *necessary* for men and women, however, because men and women do not occupy the same positions in the other half of their lives—their domestic relations. Hence neither the individual nor social cost of night work for men is so high as for women.

A woman at work in a factory, or anywhere outside her home, does not give up her household tasks. If she is married she has literally two full-time jobs when she works in the factory, for she does not earn enough to permit her to employ a servant or a housekeeper. A man does his day's work in the factory, and his job is over for the day. His wife or his sister comes home from the factory and gets his dinner and looks after the children, gets up in the morning, gets breakfast, does the housework, and goes out for another day at the factory. She does this unless she works *at night* in the factory. Then she does her housework during the day—and gets her sleep when she can.

There are, according to the Census, 2,000,000 married women in the United States gainfully occupied. Great numbers of them, mothers of little children, lead some such abnormal life as described above. The night-work laws do not solve their problem, we know. But they do lead to adjustments in industry whereby women get the day shifts, and they do serve, we believe, the greatest good of the greatest number. They can, in all cases, undoubtedly be drawn with exemptions to obviate especial hardships. . . .

All these kinds of regulatory laws have been obtainable for women because women's special needs were more evident to the public than were the needs of other workers, and there was a widespread appreciation of the importance of conserving the health of the actual and potential mothers of future generations. A similar demand for laws for men did not exist for several reasons. Chief of these was and is the fact that men in general work under much better conditions than women; where they work at night they can sleep in the day, and there are in any event no such double demands upon their energies as upon the wage-earning wife and mother; and, though men's wages are too often very low, they are never, I think we can safely say, as low as women's. . . .

But, our theoretical feminists say, "we stand on the *princi-*

ple that there should be no laws whatever that do not apply to men as well as to women." That theory is good as a theory. . . .

Conditions of life and of industry are such that while women today are working 9 hours or 10 hours or 11 hours a day in the absence of the 8-hour law, men are at this same moment, in many industries, enjoying their 8-hour day. In other words it is not the 8-hour law, but the *absence* of the 8-hour law for women, that constitutes a discrimination against them as we see it.

Similarly, women's wages are very much lower than men's—will probably average little more than half as much. Minimum wage laws bring up the lowest wages at least within striking distance of an equality with men. Instead of being discriminatory against women, the minimum wage laws lessen the discrimination that already exists.

What the feminist objection to the labor laws for women is really based on is this: The labor laws for women put women on a different *legal* basis from men so far as their jobs are concerned, and to the ultra-feminist *legal* equality means almost everything. The worker prefers *industrial* equality, which is in this case actually *defeated* by *legal* equality.

Then there are certain other contentions against the laws that are no better founded than this I have mentioned. It has been testified before the New York legislature, for instance, that the 8-hour law of the District of Columbia caused women in laundries and in restaurants to lose their jobs and be replaced by men. The authentic facts are that the 1920 Census showed almost exactly twice as many women employed in laundries as shown by the Census before the law was passed, and the proportion of women and men was exactly the same. As to waitresses, the numbers in the District of Columbia increased several times *more* than the numbers of men.

These facts are especially interesting in view of the claim loudly voiced in New York City that "thousands of women" lost their jobs as a result of the night-work law which was passed a few years ago. The Bureau of Women in Industry of the New York Department of Labor investigated this situation, and found that what really happened was that the women employees had been taken on during the war in place of men; that the company had begun dismissing the women in wholesale groups several months before the law in question was ever proposed in the legislature; that it continued this policy of dismissal between the time this law was proposed and the time it was passed; and likewise continued the policy to dismissals *after* the law was passed—giving the law as the reason for so doing. That it could have adjusted the shifts if it wanted to retain these women is scarcely open to doubt. . . .

The whole question, it seems to me, comes down to this: Shall we let women continue working longer hours than men, for less pay than men, and continue doing two jobs to their husbands' one? And is that sort of thing to continue in the name of some principle of equality? Or shall we agree that the reality of better conditions of employment is more important, both to health and to industrial equality, than is a cherished theory?

Women who are wage-earners with one job in the factory and another in the home have little time and energy left to carry on the fight to better their economic status. They need the help of other women, and they need labor laws. Such laws are a safeguard not only to women but also to the children. They give protection to the family and maintain more satisfactory standards of living. In short, they help to make the country a better place for its citizens. . . . [19]

TO MEMBERS OF THE MINNESOTA LEAGUE OF WOMEN VOTERS: A LEGISLATIVE LETTER

As we go to press, word comes from the Capitol that the introduction of the so-called "blanket" or "equal rights" bill sponsored by The Woman's Party is momentarily expected.

The object of this bill according to its supporters is to write into the law the principle of complete civil and political equality of men and women and to abolish at one stroke all remaining legal discriminations of any kind between the sexes. The League of Women Voters has no quarrel with the general object of this bill. By securing the passage of the bill making women eligible for jury service and by countless other bills secured in many states the League has been making rapid and sure advances in removing all material discriminations against women which operate to their disadvantage. The League is however absolutely opposed, both as a national organization through action of its national convention and as a state organization through action of its Legislative Council and its state convention, to the "blanket" method of legislation advocated by The Woman's Party. Such legislation we believe, after thorough study and consultation with many legal authorities, does not adequately achieve its own purpose, throws all laws relating to women and the family into a state of confusion which years of litigation may be required to straighten out, and absolutely endangers all protective legislation for women such as the limitation of hours of employment which have been enacted in the interest of the public welfare.

You will hear more of this bill! Meanwhile do not let glittering generalities and specious arguments win even momentary support for a measure which has such dangerous possibilities. Write to League office for material. [20]

Although the issue of protective legislation dominated the debate, there was also disagreement concerning the broader implications of the amendment for women and their place in society. Opponents of the Equal Rights Amendment argued that women needed special legislation because they were different from men. Women work-

ers, they suggested, would always have special problems because they were women, and they would benefit, rather than be harmed, by treatment as a separate sex group. The NWP argument, reflected in this article by Lavinia Dock, printed in the Party's Equal Rights, *rejected the view of women as an inferior caste.*

AGAINST WOMEN AS A SUB-CASTE

Reading over anew the arguments in opposition to the Lucretia Mott Amendment, one can but wonder in how far they arise from a deep-down acceptance of the idea of caste, and an inherited belief—unconscious, of course—that women do rightly and naturally belong to an inferior caste, or at least a sub-caste. . . .

The ingrained acceptance by many women themselves of an inferior caste makes the question one of grave difficulty and points more emphatically to the need of a Federal amendment proclaiming Equal Rights (that is, it does so to those who think caste is not socially wholesome or desirable) as the starting point of a broader education for the average citizen. Just as the granting of the ballot was urgently needed that women's political education might begin, so is the constitutional abolition of caste even more urgently necessary for the growth of women and men in economic intelligence and social and ethical powers. . . .

It seems sometimes to me that our trade union women are still under the shadow of the caste idea, for, while they fully respect themselves as workers, they show an indifference to, or even an impatience with, the claims made for women as a whole. They seem not at all to realize the indirect influence of the great mass of non-organized women, who are outside of industry proper, upon their own destinies as workers with definite aims and ambitions.

Wage-earning women come, mostly, from homes where the mother and wife is classified as having no occupation—is regarded as supported by her husband, a working man. Her manifold services are not allowed to have any money value. She often has inferior rights, sometimes none in questions relating to her children, or to the tiny family property accumulated with her help—the wee shop or the little farm or plot of ground or the savings in the bank or the old teapot.

When the working girl marries she returns to her mother's class—loses her prestige as an organized industrial worker and becomes an unrecognized member of an inferior caste.

Am I wrong in thinking that the dead weight of this mass is too much for my old friends to shake off, and that right there, rooted in that situation, is the first cause of lower pay for women and disregard of their welfare?

Those lower caste women, from whom the industrial woman came and to whom she will return in marriage or in old age—*they* set the standards for the employer and the exploiter.

One only realizes the magnitude of this situation when one leaves the big city, with its stimulating groups of keen,

VOL. XI, No. 2
FIVE CENTS

SATURDAY,
FEBRUARY 23, 1924

WHOSE STREETS ARE THEY?
The Law: "Streets are not safe for working women at night."
Working Woman: "Well, then, make 'em safe."

Equal Rights, *Feb. 23, 1924*

intelligent and forward-looking labor women, and begins to know the vast extent of rural, small town, middle class America. There one sees the home girls working at cheap rates which seem big to them in the little country open-shop factories, returning at night to a family circle where women's whole activity outside the home is absolutely limited to "auxiliary" service for some little church or lodge or charity; where men laborers cannot abide taking directions from a woman employer; where many, perhaps most, husbands, still refuse to permit their wives to vote; where a strict line of demarcation lies between "men's" and "women's" work (the latter by no means always the easiest).

Can the segregation of women in industry under special labor laws overcome this basic handicap of belonging to an inferior caste? Is not the first step toward safety that of lifting all women out of so ignominious a place in the world? . . . Is it credible that, the whole legal status of women being made equal with that of men, they will grow weaker instead of stronger? . . . [21]

In threatening existing protective legislation, the movement for the Equal Rights Amendment seemed to aid the conservative judges and legislators who were increasingly reluctant to condone government regulation of business and who succeeded in killing the child labor amendment. To the women who had labored so long for protective labor laws, the National Woman's Party's insistence on equality for women, even at the sacrifice of women's labor legislation, seemed like a stab in the back!

But to the NWP, issues other than protective legislation were involved. In testifying at Senate hearings on the amendment in 1931, Burnita Matthews, chairwoman of the NWP Lawyers' Council, enumerated the legal and political inequalities that would be eliminated by the ERA.

TESTIMONY BY BURNITA MATTHEWS

There are many discriminations in the laws against women. The discriminations show the need for the proposed equal rights amendment.

The woman, even in the home—that place so often designated as her "appropriate sphere"—does not share equally in the husband's authority. The father is the sole natural guardian of minor children in Alabama and Georgia. Michigan, New York, and Massachusetts are among the States where the father alone is usually entitled to the services and earnings of a minor child. In Iowa and Montana the right to recover damages for loss of a child's services and earnings in case of injury to the child belongs primarily to the father.

The Louisiana Code provides that a child owes both parents obedience, "honor, and respect," but in the case of difference between the parents, "the authority of the father prevails." . . .

In Arkansas and West Virginia, when a person dies, leaving a father and mother but no will and no descendants, the property of the decedent goes to the father to the exclusion of the mother. . . .

Over the legitimate child the father is usually given paramount rights; but over the child born out of wedlock, who is regarded by society as an outcast, the law as a general rule makes the mother the sole guardian and, contrary to the law of nature, decrees that the child has no father. Thus the male parent escapes practically all of the burdens incident to illegitimate parenthood. In Texas and Virginia, for instance, there are no laws requiring a father to contribute to the maintenance of an illegitimate child. . . .

In the eyes of the law an unmarried woman is usually regarded as able to look out for herself. If she wants to run a millinery shop or a real estate business, for example, no official inquiry is conducted as to her capacity. But as though marriage on the part of a woman indicates lack of judgment, the law in some States as soon as a woman marries places her under a disability on the theory of protection to herself from her imprudence or ignorance, and people are charged with knowledge of the dangers of a married woman's paper. Michigan and Nebraska are among the States where the power of a married woman to contract is less than that of other adult persons. In Nevada if a married woman desires to conduct a business, she has to go through a complicated court procedure and satisfy the judge as to her business capacity, but the most ignorant man, married or single, may carry on a business and no investigation is conducted as to his qualifications.

Another example is the case of Mrs. Ferguson who was elected governor of Texas. She petitioned the court to remove her disabilities as a married woman so that her contracts and acts as governor might not be called into question. The consent of her husband was required and obtained. The court found that it would be to her advantage to be able to sue and contract freely, and then entered a decree that the consent of her husband having been obtained, her disabilities were removed. . . .

The double standard of morals is recognized in practically all States. In Maryland a man may divorce his wife for being unchaste before marriage, but a divorce is not available to a woman on that ground. In Minnesota a husband whose wife is guilty of infidelity may collect damages from her paramour. On the other hand, no wife whose husband is guilty of infidelity may claim compensation from his paramour.

Under the laws of Tennessee a woman divorced for adultery and living with the adulterer is rendered incapable of disposing of any of her lands, but no such incapacity is imposed upon a man guilty of similar conduct.

In some States prostitution is regarded solely as an act of the woman and it is said that only a woman can commit prostitution. Thus women are often punished while the men who employ them go free. For instance, in New York City in 1921 a man was found in a room with two young women both nude—and he admitted having given each girl $25. Both of the girls as well as the woman in whose house the transaction occurred were convicted, but the city magistrate held that the man had committed no offense under the law.

California has held that a city ordinance penalizing any person for soliciting for prostitution has application to women but not to men, the theory of the court being that a woman only can be guilty of that act.

Eight States—Arizona, California, Idaho, Louisiana, Nevada, New Mexico, Texas, and Washington—have a community property law, under which the earnings and property acquired after marriage through the joint or individual efforts of husband and wife are usually pooled. So far as earnings and saving money is concerned, husband and wife under the community system are partners, but when it comes to spending the money, he is the head and master of the community. The husband's power to manage, control and dispose of community personal property is almost as absolute as his right over his separate property. He may exercise practically all of the powers of exclusive ownership and the wife usually has no remedy except by divorce or his death. She may witness the passing away through mismanagement or debauchery, of a family competence in which she has a kind of half interest—a right without a remedy.

In three of the community property States, Louisiana, Nevada and Texas, the general rule is that the husband may even deed away community real estate without the wife's consent. . . .

In 40 States the services of the wife to a greater or less extent belong to the husband. Therefore the first right of property which a free person enjoys; that is, the full ownership of his or her labor, is still denied the married woman.

Georgia, Vermont, and Virginia uphold the right of a husband to collect his wife's wages. Although the majority of the States permit a married woman to collect wages for work performed outside the home, the fact is that the household work and other home service devolve upon her, and this labor or service is not hers, but is legally the property of her husband. . . .

Despite the adoption of the woman suffrage amendment to the National Constitution, the political rights of women are not equal to those of men.

Women are sometimes excluded from high public offices. The Oklahoma constitution bars women from such posts as governor, lieutenant governor, secretary of state, State auditor, attorney-general, and State treasurer. Women usually outnumber men in the teaching profession, yet no woman may hold the office of superintendent of public instruction in Oklahoma.

In Wisconsin no woman may serve as clerk to a legislative committee or in any other capacity as an employee of the State legislature.

A person is sometimes appointed by the court to take charge of and distribute the estate of a decedent, compensation being allowable to such person. In a number of States, as for example, Idaho, Illinois, North Dakota, South Dakota, and Utah, a man must be preferred to a woman for appointment when both are of the same degree of kin to the decedent.

Jury service is an important part of the administration of justice, yet women are disqualified as jurors in 26 States. . . .

The United States Supreme Court has held that a State can not bar colored men from jury service, because the disbarment would brand them as an inferior class of citizens and deprive them of the equal protection of the law which is guaranteed by the National Constitution not merely to negroes, but to persons, and women are persons. Nevertheless, the court in this case, by a peculiar process of masculine reasoning, said that certain restrictions might legally be put upon jury service, such as limiting it to males. . . . [22]

Throughout the 1920's and 1930's, the Woman's Party lobbied untiringly for the Equal Rights Amendment, while its opponents, like the National Women's Trade Union League and the National Consumers' League, worked equally hard, diverting a large share of their dwindling resources to the fight against the amendment.

By the end of the 1920's, the amendment was beginning to attract more support from business and professional women, but most organized women and Progressive reformers still opposed it vehemently. In 1937, the National Federation of Business and Professional Women's Clubs

was the first major organization to break the long freeze and endorse the amendment.

By this time, the issue of protective laws for women was becoming less sensitive and controversial. New Deal labor reforms and increased unionization of women workers were slowly extending legislative protection to male and female workers alike. In 1938, for example, the Fair Labor Standards Act set up maximum hour and minimum wage limits for a large proportion of all laboring people. While some women's groups still argued the need for special protection for women, support for the Equal Rights Amendment was rising.

In the meantime, however, the fight over the amendment had contributed to the decline of the movement, sapping it of energy, nurturing personal antagonism, and dividing it in two.

A TIME OF RETRENCHMENT

The Woman's Party, despite the turmoil and division it provoked within the women's movement and the attention it focused on the Equal Rights Amendment, involved a minority of organized women. And as the years passed, it grew even smaller. Its insistence that the vote was merely a beginning and that much remained to be done for women, its talk of sweeping changes, its exclusively feminist concern, and its aggressive tone jarred both men and women. Men ridiculed the NWP, organized women attacked it, and most women stayed away from it.

Other organizations also suffered attrition as associationism waned after the mid-twenties, although they fared better than the Woman's Party. The American Association of University Women actually grew steadily after its formation in 1921. The League of Women Voters numbered about 100,000 in the early 1930's.

The League offers a strong contrast to the NWP. During its beginning years, in the early 1920's, the League toyed with direct political action, supporting and opposing candidates in a few political contests. But soon it was solidly defined as a nonpartisan, educational, and reform organization; it clearly renounced any intention of becoming a women's party. It was a moderate group, as its president, Maud Wood Park, described it, at its 1924 convention:

The League of Women Voters from the beginning has stood for step by step progress. It has chosen to be a middle-of-the-road organization in which persons of widely differing political views might work out together a program of definite advance on which they could agree. It has not sought to lead a few women a long way quickly, but rather to lead many women a little way at a time. . . . [23]

The League viewed itself primarily as a voters' organization and secondarily as a women's organization. National and state leagues worked hard for specific reforms, some of which directly affected women, many of which did not. Although the vitality and character of leagues varied from state to state (by the 1930's there were leagues in all but two states), the dominant tone throughout the country remained the moderation prescribed by Park in 1924. Through the 1930's, the League of Women Voters was mainly concerned with educating women to be informed and responsible citizens while maintaining its strict nonpartisan tone.

Among women's reform organizations, the League of Women Voters was most successful during the 1920's and 1930's. And its relative success, in contrast to the frustrations of the National Woman's Party, the slow dying of the National Women's Trade Union League, and the renunciation of reform by the General Federation of Women's Clubs, was symbolic of the state of the women's movement.

Though hardly an agent of radical change, the League was an important school of politics for women. At a time when discrimination kept women out of good jobs, higher education, government service, and politics, the League offered an opportunity to be involved, although indirectly, with public issues of concern to women. The League's relative ineffectiveness above the state and local level mirrored the general powerlessness of women in influencing and controlling the world around them. It also reflected their continuing, although diminished, interest in doing so.

In this way, the League of Women Voters symbolized the retrenchment of the women's movement that lasted until its re-emergence in the 1960's.

1930-1960: A CHANGING WORLD FOR WOMEN

During the 1930's, discrimination against women, their poverty, and their frustrations were submerged in the troubles of the whole nation. It seemed selfish, to most women and men, to distinguish women's problems from those of a whole population in economic crisis. Then, as the country began to recuperate from the Depression, its attention and energies turned toward war in Europe and Asia. Once again, injustices within the country seemed less important and less compelling than the monumental and dramatic demands of world war.

During this period, from 1930 until 1945, and during a decade of adjustment after the war, the women's movement was quiescent. Nonetheless, important changes took place in women's lives, changes that eventually contributed to a reborn and vigorous movement in the 1960's and 1970's.

Among the most significant changes were those affect-

ing women as workers. From the beginning of the century, women had constituted about one-fifth of the work force, and approximately one out of every four women worked. World War I opened more and different jobs to women, but these changes were small and short-lived. In 1910, women made up 23.4 percent of the work force; in 1920, they were 21.4 percent. Women still held the lowest-paying and least-skilled jobs, moving in large numbers into clerical work as well as domestic service and sales jobs. Moreover, black and immigrant women still worked in disproportionately large numbers. Only 43 percent of women wage earners were native-born white women; over 18 percent were black women, and the rest were immigrants or the daughters of immigrants. Married women made up about 9 percent of the female work force.

When the Depression hit, there was a predictable antagonism toward working women; they were seen as taking jobs away from men. Many unions and government agencies tried to solve unemployment by getting women out of their jobs and men into them. Some states and the federal government adopted regulations that restricted the employment of spouses. Section 213 of the federal Economic Act of 1932 limited government jobs to one member of a family and it, like state provisions, generally resulted in the dismissal of working wives. Organizations like the League of Women Voters and the National Woman's Party protested; but these and other limitations remained on the working married woman.

Professional women were hardest hit during the Depression, and the number of women teachers dropped significantly. But the necessity for women to work and their willingness to work for the lowest wages kept the proportion of women in the work force about the same. More married women worked than ever (about 35 percent of all working women were married), and a quarter of these were the primary wage earners in their families. As had long been the pattern, most working women were poor women, and more than half of the female work force was black or foreign-born.

New Deal measures to revitalize the economy resulted in labor legislation and business regulations that affected all workers, male and female. The National Recovery Administration codes regulating business practices and the Fair Labor Standards Act, legislating minimum wages and maximum hours for businesses involved in interstate commerce, supported the principle of equality for male and female workers. In practice, the new laws and regulations forced an increase in the wages of many women who had been working below the minimum wage and improved working conditions. But loopholes and exceptions in the laws and the widespread employment of women in jobs not covered by federal or state regulations meant a continuation of many inequalities and still left women the poorest-paid workers.

The New Deal encouraged and supported the growth of

unions. The resurgence of the textile unions and the emergence of the Congress of Industrial Organizations, which organized unskilled and semiskilled workers, resulted in a 300 percent increase in the number of women in unions, to 800,000. Despite these gains, overall wages decreased during the Depression, and the working woman still earned 50 to 65 percent less than the working man.

The most drastic changes in the history of working women took place during the great burst of economic expansion that accompanied World War II. The number of women working increased by more than 50 percent. In 1945, more than one out of every three women worked. Women composed 35 percent of the country's work force.

Women moved into jobs traditionally reserved for men —into heavy manufacturing, government bureaucracy, transportation, and into professions like engineering and chemistry, which had been tightly closed before the war. This upward mobility affected unskilled as well as skilled women workers, and it can be seen in the big drop in the proportion of black women working as domestic and agricultural laborers and in the increase—200 percent—in the number of black women in craft and manufacturing jobs.

The years of World War II were years of prosperity and of increasing union strength. By 1945, more than three million women were unionized, including workers in the powerful steel, automobile, and electrical unions, and many working women shared the economic benefits of a wartime economy. The National War Labor Board's policy of equal pay for equal work contributed toward better wages for women.

Nonetheless, discrimination against women continued, and differentials in pay and opportunity kept women in relatively inferior positions. To the few who were permitted into previously closed occupations—in government, in business management, and in the professions—the obstacles to fair remuneration and advancement were enormous.

With all the changes that had taken place, the profile of the working woman after World War II was very different from what it had been before. And it remained so during the following decades. More than one out of every three women in the country was a worker, and married women made up almost half of the female work force. (By the 1950's, a majority of all married women were workers.) More than 40 percent of female wage earners were over thirty-five years old, and the typical working woman was getting older. For the first time in our history, a woman worker was likely to be married and middle-aged. In addition, white educated women from middle- and upper-class backgrounds entered the work force in increasing numbers, reversing a pattern that had not changed since the century began.

Along with the boom in women's jobs during World War II came a revision in the image of the ideal woman. Magazines, films, as well as more direct recruitment literature,

applauded the capable, active woman who could manage a house, raise children, and work full-time. The picture of Rosie the Riveter, a woman in a stereotyped male job, may have been a strange one to many people, but Rosie, in her welder's hat, was drawn as a figure to be admired and imitated. No one ridiculed her wearing trousers during the war years. Similarly, for the first time in history, the wife of the country's Chief Executive offered the example of a woman engaged in traditionally masculine activities; her political involvement and travels, as well as her understanding and command of public affairs, were well publicized. Partisan ridicule of her behavior only underlined the fact that Eleanor Roosevelt was more than just the President's wife and the mother of his children.

With the end of the war, the projected image of Rosie the Riveter vanished, despite the continued participation of women in the work force. In the 1950's, a very different woman was enjoying the attention and admiration that Rosie had received, and a virtual explosion of television and other communications media gave the new idealized woman unprecedented publicity. She was a married woman and a mother of a large family. She worked as purchasing agent and general manager of a complex house, garden, and garage, usually in the suburbs. She bore heavy responsibility for the physical and psychological foundations of her four or five children's lives, as well as for her husband's career.

As always, the distance between the idealized woman and the real woman was very large. Immediately after the war, three million women did leave the work force, but more women remained in it than had been there before the war began. The most significant result of the postwar changes was a decrease in the number of women in well-paying manufacturing jobs which by and large reverted to men.

Very soon after 1945, the number of working women began to climb again and continued to do so. In 1950, women made up 29 percent of the work force, in 1960 about 33 percent, and in 1970 about 40 percent. The proportion of white women, married women, and older women working also increased. In 1960, about 60 percent of the female work force was married; almost 38 percent was forty-five years or older. One-third of working women were mothers.

Though the number and proportion of women working changed, there were few important changes in the kinds of jobs they got. Certain occupations remained "woman's work," such as clerical jobs, household service, and elementary school teaching. Those long closed to women— especially the professions—remained shut. By 1960, a smaller proportion of women held professional jobs than in 1930! On college and university campuses, for example, women made up 27 percent of the faculty and professional staff in 1930; in 1960, the proportion had dropped to 22 percent, despite a huge expansion in higher education.

In 1960, the median wage of full-time working women

was approximately 60 percent of what men earned. For part-time women workers, the disparity was almost twice as large. Differences in income occurred even in situations where women were educated and trained equally well as men. In the professions and on campuses, women consistently worked for less than men with the same degrees and qualifications. Moreover, women were earning a smaller share of university degrees than they had thirty and forty years earlier, despite the enormous growth after World War II in both the number of students and the number of institutions of higher education.

These changes in the nature of the working woman were profound. By the end of the 1950's, women were close to equaling men in numbers in the work force. At some time or other in their lives, nine out of every ten women would be in the work force. Work for wages was becoming a regular part of life for women of all classes and from all backgrounds.

While all kinds of women were entering the work force in increasing numbers, other changes, less obvious but equally important, were taking place. Foremost among them was the steady improvement in contraceptive knowledge and the widespread acceptance and practice of birth control. The birth control advocates, who started their activities in 1915 and continued them through the 1920's, began to win their battles in the 1930's. Helped by the Depression, the movement for birth control saw many of its adversaries weaken and capitulate. Slowly, the courts and the legislatures removed legal barriers. Restrictive federal laws fell into disuse. Most of the Protestant churches curtailed their opposition and slowly turned toward acceptance of contraception. The medical profession gave increasingly serious and constructive attention to the subject, and in 1937 the American Medical Association officially endorsed voluntary family planning.

Women played a leading role in the continuing birth control campaigns of the 1930's. During the decade, over a thousand women's clubs and organizations officially approved birth control, representing the collective voice of about twenty million women.[24] The number of birth control clinics increased, staffed mainly by middle-class women and funded by their efforts. At a time when the women's movement was quiet, the clinics were one of the few bridges that linked poor and working women with their more affluent sisters. For all of them, staff workers and patients, the clinics offered greater understanding and control of their own bodies and lives.

By the time that the Planned Parenthood Federation of America was founded in 1942, the most difficult battles for birth control in the United States had been fought and won; and with the development of new and improved methods of contraception after World War II, another great stride was taken.

The acceptance and spread of birth control in the period between 1930 and 1960 had very obvious and practical effects on women; there were also less obvious although equally important results. In effect, the widespread practice of contraception separated the act of sex from the act of procreation. As never before, female sexuality stood alone, undisguised and undistorted by women's reproductive function.

In the twentieth century, sex became a subject of discussion, research, and controversy. Traditional sexual mores were challenged and new ones proposed. With the improvement of contraception, women had to confront the issue and define the nature of their sexuality.

A somewhat similar change occurred concerning the nature of marriage. Since 1890, the rate of divorce had been increasing rapidly, to the consternation of the churches and other protectors of the status quo. Between 1890 and 1960, the divorce rate tripled, and, with the exception of the Depression years, the rate of divorce seemed to be steadily rising. At first, divorce was a middle-class practice; in the twentieth century it became common to all classes and groups.

Perhaps more important than the numbers was the change in attitude toward divorce and, consequently, toward marriage. Divorce laws have been revised through the century to increase the grounds for ending marriage and to make divorce simpler. The churches, which earlier had refused to remarry divorced persons, generally reversed their stand; and the number of remarriages has increased. Thus, the nature of marriage itself has been changed. Neither God nor man alone makes twentieth-century marriages, nor are they made forever.

In many ways, then, the years of the Depression and World War II witnessed changes that brought a new measure of choice and freedom to women. They gained more alternatives than they had had before—about when and how many children they would have; about where, and when, and if they would work; about whether to marry or to unmarry. However, the real meaning and full implications of these changes and new choices remained to be explored and grasped by a revived women's movement.

CHAPTER TWELVE

THE REVIVAL OF THE WOMEN'S MOVEMENT

1960's and 1970's

In the 1960's and 1970's, the women's movement in the United States revived with a vitality and impact that heralded an important phase in the long struggle for equality and dignity. The revival was part of a new period of reform that spanned the 1950's and 1960's.

From the Depression the United States had been preoccupied with economic ills, with foreign wars, and, after 1945, with its awesome rise to world power and prosperity. In the 1950's, a period of self-examination began, and soon increasing demands for internal change were heard.

Initially this reform spirit centered on the large number of black Americans who suffered economic and political deprivation in a land of plenty and democracy. But attention spread quickly to other underprivileged groups within the nation. By the 1960's, the atmosphere encouraged Americans to speak out against all forms of oppression.

Every aspect of American life came under scrutiny. Beginning with calls for disarmament and a cessation of nuclear testing, a powerful and dramatic attack was directed against the nation's foreign policy. It reached unprecedented intensity in the peace movement, which decried American participation in the war in Southeast Asia during the 1960's; and it demanded examination of national goals and values.

This reform era was unusual in many ways. People were actively involved who normally were inarticulate and politically subdued. Afro-Americans planned and executed the fight for integration of transportation and education in the South; poor people marched to Washington to demand remedies for their plight; Americans of Puerto Rican and Mexican background and American Indians added their voices to the cries of injustice and the clamor for change.

Students played a leading role in reform. Colleges and university campuses were centers of antiwar activity, of civil rights agitation, and of radical calls, not for reform, but for revolution. At the same time, television and newspapers brought the messages and activities of the protesters into almost every home in the country.

Many reformers in the 1960's were impatient and defiant. Angry marches, picketing, sit-ins, and strikes were their trademarks. Violent confrontations were not uncommon. More moderate reformers worked at and were often successful at translating some of the demands for change into legislative proposals; politicians hoped to extend and guarantee civil rights and alleviate poverty without radical revision of the country's institutions.

From the beginning, women were involved in all these reform activities. White and black women enlisted in the gamut of civil rights protest, from carefully devised nonviolent strategies against segregation to militant and revolutionary demands for black power. Young women joined political groups on college campuses, including the most militant and radical. And older women spearheaded the call for disarmament and formed a significant part of the peace movement, which soon attracted young women as well.

From their experience in reform activities, these women, like abolitionist women in the nineteenth century, learned about their own deprivation and inequality. From their concern with the needs of others, they turned to face their own.

TOWARD A REVIVAL OF THE MOVEMENT

Reflecting the general concern with discrimination and prejudice that had been aroused by civil rights agitation, President John F. Kennedy agreed to a federal study of the status of women in the United States. Prodded by labor and club women, in 1961 Kennedy set up a President's Commission on the Status of Women to investigate the "prejudice and outmoded customs [that] act as barriers to the full realization of women's basic rights"[1] and to make recommendations in areas such as employment practices in both government and the private sector, social security and tax laws, labor laws, legal treatment of women, and services needed for women, including child care.

It was the first comprehensive investigation ever made of the status of women in the United States; and it confirmed, with statistical clarity, that women, like minority groups, suffered discrimination and injustice. The Commission's report, American Women, was published in 1963. Its recommendations, while moderate compared with the demands that women would soon make for them-

selves, represented a major innovation in government policy and attitude.

RECOMMENDATIONS OF THE PRESIDENT'S COMMISSION

Education and Counseling

Means of acquiring or continuing education must be available to every adult at whatever point he or she broke off traditional formal schooling. The structure of adult education must be drastically revised. It must provide practicable and accessible opportunities, developed with regard for the needs of women, to complete elementary and secondary school and to continue education beyond high school. Vocational training . . . should be included at all of these educational levels. Where needed and appropriate, financial support should be provided by local, State, and Federal governments and by private groups and foundations. . . .

. . . Public and private agencies should join in strengthening counseling resources. . . . Institutions offering counseling education should provide both course content and ample supervised experience in the counseling of females as well as males, adults as well as adolescents.

The education of girls and women for their responsibilities in home and community should be thoroughly re-examined with a view to discovering more effective approaches. . . .

Home and Community

For the benefit of children, mothers, and society, child-care services should be available for children of families at all economic levels. . . .

Tax deductions for child-care expenses of working mothers should be kept commensurate with the median income of couples when both husband and wife are engaged in substantial employment. The present limitation on their joint income, above which deductions are not allowable, should be raised. Additional deductions, of lesser amounts, should be allowed for children beyond the first. The 11-year age limit for child-care deductions should be raised. . . .

Community programs under public and private auspices should make comprehensive provisions for health and rehabilitation services, including easily accessible maternal and child health services, accompanied by education to encourage their use.

Volunteers' services should be made more effective . . . through tapping the large reservoir of additional potential among youth, retired people, members of minority groups, and women not now in volunteer activities.

Women in Employment

Equal opportunity for women in hiring, training, and promotion should be the governing principle in private employment. An Executive order should state this principle and advance its application to work done under Federal contracts. . . .

. . . Many able women, including highly trained professionals, who are not free for full-time employment, can work part time. The Civil Service Commission and the Bureau of the Budget should facilitate the imaginative and prudent use of such personnel throughout the Government service.

Labor Standards

The federal Fair Labor Standards Act, including premium pay for overtime, should be extended to employment subject to Federal jurisdiction but now uncovered, such as work in hotels, motels, restaurants, and laundries, in additional retail establishments, in agriculture, and in nonprofit organizations.

State legislation, applicable to both men and women, should be enacted, or strengthened and extended to all types of employment to provide minimum-wage levels approximating the minimum under federal law and to require premium pay at the rate of at least time and a half for overtime. . . .

. . . The best way to discourage excessive hours for all workers is by broad and effective minimum wage coverage, both federal and state. . . .

Until such time as this goal is attained, State legislation limiting maximum hours of work for women should be maintained, strengthened, and expanded. . . .

State laws should establish the principle of equal pay for comparable work.

State laws should protect the right of all workers to join unions of their own choosing and to bargain collectively.

Security of Basic Income

A widow's benefit under the Federal old-age insurance system should be equal to the amount that her husband would have received at the same age had he lived. This objective should be approached as rapidly as may be financially feasible.

The coverage of the unemployment-insurance system should be extended. Small establishments and nonprofit organizations should be covered now through Federal action, and State and local government employees through State action. Practicable means of covering at least some household workers and agricultural workers should be actively explored.

Paid maternity leave or comparable insurance benefits should be provided for women workers; employers, unions, and governments should explore the best means of accomplishing this purpose.

Women Under the Law

Early and definitive court pronouncement, particularly by the United States Supreme Court, is urgently needed with regard to the validity under the 5th and 14th amendments of laws and official practices discriminating against women, to the end that the principle of equality become firmly established in constitutional doctrine. . . .

The United States should assert leadership, particularly in

the United Nations, in securing equality of rights for women . . . and should demonstrate its sincere concern for women's equal rights by becoming a party to appropriate conventions.

Appropriate action, including enactment of legislation where necessary, should be taken to achieve equal jury service in the States.

State legislatures, and other groups concerned with the improvement of State statutes affecting family law and personal and property rights of married women . . . should move to eliminate laws which impose legal disabilities on women.

Women as Citizens

Women should be encouraged to seek elective and appointive posts at local, State, and National levels and in all three branches of government.

Public office should be held according to ability, experience, and effort, without special preferences or discriminations based on sex. Increasing consideration should continually be given to the appointment of women of demonstrated ability and political sensitivity to policy-making positions.

Continuing Leadership

To further the objectives proposed in this report, an Executive order should:

1. Designate a Cabinet officer to be responsible for assuring that the resources and activities of the Federal Government bearing upon the Commission's recommendations are directed to carrying them out, and for making periodic progress reports to the President.

2. Designate the heads of other agencies involved in those activities to serve, under the chairmanship of the designated Cabinet officer, as an interdepartmental committee to assure proper coordination and action.

3. Establish a citizens committee, advisory to the interdepartmental committee and with its secretariat from the designated Cabinet officer, to meet periodically to evaluate progress made, provide counsel, and serve as a means for suggesting and stimulating action.[2]

Three important reforms expressed the general spirit of change and the reaction against discrimination that permeated the early 1960's. They predated the emergence of the women's movement, and only one of the measures was directly concerned with women. All three, however, would become important tools when the women's movement began its battle against sex discrimination.

The 1963 Equal Pay Act was the first federal enactment against sex discrimination. It affected all workers subject to the Fair Labor Standards Act of 1938, which meant that it excluded executive, administrative, and professional employees, as well as workers in agriculture and domestic

service. The law, to be enforced by the Department of Labor, provided the following:

THE EQUAL PAY ACT

No employer having employees subject to any provisions of this section shall discriminate within any establishment in which such employees are employed, between employees on the basis of sex by paying wages to employees in such establishment at a rate less than the rate at which he pays wages to employees of the opposite sex in such establishment for equal work on jobs the performance of which requires equal skill, effort, and responsibility, and which are performed under similar working conditions, except where such payment is made pursuant to . . . a differential based on any other factor other than sex. . . . [3]

The second law was the 1964 Civil Rights Act, of which Title VII (Section 703) contained the following provisions:

TITLE VII AND JOB DISCRIMINATION

Sec. 703 Discrimination Because of Race, Color, Religion, Sex, or National Origin

(a) It shall be an unlawful employment practice for an employer—

(1) to fail or refuse to hire or to discharge any individual, or otherwise to discriminate against any individual with respect to his compensation, terms, conditions, or privileges of employment, because of such individual's race, color, religion, sex, or national origin; or

(2) to limit, segregate, or classify his employees in any way which would deprive or tend to deprive any individual of employment opportunities or otherwise adversely affect his status as an employee, because of such individual's race, color, religion, sex, or national origin.

(b) It shall be an unlawful employment practice for an employment agency to fail or refuse to refer for employment, or otherwise to discriminate against, any individual because of his race, color, religion, sex, or national origin, or to classify or refer for employment any individual on the basis of his race, color, religion, sex, or national origin.

(c) It shall be an unlawful employment practice for a labor organization—

(1) to exclude or to expel from its membership, or otherwise to discriminate against, any individual because of his race, color, religion, sex, or national origin;

(2) to limit, segregate, or classify its membership, or to classify or fail or refuse to refer for employment any individual, in any way which would deprive or tend to deprive any individual of employment opportunities, or would limit such employment opportunities or otherwise adversely

affect his status as an employee or as an applicant for employment, because of such individual's race, color, religion, sex, or national origin; or

(3) to cause or attempt to cause an employer to discriminate against an individual in violation of this section. . . .[4]

These provisions, defining sex discrimination as an unlawful employment practice, were to be enforced by an Equal Employment Opportunity Commission (EEOC).

The third enactment was Executive Order 11246, as amended in 1967 by Executive Order 11375, which prohibited the federal government and federal contractors and subcontractors from discrimination on the basis of race, color, religion, sex, or national origin. The order was to be enforced by the Civil Service Commission in the case of discrimination by the government itself and by the Office of Federal Contract Compliance (OFCC) in cases involving businesses contracting or subcontracting federal work.

THE MOVEMENT DEVELOPS TWO CENTERS

Several factors focused the protest spirit on women and led to the revival of the women's movement: during the early 1960's, women's experience in non-feminist reform activities confirmed the picture of sex discrimination drawn by the statistics in American Women *and subsequent state and federal studies. And several influential pieces of writing strengthened the realization that women, as a sex, comprised an underprivileged group in the nation.*

As early as 1951, Helen Hacker's article "Women as a Minority Group," published in Social Forces, *introduced intellectuals to a new view of women, maintaining that women, despite their numerical dominance, had many characteristics of minority groups. In 1953, Simone de Beauvoir's* The Second Sex *was published in English. It recounted the history of women's subjection in Western civilization and analyzed the techniques and institutions that made the female the subordinate sex. In 1958, a history of the American women's movement,* Century of Struggle, *by Eleanor Flexner informed readers of a long battle for women's rights in the U.S., and in 1963, the publication of* The Feminine Mystique *by Betty Friedan concentrated attention on contemporary middle-class women.[5] Friedan examined their prevalent life style and questioned whether motherhood and housewifery were the natural and most satisfying roles for American women.*

Out of these new ideas and experiences—in an atmosphere of protest and agitation that encouraged self-expres-

sion and resistance to oppression—two centers of a revitalized women's movement developed. One grew directly out of the radical protest politics of the left; the other came out of the fight against discrimination in the power centers of the nation.

THE BATTLE AGAINST DISCRIMINATION

The work of the Kennedy Commission was followed by that of a federal Citizens' Advisory Council on the Status of Women and of similar commissions appointed within the states; the analyses and reports they produced reiterated the plight of working women and widespread discrimination against all women. By the time a third national conference of state commissions on the status of women was held in 1966, women who had taken part in the commissions' work and others who had watched their proceedings feared that nothing more than rhetoric would come from the elaborate research on women.

They resolved to act together to end sex discrimination, and in 1966 they formed the National Organization for

Women. It quickly became the largest and best-known of a series of new women's organizations.

From the beginning, NOW was a carefully structured, nationwide organization, with coordinated state and local chapters and male as well as female members. In 1966, NOW had 300 members; in 1967, 1200; and by 1974, it had grown to approximately 48,000, with 700 chapters in the United States and nine other countries.

NATIONAL ORGANIZATION FOR WOMEN (N.O.W.)

An Invitation to Join

N.O.W. is a new national organization and has been formed "To take action to bring women into full participation in the mainstream of American society NOW, exercising all the privileges and responsibilities thereof in truly equal partnership with men."

We, 300 men and women who met in Washington October 29 and 30th to constitute ourselves as the National Organization for Women, believe that the time has come for a new movement toward true equality for all women in America, and toward a fully equal partnership of the sexes, as part of the worldwide revolution of human rights now taking place within and beyond our national borders. . . .

We organize to initiate or support action, nationally, or in any part of this nation, by individuals or organizations, to break through the silken curtain of prejudice and discrimination against women in government, industry, the professions, the churches, the political parties, the judiciary, the labor unions, in education, science, medicine, law, religion and every other field of importance in American society. . . .

There is no civil rights movement to speak for women, as there has been for Negroes and other victims of discrimination. The National Organization for Women must therefore begin to speak. . . .

As an organization of individuals, not delegates or representatives, N.O.W. will be able to act promptly. As a private, voluntary, self-selected group it will establish its own procedures and not be limited in its targets for action or methods of operation by official protocol.

Membership is open to any individual who is committed to our purpose. Initial dues of $5.00 are payable to the Secretary-Treasurer.[6]

At its first national conference, in November 1967, NOW members agreed upon their objectives.

WE DEMAND:

I. That the U.S. Congress immediately pass the Equal Rights Amendment to the Constitution . . . and that such then be immediately ratified by the several States.

II. That equal employment opportunity be guaranteed to all women, as well as men. . . .

III. That women be protected by law to ensure their rights to return to their jobs within a reasonable time after childbirth without loss of seniority or other accrued benefits, and be paid maternity leave as a form of social security and/or employee benefit.

IV. Immediate revision of tax laws to permit the deduction of home and child-care expenses for working parents.

V. That child-care facilities be established by law on the same basis as parks, libraries, and public schools, adequate to the needs of children from the pre-school years through adolescence, as a community resource to be used by all citizens from all income levels.

VI. That the right of women to be educated to their full potential equally with men be secured by Federal and State legislation. . . .

VII. The right of women in poverty to secure job training, housing, and family allowances on equal terms with men, but without prejudice to a parent's right to remain at home to care for his or her children; revision of welfare legislation and poverty programs which deny women dignity, privacy, and self-respect.

VIII. The right of women to control their own reproductive lives by removing from the penal codes laws limiting access to contraceptive information and devices, and by repealing penal laws governing abortion.[7]

NOW's demand in 1967 for an Equal Rights Amendment and its assertion that abortion was a woman's right attracted considerable publicity and stirred up controversy within its own membership. Soon after this, in December 1968, the Women's Equity Action League was founded. In contrast to NOW, the League wanted to concentrate on narrower areas of discrimination and to attract professional and influential women rather than a mass membership to the women's rights cause.

WEAL

WEAL holds these truths to be self-evident:

While demonstrations and picketing may serve a certain purpose in attracting attention to the problem, WEAL believes primarily in another avenue of approach: since the present situation is the result of women's inertia, it will have to be corrected by women's action. This action must be incisive but patient, determined but diplomatic. Many of our

Formation of NOW, 1966. Betty Friedan, Kathryn Clarenbach, Anna Arnold Hedgman

political and industrial leaders will oppose us; we must exert unremitting pressure upon them—pressure of a studied, sophisticated, strategic and problem-solving nature. We must merit and obtain the support of women, women's organizations and men of good will, or we cannot succeed.

One of our hopes in organizing WEAL was to exercise a positive influence on legislation and practices regarding the work and education of women. We believe that the expertise and opinions of women need to be utilized. We must gain access to the planning and implementation levels of government and industry to press for our interests. We must keep permanent records of who is really "for us or against us" so we can act vigorously and effectively, and at strategic times.

Our primary thrust should take the direction of counseling girls toward higher career aspirations, facilitating upward mobility for all employed women, and supporting the liberation and fulfillment of women in accordance with their own aspirations and abilities.

Great concern is justified for both the individual hardships and the mass injustices and wastefulness which have been allowed to develop. Rebellion is inevitable, and WEAL stands for responsible rebellion.[8]

The same year that the Women's Equity Action League was formed, Federally Employed Women was set up to fight discrimination by the federal government, a major employer of women. Human Rights for Women was also established in 1968 to serve as a research and legal service for the anti-discrimination campaigns that were springing up in most states.

By the early 1970's, a multitude of women's pressure groups had been formed. Many of them were organized along occupational lines. Existing organizations as well, like the National Federation of Business and Professional Women's Clubs, the American Association of University Women, the Young Women's Christian Association, and

the National Council of Negro Women, turned, with new interest and enthusiasm, to women's rights issues.

The new women's rights organizations persistently pressured for effective enforcement of the three federal enactments of the 1960's. They demanded that both the Equal Employment Opportunity Commission and the Office of Federal Contract Compliance issue guidelines that would turn vague and unclear provisions of Title VII and Executive Order 11246 into clear-cut weapons against sex discrimination.

They demanded that enforcement guidelines prohibit hiring based on the classification, labeling, and advertising of jobs as "women's jobs" and "men's jobs" except in cases (termed "bona fide occupational classifications") where it was clearly necessary that sex be a requirement for the job—for example, in hiring an actress to play a woman's role.

Noting that the Office of Federal Contract Compliance required federal contractors to develop detailed plans, with specific goals and timetables, for adjusting their employment of racial minorities, they demanded that the requirement for such affirmative action programs be extended to women as well.

"N.O.W. PRESIDENT CHARGES GOVERNMENT IMPROPERLY EXCLUDES EQUAL OPPORTUNITY FOR WOMEN FROM FEDERAL COMPLIANCE PROGRAMS"

National N.O.W. President Aileen Hernandez today scored the Labor Department for weakening sex discrimination guidelines and for accepting corporate Affirmative Action Programs that do not deal with equal opportunity for women.

She called on Secretary of Labor James D. Hodgson to restore the stronger sections originally proposed for the guidelines and to announce and enforce a directive that Order No. 4 shall apply to sex discrimination by all government contractors.

At a press conference held today, Mrs. Hernandez stated: . . . "N.O.W. believes that it is essential that goals and timetables be required. N.O.W. insists that every covered Federal contractor must set appropriate goals and then direct every effort to increase materially the utilization of women at all levels and in all segments of the work force where they are underrepresented.[9]

After several years of pressure from women, in 1972, the EEOC guidelines were amended. The revised guidelines stated that women could not be denied employment merely on the presumption that they were less suited to a particular kind of job than men or because co-workers, employers, clients, or customers preferred males. The new

WOMEN'S EQUITY ACTION LEAGUE
weal
799 National Press Building
Washington, D.C. 20045

guidelines also stipulated that advertisements for job openings could not legally describe jobs as "male" and "female" jobs, express a preference for male or female applicants, or specify sex, unless sex was a bona fide qualification for the job.

Sex discrimination guidelines were also issued by the Office of Federal Contract Compliance which prohibited federal contractors and subcontractors from expressing sex preference when advertising for employees and from any discrimination in recruitment procedures. Moreover, the new guidelines, written in 1973, required federal contractors to take corrective or affirmative action to end existing sex discrimination.

The guidelines also regulated personnel policies and practices of federal contractors, realizing many of the aims of women's groups, as shown in these provisions.

OFCC GUIDELINES

§ 60-20.3 Job policies and practices.

(a) Written personnel policies relating to this subject area must expressly indicate that there shall be no discrimination against employees on account of sex. If the employer deals with a bargaining representative for its employees and there is an agreement on conditions of employment, such agreement shall not be inconsistent with these guidelines.

(b) All employees regardless of sex shall be given an equal opportunity to qualify for any job except where sex is a bona fide occupational qualification.

(c) The employer shall not make any distinction based upon sex in employment opportunities, wages, hours or other conditions of employment. Nor shall the employer make any distinction based upon sex in the granting of fringe benefits, including medical, hospital, accident, life insurance, pension and retirement benefits, profit sharing and bonus plans, credit union benefits, leave and other terms and conditions of employment. . . .

(d) Any distinction between married and unmarried persons of one sex that is not made between married and unmarried persons of the opposite sex shall be considered to be a distinction made on the basis of sex. Similarly, an employer shall not deny employment to women with young children unless it has the same exclusionary policies for men.

(e) An employer shall not make available benefits for the wives and families of male employees where the same benefits are not made available to female employees and their husbands and families; nor shall an employer make available benefits to the husbands and families of female employees which are not made available to male employees and their wives and families.

(f) The employer's policies and practices must assure comparable physical facilities including recreational facilities and other employee services to both sexes. The employer shall not refuse to hire men or women, or deny men or women a particular job because there are no restrooms or associated facilities.

(g) An employer shall not deny a female employee the right to any job that she is qualified to perform in reliance upon a State "protective" law. For example, such laws include those which prohibit women from performing certain types of occupations (e.g., a bartender); from working at jobs requiring more than a certain number of hours; and from working at jobs that require lifting or carrying more than designated weights. Such legislation has been found to result in restricting employment opportunities for men and/or women. Accordingly, it cannot be used as basis for denying employment or for establishing sex as a bona fide occupational qualification for the job.

(h)(1) Women shall not be rejected for employment, suspended from employment, or required to take leave involuntarily solely on account of the condition of pregnancy. . . . [10]

In addition to their efforts to strengthen existing legislation and executive orders, women's groups acted as watchdogs to insure compliance with existing federal regulations. In January 1970, the Women's Equity Action League filed the first of hundreds of complaints with the OFCC against academic institutions that were charged with violation of anti-discrimination rules. In June 1970, the National Organization for Women filed complaints of sex discrimination against 1300 corporations doing business with the federal government.

Throughout the country, women's rights organizations also carried out educational campaigns to inform women of their rights under existing laws and to aid them in seeking redress if their rights were being violated. Information kits and printed manuals were prepared explaining federal and local laws and clarifying procedures to follow in protesting discrimination.

In addition to enforcement work, women also lobbied and pressured for new state and federal laws against discrimination and for revision of existing legislation to broaden its provisions to include areas such as unequal social security payments for wives and widows, unequal treatment in public accommodations and housing, and inequities in education.

Subsequently, the Equal Pay Act has been amended to include executive, administrative, and professional employees. As a result of considerable work by groups such as the National Organization for Women, the Women's Equity Action League, the National Federation of Business and Professional Women's Clubs, and the American Association of University Women, Title VII of the Civil Rights Act of 1964 has been revised to cover employees of state and local governments and public and private educational institutions. And finally, after receiving support from all major women's organizations, the Equal Rights Amendment was approved by both the Senate and the House of Representatives in the spring of 1973.

STATEMENT OF DR. BERNICE SANDLER ON BEHALF OF WOMEN'S EQUITY ACTION LEAGUE

DR. SANDLER. I am Dr. Bernice Sandler of the Women's Equity Action League where I am chairman of the Action Committee for Federal Contract Compliance in Education. . . .

I come before this distinguished committee to testify on behalf of House joint resolution 208 and House resolution 916 [the Equal Rights Amendment and a federal statute carrying out recommendations of the President's Task Force on Women's Rights and Responsibilities]. I will limit my testimony mainly to the crucial area of sex discrimination in education, and to how the equal rights amendment and the Women's Equality Act would alleviate some of the dreadful injustices and inequities suffered by American women on the campus.

Since January 1970, the Women's Equity Action League (WEAL) has filed charges of sex discrimination against more than 250 universities and colleges, more than 10 percent of the Nation's institutions of higher learning.

Although we are an organization mainly of professional women, as professional women we are deeply concerned about working women and every one of our complaints has said that we request an investigation to cover all women on the campus, be they professors or women cleaning the bathrooms.

Among those charged are the University of Wisconsin, University of Minnesota, Columbia University, University of Chicago, and the entire State college and university systems of Florida, California and New Jersey.

A class action was also filed against all the medical schools. These charges are filed under Executive Order 11246, as amended. . . .

As of this date, not one of WEAL's charges has been refuted by the Department of HEW as it conducts its investigations on the campuses.

In our initial complaint, WEAL charged an industrywide pattern of sex discrimination and asked for a class action and compliance review of all universities and colleges holding Federal contracts. Accompanying our charges were more than 80 pages of documents substantiating our complaint of sex discrimination in the academic community.

Half of the brightest people in our country—half of the most talented people with the potential for the highest intellectual endeavor are women. Yet, these gifted women will find it very difficult to obtain the same kind of quality education that is so readily available to their brothers.

These women will encounter discrimination after discrimination—not once, not twice, but time after time in the very

League of Women Voters poster

academic institutions which claim to preach the tenets of democracy and fair play.

The women will face discrimination in admission where they will encounter both official and unofficial quotas; they will face discrimination when they apply for scholarships and financial assistance, including Government-financed assistance programs.

When they graduate, their own university's placement service will discriminate against them by limiting some job openings to men only.

They will be discriminated against in hiring for the faculty. If hired at all, they will be promoted far more slowly than their male counterparts, and they will most likely receive far less money than their colleagues of the other sex. And all of this is legal.

The position of women in higher education has actually been worsening; women are slowly being pushed out of the university world. For example, in 1870, women were one-third of the faculty in our Nation's institutions of higher learning. A hundred years later, women hold less than one-fourth of these positions. In the prestigious universities, the figure drops to 10 percent and less. The proportion of women graduate students is less now than it was in 1930. The University of Oregon, for example, has a lower proportion of women on its faculty than it did in 1930. The University of Chicago has a lower proportion of women on its faculty than it did in 1899.

Women are 22 percent of the graduate students in the Graduate School of Arts and Sciences at Harvard University. But of the 411 tenured professors at the Graduate School of Arts and Sciences at Harvard University, only one is a woman, and that is in a chair that can only be held by a woman.

At the University of Connecticut, a State-supported institution, women are 33 percent of the instructors but only 4.8

percent of the full professors. On the University of Massachusetts campus at Boston, also a State-supported institution, there are 65 women faculty, but only two have tenure. . . .

Even when women are hired they generally remain at the bottom of the academic hierarchy. The higher the rank, the fewer the women. . . . In a typical study of the 188 major departments of sociology, Dr. Alice Rossi, a noted sociologist, found that women accounted for:

30 percent of the doctoral candidates;
27 percent of the full-time professors;
14 percent of the assistant professors;
9 percent of the associate professors;
4 percent of the full professors;
less than 1 percent of the departmental chairmen. . . .

Apparently women are somehow "qualified" to earn doctoral degrees, but are not considered "qualified" to teach once they have earned these degrees. . . .

Where do these qualified women go, for it is clear that very few of them will ever teach in the major universities and colleges. Do they marry and give up their careers? This is another academic myth: 91 percent of the women with doctorates are working. . . .

Many women end up teaching on the faculty of junior colleges and community colleges where they comprise about 40 percent of the faculty, and where the pay, status, and research opportunities are substantially less than in the major universities. . . .

Undoubtedly, the percentage of degrees awarded to women would still be higher if the discriminations based on sex were eliminated. Official and unofficial quota systems for women are widespread. . . .

Girls need far higher grades for admission to many institutions. Numerous studies have shown that between 75 and 95 percent of the well-qualified students that do not go on to college are women. And discrimination is one of the major reasons why. In graduate school, the quota system is even more vicious. At Stanford, for example, the proportion of women students has declined over the last 10 years, even though more and equally or better qualified women have applied for admission to graduate school. One out of every 2.8 men who applied [was] accepted; only one woman out of every 4.7 female applicants was accepted. The percentage of women with M.D. degrees is the same today as it was 50 years ago when women first won the right to vote. In the Soviet Union 75 percent of the physicians are women; in our country it is barely 7 percent. . . .

In every salary study that I know of, whether it is nationwide, limited to a single campus or limited to a single profession, academic women earn less than academic men, and the gap is widening. . . .

As more and more information has been collected, there is no question whatsoever of a massive, pervasive, consistent, and vicious pattern of discrimination against women in our universities and colleges. . . .

The situation at the elementary and secondary school level is equally shocking. Although nearly half of the teachers in secondary schools are women, it has become almost impossible for a woman—no matter how well qualified—to become principal of a high school. Only 4 percent of the high school principalships are held by women. Since 1928 the number of women elementary school principals has dropped from 55 percent to 22 percent.

Men are only 12 percent of the elementary school teachers, but they account for 78 percent of the elementary school principals. Of the 13,000 school district superintendents only two are women. And education is supposed to be a woman's field! . . .

Executive Order 11246 as amended, under which WEAL is filing its charges of sex discrimination, is at best an administrative remedy for such discrimination. Unfortunately, the actual rules and regulations adopted by the Department of Labor to implement the order arbitrarily restrict the effectiveness and activities of the Office of Federal Contract Compliance by requiring far less in the way of affirmative action from State-supported institutions than that required of privately supported institutions. . . .

Let us not forget too, that the executive order does not have the status of law. It can be amended or suspended at the pleasure of a particular administration. Furthermore, any institution that wanted to continue discrimination is legally free to do so if it gives up its Government contracts.

There are simply no laws whatsoever that forbid universities and colleges from continuing their vicious patterns of discrimination against women. The executive order is the only weapon that women now have in legally fighting sex discrimination in education. Yet until WEAL filed its complaints, the Department of Labor and all other compliance agencies of the United States Government shamelessly ignored all aspects of the executive order that pertained to sex discrimination. In the absence of constitutional and statutory mandates, such inaction is almost predictable.

New legislation, including the equal rights amendment, is necessary if women are to be accorded the fair treatment that is the birthright of their brothers. Existing legislation, including the 14th amendment, has been woefully inadequate, particularly in the area of education.[11]

Women also played an important part in carrying the fight against sex discrimination into the state and federal courts. As appellants, lawyers, volunteer research teams, and fund raisers, individually and through women's organizations and civil rights organizations, they have challenged discrimination against women. In numerous court cases, they have fought (and are still fighting) discriminatory statutes and practices and have sought judicial confirmation of the view that the use of sex as a classification in laws is discriminatory and unconstitutional.

Almost 100 years after the Supreme Court of the United States denied women the right to vote under the Fourteenth Amendment (in the case of Minor v. Happerstett*),* the Court has declared some state laws unconstitutional because they discriminate against women. Conspicuous among the gains achieved in the courts were the decisions handed down by the Supreme Court in January 1973 in Roe et al. v. Wade and Doe v. Bolton. As a result of these rulings, state laws prohibiting abortion have been radically restricted, and women have gained a greater measure of control over their own reproductive capacities and, consequently, over their own lives.

THE RADICAL SECOND CENTER

By and large, the early fight against sex discrimination in the courts and legislatures was the work of white middle-class women (and some men), often married, middle-aged, and with working experience. In mass-membership organizations like the National Organization for Women and in groups with smaller constituencies like the Women's Equity Action League, much of the leadership came from women with professional training or experience as educators.

The new organizations were traditionally structured, with elected officers, national conventions, and specific goals. Their emphasis on political and legal reforms, their goal of equality, as well as their middle-class membership, were reminiscent of earlier women's rights activity; to the casual observer, it appeared that the women's movement of the 1970's was following a path marked out for it a century ago.

However, at the same time that the traditionally structured women's rights groups were fighting sex discrimination, another center of women's activity was developing independently.

Here, too, most of those involved were white and middle-class. But in contrast to the large number of married and professional women in the structured groups, they were younger and mostly unmarried. Often the women were college or graduate school students, with little working experience. Most of them had taken part in the political protest activity and intellectual ferment of the 1960's, either in the peace movement, civil rights organizations, or the groups that made up the New Left on the country's campuses.

In several ways, their membership in protest politics led them directly into the women's movement. In the first place, through this experience, women discovered in

Abortion Demonstration, New York, 1972

themselves unknown reservoirs of courage, ability, and determination. In organizations like the Student Nonviolent Coordinating Committee and Students for a Democratic Society, women carried out community action programs, setting up library facilities or day-care centers and aiding welfare mothers. They worked in the South in campaigns to register black voters. Along with men, they often encountered hostility and obstruction, and, in voter registration work, violence and physical danger.

At the same time, women's experiences in the New Left revealed definite limits to their participation and pointed up their own inequality. Like their foremothers in the nineteenth century, who had also lived in an era of reform and who had plunged enthusiastically into the fight for abolition and temperance, these women discovered that, along with their general inequality, they were unequal within the radical protest organizations. While some women had the opportunity to organize and initiate projects, many women were not in leadership positions; generally they played supportive rather than decision-making roles. They were, in large measure, the clerical staff and the coffee makers.

Unknown to each other, small groups of women within several radical protest organizations began to meet to air their discontent and to discuss and write about its causes and its remedies. These small informal meetings were the genesis of an important part of the contemporary women's movement.

In November 1965, the following memo, written by two female members of the Student Nonviolent Coordinating Committee, was circulated among women in radical protest groups. It was one of the first of many statements concerning women's place in protest politics and in the world; it turned out to be a call for a revived women's movement.

"A KIND OF MEMO FROM CASEY HAYDEN AND MARY KING TO A NUMBER OF OTHER WOMEN IN THE PEACE AND FREEDOM MOVEMENTS"

November 18, 1965

We've talked a lot, to each other and to some of you, about our own and other women's problems in trying to live in our personal lives and in our work as independent and creative people. In these conversations we've found what seems to be recurrent ideas or themes. Maybe we can look at these things many of us perceive, often as a result of insights learned from the movement:

• Sex and caste: There seem to be many parallels that can be drawn between treatment of Negroes and treatment of women in our society as a whole. But in particular, women

we've talked to who work in the movement seem to be caught up in a common-law caste system that operates, sometimes subtly, forcing them to work around or outside hierarchical structures of power which may exclude them. Women seem to be placed in the same position of assumed subordination in personal situations too. It is a caste system which, at its worst, uses and exploits women. . . .

Many people who are very hip to the implications of the racial caste system, even people in the movement, don't seem to be able to see the sexual caste system and if the question is raised they respond with: "That's the way it's supposed to be. There are biological differences." Or with other statements which recall a white segregationist confronted with integration.

• Women and problems of work: The caste system perspective dictates the roles assigned to women in the movement, and certainly even more to women outside the movement. Within the movement, questions arise in situations ranging from relationships of women organizers to men in the community, to who cleans the freedom house, to who holds leadership positions, to who does secretarial work, and who acts as spokesman for groups. Other problems arise between women with varying degrees of awareness of themselves as being as capable as men but held back from full participation, or between women who see themselves as needing more control of their work than other women demand. And there are problems with relationships between white women and black women.

• Women and personal relations with men: Having learned from the movement to think radically about the personal worth and abilities of people whose role in society had gone unchallenged before, a lot of women in the movement have begun trying to apply those lessons to their own relations with men. Each of us probably has her own story of the various results, and of the internal struggle occasioned by trying to break out of very deeply learned fears, needs, and self-perceptions, and of what happens when we try to replace them with concepts of people and freedom learned from the movement and organizing.

• Institutions: Nearly everyone has real questions about those institutions which shape perspectives on men and women: marriage, child rearing patterns, women's (and men's) magazines, etc. People are beginning to think about and even to experiment with new forms in these areas.

• Men's reactions to the questions raised here: A very few men seem to feel, when they hear conversations involving these problems, that they have a right to be present and participate in them, since they are so deeply involved. At the same time, very few men can respond non-defensively, since the whole idea is either beyond their comprehension or threatens and exposes them. The usual response is laughter. That inability to see the whole issue as serious, as the strait-jacketing of both sexes, and as societally determined often shapes our own response so that we learn to think in their terms about ourselves and to feel silly rather than trust our inner feelings. . . .

• Lack of community for discussion: Nobody is writing, or organizing or talking publicly about women, in any way that reflects the problems that various women in the movement come across and which we've tried to touch above. . . .

The reason we want to try to open up dialogue is most subjective. Working in the movement often intensifies personal problems, especially if we start trying to apply things we're learning there to our personal lives. Perhaps we can start to talk with each other more openly than in the past and create a community of support for each other so we can deal with ourselves and others with integrity and can therefore keep working.

Objectively, the chances seem nil that we could start a movement based on anything as distant to general American thought as a sex-caste system. Therefore, most of us will probably want to work full time on problems such as war, poverty, race. The very fact that the country can't face, much less deal with, the questions we're raising means that the movement is one place to look for some relief. . . . We've talked in the movement about trying to build a society which would see basic human problems (which are now seen as private troubles), as public problems and would try to shape institutions to meet human needs rather than shaping people to meet the needs of those with power. To raise questions like those above illustrates very directly that society hasn't dealt with some of its deepest problems and opens discussion of why that is so. (In one sense, it is a radicalizing question that can take people beyond legalistic solutions into areas of personal and institutional change.) The second objective reason we'd like to see discussion begin is that we've learned a great deal in the movement and perhaps this is one area where a determined attempt to apply ideas we've learned there can produce some new alternatives.[12]

Increasingly troubled by their second-class membership in the radical left, women tried on several occasions to get men to recognize the situation and change it. They were usually rebuffed. A few times they gained a sympathetic statement from the organization, but nothing more. As part of this effort to change their role within the New Left, a group of women asked to deliver a statement at an anti-war demonstration in Washington, D.C., in January 1969. One of the group, Ellen Willis, wrote the following description of the episode.

WILLIS'S REPORT

Dave Dellinger introduces the rally with a stirring denunciation of the war and racism.

'What about women, you schmuck,' I shout.

'And, uh, a special message from women's liberation,' he adds.

Our moment comes. [Women from both New York and Washington planned a feminist statement.] M., from the Washington group, stands up to speak. This isn't the protest against movement men, which is the second on the agenda, just fairly innocuous radical rhetoric—except that it's a good-looking woman talking about women. The men go crazy. 'Take it off!' 'Take her off the stage and fuck her!' They yell and boo and guffaw at unwitting double entendres like 'We must take to the streets.' When S. (Shulamith Firestone), who is representing the New York group, comes to the mike and announces that women will no longer participate in any so-called revolution that does not include the abolition of male privilege, it sounds like a spontaneous outburst of rage (rather than like a deliberate statement of the politics of women's liberation).

By the time we get to the voter card business, I am shaking. If radical men can be so easily provoked into acting like rednecks (a women's liberation group at the University of North Carolina was urinated on by male hecklers at a demonstration) what can we expect from others? What have we gotten ourselves into?

Meanwhile Dellinger has been pleading with us to get off the stage, 'for your own good.' Why isn't he telling them [the men] to shut up?[13]

The contradiction between the egalitarianism and emphasis on individual self-development in the ideology of the New Left and the treatment of women became increasingly disturbing. Between 1967 and 1969, small groups of women (ranging in size from ten to thirty members) started to meet regularly; some separated themselves completely from the mixed groups, others remained attached to them. They met in Boston, Chicago, Detroit, Gainesville, Los Angeles, New York, San Francisco, Seattle, and elsewhere. They debated the validity of forming a separate women's movement and giving women's issues priority over other political and economic causes. In their meetings and writings, they wrestled with the question of whether a women's movement could be justified.

In 1967, women in Chicago announced their decision to organize "a movement for woman's liberation."

"CHICAGO WOMEN FORM LIBERATION GROUP"

To the Women of the Left:

Below is a Preliminary Statement of Principles used as a working paper by a group of Chicago women. Most of us, tho not all, are of the Movement. A few, very few, are in SDS.

We have been meeting weekly for the last two months to discuss our colonial status in this society and to propound strategy and methods of attacking it. Our political awareness of our oppression has developed thru the last couple years as we sought to apply the principles of justice, equality, mutual respect and dignity which we learned from the Movement to the lives we lived as part of the Movement; only to come up against the solid wall of male chauvinism.

Realizing that this is a social problem of national significance not at all confined to our struggle for personal liberation within the Movement we must approach it in a political manner. Therefore it is incumbent on us, as women, to organize a movement for woman's liberation.

Women must not make the same mistake the blacks did at first of allowing others (whites in their case, men in ours) to define our issues, methods and goals. Only we can and must define the terms of our struggle.

The time has come for us to take the initiative in organizing ourselves for our own liberation. It is for that purpose that this group came together and this Statement was written.

While we welcome inquiries and assitance from all concerned persons this organization and its sister chapter now forming in New York are open only to women. Any woman who would like to join us or who would like help in organizing a local group should write or call. The liberation of women cannot be divorced from the larger revolutionary struggle.

Statement of Radical Women

. . . Specifically, it is imperative that we unite behind the following points as a beginning step towards full and equal participation of women in our society.

1. As women are 51% of the population of this country, they must be proportionally represented on all levels of society rather than relegated to trivial functions that have been predetermined for them. Particularly they must be allowed to assume full participation in the decision-making processes and positions of our political, economic and social institutions.

2. We condemn the mass media for perpetuating the stereotype of women as always in an auxiliary position to men, being no more than mothers, wives or sexual objects. We specifically condemn the advertising concerns for creating the myths about women solely to profit from them as consumers. Furthermore, we call for a boycott of the thriving women's magazines. . . .

3. There must be total equality of opportunity for education. . . .

4. Equal employment opportunities must be enforced. This includes equal pay for equal work, no discrimination on the basis of women's childbearing functions, and open access to all jobs, particularly managerial and policy making positions.

5. The labor movement and all labor organizations, unions and groups must admit women on an equal basis to all executive and policy levels while encouraging women to assume leadership roles in their organizations. There must be a concerted effort to organize and unionize those low-pay-

ing, servile occupations in which women are primarily employed.

6. Women must have complete control of their own bodies. This means (a) the dissemination of birth control information and devices, free of charge by the state, to all women regardless of age and marital status; (b) the availability of a competent, inexpensive medical abortion for all women who so desire.

7. The structure of the family unit in our society must be reconsidered and the following institutional changes must be incorporated: (a) a fundamental revamping of marriage, divorce and property laws and customs which cause an injustice to or a subjection of either sex; (b) the equal sharing by husbands and wives of the responsibility for maintaining the home and raising the children; (c) the creation of communal child care centers which would be staffed by women and men assuming equal responsibility and controlled by the adults and children involved in the center; (d) the creation of non-profit-making food preparation centers conveniently located in all communities.

8. We must fight against male domination in all aspects of society and correct the entrenched assumption of superiority on which it thrives, recognizing that the right to define is the most powerful characteristic of any ruling group. . . .

We recognize that women are often their own worst enemies because they have been trained to be prejudiced against themselves. Women must become conscious of the fact that they represent the largest "minority" group in this country and as such are subject to the same segregation, discrimination and dehumanizing influences as other dominated peoples. We know that to become truly free, we must abdicate the superficial privilege which has been purposely substituted for equality and replace it with an equal share of responsibility for taking power in our society.

We believe these minimal demands for equality and full participation in a society that is based on one group victimizing another cannot be met without a restructuring of that society. . . .

We are conscious that reform may not be the most direct route towards that social restructuring. However, women are a widely dispersed group with little recognition of their common oppression. We hope our words and actions will help make women more aware and organized in their own movement through which a concept of free womanhood will emerge.

Towards this end, we identify with those groups now in revolutionary struggle within our country and abroad. Until the movement recognizes the necessity that women be free and women recognize the necessity for all struggles of liberation, there can be no revolution.[14]

In June 1968, Beverly Jones and Judith Brown wrote a lengthy paper, widely read in protest groups, that called on *radical women to form a Female Liberation Movement and outlined its prospective course of action.*

"TOWARD A FEMALE LIBERATION MOVEMENT"

. . . 1. People don't get radicalized (engaged with basic truths) fighting other people's battles.

2. The females in SDS [i.e., those not sympathetic to a woman's movement] essentially reject an identification with their own sex and are using the language of female power in an attempt to advance themselves personally in the male power structure they are presently concerned with.

3. . . . for at least two reasons radical females do not understand the desperate condition of women in general. In the first place, as students they occupy some sexy, sexless, limbo area where they are treated by males in general with less discrimination than they will ever again face. And in the second place, few of them are married or if married have children.

4. For their own salvation and for the good of the movement, women must form their own group and work primarily for female liberation. . . .

Women who would avoid or extricate themselves from the common plight I've described and would begin new lives, new movements, and new worlds, must first learn to acknowledge the reality of their present condition. They have got to reject the blind and faulty categories of thought foisted on them by a male order for its own benefit. . . .

The first step, then, is to accept our plight as a common plight, to see other women as reflections of ourselves, without obscuring, of course, the very real differences intelligence, temperament, age, education, and background create. . . .

Having accepted our common identity the next thing we must do is to get in touch with each other. I mean that absolutely literally. Women see each other all the time, open their mouths and make noises, but communicate on only the most superficial level. We don't talk to each other about what we consider our real problems because we are afraid to look insecure, because we don't trust or respect each other, and because we are afraid to look or be disloyal to our husbands and benefactors. . . .

I cannot make it too clear that I am not talking about group therapy or individual catharsis (we aren't sick, we are oppressed). I'm talking about movement. Let's get together to decide in groups of women how to get out of this bind, to discover and fight the techniques of domination in and out of the home. To change our physical and social surroundings to free our time, our energy, and our minds—to start to build for ourselves, for all mankind, a world without horrors. . . .

1. Women must resist pressure to enter into movement activities other than their own. There cannot be real restructuring of this society until the relationships between the sexes are restructured. . . .

2. Since women in great measure are ruled by the fear of physical force, they must learn to protect themselves. Women who are able ought to take jujitsu or karate until they are proficient in the art. Certainly they ought to organize and enroll their daughters in such courses. . . .

3. We must force the media to a position of realism. Ninety percent of the women in this country have an inferiority complex because they do not have turned-up noses, wear a size ten or under dress, have "good legs," flat stomachs, and fall within a certain age bracket. According to television no man is hot for a middle-aged woman. If she is his wife he may screw her but only because he is stuck with her. More important than that, women are constantly portrayed as stupid. The advertisements are the worst offenders. . . . From such stuff is our self-image created, the public and accepted image of women. . . . Let's not simply boycott selected products; let's break up those television shows and refuse to let them go on until female heroines are portrayed in their total spectrum. . . .

4. Women must share their experiences with each other until they understand, identify, and explicitly state the many psychological techniques of domination in and out of the home. These should be published and distributed widely until they are common knowledge. No woman should feel befuddled and helpless in an argument with her husband.

Notes from the Second Year: Women's Liberation
Major Writings of the Radical Feminists

She ought to be able to identify his stratagems and to protect herself against them, to say, you're using the two-cop routine, and premature apology, the purposeful misunderstanding, etc.

5. Somebody has got to start designing communities in which women can be freed from their burdens long enough for them to experience humanity. Houses might be built around schools to be rented only to people with children enrolled in the particular school, and only as long as they were enrolled. This geographically confined community could contain cheap or cooperative cafeterias and a restaurant so that mothers would not have to cook. . . . These geographic school complexes could also contain full-time nurseries. They could offer space for instrument, dance, and self-defense lessons. In other words, a woman could live in them and be relieved of cooking, childcare for the greater part of the day, and chauffeuring. . . .

6. Women must learn their own history because they have a history to be proud of and a history which will give pride to their daughters. . . . To keep us from our history is to keep us from each other. To keep us from our history is to deny to us the group pride from which individual pride is born. To deny to us the possibility of revolt. Our rulers, consciously, unconsciously, perhaps intuitively, know these truths. That's why there is no black or female history in high school texts.
. . . Courageous women brought us out of total bondage to our present improved position. We must not forsake them but learn from them and allow them to join the cause once more. The market is ripe for feminist literature, historic and otherwise. We must provide it.

7. Women who have any scientific competency at all ought to begin to investigate the real temperament and cognitive differences between the sexes. . . .

8. Equal pay for equal work has been a project poo-pooed by the radicals but it should not be because it is an instrument of bondage. If women, particularly women with children, cannot leave their husbands and support themselves decently, they are bound to remain under all sorts of degrading circumstances. In this same line college entrance discrimination against females, and job discrimination in general, must be fought, no matter what we think about the striving to become professional. A guaranteed annual income would also be of direct relevance to women.

9. In what is hardly an exhaustive list, I must mention abortion laws. All laws relating to abortion must be stricken from the books. Abortion, like contraceptives, must be legal and available if women are to have control of their bodies, their lives, and their destiny. . . . [15]

The earliest of the separate women's liberation groups were influential in spite of their small size. Using the network of mimeographed journals, newsletters, private correspondence, and personal contact that existed among New Left groups, and adding their own newsletters and journals to it, the small women's groups spread their ideas and experiences across the country.

The mimeographed Voice of the Women's Liberation Movement *was the first of the newsletters. Its first issue, printed in Chicago, in March 1968, contained an editorial, concluding with this call for organization.*

"WHAT IN THE HELL IS WOMEN'S LIBERATION ANYWAY"

. . . The time has come for us to take the initiative in organizing ourselves for our own liberation, and in organizing all women, around issues which directly affect their lives, to see the need for fundamental social change. . . .

While we are aware that men are not free either, we, as women, have special problems, within and without the Movement, which we must talk about among ourselves. Only women can define what it means to be a woman in a liberated society and we cannot allow others, by our inaction, to do this for us. It is up to us to meet the challenge to define, and organize, ourselves.[16]

In June 1968, Notes from the First Year *was printed in New York, and in October 1968, the first issue of a Boston*

journal, A Journal of Female Liberation: No More Fun and Games, *was published. Many others followed, including* Notes from the Second Year, Off Our Backs, It Ain't Me Babe, Women—A Journal of Liberation.

During 1968, the number of independent and semi-independent small women's groups grew. Despite geographical separation, they reached out to each other, writing to share their developing ideas and attitudes and in August 1968, twenty women from seven states and Washington, D.C., met at Sandy Springs, Maryland to discuss common problems.

Three months later, in November 1968, more than 200 members from small women's groups met in Chicago for their first national meeting; the second center of the women's movement had taken shape.

SMALL WOMEN'S GROUPS

Small women's groups grew in number during 1969 and 1970, as existing groups expanded and subdivided and as new ones were formed. Extensive publicity attracted many women into the small groups; some existing groups actively

---

SAN FRANCISCO WOMEN'S CONFERENCE: January 18, 1969

10 A.M. - 4 P.M.

Howard Presbyterian Church (Oak & Baker)

A conference for women only:

There will be an all day conference for women interested in Women's Liberation in San Francisco. Members of existing groups have arranged this meeting to meet each other and welcome any interested women to attend all or part of the conference.

The agenda includes morning workshops, informal lunch (bring your own; coffee and tea will be available), and afternoon general discussion. Workshops will be on the following topics (plus any others that may be suggested: 1) Marriage
2) Abortion and post abortion
3) Problems of working women
4) Women in educational institutions
5) Problems & possibilities of raising children
6) Writers workshop - developing an ideology
7) Women under capitalism

The afternoon will be devoted to a dialogue about the personal and political approaches to Women's Liberation.

Our goal is to meet other women and begin a discussion of the ways to the full liberation of ourselves and all people.

WOMEN are coming together in Atlanta on August 10 - 13 1971

How much can we learn from each other?
How close can we come to each other?
How high can we go together?

Experiencing, creating, sharing, planning with sisters from all over Amerika and abroad to discover on what level we can relate, to exchange practical life-centered skills, and to discuss in what ways individual frustration is a product of our patriarchal political system-octopus with a thousand arms that strangles us all.

Workshops are being planned on such topics as health care, self-defense, street theater, silk screening, backing and other crafts, video, day care, and abortion.

Music, video tapes, movies, theater by Earth Onion and others, a make your own music celebration, smiling and dancing are also on the agenda, SO FAR!

We'd like to get it together in small groups to work out a political analysis of Women's proposals and demands for the fall offensive and beyond. We should also try to clarify women's relationship to the Vietnamese struggle, the peace treaty, and the class structure....

It's a time to create situations instead of submitting to them, to stir up controversy and shake people out of their complacency about the war and women's rights, and to raise a high level of consciousness among ourselves. It promises to be a learning, loving, changing experience for us all.

Let's DO IT!

recruited new members and some set up new units for new members. Because they were informally organized and valued privacy, it is difficult to estimate how many women were involved in the groups; by 1970 [17] at least twenty newsletters and magazines were being printed by small groups, and it seems likely that at least ten thousand, and probably tens of thousands of women were participating.

There were many paths into this center of the movement. As the radical political activities of the 1960's waned in the 1970's, many women joined who had no earlier experience in protest politics. Throughout the country, women organized conferences which attracted new recruits to the movement, sparked interest in women's issues, and offered a way to participate in the work of the groups.

Those who came to the women's movement from the protest politics of the 1960's brought with them a variety of political and philosophical outlooks. Most of them had been steeped in a humanitarian egalitarianism; they had a horror of elitism, a distrust of authority, and an antipathy toward hierarchy. Many had been Marxists. Most saw themselves as enemies of all injustice. Some had lost faith in gradual reform and believed revolutionary change was necessary. For all, struggle and confrontation had been regular fare for several years. Because of this, the aims of the small women's groups differed significantly from those of the other center of the movement. The small groups called for far-reaching and radical change in almost all aspects of American society, while structured groups, like the National Organization for Women and the Women's Equity Action League, aimed at specific legislative and legal reforms and did not, at that time, directly challenge the institutional framework of American society.

Piecemeal or gradual reform seemed inadequate to the small groups, which were involved, instead, in analyzing social forces and institutions and in developing an ideological foundation for the women's movement. Concern with ideology grew, in part, out of efforts to justify separating from the New Left and concentrating on women's issues. For those, for example, who had once accepted a Marxist point of view and the primacy of class struggle, giving priority to fighting the oppression of women (and considering women as one group despite differences of class among them) necessitated revision or renunciation of Marxist ideas. For the civil libertarians who had campaigned against racial injustice, it was necessary to weigh the plight of women of all races against the needs of black Americans.

The major task of the small groups in the early 1970's was analysis, but they did not ignore action. Here, too, the small groups differed from the larger structured organizations, which relied mainly on traditional pressure techniques—letter writing, petitioning, lobbying, and testifying before government committees and agencies. Small-group action was in the protest tradition of the New Left and consisted of dramatic demonstrations intended to catch public attention and focus it on women's issues. "Zap" actions, as they were called, took place at the Miss America beauty pageant in Atlantic City, New Jersey, at bridal fairs in San Francisco and New York, and on Wall Street in New York City.

Miss America Demonstration, Atlantic City, 1968

ARE YOU THE MISS AMERICA TYPE?

1. Are there times when you don't feel like smiling?
2. Would you be comfortable wearing heels and a bathing suit?
3. Are your measurements 36-24-36?
4. Are you White, Anglo-Saxon, Protestant?
5. Can you confide in your father?
6. Are you a virgin?
7. Is your highest goal to fulfill the roles of Wife and Mother?
8. Did you go to "Charm" school?
9. Are all your girlfriends envious of you?
10. Has Revlon, General Motors and General Electric given you the good life?
11. Can you afford the latest fashions, appliances, cars, etc.?

---If you answer "No" to any of the above, then you can't be MISS AMERICA.

WHERE DID YOU FAIL???

So you're not Miss America. But think about this: Can the bland, narrow standards by which Miss America is judged truly measure your value to yourself and to others? You're beautiful because you are; whatever your size, shape, or color may be. Your own personality is great -- no charm school in the world could improve it. You don't have to compete with your sisters to prove you're worthy as a woman -- womanhood is whatever and whoever you are.

"WOMEN'S LIBERATION" -- JOIN US!

Zap actions usually involved a broad statement of protest, but abortion soon became a specific objective of small-group action. To gain support and numbers in their abortion fight, the groups formed temporary coalitions and enlisted other women in Zap attacks on abortion legislation and calls for repeal of state abortion laws.

During 1969, much analysis and ideological formulation took place in New York City, where several groups had been formed. The earliest of them, New York Radical Women, was set up in 1967, and out of it evolved several others, among them Redstockings and WITCH. In 1968, the Feminists was formed by a splinter group from the New York NOW. In December 1969, New York Radical Feminists was set up by women who had been in the earlier groups.

At their meetings, these groups searched for new political and philosophical theories that could explain women's oppression and point the way to change. Their conclusions, issued as manifestos and declarations of principles, spread throughout the country. For by 1969 and 1970, the network that linked small women's groups in cities and campuses throughout the country was surprisingly efficient, though informal. Ideas and experiences were quickly communicated and shared despite the barriers of distance.

The Redstockings Manifesto, issued in July 1969, began with this statement, which declared sex oppression to be the first and fundamental form of domination.

REDSTOCKINGS MANIFESTO

I. After centuries of individual and preliminary political struggle, women are uniting to achieve their final liberation from male supremacy. Redstockings is dedicated to building this unity and winning our freedom.

II. Women are an oppressed class. Our oppression is total, affecting every facet of our lives. We are exploited as sex objects, breeders, domestic servants, and cheap labor. We are considered inferior beings, whose only purpose is to enhance men's lives. Our humanity is denied. Our prescribed behavior is enforced by the threat of physical violence.

Because we have lived so intimately with our oppressors, in isolation from each other, we have been kept from seeing our personal suffering as a political condition. This creates the illusion that a woman's relationship with her man is a matter of interplay between two unique personalities, and can be worked out individually. In reality, every such relationship is a *class* relationship, and the conflicts between individual men and women are *political* conflicts that can only be solved collectively.

III. We identify the agents of our oppression as men. Male supremacy is the oldest, most basic form of domination. All other forms of exploitation and oppression (racism, capitalism, imperialism, etc.) are extensions of male supremacy; men dominate women, a few men dominate the rest. All power structures throughout history have been male-dominated and male-oriented. Men have controlled all political, economic and cultural institutions and backed up this control with physical force. They have used their power to keep women in an inferior position. *All men* receive economic, sexual, and psychological benefits from male supremacy. *All men* have oppressed women.

IV. Attempts have been made to shift the burden of responsibility from men to institutions or to women themselves. We condemn these arguments as evasions. Institutions alone do not oppress; they are merely tools of the oppressor. To blame institutions implies that men and women are equally victimized, obscures the fact that men benefit from the subordination of women, and gives men the excuse that they are forced to be oppressors. On the contrary, any man is free to renounce his superior position provided that he is willing to be treated like a woman by other men.

We also reject the idea that women consent to or are to blame for their own oppression. Women's submission is not the result of brainwashing, stupidity, or mental illness but of continual, daily pressure from men. We do not need to change ourselves, but to change men.

The most slanderous evasion of all is that women can oppress men. The basis for this illusion is the isolation of individual relationships from their political context and the tendency of men to see any legitimate challenge to their privileges as persecution. . . . [18]

From the Feminists came an attack upon a "sex-role system" that assigned and restricted males and females to different roles in society and was seen to be the basis for all women's oppression. The Feminists called for revision of the institutions that reinforced the sex-role system, and in doing so, expanded women's issues into all aspects of human relationships.

"THE FEMINISTS PROGRAMMATIC ANALYSIS"

. . . We seek the self-development of every individual woman. To accomplish this we must eliminate the institutions built on the myth of maternal instinct which prevent her self-development, i.e., those institutions which enforce the female role.

We must destroy love (an institution by definition), which is generally recognized as approval and acceptance. Love promotes vulnerability, dependence, possessiveness, susceptibility to pain, and prevents the full development of woman's human potential by directing all her energies outward in the interests of others. The family depends for its maintenance on the identification by the woman of her own desires and needs with the desires and needs of the others. Motherhood provides blind approval as a bribe in return for which the mother expects to live vicariously through the child. Between husband and wife love is a delusion in the female that she is both a giver and a receiver, i.e., she sacrifices to get approval from the male. Love is a self-defense developed by the female to prevent her from seeing her powerless situation: it arises from fear when contact with reality provides no alternative to powerlessness. It is protection from the violence of violations by other men. Heterosexual love is a delusion in yet another sense; it is a means of escape from the role system by way of approval from and identification with the man, who has defined himself as humanity (beyond role)—she desires to be him. The identification of each woman's interests with those of a man prevents her from uniting with other women and seeing herself as a member of the class of women.

All contributions to society which do not add to the individual's unique development must be shared equally, e.g., all "wifely" and "motherly" duties. Child-rearing to the extent to which it is necessary is the responsibility of all; children are part of society but they should not be possessed by anyone. Extra-uterine means of reproduction should be developed because the elimination of pain is a humane goal. Marriage and the family must be eliminated. . . .

We must destroy the institution of heterosexual sex which is a manifestation of the male-female role. Since physical pleasure can be achieved in both sexes by auto-erotic acts, sex as a social act is psychological in nature; at present its psychology is dominance-passivity. One of the ways the female is coerced into sexual relations with the male is by means of satisfying her supposed need to bear children. When reproduction had to be controlled, the myth of vaginal orgasm was created so that the female would remain sexually dependent on the male. The myth of vaginal orgasm stresses intercourse as a primary means of sexual gratification and this emphasis on the genital area and the vagina in particular reinforces the definition of the female as child-bearer even when contraceptives are used to avoid pregnancy.

It is in the interest of the male in the sexual act to emphasize the organ of reproduction in the female because it is the institution of motherhood, in which the mother *serves* the child, which forms the pattern (submission of her will to the other) for her relationship to the male. . . .

Rape is the simplest and most blatant form of the male wantonly forcing his will on the female. Rape occurs whenever a woman unwillingly submits to the sexual advances of a man. In courtship and marriage, rape is legalized because sexual relations are part of the marriage contract.

Prostitution was created by men as the terrifying alternative to the institution of marriage. The other so-called "alternatives" devised by men are modeled on the principles of prostitution—the principles of debasement and deprivation. Thus, the essence of the female (by male definition) is seen to be that of a sexual object, and is the only means through which she can survive. No female is permitted to maintain existence outside her sex-object/motherhood definition. All work for women in the public area must involve only attitudes and skills applicable to her home functions.

Political institutions such as religion, because they are based on philosophies of hierarchical orders and reinforce male oppression of females, must be destroyed.

The elimination of these institutions requires a program understood in terms of stages. Each stage takes into account the interrelationship of all the institutions and therefore calls for simultaneous attacks on all of them. The strategy requires that all avenues of escape from our destruction of the male role and role system be closed. The web of institutions which must be dealt with are: marriage (and the family—child-bearing and child-rearing), the destruction of which requires the simultaneous destruction of prostitution (and "free" love) and exclusively heterosexual sex; the provision for a real alternative for the female (e.g., guaranteed equal annual income); and a program of reparations (e.g., preferential education and employment).[19]

———

In December 1969, New York Radical Feminists adopted this manifesto, which maintained that psychological need, rather than economic relationships, was the main well-spring of male dominance and which analyzed the way in which social institutions—such as marriage and the family —reinforced the oppression of women.

"POLITICS OF THE EGO: A MANIFESTO FOR N.Y. RADICAL FEMINISTS"

Radical feminism recognizes the oppression of women as a fundamental political oppression wherein women are categorized as an inferior class based upon their sex. It is the aim of radical feminism to organize politically to destroy this sex class system.

As radical feminists we recognize that we are engaged in a power struggle with men, and that the agent of our oppression is man insofar as he identifies with and carries out the supremacy privileges of the male role. For while we realize that the liberation of women will ultimately mean the liberation of men from their destructive role as oppressor, we have no illusion that men will welcome this liberation without a struggle.

Radical feminism is political because it recognizes that a group of individuals (men) have organized together for power over women, and that they have set up institutions throughout society to maintain this power.

A political power institution is set up for a purpose. We

believe that the purpose of male chauvinism is primarily to obtain psychological ego satisfaction, and that only secondarily does this manifest itself in economic relationships. For this reason we do not believe that capitalism, or any other economic system, is the cause of female oppression, nor do we believe that female oppression will disappear as a result of a purely economic revolution. The political oppression of women has its own class dynamic; and that dynamic must be understood in terms previously called "non-political"—namely the politics of the ego.

Thus the purpose of the male power group is to fulfill a need. That need is psychological, and derives from the supremacist assumptions of the male identity—namely that the male identity be sustained through its ability to have power over the female ego.

As women we are living in a male power structure, and our roles become necessarily a function of men. The services we supply are services to the male ego. We are rewarded according to how well we perform these services. Our skill —our profession—is our ability to be feminine—that is, dainty, sweet, passive, helpless, ever-giving and sexy. In other words, everything to help reassure man that he is primary. If we perform successfully, our skills are rewarded. We "marry well"; we are treated with benevolent paternalism; we are deemed successful women, and may even make the "women's pages."

If we do not choose to perform these ego services, but instead assert ourselves as primary to ourselves, we are denied the necessary access to alternatives to express our self-assertion. Decision-making positions in the various job fields are closed to us; politics (left, right or liberal) are barred in other than auxiliary roles; our creative efforts are *a priori* judged not serious because we are females; our day-to-day lives are judged failures because we have not become "real women."

Rejection is economic in that women's work is underpaid. It is emotional in that we are cut off from human relationships because we choose to reject the submissive female role. We are trapped in an alien system, just as the worker under capitalism is forced to sell his economic services in a system which is set up against his self-interest. . . . [20]

A conspicuous difference between the two centers of the movement was in their form. The more radical women generally opposed the establishment of large, traditionally organized groups, precisely the kind that NOW and WEAL were. Their small, unstructured groups, limited in size and not formally connected with each other, were deliberately and purposefully set up this way.

They believed that structured, hierarchical organizations promoted inequality and domination and reflected patriarchal relations. Small groups, it was thought, would encourage full and equal participation of all members and avoid

the necessity for leaders; thus, they would promote egalitarianism and collective or communal relationships. It was also hoped that forming many small groups would prevent serious splits and schisms in the movement, since new groups could easily spin off or be created to accommodate new and different ideas.

Consequently, as more members were attracted, the original groups subdivided or encouraged the formation of separate groups. In this way, the number of women who met together was usually kept within a range of ten to thirty.

The small groups experimented with leaderless meetings, the use of lots for assignments, and anonymous or collective authorship. Their desire to encourage the self-development of every member inspired many innovations; among them were the experiments of the Feminists.

A LOT SYSTEM

The Feminists is an organization without officers which divides work according to the principle of participation by lot. Our goal is a just society all of whose members are equal. Therefore, we aim to develop knowledge and skills in all members and prevent any one member or small group from hoarding information or abilities.

Traditionally official posts such as the chair of the meeting and the secretary are determined by lot and change with each meeting. The treasurer is chosen by lot to function for one month.

Assignments may be menial or beyond the experience of a member. To assign a member work she is not experienced in may involve an initial loss of efficiency but fosters equality and allows all members to acquire the skills necessary for revolutionary work. When a member draws a task beyond her experience she may call on the knowledge of other members, but her own input and development are of primary importance. The group has the responsibility to support a member's efforts, as long as the group believes that member to be working in good faith. A member has the duty to submit her work for the group—such as articles and speeches—to the group for correction and approval.

In order to make efficient use of all opportunities for writing and speaking, in order to develop members without experience in these areas, members who are experienced in them are urged to withdraw their names from a lot assigning those tasks. Also those members, experienced or inexperienced, who have once drawn a lot to write or speak must withdraw their names until all members have had a turn.

The system of the lot encourages growth by maximizing the sharing of tasks, but the responsibility for contributions rests ultimately with the individual. One's growth develops in proportion to one's contributions. [21]

GONSGIOUSNESS RAISING AND SISTERHOOD

Full participation and leaderless meetings were not the only benefits of limiting the size of the small groups. It also encouraged openness and personal discussion and created an atmosphere of camaraderie, trust, and ease.

As women shared their experiences and feelings and analyzed them together, they discovered that what each woman had considered personal experiences (and personal problems) were, in large measure, experiences and problems common to other women in the group and to most women. To a great extent, their "personal" experiences were the result of being female in American society. The political implications of this discovery of common problems became apparent: women constituted a caste, tied together by their sex. What had seemed at first only the personal experiences of individuals were now regarded, in the small groups, as the political experiences of all women.

The recognition of common problems and the process of relating personal life to women's condition were seen as an important step in achieving freedom for women. This consciousness raising, as it was called, became a unique and important contribution of the small groups to the developing movement.

During 1969, Redstockings in New York was one of the first groups to experiment seriously with consciousness raising as a component of the women's movement. In its Manifesto, Redstockings stressed the importance of personal experience.

PERSONAL EXPERIENCE

V. We regard our personal experience, and our feelings about that experience, as the basis for an analysis of our common situation. We cannot rely on existing ideologies as they are all products of male supremacist culture. We question every generalization and accept none that are not confirmed by our experience.

Our chief task at present is to develop female class consciousness through sharing experience and publicly exposing the sexist foundation of all our institutions. Consciousness-raising is not "therapy," which implies the existence of individual solutions and falsely assumes that the male-female relationship is purely personal, but the only method by which we can ensure that our program for liberation is based on the concrete realities of our lives.

The first requirement for raising class consciousness is honesty, in private and in public, with ourselves and other women.[22] . . .

In November 1968, "A Program for Consciousness-Raising" was presented to the National Women's Liberation Conference by Kathie Sarachild.

This is a consciousness-raising program for those of us who are feeling more and more that women are about the most exciting people around, at this stage of time, anyway, and that the seeds of a new and beautiful world society lie buried in the consciousness of this very class which has been abused and oppressed since the beginning of human history. It is a program planned on the assumption that a mass liberation movement will develop as more and more women begin to perceive their situation correctly and that, therefore, our primary task right now is to awaken "class" consciousness in ourselves and others on a mass scale. The following outline is just one hunch of what a theory of mass consciousness-raising would look like in skeleton form.

I.   The "bitch session" cell group
A. Ongoing consciousness expansion
  1. Personal recognition and testimony
    a. Recalling and sharing our bitter experiences
    b. Expressing our feelings about our experiences both at the time they occurred and at present
    c. Expressing our feelings about ourselves, men, other women
    d. Evaluating our feelings
  2. Personal testimony—methods of group practice
    a. Going around the room with key questions on key topics
    b. Speaking our experience—at random
    c. Cross examination
  3. Relating and generalizing individual testimony
    a. Finding the common root when different women have opposite feelings and experiences
    b. Examining the negative and positive aspects of each woman's feelings and her way of dealing with her situation as a woman
B. Classic forms of resisting consciousness, or: How to avoid facing the awful truth
  1. Anti-womanism
  2. Glorification of the oppressor
  3. Excusing the oppressor (and feeling sorry for him)
  4. False identification with the oppressor and other socially privileged groups
  5. Shunning identification with one's own oppressed group and other oppressed groups
  6. Romantic fantasies, utopian thinking and other forms of confusing present reality with what one wishes reality to be
  7. Thinking one has power in the traditional role—can "get what one wants," has power behind the throne, etc.
  8. Belief that one has found an adequate personal solution or will be able to find one without large social changes

9. Self-cultivation, rugged individualism, seclusion, and other forms of go-it-alonism
10. Self-blame!!
11. Ultra-militancy; and others??

C. Recognizing the survival reasons for resisting consciousness

D. "Starting to Stop"—overcoming repressions and delusions
  1. Daring to see, or: Taking off the rose-colored glasses
    a. Reasons for repressing one's own consciousness
      1) Fear of feeling the full weight of one's painful situation
      2) Fear of feeling one's past wasted and meaningless (plus wanting others to go through the same obstacles)
      3) Fear of despair for the future
    b. Analyzing which fears are valid and which invalid
      1) Examining the objective conditions in one's own past and in the lives of most women throughout history
      2) Examining objective conditions for the present
    c. Discussing possible methods of struggle
      1) History of women's struggle and resistance to oppression
      2) Possibilities for individual struggle at present
      3) Group struggle
  2. Daring to share one's experience with the group
    a. Sources of hesitancy
      1) Fear of personal exposure (fear of being thought stupid, immoral, weak, self-destructive, etc. by the group)
      2) Feeling of loyalty to one's man, boss, parents, children, friends, "the Movement"
      3) Fear of reprisal if the word gets out (losing one's man, job, reputation)
      4) Fear of hurting the feelings of someone in the group
      5) Not seeing how one's own experience is relevant to others, or vice versa
    b. Deciding which fears are valid and which invalid
    c. Structuring the group so that it is relatively safe for people to participate in it

E. Understanding and developing radical feminist theory
  1. Using above techniques to arrive at an understanding of oppression wherever it exists in our lives—our oppression as black people, workers, tenants, consumers, children, or whatever as well as our oppression as women
  2. Analyzing whatever privileges we may have—the white skin privilege, the education and citizenship of a big-power (imperialist) nation privilege, and seeing how these help to perpetuate our oppression as women, workers

F. Consciousness-raiser (organizer) training—so that every woman in a given bitch session cell group herself becomes an "organizer" of other groups. . . .

  1. The role of the consciousness-raiser ("organizer")
    a. Dares to participate; dares to expose herself, bitch
    b. Dares to struggle
  2. Learning how to bring theory down to earth
    a. Speaking in terms of personal experience
  3. Learning to "relate"
    a. To sisters in the group
    b. To other women
    c. Friends and allies
    d. Enemies
  4. Particular problems of starting a new group

II. Consciousness-raising Actions
A. Zap actions
  1. Movie benefits, attacks on cultural phenomena and events, stickers, buttons, posters, films
B. Consciousness programs
  1. Newspapers, broadsides, storefronts, women's liberation communes, literature, answering mail, others . . . ??
C. Utilizing the mass media

III. Organizing
A. Helping new people start groups
B. Intra-group communication and actions
  1. Monthly meetings
  2. Conferences[23]

Consciousness raising, which revealed the political implications inherent in one's own life, was a valuable process for educating women and enlisting them into the movement. As information about the technique spread, many new groups were set up for the express purpose of experimenting with it. Through these consciousness-raising groups, many women were introduced to the movement and eventually became involved in its other activities.

Closely tied in with consciousness raising—which translated the individual experience into a collective women's experience—was the growing emphasis on the concept of "sisterhood." It asserted that a bond existed among women because of their womanhood which linked them together, despite differences of class, color, and religion. Soon "sisterhood" was a basic part of the movement ideology, as expressed here in the Redstockings Manifesto.

THE IDEA OF SISTERHOOD

VI. We identify with all women. We define our best interest as that of the poorest, most brutally exploited woman. We repudiate all economic, racial, educational or status privileges that divide us from other women. We are determined to recognize and eliminate any prejudices we may hold against other women.

We are committed to achieving internal democracy. We will do whatever is necessary to ensure that every woman in our movement has an equal chance to participate, assume responsibility, and develop her political potential.

VII. We call on all our sisters to unite with us in struggle.

We call on all men to give up their male privileges and support women's liberation in the interest of our humanity and their own.

In fighting for our liberation we will always take the side of women against their oppressors. We will not ask what is ''revolutionary'' or ''reformist,'' only what is good for women.

The time for individual skirmishes has passed. This time we are going all the way.[24]

Passion and militancy distinguished the early small groups from the large structured organizations which, like Women's Equity Action League, hoped to achieve reform not by confrontation but by education, persuasion, and legislative and court action. In asserting that personal feelings and experiences were political, the small groups maintained a high level of emotionalism and they kept alive the spirit of protest and indignation that had characterized the New Left in the 1960's but which was fading elsewhere as the 1970's began. Moreover, the anger directed at the men of the New Left during the late 1960's was multiplied and extended to all men who supported and accepted institutionalized oppression of women.

By the 1970's, it appeared that a distinct center of the women's movement had developed in the small groups. Their interest in analysis and ideology, their calls for radical change in all aspects of society, their use of theatrical protest and Zap action, their preference for informal and unstructured groups, and their emphasis on emotion and consciousness—in contrast to the structured organizations—seemed to point toward continuing development of two separate wings of the movement. One talked of women's rights; the other of women's liberation.

THE MOVEMENT IN THE SEVENTIES: TWO CENTERS FORM ONE MOVEMENT

As the movement evolved in the 1970's, many of the differences that seemed to divide it in two disappeared or blurred, and the movement grew to encompass both the

small and the large, the structured and the amorphous, the conservative and the radical, the persuasive and the belligerent. The women's movement became, in effect, a huge umbrella under which all stood together.

Although the two centers were never linked in any formal way, women from both found themselves working together on certain projects. In 1970, for example, they planned and participated in a national demonstration celebrating the anniversary of woman suffrage and publicizing contemporary demands for change. In several states, campaigns against existing abortion laws enlisted so-called women's-liberationists as well as women's-righters.

Women's Strike for Equality, Aug. 26, 1970

The constant interchange of ideas and information that occurred within the movement was particularly important in diminishing differences. The regular media—television, radio, magazines, and books—decided that the women's movement was news and gave it attention. A great deal of this attention was inaccurate and hostile; newsmen, in a tradition that was as old as the women's movement, often portrayed the movement as ludicrous and neurotic. Nonetheless, the media did help diverse groups know about each other, quickly and regularly, and kept the movement informed about itself.

Building on the New Left network, an extensive communication system also developed within the movement during the early 1970's. More than a hundred journals and newspapers were published. Reprint services and women's printing presses were set up. Many organizations published regular and special newsletters for their members. Women's centers, health groups, and child-care centers issued literature explaining themselves. In 1972, women began publishing Ms. Magazine, *a mass-audience national maga-*

zine. A profusion of books and studies followed in the wake of the developing movement.

Women's centers also served to tie together diverse and separate groups. Located in a YWCA, on a college campus, or in a community building, these centers became sources of information about the activities of women in the community. Although many centers were started for a specific purpose (abortion counseling, for example), as their numbers multiplied throughout the country (today there are at least 500 centers) their functions also increased. They offered information about job opportunities, employment discrimination, and contraception. Centers served as referral agencies, directing women to legal or medical aid; some centers gave rape counseling; others ran their own abortion clinics. The women's center provided information about movement organizations; in many communities, it channeled interested women into consciousness-raising groups.

Sometimes the women's center brought several groups together to coordinate their efforts for a specific local project, such as setting up a child-care center or studying employment or housing practices in the area. In general, the women's center brought women together, kept them in touch with each other, informed them about each other's work, and fostered a sense of unity.

As the years passed, the groups themselves changed in ways that decreased the differences between them. Many of the ideas that came out of small-group discussions were incorporated into articles which were widely reprinted and read, such as "Female Liberation as the Basis for Social Revolution" (by Roxanne Dunbar), " 'Kinder, Küche, Kirche' as Scientific Law: Psychology Constructs the Female" (Naomi Weisstein), "The Myth of the Vaginal Orgasm" (Anne Koedt), "The Politics of Housework" (Pat Mainardi), and "The Woman Identified Woman" (Radicalesbians).[25]

These and other writings at first seemed radical and tangential to more moderate and traditional groups; but this changed as the moderate groups accepted many aspects of small-group analysis and theory. The subject of female sexuality, for example, and its role in heterosexual and homosexual relations, a concern of many small groups, gradually gained attention from other women who at first had considered it an irrelevant and nonpolitical issue.

As a result of the flow of ideas from small groups into more traditional groups, the entire movement became more analytical about what it was doing, relating the struggle for women's rights and reform to social theory, seeing itself in historical perspective, and broadening the definition of women's issues.

At the same time, the small groups themselves were changing. There was a general decrease in nonfeminist protest politics in the country after the 1960's and an increasing interest in electoral politics. This, plus the influx of many new members into the small groups, weakened ties with the New Left.

In addition, the success of the larger, traditional organizations in battling discrimination in the courts and legislatives chambers raised hopes for achieving change through education and reform among many who had despaired at such gradualism in the 1960's. Many small groups turned to action programs, passing from consciousness raising and theory to attack specific institutional problems.

After 1970, for example, women's groups, large and small, supported the Equal Rights Amendment and worked for its passage. In the spring of 1973, the amendment finally gained approval from both houses of Congress, and the fight for the ERA was transferred to the individual states, where a united movement rallied to its support.

Many small-group experiments in unstructured and leaderless organization had foundered over the years, and when small groups turned to political action, many also adopted more conventional forms and procedures. However, their commitment to egalitarianism, the emphasis on the development of each woman, and the opposition to hierarchy remained, a product of the heritage from the New Left and a consequence of sisterhood.

ORGANIZATIONS MULTIPLY

In the 1970's the number and diversity of organizations in the movement multiplied many times. Traditionally structured organizations as well as small informal groups were established to operate nationally, in the states, and in local communities. A recent study estimates that between eighty and one hundred thousand women had joined these organizations and groups by early 1973.[26]

Most numerous of these were consciousness-raising groups, usually made up of between five and twelve women, some sponsored by existing organizations, others springing up without any encouragement. They met in factories, offices, neighborhoods, schools, and campuses. The groups had varying life spans, but they often generated similar groups and frequently converted their members into active movement workers.

Women organized along occupational lines. Lawyers, doctors, sociologists, historians, chemists, teachers, and others set up groups to work against discrimination and to increase opportunities within their professions. Working women formed a variety of organizations, ranging from women's caucuses within existing unions to factory child-care committees.

Groups were formed for specific purposes—to teach women self-defense techniques, to improve and change health care, to change the churches, or to influence the way in which women are portrayed in children's books and in school curricula. Women organized to represent special interests. Welfare women were one of the earliest to come together.

Women united on ethnic, racial, and religious lines, on the basis of their sexual preference, marital status, and age.

And while new groups were being formed, many existing organizations were drawn into movement activities. Organizations like the League of Women Voters, The National Council of Negro Women, women's church societies endorsed the Equal Rights Amendment and turned their attention more and more to women's issues.

Minority women were among those who formed new organizations during the 1970's. In 1973, for example, the National Conference of Puerto Rican Women was established. Black women, too, were drawn into the movement. Movement issues that touched directly upon their lives as minority women and often as poor women—such as job discrimination, abortion, day care, educational opportunities, and the welfare system—were of special concern to them. However, black women's organizations extended their objectives beyond women's issues and, in a tradition that goes back to the nineteenth-century club movement, they included the needs of the entire black community within the scope of their groups.

In 1973, Black Women Organized for Action was

formed in San Francisco. As a Bay Area organization, BWOA published a monthly newsletter, what it is, ran a publishing firm, the Sapphire Publishing Company, and carried out an action program that involved black women in all facets of public life.

BLACK WOMEN ORGANIZED FOR ACTION

Who Are Black Women Organized for Action?

Old sisters, young sisters, skinny sisters, fat sisters . . . the poor and the not so poor . . . you and me . . . from blue black to high yellow. A bouquet of BLACK WOMEN—action oriented, composed of feminists and non-feminists concerned with the political and economic development of a total Black community. . . .

Statement of Purpose

We are *Black,* and therefore imbedded in our consciousness is commitment to the struggle of Black people for identity and involvement in decisions that affect our lives and the lives of generations of Black people who will follow us.

We are *Women,* and therefore aware of the blatant waste of the talents and energies of Black Women because this society has decreed a place for us.

We are *Organized,* because we recognize that only together, by pooling our talents and resources can we make major change in the institutions which have limited our opportunities and stifled our growth as human beings.

We are *For Action,* because we believe that the time for rhetoric is past; that the skills of Black women can best be put to use in a variety of ways to change the society; that, in the political world in which we live, involvement for Black women must go beyond the traditional fundraising and into the full gamut of activities that make up the political process which affects our lives in so many ways.[27]

The first national black feminist organization was also formed in 1973, and it issued this statement of purpose.

THE NATIONAL BLACK FEMINIST ORGANIZATION

The distorted male-dominated media image of the Women's Liberation Movement has clouded the vital and revolutionary importance of this movement to Third World women, especially black women. The Movement has been characterized as the exclusive property of so-called white middle-class women and any black women seen involved in this Movement have been seen as "selling out," "dividing the race," and an assortment of nonsensical epithets. Black feminists resent these charges and have therefore established The National Black Feminist Organization, in order to address ourselves to the particular and specific needs of the larger, but almost cast-aside half of the black race in Amerikkka, the black woman.

Black women have suffered cruelly in this society from living the phenomenon of being black and female, in a country that is *both* racist and sexist. There has been very little real examination of the damage it has caused on the lives and on the minds of black women. Because we live in a patriarchy, we have allowed a premium to be put on black male suffering. No one of us would minimize the pain or hardship or the cruel and inhumane treatment experienced by the black man. But history, past or present, rarely deals with the malicious abuse put upon the black woman. We were seen as breeders by the master; despised and historically polarized from/by the master's wife; and looked upon as castraters by our lovers and husbands. The black woman has had to be strong, yet we are persecuted for having survived. We have been called "matriarchs" by white racists and black nationalists; we have virtually no positive self-images to validate our existence. Black women want to be proud, dignified, and free from all those false definitions of beauty and womanhood that are unrealistic and unnatural. *We,* not white men or black men, must define our own self-image as black women and not fall into the mistake of being placed upon the pedestal which is even being rejected by white women. It has been hard for black women to emerge from the myriad of distorted images that have portrayed us as grinning Beulahs, castrating Sapphires, and pancake-box Jemimas. As black feminists we realized the need to establish ourselves as an independent black feminist organization. Our aboveground presence will lend enormous credibility to the current Women's Liberation Movement, which unfortunately is not seen as the serious political and economic revolutionary force that it is. We will strengthen the current efforts of the Black Liberation struggle in this country by encouraging *all* of the talents and creativities of black women to emerge, strong and beautiful, not to feel guilty or divisive, and assume positions of leadership and honor in the black community. We will encourage the black community to stop falling into the trap of the white male Left, utilizing women only in terms of domestic or servile needs. We will continue to remind the Black Liberation Movement that there can't be liberation for half the race. We must together, as a people, work to eliminate racism, from without the black community, which is trying to destroy us as an entire people; but we must remember that sexism is destroying and crippling us from within.[28]

Within El Partido de la Raza Unida (the Party of the United People, formed in 1970 by men and women with Spanish surnames), a feminist bloc was formed to give expression to the opinions and needs of women within the organization. The demands of the women, known as the Chicana

Caucus, were formalized and presented to the national convention of La Raza in 1972 in the following statement.

SOME DEMANDS OF CHICANA WOMEN

We, as *Chicanas,* are a vital part of the *Chicano* community. (We are workers, unemployed women, welfare recipients, housewives, students.) Therefore, we demand that we be heard and that the following resolutions be accepted.

Be it resolved that we, as *Chicanas,* will promote *la hermanidad* [sisterhood] concept in organizing *Chicanas.* As *hermanas,* we have a responsibility to help each other in problems that are common to all of us. . . .

Be it also resolved, that we as *Raza* must not condone, accept, or transfer the oppression of *La Chicana.*

That all *La Raza* literature should include *Chicana* written articles, poems, and other writings to relate the *Chicana* perspective in the *Chicano* movement.

That *Chicanas* be represented in all levels of *La Raza Unida* party and be run as candidates in all general, primary, and local elections.

Jobs

Whereas the *Chicana* on the job is subject to unbearable inhumane conditions, be it resolved that:

Chicanas receive equal pay for equal work; working conditions, particularly in the garment-factory sweatshops, be improved; *Chicanas* join unions and hold leadership positions within these unions; *Chicanas* be given the opportunity for promotions and be given free training to improve skills; there be maternity leaves with pay.

Prostitution

Whereas prostitution is used by a corrupt few to reap profits for themselves with no human consideration for the needs of *mujeres,* and *whereas* prostitutes are victims of an exploitative economic system and are not criminals, and *whereas* legalized prostitution is used as a means of employing poor women who are on welfare, be it resolved that:

(1) those who reap profits from prostitution be given heavy prison sentences and be made to pay large fines;

(2) that *mujeres* who are forced to prostitution not be condemned to serve prison sentences;

(3) that prostitution not be legalized.

Abortions

Whereas we, as *Chicanas,* have been subjected to illegal, dehumanizing, and unsafe abortions, let it be resolved that we endorse legalized medical abortions in order to protect the human right of self-determination. . . .

Community-Controlled Clinics

We resolve that more *Chicano* clinics (self-supporting) be implemented to service the *Chicano* community. . . .

Child-Care Centers

In order that women may leave their children in the hands of someone they trust and know will understand the cultural ways of their children, be it resolved that *Raza* child-care programs be established in *nuestros barrios.* . . . [29]

GOALS OF THE MOVEMENT: ECONOMIC CHANGE

As the movement developed in the 1970's, the agitation, lobbying, and educational work of its many components constituted an assault upon the major institutions of American society and a sweeping demand for change.

In various ways, the movement attacked the widespread poverty of women and demanded for them a fair share of the nation's wealth. In its struggles against job discrimination and for educational opportunities, the movement called for an end to the economic exploitation of females. To improve their economic status, women established and supported their own businesses (as diverse as printing shops, art galleries, and legal firms).

Among the many aspects of women's economic inferiority that came under scrutiny were the welfare system and its effect upon women, the absence of government regulations protecting household workers, and prostitution as a form of economic exploitation. The movement attacked the unpaid labor of wives as houseworkers and child rearers and sought a measure of social security coverage for housewives.

Added together, these efforts to end women's economic inferiority constituted a major challenge to existing economic institutions.

In 1974, the Coalition of Labor Union Women was founded to improve the condition of working women in unions and to organize non-unionized workers. Representing fifty-eight trade unions, in an atmosphere of enthusiasm more than three thousand women set up a new national organization, provided for the formation of local chapters, adopted a set of guidelines, and established a number of governing committees. It issued this statement of purpose.

LABOR UNION WOMEN

Of the 34 million women in the work force—little more than 4 million women are members of unions. It is imperative that within the framework of the union movement we take aggressive steps to more effectively address ourselves to the critical needs of 30 million unorganized sisters and to make our unions more responsive to the needs of all women, especially the needs of minority women who have traditionally been singled out for particularly blatant oppression. . . .

The primary purpose of this new national coalition is to unify all union women in a viable organization to determine, first—our common problems and concerns and, second—to develop action programs within the framework of our unions to deal effectively with our objectives. Through unity of purpose, the Coalition of Labor Union Women will seek to accomplish these goals. We recognize that our struggle goes beyond the borders of this nation and seek to link up with our working sisters and brothers throughout the world through concrete action of international workers' solidarity.

Organizing Unorganized Women

. . . The Coalition of Labor Union Women seeks to promote unionism and to encourage unions to be more aggressive in their efforts to bring unorganized women under collective bargaining agreements, particularly in those areas where there are large numbers of unorganized and/or minority women. . . .

Affirmative Action in the Work Place

Employers continue to profit by dividing workers on sexual, racial and age lines. . . . The Coalition will seek to encourage women, through their unions, to recognize and take positive action against job discrimination in hiring, promotion, classification and other aspects of work. Women must learn what their rights are under the law. We must become more knowledgeable of the specifics of collective bargaining; and of the contract clauses and workplace practices which discriminate against us. . . . We seek to educate and inspire our union brothers to help achieve affirmative action in the work place.

Political Action and Legislation

It is imperative that union women, through action programs of the Coalition become more active participants in the political and legislative processes of our unions. . . . Whenever or wherever possible, CLUW urges union women to seek election to public office or selection for governmental appointive office at local, county, state and national levels.

Participation of Women Within Their Unions

The Coalition seeks to inspire and educate union women to insure and strengthen our participation, to encourage our leadership and our movement into policy-making roles within our own unions and within the union movement in all areas. The Coalition supports the formation of women's

Gloria Steinem, Bella Abzug, Shirley Chisholm, Betty Friedan at National Women's Political Caucus News Conference. Washington, D.C., July 12, 1971

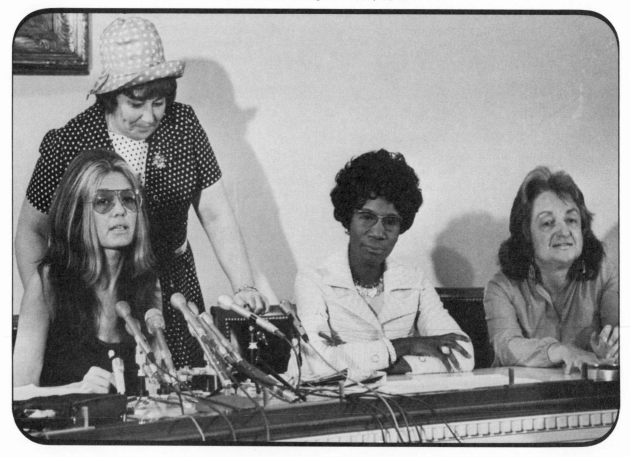

committees and women's caucuses within labor unions at all levels, wherever necessary. Additionally the Coalition will encourage democratic procedures in all unions.[30]

POLITICAL POWER

Seeking more power for women in the political life of the country, the contemporary movement has rejected the token role of women in the major political parties and has demanded a significant increase in the number of women on party committees and an effective role for them in determining party policies and goals.

Women's organizations have encouraged and supported female candidates for elective office. They have worked to arouse and organize women voters to support or oppose male candidates on the basis of their stands on issues of importance to women.

In July 1971, the National Women's Political Caucus was established by a nonpartisan group of women. Its goal was to unite women of different political convictions and backgrounds, to bring them together on the basis of common interests as women, and to organize them into an effective political force. Since 1971, Women's Political Caucuses have been set up in all but two states, in every major city, and in thousands of small communities. Women's Caucuses have also been formed within established political groups, including the major parties.

NATIONAL WOMEN'S POLITICAL CAUCUS: STATEMENT OF PURPOSE

• We believe that women must take action to unite against sexism, racism, institutional violence and poverty. We will:

• Rally national and local support for the campaigns of women candidates—federal, state, and local—who declare themselves ready to fight for the rights and needs of women, and of all under-represented groups.

• Confront our own party structures, and, when necessary, cross party lines or work outside formal political parties in support of such women.

• Train women to organize caucuses on a state and local level.

• Reform party structure to assure women of all ages, races and socio-economic groups equal voice in decision-making and selection of candidates at all levels—federal, state, county and precinct.

• Register new women voters and encourage women to vote for women's priorities.

• Raise women's issues in every election and publicize the records on such issues of all male and female candidates, so

that they shall be made to rise or fall on their position and action for human equality.

• Give active support only to those candidates for public or party office, whether male or female, who support women's issues and employ women in a decision-making position on their administrative and campaign staffs.

• Monitor the selection of delegates to the presidential nominating conventions for the purpose of challenging those delegations where the number and qualifications of the women delegates are unacceptable.

• Insist that there be no token female representation, that the women selected to give equal voice to women actually represent the views of women, and not merely to echo the unacceptable views of men.

• Draft and support legislation to meet the needs of women.

• Form coalitions with other oppressed groups and all humane groups which share the goals of fighting against racism, sexism, violence and poverty.[31]

NATIONAL WOMEN'S POLITICAL CAUCUS: ORGANIZING PROCEDURES

How to Begin

Individuals and groups should begin organizing immediately. If your state has a temporary coordinator . . . contact her. If not, check with the national office for names of others in your state who are interested or already at work. Begin by contacting women from existing political, social, and community groups so as to involve broad spectrums of interest and experience. . . . There are groups who might be dismissed as uninterested—try them first. Attempt to reach women who haven't been active at all—people who have been isolated in their homes, people in poverty, people at work. . . .

One Way to Launch a Caucus

Any number of methods might be used to bring together a local or state caucus. The following is a method already used in one state.

After contacting representatives . . . of organizations . . . arrange for a kick-off press conference to announce the establishment of a caucus and/or a state organizing meeting date. The objective is to give wide coverage to the formation of an NWPC which can communicate to women throughout an area or state. . . .

Hold the conference in the state capital, county seat, or some central location. Use written notices, followed up by a phone call, to invite local and state newspaper reporters and media. Also invite elected women officials, representatives of organizations contacted, and anyone else who might be interested. . . .

Once You Have Begun

After you have started a Caucus, make sure that your organizing activities continue to reach a broad cross-section of women in your state or community. Build a good relationship with the press and use publicity to create a climate of change and acceptance. Let the Caucus act as a catalyst for local and state action. The Caucus has a global job to do, but it is a job that MUST begin with the selection of specific and realizable goals at the *local* level. . . .

Ideally, you should work to enlist an organizer in every significant political unit—a person who has the time and energy to spend on the gut-work of politics:

—organizing door to door canvassing drives

—registering new voters

—working on fund raising

—involving new people, and

—communicating the long-range goals of the Caucus and following up contacts with specific short-range activities.

You can start electoral activities with involvement in local races. . . .

Electoral politics is one way to focus Caucus activity. Lobbying is another and should also be carefully planned. . . . Although the national office will keep you informed of legislative developments in Washington and will provide general position statements, it is important for the Caucus to establish contacts in all state legislatures and councils who will monitor legislation and keep information flowing to members. States might want to prepare a packet for lobbying state legislatures, with names of key committee members, outlines of Caucus positions, and suggestions for personal visits, phone calls, and letter writing. Lobbying is the steady application of pressure; as the Caucus builds its organization its capacity for applying pressure will increase. But, in lobbying, one letter from one individual counts too. It is the task of the Caucus to inform women on the issues—local, state, and national—and to help them act on the information.[32]

SOCIAL CHANGE

Since the late 1960's, radical segments of the contemporary movement have demanded drastic and extensive social change: they have attacked traditional heterosexual relations as exploitative of women, challenged women's roles as mothers and wives, and rejected the nuclear family. Indirectly, and less dramatically, more moderate components of the movement have also called for social reform. In demanding an end to sex discrimination and in striving for women's economic independence, the current movement has, in fact, challenged a social system that rests upon women's economic dependency and inferiority. Thus, the original, apparently limited and moderate demands of organizations like the National Organization for Women for equal rights in employment and education have, over the years, been understood to carry profound implications for society: social institutions, like the nuclear family, which have been built upon women's economic

No More Fun and Games, *July 1971*

dependence and subjection, must of necessity change when that dependence and subjection disappear.

Among the earliest objectives of the current movement was the demand for reproductive freedom: women fought for their right to abortion and for safe and accessible abortion facilities; they continued the demand for reliable contraception; they attacked the concept and practice of forced sterilization; they organized to protect themselves against rape. Collectively, these efforts aimed to give women control over their own bodies and over reproduction, both of which traditionally have been regulated by civil and religious laws written by men.

The contemporary movement also sought changes in the system of child care, lobbying for government support for public child-care centers; it established cooperative centers of its own, and challenged the view that child care is a private and necessarily female responsibility.

The movement also focused on the process by which society prepares women (and men) for traditional sex roles and behavior; and it has tried to change the image of women that functions as an example of admirable and acceptable female behavior and plays an important part in the socialization of children.

Thus, women's groups have opposed the usual portrayal of women in the popular media, in children's literature, and in the historical record. They have rejected the image of women as primarily and necessarily sexual objects for men, as mothers of children, and as passive observers in human history. And they have tried, through pressure on the advertising industry, publishers, and educators, to promote a new image.

Unlike earlier phases of the women's movement, the contemporary movement directly and explicitly confronted the subject of sex. It has examined, discussed, and debated the nature of female sexuality and heterosexual and homosexual relationships. Beginning in the consciousness raising groups, the exploration of female sexuality was also stimulated and provoked by the ideas of radical lesbian women within the movement. Arguing that private heterosexual relations inevitably reflected the power relationships of the larger society and necessarily exploited women, radical lesbians proposed that only homosexuality could provide women with sexual relations that were not oppressive and exploitative.

In response to problems discussed in consciousness raising and to the radical lesbian analysis, the contemporary movement commenced a serious exploration into the nature of female sexuality, the most widespread discussion of the subject in modern times. It has questioned contempo-

rary views of women's sexuality, called for new biological and psychological research, and exposed hidden assumptions about female sexuality that underlay the functioning of institutions such as marriage, the family, the church, and the school.

This concern with female sexuality attracted the attention of the media, which focused upon disagreements between radical lesbians and heterosexual women and emphasized the most spectacular aspects of a broad and serious examination. The media also ignored a large area of agreement about sex within the movement. For in attacking the sex-role system (which defines both women and men and limits them accordingly to certain roles, relationships, and behavior), in seeking control over their own bodies and over reproduction, in fighting prostitution and rape, the contemporary women's movement has repudiated a double standard for sexual behavior and has claimed a new area of freedom for women—sexual freedom.

Women's groups have worked to change the stereotype of feminine behavior, attacking the common portrayal of women in books, in magazines, on television, and in adver-

"Hire him. He's got great legs."

If women thought this way about men they would be awfully silly.

When men think this way about women they're silly, too.

Women should be judged for a job by whether or not they can do it.

In a world where women are doctors, lawyers, judges, brokers, economists, scientists, political candidates, professors and company presidents, any other viewpoint is ridiculous.

Think of it this way. When we need all the help we can get, why waste half the brains around?

Womanpower. It's much too good to waste.

For information: NOW Legal Defense and Education Fund, Box PSAC, 9 West 57 Street, New York, New York 10019

tisements. In contrast, they promote a view of women that emphasizes their ability to function successfully in what has been man's world.

The attempt to create a new image of women has taken many shapes, among them an advertising campaign by NOW and studies of children's school books.

The campaign against abortion laws began almost as soon as the women's movement revived in the late 1960's. Small groups as well as some of the structured organizations lobbied against restrictive abortion laws.

In March 1969, Redstockings in New York held an unusual public meeting, at which twelve women calmly described their own experiences with abortion to a large audience. It was a startling way to demonstrate that women had knowledge about abortion and the right to be concerned with abortion laws, both of which had often been denied by male legislators.

Slowly, through this kind of action, through mass demonstations, and by hard, patient lobbying and testimony, women made abortion a public issue and a women's issue. In 1971, the Women's National Abortion Coalition was formed to unite all the separated and varied efforts under one aegis.

WOMEN'S NATIONAL ABORTION CONFERENCE

. . . We believe that the most democratic way we could launch a national campaign for the repeal of all abortion laws would be to move quickly to hold a national women's conference on abortion. We want to gather the growing numbers of women who are eager to get involved—Black, Chicana, Latina, Asian, Puerto Rican and Native American women, campus women, gay women, high school students, housewives, professional, welfare and working women, young women and older women, women from churches, political organizations, trade unions, the military and communities across the country—and together decide on a course of action that can best win the repeal of all abortion laws with no forced sterilization. We will also be concerned with the repeal of restrictive contraception laws that exist in 30 states.

At a national conference we can both share information and experiences and discuss proposals for action. Women

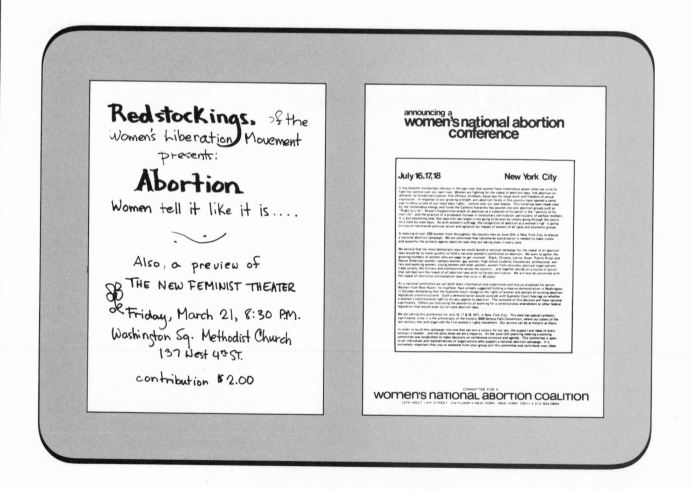

effort to increase control over their own bodies and lives. With the specific needs of women in mind, they established feminist health centers to provide health and medical services as well as counseling and referrals.

FEMINIST WOMEN'S HEALTH CENTER

The FEMINIST WOMEN'S HEALTH CENTER is a non-profit corporation that was formed to provide high quality medical care at reasonable prices for all women. We are presently involved in community educational programs as well as providing the facilities where the finest medical care possible in the most supportive atmosphere can be provided. . . .

Self-Help Clinic

The SELF-HELP CLINIC is a meeting where women learn self-examination and share experiences about health care. . . . Through education women can learn how to take a more active part in medical examinations and make each doctor's visit more profitable for themselves as well as for the doctor.

Pregnancy Screening

Free PREGNANCY SCREENING is available for all women. We feel it is important for women to determine pregnancy as soon as possible. . . .

Pregnancy Counseling

For interested women, information about abortion, childbirth, and birth control is available. Alternatives are explained. The ultimate decision is in the hands of the women.

Referrals

There is a complete referral list for women interested in finding a gynecologist, an obstetrician, a pediatrician, or any type doctor or clinic.

The Abortion Clinic

The Feminist Women's Health Center's Women's Choice Clinics will be more than a facility for doing abortions. When a woman dials our number, . . . she will be greeted by a woman knowledgeable about abortions and sympathetic to her situation and willing to offer as much or as little information as desired. Through this phone conversation women will be scheduled for free pregnancy screening if necessary or for an abortion. The woman will be accompanied through the entire process including the abortion itself by a woman counselor.

The health center will also arrange for transportation and childcare etc. It is our strong feeling that much of the difficulty in obtaining an abortion can be effectively dealt with in a practical way.

The abortion a woman receives is non-traumatic, done under local anesthetic with a flexible plastic cannula which entails a minimal amount of dilatation. For women requiring

From Feminist Health Center pamphlet

from New Haven, for example, have already suggested holding a massive demonstration in Washington in October demanding that the Supreme Court recognize the rights of women and declare all existing abortion legislation unconstitutional. Such a demonstration would coincide with Supreme Court hearings on whether a woman's constitutional right to privacy applies to abortion. The outcome of this decision will have national significance. Others are discussing the possibility of working for a constitutional amendment or other federal legislation that would wipe out all state abortion laws.

We are calling this conference for July 16, 17 & 18, 1971, in New York City. This date has special symbolic significance, since it is the anniversary of the historic 1848 Seneca Falls Convention, where our sisters of the last century met and organized the first women's rights movement. Our actions can be as historic as theirs. . . . [34]

In many states, women organized to introduce changes and innovations into traditional health care as part of the

Rhogam it is included in the price as well as all medication, aftercare information and check-up, and birth control.

Women's Clinic

The FEMINIST WOMEN'S HEALTH CENTER WOMEN'S CLINIC deals generally with the needs of the women in the community. We provide general screening services for venereal disease, sickle cell anemia, pap smears, pregnancy, vaginal infections, birth control, etc. If diagnosis warrants a treatment not available through our services, we have referrals for the needed treatment.

Family Planning as a Community Educational Experience

The Feminist Women's Health Center offers two types of Family Planning. The first is the conventional form, one doctor spending approximately fifteen minutes per woman on an individual basis. The second is a form of Family Planning conceived by Carol Downer of Los Angeles. Women meet in groups and experience a self-help clinic. Women learn to use the speculum and share experiences about health care and birth control. The doctor inserts IUD's in groups and women are there to see how it happens and also to lend support, if necessary, to the patient. Diaphragms are fitted and pills are prescribed. Often times these women form on-going self-help clinics and follow closely what happens to their bodies.

Sterilization

We feel that each individual has the right to decide whether or not to have children as well as the number of children. We offer counseling and referral for anyone interested in voluntary sterilization.[35]

to be a self-defined individual. We declare the necessity for all women to discover and use the potentials and resources which exist in themselves and each other. We assert the right of every woman to express herself with her body, intellect and emotions as the complete human being that society has discouraged her from being. We assert the right of every woman to express her sexuality in any way she chooses as an affirmation of her individuality. We declare our intention to confront and disarm the attitudes and institutions that attempt to limit these rights.

We foresee the day when all individuals are free to define themselves in a non-sexist society. However, our present oppression as Lesbians and as women, makes it imperative that we not content ourselves with this utopian vision. Because the achievement of our liberation as gay people would leave us still oppressed as women, we recognize that our primary strength is in feminism. Feminism is not so much a given set of specific issues as it is a way of life which considers as primary our identities as women. As Lesbian-feminists the focus of all our thoughts and actions centers on our identities as Lesbian women. Now we must dedicate our energies primarily to discovering ourselves and our special causes, and, acting as our own spokeswomen, to promoting ourselves everywhere, at all times, as Lesbian women. To this end, it is crucial that we function as an organization distinct from both the gay and feminist movements, unique unto ourselves, yet making coalitions with groups on gay and feminist issues specifically as they relate to our Lesbian identities.

Our feminism and our Lesbianism fuse in our love and respect for women. We are determined to live as we see fit, with other women, in pride and dignity.[36]

SEXUAL FREEDOM

During the 1970's, homosexuals, male and female, began an open struggle against legislation that restricted and discriminated against them. Feminist lesbians, protesting dual discrimination as lesbians and as women, organized to work for freedom of sexual preference. Through political pressure and agitation and a campaign to create public understanding, they sought legal changes, protection of their civil rights, and changing attitudes toward lesbianism.

One of many organizations formed was Lesbian Feminist Liberation. Its 1973 constitution had this preamble:

CONSTITUTION OF LESBIAN FEMINIST LIBERATION

We, Lesbian Feminist Liberation, dedicate ourselves to promoting our identities as Lesbians and combating sexism as it manifests itself in heterosexual chauvinism and male supremacy.

We as Lesbian-feminists assert the right of every woman

Lesbians also called for support from the women's movement. They received a mixed response. In 1970, the National Organization for Women was divided between those who feared the controversial issue would hurt the movement and cripple its effectiveness and those who pressed for support of lesbians and a clear defense of freedom of sexual preference.

As the years passed, the organized women's movement slowly extended more support to lesbians. In 1971, the National Conference of NOW adopted this resolution.

Be it resolved that a woman's right to her own person includes the right to define and express her own sexuality and to choose her own lifestyle.[37]

In 1973, the National Conference of NOW adopted the following:

RESOLUTION ON SEXUALITY AND LESBIANISM

Whereas, women have the basic right to develop to the maximum their full human sexual potential, and

Whereas, diversity is richly human and all women must be able to freely define and to express their own sexuality and to choose their own life style, and

Whereas, NOW's public relations and communications have omitted references to the unified efforts of women of traditional and diverse sexual experience, and

Whereas, Lesbians have formed a caucus in NOW to communicate openly, without fear and hostility, and

Whereas, the threat traditionally felt from Lesbianism must no longer be a barrier to open communication between all people, and

Whereas, we recognize that women are all oppressed by one common oppression, and therefore, surely we must not oppress one another for any reason;

Therefore be it resolved that a statement adopting the sense of this resolution be included in all appropriate NOW publicatons and policy statements; and,

Be it further resolved that NOW actively introduce and support civil rights legislation designed to end discrimination based on sexual orientation and to introduce with legislation to end discrimination based on sex the phrase ''sexual orientation'' in areas such as, but not limited to, housing, unemployment, credit, finance, child custody and public accommodations. [38]

In February 1975, Ms. *magazine published this petition for sexual freedom which was signed by more than one hundred prominent women representing diverse fields and interests, such as Congresswomen Bella S. Abzug and Shirley Chisholm, actresses Joanne Woodward and Lily Tomlin, writers Anaïs Nin and Joyce Carol Oates, scholar Margaret Mead, and the Reverend Carter Heyward.*

"A PETITION FOR SANITY"

We, the undersigned, wish to state publicly our opposition to an archaic practice that is still alive in this country: the attempt by government to interfere in the sexual lives of consenting adults, and the failure by government to protect the civil rights of people who suffer such interference from others.

We believe all people to have common cause in eliminating this practice. Though laws and regulations governing private sexual behavior tend to be selectively enforced against lesbians and male homosexuals—particularly from poor, minority and politicaly unpopular groups—they potentially affect every person, regardless of personal power or sexual orientation. Not only do these laws and regulations leave privacy and individual freedom to the whim of employers and legislators, landlords and judges, but their enforcement results in a tragic waste of human talent. Even when not enforced, their existence serves to inhibit the free choice of lifestyle.

Therefore, we urge every person, regardless of race, age,

class, sex or sexual orientation, to join us in establishing this fundamental right to privacy and individual freedom.

As feminists, we sign this petition for one additional reason. In the history of women's struggle for self-determination, it has been a painful fact that almost any woman who did not choose to play a traditional or secondary role might find herself labeled a lesbian, and restricted in her efforts for fear of the effects of that label. Indeed, even the Women's Movement itself has sometimes been divided and weakened by this fear. Therefore, we must unite on the issue of *all* women's rights to a free choice of lifestyle regardless of sexual orientation. Only when the word *lesbian* has lost its power to intimidate and oppress, when it is as positive as other human choices, can each individual woman be fearless and free.

As women and as feminists, we pledge to work toward the following goals which we believe will benefit all citizens:

1. The repeal of all regulations and the elimination of institutional practices that limit access to employment, housing, public accommodations, credit, government or military service and child custody because of sexual orientation.

2. The repeal of all laws that make sexual acts between consenting adults criminal.

3. The passage of legislation that will guarantee each individual's rights, regardless of sexual orientation, so that those who suffer discriminaion for that reason will have the same access to redress as do the victims of discrimination because of race, sex, religion or national origin.

4. The creation of a social climate in which lifestyles may be freely chosen.

THIS STATEMENT AND ITS LIST OF SIGNERS WILL BE SENT TO THE UNITED STATES CONGRESS, STATE LEGISLATURES, AND THE WHITE HOUSE; TO NATIONAL GROUPS ALREADY FIGHTING FOR SUCH CHANGES; AND TO WOMEN'S GROUPS IN OTHER COUNTRIES THAT MAY BE ORGANIZING SIMILAR CAMPAIGNS. IF YOU WOULD LIKE TO BE INCLUDED, PLEASE FILL IN THE SPACE BELOW AND SEND TO WOMEN'S PETITION FOR SANITY, MS. MAGAZINE, 370 LEXINGTON AVENUE, NEW YORK, NEW YORK 10017. . . . [39]

THE CONTEMPORARY MOVEMENT

Within less than a decade, the contemporary women's movement has developed and changed with surprising rapidity. This is illustrated by the history of NOW, formed in 1966. Then, NOW was concerned primarily with legislative and judicial reforms to combat discrimination against women in education and employment. NOW members hesitated and debated before affirming that abortion was a women's rights issue and adding abortion reform to its objectives. In contrast, in 1973, NOW had task forces working in the following areas: women and the arts; child care; employment discrimination; discrimination in educa-

tion; discrimination in consumer finance; the relationship between education and women's roles; the portrayal of women by the media; women's health and control of their bodies; women and unions; marriage, divorce, and family relations; the masculine mystique; minority women and women's rights; older women; women in politics; women and poverty; rape; religion, reproduction, and population; sexuality and lesbianism; women and sports; women as stockholders; women and taxes; and women as volunteers.

At their national conventions in 1973 and 1974, NOW members adopted resolutions such as these:

RESOLUTION ON POVERTY

Whereas, NOW has consistently affirmed its commitment to improving the economic "survivability" of women by adopting resolutions on equal pay, minimum wages, child care, welfare, job expansion, etc., at each national conference, and

Whereas, poverty is a "woman's issue" (since nearly two-thirds of those living in poverty are women) . . .

Whereas, resolutions without implementing action do nothing to change the desperate plight of women,

Therefore be it resolved that the National Conference designate 1973 as NOW's Action Year Against Poverty, during which all NOW chapters, task forces (national and local) and members are strongly urged to focus their activities on strategies and actions to dramatize the problems of women in poverty and effect meaningful changes in the economic status of all women, and . . .

Be it further resolved that the top four legislative priorities for NOW in 1973 be

a) Revision of the Fair Labor Standards Act and similar state laws to provide for a minimum wage of at least $2.50 per hour, and extension of coverage under FLSA to include all workers, including domestics. . . .

b) Passage of a comprehensive child development program. . . .

c) A complete overhaul of the welfare program to provide for federalization of welfare in order to eliminate variations in requirements and payments, assurances that no custodial guardian or parent of pre-school or school age children will be required to work outside of the home and provision of supportive services including realistic job training.

d) Passage of legislation to provide for a full employment program for the U.S. in which private industry and the public sector expand opportunities for work for all. . . . [40]

RESOLUTION ON NEEDS OF MINORITY PERSONS

Whereas, it is vital to the future growth and development of the organization to broaden its areas of concern in order to include those who are *doubly* oppressed,

Whereas, the present image of NOW is not perceived by minority persons as that of an organization working toward objectives relevant to their needs and concerns, and

Whereas, this image is a critical factor alienating many members of minority groups from this organization, and

Whereas, NOW's Statement of Purpose clearly defines the organization's dedication to work on behalf of all those who are oppressed,

Therefore be it resolved that a national organizational effort be mounted immediately within NOW on behalf of the needs of *all* minority persons, and that the following actions be undertaken towards the immediate elimination of structures, policies, and practices within NOW which tend to inhibit the participation of minority persons. The following affirmative action program is therefore recommended:

1) NOW should again condemn the policies of the Nixon administration as not being in the interest of minorities.

2) NOW should actively protest the dismantling of the OEO programs and the massive budgetary cuts to social service programs.

3) NOW, at both national and local levels, should take whatever action necessary to apply effective pressure upon state and local governments to implement the distribution of revenue-sharing funds for social services.

4) NOW, at both the national and local levels, should institute a sliding scale, starting with $0.00, for the payment of dues and conference fees to facilitate the participation of [people of] lower economic status and the working poor.

5) Local NOW chapter meetings should be held accessible to minority persons with limited mobility and transportation.

6) Local NOW chapter meetings should include facilities for child care.

7) A deliberate effort should be undertaken to recruit minority members.

8) In support of Mexican-American sisters, NOW should endorse the United Farm Workers' Boycott of California-Arizona lettuce and Guild Brandy. . . . [41]

RESOLUTION ON SPORTS

Be it resolved that NOW opposes and actively works to eliminate all forms of discrimination against women and girls in recreation and sport, including school/college/community physical education and recreation programs and facilities, school/college/community sponsored or recognized athletic and recreation programs, amateur and professional athletics, and media coverage and employment, and that a Task Force be created to establish goals and actions to implement sports policies, and

Be it further resolved that NOW actively support the efforts of women engaged in or seeking employment in professional athletics or an occupation (such as media coverage of sport activities) to secure equal pay, prize money, status, self-determination, policy-making positions, promotional opportunities, and equal and unbiased media coverage of women's sports actvities by both women and men and furthermore, that NOW actively work to change the currently existing negative image of women engaged in sports as created and perpetuated by the media and advertising fields.[42]

RESOLUTION ON OLDER WOMEN

Whereas, sexism is compounded with ageism as a woman grows older, and women experience the negative effects of age discrimination at an earlier age, so that there is a double standard of aging in our society . . .

Whereas, women live longer than men (average life expectancy for males is 67 years, for females, 74 years) and women greatly outnumber men in later years (1,000 elderly women to 722 men), and the outlook is for continued growth of the older population, with a declining ratio of men to women . . .

Whereas, technological and social changes continue to erode the jobs, status and social role of older persons, especially women (such as the decline of the family farm and extended family), thereby increasing the dependency of older persons, with the consequent feeling of uselessness . . .

Whereas, aging is a hush-hush subject except as a "social problem" . . .

Whereas, many older women who accepted the social dictum of marriage as a career now find themselves suddenly forced to fend for themselves, or are threatened with that eventuality . . .

Whereas, jobs are as important to older people as to any other segment of the population and for the same reasons. . . . And older women experience virulent job discrimination . . .

Whereas, menopause is another hush-hush subject that has been brushed aside by the male-dominated medical profession, and myths of raging hormones go unchallenged by research (except recently by feminists) . . .

Whereas, the sexuality of middle-aged and elderly women has been consistently denied, ignored, derided, feared, and poorly understood. It is socially acceptable for older men to pair off with younger women, while the reverse is ridiculed (despite the fact that male sexuality is known to peak at a much younger age than female sexuality). Moral standards for sexual behavior have changed for everyone except older women, while, at the same time, many women are forced, against their will, to live without benefit of marriage, because of social security penalties and punitive wills. While the bachelor is sought after, the "spinster" is still shunned . . .

Whereas, in order to achieve our feminist goals we need to build a personhood that crosses age barriers and bridges generation gaps, as well as one that helps to overcome racial, ethnic, religious and class differences, all of which serve to keep us separate and powerless . . .

Whereas, we will all get old, if we live so long . . .

BE IT THEREFORE RESOLVED

That we affirm the positive values that maturity brings, the relevance of our life experience, and we are detemined to combat ageism in its many manifestations . . .

That we support more equitable social security for women. While we work for immediate increases and against inequities, we advocate more basic changes, such as recognition of the financial value of non-paid work in the home and community by allowing women to accumulate credits under the social security system in their own names (women should be eligible for income maintenance because they have earned it, not because they are dependents) . . .

That we demand the right to earn a livelihood and to be economically independent. We will combat age discrimination in employment by working for enforcement of existing legislation (such as the Age Discrimination in Employment Act of 1967) while working to include proscriptions against age discrimination in other legislation designed to provide equal opportunity for all persons . . .

That we demand government funded programs providing decent jobs for older women to replace women now exploited as volunteers . . .

That we recognize and encourage as many choices for older women as for any others: in housing, in life style, in sex, in sexual orientation, in education, in recreation.

That we recognize that many older women have invested years of (non-paid) labor in marriage, with expectation of social and economic security in their futures. We will work to protect their interests as divorce laws and customs change, so that they do not become victims of unwelcomed "liberation" . . .

That we will work for a more humane health delivery system that will value a person's well-being at any age. Specifically, we seek alternatives to profit-run nursing homes, and meanwhile will work for more stringent regulations of current ones. We seek financially supported research by feminists on menopause, preventive medicine and creative aging . . .

That we demand a voice in all the institutions that "serve" us, and treatment as full human beings, without condescension . . .

That we strongly urge local chapters to organize local task forces to raise the consciousness both inside and outside of NOW to the problems of ageism and the older women, as well as to implement programs based on the above,

That we demand that the Board designate an employee of the National Office to work full time on implementing the

U.S. DEPARTMENT OF LABOR
EMPLOYMENT STANDARDS ADMINISTRATION

WOMEN'S BUREAU
WASHINGTON, D.C. 20210

Employed Women in Selected Occupations
1973 Annual Averages

Occupations	Employed women (in thousands)	Percent distribution	Women as percent of total employed
Total	32,446	100.0	38.4
White collar workers	19,681	60.7	48.7
Professional and technical	1/ 4,711	1/ 14.5	40.0
Accountants	162	0.5	21.6
Computer specialists	56	0.2	16.5
Librarian, archivists & curators	122	0.4	82.1
Personnel & labor relations workers	104	0.3	33.7
Physicians	62	0.1	12.2
Registered nurses	805	2.5	97.8
Health technologists & technicians	236	0.7	71.5
Social workers	161	0.5	60.8
Teachers, college & university	133	0.4	27.1
Teachers, Exc. college & univ.	2,030	6.3	69.9
Elementary school teachers	1,094	3.4	84.5
Kindergarten & prekindergarten teachers	13	0.6	97.9
Secondary school teachers	565	1.7	49.5
Engineering & science tech	87	0.3	10.2
Writers, artists & entertainers	312	1.0	33.6
Managers and Administrators	1/ 1,590	1/ 4.9	18.4
Bank officials & financial mgr.	99	0.3	19.4
Buyers & purchasing agents	95	0.3	25.1
Restaurant, cafeteria & bar managers	160	0.5	32.4
Sales managers & deparment heads, retail trade	94	0.3	28.9
School administrators	90	0.3	29.0
Sales Workers	1/ 2,240	1/ 6.9	41.4
Hucksters and peddlers	166	0.5	77.2
Insurance agents, brokers & underwriters	61	0.2	12.9
Real estate agents & brokers	142	0.4	36.4
Sales clerks, retail trade	1,561	4.8	69.0
Clerical Workers	1/ 11,140	1/ 34.3	76.6
Bank tellers	293	0.9	89.9
Billing clerks	137	0.4	83.0
Bookkeepers	1,466	4.5	88.3
Cashiers	900	2.8	86.7
Counter clerks, exc. food	266	0.8	76.2
Estimators & investigators, nec.	164	0.5	49.5
File clerks	245	0.8	86.3
Computers & peripheral equip. operators	87	0.3	40.3
Keypunch operators	230	0.7	90.9
Payroll & timekeeping clerks	143	0.4	72.2
Postal clerks	81	0.2	26.9
Receptionists	431	1.3	96.9
Secretaries	3,037	9.4	99.1
Shipping & receiving clerks	66	0.2	14.4
Statistical clerks	204	0.6	68.5
Stock clerks & storekeepers	120	0.4	25.2
Teachers aids, exc. school monitors	207	0.6	90.4
Telephone operators	372	1.1	95.7
Typists	999	3.1	96.6

Blue Collar Workers	5,243	16.2	17.6
Craft and kindred workers	1/ 463	1/ 1.4	4.1
Blue collar worker supervisors, n.e.c.	109	0.3	7.5
Printing craft workers	68	0.2	17.0
Operatives	1/ 4,482	1/ 13.8	31.4
Assemblers	600	1.8	49.7
Checkers, examiners & inspectors, Manufacturing	377	1.2	49.5
Clothing ironers & pressers	118	0.4	77.1
Laundry & dry cleaning operators, n.e.c.	112	0.3	63.3
Packers & wrappers, n.e.c.	420	1.3	61.5
Sewers and stitchers	891	2.7	95.5
Textile operatives	240	0.7	56.9
Bus drivers	97	0.3	36.6
Nonfarm laborers	1/ 299	1/ 0.9	6.9
Stockhandlers	130	0.4	17.3
Service Workers	7,008	21.6	63.0
Private Household Workers	1/ 1,330	1/ 4.1	98.3
Child care workers	532	1.6	98.3
Cleaners and servants	631	1.9	98.3
Service workers, exc. private household	1/ 5,678	1/ 17.5	58.1
Cleaning service workers	707	2.2	34.1
Lodging quarters cleaners	196	0.6	96.6
Building interior cleaners, n.e.c.	358	1.1	54.2
Janitors and sextons	153	0.5	12.6
Food service workers	2,370	7.3	69.7
Bartenders	65	0.2	30.2
Cooks	555	1.7	59.8
Dishwashers	74	0.2	37.8
Food counter & fountain workers	254	0.8	80.9
Waiters and waiter's assistants	1,082	3.3	82.9
Health service workers	1,398	4.3	87.6
Health aids & trainees, exc. nursing	150	0.5	82.4
Nursing aids, orderlies & attendants	790	2.4	83.9
Practical nurses	345	1.1	96.4
Personal service workers	1,140	3.5	73.9
Child care workers	342	1.1	95.5
Hairdressers and cosmetologists	458	1.4	91.8

Farm Workers	513	1.6	16.9
Farmers and farm managers	1/ 103	1/ 0.3	6.2
Farm laborers and supervisors	411	1.3	30.2
Farm laborers, wage workers	137	0.4	11.1
Farm laborers, unpaid family workers	270	0.8	66.3

Source: U.S. Department of Labor, Bureau of Labor Statistics (unpublished)
1/ Totals include women employed in occupations not separately listed

mandate of NOW conferences on women in poverty resolutions, including older women.[43]

RESOLUTION ON TRADITIONALLY FEMALE JOBS

. . . be it resolved . . .

That the National Organization for Women particularly focus on improving the image of and status of women who choose to work in the home by action such as:

1) Designing legislation which would guarantee all homemakers, married and unmarried, female or male —an income,

2) Designing legislation which would guarantee that homemakers receive social security benefits in their own right rather than receiving a portion of their spouse's (which they can't even collect if divorced, unless they had been married 20 years before the divorce),

3) Designing public education programs which would teach that working in the home is a vocation which requires not only hard work but also managerial, technical and nurturing skills, thereby refuting the image of the homemaker presented by the media, and

4) Educating employers to recognize that women who return to work after spending some years working in the home are not inexperienced and unskilled.[44]

RESOLUTION ON RAPE

Resolved, by the National Organization for Women, as follows:

A. Review of the existing rape laws have found these laws to deter rather than facilitate convictions of rapists by:

1. Protecting the rights of the accused more than they seek to protect the physical integrity and freedom of movement of victims themselves.

2. Being overly solicitous of the accused, and overly suspicious of the complainant.

3. Containing overly stringent rules of evidence which impede convictions, by:

  a. containing "consent" standards which define rape in terms of the victim's frame of mind;

  b. regarding the nonmarital sexual activity of the accused as being irrelevant, yet allowing the impugning of the victim's credibility based on such activity.

4. Imposing penalties not in keeping with the particular acts of the crime, thus deterring judges and juries from convicting.

5. Placing a web of formal and informal restraints upon police and prosecutors in pursuing and obtaining the prosecution and conviction of rapists.

B. Reevaluation and restructuring of rape laws being indisputedly necessary, we propose the following model legislative and procedural changes. . . .

GOAL: To revise the present laws which overwhelmingly favor the defendant; impede convictions; allow victims, as witnesses, to be treated in a manner which is both humiliating and damaging to their emotional health; and which further discourages victims from reporting the crime to the officials.

1. To revise the present rules of evidence which places the victim in the position of being on trial, instead of the accused.

2. To eliminate the life imprisonment penalty except in cases where the victim met with death, permanent bodily injury, permanent mental impairment, and in cases of conviction for the third offense, and

   a) To attain a general lowering of penalties, except in gang rapes, to fit the severity of the crime, thus making convictions more possible. . . .

   b) To require that parole be granted only after the serving of one year for the first offense and five years for the second offense, with intensive rehabilitative counseling. In the absence of such counseling, a term of not less than four years must be served prior to the granting of parole.

3. To redefine "rape" to include oral and anal sodomy and penetration by instrument or device, thereby protecting women from any form of sexual humiliation and extending equal protection under the rape laws to men as well as women.

4. To broaden the law to permit the prosecution for rape by a spouse in the case of non-consent of a spouse to sexual intercourse, when the couple are living separate and apart and one has filed for a divorce or separate maintenance. . . . [45]

[The resolution also contained a proposal for methods of action and a model rape law.]

———

Together in the women's movement today are a large number of different women's organizations as well as mil-lions of individual women who are linked to the movement by modern communications media and who can participate without joining organizations. In earlier times, organizational membership and activity was necessarily the principal means of carrying on the struggle for equality and independence. Women needed the confidence and mutual support that groups afforded, and there were few alternatives to organized action. Today, the mass media not only spread information about the movement very widely and with great rapidity, but also put women in touch with movement leaders and spokespersons and show ways in which any individual can take a stand on women's issues in everyday life, at home and at work.

There are many different points of view and many different emphases within the contemporary movement. There are, for example, those who believe that equality for women can be achieved only by ending capitalism, or the family structure, or women's role as childbearers, or all heterosexual sex. In contrast, there are those who support specific limited reforms, who oppose economic discrimination, support free abortions, or work for vocational education for women, but who staunchly defend the nuclear family, women's role as mothers and housewives, or the existing economic system.

Thus far, there has been room for such diverse views—and many others. The multiplicity of organizations and groups, the ease with which new ideas are exchanged, and a changing and growing ideology have broadened rather than narrowed the scope of the movement. Thus, despite its complexity and lack of unanimity, the current movement seemed to operate in the early 1970's as an effective coalition, propelled in part by a strong sense of common cause and an exhilarating feeling of sisterhood. But this most recent phase of the women's movement is less than a decade old, and its accomplishments as well as its history await the future.

NOTES
BIBLIOGRAPHY
ACKNOWLEDGMENTS

NOTES

Chapter One

1. Anna Hallowell, *James and Lucretia Mott: Life and Letters* (Boston: Houghton Mifflin, 1896), p. 445.

2. Keith E. Melder, *The Beginnings of the Women's Rights Movement in the United States: 1800–1840* (Ann Arbor, Mich.: University Microfilms, 1974), p. 147.

3. *Fourth Annual Report of the Philadelphia Female Anti-Slavery Society, January 11, 1838* (Philadelphia: Merrihew and Gunn, 1838), pp. 13–16.

4. *The Liberator,* October 15, 1836.

5. *The Liberator,* January 2, 1837.

6. *Human Rights,* reprinted in *The Liberator,* January 21, 1837.

7. *The Liberator,* August 4, 1837.

8. *The Liberator,* June 16, 1837.

9. *National Enquirer,* reprinted in *The Liberator,* March 4, 1837.

10. *New York Commercial Advertiser,* May 17, 1837, reprinted in *The Liberator,* June 2, 1837.

11. *Fourth Annual Report of the Philadelphia Female Anti-Slavery Society,* pp. 4–6.

12. Letter, dated May 6, 1837, printed by permission of the Western Reserve Historical Society, Cleveland, Ohio.

13. Angelina Grimké, *An Appeal to the Christian Women of the South* (New York: American Anti-Slavery Society, 1836), pp. 16–19, 21, 22.

14. "Pastoral Letter of the General Association of Massachusetts to the Congregational Churches under Their Care," reprinted in *The Liberator,* August 11, 1837.

15. John Quincy Adams, *Speech of John Quincy Adams of Massachusetts, upon the Right of the People, Men and Women to Petition; on the Freedom of Speech and of Debate in the House of Representatives of the United States; . . . and the Petitions of More Than One Hundred Thousand Petitioners, Relating to Annexation of Texas to This Union* (Washington, D.C.: Gates and Seaton, 1838), pp. 65, 67–8.

16. *The Liberator,* August 25, 1837.

17. Sarah Grimké, *Letters on the Equality of the Sexes and the Condition of Women* (Boston: Isaac Knapp, 1838), Letter I, July 11, 1837, p. 8; Letter II, July 17, 1837, p. 10; Letter III, July, 1837, pp. 12–21.

18. *The Liberator,* March 2, 1838.

19. *Boston Gazette,* March 8, 1838, reprinted in *The Liberator,* March 9, 1838.

20. *Boston Reformer,* reprinted in *The Liberator,* March 9, 1838.

21. *Pittsburgh Manufacturer,* May 11, 1838, reprinted in *The Liberator,* March 9, 1838.

22. From *The Report of the New England Anti-Slavery Society Convention,* printed in *The Liberator,* June 22, 1838.

23. *The Liberator,* July 27, 1938.

24. Elizabeth Cady Stanton, Susan B. Anthony, and Matilda Joslyn Gage, eds., *History of Woman Suffrage,* Vol. I (New York: Fowler & Wells, 1881), p. 58. Referred to hereafter as HWS I.

25. Elizabeth Cady Stanton, *Eighty Years and More: Reminiscences 1815–1897* (1898; reprinted, New York: Schocken Books, 1971), p. 83.

26. *The Lily,* January 1, 1848.

27. *The Lily,* June 1853, reprinted in HWS I, p. 475.

28. HWS I, pp. 494–6.

Chapter Two

1. *Seneca County Courier,* July 14, 1848, reprinted in HWS I, p. 67.

2. *Report of the Woman's Rights Convention Held at Seneca Falls, N.Y., July 19th & 20th, 1848* (Rochester: John Dick, 1848), pp. 5–7.

3. *Report of the Woman's Rights Convention . . . ,* pp. 4, 5, 9.

4. *Daily Advertiser* (Rochester), August 8, 1848; in Elizabeth Cady Stanton Scrapbook, Manuscripts Division, Library of Congress, Washington, D.C.

5. *Proceedings of the Woman's Rights Convention, Held at the Unitarian Church, Rochester, N.Y., August 2, 1848* (New York: Robert J. Johnston, 1870), p. 15.

6. *Mechanic's Advocate* (Albany), reprinted in HWS I, 802–3.

7. *Public Ledger and Daily Transcript* (Philadelphia), reprinted in HWS I, pp. 804–5.

8. *Rochester Daily Advertiser,* reprinted in HWS I, pp. 803–4.

9. HWS I, pp. 103–4. According to Keith Melder, the Salem call was printed in the *Anti-Slavery Bugle* (Ohio), March 30, 1850.

10. HWS I, pp. 221–2.

11. HWS I, p. 118.

12. *Proceedings of the Woman's Rights Convention, Held at Worcester . . . , 1850 (Boston: Prentiss & Sawyer, 1851), pp. 7, 8, 10.*

13. HWS I, pp. 108–10.

14. HWS I, pp. 165–7.

15. *Proceedings of the Woman's Rights Convention, Held at Worcester . . . , 1851* (New York: Fowler & Wells, 1852), pp. 36–45.

16. HWS I, pp. 515–17.

17. *Proceedings of the Woman's Rights Convention, Held at Worcester . . . , 1851,* p. 18.

18. Massilon, Ohio, Convention, 1852, printed in HWS I, p. 817.

19. Woman's Convention, Westchester, Pennsylvania, 1852, printed in HWS I, p. 356.

20. New York Woman's Rights Convention, 1853, printed in HWS I, pp. 581–2.

21. Massilon, Ohio, convention, 1852, printed in HWS I, p. 817.

22. HWS I, pp. 588–9.

23. HWS I, pp. 562–3.

24. New York Woman's Rights Convention, 1853, printed in HWS I, pp. 581–2.

25. New York Woman's Rights Convention, 1853, printed in HWS I, p. 582.

26. *Proceedings of the National Women's Rights Convention, Held at Cleveland, Ohio, October, 1853* (Cleveland: Gray, Beardsley, Spear, and Co., 1854), p. 23. (Although the convention's name usually had the singular form "Woman's," occasionally—as here—the plural form was used.)

27. Ida Husted Harper, *The Life and Work of Susan B. Anthony,* 3 vols. (Indianapolis and Kansas City: Bowen Merrill Co. and the Hollenbeck Press, 1898–1908), I, p. 67. Hereafter referred to as Harper, with the appropriate volume number.

28. HWS I, pp. 716–17.

29. Harper II, p. 116.

30. *Proceedings of the Woman's Rights Convention . . . 1851,* pp. 12–13.

31. HWS I, pp. 168–70.

32. HWS I, p. 194.

33. *The Chronotype* (Council Bluffs, Nebraska), January 16, 1856, courtesy of the Nebraska State Historical Society.

34. *Daily Star* (Syracuse, New York), September 11, 1852, reprinted in HWS I, pp. 852–3.

35. *New York Herald,* September 7, 1853, reprinted in HWS I, pp. 556–7.

36. *Albany Register,* March 1856, reprinted in HWS I, pp. 629–30.

37. *Atlas and Daily Bee,* reprinted in *Report of the Woman's Rights Meeting at Mercantile Hall, May 27, 1859* (Boston: S. Urbino, 1859).

38. *The Nebraskan* (Omaha), January 9, 1856, courtesy of the Nebraska Historical Society.

39. *The North Star,* July 28, 1848, editorial by Frederick Douglass, reprinted in HWS I, pp. 74–5.

Chapter Three

1. Elizabeth Cady Stanton, Susan B. Anthony, and Matilda Joslyn Gage, eds., *History of Woman Suffrage,* Vol. II (New York: Fowler & Wells, 1882), p. 92. Referred to hereafter as HWS II.

2. HWS II, p. 92.

3. The Constitution of the United States of America, Amendment XIV, Section 2.

4. *New York World,* November 1866, reprinted in Harper I, p. 264.

5. Harper I, p. 276.

6. HWS II, pp. 235–7.

7. HWS II, pp. 259–61. The reminiscences were written in a letter to Susan B. Anthony in 1882.

8. HWS II, p. 285.

9. *The Sun,* July 7, 1868, reprinted in *The Revolution,* July 16, 1868.

10. *Chicago Republican,* reprinted in Harper I, p. 306.

11. *The Revolution,* July 30, 1868.

12. *New York News,* reprinted in *The Revolution,* July 30, 1868.

13. The Constitution of the United States . . . Article XV.

14. *The Revolution,* February 5, 1868.

15. *The Revolution,* March 19, 1868.

16. *The Revolution,* February 4, 1869.

17. *The Revolution,* May 28, 1868.

18. *The Revolution,* June 18, 1868.

19. *The Revolution,* May 14, 1868.

20. *Woman's Journal,* March 11, 1899.

21. *The Revolution,* May 14, 1868.

22. HWS II, pp. 310–11.

23. *The Revolution,* April 10, 1868.

24. *The Revolution,* June 11, 1868.

25. *The Revolution,* March 19, 1868.

26. *The Revolution,* March 19, 1868.

27. *The Revolution,* July 22, 1869.

28. *The Revolution,* June 24, 1869, by Parker Pillsbury.

29. *The Revolution,* August 27, 1868, by Eleanor Kirk.

30. HWS II, pp. 380–92.

Chapter Four

1. Andrew Sinclair, *The Better Half: The Emancipation of the American Woman* (New York: Harper & Row, 1965), p. 194.

2. *The Woman's Journal,* December 3, 1870.

3. *The Revolution,* August 27, 1868.

4. *The Revolution,* October 3, 1870.

5. *The Revolution,* September 15, 1870.

6. *The Revolution,* July 14, 1870.

7. Paulina Wright Davis, *A History of the National Woman's Rights Movement for Twenty Years . . . from 1850 to 1870* (New York: Journeymen Printers' Co-operative Association, 1871), pp. 62–83.

8. *The Revolution,* November 24, 1870.

9. *The Woman's Journal,* December 3, 1870.

10. HWS II, pp. 389–90.

11. Davis, *A History of the National Woman's Rights Movement . . . ,* pp. 117–18.

12. The circular was reprinted in *Woodhull & Claflin's Weekly,* December 2, 1871.

13. "A Speech on the Principles of Social Freedom," *Woodhull & Claflin's Weekly,* August 16, 1873.

14. *Golden Age,* reprinted in *Woodhull & Claflin's Weekly,* December 16, 1871.

15. HWS II, p. 809.

16. HWS II, pp. 810–11.

17. *Woodhull & Claflin's Weekly,* November 2, 1872.

18. Reprinted in the *Brooklyn Eagle.* See Scrapbook of Beecher-Tilton Scandal, New York Public Library.

19. Letter to Mrs. Campbell, April 10, 1875, in Lois Merk, *Massachusetts and the Woman Suffrage Movement,* 2 vols. (Cambridge, Mass.: General Microfilm Co., 1961), N. 200.

20. Letter from Newbury, Vermont, June 12, 1889. Blackwell Family Papers, Box 8, Library of Congress.

21. *New York Tribune,* reprinted in Elizabeth Cady Stanton, Susan B. Anthony, and Matilda Joslyn Gage, eds., *History of Woman Suffrage,* Vol. III (New York: Charles Mann, 1887), p. 42. Referred to hereafter as HWS III.

22. Susan B. Anthony and Ida Husted Harper, eds., *History of Woman Suffrage,* Vol. IV (Indianapolis: The Hollenbeck Press, 1902), pp. 58–59. Referred to hereafter as HWS IV.

23. From "Report of the Executive Committee," reprinted in HWS IV, pp. 75–7.

24. *The Woman's Journal,* February 5, 1881.

25. *The Woman's Journal,* April 26, 1890.

26. HWS IV, p. 263.

27. HWS IV, pp. 263–64.

Chapter Five

1. Reprinted in Eliza (Mother) Stewart, *Memories of the Crusade: A Thrilling Account of the Great Uprising of the Women of Ohio of 1873, against the Liquor Crime . . .* (Columbus, Ohio: W. G. Hubbard & Co., 1889), pp. 96–100.

2. *Minutes of the Woman's National Christian Temperance Union . . . Annual Meeting, . . . 1877* (Cincinnati: A. H. Pugh, 1877), p. 12. (In later years the plural form, "Women's," became more common, but originally it was "Woman's.")

3. *Minutes of the National Woman's Christian Temperance Union . . . Annual Meeting, . . . 1883* (Cleveland: Home Publishing Co., 1883), pp. 46–7.

4. Mary Earhart Dillon, *Frances Willard: From Prayers to Politics* (Chicago: University of Chicago Press, 1944), p. 153.

5. Frances Willard, *Home Protection Manual . . .* (New York: "The Independent" Off., 1879), p. 7.

6. Frances E. Willard, *Woman and Temperance, or the Work and Workers of the Woman's Christian Temperance Union* (Hartford, Conn.: Park Publishing Co., 1884), pp. 457–9.

7. *Minutes of the Woman's National Christian Temperance Union . . . 1881* (Brooklyn: Union Argus Steam Printing, 1881), p. 43.

8. Frances Willard, *Home Protection Manual . . . ,* pp. 13, 17.

9. *The Woman's Journal,* October 27, 1883, letter from C. S. Talcott.

10. *The Woman's Journal,* November 21, 1891.

11. *Minutes of the National Woman's Christian Temperance Union . . . 1885* (Brooklyn: Martin and Niper, 1885), p. 62.

12. *Minutes of the National Woman's Christian Temperance Union . . . 1887* (Chicago: Woman's Temperance Publication Association, 1887), pp. 89–91.

Chapter Six

1. HWS IV, p. 40. Speech by Susan B. Anthony to Senate Committee on Woman Suffrage, March 7, 1884.

2. *The Woman's Journal,* June 4, 1881. Speech by Henry B. Blackwell to the New England Woman Suffrage Association's annual meeting, May 1881.

3. HWS II, pp. 496–7. Report by Isabella Beecher Hooker to a National Woman Suffrage Association meeting, May 11, 1871.

4. HWS II, pp. 934–5.

5. *Evening Express* (Rochester), reprinted in Harper II, p. 995.

6. *Boston Transcript,* reprinted in HWS II, p. 935.

7. *New York Commercial Advertiser,* reprinted in Harper II, pp. 993–4.

8. *An Account of the Proceedings on the Trial of Susan B. Anthony, on the Charge of Illegal Voting, at the Presidential Election in Nov., 1872 . . .* (Rochester: Daily Democrat & Chronicle Book Print, 1874), p. 66.

9. *Account of . . . the Trial of Susan B. Anthony . . . ,* pp. 81–5.

10. *Minor* v. *Happerstett,* Supreme Court of the United States, 1874, 88 U.S. (21 Wallace) 162, 22 L. Ed. 627.

11. HWS II, p. 603.

12. *Bradwell* v. *Illinois,* Supreme Court of the United States, 1873, 83 U.S. (16 Wallace) 130, 141.

13. HWS III, pp. 58–9.

14. HWS III, pp. 58–9.

15. HWS III, pp. 134–5.

16. *The Woman's Journal,* June 3, 1882.

17. *The Woman's Journal,* July 22, 1882.

18. *The Woman's Journal,* October 24, 1874.

19. Alice Stone Blackwell, *Lucy Stone: Pioneer of Woman's Rights* (Boston: Little, Brown & Co., 1930), pp. 239–40.

20. *The Woman's Journal,* February 5, 1881.

21. *Terre Haute Express,* February 12, 1879, reprinted in Harper I, p. 503.

22. Elizabeth Cady Stanton Scrapbooks, III, 1870–1878, Manuscripts Division, Library of Congress, Washington, D.C.

Chapter Seven

1. Jennie C. Croly, *History of the Woman's Club Movement in America* (New York: Henry G. Allen & Co., 1898), p. 24.

2. *Syracuse Daily Journal,* October 14, 1875, reprinted in Dillon, *Frances Willard . . . ,* p. 137.

3. *The Woman's Journal,* October 11, 1873.

4. *Historical Account of the Association for the Advancement of Women* (Dedham, Mass.: Transcript Steam Job Print, 1893), p. 5.

5. *The Woman's Journal,* November 21, 1891. Report of a Supplemental Woman's Congress in St. Paul, Minnesota, October 1871.

6. Mildred White Wells, *Unity in Diversity: The History of the General Federation of Women's Clubs* (General Federation of Women's Clubs, 1953), p. 26.

7. Wells, *Unity in Diversity,* p. 198.

8. *General Federation of Women's Clubs Magazine,* August 1914, p. 23.

9. Letter dated 1903, quoted in Wells, *Unity in Diversity,* p. 37.

10. Agnes L. Peterson, "Women Inspectors for Women at Work," *General Federation of Women's Clubs Magazine,* October 1914, p. 36.

11. New York Public Library collection.

12. New York Public Library collection.

13. *General Federation of Women's Clubs Magazine,* June 1915, p. 27.

14. *General Federation of Women's Clubs Magazine,* September 1914, p. 17.

15. "Address of Josephine St. P. Ruffin, President of the Conference," *The Woman's Era,* II, No. 5 (September 1895), 14–15, courtesy of the Smith College Library.

16. Letter dated June 16, 1899, Mary Church Terrell papers, Box 39, Manuscripts Division, Library of Congress, Washington, D.C.

17. Mary Church Terrell papers, Box 1. The question marks indicate words that were unclear in the original.

18. Mary Church Terrell papers, Box 1.

19. *National Association Notes,* February 1902.

20. Ida B. Wells Barnett, *Southern Horrors,* 1892 (reprinted as part of a collection of pamphlets; New York: Arno Press, 1969), pp. 13–15.

Chapter Eight

1. John B. Andrews and W. D. P. Bliss, *History of Women in Trade Unions.* Report on Condition of Woman and Child Wage Earners in the United States, vol. IX. U.S. Senate Document 645, 61st Congress, 2nd Session (Washington, D.C.: Government Printing Office, 1910), pp. 23–24.

2. *National Gazette* (Philadelphia), January 7, 1829, reprinted in Andrews and Bliss, *History of Women in Trade Unions,* p. 23.

3. *Mechanics' Free Press,* January 17, 1829, reprinted in Andrews and Bliss, *History of Women in Trade Unions,* p. 23.

4. *The Man,* February 22, 1834, and the *Boston Transcript,* February 18, 1834, reprinted in Andrews and Bliss, *History of Women in Trade Unions,* p. 28.

5. "Report on the Special Committee on Hours of Labor," House Report No. 50, *Massachusetts General Court Legislative Document 1845,* House 1–65, pp. 2–4.

6. *Pittsburgh Daily Commercial Journal,* August 1, 1848, reprinted in Andrews and Bliss, *History of Women in Trade Unions,* pp. 64–65.

7. "Report of the General Master Workman, Terence V. Powderly," *Proceedings of the General Assembly of the Knights of Labor of America, 1888* (Philadelphia: Journal of United Labor Print, 1889).

8. "Report of the General Investigator of Woman's Work and Wages," *Proceedings . . . Knights of Labor . . . 1888,* pp. 1–15.

9. Dorothy Richardson, *The Long Day: The Story of a New York Working Girl,* reprinted in *Women at Work,* William L. O'Neill, ed. (Chicago: Quadrangle Books, 1972).

10. From *The Call,* reprinted in *ILGWU News-History: 1900-1950—The Story of the Ladies' Garment Workers,* edited by Max D. Danish and Leon Stein (New York: ABCO Press, 1950), Chapter 3, pp. 1–2.

Chapter Nine

1. *Proceedings of the Twenty-First Annual Convention of the National-American Woman Suffrage Association, Grand Rapids, Mich., 1899* (Warren, Ohio: Press of Perry the Printer, 1899), p. 58.

2. *Proceedings of the Twenty-First Annual Convention . . . ,* p. 59.

3. *Proceedings of the Twenty-First Annual Convention . . . ,* p. 61.

4. Reprinted in *The Woman's Journal,* March 28, 1903.

5. *The Woman's Journal,* April 4, 1903.

6. *The Woman's Journal,* April 25, 1903.

7. Mary Church Terrell papers, Box 3, Manuscripts Division, Library of Congress, Washington, D.C.

8. Sarah Grimké, *Letters on the Equality of the Sexes . . . ,* Letter VIII, "On the Condition of Women in the United States, 1837," pp. 50–51.

9. HWS I, p. 78.

10. HWS I, p. 809.

11. *The Revolution,* February 19, 1868.

12. *The Revolution,* April 2, 1868.

13. Harper II, pp. 996–1003, speech abstracted by Harper.

14. HWS IV, p. 122, National Woman Suffrage Association resolution, 1887.

15. Harper III, p. 1162.

16. *Proceedings of the . . . Annual Convention of the National American Woman Suffrage Association . . . 1893,* p. 84.

17. *The Woman's Journal,* November 3, 1894.

18. *The Woman's Journal,* February 20, 1904. Catt speech at 1904 NAWSA convention.

19. *The Woman's Journal,* December 22, 1894.

20. *The Woman's Journal,* March 28, 1908. Addams speech at Boston University.

21. *The Woman's Journal,* April 11, 1911.

22. *The Woman's Journal,* June 24, 1911.

23. *The Woman's Journal,* July 13, 1912, by Harriet Burton Laidlaw.

24. Grace Hannah Wilson, *The Religious and Educational Philosophy of The Young Women's Christian Association . . .* (New York: Teachers' College, Columbia University, Bureau of Publications, 1933), p. 5.

25. Wilson, *The Religious and Educational Philosophy . . . ,* p. 32.

26. Gladys Boone, *The Women's Trade Union Leagues in Great Britain and the United States of America* (New York: Columbia University Press), p. 250.

27. Boone, *The Women's Trade Union Leagues . . . ,* p. 250.

28. National Women's Trade Union League, *Convention Handbook,* 1909 (Chicago: Allied Printers, 1909), pp. 12–17.

29. Boone, *The Women's Trade Union Leagues . . . ,* pp. 113–14.

30. Robin Miller Jacoby, "The Women's Trade Union League and American Feminism," unpublished paper.

31. *Life and Labor,* January 1919, pp. 15–16.

32. National Consumers' League, *First Quarter Century 1899–1924,* p. 1.

33. *General Federation of Women's Clubs Magazine,* November 1916, p. 43.

34. Agnes De Lima, *Night-Working Mothers in Textile Mills, Passaic, New Jersey* (National Consumers' League and the Consumers' League of New Jersey, 1920), pp. 6–17.

35. Paper of the National Consumers' League, Manuscripts Division, Library of Congress, Washington, D.C. The contract is reprinted in Maud Nathan, *The Story of an Epoch-making Movement* (Garden City, N.Y.: Doubleday, Page & Co., 1926), pp. 225–228.

36. *Muller* v. *State of Oregon,* Supreme Court of the United States, 1907, 208 U.S. 412.

37. *The Woman's Journal,* July 22, 1905.

Chapter Ten

1. Harriot Stanton Blatch, ed., *Two Speeches by Industrial Women.* A copy of this pamphlet is in Harriot Stanton Blatch's Scrapbook, Vol. I., Library of Congress, Manuscripts Division, Washington, D.C.

2. *The New York Times,* August 11, 1914.

3. Inez Haynes Irwin, *The Story of the Woman's Party: Uphill with Banners Flying* (New York: Harcourt, Brace and Co., 1921), p. 75.

4. *The Suffragist,* January 24, 1914.

5. *The Suffragist,* September 19, 1914. Report by Jessie Hardy Stubbs.

6. *The Suffragist,* October 3, 1914. Report by Doris Stevens.

7. *The Suffragist,* October 10, 1914. Report by Lola Trax.

8. *The Suffragist,* October 21, 1916.

9. *The Suffragist,* October 21, 1916. "Dodgers" used in campaign against Wilson, 1916.

10. Irwin, *The Story of the Woman's Party,* p. 127.

11. *The New York Times,* December 6, 1916.

12. *The Suffragist,* April 21, 1917.

13. *The New York Times,* July 21, 1917.

14. Irwin, *The Story of the Women's Party,* pp. 207, 236–37.

15. *The Boston Journal,* August 20, 1917, reprinted in Doris Stevens, *Jailed for Freedom* (New York: Boni and Liveright, 1920), p. 138.

16. *St. Paul Daily News,* July 28, 1917, reprinted in *The Suffragist,* August 11, 1917.

17. Reprinted in *The Suffragist,* August 11, 1917.

18. *Telegram* (Lawrence, Mass.), December 3, 1917, reprinted in *The Suffragist,* December 15, 1917.

19. *The Suffragist,* December 1, 1917.

20. *The Suffragist,* December 1, 1917.

21. "Report of the Church Work Committee," *Proceedings of the Forty-fourth Annual Convention of the National American Woman Suffrage Association* (New York: National American Woman Suffrage Assoc., 1912), pp. 55–57.

22. News release dated May 18, 1915, Carrie Chapman Catt papers, Box 2, New York Public Library Manuscripts Collection.

23. *The New York Times,* November 13, 1917.

24. Catt papers, Box 1, Letters, New York Public Library.

25. Wilson's letter to Pou and reply to Gardener in Catt papers, Box 1, New York Public Library.

26. National American Woman Suffrage Association papers, Box 48, Manuscripts Division, Library of Congress, Washington, D.C. The copy of the letter is not dated, and a penciled "1918" is obviously incorrect.

27. Reprinted in Eleanor Flexner, *Century of Struggle: The Woman's Rights Movement in the United States* (Cambridge: Belknap Press of Harvard University Press, 1959), pp. 280–81.

28. *The New York Times,* January 10, 1918.

29. United States *Congressional Record,* Vol. 56, pt. 11 (Washington, D.C.: U.S. Government Printing Office, 1918), pp. 10928–10929.

30. The Constitution of the United States . . . , Article XIX.

Chapter Eleven

1. "Minutes of the Women's Joint Congressional Committee, March 1921," Women's Joint Congressional Committee Records, Box 6, Manuscripts Division, Library of Congress, Washington, D.C.

2. *Good Housekeeping,* April 1920, pp. 19–20.

3. Mary Ware Dennett, *Birth Control Laws: Shall We Keep Them, Change Them, or Abolish Them?* (New York: Frederick H. Hitchcock, 1926), p. 68.

4. *The Birth Control Review,* December 1921, p. 18.

5. Caroline Robinson, *Seventy Birth Control Clinics: . . .* (Baltimore: Williams and Wilkins Co., 1930).

6. Dennett, *Birth Control Laws . . . ,* pp. 272–76.

7. *The Birth Control Review,* May 1926, p. 172.

8. Margaret Sanger, *Women and the New Race* (New York: Brentano's, 1920), pp. 94–96.

9. Dennett, *Birth Control Laws . . . ,* p. 192.

10. Charles A. Selden, "The Most Powerful Lobby in Washington . . . ," *Ladies' Home Journal,* April 1922, p. 5.

11. *The Woman Citizen,* March 22, 1924, pp. 9, 29.

12. This copy of the poem was found in a "Confidential Report," Women's Joint Congressional Committee Records, Box 6, Library of Congress, Washington, D.C.

13. *Dearborn Independent,* March 15, 1924.

14. *The Woman Patriot,* February 1, 1923. Originally printed in the *Press-Herald* (Portland), January 30, 1923.

15. John H. Edgerton, "Protect American Womanhood Against Degrading Propaganda" (National Association of Manufacturers, 1926). Speech delivered at a Conference on Women in Industry, U.S. Department of Labor, Washington, D.C., January 19, 1926.

16. *The Woman Citizen,* June 1927.

17. *Equal Rights,* February 17, 1923.

18. *Ladies' Home Journal,* September 1922, p. 7.

19. *Good Housekeeping,* September 1925, pp. 52, 53, 159, 163, 164, 166, 169, 170, 173, 176, 179, 180.

20. *The Woman Voter* (Minneapolis, Minn.), February 15, 1923.

21. Lavinia Dock, "A Sub-Caste," *Equal Rights,* May 31, 1924.

22. *Equal Rights: Hearings Before a Subcommittee of the Committee on the Judiciary.* U.S. Senate, 71st Congress, 3rd session, January 1, 1931, pp. 5–11.

23. *The Woman Citizen,* May 3, 1924, p. 10.

24. Lawrence Lader, *The Margaret Sanger Story and the Fight for Birth Control* (Garden City, N.Y.: Doubleday & Co., Inc., 1955.

Chapter Twelve

1. "Executive Order 10980, Establishing the President's Commission on the Status of Women," reprinted in *American Women: Report of the President's Commission on the Status of Women, 1963* (Washington, D.C.: U.S. Government Printing Office, 1963), p. 76.

2. *American Women,* pp. 13, 15, 17, 20–23, 26, 30, 32, 36–37, 38, 42–43.

3. 29 U.S.C. § 206 (d)(1)(1964).

4. 78 Stat. 25.3, 42 U.S.C. 20008 *et seq.* (1964).

5. Helen Hacker, "Women as a Minority Group," *Social Forces,* October 1951; Simone de Beauvoir, *The Second Sex* (New York: Alfred A. Knopf, 1953); Eleanor Flexner, *Century of Struggle* (Cambridge, Mass.: Belknap Press of Harvard University Press, 1959); Betty Friedan, *The Feminine Mystique* (New York: W. W. Norton & Co., 1963).

6. National Organization for Women, Washington, D.C., 1966.

7. National Organization for Women, *NOW Bill of Rights,* Washington, D.C., 1967.

8. Women's Equity Action League flyer.

9. National Organization for Women, news release, June 25, 1970.

10. *Federal Register,* Vol. 3, No. 247, December 27, 1973.

11. *Equal Rights for Men and Women, 1971: Hearings Before Subcommittee No. 4 of the Committee on the Judiciary, House of Representatives . . . 1971.* Serial No. 2 (Washington, D.C.: U.S. Government Printing Office, 1971), pp. 263–272.

12. The memo was reprinted in *Liberation* (April, 1966). In an unpublished paper, "Racial Revolt and Sexual Consciousness: Women in the Civil Rights Movement, 1960–1965," Sara M. Evans writes that the position of women in SNCC deteriorated after 1965, compounded by racial tensions between black and white women and by the move toward ejection of all whites, male and female, from the organization. Evans sees the memo as an outgrowth of this complex of tensions and disappointments on the part of the white women in SNCC.

13. Celestine Ware, *Women Power: The Movement for Women's Liberation* (New York: Tower Publications, 1970), pp. 36–37.

14. Statement issued by Chicago Radical Women, printed in *New Left Notes,* November 13, 1967.

15. Beverly Jones and Judith Brown, "Toward a Female Liberation Movement" (Boston: New England Free Press, June 1968).

16. *Voice of the Women's Liberation Movement,* March 1968.

17. Maren Lockwood Carden, in *The New Feminist Movement* (New York: Russell Sage Foundation, 1974), p. 64, estimates that there were small women's groups in at least forty cities by the end of 1969.

18. "Redstockings Manifesto," July 7, 1969. Complete text available in Leslie Tanner, ed., *Voices from Women's Liberation* (New York, Signet, 1971).

19. The Feminists, "A Programmatic Analysis," August 15, 1969.

20. New York Radical Feminists, December 1969.

21. The Feminists, "Organizational Principles and Structure," August 22, 1969.

22. "Redstockings Manifesto," July 7, 1969.

23. "A Program for Feminist Consciousness Raising," *Notes from the Second Year: Women's Liberation* (New York, 1970), 78–80. The author, Kathie Sarachild, wishes to state that for a fuller explanation of the role of consciousness-raising, and one that is very different from the small-group interpretation advanced in this book, the reader should see *Feminist Revolution,* published by Redstockings in 1975 (P.O. Box 413, New Paltz, New York 15261). In *Feminist Revolution,* you will also find an approach to history at odds with the one presented in this book.

24. "Redstockings Manifesto," July 7, 1969.

25. Dunbar, Mainardi, and Weisstein reprinted in Robin Morgan, ed., *Sisterhood Is Powerful: An Anthology of Writings from the Women's Liberation Movement* (New York: Random House, 1970); Koedt and Radicalesbians in Anne Koedt, Ellen Levine, Anita Rapone, eds., *Radical Feminism* (New York: Quadrangle, 1973).

26. Carden, *The New Feminist Movement,* p. 140.

27. Black Women Organized for Action, flyer.

28. National Black Feminist Organization, reprinted in *Ms.,* May 1974, p. 99.

29. Demands originally presented September 1972, reprinted in *Ms.,* December 1972, p. 128.

30. Coalition of Labor Union Women, "Statement of Purpose," March 23–24, 1974.

31. National Women's Political Caucus, "Statement of Purpose," Washington, D.C., July 11, 1971.

32. National Women's Political Caucus, "Organizing Information," Washington, D.C., Fall 1971.

33. National Organization for Women, Washington, D.C., 1966.

34. Committee for a Women's National Abortion Coalition, flyer, 1971.

35. Feminist Women's Health Center, Los Angeles, California, brochure.

36. Lesbian Feminist Liberation, Constitution, 1973.

37. National Organization for Women, "Program for NOW: Task Forces Summaries," January 1974.

38. "Resolutions of the 1973 National Conference of NOW," printed in *NOW acts,* Vol. 6, No. 1.

39. *Ms.,* February 1975, pp. 80–81.

40. "Resolutions of the 1973 National Conference of NOW."

41. *Ibid.*

42. *Ibid.*

43. National Organization for Women, Resolutions adopted at the National Conference in 1974.

44. *Ibid.*

45. *Ibid.*

BIBLIOGRAPHY

The selective bibliography below is offered to readers who want to delve further into the history of the women's movement in the United States. Those interested in research in women's history should become familiar with the outstanding collections at Radcliffe and Smith Colleges, the New York Public Library, and the Library of Congress, which include a wealth of private papers and organization records. Other university and public libraries, as well as state historical societies, also offer abundant source material for scholarly research.

For the serious reader and scholar who cannot take advantage of special collections of primary materials, there is a considerable amount of printed source material accessible in libraries across the country. Copies of the *History of Woman Suffrage,* in six volumes, edited by Elizabeth Cady Stanton, Susan B. Anthony, Matilda Joslyn Gage, and Ida Husted Harper, can often be found; they contain primary data of great interest and usefulness, although rather haphazardly organized. Similarly, Ida Husted Harper's three-volume *Life and Work of Susan B. Anthony* reprints material such as speeches, letters, newspaper articles, and resolutions that covers the lengthy period of Anthony's life and active participation in women's affairs. In addition, many libraries have copies of the printed minutes and proceedings of women's groups—of the early women's rights conventions, the National Woman Suffrage Association, the American Woman Suffrage Association, the Women's Christian Temperance Union, the National American Woman Suffrage Association, the National Consumers' League, the National Women's Trade Union League, the General Federation of Women's Clubs, the League of Women Voters, and numerous other women's associations and organizations. Most of these groups, moreover, issued regular publications which can often be found in libraries' general collections. Thus, the reader may be able to read *The Revolution, The Woman's Journal,* the GFWC *Magazine, Life and Labor, The Suffragist, Equal Rights,* and *Woman Citizen,* as well as more recent journals.

A three-volume reference work by Janet Wilson James and Edward T. James, *Notable American Women, 1607–1950* (Cambridge, Mass.: Harvard University Press, 1970), is available in libraries throughout the country, and offers a thorough and careful biographical introduction to the lives and work of movement activists. Various biographies and autobiographies can be found to supplement the basic information provided in James and James.

While the history of women in the United States, and with it the history of their reform efforts, has long been neglected, it is finally beginning to attract its proper share of attention from scholars and writers. Specialized journals such as *Women's Studies* and *Feminist Studies* are being published, and even traditional historical journals, like the *Journal of American History* and *American Historical Review,* nowadays include articles and reviews of books relevant to study of the women's movement.

The chief problem with material concerning the contemporary movement is that it is at once all around us and for the most part inaccessible. There exists a profusion of printed material issued both by contemporary women's groups and about them, but comparatively little of it has been collected, organized, and analyzed. Several printed collections are listed in section IX below. Library collections are few. Part of the collection of the Women's History Research Center, Berkeley, California, consisting of many journals and newsletters, has been microfilmed by Bell and Howell and sold to libraries under the title *Herstory.* One recent and encouraging development is that many women's centers are now beginning to serve as repositories and collectors of contemporary documents. Usually, their material is easily available to readers.

Scholars and curious readers alike will find much useful information in Albert Krichmar's *The Women's Rights Movement in the United States, 1848–1970: A Bibliography and Sourcebook* (Metuchen, N.J.: Scarecrow Press, Inc., 1972).

The list that follows is by no means complete or definitive; it is offered as an introduction and a guide.

I. GENERAL

1. Lois Banner, *Women in Modern America: A Brief History* (New York: Harcourt Brace Jovanovich, 1974).

2. William Henry Chafe, *The American Woman: Her Changing Social, Economic, and Political Roles, 1920–1970* (New York: Oxford University Press, 1972).

3. Eleanor Flexner, *Century of Struggle: The Woman's Rights Movement in the United States* (Cambridge, Mass.: Belknap Press of Harvard University Press, 1959).

4. Oliver O. Jensen, *The Revolt of American Women: A Pictorial History of the Century of Change from Bloomers to Bikinis—From Feminism to Freud* (New York: Harcourt, Brace, 1952).

5. Aileen S. Kraditor, *Up from the Pedestal: Selected Writings in the History of American Feminism* (Chicago: Quadrangle Books, 1968).

6. Gerda Lerner, *Black Women in White America: A Documentary History* (New York: Pantheon Books, 1972).

7. William L. O'Neill, *Everyone Was Brave: The Rise and Fall of Feminism in the United States* (Chicago: Quadrangle Books, 1969).

8. William L. O'Neill, *The Woman Movement: Feminism in the United States and England* (Chicago: Quadrangle Books, 1971).

9. Robert E. Riegel, *American Feminists* (Lawrence, Kan.: University of Kansas Press, 1963).

10. Anne F. Scott, *The Southern Lady: From Pedestal to Politics, 1830–1930* (Chicago: University of Chicago Press, 1970).

11. Andrew Sinclair, *The Better Half: The Emancipation of the American Woman* (New York: Harper and Row, 1965).

12. June Sochen, *The New Feminism in Twentieth-Century America* (Lexington, Mass.: D. C. Heath and Co., 1971).

13. Leslie B. Tanner, ed., *Voices from Women's Liberation* (New York: New American Library, 1971).

II. ORIGINS OF THE WOMEN'S MOVEMENT

1. Otelia Cromwell, *Lucretia Mott* (Cambridge, Mass.: Harvard University Press, 1958).

2. Louis Filler, *The Crusade Against Slavery, 1830–1860* (New York: Harper & Brothers, 1960).

3. Sarah Grimké, *Letters on the Equality of the Sexes and Condition of Women* (Boston: Isaac Knapp, 1838).

4. Anna Hallowell, *James and Lucretia Mott: Life and Letters* (Boston: Houghton Mifflin & Co., 1896).

5. Aileen Kraditor, *Means and Ends in American Abolitionism: Garrison and His Critics on Strategy and Tactics, 1834–1850* (New York: Random House, 1967).

6. Gerda Lerner, *The Grimké Sisters from South Carolina: Pioneers for Woman's Rights and Abolition* (New York: Houghton Mifflin & Co., 1967).

7. Mary Elizabeth Massey, *Bonnet Brigades: American Women and the Civil War* (New York: Alfred A. Knopf, 1966).

8. Keith E. Melder, *The Beginnings of the Women's Rights Movement in the United States, 1800–1840* (Ann Arbor, Mich.: University Microfilms, 1974).

9. Victoria Ortiz, *Sojourner Truth, A Self-Made Woman* (New York: J. B. Lippincott, 1974).

10. Elizabeth Cady Stanton, *Eighty Years and More: Reminiscences, 1815–1897* (1898; repr. New York: Schocken Books, 1971).

III. EARLY YEARS, 1848–1890

1. Alice Stone Blackwell, *Lucy Stone: Pioneer of Woman's Rights* (Boston: Little, Brown & Co., 1930).

2. Dexter C. Bloomer, *Life and Writings of Amelia Bloomer* (Boston: Arena Publishing Co., 1895).

3. Paulina Wright Davis, *A History of the National Woman's Rights Movement for Twenty Years . . . from 1850 to 1870* (New York: Journeymen Printer's Co-operative Association, 1871).

4. Ida Husted Harper, *The Life and Work of Susan B. Anthony,* 3 vols. (Indianapolis and Kansas City: Bowen Merrill Co. and the Hollenbeck Press, 1898–1908).

5. Elinor Hays, *Morning Star: A Biography of Lucy Stone, 1818–1893* (New York: Harcourt Brace & World, 1961).

6. Johanna Johnston, *Mrs. Satan: The Incredible Saga of Victoria C. Woodhull* (New York: Putnam, 1967).

7. Alma Lutz, *Susan B. Anthony: Rebel, Crusader, Humanitarian* (Boston: Beacon Press, 1959).

8. Lois Bannister Merk, *Massachusetts and the Woman Suffrage Movement,* 2 vols. (Cambridge, Mass.: General Microfilm Co., 1961).

9. Louise R. Noun, *Strong-minded Women: The Emergence of the Woman-Suffrage Movement in Iowa* (Ames, Iowa: Iowa State University Press, 1969).

10. Emanie Sachs, *The Terrible Siren: Victoria Woodhull* (New York: Harper, 1928).

11. Robert Shaplen, *Free Love and Heavenly Sinners* (New York: Alfred A. Knopf, 1954).

12. Elizabeth Cady Stanton, Susan B. Anthony, Matilda Joslyn Gage, and Ida Husted Harper, eds., *History of Woman Suffrage,* vols. I–IV (New York, Rochester, and Indianapolis: Fowler & Wells, Charles Mann, and Hollenbeck Press, 1881–1902).

13. Theodore Stanton & Harriot Stanton Blatch, eds., *Elizabeth Cady Stanton as Revealed in Her Letters, Diary, and Reminiscences,* 2 vols. (New York: Harper & Bros., 1922).

14. Yuri Suhl, *Ernestine Rose and the Battle for Human Rights* (New York: Reynal & Co., 1959).

IV. RACE, CLASS, ETHNICITY, AND THE WOMEN'S MOVEMENT

1. Jane Addams, *Twenty Years at Hull House* (New York: Macmillan, 1910).

2. Ida B. Wells Barnett, *On Lynchings: Southern Horrors; A Red Record; Mob Rule in New Orleans* (a collection of pamphlets, 1892–1900; repr. New York: Arno Press, 1969).

3. Sylvia G. L. Dannett, *Profiles of Negro Womanhood,* vol. I, 1619–1900 (Chicago: Educational Heritage, Inc., 1964).

4. Allen F. Davis, *Spearheads for Reform: The Social Settlements and the Progressive Movement, 1890–1914* (New York: Oxford University Press, 1967).

5. Elizabeth L. Davis, *Lifting as They Climb: The National Association of Colored Women* (n.p.: National Association of Colored Women, 1933).

6. Alfreda Duster, ed., *Crusade for Justice: The Autobiography of Ida B. Wells* (Chicago: University of Chicago Press, 1970).

7. John Gibson, J. L. Nichols, and William H. Cragman, *Progress of a Race* (Naperville, Ill.: J. L. Nichols & Co., 1920).

8. Emma Goldman, *Living My Life,* 2 vols. (New York: Dover Press, 1970).

9. Margaret V. Holt, *Mary McLeod Bethune: A Biography* (New York: Doubleday & Co., 1964).

10. Aileen Kraditor, *The Ideas of the Woman Suffrage Movement, 1899–1929* (New York: Columbia University Press, 1965).

11. Gerda Lerner, *Black Women in White America: A Documentary History* (New York: Pantheon Books, 1972).

12. Monroe Alphus Majors, *Noted Negro Women: Their Triumphs and Activities* (Chicago: Donohue & Henneberry, 1893).

13. Emma Gelders Sterne, *Mary McLeod Bethune* (New York: Alfred A. Knopf, 1969).

14. Mary Church Terrell, *A Colored Woman in a White World* (Washington, D.C.: Ransdell, Inc., 1940).

V. WORKING WOMEN AND THE WOMEN'S MOVEMENT

1. Elizabeth Abbott, *Women in Industry: A Study in American Economic History* (New York: D. Appleton & Co., 1910; repr. Arno Press, 1969).

2. John B. Andrews and W. D. P. Bliss, *History of Women in Trade Unions,* Report on Condition of Woman and Child Wage Earners in the United States, vol. IX. U.S. Senate Document 645, 61st Congress, 2nd Session (Washington, D.C.: Government Printing Office, 1910).

3. Gladys Boone, *The Women's Trade Union Leagues in Great Britain and the United States of America* (New York: Columbia University Press, 1942; repr. Arno Press, 1968).

4. Sophonisba Breckenridge, *Women in the Twentieth Century: A Study of Their Political, Social and Economic Activities* (New York: McGraw-Hill Book Co., 1933).

5. Mary Dreier, *Mary Dreier Robins: Her Life, Letters and Work* (New York: Island Press Cooperative, 1950).

6. Charlotte Perkins Gilman, *Women and Economics: The Economic Factor Between Men and Women as a Factor in Social Evolution,* ed. Carl Degler (New York: Harper and Row, 1966).

7. Josephine Goldmark, *Impatient Crusader: Florence Kelley's Life Story* (Urbana, Ill.: University of Illinois Press, 1953).

8. Alice Henry, *The Trade Union Woman* (New York: D. Appleton & Co., 1915).

9. Hannah Josephson, *The Golden Threads: New England's Mill Girls and Magnates* (New York: Duell, Sloan and Pearce, 1949).

10. Lucy Larcom, *A New England Girlhood, Outlined from Memory* (Boston: Houghton Mifflin & Co., 1889).

11. Louis Levine, *The Women's Garment Workers Union: A History of the International Ladies Garment Workers Union* (New York: n.p., 1924).

12. Annie Nathan Meyer, *Woman's Work in America* (New York: Henry Holt, 1891).

13. Maud Nathan, *The Story of an Epoch-making Movement* (Garden City, N.Y.: Doubleday & Co., 1926).

14. William L. O'Neill, ed., *Women at Work; including The Long Day . . .* (Chicago: Quadrangle Books, 1972).

15. Rose Schneiderman, *All for One* (New York: Paul S. Eriksson, 1967).

16. Robert Smuts, *Women and Work in America* (New York: Columbia University Press, 1959).

17. Helen L. Sumner, *History of Women in Industry in the United States,* Report on Condition of Woman and Child Wage Earners in the United States, vol X, U.S. Senate Document 655, 61st Congress, 2nd Session (Washington, D.C.: Government Printing Office, 1910).

VI. CLUBS, ASSOCIATIONS, AND THE WOMEN'S MOVEMENT

1. Sophonisba Breckenridge, *Women in the Twentieth Century: A Study of Their Political, Social and Economic Activities* (New York: McGraw-Hill Book Co., 1933).

2. Jennie C. Croly, *History of the Woman's Club Movement in America* (New York: Henry G. Allen & Co., 1898).

3. Mary Earhart Dillon, *Frances Willard: From Prayers to Politics* (Chicago: University of Chicago Press, 1944).

4. Genevieve Fox, *The Industrial Awakening and the Young Women's Christian Association* (New York: Young Women's Christian Associations, 1920).

5. Inez Haynes Irwin, *Angels and Amazons: A Hundred Years of American Women* (Garden City, N.Y.: Doubleday & Co., 1934).

6. Mary Church Terrell, *A Colored Woman in a White World* (Washington, D.C.: Ransdell Inc., 1940).

7. Mildred White Wells, *Unity in Diversity: The History of the General Federation of Women's Clubs* (General Federation of Women's Clubs, 1953).

8. Frances E. Willard, *Glimpses of Fifty Years: The Autobiography of an American Woman* (Chicago: Woman's Temperance Publication Association, 1889; repr. Source Book Press, 1970).

9. Frances E. Willard, *Woman and Temperance, or the Work and Workers of the Woman's Christian Temperance Union* (Hartford, Conn.: Park Publishing Co., 1884).

10. Elizabeth Wilson, *Fifty Years of Association Work among Young Women, 1866–1916: A History of Young Women's Christian Associations in the United States of America* (New York: National Board of the Young Women's Christian Association of the U.S. of A., 1916).

11. Grace Hannah Wilson, *The Religious and Educational*

Philosophy of the Young Women's Christian Association (New York: Teachers College, Columbia University Bureau of Publications, 1933).

VII. SUFFRAGE

1. Harriot Stanton Blatch and Alma Lutz, *Challenging Years: The Memories of Harriot Stanton Blatch* (New York: Putnam's Sons, 1940).

2. Carrie Chapman Catt and Nettie R. Shuler, *Woman Suffrage and Politics: The Inner Story of the Suffrage Movement* (New York: Charles Scribner's Sons, 1923; repr. Seattle: University of Washington Press, 1969).

3. Abigail S. Duniway, *Path Breaking: An Autobiographical History of the Equal Suffrage Movement in Pacific Coast States* (Portland, Ore.: James, Kerns, & Abbott Co., 1914; repr. New York: Schocken Books, 1971).

4. Alan P. Grimes, *The Puritan Ethic and Woman Suffrage* (New York: Oxford University Press, 1967).

5. Inez Haynes Irwin, *The Story of the Woman's Party: Uphill with Banners Flying* (New York: Harcourt Brace & Co., 1921).

6. David Morgan, *Suffragists and Democrats: The Politics of Woman Suffrage in America* (

7. National American Woman Suffrage Association, *Victory: How Women Won It; the Centennial Symposium, 1840–1940* (New York: Wilson, 1940).

8. Anna Howard Shaw, *The Story of a Pioneer* (New York: Harper, 1915).

9. Doris Stevens, *Jailed for Freedom* (New York: Boni and Liveright, 1920).

VIII. FROM 1920 TO THE FIFTIES

1. Mary Anderson, *Woman at Work: The Autobiography of Mary Anderson as Told to Mary N. Winslow* (Minneapolis: University of Minnesota Press, 1951).

2. William Chafe, *The American Woman: Her Changing Social, Economic and Political Roles, 1920–1970* (New York: Oxford University Press, 1972).

3. Mary Louise Degen, *History of the Woman's Peace Party* (Baltimore: Johns Hopkins Press, 1939).

4. Mary Ware Dennett, *Birth Control Laws: Shall We Keep Them, Change Them or Abolish Them?* (New York: Frederick H. Hitchcock, 1926).

5. Betty Friedan, *The Feminine Mystique* (New York: W. W. Norton & Co., Inc., 1963).

6. David Kennedy, *Birth Control in America: The Career of Margaret Sanger* (New Haven, Conn.: Yale University Press, 1970).

7. J. Stanley Lemons, *The Woman Citizen: Social Feminism in the 1920's* (Urbana, Ill.: University of Illinois Press, 1973).

8. William O'Neill, *Everyone Was Brave: The Rise and Fall of Feminism in America* (New York: Quadrangle Books, 1969).

9. Margaret Sanger, *An Autobiography* (New York: W. W. Norton & Co., 1938).

10. June Sochen, *The New Woman: Feminism in Greenwich Village, 1910–1920* (New York: Quadrangle Books, 1972).

IX. THE CONTEMPORARY MOVEMENT

1. *American Women, Report of the President's Commission on the Status of Women, 1963* (Washington, D.C.: Government Printing Office, 1963).

2. Toni Cade, *The Black Woman: An Anthology* (New York: New American Library, 1970).

3. Maren Lockwood Carden, *The New Feminist Movement,* (New York: Russell Sage Foundation, 1974).

4. *Equal Rights for Men and Women, 1971: Hearings Before Subcommittee No. 4 of the Committee on the Judiciary, House of Representatives . . . 1971,* Serial No. 2 (Washington, D.C.: Government Printing Office, 1971).

5. Vivian Gornick and Barbara K. Moran, eds., *Woman in Sexist Society: Studies in Power and Powerlessness* (New York: Basic Books, 1971).

6. Judith Hole and Ellen Levine, *The Rebirth of Feminism* (New York: Quadrangle Books, 1972).

7. Anne Koedt, Ellen Levine, and Anita Rapone, eds., *Radical Feminism* (New York: Quadrangle, 1973).

8. Robert Jay Lifton, ed., *The American Woman* (Boston: Houghton Mifflin, 1965).

9. Robin Morgan, ed., *Sisterhood Is Powerful: An Anthology of Writings from the Women's Liberation Movement* (New York: Random House, 1970).

10. Joan Robins, *Handbook of Women's Liberation* (North Hollywood, Calif.: National Organization for Women Library Press, 1970).

11. Roberta Salper, ed., *Female Liberation: History and Current Writings* (New York: Alfred A. Knopf, 1971).

12. Leslie Tanner, *Voices from Women's Liberation* (New York: New American Library, 1971).

13. Celestine Ware, *Woman Power: The Movement for Women's Liberation* (New York: Tower Publications, 1970).

ACKNOWLEDGMENTS

The illustrations in this book came from many people and places, to all of whom grateful thanks are extended. The sources, with abbreviated illustration titles, are listed below:

AMERICAN ANTIQUARIAN SOCIETY

Call to the Eighth National Woman's Rights Convention

BROWN BROTHERS

"What Will Save the Home"
Rose Schneiderman

FEMINIST WOMEN'S HEALTH CENTER
  (Berkeley, California)

Pamphlet drawing

FAITH FLAGG

"We Couldn't Afford a Doctor"
"Should There Be Labor Laws for Women?"

GFWC MAGAZINE

GFWC *Bulletin* cover and contents
Parliamentary Usage ad
Consumer's Conscience Masthead

INTERNATIONAL HERALD TRIBUNE

"Progress of Women's Rights in Kansas"
"The Type Has Changed"

BETTYE LANE

Abortion Demonstration, 1972
Women's Strike for Equality

LEAGUE OF WOMEN VOTERS

ERA "Yes" poster

LIBRARY OF CONGRESS

Angelina and Sarah Grimké
Elizabeth Cady Stanton
Susan B. Anthony
Ernestine Rose
Frederick Douglass
Lucy Stone
Susan B. Anthony
Elizabeth Cady Stanton and daughter Harriot
"Will the Federal Suffrage Amendment" flyer

"Don't Vote for a Clown" flyer
Alice Paul
"Women of Colorado"
Mary A. Nolan
Carrie Chapman Catt
"Spider Web" Chart
Woman Patriot masthead
Alva Belmont

NATIONAL CONSUMERS' LEAGUE

Label

NEW YORK DAILY NEWS

Formation of NOW, 1966

NEW-YORK HISTORICAL SOCIETY

"Ye May Session"
"The Fe'he Males"
Amelia Bloomer
Revolution statement of purpose
Front page *Woodhull & Claflin's Weekly*
The Beecher-Tilton Case
"Free Love"

NEW YORK PUBLIC LIBRARY

Astor, Lenox and Tilden Foundations:

Liberator Masthead
Title page, Anti-Slavery Convention of American Women
1837 Appeal to Women
Lily Masthead
Title page, Report of Seneca Falls Convention
Cartoon of Seneca Falls Meeting
Sojourner Truth
"Ladies Dress Reform Meeting"
"Lady Clerks Leaving the Treasury Department"
Anna E. Dickinson
Mrs. E. Cady Stanton
"Congressional Pests"
Olympia Brown
"The Cincinnati Convention"
Title page and inscription of *History of Woman Suffrage*
"George Francis Train in Court"
Revolution masthead
Woman's Journal masthead
Woman's Journal announcement
Victoria Woodhull

NEW YORK PUBLIC LIBRARY (cont'd).

"Women's Whisky War in Ohio"
Frances Willard
Home Protection Manual, title page
Glimpses of Fifty Years, title page
"Suffragists at the House of Representatives"
Anthony votes
Trial of Susan B. Anthony, title page
Virginia Minor
Myra Bradwell
NAWSA Declaration of Rights
Ohio Woman Suffrage press clipping
General Federation Bulletin and Cover
Southern Horrors, title page
Parliamentary Usage ad
"Shoemakers' Strike in Lynn"
"Lady Strikers to the Chowder Party"
"Servant Girls Writing Advertisements"
"The Great Fire in Boston"
Vignettes from *Life in New York*
New York Employment Bureau
Woman's Journal page
Proceedings of NAWSA Convention
Suffragist covers
"Women First" cartoon
Birth Control Review, cover and cartoon
Equal Rights covers
NWTUL Convention handbook and labels
Life and Labor masthead and cover
Woman Citizen covers

Picture Collection:

Lucretia Mott
Margaret Sanger
"New York—Scene of the Woman's Temperance Convention"

*Schomberg Center for Research in Black Culture,
Astor, Lenox and Tilden Foundations:*

Mary Church Terrell

NEW YORK TIMES

"Suffrage Army on Parade" headlines
"Wilson Backs Amendment" headlines

MARTIN SHULMAN

Miss America Demonstration

SOPHIA SMITH COLLECTION, SMITH COLLEGE

Executive Committee, Philadelphia Anti-Slavery Convention,
1851
Jane Addams

UNDERWOOD

Florence Kelley

WIDE WORLD PHOTOS

Gloria Steinem, Bella Abzug, Shirley Chisholm, Betty Friedan

*The following individuals, publications, and organizations have
kindly given permission to reprint the material indicated:*

C. C. CATT PAPERS (Manuscripts and Archives Division, The New York Public
Library. Astor, Lenox and Tilden Foundations)

"Mrs. Catt's Views on Heckling President Wilson"

DA CAPO PRESS

Two articles from their reprint edition of the *Birth Control
Review:*
Principles and Aims of the American Birth Control League.
December 1921
Report of Los Angeles Mothers Clinic Association. May 1926

WILLARD F. DAY and C. C. CATT PAPERS (The New York Public Library)

Letter to President Wilson from Helen Gardener, May 10, 1917

FEMINIST WOMEN'S HEALTH CENTER

Feminist Women's Health Center brochure

GENERAL FEDERATION OF WOMEN'S CLUBS MAGAZINE

1914 GFWC Resolutions. August 1914
"New Mexico Women Active." September 1914
"Women Inspectors for Women at Work," by Agnes L.
Peterson. October 1914
GFWC Legislative Reports. June 1915
"The Consumer's Conscience," by Maud Nathan, November
1916

GENERAL MICROFILM COMPANY

Letter from Lucy Stone, April 10, 1875

GOOD HOUSEKEEPING

"We Couldn't Afford a Doctor," by Anne Martin
"Should There Be Labor Laws for Women?" by Rita Dorr and
Mary Anderson

HARCOURT, BRACE & WORLD

Valentines from the Union
Banners Quoting Wilson

CASEY HAYDEN-BOYCE

"A Kind of Memo from Casey Hayden and Mary King . . . "

LADIES HOME JOURNAL

"Women as Dictators," by Mrs. O. H. P. Belmont. September
1922. © September 1922, Curtis Publishing Company

LESBIAN FEMINIST LIBERATION

Constitution of Lesbian Feminist Liberation

LITTLE, BROWN & COMPANY

Letter from Lucy Stone to Margaret Campbell, 1874

MS. MAGAZINE

The National Black Feminist Organization, Statement of Purpose
Some Demands of Chicana Women
"A Petition for Sanity"

THE NEW YORK TIMES

Editorial Comment on League Activity: "The foxes have holes . . . " August 11, 1914
"Hang Suffrage Banner as President Speaks." December 6, 1916
Banners for the Russian Mission, from an article describing suffragist demonstration. July 21, 1917
"Mrs. Catt Assails Pickets." November 13, 1917
Statement of House Suffrage Committee. January 10, 1918

NATIONAL ORGANIZATION FOR WOMEN

An Invitation to Join
Statement of Objectives
"N.O.W. President Charges Government . . . "

Resolution on Sexuality and Lesbians
Resolutions on Poverty, Needs of Minority Persons, Sports, Older Women, Traditionally Female Jobs, Rape

REDSTOCKINGS

Redstockings Manifesto

KATHIE SARACHILD

A Program for Consciousness-raising

TODAY'S EDUCATION—CAROL JACOBS and CYNTHIA EATON

"Evaluating Sexism in Readers"

TOWER PUBLICATIONS

Willis's Report

WESTERN RESERVE HISTORICAL SOCIETY

Letter from Eliza Ann Griffith, May 6, 1837

INDEX

A Note About the Type

The text of this book was set in Roma, a computer version of
Optima, a typeface designed by Hermann Zapf from 1952-55
and issued in 1958. In designing Optima, Zapf created a truly
new type form—a cross between the classic roman and a
sans-serif face. So delicate are the stresses and balances in
Optima that it rivals sans-serif faces in clarity and freshness and
old-style faces in variety and interest.

Composed by CompuComp Corporation, Montreal, Canada.
Printed and bound by The Colonial Press, Clinton,
Massachusetts.

The book was designed by Susan Mitchell.

 KALAMAZOO VALLEY
COMMUNITY COLLEGE
LIBRARY

KALAMAZOO VALLEY
COMMUNITY COLLEGE
LIBRARY